VOLUME 2:
EAST ASIA
AND THE PACIFIC

ECHOES of ARARAT

A COLLECTION OF OVER 300 FLOOD LEGENDS
FROM EAST ASIA AND THE PACIFIC

Nick Liguori and Valdis Gauss

First printing: February 2026

Master Books, P.O. Box 726, Green Forest, AR 72638

Master Books® is a division of the New Leaf Publishing Group, LLC

ISBN: 978-1-68344-413-8
ISBN: 979-8-90092-000-9 (digital)

Library of Congress Number: 2025949387

Cover design: Diana Bogardus

Interior Design: Terry White

Please consider requesting that a copy of this volume be purchased by your local library system.

Printed in the United States of America

Please visit our website for other great titles: www.masterbooks.com

Contact details: The authors can be reached at nicholasliguori@gmail.com and gaojiajo@gmail.com.

TABLE OF CONTENTS

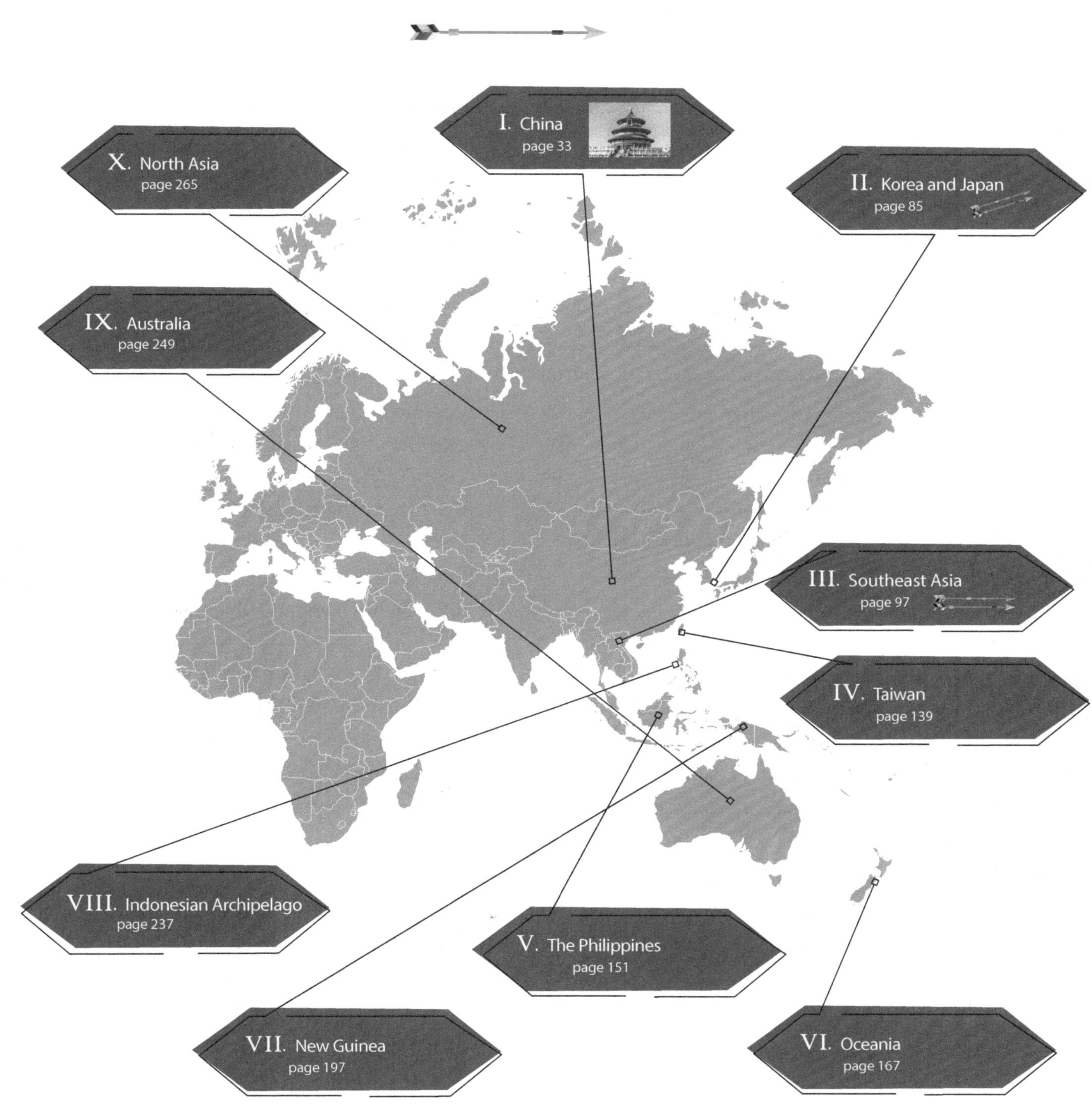

TABLE OF CONTENTS (continued)

ENDORSEMENTS

"Nick has meticulously scanned every available source to compile this masterpiece! In doing so, he has been given the unique blessing of portraying some of God's previously hidden works of how He preserved a witness for Himself among many of the peoples of the world. I hope this precious book is widely read as it will enlighten and encourage Christians everywhere in the faith, and challenge those who are not yet believers to view the world in light of God's power and grace."

—Paul Hattaway, Director of Asia Harvest and author of works such as *Operation China, Heavenly Man*, and the *China Chronicles* series

"Noah's Flood is the most significant event in earth history since God's work of creation in Genesis 1. For 200 years most geologists have been blind to the overwhelming geological evidence of Flood because of their naturalist worldview. By diligent research, the authors have carefully documented more compelling evidence for the global Flood, this time from the historical memory of people groups all over Asia."

—Dr. Terry Mortenson, author with Answers in Genesis and editor of *Coming to Grips With Genesis* and *Searching for Adam: Genesis & the Truth About Man's Origin.*

"This relentless international search, into every tribal, ethnic and historic corner of our world and epoch, has irrefutably shown Genesis to be accurate, and that we are all, after all, descended from one family."

—Stan Avery, pastor, missionary, and director of Unreached Villages

"One of the more important research projects I've ever seen. *Echoes of Ararat* shows an incredible worldwide pattern of evidence to Creation, the Flood, and the Tower of Babel."

—Tim Mahoney, Investigative Filmmaker and Producer of *The American Miracle, Patterns of Evidence: Exodus, The Moses Controversy,* and *Journey to Mount Sinai*

"I wholeheartedly endorse this second volume of *Echoes of Ararat.* Liguori and Gauss have done a wonderful job documenting how Genesis is the true origin story of all ancient cultures. What's more, they have also provided an incredible resource for evangelism and missionary work all around the world. Your confidence in God's historical and inspired Word will only grow by reading this!"

—Caleb Harrelson, pastor and evangelist

"*Echoes of Ararat* is a great book for evangelism. Within the ancient history of hundreds of cultures is the knowledge of Genesis: Creation, sin, and Noah's Flood. Christianity is not just a white European religion; the forefathers of these ancient cultures from around the world knew the God of the Bible!"

—Julie Von Vett, missionary and author of works such as *Have You Considered?* and *Without Excuse: The Compelling Evidence for Creation*

INTRODUCTION

A Brief Overview

In my first volume, I documented the wealth of evidence showing that tribes and nations all over the world really do know of Noah's Flood. It is recounted in their traditions. It is depicted in their ancient paintings and rock carvings in Mexico, the southwestern U.S., and Venezuela. It is commemorated in their sacrifices, festivals, and songs. It is seared into the collective memory of the ancestors of nations all over the world. We learned of the impressive Flood traditions of the Mandans, the Cherokee, the Lakota, the Ottawa, the Inuit peoples of the Arctic, the Mexican nations, the jungle tribes of South America, and many others. In total, more than 330 indigenous people groups from North and South America possess such memories of this Flood, and they correspond to the Genesis Flood account in particular.

Now, in a long-overdue *Volume 2*, we will turn our attention to the Eastern Hemisphere. We will trace the knowledge of Noah's Flood, and of other events from Genesis chapters 1 to 11, across Asia and the Pacific Islands. We will see that just as the Native Americans bear witness to the truth of the Genesis Flood, so do their Asian, Pacific Islander, and Australian counterparts commemorate this unforgettable event in their ancient traditions and texts. Indeed, it is a memory which unites all these people groups and transports us to the most ancient past.

Thus, we will hear from the Han Chinese and over 40 ethnic minorities of China,[1] as they recount the memory of that Flood that destroyed the world, and of the floating vessel that landed on a high mountain. We will press south into Vietnam, Thailand, and Burma, where over 50 tribes recall that great Flood, a warning that was given in advance, a floating vessel (either made of wood, or a giant gourd or pumpkin) which enabled one, two, three, or eight people to survive. They also recall the high mountain of landing, a bird which brought good news of the Flood's end, and often a Tower of Babel event that occurred afterward. We will find traditions of that same Flood in Mongolia, in Siberia, in Korea, Japan, the Ryukyu Islands, and Taiwan.

Crossing the sea and arriving at the Indonesian Archipelago, we will hear the memory of that same event from the Austronesian-language peoples in the jungles of Java, Sumatra, Borneo, and other islands. On the island of New Guinea, where some anthropologists have assured us that the Flood is absent from native traditions, we will find quite the opposite. The memory of Noah's Flood is not only alive and well in New Guinea, but present in numbers not seen on par with any part of the world! The aborigines of Australia also know of the Flood and the Ark, for their ancestors, like the rest of humanity, were on that Ark. And from Polynesia, New Zealand, and other Pacific islands, we will hear some of the most carefully preserved traditions of the Flood and of Creation to be found anywhere on earth.

Why I Wrote this Book

I (Nick) had no intention of writing a book at first. However, once a certain set of events took place, it was inevitable.

One evening in November, 2015, I was reclining while reading a new book that had just come in the mail. It was called *The Popular Handbook of Archaeology and the Bible*, by Joseph Holden and Norman Geisler (who is now with the Lord). I was enjoying every page of this book. It is a riveting book which introduced me to many archeological evidences and historical discoveries confirming the Bible, such as the Ketef Hinnom Silver Scrolls, the Nazareth Inscription, and the discovery of Sodom on the east side of the Jordan River.

But as I continued reading, I came to a chapter about evidences for the early chapters of Genesis. There, I came to a statement which seemingly leapt out of the page at me. It was a simple and unadorned statement, yet so potent and intriguing that I could not get it out of my mind:

> "There are numerous flood stories from different geographical regions and ethnic backgrounds. If the Flood actually occurred, this is what one would expect to see in the historical-archeological record. Such an event surely would leave a lasting impression on the human psyche and demand an explanation from those who heard about it."[2]

1. The number is even greater if we count some of the tribes of northern China, such as the Manchu and Oruqen, which we have instead placed in the chapter on North Asia (Siberia and Mongolia). Many ethnic groups, of course, cross modern national boundaries.
2. Joseph M. Holden and Norman Geisler, *The Popular Handbook of Archaeology and the Bible* (Eugene, OR: Harvest House, 2013), p. 209.

Flood legends from all across the world? And they describe the same event recorded in Genesis? I understood the impact of that statement. I knew that if true, it represented one of the most compelling exhibits of the truth of Genesis that could be imagined.

This wasn't the first time I had heard such a statement about Flood legends confirming Genesis. I had read Josephus' *Antiquities*. I had heard from many people that there are large volumes of Flood legends from tribes and nations around the world. I had even heard that there are "hundreds" of Flood legends.

But this time, my curiosity was piqued more than ever before. I had to learn more. "Is it true that there are hundreds of Flood legends? Where can I learn more?" It launched me on a quest, because I knew what was at stake. I knew what they were teaching on college campuses and in public schools, and it wasn't a biblical worldview rooted in Genesis. I knew that if this (and other evidences for Genesis) was true, then people needed to know about it.

So I began researching and collecting books. I expected that I would find books documenting hundreds of these Flood traditions. But that is not what I found at all. To be fair, some of these books were quite good in their own way, but nothing like a comprehensive collection of Flood traditions. There was some quality material, but it was piecemeal, limited in scope. Where were the "hundreds" of Flood legends? On the other hand, many sources were poorly documented, based on second-hand information, or unverifiable altogether. I recognized this as a problem.

At the same time, I knew that there were many hundreds of tribes, nations, and people groups across the world. What did they believe? Did their histories contain a memory of Noah's Flood? I grew up in eastern Pennsylvania, home to the Lenape people long ago. What did they believe? I now lived in Virginia, once home to the Powhatan confederacy. What did they believe?

These questions drove me to search for original, early sources. I began locating sources with the earliest, most reliable information on these tribes—often sources from the 1800s, 1700s, 1600s, or even earlier. I was amazed at what I found. As I reflect back on that period of research, two things stand out to me. First, the sheer number of tribes possessing Flood stories. I found more of these than I ever imagined: over 330 in North and South America! Second, the impossibility of what I was finding. I mean impossibility from a secular viewpoint. I was frequently stunned to read a book on a certain tribe's history and find therein a clear memory of the Flood of Noah. And I would ask myself, "What is the Genesis Flood doing in the Cherokee nation's history?" "What is the Genesis Flood doing in the Apache nation's history? In the Nez Perce nation's history? In the Ottawa nation's history?"

As I said above, I never intended to write a book. But in light of the gap of information, the volume of evidence I found, and the gravity of importance it possesses, I was compelled to write. People needed to know that there is vast evidence for Genesis from histories around the world.

At the same time, there were several secular narratives about these Flood stories. "Moses stole the Flood story." "It was only a local flood." "Christian missionaries influenced their traditions." Sadly, I saw that secularists were controlling the narratives. Yet I could see that these narratives were false and perilously misleading. These false narratives needed to be exposed for the sake of the truth. Did not Paul say the same thing? It was not without reason that he wrote this to the Corinthians:

> "We destroy arguments and every lofty opinion raised against the knowledge of God, and take every thought captive to obey Christ."
> (2 Corinthians 10:5 ESV)

Introducing Co-author, Valdis Gauss

This second book was much more challenging to write than the first. The first *Volume* covered North and South America, but the second Volume, covering the entire Pacific and most of Asia, was larger in scope geographically, demographically, and historically.[3]

Also, *Volume 2* was much more challenging linguistically. Consider the fact that *Volume 1*, which covered North and South America, was mostly a matter of consulting English and Spanish sources, both very accessible to me. For *Volume 2*, however, many texts and traditions could only be accessed through Chinese, French, Japanese, Russian, Vietnamese, and other language sources. I had begun learning French for this reason, but that is only one of the languages required. Besides that, I now had a second child, and less time with which to research and write (to say nothing of the fact that I have a full-time job). I was staring at a task many times more difficult than *Volume 1*.

At that time, a godsend arrived in the person of Valdis Gauss, an Assistant Professor and researcher at National Taitung University. Not only did Valdis write his PhD dissertation on the Formosan deluge myths, but he is also arguably the leading expert in the world on the Flood and creation stories of Taiwan's aboriginal tribes. I encourage you to read Valdis' works, *The Formosan Great Flood Myths* and *The Formosan Primary Anthropogenic Myths, Genesis and the Creation of Man.* His publications are listed in full on ResearchGate.net. Valdis' BA in Linguistics and MA in TESOL facilitated his acquisition,

3. Originally, my plan was to include India in this volume as well. However, the amount of evidence that Valdis and I found (which is a happy problem) necessitated that we cut India from this volume and reserve it for the third volume.

to various levels, of Mandarin, German, Japanese, and Spanish, among other languages. He is also a master researcher, and he made me better. I could not imagine anyone more equipped to help me with this task than he, and I am grateful to God for sending Valdis my way. This book would not have reached a successful completion without Valdis' contribution.

I and We

As you read this book, you will encounter "I" and "We" statements. In the case of "I", you may be wondering which of us is speaking. We will often clarify with an "I (Nick)" or "I (Valdis)". However, if no parenthetical clarification is given (for it becomes unwieldy to always add this), you may assume "I" means Nick. These differences in voice occur simply because, of practical necessity, one or the other of us took the lead on a particular section or chapter. We hope that you will enjoy this work that we have completed together.

Theological Context

Now we have to establish the context in which this book matters. I am speaking at the moment to Christians, those who believe the Bible. To my surprise, some have expressed confusion about why a book like this should be written. "Who cares if Genesis is true?" "What does it matter if the Flood really happened, or if it was global or local?" "Why don't we just focus on the Gospel? Let's keep the focus on Jesus."

But to make this objection is to assume a couple things. First, it assumes that teaching on Genesis and Jesus are mutually exclusive. This is false biblically, for the same reason that it's false to say "Pouring a foundation is a waste of time. It only delays the construction of the house." Try building a house upon clay, with no foundation. The fact is, the book of Genesis provides the worldview which is foundational to Christianity and the Gospel. *Echoes of Ararat Volume 2* provides evidence confirming Genesis and this biblical worldview.

Sound doctrine, such as a proper view of Genesis, does not distract from Jesus (2 Timothy 4:1-5, Titus 1:9-13, Jude 3). It actually magnifies Jesus! It gives more focus, not less, to the cross of Christ. What really takes the attention off Jesus and makes Him less relevant is the denial of the truth of Genesis, and the doubts this causes. Remember the words of Jesus: "If I have spoken to you of earthly things and you do not believe, how will you believe if I speak of heavenly things?" (John 3:12). Today we have an epidemic of people who cannot believe Jesus on heavenly things because they do not believe Jesus about earthly things, especially in Genesis. At the same time, we have forgotten the prediction of Peter that in later times, people will reject two things—biblical Creation and Noah's Flood—and that this will lead to them rejecting Jesus Himself (2 Peter 3:5-6). This insightful statement by Peter points us to a raw and undeniable fact of experience: denial of Genesis breeds unbelief.

> "For this they willfully forget: that by the word of God the heavens were of old, and the earth standing out of water and in the water, by which the world that then existed perished, being flooded with water." (2 Peter 3:5-6 NKJV)

Second, it assumes that you can discard Noah's Flood without impacts to the Garden of Eden and the doctrine of the Fall. But you cannot. Now to begin with, it should be very evident to all that biblically we cannot afford to lose Adam and the Garden of Eden (Romans 5:12-19, 1 Corinthians 15:21-22, Romans 8:2,19-23, Luke 3:23-38, Romans 7:5-14). Lose the first Adam, and you lose the Second Adam. Lose the Garden of Eden, and you lose Calvary. Lose the Curse, and you lose the Cross. Lose the law of sin and death, and you lose the Resurrection. Lose the protoevangelium (Gen. 3:15), and you lose the Gospel.

But what does the Genesis Flood have to do with the Garden of Eden, you ask? First, to introduce myth into the Flood narrative—chapters 6 through 9 of Genesis—is to introduce myth into that which is prior: chapters 1 through 3. How can you defend Genesis 1 through 3 to your children and an unbelieving world, when you have already surrendered Genesis 6 through 9? Secondly, the testimony of the geologic record would utterly destroy the doctrine of the law of sin and death if we did not have the global and destructive Flood of Genesis. In that case, we would not have a mechanism to account for the death, destruction, carnivory, disease, and suffering plainly visible in the fossil record.

The Book of Genesis provides the worldview which is foundational to Christianity and the Gospel.

I will now cross-examine the objector. When were these fossil-bearing rocks laid down: before or after Adam sinned? Having denied the Genesis Flood, how can you avoid the geological conclusion that these fossils were laid down before Adam and Eve? That is, if you can even sustain that Adam and Eve were real people at all. How then can it be true, as Genesis 3 says, that Adam's sin brought death, animal carnivory, and natural evil into the world if these evils already existed before him? Did Adam travel back in time and plant fossils? Or how will you explain the statement of Genesis 3:17-18, where God tells Adam that the ground is now cursed and will produce thorns and thistles? According to your interpretation of the rock layers, wouldn't these rock layers containing thorns and thistles predate mankind? How will you avoid reducing Genesis 3 to myth?

Now it is not at all the case that thorns, thistles, carnivory, and natural evil predate Adam. They absolutely do not. The truth of the Genesis Flood offers a different interpretation of the fossil record and one which actually has much more explanatory power and consistency than the secular view. (See "Geological and Scientific Context" in the following pages, along with the recommendations for further study in Appendix D). When we embrace Genesis and the Genesis Flood, then it follows that these fossil-bearing rocks are Flood rocks, and therefore were deposited after Adam sinned.

> Although this book devotes enormous attention to the Flood and Noah's Ark, I am actually contending for something much more important: I am contending for Adam, for Genesis 3, and for Romans 5 and 6!

What I am saying, however, is that to lose the biblical teaching of the Flood—to which God devoted four entire chapters in Scripture, and which Peter predicted would be denied in the future, at great peril (2 Peter 3:3-7)—is to also lose Adam and Eve and the doctrine of the Fall (sin-death causality). To lose Adam and the Fall (sin-death causality) is to lose the Gospel itself, according to Romans 5.

The law of sin and death (Romans 6:23), which is foundational to the Gospel itself, is the most important reason why the truth of the Flood matters. We could also add 2) the doctrine of the inerrancy and authority of Scripture, 3) the ability to answer the problem of evil (theodicy), and 4) the character of God. All these are at stake.

Summary of Theological Context

Although this is a book mainly about the Genesis Flood and tribal traditions of that Flood, I am not merely contending for the truth of the Flood. I am also contending for the Garden of Eden! Why the Garden of Eden? Because the Garden has to do with 1) our identity as the descendants of Adam and Eve who were created by God, and 2) the law of sin and death (that death is the consequence of sin), which is the basis for the Gospel of Jesus.

While this book devotes enormous attention to the Flood and Noah's Ark, I am actually contending for something much more important, even if indirectly: I am contending for Adam, for Genesis 3, and for Romans 5 and 6! Whether one realizes it or not, the Flood has implications for the truth of Adam and of the law of sin and death, upon which the Gospel is predicated in Romans 5 and 6, and other passages.

> For as by one man's disobedience many were made sinners, so also by one Man's obedience many will be made righteous. (Romans 5:19 NKJV)

> For the wages of sin is death, but the gift of God is eternal life in Christ Jesus our Lord. (Romans 6:23 NKJV)

In short, if we mythologize Genesis, we are left with a mythical Creation, a mythical Garden of Eden, a mythical Adam, a mythical Fall, a mythical sin problem, and a mythical Savior Jesus offering us a mythical hope. On the other hand, if we have true history in Genesis, then we have a true Adam, a true Garden of Eden, a true Fall into sin and death, a true flood that testifies of God's judgment and His righteousness, a true and profound existential need for forgiveness and right status with God, and a true Savior Jesus, who offers us a true hope and true eternal life. That is why this book has been written.

Geological and Scientific Context

Despite all the effort we have poured into collecting Flood legends and showing that they confirm the account in Genesis, this effort would all be for naught if, at the end of the day, we could not answer the following question in the affirmative: Scientifically, is the Genesis Flood consistent with the geological data? Can it account for the geologic and fossil evidence?

It will come as a surprise to some, but the answer is absolutely affirmative. And let me be absolutely clear: the modern creationist view far surpasses the evolutionary view in credible explanatory power.

Now historically, we know the 19th century was a crucial period when Christian and theistic perspectives in the scientific fields of geology and biology were abandoned in favor of a new evolutionary, uniformitarian, and materialistic perspective. This shaped the nature of the debate in the 20th century, and today in the 2020s.

This evolutionary materialistic paradigm still appears to be in power. However, it has never been weaker and more vulnerable than it is today, with high-ranking defections and an ever-growing number of vocal opponents. Meanwhile, the traditional biblical perspective, assumed to be dead, is very much alive, and is represented by thousands of PhD and Masters level scientists producing formidable work.

A very compelling and persuasive case for biblical creationism is now being made on scientific grounds, with an ever-growing array of evidences from diverse disciplines. Not only is the modern creationist perspective able to answer evolutionary arguments (See Creation Ministries International with their over

15,000 online articles and resources. Answers in Genesis and Institute for Creation Research are producing prolific work as well), but creationism is increasingly demonstrating positive, predictive power.

It is well-documented how the field of geology abandoned any embrace of the Noahic Flood in the early 1800s. By the early 1830s, very few geologists still held to the Flood in the literal sense of Genesis. Now, it turns out that shift was largely attributable to certain geological arguments which were very convincing, championed by James Hutton, Charles Lyell, and others. Terry Mortenson, who has studied the history of geology extensively, has identified several arguments on the basis of which Lyell's view won the day.[4]

To a geologist in the 1830s, these arguments seemed irresistible. However, today such arguments are highly answerable, thanks to the work and progress of many PhD geologists such as Andrew Snelling, Timothy Clarey, Steven Austin, John Whitmore, and John Baumgartner. For example, it is now known that marine fossils are found at every level of the geologic column. Where terrestrial fossils are found, they occur in the same layers as marine fossils. Sharks and deep-sea coelacanth fish are found in the same layers as dinosaurs and other terrestrial species! These layers are also massive in scope: extending across entire nations, even continents and multiple continents. What could have deposited these layers but a global Flood? These layers also bear many indications that they were laid down rapidly, one after another in a matter of days and weeks, not millions of years. These include a lack of internal bioturbation, lack of erosional channels, and knife-edge boundaries—all of which would be obliterated if they were exposed for long eons, yet these features are exactly what we would expect if the global Flood is a fact! In 2023, Andrew Snelling published the results of a comprehensive investigation, showing that bent and folded layers in the Southwest US were deformed rapidly, not over millions of years, and while the sediments were still wet and uncemented.[5]

Of course, secular geologists have updated their arguments since the early 19th century. Chiefly, these arguments have to do with the differences in types of species found at different levels in the geologic column. However, again thanks to the progress of modern creationism in geology and paleontology, these arguments are highly answerable, and subject to devastating counterarguments.[6] This is not to say that creationist geology has answered every single question with finality, but the progress made in the last few decades has been more than promising, and frankly amazing.

With many thanks to the work and insight of our leading creationist geologists and paleontologists, Tables 1 through 3 in the following pages give just a taste of the superior explanatory power of the biblical view. The reports of the death of biblical creationism have been greatly exaggerated.

The situation, therefore, is very ironic. The evolutionary, conventional perspective has achieved historic victories and has amassed great influence, resources, and manpower. However, it has always been built on a faulty foundation. Even now there are many and major problems in this model, and many who once espoused evolutionary teaching are defecting. Evolutionary geology is, I contend, a theory assumed to possess all power, but with little real power.

On the other hand, the biblical creationist, Flood-based geologic perspective is assumed by many to be utterly powerless, yet it possesses all the power of the truth, for "we can do nothing against the truth, but only for the truth" (2 Corinthians 13:8). The biblical creationist view suffered early setbacks and lacked capable defenders in the early 19th century. This continued until the second half of the 20th century. Public advocacy for the biblical origin narratives has long been deprived of resources, funding, and manpower. And despite all that, I contend (and others smarter than me) that it was true all along. Today, biblical creation and Flood-based geology is capably represented by highly qualified scientists who are performing top-rate field work and publishing compelling new discoveries and answers.

4. "First, the primitive rocks were covered by at least two miles of secondary and tertiary strata, in which was seen evidence of slow gradual deposition during successive periods of calm and catastrophe. Second, some strata were clearly formed from the violent destruction of older strata. Third, different strata contained different fossils; it was especially noted that strata with terrestrial and fresh-water shells alternate with those containing marine shells, and that strata nearest the surface contained land animals mixed with marine creatures. Fourth, generally speaking, the lower the strata were, the greater was the difference between fossil and living species, which to old-earth geologists implied many extinctions as a result of a series of revolutions over a long time. Fifth, the evidence that faults and dislocations occurred after the deposition and induration of many strata implied a lapse of time between the formation of the various strata. Finally, there was the fact that man was apparently only found fossilized in the most recent strata." Terry Mortenson, "British scriptural geologists in the first half of the nineteenth century: part 1." *Journal of Creation*, vol. 11, no. 2 (1997), pp. 231-232.
5. Andrew Snelling, "The Carbon Canyon Fold, Eastern Grand Canyon, Arizona," *Answers Research Journal*, vol. 16 (2023), pp. 1-124. Snelling, "The Monument Fold, Central Grand Canyon, Arizona," *Answers Research Journal*, vol. 16 (2023), pp. 301-432.
6. See, for example, *Carved in Stone* by Timothy Clarey, *Earth's Catastrophic Past* (2 vols.) by Andrew Snelling, and *Grand Canyon: A Different View* by Tom Vail.

Table 1 - The Geologic Record in General: Does it Confirm or Deny Genesis?		
YES = Can Account For **NO = Cannot Account For**	**View**	
	Biblical view (the Genesis Flood account is true)	**Secular view (billions of years, evolution, uniformitarianism)**
Most of the earth is covered in sedimentary rock layers, which are several thousand feet thick in many places.	**YES**	**POSSIBLE**
The geologic column has order. Each layer contains certain fossils and has a certain composition, and is differentiated from adjacent layers	**YES**	**POSSIBLE**
The earth's sedimentary layers are frequently bent, folded, and curved, with tight radii. Yet these deformed layers are not cracked or metamorphosed! This indicates they were displaced while still soft, prior to cementing.[7]	**YES**	**NO**
The finely laminated shales, mudstone, and limestone layers that we find all over the world can only be formed by moving water, as laboratory experiments have shown.[8]	**YES**	**NO**
These finely laminated sedimentary layers, furthermore, are not small or local in extent. They are enormous, spanning across thousands of square miles, and even across continents! Their thickness ranges from a few feet to several hundred feet! These layers are without modern parallel!	**YES**	**NO**
Bioturbation quickly destroys laminated sediment layers, creating homogeneity. The only way for laminated layers to be preserved is to be rapidly buried at sufficient depths to escape burrowers and other causes of bioturbation. Yet the rule in the geologic record is that all sediments are laminated, consisting of distinct layers stacked on top of one another. These deposits have no modern parallel.	**YES**	
Rock layers have knife-edge, flat boundaries with adjacent layers, indicating they were deposited one right after the other. There is no long-term erosion or bioturbation at layer boundaries.	**YES**	**NO**
The uniformitarian view, based on present-day processes, would anticipate fossilization to be extremely rare, and for the few fossils found to be poorly preserved. Yet fossils are not only abundant, but well-preserved!	**YES**	**NO**

7. Steven A. Austin and J. D. Morris, "Tight folds and clastic dikes as evidence for rapid deposition and deformation of two very thick stratigraphic sequences," *Proceedings of the First International Conference on Creationism* (Pittsburgh: Creation Science Fellowship, 1986), pp. 3-13. Andrew Snelling, "The Carbon Canyon Fold, Eastern Grand Canyon, Arizona," *Answers Research Journal*, vol. 16 (2023), pp. 1-124. Snelling, "The Monument Fold, Central Grand Canyon, Arizona," *Answers Research Journal*, vol. 16 (2023), pp. 301-432.
8. Andrew Snelling, "Sedimentation experiments: Nature finally catches up!" *Journal of Creation*, vol. 11, no. 2 (1997), pp. 125-126.

(continued) Table 1 - The Geologic Record in General: Does it Confirm or Deny Genesis?		
	View	
YES = Can Account For **NO = Cannot Account For**	**Biblical view (the Genesis Flood account is true)**	**Secular view (billions of years, evolution, uniformitarianism)**
In the geologic column we find polystrate trees (tree trunks which vertically traverse multiple layers) and other polystrate fossils! Polystrate trees are even found inverted. Some inverted polystrate trees are even found directly above or below upright polystrate trees![9]	**YES**	**NO**
The rule in the fossil record is that all classes of organisms appear suddenly, as opposed to gradual transition from one type of organism to another.	**YES**	**NO**
Clastic dikes, in which sand has been injected into a fault zone (like toothpaste) from an adjacent sandstone layer, show evidence of injection while still soft and uncemented. These include laminated flow structures within the dikes, the existence of even very small clastic dikes a fraction of an inch wide, and a lack of fine matrix or broken sand grains which might be expected if it were already lithified. These occur even in Cambrian sandstones![10]	**YES**	**NO**
Vertical, upright fossils are found in layers which are not local deposits, but vast deposits which stretch for thousands of miles and even across continents	**YES**	**NO**
Reptile and amphibian tracks and footprints are found in the rock column slightly below (and conventionally millions of years before) their associated body fossils![11]	**YES**	**NO**
In the groups of organisms that are most well-documented in the fossil record (such as shallow marine invertebrates), there are no potential intermediates. In the less-documented groups of organisms (e.g., mammals and reptiles) evolutionists have proposed intermediates, but the Flood model and subsequent ice age can account for these as well.[12]	**YES**	**NO**
Verdict:	**The geologic record confirms the Flood as described in Genesis**	

9. Paul Price, "How the Joggins polystrate fossils falsify long ages." https://creation.com/joggins-polystrate-fossils 16 Apr. 2020. Retrieved 27 Oct. 2021. Tasman Walker, "Chapter 5. The Geologic Record," ed. Robert Carter, in *Evolution's Achilles Heels* (Powder Springs, GA: Creation Book Publishers, 2014), p. 173.
10. Austin and Morris, "Tight folds and clastic dikes," pp. 10-13.
11. Thomas Purifoy Jr. "Why are fossil footprints curious evidence for the Flood?" *Is Genesis History?* https://isgenesishistory.com/fossil-footprints-curious-evidence-flood/ Retrieved 31 Oct. 2021.
12. Kurt P. Wise, "The Fossil Record." Presentation at the *Is Genesis History? Conference*, June 19-23, 2017, Dickson, Tennessee. Retrieved from: https://youtu.be/wKuFQLkFW7o. Dr. Wise was a student of the famous paleontologist Stephen Jay Gould at Harvard University.

Table 2 – Trilobites and Other Features in the Paleozoic (Oldest) Sedimentary Layers: Do They Confirm or Deny Genesis?		
	View	
YES = Can Account For **NO = Cannot Account For**	**Biblical view (the Genesis Flood account is true)**	**Secular view (billions of years, evolution, uniformitarianism)**
Trilobites first appear in the Cambrian sedimentary layers, mostly terminate above the Devonian layers, and are not found at all above the Permian layers.	**YES**	**YES**
The earliest fossil evidence we find of trilobites are not their shells, but their tracks! Their tracks are found at the very base of the Cambrian layer. Their shells are found higher, and conventionally tens of millions of years later, than their tracks. This makes sense from a Genesis Flood perspective, but not from an evolutionary / uniformitarian perspective. Furthermore, their shells are made of limestone and should be easier to preserve than their tracks. Yet their shells are only found higher in the record. [13]	**YES**	**NO**
Trilobites have perhaps the most sophisticated optical system of any organism. Phacopid trilobites have two "hyper-compound eyes" with hundreds of lenses wrapping around much of the head, providing unparalleled peripheral vision horizontally and vertically.[14] Yet they occur in early Cambrian layers, without precedent in underlying rock!	**YES**	**NO**
Evolution predicts that diversity (the number of species) must increase before disparity (how different the species are). Yet the fossil record continually shows high disparity at the beginning, before we get any diversity![15]	**YES**	**NO**
In the Cambrian layers we find what is widely known as the Cambrian Explosion. The lowest strata show highly complex, highly distinct, separate types of organisms, and yet with very little diversification within these types! They show up all of a sudden, as it were!	**YES**	**NO**

13. Kurt P. Wise, "Tracks but no Trilobites." (1 Oct. 2012). Retrieved 31 Oct. 2021 from https://answersingenesis.org/extinct-animals/five-tracks-but-no-trilobites/
14. Joanna Thompson, "This trilobite was equipped with a 'hyper-eye' never seen before in the animal kingdom." *Live Science*. Retrieved 30 October, 2021 from https://www.livescience.com/trilobite-eyes
15. Kurt P. Wise, "The Fossil Record." Presentation at the *Is Genesis History? Conference*. For example, the Burgess Shale is among the earliest sedimentary rocks containing arthropod fossils. Of non-trilobite arthropods, it contains 21 different species of arthropods, and they represent 20 different classes of arthropods! In other words, at the first layer where you find arthropods at all, you find 20 different classes all at once. That is huge disparity, even more disparity than we find in present arthropods (only 5 classes have survived)! Yet it is very low diversity: only 1 more species than classes! That is the opposite of what evolution predicts! This is the same thing we see, for example, with echinoderms: very high disparity when they first appear in the fossil record, even higher disparity than echinoderms in the present, and very low diversity.

(continued) Table 2 – Trilobites and Other Features in the Paleozoic (Oldest) Sedimentary Layers: Do They Confirm or Deny Genesis?		
YES = Can Account For NO = Cannot Account For	View	
	Biblical view (the Genesis Flood account is true)	Secular view (billions of years, evolution, uniformitarianism)
A study of the phylogeny of 144 classes or phyla showed that, in 95% of cases, the predicted evolutionary order does not match the actual order in the fossil record. The other 5% can be attributed to cases where the predicted order is sea-to-land, but this is also predicted by the Flood model.[16] Another study documented 250 out-of-order fossils.[17]	YES	NO
We find fossilized trilobite queues! These indicate instantaneous burial. Yet they occur in vast sedimentary layers spanning thousands of miles.[18]	YES	NO
Paleozoic rock layers are vast in geographic extent, stretching across multiple states and even different countries! Such deposits are without modern parallel, but would be anticipated by a global Flood.	YES	NO
Verdict:	Trilobite fossils and Paleozoic rock layers confirm the Flood as described in Genesis	

Table 3 - Dinosaurs and Other Features in the Mesozoic (Middle) Rock Layers: Do They Confirm or Deny Genesis?		
YES = Can Account For NO = Cannot Account For	View	
	Biblical view (the Genesis Flood account is true)	Secular view (billions of years, evolution, uniformitarianism)
Dinosaur fossils are found in Mezozoic sedimentary layers, but have not been found in overlying layers	YES	YES
Based on the Genesis Flood account and its chronology, we do not necessarily expect to find humans and dinosaurs buried in the same layers[19]	YES	

16. Kurt P. Wise, *First appearances of higher taxa: a preliminary study of order in the fossil record.* N.D. Unpublished study.
17. John Woodmorappe, "An anthology of matters significant to creationism and diluviology," *Creation Research Society Quarterly*, vol. 18, no. 4 (1982), pp. 210-214.
18. Philip Robinson, "Trilobite Conga Line vs Evolutionary Timeline," *Creation*, vol. 42, no. 3 (July 2020). Retrieved 30 October 2021 from https://creation.com/trilobite-conga-line
19. Humans likely lived in the highlands of the pre-Flood world, whereas dinosaurs lived in lower elevations.

(continued) **Table 3 - Dinosaurs and Other Features in the Mesozoic (Middle) Rock Layers: Do They Confirm or Deny Genesis?**

YES = Can Account For NO = Cannot Account For	View	
	Biblical view (the Genesis Flood account is true)	**Secular view (billions of years, evolution, uniformitarianism)**
The earliest records of dinosaurs in the geologic column are not their body fossils but their footprints! They are found conventionally tens of millions of years earlier than dinosaur body fossils. This fits perfectly with a Genesis Flood scenario, but not with the secular view, since dinosaur bones should be easier to preserve than fragile footprints.	**YES**	**NO**
Analysis of footprints found in Coconino sandstones points to these footprints having been made underwater rather than on surface sand.	**YES**	**NO**
Soft tissue, red blood cells, and DNA have been found preserved in dinosaur fossils, which could not possibly have survived for millions of years.[20]	**YES**	**NO**
Dinosaur bones contain measurable amounts Carbon 14. Carbon 14 should not be traceable beyond 100,000 years.	**YES**	**NO**
Carbon 14 dates for fossils found in lower layers are consistent with dates for fossils in higher layers.	**YES**	**NO**
Dinosaur fossil graveyards occur in vast sedimentary deposits such as the Morrison Formation, stretching from New Mexico to Canada, over 700,000 square miles! These deposits themselves have no modern parallel and cannot be accounted for by local floods.	**YES**	**NO**
The Book of Job makes clear references to both a land dinosaur (likely a sauropod) and a marine reptile (likely a plesiosaur), indicating that they were alive in biblical times! (Job 40-41)	**YES**	**NO**
Historical evidence from nations all over the world—from Peru to China, from England to Cambodia—including drawings and descriptions of dinosaurs, indicates that mankind lived contemporaneously with dinosaurs in the past.[21]	**YES**	**NO**

20. Jeffrey M. Tomkins, "The Fossils Still Say No: Capping a Cretaceous Conundrum." (31 August, 2021). Retrieved 30 October, 2021 from https://www.icr.org/article/the-fossils-still-say-no-cretaceous-conundrum/
21. See Vance Nelson's work, *Dire Dragons* (2018).

(continued) **Table 3 - Dinosaurs and Other Features in the Mesozoic (Middle) Rock Layers: Do They Confirm or Deny Genesis?**

YES = Can Account For NO = Cannot Account For	View	
	Biblical view (the Genesis Flood account is true)	**Secular view (billions of years, evolution, uniformitarianism)**
Human footprints have apparently been found by professional scientists in the same rock layers as dinosaurs.[22]	**YES**	
Dinosaur fossils are found buried next to marine fossils including sharks and deep-sea coelacanth fish	**YES**	**NO**
Dinosaurs appear immediately in the fossil record in about 20 distinct groups, without precedent in lower rock layers.	**YES**	**NO**
Other classes of dinosaurs appear in higher rock layers, again without precedent or intermediates.	**YES**	**NO**
Grass—which is not supposed to have existed at the time of dinosaurs—has been found in dinosaur stools and stomachs[23]	**YES**	**NO**
Dinosaur fossils are frequently found with their heads arched back and tails arched—a position which is associated with drowning.	**YES**	**NO**
In the fossil record, dinosaurs are found fighting each other, or sitting on nests of eggs, indicating very rapid burial in water.	**YES**	**NO**
Preserved blood vessels in dinosaur fossils show blot clotting, which unmistakably points to death by drowning. Yet these fossils occur in vast deposits which cannot be explained by river transport or a local flood, indicating they were drowned in a much larger flooding event.[24]	**YES**	**NO**
Dinosaur fossils are found in layers that stretch across whole continents, and with no signs of erosion between adjacent layers.	**YES**	**NO**

22. Henry R. Schoolcraft and Thomas H. Benton, "Remarks on the Prints of Human Feet, Observed in the Secondary Limestone of the Mississippi Valley," *The American Journal of Science and Arts*, vol. 5 (New Haven, CT: S. Converse, 1822), pp. 223–231. "Human-Like Tracks in Stone are Riddle to Scientists," *The Science News Letter*, vol. 34, no. 18, 29 October 1938, pp. 278–279.
23. David Catchpoole, "Grass-eating dinos: A 'time-travel' problem for evolution," *Creation*, vol. 29, no. 2 (2007), pp. 22-23. https://creation.com/grass-eating-dinos
    Jeff Hecht, "Dino droppings reveal prehistoric taste for grass," *New Scientist*, Vol. 188 (2005). https://www.newscientist.com/article/mg18825274-400-dino-droppings-reveal-prehistoric-taste-for-grass/
24. Mark Armitage and Jim Solliday, "UV Autofluorescence Microscopy of Dinosaur Bone Reveals Encapsulation of Blood Clots within Vessel Canals," *Microscopy Today*, vol. 28, no. 5 (September 2020), pp. 30-38. https://dstri.org/wp-content/uploads/2020/09/2armitage_MicroToday.pdf

(continued) Table 3 - Dinosaurs and Other Features in the Mesozoic (Middle) Rock Layers: Do They Confirm or Deny Genesis?		
	View	
YES = Can Account For **NO = Cannot Account For**	**Biblical view (the Genesis Flood account is true)**	**Secular view (billions of years, evolution, uniformitarianism)**
Dinosaur bones occur in graded fossil beds, such as the Morrison Formation of the western US, which can only be explained by transport by water and rapid deposition of the entire sediment package	**YES**	**NO**
Verdict:	**Dinosaur fossils and Mesozoic rock layers confirm the Flood as described in Genesis**	

Anthropological Context

An Ancient Argument

The discovery of the knowledge of Noah's Flood among so many nations by no means starts with this book. Nor does the argument for the truth of the Genesis Flood from similar traditions around the world begin with this book. It is an ancient argument, and one which is well-founded and has stood the test of time. Josephus, a Roman-Jewish historian, made this same argument in the first century A.D., citing much older material:

> "Now all the writers of barbarian histories make mention of this flood and of this ark; among whom is Berosus the Chaldean; for when he is describing the circumstances of the flood, he goes on thus: "It is said there is still some part of this ship in Armenia, at the mountain of the Cordyaeans; and that some people carry off pieces of the bitumen, which they take away, and use chiefly as amulets for the averting of mischiefs. Hieronymous the Egyptian, also, who wrote the Phoenician Antiquities, and Mnaseas, and a great many more, make mention of the same. Nay, Nicolaus of Damascus, in his ninety-sixth book, hath a particular relation about them, where he speaks thus: "There is a great mountain in Armenia, over Minyas, called Baris, upon which it is reported that many who fled at the time of the Deluge were saved; and that one who was carried in an ark came on shore upon the top of it; and that the remains of the timber were a great while preserved. This might be the man about whom Moses, the legislator of the Jews wrote."[25]

The main thesis of this book is an ancient argument. In fact, for most of history the truth of this global Flood was not even questioned! The Flood was acknowledged even by those who did not hold to a Judeo-Christian worldview. It is only in the past 250 years or so that the truth of the Flood has been increasingly questioned.

Opposing Argument #1: Geological Argument

The nonbelieving community has not been silent. Counterarguments had to be developed to resist the force of the cumulative testimony of distant nations with their Flood traditions. There are a handful of arguments that recur. The first one may be called the *geological argument*, which goes like this: *"However universal flood stories might be, they are nevertheless mythical. Our current understanding of geology informs us that there is no evidence of a global flood. Therefore, these Flood stories must be flatly rejected on geological grounds."*[26]

Now, from the standpoint of consensus, the geological argument is reputed to be strong. But so is an emperor with no clothes! Upon critical examination, this argument is not strong at all. We have addressed this argument in the previous pages, and Tables 1 through 3 provide many forms of evidence that the biblical view of geology, and not the evolutionary, uniformitarian one, is true.[27]

> "All the writers of barbarian histories make mention of this flood and of this ark" (Josephus)

The rocks cry out that there was a global Flood and demonstrate that God's Word is true!

#2: Natural / Psychological Origin Argument

Many secular anthropologists do not invoke geology, instead making an anthropological argument. We may call this second argument the *natural / psychological origin argument*. It states that "These Flood traditions arose by environmental factors and/or human thought patterns, perhaps an attempt to explain the world around them. Their resemblance with the Genesis Flood account is therefore not an indication that such a Flood really occurred, but a reflection of a common human experience."

On the surface, this argument seems reasonable and plausible. It has a certain elegance that seems promising in explanatory value. The problem is, it does not fit the data, which are the Flood traditions we possess! It cannot account for the specific and multi-faceted similarities that continually recur in Flood texts. Otherwise, how do we explain the recurring specific details such as an old man who is warned of a coming Flood, a Flood that is sent because of human evil and violence, and the preparation of an enormous floating vessel? Do these details arise by chance, all over the world among cultures who were separated geographically, linguistically, religiously, and otherwise?

What about the detail that this Ark landed on a high mountain, and the survivors later came down and repopulated the earth? What about the two birds which were sent in search of dry land, the return of one bird with something in its beak, and the sign this indicated

25. Josephus, *Antiquities of the Jews*, in *The Works of Josephus*, trans. William Whiston (Peabody, MA: Hendrickson, 1987), 1.3.6.
26. For example, Stephen Jay Gould wrote that "Geology proclaimed no worldwide flood but rather a long sequence of local events." Stephen Jay Gould, "Creationism: Genesis vs. Geology,", in *The Flood Myth*, ed. Alan Dundes (Berkeley: University of California Press, 1988), pp. 433.
27. For much more information, see *Carved in Stone* by Timothy Clarey, *Earth's Catastrophic Past* by Andrew Snelling, and *Grand Canyon: A Different View* by Tom Vail et. al.

that the Flood was coming to an end? What about Noah's burnt offering sacrifice and a tower of confusion event afterward? Can a natural / psychological origin argument explain these similarities in detail? No, of course it cannot explain these things.

#3: Local Flood Argument

The third argument (local flood) is much like the second. It goes something like this: *"A local flood occurred and gave rise to Flood legends which were later told in a wider geographical part of the world. This could be the Black Sea Flood or a particularly devastating flood in Mesopotamia. Additional floods in other parts of the world (e.g., Australia, the Yellow River in China, or Pacific Islands) could be the inspiration behind Flood stories in other parts of the world. Thus, there was not one global flood, but many local floods."*[28]

Similar to the second argument, this local flood argument has a certain veneer of plausibility. After all, local flooding does happen. That plausibility evaporates, however, as soon as we examine the evidence. Contrary to the desires of some, there is an inherent unity in these Flood stories told around the world. There are elements that recur. There is a similarity both in general outline and specific details. How then do multiple local floods from different parts of the world produce a story that is so similar in unnecessary details? No, it is one story that has pervaded the whole world.

Now I am not here to deny that the Black Sea Flood took place, or that any other local flood took place. Quite the opposite. I believe in the global Flood, and because of that I believe in many local floods as well.[29]

However, what I am objecting to is the notion that the Black Sea Flood, or any other local flood, could inspire people all over the world to believe there was a global flood, if in fact there was no global flood. In other words, I am not falling for the bait and switch.

Suppose the Black Sea Flood had left a strong impression on some people from Anatolia (modern-day Turkey). Would they then develop a flood story in global terms, about the preparation of an Ark, the boarding of animals and birds, the lifting of this Ark by waters that carried it above even the mountains, its landing on a high mountain, the sending of birds in search for life, and other details which contradict the actual event? Would they take this news across the whole world? Would they succeed in convincing hundreds of tribes, each with their own strange language, and with their own traditions that they are zealous to preserve, to embrace a new tradition that such a global flood really took place? Would they persuade tribes that had no knowledge of this flood to adopt it and consider it sacred? We are unable to believe such a story.

#4: Christian / Missionary Influence

The fourth argument alleges that missionary influence is at work in these Flood traditions which so remarkably parallel Genesis. It goes something like this. *"If these Flood traditions closely resemble Genesis, it is because of the influence of Christian missionaries (or others). In other words, the tribes did not originally have these Flood traditions, but missionaries got there early and taught local tribes about Noah's Flood and then the tribes adopted or adapted this story, making it their own."*

I will certainly grant that we sometimes find narratives in which Christian influence is a factor. References to Noah, Satan, Jesus, Mary, or other biblical names often occur in such cases and are clear indicators of influence. Historical evidence of missionary activity often validates such suspicions of outside influence. But this is precisely the type of material we have rejected from this book entirely! After all, we have very little interest in later, inauthentic traditions, but rather in ancient, authentic ones! The latter is the type of material we have relentlessly pursued in writing this book.

And yet after that screening stage, hundreds of Flood texts remain, which this argument does not have the power to deal with. Why? Because the argument was never built on data in the first place. Rather, this argument is the expression of a desire, a wish: an anti-biblical desire for original, authentic Flood traditions confirming Genesis not to exist. For if they are proven to exist, then we have to deal with Genesis and the God it reveals.

Let's elaborate now. It is time to put away the argument of missionary influence once and for all. This argument fails for several reasons. First, many of the Flood texts and artifacts predate the existence of missionaries and

28. Exemplary of this is a statement from Dorothy Vitaliano: "Flood traditions are nearly universal ... mainly because floods in the plural are the most universal of geologic catastrophes." Dorothy Vitaliano, *Legends of the Earth: Their Geologic Origins* (Bloomington, IN: Indiana University, 1973), p. 178.
29. Noah's Flood involved catastrophic plate tectonics on a global, unprecedented scale. This upheaval and violent tectonic activity did not simply "stop on a dime" after the Flood. A pendulum, once it is set in motion, takes time to come to rest. In the same way, we can expect that the Flood set in motion powerful tectonic, hydrologic, volcanic, and meteorologic processes which had to slowly return to a state of equilibrium. This recovery period must have taken centuries! Importantly, we can expect that the Flood left many wet sediment deposits which could have easily been breached by lakes and seas in the same way that a dam is broken. The breaching of a wall of sediment by a large lake or water flow, after Noah's Flood, is a perfect recipe for a local flood. This is precisely the condition to which we would attribute the formation of the Grand Canyon and the Lake Missoula flood, according to the great work of our creationist geologists.

predate the birth of Christ! Recall Josephus and the ancient sources he cites, adding that "all barbarian histories make mention of this Flood and of this Ark." What "missionaries" could have possibly influenced these "barbarians" in the most ancient past? We also have Flood accounts predating Christ from India, from Chinese classic texts, from Chinese and Indian minorities, and other places. We have a pyramid dedicated to the Flood in Cholula, Mexico, built over 2,000 years ago. How can it be "missionary influence" if there were no missionaries?

Or consider the ancient Mayan Popol Vuh text, and the ancient paintings of the Aztecs and other Mexican tribes, which predate the arrival of European powers by at least several centuries. Or the ancient rock carvings in Arizona and South America which depict this Flood.[30] Exactly how are missionaries responsible for these?

Second, the argument of missionary influence assumes there was a period of time between the arrival of missionaries and when these Flood stories were finally recorded. That is simply not the case! Many of these traditions were recorded immediately, as soon as they could linguistically be accessed. Such as that recorded in Cuba in 1493, within one year of discovery of that island by the Spanish, or the very early material we have from the Polynesian Islands, and various other parts of the world. Or hear the words of Myron Eells, regarding the tribes of the Pacific Northwest: "When the earliest missionaries came among the Spokanes, Nez Perces, and Cayuses, who with the Yakimas live in the eastern part of the Territory, they found that those Indians had their tradition of a flood, in which one man and wife were saved on a raft. Each of those three tribes also, together with the Flathead tribes, has their separate Ararat in connection with this event."[31] It was "the earliest missionaries," not the latest, who recorded these things. There simply was no time for influence to have possibly occurred.

Third, even in cases where some time passed (say, a generation or two) between contact and recording, the argument from missionary influence assumes these tribes were easily influenced to abandon or alter their sacred traditions. I think this is rather insulting to these foreign cultures, and it is simply not true, as we will show momentarily.

To put it another way, the proponent of this argument assumes that knowledge of this Flood is "shallow," new, embraced only recently. But it is actually deeply rooted! They are like one who attempts to pull a small weed from the ground, but they are actually pulling on a mighty tree! And it will not be uprooted, for the ways in which the Flood is commemorated by tribes and nations give evidence of deep-rootedness, sacredness, and antiquity. This will be abundantly clear in this book, as in *Volume 1*.

They are like one who attempts to pull a small weed from the ground, but they are actually pulling on a mighty tree! And it will not be uprooted, for the ways in which the Flood is commemorated by tribes and nations give evidence of deep-rootedness, sacredness, and antiquity.

To give a few examples, we will learn of annual sacrifices and memorials held in honor of the Flood, which the natives insisted were observed for thousands of years! Chants, songs, and poems commemorating the Flood, performed solemnly, and with ancient words testifying to the antiquity of these practices. Taboos, proverbs, and sayings which stem from their knowledge of the Flood, which every member of the tribe could easily recite. We have also learned of tribes which made yearly pilgrimages to a mountain where they said the "great canoe" landed, gathering there with neighboring tribes to remember their ancestors' deliverance from the Flood. They were deeply convinced their local mountain was where the canoe landed. Others held the turtle dove, bluebird, or other bird in highest honor, even instructing their dogs to do them no harm, "because this bird notified our ancestor that the Flood was over."

You see, the Flood wasn't just another story to these tribes. It was sacred! And it was deeply rooted in their beliefs. To many tribes, like the Incans and Lenape, the Flood was even part of their identity and pedigree!

But let's suppose, for the sake of argument, that Christian missionary influence on native traditions was successful. Even if you could win over the elders of the tribe and get them to adopt a Flood story, one with parallels to Genesis but also native undertones and variations—I ask then, could you really produce this kind of material I have just mentioned? Could you get them to say that have been meeting on this mountain for hundreds or thousands of years to remember this Flood and to offer sacrifices to God? Could you get them to believe they must make a sacrifice to the waters to avoid another global Flood? Could you get them to sing native-sounding songs of the Flood? To refer frequently and naturally to their great ancestor "Trow," "Bok Seugucur," or any other local name for Noah? Or could you make the knowledge of this Flood so organic and implicit, that they sang about it in their weddings, like the Miao? In beautiful ballads, like the Axi? Could you do this a thousand times over all across the world? Certainly not!

30. In connection with all the material mentioned here from North and South America, see my previous book, *Echoes of Ararat* (*"Volume 1"*).
31. Rev. Myron Eells, "Traditions of the Deluge Among the Tribes of the North-West," *The American Antiquarian and Oriental Journal*, vol. 1 (1878), p. 70.

Fifth, it cannot account for the great consistency that we find among tribes that are linguistically or historically related. Their Flood traditions are typically consistent, not only in their matches with Genesis but also their peculiar differences! These differences themselves are signs of authenticity, and yet the differences are consistent among language families and regions. How is it possible for Christian missionaries to have influenced the Flood story among, say, 10 to 20 different tribes of a given language family, in the same peculiar way? Can anyone really deny the authenticity of dozens of Vietnamese and Southeast Asian Flood stories which are essentially the same story? Can anyone really deny the authenticity of dozens of Chinese Flood stories, which are so consistent with one another? What about New Guinean and North American versions? No. This consistency is evidence of authenticity and originality.

Sixth, related to the point above, this argument does not account for the clearly native material that characterizes these Flood traditions. These traditions contain a weight of native material (at odds with the Bible) and other internal evidence that demonstrates they are not the result of missionary teaching or influence.

Seventh, it does not account for the finding of Flood traditions among very isolated tribes—those with great geographical, linguistic, and cultural barriers to outsiders.

Eighth, it does not account for the fact that, as researchers, we have actively screened out versions where obvious Christian influence took place.[32]

Ninth, this objection requires special pleading. If missionaries influenced local traditions, why do we not find several hundred versions of other well-known biblical accounts, such as the virgin birth, the Trinity, the death and resurrection of Jesus, David and Goliath, the Exodus, and so forth? Why is the Flood—along with (to a lesser degree) Creation, the Garden of Eden, and the Tower of Babel—the only biblical event that these tribes know about? Why do they only know the first 11 chapters of Genesis, and nothing else of the Bible? Or what kind of terrible missionary would only teach his hearers about the Flood? Only a fictitious missionary.

In the end, the missionary influence argument requires calling too many people liars. A position that dismisses hundreds of expert witnesses as "liars" for its own sake and self-preservation is no commendable position. Moreover, it requires a grand conspiracy: a conspiracy which also requires time-travel and other miracles, for which reasons it must be rejected.

#5: Babylonian Borrowing

A fifth and very prominent argument is that of borrowing from an earlier Babylonian story. This argument essentially states that "*Moses (or whoever wrote Genesis) plagiarized a flood story from an earlier, Babylonian source—likely the Epic of Gilgamesh, which itself is mythical in content.*"[33]

I have refuted the Babylonian borrowing argument at length in Appendix A: "The Myth of the Flood Myth." In that article I summarize the problems with this argument as follows:

1. This argument relies on the post hoc, ergo propter hoc fallacy (after this, therefore because of this). In making this assumption, they do not account for the possibility that there is a document which predates both Genesis and the *Epic of Gilgamesh* (or other Babylonian cognates), to which Moses (the author of Genesis) had access.
2. They do not account for the fact that Moses tells us explicitly that he had sources.[34]
3. Genesis itself provides strong internal evidence of the sources of Moses' writing: they are ancient sources from the patriarchs themselves, including Joseph, Jacob, Isaac, Abraham, and even Noah!
4. This argument is contradicted by historical trends from the ancient Near East, which point to simpler accounts giving rise to more complex, embellished ones—rather than the reverse. This points to Genesis as containing the original account, and the *Epic of Gilgamesh* as a later account.
5. This argument is contradicted by flood traditions from across the world, which are ancient and original, and agree with Genesis rather than the Babylonian version. Specifically, these foreign traditions agree with Genesis, and not the Babylonian version, on several particular points such as the sending of birds, the cause of the flood, and the type and shape of floating vessel.
6. Unlike the Babylonian version, the Genesis account stands up to scrutiny, and finds confirmation from multiple fields of science such as geology, naval design, and paleontology. This attests to its authenticity. After all, a false testimony will fall apart under critical cross-examination, but a true testimony holds up.

In short, the Babylonian borrowing argument relies on fallacious reasoning, popular misconceptions about

32. For example, some recorded Flood traditions contain word-for-word quotes from Genesis, or contain the words "Noah", "Jesus", "the Trinity", etc. The signs of missionary influence are generally obvious.
33. See, for example: *The Flood Myth*, ed. Alan Dundes (Berkeley: University of California Press, 1988), pp. 3-4. Sir James George Frazer, *"The Great Flood,"* in *The Flood Myth* (Berkeley: University of California Press, 1988), p. 120.
34. Among others, see Genesis 5:1 which refers to a "book," and see the 11 uses of the Hebrew word *toledot*, which means genealogy, family record, or history.

Genesis, and cannot survive careful examination. For these reasons, this argument should be retired once and for all.

#6: Anthropologically Global but Geographically Local

But could someone modify the local flood argument and posit an anthropologically global but geographically local flood? Some within the Christian world (though contrary to Scripture) have proposed this, such as Hugh Ross with Reasons to Believe. The idea is that at one point, all people lived in one place and experienced a flood that was "universal" from their perspective, but geologically local. There are many problems with such a notion:

Scripture militates against it. For example, Genesis 7:17-24 leaves absolutely no room for a local flood interpretation.

1. There is no geological evidence in Mesopotamia of such a large local flood. Nor can another part of the world be proposed, for the geographic descriptions in Genesis require a landing in northern Mesopotamia or its immediate vicinity.
2. It is not sufficient for the Flood to be anthropologically global. It must be zoologically global, according to Genesis! No local flood can be zoologically universal, and if it cannot, then the Bible rejects it as false.
3. This view calls God a liar. In Genesis 9:9-17, He gave the rainbow as a sign of promise that He would never again destroy the world with a flood. But if that were a local flood, then God lied, for there have been many deadly and destructive floods on a local scale. But God is no liar, for He spoke of a global Flood.
4. A local flood interpretation of the Genesis Flood lacks internal consistency. How was it a local flood if the waters were "fifteen cubits" above the mountains, according to Genesis 7:20? Why did birds need to be taken aboard the Ark? Why was the construction of the Ark necessary at all? What kind of local flood lasts 370 days and strands a boat near the top of a mountain? And why, thousands of years later, does the Apostle Peter say that God destroyed the world that existed at that time with the Flood, if in fact only a small geographical part of the world was flooded? (2 Peter 3:6)

#7: Universal Myth

But wouldn't it be possible to modify the previous argument in the following way? *"The flood story is a universal myth.*[35] *Sure, every nation knows this story. It goes back a long time. But it's just that: a story. There's not a shred of truth to it."*

This argument has a coherency problem, because it grants the truth of data which will undo the position itself. What do I mean by that? The one who makes this argument holds to an evolutionary view of history. He holds that humans evolved over long periods of time, beginning from an ape-like ancestor and progressing into modern humans.

However, he is also granting that Flood stories are genuine and original. But these Flood texts go back to one original story from one place. Given the universal scope of Flood stories, they must go back to the very cradle of humanity. But from the evolutionist's point of view, this puts the Flood story back at the point when humans diverged from an ape-like ancestor. This means that if we traveled back in time, we would find ape-like human ancestors recounting the story of the Genesis Flood! Is the evolutionist prepared for this? Ape-men telling about the Ark, the warning from God, the sin that prompted the Flood, the boarding of animals, the lifting of the Ark high upon the waters, the landing on a mountain, the sending of a raven and a dove, a sacrifice to God, and the repopulation of the earth. After all, these are recurring themes worldwide, which must be in the original. Therefore, if even "ape-men" (created by the imagination of evolutionists) would testify to the truth of Genesis, how will the evolutionist argue that Genesis is not true?

Second, how did the Flood story get going in the first place? For a story like the Flood to be told so universally, it had to be believed. That means that if, at any time, these first humans traveled and met other people who were not descended from the Flood survivors, the story would be exposed as untrue and abandoned.

The Flood story has to do with death and decimation of a previously much larger population by watery destruction. But we have just stated that the Flood story must have been present at the very cradle of humanity. Then in what sense was there a larger, earlier population prior to this cradle? This is beginning to sound more and more like Genesis. Is the evolutionist prepared to accept these consequences?

Third, the evolutionist is about to lose the prized doctrine of "Out of Africa." African Flood stories do not show any signs of centrality, whereas Genesis does. Therefore, this Flood story—and humanity with it—must not originate in Africa. It is not "Out of Africa," but "Out of Mesopotamia," the exact place that Genesis says humanity fanned out from after Babel. The evolutionist pays a heavy price, and we come still nearer to the biblical testimony of history.

35. Refer to our definition of terms later in this introduction regarding "myth" and "legend."

Fourth, the evolutionist has a time problem. How will Flood traditions with such specific details be preserved, through oral transmission, over long ages of time? It is one thing to say—as I am doing—that Flood stories were preserved for over 4,000 years. It is another to claim they survived for well over 100,000 years according to the evolutionist's required timeframe. Indeed, it is with difficulty that Flood texts have been passed down even for 4,000 years! Some of these barely survived as fragments, and some are so worn down as to be barely recognizable. To ask imperfect human beings to pass them down for at least another 100,000 years strains credibility.

It is a major thrust of this book that Tower of Babel stories are just as real and original as Flood stories.

Fifth, a most terrifying problem for those who would advance the "universal myth" argument comes from an unexpected and overlooked source: the Tower of Babel story. Now, if we accept that Flood stories are real and original, we can hardly deny that Tower of Babel stories are authentic as well. This book will present dozens of them. There are not fewer than 60 Tower of Babel stories worldwide. To be clear: these are just the ones we have found. No doubt, many more were lost. In fact, it is a major thrust of this book that Tower of Babel stories are just as real and original as Flood stories.

Now if Tower of Babel stories are authentic and universal, then they go back to the birthplace of humanity just like Flood stories. But what is the Tower of Babel story? It has to do, of course, with a great tower construction project which was started. As the tower grew taller, God brought it to nothing, changed the language of the audacious builders, and the families of the earth were scattered.

Now where is the coherence in a Tower of Babel story, about scattering and separation, in a cradle of humanity that is, by definition, neither scattered nor separated? How in the world does such a story get going in the first place? It is the height of absurdity and self-contradiction. Who would tell such a story? Unless Genesis is true.

You see, the "universal myth" argument undoes itself on account of what it grants. Unless the evolutionist is prepared to admit that the Tower of Babel event actually happened, in which case it is no longer universal myth, but universal truth.

We can come at this from another angle. 19th and early 20th century secularists who denied the authenticity of Flood traditions matching Genesis knew something. They knew that it would be fatal to their denial of Genesis to admit the authenticity of Flood legends. And they were correct. That is why they resisted so strenuously the affirmation of authenticity of Flood stories which matched Genesis. "Missionary influence!" "Christian teaching!" they proclaimed, in hope against hope.

Modern secularists, however, are increasingly retreating from this claim, because it is increasingly absurd to deny the authenticity of Flood traditions.[36] They are changing their tune, from "missionary influence" to "original myth," not willingly, but reluctantly. And in part, they are to be commended for that admission, for they are correct that these Flood traditions can no longer be denied their genuineness.

The problem is that they are denying the consequences of their retreat. Who can retreat in a fierce battle without suffering losses? They are retreating at great cost, because the admission of authenticity of these traditions has consequences, and the consequences are the undermining of their "universal myth" position—a consequence that their predecessors fought desperately to avoid. You see, both the early secularists and the modern secularists are correct about something. The problem is they are correct in a way that cancels out each other's positions.

Positive Analytical and Predictive Value

This book is about more than refutation of anti-biblical arguments against Flood legends. This book is about the positive explanatory power of Genesis and the biblical worldview. First of all, tribal traditions from around the world clearly support Genesis. This is one more piece of evidence inviting us to read Scripture and take God at His Word which is trustworthy.

But second, there are a great many recurring themes or motifs in tribal traditions all over the world. Now if there were some paradigm which united them and made sense of them, that would be of extraordinary anthropological value. For example, what if we had a paradigm that could explain not only Flood stories, but also fire fetching stories, earth diver stories, incestuous union stories, and sky woman stories? What if we had a paradigm which could explain forbidden fruit / tree stories, raven stories, brothers quarreling stories, and "shooting the sun" stories?

We have such a paradigm in the Genesis view of history. But having dismissed it long ago, Genesis has been lost to the secular anthropological community as an explanatory tool. Nevertheless, God's Word remains true. The book of Genesis has the power to explain traditions of many types that we find all over the world. This is a bold assertion which we will further develop in

36. See for example: E. J. Michael Witzel, *The Origin of the World's Mythologies* (Oxford: Oxford University Press, 2012), pp. 178-179.

Appendix B of this book. Indeed, the book of Genesis turns out to be a unique key for unlocking knowledge in several fields, which many of our creationist geologists, biologists, geneticists, paleontologists, and Hebrew scholars are finding out.[37]

At the same time, we speak confidently to our secular, evolutionary anthropologists who may be reading this book. We warmly offer an alternative, which we believe is more consistent, more satisfying, and offers a more predictive view of human history, of comparative folklore, of genetics, and of linguistics.[38] This is nothing to boast about on our part, for we have done little more than embrace the meaning of Genesis and apply its logical consequences.

More About Sources and Terminology

The Sources

The ultimate sources for the material contained in this Volume are the representatives of the tribes and nations who have lived in Asia and the Pacific from ancient times. Their histories and oral traditions have been recorded in a variety of settings, by a variety of individuals, at times ranging from 1,000 years before Christ to the present century. Those who recorded the information are historians, scientists, indigenous writers themselves, government officials, missionaries, ethnographers, and many others. As to the Flood traditions themselves, some are clearer than others. Some bear uncanny, specific resemblances to the Genesis account. Other Flood traditions are vague or fragmentary (yet even these have value, as we will see). Much has already been lost, due to the decimation of entire cultures, and due to imperfect oral transmission and memory.

We are thankful to the various historians and researchers whose work has made this volume possible, and who have provided very helpful leads in locating original sources. Many of these have been documented already. Others we found through an extensive research process, whether online or in libraries, or in rare books obtained from foreign countries. Overall, the goal of this book was to assemble all of the relevant material so that it could be evaluated in a comprehensive manner.

We considered it very important to locate primary sources, which give the earliest and most direct access available to the information in question. Also, it was essential that the oral traditions of the Flood be aboriginal in origin, rather than influenced by Christian or European ideas. We screened out and discarded those Flood traditions which had obvious signs of influence by settlers and missionaries. For instance, any oral traditions with biblical names such as Noah, Jesus, and the Holy Spirit obviously bear the marks of Christian influence, and were thus discarded.

Overall, this process of researching netted 300 people groups from East Asia and the Pacific with Flood or other Genesis-related stories.[39] Now if we love the truth, we must ask ourselves one important question: Why? Why are there so many native, oral traditions that sound so similar to the Genesis Flood? We contend that the only explanation that can truly account for all these flood traditions, which are so similar to the Genesis account, is that the Flood happened, just as Genesis says.

"Myth" and "Legend"

A word about terminology: In this book we are using "myth" and "legend" in the popular, colloquial sense, and not in the sense used in the anthropological and folklore community.

"Myth," as we are using the term, means a story that is untrue or fictional. Since we believe the global Flood to be a true, historical event, we have chosen not to refer to indigenous accounts as "Flood myths," in order to avoid confusion for the reader. However, we would not be wrong if we used the term "Flood myth" in a purely academic context, where myths are understood as "stories of the beginning" according to Mineke Schipper[40]: stories of how something (the world, humanity, or anything else) came into being, and even why they came into being.

"Legend," as we are using the term, simply means a story that has been passed down from generation to generation, without making a judgment as to its truth or historicity. Therefore, we are using the word "legend" synonymously with "tradition." This is to be

37. In general, see the most recent *Proceedings of the 9th International Conference on Creationism*, held in 2023 at Cedarville University. On geology, see *Carved in Stone* by Timothy Clarey (Dallas: ICR, 2020). On genetics and biology, see *Traced* by Nathaniel Jeanson (Green Forest, AR: Master Books, 2022) and the ongoing work of biologist Robert Carter. On paleontology, see Kurt P. Wise, "The Fossil Record." Presentation at the Is Genesis History? Conference, June 19-23, 2017, Dickson, Tennessee. https://youtu.be/wKuFQLkFW7o On Hebrew insights, see: William D. Barrick, "Exegetical Analysis of Psalm 104:8 and Its Possible Implications for Interpreting the Geological Record," *Proceedings of the International Conference on Creationism*, vol. 8 (2018).
38. On the mounting list of problems with the "Out of Africa Model", or OoAM, and positive evidence for the biblical creation timeline, see: Jeff Tomkins, "Out of Babel—not Africa: genetic evidence for a biblical model of human origins," *Journal of Creation*, vol. 34, no. 1 (April 2020). Retrieved from: https://creation.com/genetics-supports-a-biblical-model-of-human-origins
39. Often we find than one Flood text per tribe. For example, consider the 220 Formosan Flood texts found by Valdis among 17 tribes in Taiwan! See: Valdis Gauss, *The Formosan Great Flood Myths: An Analysis of the Oral Traditions of Ancient Taiwan* (Edwin Mellen Press, 2022).
40. Mineke Schipper, "Humanity's Beginnings in Creation and Origin Myths from Around the World," *China's Creation and Origin Myths* (Brill: Boston, 2011), pp. 3-4.

distinguished from the more technical definition of legend, which is a story based on some real person or event, but with a level of exaggeration, fiction, or distortion. Now we would be the first to admit that the "Flood legends" which we find around the world have, generally, some fanciful or erroneous elements mixed in, or some distortion, on top of an otherwise true account of the global Flood. However, by the mere use of the term "legend" we are not making a judgment as to a text's accuracy or error.

Recognizing that "legend" can be a bit confusing as to its meaning, we have limited its frequency of use in the pages that follow. We have much more frequently used "tradition," which by all accounts is certainly a more neutral term. "Tradition" also seems to more properly reflect the sacredness and great care with which the memory of the Flood has been passed down, as opposed to fairy tales and other stories.

Whether we use the term "tradition," "legend," "account," or any other term, we would be quick to add that Genesis is the only inerrant and infallible record of that event. This conviction of ours comes from the Word of God itself. Yet we would add that comparative analysis will confirm that conviction as well, and we believe that is demonstrated in the rest of this book, as it is in *Volume 1*.

A Guide to this Volume

The more than 300 Flood traditions and other Genesis-related traditions in this volume come from all over East Asia and the Pacific, including Indonesia, Australia, Taiwan, the Philippines, Japan, and Polynesia. They are organized by regions, beginning in China, and proceeding to other parts of the Orient in turn.

We would also encourage the reader to check out the material in the appendices, which contains further information on related topics. These include:

- Appendix A: The Myth of the Flood Myth: Refuting the Claim that Genesis Borrows from a Babylonian Source
- Appendix B: Variant Flood Themes and Their Common Source
- Appendix C: Bibliography
- Appendix D: Recommendations for Further Study
- Appendix E: Topical Index

While the Flood is the primary subject addressed in the traditions contained in this volume, it is by no means the only one. You will find many traditions of the Tower of Babel, Creation, the Garden of Eden, and even Cain and Abel!

Furthermore, we are convinced with Paul that "God has not left Himself without witness in any nation on earth." (Acts 14:17) Therefore, we have collected many "altars to an unknown god" (Acts 17:23), or cultural features which can serve (or have served) as bridges of understanding, leading to acceptance of the Gospel in foreign cultures. We are passionate about the advance of the Gospel around the world, including among all the tribes and regions embraced by this book. There are also several moving stories about the work of Jesus and the advance of the Gospel in various nations.

We hope you find the content of this book interesting. We pray that this book increases your faith in God and your confidence in the scriptures, beginning with the first and very formative book of Genesis. Genesis, like so many books of the Old Testament, prophesied of the coming Savior of the world, God in the flesh—Jesus, who would come to make atonement for sin and provide the way to a right relationship with God.

Finally, in the same way that Jesus acknowledged the global Genesis Flood (Matthew 24:37-39), it is important that we acknowledge it too. As we have noted previously, denial of the Bible's message about historical, earthly things (including the global Flood) leads to denial of the Bible's message about spiritual things. Let us heed the warning of Jesus, the ultimate author of all the Bible, who said the following:

> "If I told you earthly things and you do not believe, how will you believe if I tell you heavenly things?" (John 3:12)

THE GENESIS FLOOD ACCOUNT

The Book of Genesis, Chapters 6 – 8, and portions of Chapters 9 and 11 (LSB translation):

Chapter 6 (Pre-Flood)

Now it happened, when men began to multiply on the
face of the land, and daughters were born to them, **2**
that the sons of God saw that the daughters of men
were good in appearance; and they took wives for
themselves, whomever they chose. **3** Then Yahweh said,
"My Spirit shall not strive with man forever because he
indeed is flesh; nevertheless his days shall be 120 years."
4 The Nephilim were on the earth in those days, and
also afterward, when the sons of God came in to the
daughters of men, and they bore children to them. Those
were the mighty men who were of old, men of renown.
5 Then Yahweh saw that the evil of man was great on the
earth, and that every intent of the thoughts of his heart
was only evil continually. **6** And Yahweh regretted that
He had made man on the earth, and He was grieved
in His heart. **7** And Yahweh said, "I will blot out man
whom I have created from the face of the land, from man
to animals to creeping things and to birds of the sky;
for I regret that I have made them." **8** But Noah found
favor in the eyes of Yahweh. **9** These are the generations
of Noah. Noah was a righteous man, blameless among
those in his generations; Noah walked with God. **10**
And Noah became the father of three sons: Shem, Ham,
and Japheth. **11** Now the earth was corrupt before God,
and the earth was filled with violence. **12** And God saw
the earth, and behold, it was corrupt; for all flesh had
corrupted their way upon the earth. **13** Then God said to
Noah, "The end of all flesh has come before Me; for the
earth is filled with violence because of them; and behold,
I am about to destroy them with the earth. **14** Make for
yourself an ark of gopher wood; you shall make the ark
with rooms, and you shall cover it inside and out with
pitch. **15** Now this is how you shall make it: the length
of the ark 300 cubits, its breadth 50 cubits, and its height
30 cubits. **16** You shall make a window for the ark, and
complete it to one cubit from the top; and set the door
of the ark in the side of it; you shall make it with lower,
second, and third decks. **17** As for Me, behold I am
bringing the flood of water upon the earth, to destroy all
flesh in which is the breath of life, from under heaven;
everything that is on the earth shall breathe its last.
18 But I will establish My covenant with you; and you
shall enter the ark—you and your sons and your wife
and your sons' wives with you. **19** And of every living
thing of all flesh, you shall bring two of every kind into
the ark, to keep them alive with you; they shall be male
and female. **20** Of the birds after their kind, and of the
animals after their kind, of every creeping thing of the
ground after its kind, two of every kind will come to you
to keep them alive. **21** As for you, take for yourself some
of all food which is edible, and gather it to yourself; and
it shall be for food for you and for them." **22** Thus Noah
did; according to all that God had commanded him, so
he did.

Chapter 7 (Early Flood)

Then Yahweh said to Noah, "Enter the ark, you and all
your household, for you alone I have seen to be righteous
before Me in this generation. **2** You shall take with you
of every clean animal by sevens, a male and his female;
and of the animals that are not clean, two, a male and
his female; **3** also of the birds of the sky, by sevens, male
and female, to keep their seed alive on the face of all the
earth. **4** For after seven more days, I will send rain on
the earth forty days and forty nights; and I will blot out
from the face of the land every living thing that I have
made." **5** And Noah did according to all that Yahweh had
commanded him. **6** Now Noah was six hundred years
old when the flood of water came upon the earth. **7** Then
Noah and his sons and his wife and his sons' wives with
him entered the ark because of the water of the flood.
8 Of clean animals and animals that are not clean and
birds and everything that creeps on the ground, **9** by
twos they came to Noah into the ark, male and female,
as God had commanded Noah. **10** Now it happened
after the seven days, that the water of the flood came
upon the earth. **11** In the six hundredth year of Noah's
life, in the second month, on the seventeenth day of the
month, on this day all the fountains of the great deep

split open, and the floodgates of the sky were opened.
12 Then the rain came upon the earth for forty days and
forty nights. **13** On this very day Noah and Shem and
Ham and Japheth, the sons of Noah, and Noah's wife and
the three wives of his sons with them, entered the ark, **14**
they and every beast after its kind, and all the cattle after
their kind, and every creeping thing that creeps on the
earth after its kind, and every bird after its kind—every
fowl, every winged creature. **15** So they came to Noah
into the ark, by twos of all flesh in which was the breath
of life. 16 And those that entered, male and female of all
flesh, entered as God had commanded him; and Yahweh
closed it behind him. **17** Then the flood came upon the
earth for forty days, and the water multiplied and lifted
up the ark, so that it rose above the earth. **18** And the
water prevailed and multiplied greatly upon the earth,
and the ark went on the surface of the water. **19** And
the water prevailed more and more upon the earth, so
that all the high mountains under all the heavens were
covered. **20** The water prevailed fifteen cubits higher, and
the mountains were covered. **21** And all flesh that moved
on the earth breathed its last, that is birds and cattle and
beasts and every swarming thing that swarms upon the
earth, as well as all mankind. **22** All in whose nostrils
was the breath of the spirit of life—of all that was on
the dry land—died. **23** Thus He blotted out every living
thing that was upon the face of the land, from man to
animals to creeping things and to birds of the sky, and
they were blotted out from the earth; and only Noah
remained, and those that were with him in the ark. **24**
And the water prevailed upon the earth 150 days.

Chapter 8 (Late Flood)

Then God remembered Noah and all the beasts and all
the cattle that were with him in the ark; and God caused
a wind to pass over the earth, and the water subsided.
2 Also the fountains of the deep and the floodgates
of the sky were closed, and the rain from the sky was
restrained; **3** and the water receded from the earth, going
forth and returning, and at the end of 150 days the water
decreased. **4** In the seventh month, on the seventeenth
day of the month, the ark rested upon the mountains
of Ararat. **5** Now the water decreased steadily until the
tenth month; in the tenth month, on the first day of the
month, the tops of the mountains appeared. **6** Then it
happened at the end of forty days, that Noah opened the
window of the ark which he had made; 7 and he sent out
a raven, and it went out flying back and forth until the
water was dried up from the earth. **8** Then he sent out a
dove from him, to see if the water was abated from the
face of the land; **9** but the dove found no resting place
for the sole of its foot, so it returned to him into the ark,
for the water was on the surface of all the earth. Then he
stretched out his hand and took it and brought it into
the ark to himself. **10** Then he waited yet another seven
days; and again he sent out the dove from the ark. **11**
And the dove came to him toward evening, and behold,
in its beak was a freshly picked olive leaf. So Noah knew
that the water was abated from the earth. **12** Then he
waited yet another seven days and sent out the dove; but
it did not return to him again. **13** Now it happened in
the six hundred and first year, in the first month, on the
first of the month, the water was dried up from the earth.
Then Noah removed the covering of the ark and looked,
and behold, the surface of the ground was dried up. **14**
In the second month, on the twenty-seventh day of the
month, the earth was dry. **15** Then God spoke to Noah,
saying, **16** "Go out of the ark, you and your wife and
your sons and your sons' wives with you. **17** Bring out
with you every living thing of all flesh that is with you,
birds and animals and every creeping thing that creeps
on the earth, that they may swarm on the earth, and that
they may be fruitful and multiply on the earth." **18** So
Noah went out, and his sons and his wife and his sons'
wives with him. **19** Every beast, every creeping thing,
and every bird, everything that moves on the earth, went
out by their families from the ark. **20** Then Noah built
an altar to Yahweh and took of every clean animal and
of every clean bird and offered burnt offerings on the
altar. **21** And Yahweh smelled the soothing aroma; and
Yahweh said to Himself, "I will never again curse the
ground because of man, for the intent of man's heart is
evil from his youth; and I will never again strike down
every living thing as I have done. **22** While all the days
of the earth remain, Seedtime and harvest, And cold and
heat, And summer and winter, And day and night Shall
not cease."

Chapter 9 (Post-Flood)

And God blessed Noah and his sons and said to them,
"Be fruitful and multiply, and fill the earth. **2** And the
fear of you and the terror of you will be on every beast of
the earth and on every bird of the sky; with everything
that creeps on the ground, and all the fish of the sea, into
your hand they are given. **3** Every moving thing that is
alive shall be food for you; as with the green plant, I give
all to you. **4** However, flesh with its life, that is, its blood,
you shall not eat. **5** Surely I will require your lifeblood;
from every living thing I will require it. And from every
man, from each man's brother I will require the life of
man. **6** Whoever sheds man's blood, By man his blood
shall be shed, For in the image of God He made man. **7**
As for you, be fruitful and multiply; Swarm on the earth
and multiply in it." **8** Then God spoke to Noah and to his
sons with him, saying, **9** "As for Me, behold, I establish
My covenant with you and with your seed after you; **10**

and with every living creature that is with you, the birds, the cattle, and every beast of the earth with you; of all that comes out of the ark, even every beast of the earth. **11** Indeed I establish My covenant with you; and all flesh shall never again be cut off by the water of the flood, and there shall never again be a flood to destroy the earth." **12** Then God said, "This is the sign of the covenant which I am giving to be between Me and you and every living creature that is with you, for all successive generations; **13** I put My bow in the cloud, and it shall be for a sign of a covenant between Me and the earth. **14** And it will be, when I bring a cloud over the earth, that the bow will be seen in the cloud, **15** and I will remember My covenant, which is between Me and you and every living creature of all flesh; and never again shall the water become a flood to destroy all flesh. **16** So the bow shall be in the cloud, and I will look upon it, to remember the everlasting covenant between God and every living creature of all flesh that is on the earth." **17** And God said to Noah, "This is the sign of the covenant which I have established between Me and all flesh that is on the earth." **18** Now the sons of Noah who went out of the ark were Shem and Ham and Japheth; and Ham was the father of Canaan. **19** These three were the sons of Noah, and from these the whole earth was scattered abroad.

Chapter 11 (Tower of Babel)

Now the whole earth had the same language and the same words. **2** And it happened as they journeyed east, that they found a plain in the land of Shinar and settled there. **3** Then they said to one another, "Come, let us make bricks and burn them thoroughly." And they had brick for stone, and they had tar for mortar. **4** And they said, "Come, let us build for ourselves a city, and a tower whose top will reach into heaven, and let us make for ourselves a name, lest we be scattered over the face of the whole earth." **5** Then Yahweh came down to see the city and the tower which the sons of men had built. **6** And Yahweh said, "Behold, they are one people, and they all have the same language. And this is what they have begun to do. So now nothing which they purpose to do will be impossible for them. **7** Come, let Us go down and there confuse their language, so that they will not understand one another's language." **8** So Yahweh scattered them from there over the face of the whole earth; and they stopped building the city. **9** Therefore its name was called Babel, because there Yahweh confused the language of the whole earth; and from there Yahweh scattered them over the face of the whole earth.

Section I

Daocheng Yading, Sichuan, China

CHINA

We will begin this chapter with the Han Chinese, the majority people who make up 92% of China's population of 1.4 billion souls. The Han Chinese possess an array of literature, archeology, and other material containing echoes of Genesis and of the God of the Bible.

Next we will come to China's ethnic minorities. Some 4,000 years ago, when the founders of the Chinese nation arrived and settled on the Yellow River in modern-day Shaanxi Province, they found that they were not alone. There were other peoples living in that land. Some of these, such as the Miao and the Di-Qiang, are still among the Han Chinese today as ethnic minorities.

Tribes of the Region

1. Han Chinese
2. Miao
3. Black Miao
4. Gha-Mu
5. Ch'uan Miao
6. Nosu
7. Yinuo Nosu
8. Daliangshan Nosu
9. Zhuang
10. Bouyei
11. Jino
12. Derung
13. Lisu
14. Tai Kao
15. Tai Mao
16. Younuo
17. Naxi
18. Yao
19. Pai Yao
20. Tibetan Tradition
21. Axi
22. Sani
23. Dong
24. Wa
25. Kucong
26. Li
27. Mulao
28. Tujia
29. Maonan
30. Dai
31. Hani
32. Anong
33. Shui
34. Gelao
35. Bai
36. De'ang
37. Pumi
38. Achang
39. Bonan
40. Bulang
41. Monba
42. Lhoba
43. Qiang
44. She

What did these early inhabitants of the Far East believe concerning ancient human history? Did they know of Noah's Flood? Is biblical history their history as well?

Indeed. As we will see, the Miao tribe tell of a man who, prior to the Flood, was instructed by God "to build a boat made of wood, and to take his sister with him, along with a male and female of every kind of animals, also to take food for all, and two seeds of every kind of flower, tree, and grain." The Nosu said that a pair survived the Flood inside a floating wooden chest, which landed on a mountain called Moutou, and that the singing of a chicken alerted them it was safe to come out. Another division of the Nosu said that "the boat landed in the snowy mountains of Tibet." Those living near Xichang said a brother and sister made a wooden ark and used tree sap to render it waterproof. After the Flood, their vessel landed at Olou Mountain.

"In ancient times," declared the Zhuang people of southern China, "the ancestors said that a flood covered the entire earth," and "only two relatives survived: a woman and a man." The Bouyei refer to an "enormous gourd" in which two siblings, Daekdou and Dadaeu, survived during the Flood. The Jino people speak of a twin brother and sister, Mahei and Maniu, who were placed in a hollow tree by their parents. The Dulong people have a carefully preserved chant, called a Mangrong, in which a memory of the Flood is preserved. Another chant tells of the Tower of Babel. "They said, 'Let's build a sky supporter stone house [tower] that the flood water can't reach.' When the stones were stacked, they fell down and scattered all over, and then the people came to not understand each other's speech, so they split up from there."

The Lisu people are so keenly aware of the Flood they even recount it in their weddings. Their tradition tells, "The Heavenly Lord was angry with the people." He foretold what was coming to a certain man, telling him to take his sister with him in a giant gourd. Afterwards, a pair of birds announced the Flood was over, and the siblings found they had landed on a mountain. According to the Tai Kao people, a giant pumpkin was the means of escape during a "divinely decreed flood that drowned all the other inhabitants of the earth because of their wickedness."

It was during the 10th generation of humanity that the Flood occurred, say the Naxi people. This is the same number of generations as we find in Genesis, from Adam to Noah. They say the Flood was sent because of unlawful, incestuous marriages, or in another version, because of a crime committed against the gods. Only a righteous man named Liwei escaped, having been forewarned and told to prepare a floating drum. Long ago, human beings broke heaven's laws, said the Yao people. A boy and his sister were instructed to enter a giant calabash when the Flood began. The A-Hsi tribe have preserved, in their sacred traditions set to verse, a memory of the creation of the first woman from a rib taken from the first man. They have an impressive memory of the Genesis Flood as well, beginning with a warning that "the Lord of Heaven is going to send a great flood. Each should quickly prepare something whereby to escape the flood."

"The mountains were submerged in water," said the Kam people of southern China. "Brother and sister survived by floating in the huge gourd that had grown from Lightning's tooth." The Wa people of southwest China remember the Flood in their creation story, saying that a few people survived the Flood inside a cave. According to the Kucong people, the siblings named Dansou and Danlou "lay down inside a huge gourd and escaped the disaster of the Flood."

The Li people, natives of Hainan Island, say an old man warned two families of a coming Flood and gave them a special pumpkin seed which grew a house-sized pumpkin. They placed their children inside it, along with many animals, and the pumpkin floated during the Flood which lasted ten years. The pumpkin landed at the top of Wuzhi Mountain. Then "Lao Xian and He Fa heard the rooster's crow and knew that everything was safe outside." "It rained for three years and six months," said the Mulao tribe, who maintained that the vessel was a giant calabash gourd which landed on a mountain.

According to the Maonan, the Flood which carried the massive gourd to the top of a mountain lasted 360 days, only 10 short of the biblical 370.

"The water flooded the earth for a hundred days," said the Dai people. They pointed to Pizahu Mountain as the place where a small remnant of people and animals survived. "No one escaped this disaster except two siblings, Zuo Luo and his sister Zuo Bei, who survived by hiding inside a gourd," we are told by the Hani tribe. The Anong and Shui versions are similar. According to the Gelao people, an old man instructed a man to cut cedar wood, build an enclosed wooden vessel, cover it with paint, and bring his sister on board, along with two baby chicks. These are no doubt a memory of Noah's raven and dove.

"Only two siblings survived the Flood," said the Bai tribe, enclosed in a golden drum, which was later pulled to land by two birds. The Pumi people tell that it was a crow which warned of the coming Flood. The De'ang, Achang, Tujia, and many other tribal groups of China have their traditions of this Flood, as we will see in this chapter. A few tribes which straddle China's northern border with Mongolia and Russia will be treated later in the North Asia chapter.

The Dragon and the Siblings

We have mentioned above a "Thunder God" or "Lightning," who figures prominently in many Chinese Flood stories. Who is he? They identify this Thunder God as a dragon. But take note: this dragon is not as innocent and sympathetic as he is sometimes portrayed in these traditions. He also shows up in other cultures outside China as well. He is the shapeshifting masalai serpent-man of New Guinean traditions. He is the evil serpent that Nanabozou shoots in North American Flood stories. He is the serpent who tempts a woman in South American Flood stories. He is the great horned serpent Quetzalcoatl of aboriginal Mexico. He is the serpent frequently found in "loss of immortality" stories. He is none other than the serpent of Genesis 3, Satan himself.

Likewise, the "brother and sister" or "twin siblings", who experience shame but ultimately marry, are a memory of Adam and Eve. We will see that the Garden of Eden story has become mixed with the Flood story in many of their traditions, a fact which we analyze further in Appendix B.

Therefore, to answer our original question: these tribes of China most certainly have a memory of the events recorded in Genesis. Biblical history is China's history. And the Bible's promised Savior, Jesus, is China's Savior. Indeed, many millions of Chinese already know Him as their Savior.

Therefore, to answer our original question: these tribes of China most certainly have a memory of the events recorded in Genesis. Biblical history is China's history. And the Bible's promised Savior, Jesus, is China's Savior. Indeed, many millions of Chinese already know Him as their Savior.

Master Thunder

1

HAN CHINESE

The Bronze Sacred Tree of Sanxingdui

Although most of this book will deal with the Flood, we will begin our journey with one of the first events recorded in the book of Genesis: the Garden of Eden. One of the most memorable scenes in all of Scripture takes place here. I am referring to the time that Satan, in the form of a serpent, enticed Eve to take the forbidden fruit from the Tree of the Knowledge of Good and Evil. Her husband Adam immediately followed in this act of disobedience. Without question, this was one of the most important, and most tragic, moments in all of human history.

Yet how many people are aware that this same event has been found recorded in China? We are referring to an artifact known as the Bronze Tree of Sanxingdui, which depicts a memory of the Tree of the Knowledge of Good and Evil, and of the Serpent, and of the temptation that took place there.

This artifact was found in 1986 when Chinese archeologists excavated a pit in Guanghan, Sichuan Province. Here they found hundreds of ancient artifacts, which are estimated to be at least 3,000 years old. But the most striking of all is this bronze tree which bears a haunting resemblance to the Tree of the Knowledge of Good and Evil!

The significance of this Bronze Sacred Tree, and what it represents, is even greater when we consider that it fits perfectly with the Sang Tree of Chinese mythology. It is represented, in the most ancient Chinese pictographs, as a source of death, an object of temptation, and is associated with a serpent.

What exactly is this Bronze Tree? Here we are indebted to Stephen Brennecke, who has closely studied this artifact. He describes it thus:

> "The Bronze Tree stands 3.95 m tall, rising almost 3.65 m from its circular base to the top of its branches. As such, it is a life-size fruit tree. Viewed from above, the branches radiate from the central trunk. When viewed from the side, the branches grow out from the trunk in an upward direction and then arch over in a uniform manner, bending down toward the ground. Each branch terminates in one piece of fruit which is cloaked in ornate, cast-bronze leaves."[1]

The Bronze Sacred Tree of Sanxingdui

It is a fruit tree. But not just any fruit tree. As Brennecke writes, "Strikingly, the leaves near the fruit on the majority of these branches are cast in the shape of large, menacing knives!"[2]

But what makes this strange tree even more haunting is the creature that makes its home there. A long snake stretches down from the upper portions of the tree. Reaching the ground, its neck is arched and its raised head looks straight. It has two horns on its head, and large menacing eyes. The serpent touches the ground with two small feet, attached to front shoulders!

Brennecke adds, "Some of the serpent is missing, but the pieces that have been recovered include a

1. Stephen Brennecke, "The Bronze Tree of Sanxingdui," *Journal of Creation*, Vol. 20, no. 2 (August, 2006), pp. 8-10. Retrieved from: https://creation.com/the-bronze-tree-of-sanxingdui-genesis-artefact Accessed 22 Feb. 2022.
2. Ibid.

tail-like limb that terminates in a long knife."[3] We see then that there is some connection between this snake and the tree.

What kind of serpent is this, that has feet to walk upon? Nature knows of no such snake, nor any other creature like that. And what kind of fruit tree is so dangerous as to be depicted with knives for leaves?

Genesis knows of this Serpent, and of this Forbidden Tree. And in amazing confirmation of that account in Genesis, so did the ancient Chinese, some 5,000 miles away from Israel.

Detail of The Bronze Tree

But let's continue and notice another detail: a human hand! "The hand is complete with an opposable thumb, anatomically correct rows of knuckles, and detailed fingernails," Brennecke adds.[4] I would add that the hand seems to be that of a woman, on account of its slender proportions and feminine appearance.

What is the hand doing? It is reaching for the tree. Again, does Genesis know of such an event involving a forbidden tree and an evil serpent and a woman taking something from the tree? Yes, it most certainly does.

Finally, let's think about this from the designer's perspective. Clearly an enormous amount of time and effort was spent crafting this massive Bronze Tree. What did the artists intend to represent, and why? Brennecke summarized it well:

> "When we ponder the combination of these factors, it is clear that the artists have not only created a particular tree, they have also captured a specific moment in time; arguably the second most important moment in human history after creation. The Sanxingdui Bronze Tree depicts the last moments of human innocence before God. In the boughs of the tree we see the forbidden fruit, and none has yet been taken. The serpent that will help bring about the downfall of man is there in its pre-cursed state. It is symbolized as bringing death, with his knife-like tail."[5]

The discovery of the knowledge of the Garden of Eden in China points to a shared history between the Hebrews and the Chinese.

The significance of this Bronze Sacred Tree is further amplified when we consider that it fits perfectly with what is known as the "Sang Tree" in Chinese mythology.[6] It is represented, too, in the most ancient Chinese pictographs, as we will see. These pictographs depict such a tree as the source of death, an object of temptation, which is often associated with a serpent.

What is the Tree of the Knowledge of Good and Evil doing in China? This parallel between Genesis and ancient China is a stunning discovery which will not easily be explained away. It points to a knowledge of our most ancient past shared by the Hebrews and the Chinese. But we have only scratched the surface.

3. Ibid.
4. Ibid.
5. Ibid.
6. Ginger Tong Chock, *Genesis in Ancient China* (Honolulu: Eastward Garden, 2015), pp. 103-105.

China's Ancient Pictographic Script

If you've ever seen the Chinese written script before, you know how different it is from most other languages in the world. Indeed, the Chinese written script is truly one of a kind. Chinese characters (words) consist of several symbols known as radicals or roots. These radicals are combined into one character, forming a word. This technique allows complex ideas to be conveyed in a single character.

Since at least the early 1900s, Chinese scholars have scrutinized and investigated how this written script was invented, the composition of these characters, and the origin of the root symbols. By the 1940s, a Chinese pastor known as C. H. Kang began to notice similarities between the written characters and the book of Genesis. First, he noticed that the character 船 meaning "large boat" is composed of three roots meaning "vessel," "eight," and "mouths." Then he saw that the character 造 for "create" is made up of 1) earth or mud, 2) a mouth, 3) movement or life, and 4) able to walk.[7] He eventually wrote a small book in 1950, further documenting these parallels between the Chinese script and Genesis. He would later work with Ethel Nelson to publish *The Discovery of Genesis* (1979), a groundbreaking book which brought these Chinese parallels with Genesis to a larger audience.[8]

But China has an even older written script. This "oracle bone script" was first discovered around 1899 at Anyang, Henan Province. The archeologists found bones and tortoise shells engraved with characters written in a different style, which would turn out to be China's most ancient script ever discovered!

Ethel Nelson began to study these ancient oracle bone characters to see whether these connections with Genesis still held true. Other researchers too, including Ginger Tong Chock, Richard Broadberry, and Chan Kei Thong, have published important books on the subject of oracle bone characters in the last two decades.[9]

Remarkably, when we come to China's most ancient (oracle bone) script, the parallels with Genesis are even stronger than later scripts! This is because the oracle bone characters are more pictographic than later Chinese scripts.[10]

Pictographs and Their Meaning

When we examine China's oracle bone script, we are dealing with pictographic characters composed of several root symbols. The key question is, Is there any logic or meaning at all to why they are composed in the way that they are? And what is the relationship between these roots and the words that they combine to form? We are arguing that, indeed, there is a meaning and logic to how these characters are composed, but this meaning includes a knowledge and awareness of the events of Genesis! Many of these characters, as we will see, demonstrate an awareness of the events of Genesis. On the other hand, if we insist the ancient Chinese inventors of this script had no knowledge of Genesis 1 through 11, many of these characters have no discernible logic to their composition.

> There is a meaning and logic to how these characters are composed, but this meaning includes a knowledge and awareness of the events of Genesis!

Now for the following analysis I am entirely indebted to Ethel Nelson, Ginger Tong Chock, Chan Kei Thong, and Richard Broadberry for their excellent work.

---

7. C.H. Kang and Ethel Nelson, *The Discovery of Genesis in China* (St. Louis: Concordia, 1979), pp. xii-xiii.
8. C. H. Kang and Ethel Nelson, *The Discovery of Genesis* (St Louis: Concordia Publishing House, 1979).
9. Specifically, see: Ethel Nelson, *The Discovery of Genesis*; Chan Kei Thong, *Faith of Our Fathers*; Nelson and Richard Broadberry, *Genesis and the Mystery Confucius Couldn't Solve;* Ginger Tong Chock, *Genesis in Ancient China;* Nelson, Broadberry, and Chock, *God's Promise to the Chinese.*
10. Ethel Nelson, Richard Broadberry, and Ginger Tong Chock, *God's Promise to the Chinese*, p. 22.

They have addressed this subject thoroughly in their publications.[11] I merely present a handful of examples, beginning with Table 4.

Consider the character "covet" from Table 4. This graph pictures a woman between two trees. So the operative question we want to ask is, "When was the first time coveting happened?" The biblical answer to that question is found in Genesis 3:6. "Then the woman saw that the tree was good for food, and that it was a delight to the eyes, and that the tree was desirable to make one wise, so she took from its fruit and ate" (LSB). And this exactly corresponds to what the Chinese character illustrates! This also confirms the significance of the bronze tree statue we just discussed.

Similarly, consider the graph "deny, negate." It pictures a serpent among two trees. The operative question is, "What was the first time a denial or negation occurred?" The biblical answer is found in Genesis 3:4-5. "The serpent said to the woman, "You surely will not die! For God knows that in the day you eat from it your eyes will be opened, and you will be like God, knowing good and evil." (LSB) This exactly corresponds to what the character represents.

Or again, the graph for "death" pictures a mouth or mouths next to a divine tree, known in China as the Sang Tree, the forbidden tree. So we ask, What was the first time death happened? The biblical answer is found in Genesis 2:16-17. "From any tree of the garden you may surely eat; but from the tree of the knowledge of good and evil, you shall not eat from it; for in the day that you eat from it you will surely die." (LSB) This is exactly what the character for "death" represents.

Table 4: Ancient Chinese Pictographs with Genesis Parallels

Character	Composition	Operative Question (1st Instance)	Operative Answer (1st Instance)	Scripture Parallel
Deny, Negate	= Two Trees + Serpent	When was the first denial?	The first denial was made by the serpent, at the place of two trees. He contradicted what God said about the two trees.	The serpent said to the woman, "You surely will not die! For God knows that in the day you eat from it your eyes will be opened, and you will be like God, knowing good and evil." (Gen. 3:4-5)

11. On this subject, see the following books: *God's Promise to the Chinese* by Ethel Nelson, Ginger Tong Chock, and Richard Broadberry; *Faith of our Fathers* by Chan Kei Thong; *Genesis and the Mystery Confucius Couldn't Solve* by Ethel Nelson and Richard Broadberry; and *Genesis in Ancient China* by Ginger Tong Chock.

Character	Composition	Operative Question (1st Instance)	Operative Answer (1st Instance)	Scripture Parallel
 Suitable, Prepare	= Hand + Woman	What was the first thing made suitable?	By the hand of God, he made the woman, a suitable companion for the man	There was not found a helper suitable for Adam. So the Lord God caused a deep sleep to fall upon the man, and he slept; then He took one of his ribs and closed up the flesh at that place. The Lord God fashioned into a woman the rib which He had taken from the man, and brought her to the man. (Gen. 2:20-22)
 Covet	= Woman + Between Two Trees	When was the first act of coveting?	When the woman coveted, at the place of two trees	When the woman saw that the tree was good for food, and that it was a delight to the eyes, and that the tree was desirable to make one wise, she took from its fruit and ate. (Gen. 3:6)
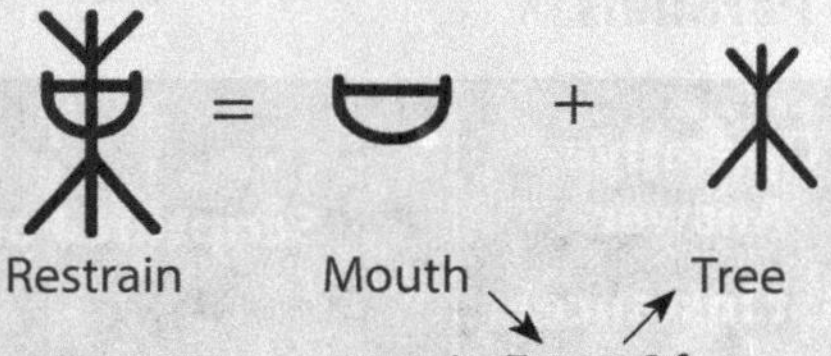 Restrain	= Mouth + Tree; In Front Of	When was the first time someone had to exercise restraint?	In the Garden, they were told not to eat from a certain tree	You shall not eat from the tree of the knowledge of good and evil, for in the day that you eat of it you shall surely die (Gen. 2:17)
 Rest, to Rest in	= House + Seven	Why do we rest?	We rest on the seventh day, because God also rested from His works on the seventh day	Then God blessed the seventh day and sanctified it, because in it He rested from all His work which God had created and made. (Gen. 2:3)
 Perish, Death, Destruction	= *Sang* tree (divine tree) + Mouth	When did death first occur?	Death began when the first couple ate from the forbidden Sang tree	When the woman saw that the tree was good for food, and that it was a delight to the eyes, and that the tree was to be desired to make one wise, she took of its fruit and ate, and she also gave some to her husband who was with her, and he ate. (Gen. 3:6)

Character	Composition	Operative Question (1st Instance)	Operative Answer (1st Instance)	Scripture Parallel
𢦏 Foreigner, Kill	= S *Curved, snakelike* + 大 Noble Man	Who was the first foreigner who killed?	Long ago, the devil disguised himself as a serpent, yet spoke as a man, and brought death to our ancestors.	The serpent said to the woman, "You surely will not die! For God knows that in the day you eat from it your eyes will be opened, and you will be like God, knowing good and evil." (Gen. 3:4-5)

Concerning "covet," Chan writes: "The composition of this character is even more interesting when one recalls that in ancient China, women had no place in society: they were not involved in public affairs; they had no role in social transactions; in some cases, they were not even allowed to leave their rooms. Yet, the ancient Chinese chose to use the character for "woman" rather than the one for "man" in constructing this "covet" character. This shows that the ancient Chinese had some knowledge of the story of the first act of disobedience against God, which resulted in sin entering the world."[12] Biblically, we would add that the woman was not solely responsible for sin and death entering the world, but Adam also sinned and bore responsibility (Genesis 3).

Concerning "restrain," Chan observes: "If we were to devise a character today to mean "restrain," we probably would try to depict two hands tied together. Yet, that is not at all how this character is written. In fact, it is a "mouth," superimposed over a "tree." This Chinese character further confirms the Genesis account described above. It refers to the first restraint placed on man, that is, when God told Adam, "Do not eat from the Tree of the Knowledge of Good and Evil."[13]

The parallels with Genesis in these Chinese characters are unmistakable. This information is routinely compelling to those from China, and is even being advocated by a growing number of scholars from China and within China.[14] Work on this subject continues, and will likely yield more examples of characters which presuppose knowledge of Creation, the Garden, and the Flood in ancient China.

In the end, there is only one way to explain these discoveries: that when the early Chinese first invented their written language, they represented ideas by anchoring them in events they still remembered, from the Garden of Eden.

Chinese Flood Accounts

That is all well and good, but what about the Flood? Perhaps you have heard claims that China knows nothing of the Flood, or that China knows only of a local flood.

12. Chan, *Faith of Our Fathers*, p. 58.
13. Chan, *Faith of our Fathers*, pp. 56-57.
14. In addition to some of the scholars cited above, see: Kui Shin Voo and Larry Hovee, "The Lamb of God Hidden in the Ancient Chinese characters," *CEN Technical Journal*, vol. 13, no. 1 (1999). Retrieved from: https://creation.com/images/pdfs/tj/tjv13n1chinese_lamb.pdf

In the previous volume, we learned that the oral histories of Native American tribes often begin with a flood. Similarly, near the beginning of China's *Shoo King*, or "Book of History," a flood is described:

> "See! The floods assail the heavens." The emperor [Yao] said, "Oh! Chief of the four mountains, destructive in their overflow are the waters of the inundation. In their vast extent they embrace the mountains and overtop the hills, threatening the heavens with their floods, so that the inferior people groan and murmur."[15]

But there is much debate about whether this flood was global or local in scope. Many people are persuaded that a local flood of the Yellow River is in view, because elsewhere in the *Chinese Classics* the Yellow River is identified as its cause. Also, it refers to the cutting of drainage channels as the wise solution enacted by Emperor Yu, which seems to imply a local event.

On the other hand, much of the language in this account implies a global Flood: waters overwhelming the mountains, threatening the heavens, and remaining at such heights for considerable time. Such descriptions can hardly apply to a local flood.

But what has long been absent from discussions of the extent of the Chinese flood is a comparative analysis of this Flood text in the context of other closely related Flood texts from cultures in East Asia and the Pacific. It was this comparative analysis that convinced me of the global scope of China's flood, for a very similar flood story is told by other tribes and nations, yet always identified as a global flood! We will especially see this when we come to the minority tribes of China and the tribes of Taiwan. As we proceed, keep an eye out for Flood stories similar to the Han version. They are always describing a global Flood.

The Flood Account of Nu Kua and Fu-hi

We have another Han Chinese account of the Flood in a work called the Huainanzi, and derivative accounts. This text involves a goddess named Nu Kua, who is often paired with a wise man named Fu-hi:

> "Going back to more ancient times, the four pillars were broken; the nine provinces were in tatters. Heaven did not completely cover [the earth]; Earth did not hold up [Heaven] all the way around [its circumference]. Fires blazed out of control and could not be extinguished; water flooded in great expanses and would not recede. Ferocious animals ate blameless people; predatory birds snatched the elderly and the weak. Thereupon, Nüwa smelted together five-colored stones in order to patch up the azure sky, cut off the legs of the great turtle to set them up as the four pillars, killed the black dragon to provide relief for Ji Province, and piled up reeds and cinders to stop the surging waters. The azure sky was patched; the four pillars were set up; the surging waters were drained; the province of Ji was tranquil; crafty vermin died off; blameless people [preserved their] lives."[16]

The statement that "Nüwa smelted together five-colored stones in order to patch up the azure sky" is an echo of the rainbow established by God: "I set My bow in the cloud, and it shall be for a sign of a covenant between Me and the earth." (Gen. 9:13) Indeed, this memorial of the rainbow from Genesis 9 can be seen even in the Chu Silk Manuscript. The relevant section of this manuscript dates to at least the 300s B.C. "In the manuscript," as Kao Lifeng summarizes, "the emperor of heaven made five wooden pillars in five colors to

15. "The Shoo King," trans. James Legge, part 1 (The Canon of Yao), in *The Chinese Classics, vol. 3*, part 1 (London: Trubner & Co., 1865), p. 24. This flood is also attested in the Shi King (Book of Odes): "The She King," trans. James Legge, Part 4, Book 3, Ode 4. In *The Chinese Classics, vol. 4*, part 2 (London: Trubner & Co., 1871), pp. 638-639. For more regarding the actions of Yu, see Part 3, Book 1, Ode 10; Part 2, Book 6, Ode 6; Part 3, Book 3, Ode 7, verse 1.
16. John S. Major et al., *The Huainanzi: A Guide to the Theory and Practice of Government in Early Han China* (New York: Columbia University Press, 2010), p. 224.

protect and support the heavenly dome in order to maintain the cosmic order. One of the pillars stood in the central part of heaven and the others in the four poles respectively."[17]

Note the global—indeed, celestial—scope of this Flood!

Chinese Pictographs Corresponding to the Flood

Earlier we observed that the events of Creation and the Garden of Eden are memorialized in China's earliest pictographic script. Is the Flood also preserved in these characters?

Indeed, it is. Again we have Nelson, Chock, and Broadberry to thank for these findings.[18] Consider the two characters shown below. The first means "in the beginning." It is pictured by "disaster" or "rising water" right below the "sun."

The second means "boat", and is constituted of three radicals, which mean "vessel," "eight," and "mouths" (people). What a remarkable way to convey the idea of "boat": a vessel carrying eight people. As it is written in Genesis 7:7, "Then Noah and his sons and his wife and his sons' wives with him entered the ark because of the water of the flood."

Character	Composition	Operative Question (1st Instance)	Operative Answer (1st Instance)	Scripture Parallel
In the Beginning	= Disaster, Rising Water + Sun	What was it like in the beginning?	Long ago, a flood raged upon the earth and nearly reached the heavens.	The water prevailed more and more upon the earth, so that all the high mountains everywhere under the heavens were covered. (Gen 7:19)
船 Boat	= 舟 Vessel + 八 Eight + 口 Mouth, People	What was the first boat?	Long ago, eight people floated inside a vessel	Then Noah and his sons and his wife and his sons' wives with him entered the ark because of the water of the flood. (Gen. 7:7)

Creation (Genesis 1)

> "In the beginning God created the heavens and the earth. The earth was formless and void, and darkness was over the surface of the deep, and the Spirit of God was moving over the surface of the waters. Then God said, "Let there be light"; and there was light. God saw that the light was good; and God separated the light from the darkness. God called the light day, and the darkness He called night. And there was evening and there was morning, one day." (Genesis 1:1-5)

The first chapter of Genesis is among the most frequently attacked passages of Scripture by secularists and unbelievers. Yet remarkably, it finds confirmation from an unexpected source: the far-eastern nation of China.

17. Kao Lifeng, "Sacred Order: Cosmogonic Myth in the Chu Silk Manuscript", in *China's Origin and Creation Myths*, eds. Mineke Schipper, Ye Shuxian and Yin Hubin (Boston: Brill, 2011), p. 126.
18. See *The Discovery of Genesis in China* by Ethel Nelson and C. H. Kang, and *God's Promise to the Chinese* by Nelson, Broadberry, and Chock.

Let us first consider the *Collected Statutes of the Ming Dynasty*.[19] This records a song called the "Zhong He" or Song of Central Peace, which was sung at the Border Sacrifice. This was an ancient song that went back long before the Ming Dynasty, and which told of God's work in Creation. The Chinese had not forgotten God after Babel. Notice the echoes of Genesis 1 in what follows.

> "Of old in the beginning, there was the great chaos, without form and dark. The five planets had not begun to revolve, nor the two lights to shine. In the midst of it there existed neither form nor sound. You, O spiritual Sovereign, came forth in Your sovereignty, and first did separate the impure from the pure. You made heaven; You made earth; You made man. All things became alive with reproducing power."[20]

And another ancient song has similar parallels to Genesis 1 and is a monument to monotheism. *The Yuan He* or "Song of Beginning Peace," which was also part of the Border Sacrifice, went like this:

> "Lord Di, when you separated the Yin and the Yang [i.e. the heavens and the earth], Your creative work had begun. You did produce, O Spirit, the seven elements [i.e. the sun and the moon and the five planets]. Their beautiful and brilliant lights lit up the circular sky and square earth. All things were good. I, Your servant, thank You fearfully and, while I worship, present this memorial to You, O Di, calling You Sovereign."[21]

Third, a document called the Record of Threes and Fives, written in the 200s A.D. (during the Han Dynasty), contains several statements with Genesis 1 parallels. These occur at the beginning of its "Pan Gu" narrative. Pan Gu, according to the Chinese, is the first man ever created. And just as there are ten generations from Adam to Noah, there are ten generations from Pan Gu to Fuxi. The Record of Threes and Fives recalls Creation, the creation of the world and the universe is described in the following terms [bracketed contents mine]:

> "Heaven and earth were once inextricably comingled as a formless mass, from which Pan Gu originated." [Compare with Genesis 1:2, "The earth was formless and void"]
>
> "After 18,000 years this formless mass split apart into bright and light ... dark and heavy." [Compare with Genesis 1:4, "God separated the light from the darkness"]
>
> "After another 18,000 years, heaven daily increased 10 feet in height, thus creating the space between the waters of the earth and the clouds."[22] [Compare with Genesis 1:7-8, "God made the expanse, and separated the waters which were below the expanse from the waters which were above the expanse; and it was so. God called the expanse heaven."]

"That the Chinese at an early period in their history possessed a purer faith than their now popular one, is shown by their earliest books." (Charles Forbes, *The Native Races of British Burma*, p. 264)

19. The Ming Dynasty was in power from 1368 to 1644 A.D., but the songs cited here are much older. The Mings were anxious to restore the worship of Shang Di (discussed in the following pages) which had languished and been corrupted by previous dynasties. Thus, at the beginning of their reign in 1366 A.D., the Mings appointed two committees to "to investigate all subjects pertaining to rites and music." As a result, they restored and re-implemented the songs and the worship and all other aspects of the Border Sacrifice, which were addressed to the worship of Shang Di.
20. *Collected Statutes of the Ming Dynasty*, vol. 82, p. 28. As translated in: Chan, Faith of Our Fathers, pp. 130-131. See also: James Legge, *The Notions of the Chinese Concerning God and Spirits* (Hong Kong, 1852), p. 28.
21. Chan, *Faith of Our Fathers*, p. 132.
22. As summarized in: Ethel Nelson, Richard Broadberry, and Ginger Tong Chock, *God's Promise to the Chinese*, pp. 111-112.

The Angels Guarding the Way

The following quotation comes from an ancient record of the Zhou dynasty (1122-781 B.C.):

> "Because man sinned in ancient times, the God of heaven ordered Chung and Li to block up the way between heaven and earth."[23]

This statement is reminiscent of God's expulsion of Adam and Eve from the Garden, when He stationed two angels to block the entrance:

> "He [God] drove the man out; and at the east of the garden of Eden He stationed the cherubim and the flaming sword which turned every direction to guard the way to the tree of life." (Genesis 3:24 LSB)

Cain and Abel

What about the passage of Cain and Abel in Genesis 4? Do the Chinese have any memory of that? Yes, their written script preserves a memory of that event.

We have Nelson, Chock, and Broadberry again to thank for the following observation. Consider the ancient Chinese character meaning "cruel," "violent" or "fierce." It is composed of three roots representing "elder brother," "mark," and "person."[24] Again, the operative question we ask is, what was the first cruel or violent act? The Chinese pictograph matches the event recorded in Genesis history.

The term "Shang Di," referring to Almighty God, is used 174 times in the *Chinese Classics*, according to sinologist William Medhurst

Table 2: Chinese Pictograph with Parallels to Cain and Abel

Character	Composition	Operative Question (1st Instance)	Operative Answer (1st Instance)	Scripture Parallel
Cruel, Violent, Fierce	= Elder Brother + Mark + Person	What was the first cruel, violent, or fierce act?	The murder of innocent Abel by his older brother Cain	And it came about when they were in the field, that Cain rose up and killed his brother Abel. … And the Lord put a mark on Cain (Gen 4:8,15)

> "Cain spoke to Abel his brother. And when they were in the field, Cain rose up against his brother Abel and killed him." (Genesis 4:8 ESV)

It is still more remarkable when we notice the symbol "mark" in this character, and we recall that God placed a mark on Cain:

> "And the Lord put a mark on Cain, lest any who found him should attack him." (Genesis 4:15 ESV)

We will see in later chapters of this book that many tribes in Asia and around the world retain a memory of Cain and Abel.

23. Kung Kuang Lang, *1985. P'ing An We P'u* (Taipei: *Decision Magazine*, 1985), p. 15. As quoted in: Kui Shin Voo and Larry Hovee, "The Lamb of God Hidden in Ancient Chinese Characters," *Journal of Creation*, vol. 13, no. 1 (April 1999), p. 82. See also: Ethel R. Nelson and Richard E. Broadberry, *Genesis and the Mystery Confucius Couldn't Solve*, p. 81.
24. Nelson, Broadberry, and Chock, *God's Promise to the Chinese*, p. 62.

The God of China

We will close our discussion of the Han Chinese by considering the following question: Who did the Chinese worship in ancient times? In the earliest centuries of China's history, who did they worship and what was their religion?

China did not follow Buddhism, which entered the land in the 1st century B.C. from India. Nor did they follow Taoism, which emerged in the 3rd or 4th century B.C. Neither did they worship other gods or household idols in earliest times.

From its earliest days as a nation, China was monotheistic. They worshiped the God of Heaven—known as Shang Di in their language, which means "Heavenly Ruler." As Confucius (551-479 B.C.) himself wrote: "The ceremonies of the celestial and terrestrial sacrifices are those by which men serve Shang Di."[25]

China was originally monotheistic. This may seem shocking to many readers, but it is the truth documented at length by the 19th century Sinologist James Legge, and established by all the Chinese classics, such as the *Shoo King* ("Book of History"). The *Shoo King* records of Emperor Yu, the first emperor of China's first dynasty (the Xia), that "when his House was at its strength, he sought for able men to honor Shang Di [God]."[26] And of Emperor Shun, one of China's first emperors, it says that "he sacrificed to Shang Di."[27]

The Chinese recognized Shang Di as the Creator, the One who made the heavens, the earth, mankind, and all life. He is omnipotent, omniscient, sovereign, and yet benevolent and merciful. The *Li Ki* ("Book of Rites"), another of the Chinese classics, says that "Shang Di is revered because His will extends to the nine limits [everywhere],"[28] and that "our King Wan wisely served God, and God crowned him with great favor."[29]

The Yi King ("Book of Changes"), the *Analects of Confucius*, and the other Classics testify to the original monotheism of China.[30] *The Shi King* ("Book of Poetry") is almost overflowing with statements about God, referring to Him as "the bright and glorious God," [31] and "the great and sovereign God." A monument to monotheism, the Shi King contains poems with statements such as "How vast is God, the ruler of men below!"[32] and "Great is God, beholding this lower world in majesty."[33]

There can be no doubt that Shang Di is honored as the Creator God in the Chinese Classics. In fact, William Medhurst, a distinguished sinologist of the mid-19th century counted 174 references to Shang Di in the Chinese Classics![34]

The Li Ki prescribed that all people in China should worship the God of Heaven (Shang Di). "All the people under the sky, within the nine provinces, must, without exception, do their utmost to contribute to the sacrifices: to God dwelling in the great heaven." All people were commanded to supply offerings, which were "for the worship of God dwelling in the great heaven."[35]

Sadly, over time sacrifices began to be offered to ancestors and to lesser spirits. Eventually, the worship of the Creator Shang Di waned and was neglected. Today, Beijing's official position is one of communistic atheism.

---

25. Confucius, *Doctrine of the Mean*, chapter 19, verse 6.
26. "Shoo King," trans James Legge, *The Chinese Classics, vol. 3, part 2* (London: Trubner, 1865), p. 511.
27. "Shoo King," trans James Legge, *The Chinese Classics, vol. 3, part 1* (London: Trubner, 1865), pp. 33-34.
28. The Li Ki, Confucius, Xian Ju, verse 29. As translation appears in: Chan Kei Thong, *Faith of our Fathers* (Shanghai: Publishing Group Orient, 2006), p. 93.
29. "The Li Ki," trans. James Legge, *The Sacred Books of the East*, ed. F. Max Muller, vol. 28 (Oxford: Clarendon, 1885), p. 339.
30. See, for example: "The Yi King," trans., *The Sacred Books of the East, vol. 16* (Oxford: Clarendon Press, 1882), p. 287. "The Doctrine of the Mean," trans. James Legge, *The Chinese Classics, vol. 1* (London: Trubner, 1861), p. 268.
31. "The She King," trans. James Legge, *The Chinese Classics, vol. 4, part 2* (London: Trubner, 1871), p. 583.
32. *Ibid.*, p. 505.
33. "The She King," pp. 448-452.
34. W. H. Medhurst, *A Dissertation on the Theology of the Chinese* (Shanghai: Mission Press, 1847), pp. 272-273.
35. *Ibid.*, p. 309.

With regard to the Chinese Classics, which are so foundational to China's history, many modern translations have actually purged references to God! This is especially true for versions printed in China. As Dr. Chan Kei Thong writes, "This is one reason why so many Chinese themselves, even scholars of these texts, are ignorant of the truth of the prevalence and the dominance of the belief in Shang Di in ancient times."[36]

The Knowledge of God Preserved for a While After Babel

"Have ever the Chinese, during the four thousand years over which their history extends, fashioned an image of Shang-Te? They have not." (James Legge)

After Noah and the seven others with him exited the Ark, humanity was repopulated from Noah's three sons and their wives. They worshiped the God who saved them aboard the Ark, and they offered sacrifices to Him. They passed down the knowledge of God to their descendants, and this was preserved for some time. A logical consequence of this is original monotheism, a subject treated in depth by Wilhelm Schmidt elsewhere.[37] Inevitably, however, the worship of God was corrupted and lost over time, as the knowledge of the truth was exchanged for that which the sinful human heart preferred (see Romans 1). In China too, other objects of worship and sacrifice were added, such as offerings to ancestors, and the worship of God was neglected over time.

China's Border Sacrifice

> "Today the Temple and Altar of Heaven (Tian Tan) in Beijing are prime tourist attractions. However, few people in the surging crowds that clamber over the worn marble steps even concern themselves with wondering about the origin and meaning of the great Border Sacrifice that used to be performed there. But centuries ago, the important ceremony that inspired the construction of these beautiful edifices was recognized by Confucius as representing perhaps the emperor's single most responsible act of obedience to the ultimate Ruler of all, the Supreme God in Heaven, Shang Di." (Nelson, Broadberry, and Chock, in *God's Promise to the Chinese*)[38]

The ancient Chinese not only knew about God, but also understood that they should sacrifice to Him–in the same way that Abel, Noah, and Job offered sacrifices to God. The Chinese Classics refer to these sacrifices, the most important of which was the Border Sacrifice, which they offered once a year on the winter solstice:

> "For more than 4,000 years the reigning emperors of China traveled annually to the border of their country or to the imperial city. There, on an outdoor altar, they sacrificed and burned young unblemished bullocks to their God, Shang Di, whose name means literally the God above, or Supreme God."[39]

It is ironic that in Beijing—the capital of atheistic communism in East Asia—stands a magnificent complex known as the Altar of Heaven, a monument to the worship of Shang Di in China!

36. Chan Kei Thong, *Faith of our Fathers* (Shanghai: Publishing Group Orient, 2006), p. 88.
37. See *The Origin and Growth of Religion* by Wilhelm Schmidt and, for those able to read German, his 12-volume work, *Der Ursprung der Gottesidee* (The Origin of the Idea of God).
38. Ethel R. Nelson, Richard E. Broadberry, and Ginger Tong Chock, *God's Promise to the Chinese* (Dunlap, TN: Read Books Publisher, 1997), pp. 5-6.
39. Nelson, Broadberry, and Chock, *God's Promise to the Chinese*, p. 1.

Among the many references to the Border Sacrifice in the Classics, the *Li Ki* tells that "the ancient kings sacrificed to God in the suburb of the capital,"[40] and "the son of Heaven [the emperor] sacrificed to God."[41] Concerning its importance, the *Li Ki* tells that "Sacrifice is the greatest of all things."[42] Confucius, whom we have previously quoted in this regard, famously stated that the emperor who understands the sacrifices and their meaning "would find the government of a kingdom as easy as to look into his palm."[43]

Hall of Prayer at the Altar of Heaven Complex

In earliest times, this sacrifice was performed at Mount Tai in what is now Shandong Province. According to the Historical Records of Grand Historian Qima Sian (c. 145-87 B.C.), it was the emperor Huang Di who first built an altar at Mount Tai for the worship of Shang Di.[44] The location of this sacrifice changed over the centuries. As recently as 1911 A.D., before the Qing Dynasty was overthrown, it was performed in Beijing at the Altar of Heaven complex, a spectacular site dedicated to the worship of Shang Di. Today, one may take a tour of the Altar of Heaven complex, with its beautiful Prayer Hall, Imperial Vault of Heaven, and the Altar Mound where the sacrifice was offered to God.[45]

How ironic that in Beijing—the capital of atheistic communism in East Asia—stands a magnificent complex known as the Altar of Heaven, a monument to the worship of God in China!

Concerning this "Shang Di," James Legge once stated rhetorically, "Have ever the Chinese, during the four thousand years over which their history extends, fashioned an image of Shang-Te? They have not."[46] Indeed, there is no image, no idol, no statue of Shang Di to be found anywhere at the Altar of Heaven site. There is only found this one thing in the Imperial Vault, which is at the center of the Altar of Heaven: a tablet on display which reads, Huang Tian Shang Di, which means, "Supreme Lord of the Great Heaven." As Chan explains:

> "Once inside the Imperial Vault, the emperor presented himself before a tablet inscribed with the Name Above All Names in China (Huang Tian Shang Di, meaning, Supreme Lord of the Great Heaven). With his face to the floor, China's emperor—the most powerful man in the most powerful nation of the world at that time—humbled himself to worship and burn incense to Shang Di. He accorded Shang Di the highest honor by kneeling three times and kowtowing three times with each kneeling, for a total of nine kowtows. Kowtowing is but an outward expression of an inner attitude of humility shown by the emperor only before Shang Di."[47]

"His response is typical of most Chinese today, who think of the dragon as part of their culture, while knowing nothing of Shang Di." (Chan Kei Thong)

Chan also related a personal exchange he had during one visit to the Altar of Heaven:

> "I encountered an old man standing before the Imperial Vault of Heaven. He was having difficulty reading the tablet bearing the name of the Most High God, and when I read it to him, he expressed surprise. 'I did not know that our ancestors used to worship Shang Di,' he said. His response is typical of most Chinese today,

40. "The Li Ki," trans. James Legge, *The Sacred Books of the East*, ed. F. Max Muller, vol. 28 (Oxford: Clarendon, 1885), p. 385.
41. *Ibid.*, p. 218.
42. *Ibid.*, p. 244.
43. "The Doctrine of the Mean," trans. James Legge, *The Chinese Classics, vol. 1* (London: Trubner, 1861), p. 268.
44. Chan, *Faith of our Fathers*, p. 234.
45. For more information on this site, I encourage you to read *Faith of Our Fathers* by Chan Kei Thong and *God's Promise to the Chinese* by Ethel Nelson, Richard Broadberry, and Ginger Tong Chock.
46. James Legge, *The Notions of the Chinese Concerning God and Spirits* (Hong Kong, 1852), p. 32.
47. Chan, *Faith of Our Fathers*, pp. 125-126.

who think of the dragon as part of their culture, while knowing nothing of Shang Di."[48]

As Chan says, many Chinese today are unaware that their ancestors originally worshiped Shang Di. This God is the same God as their earliest ancestors worshiped—along with the other descendants of Noah, Shem, Ham, and Japheth—when they were living at the Plain of Shinar in Mesopotamia (Genesis 11:2). Indeed, the Border Sacrifice is probably the remnant of an annual most holy sacrifice offered to God in Mesopotamia, which the Chinese patriarchs carried with them as they departed from Babel and traveled eastward across Asia more than 4,000 years ago. There are many cultures which have preserved (with varying degrees of integrity) an annual sacrifice to God, in similar fashion to China.

In conclusion, the Apostle Paul declared long ago that God has not left Himself without witness in any nation on earth. This was true in the cities of Anatolia where Paul visited (Acts 14:17). It was true in Athens (Acts 17:23-28). And it is certainly true of China, for we find many witnesses to Him in China.

> "Therefore having overlooked the times of ignorance, God is now declaring to men that all people everywhere should repent, because He has fixed a day in which He will judge the world in righteousness through a Man [Jesus] whom He has appointed, having furnished proof to all men by raising Him from the dead." (Acts 17:30-31)

> "In 1990, a graduate student from communist China—raised on atheistic evolution—asked me the following question: "Why should I believe in the Bible God, the Bible is true, and God is fair, when China was never given Bible truth about God to believe?" Simply put, this young man was asking: "Why should I believe in your Bible's God?" and "Why should I believe in your God's Bible?"

> Recalling that I learned somewhere that the Chinese character for "flood" somehow contained the symbol for "eight," I asked my Chinese friend to write out the Chinese word for flood, and to describe what its component symbols represented. As indicated above, his description of flood included the number eight—a fact he had no explanation for, other than he guessed that it might have once been a phonetic symbol, similar to how "4" can be shorthand for "for" or "8" for "ate."

> Then I read 1 Peter 3:20 to him and pointed out how Genesis 6–10 reports that exactly eight humans survived the global Flood, a fact that perfectly made sense of the Chinese pictographs. Then, he added that the Chinese character for "boat" also contained the number eight, and he began to realize that his own language contained latent clues that the Bible's early history was once well known to the Chinese people.

> After further discussion about how the biblical God is a loving shepherd who seeks to secure wandering sheep into His heavenly sheepfold (Psalm 23; Luke 15; John 10), my friend concluded that, long ago, the Chinese people had known the truth about the God of the Bible, including the early history of God's dealings with mankind as Genesis records, but that somehow this precious truth had been lost or wasted. During the wee hours of the morning, with joy in knowing that God had caringly revealed Himself to the Chinese people, my friend trusted Christ as his personal Savior, and he has enjoyed belonging to Him since (Luke 15:7; Romans 4:3; Luke 10:20)." (Dr. James Johnson)[49]

---

48. *Ibid.*, p. 264.
49. James J. S. Johnson, "Genesis in Chinese Pictographs," *Acts & Facts*, vol. 44, no. 3 (2015), p. 20.

The *Shu King* or "Book of Documents" records that when the ancestors of the Han Chinese first entered China, they encountered other tribes and people groups who had already settled there. Prominent among these were the Miao (or Hmong) people. Unlike the Chinese, who often referred to themselves as "the black-haired people,"[50] the Miao were noted for their comparatively blonde, light brown, and red hair, and other physical features. This has led some to suggest an Indo-European origin for the Miao. However, the Miao speak a Hmong-Mien language, with no connection to Indo-European.

Chinese girl wearing traditional costume

The Miao have preserved many of their traditions and ancient genealogies by means of songs in couplet form.[51] In one of these traditions occurs a memory of the Tower of Babel, which François Savina recorded from them around the year 1910:

> "People became very numerous upon the earth. They tried to climb up to heaven by means of stairs. But the Lord of heaven observed this and struck down all those who had climbed.
>
> Previously, all mankind spoke the same language. After that day, each family spoke a different language. People could no longer understand one another, and had to separate. This was the origin of all the languages that are in the world today."[52]

They also speak of a former homeland, prior to their settling in western China. They describe it as a very cold, northerly place:

> "The Miao (Hmong) multiplied rapidly, and soon became a powerful nation. The place where the Miao settled first was the opposite of the place where they now live. It was a land of long winters and long nights (dark for six months). The people were small, and the trees were minuscule. The water was frozen, and the ground was covered in snow. Everyone was covered in furs.
>
> The first ruler of the Miao was a child who had nursed from his mother's breast for three years. He lived in a massive golden palace. He ruled many peoples. The Miao had close relations with a western people called the Si-Txoa."[53]

They tried to climb up to heaven by means of stairs. But the Lord of heaven observed this and struck down all those who had climbed. Previously, all mankind spoke the same language. After that day, each family spoke a different language.

In regard to Creation, the Miao have a tradition with several parallels to Genesis, including a 7-day creation week and a world that was initially perfect:

50. Edouard Biot, *Le Tcheou-li: ou, Rites des Tcheou, vol. 1* (Paris, 1851), p. v.
51. Samuel Clarke, *Among the Tribes of South-west China* (London: Morgan & Scott, 1911), p. 49. Clarke wrote: "They have plenty of legends handed down from earlier times. Who composed these legends no one knows; they are taught by the older people to the girls and boys. Many of them are in verse, five syllables to a line, the stanzas being of unequal length, one stanza interrogative and one responsive. These are sung or recited at their festivals by two persons or two groups, generally one group of young men and one group of young women."
52. Savina, *Histoire des Miao*, pp. 246-247.
53. *Ibid*.

"The Lord of heaven created the heavens and the earth in seven days. He created the heavens first and the earth afterwards. The earth was beautiful, and it gave its fruits without labor. The earth was covered in flowers as large as baskets. But the sky was still without stars. The Lord of heaven created ten suns and nine moons to illuminate the sky—along with an infinite number of stars.

... Once the earth was dry, the Lord of heaven created plants, each according to its kind. Then He created trees, each according to their kind, and then animals, each according to their kind. Lastly, He created man. The Lord of heaven also created forests on the moon, at the same time."[54]

The Miao also are well-informed about the Flood. Their Flood account features a divine figure who disturbs the work of two brothers who are working in the field. He tells them they are "working in vain", and gives forewarning of a deadly flood. The younger brother is described as kind and the older brother as violent–possibly a memory of Cain and Abel (Genesis 4:1-15):

> The Lord of heaven created the heavens and the earth in seven days. He created the heavens first and the earth afterwards.

"People lived on the earth for 9,000 years. That year, two brothers who worked in the same field noticed that someone came by night and undid all the work which they did that day. The next day, they stayed on the lookout. They watched as an old man came and filled in the furrows that they had dug. The older brother wanted to kill the old man immediately, but the younger wanted to first ask the old man why he was doing this. So they asked him, and the old man told them they were working in vain. That they would not be able to eat from that which they were sowing in the field, because that same year, in the seventh month, the whole surface of the earth would be covered by water. The two brothers realized that this old man was none other than the Lord of heaven."[55]

> The old man told them they were working in vain. ... that same year, in the seventh month, the whole surface of the earth would be covered by water.

Regarding what they must do, the tradition continues:

"They asked him what they must do to survive and not drown. To the older brother, who was a violent person, the Lord of heaven told him to construct a boat of iron. To the younger brother, who was gentle, he

54. François M. Savina, *Histoire des Miao* (Hong Kong: Société des Missions Étrangères, 1924), pp. 243-244.
55. Savina, *Histoire des Miao*, pp. 245-246. To expand, their Flood tradition also adds: "The Lord of heaven, upon seeing them, asked them why they were going up to the sky. The brother and sister immediately responded: "the water has covered all the surface of the earth and it is no longer habitable." The Lord of heaven, on hearing these words, leaned over the earth and saw that it really was completely covered with water. Then he sent a dragon over the earth to dry it out. The dragon had the form of a rainbow. The water went down, and the drum went down with it. The drum came back down to the earth at the end of 50 days. The earth was still wet and soggy. A huge eagle came and landed near the drum. It carried the brother and sister on its wings and set them on a place that was dry. The eagle, however, did not find any food upon the earth. The brother and sister, to show him their gratitude, gave him some of their own flesh to eat. They each gave him three pieces of their flesh, taken behind the head, under their arms, and below their knees. This was the origin of the hollow of the back of the head, the armpits, and the knees.
After this, the brother and sister began to cultivate the earth and to sow the grain seeds which they had taken in the drum. The brother was still young, but the sister was already grown. When the brother had grown up, he told his sister that he wanted to marry her. She refused to go along with her brother's desire, however. Then he told her that the heavens wanted them to marry. He added that she was the only woman on the earth. Then the two of them resolved to consult the will of the Master of heaven on the matter. First, they each rolled a stone from the top of the mountain down to the plain. The two stones came to rest together. Next, they each threw a needle into the air. The two needles stuck together and fell to the earth together. Finally, they threw two pieces of metal into the air, and these also stuck together as they fell. The will of heaven was thus understood, and the brother and sister married."

instructed him to build a boat made of wood, and to take his sister with him, along with a male and female of every kind of animals, also to take food for all, and two seeds of every kind of flower, tree, and grain.

The two brothers did as the Lord of Heaven had ordered them. In the seventh month, rains poured down for four days and four nights. The older brother's boat of iron sunk, while the younger brother's boat of wood floated with everything in it. … When all the water had drained out, the brother and sister got out of their boat. They saw that all mankind had died and their bodies were laying on the wet earth."[56]

He instructed him to build a boat made of wood, and to take his sister with him, along with a male and female of every kind of animals, also to take food for all, and two seeds of every kind of flower, tree, and grain.

Lastly, they have an account of a rooster crowing to make the sun return after a long period of darkness. This seems to be a distant memory of Noah's dove which returns with an olive leaf (Genesis 8:8-11):

"… there was a continual night and no day. Thus, people lived seven years in thickest darkness. The people begged the sun and the moon to return, but they would not even listen to them. The tiger also entreated them to return, but in vain. Finally, after seven long years had already passed, a rooster was able to make the sun and moon return by crowing seven times.

Ever since that time, roosters have had a crest upon their heads. The Lord of heaven gave this to them in reward for making the sun and moon reappear after seven years of absence."[57]

China is in the Bible (Isaiah 49:12)

Is the great nation of China mentioned anywhere in the Bible? Indeed it is, in the midst of a passage of great prophetic significance in the book of Isaiah:

"Behold, these will come from afar;
And behold, these will come from the north and from the west,
And these from the land of Sinim." (Isaiah 49:12 LSB)

"The land of Sinim" is a reference to China. For a biblical and scholarly defense of this identification of "Sinim" as China, see Dr. Raanan Eichler's excellent work, "China is in the Bible."[58]

One subgroup of the Miao are known to the Han Chinese as the Hei Miao ("Black Miao") for the color of dress that their women wore. Sometime in the late 1800s they shared their account of the Flood with Samuel Clarke. This tradition replaces Noah's Ark with a huge gourd, hollowed out and prepared before the Flood. And similar to the Miao tradition above, there is an element of two brothers quarreling, reminiscent of Cain and Abel:

"In the Heh [Black] Miao metrical version of the Flood, that catastrophe was in consequence of a quarrel between the two brothers A F'o and A-Zie. F'o means "thunder," but as we have just mentioned above, we do not know what Zie means. These two fell out about the division of the

56. *Ibid.*
57. François M. Savina, *Histoire des Miao* (Hong Kong: Société des Missions Étrangères, 1924), p. 244.
58. Ranaan Eichler, "China is in the Bible," *Vetus Testamentum*, vol. 74, no. 1 (2023), pp. 60-77. https://doi.org/10.1163/15685330-bja10124

family possessions, a very common source of ill-feeling among the Miao and others. Thunder evidently lived above, probably in heaven, and A-Zie lived on earth. When Thunder threatened to destroy the earth with a deluge, A-Zie hollowed out a large gourd for himself, and collected a hundred kinds and a thousand sorts of seeds, and put them in a smaller gourd.

After the Flood, when the earth dragon had swallowed up all the water, and the hill dragon all the mist, the earth was again habitable. As all the people on the earth had been destroyed, and they were the only persons surviving, A-Zie asked his sister to be his wife. How this sister had been preserved is not clear in the Heh Miao version."[59]

When Thunder threatened to destroy the earth with a deluge, A-Zie hollowed out a large gourd for himself, and collected a hundred kinds and a thousand sorts of seeds, and put them in a smaller gourd.

4

GHA-MU

Another division of the Miao are the Gha-Mu or Hua Miao ("Small Flowery Miao") who live mainly in Yunnan and Guizhou Provinces. A Gha-Mu source related their account of the Flood to one of Samuel Clarke's contemporaries in the late 1800s. It begins with two brothers noticing that their work in the field was undone by a stranger.[60] This theme recurs in southwest China, and we believe it to be a distorted memory of the Garden of Eden, possibly recalling also the introduction of suffering and grueling labor into the world (Genesis 3:17-19). Then a warning of the coming Flood is given:

"She then told them it was useless for them to waste time in plowing land as a great flood was coming to drown the world. She then advised the younger brother, because he had been kind to her and prevented the elder brother killing her, to save himself in a huge wooden drum. He was to cut down a tree, hollow it out from the bottom upwards, and nail a piece of skin over the opening. She told the elder brother, because he had wished to kill her, to make for himself an iron drum. They were each to retire into their respective drums when the flood came.[61]

In many Flood traditions of China and Southeast Asia, the floating vessel is a hollowed-out gourd or a pumpkin. However, in this version it is a wooden vessel, namely, a hollowed-out tree:

She then advised the younger brother … to save himself in a huge wooden drum. He was to cut down a tree, hollow it out from the bottom upwards, and nail a piece of skin over the opening.

"When the flood came and the waters rose, the younger brother invited his sister to take refuge in his drum, and she did so. The elder brother was drowned in his iron drum, but the younger brother and his sister were safely preserved in the wooden one. The waters rose half-way up to heaven, and so high were the brother and sister carried in the hollow tree. With the rush of water they were carried hither and thither, and the tree at length was seen by one of the Genii of heaven, who thought it was some huge creature with as many horns as the tree had branches. He was very much alarmed, and said: "I have only twelve horns, but this thing has many more; whatever shall I do?"

59. Clarke, *Among the Tribes in South-west China*, pp. 43-44.
60. "Two brothers plowed a field one day, and the next morning found the soil all replaced and smoothed over as if it had never been disturbed. This happened four times, and being greatly perplexed they decided to plough the field over once more and observe what happened. In the middle of the night while the brothers were watching, one on one side of the field and one on the other side, they saw an old woman descend from heaven with a board in her hand, who, after replacing the clods of earth, smoothed them with the board. The elder brother at once shouted to the younger one to come and help him to kill the old woman who had undone all their work. But the younger brother suggested that they should first ask her why she did this and put them to so much trouble. So they asked the old woman why she had acted so, and made them labor in vain." Clarke, *Among the Tribes in South-west China*, pp. 50-51.
61. Clarke, *Among the Tribes in South-west China*, p. 51.

Thereupon he cried out for the dragon, lizards, tadpoles, and eels to clear out the channels and make holes for the waters of the flood to recede, and thus deliver him from the monster with so many horns."[62]

Comparative Insights Into China's Flood Account

Notice in the above text a similarity with the Han Chinese account of how the Flood was brought to an end. In the Hua Miao account, reptiles and aquatic creatures carve out drainage channels. In the Han Chinese version, recorded in the Shu King and the Shi King, the emperor Yu directs the people to carve out drainage channels. They are certainly describing the same event!

Yet we will see that several other tribes, in China and even beyond China, have a similar detail about the carving out of drainage channels or the removing of an impediment to drainage. They are similar to China's account. Yet they always occur in the context of a global Flood story!

This lends evidence to the view that the Shu King envisions not merely a local flood, but the global Flood, for this same story occurs among other tribes and nations, but always in the context of a global Flood.

Yet all of these accounts are but memories of that event described in Genesis 6-9. And the three leaders of China who battled against the Flood–Gun, Shun, and Yu–are likely a memory of the three times that Noah sent a bird in search of dry land: the raven, the dove, and the dove again.

Continuing, we read that the efforts of the animals were at last successful. The floating vessel comes to rest, like Noah's Ark, on a high and rocky place:

"Through the efforts of the dragon and his crew, and after twenty days the waters subsided, and the hollow tree stuck half-way down a steep and dangerous precipice."[63]

Finally, the story goes on to tell that the brother proposed to his sister that they should be man and wife, that they might repopulate the earth. At first she was unwilling, but through a series of tests which the brother passed by trickery, she agreed to the proposal.

The three leaders of China who battled against the Flood–Gun, Shun, and Yu–are likely a memory of the three times that Noah sent a bird in search of dry land: the raven, the dove, and the dove again.

5

CH'UAN MIAO

The Ch'uan Miao (or Magpie Miao) of Szechuan Province have a Flood tradition very similar to the Gha-Mu, which they told to David Graham in the 1920s or 1930s. The main difference is they replace the old woman with an old man.[64] "The Ya-ch'io [Magpie] Miao, three or four days south of Kweiyang [Guiyang], also tell the Story of the Flood," Samuel Clarke explained. "They also tell of a brother and sister, the only survivors, who were saved in a huge bottle gourd they had hollowed out for themselves. They also tell the story of the millstones, but as the second test they mention two trees. If both bore fruit, they would marry; if one

62. *Ibid.*, pp. 51-52.
63. *Ibid.*, p. 52.
64. David Crockett Graham, "Songs and Stories of the Ch'uan Miao," *Smithsonian Miscellaneous Collections*, vol. 123, no. 1 (Washington: Smithsonian, 1954), pp. 179-180.

bore fruit and the other did not, they would not marry. Finally, they married and had two children …"[65]

> In connection with the above Flood tradition, Clarke mentions that the Magpie Miao people called the man who survived Bu-i, and his sister's name Ku-eh. But when speaking in Chinese they called the man Fu-hsi, a name which he speculates is the Chinese Noah. He further writes:
>
> "According to Chinese mythology, P'an-ku was the first man, but Fu-hsi was also the first man of another epoch, and it is worthy of note that there were ten generations between Pan-ku and Fu-hsi [the same number of generations as between Adam and Noah]. The time of Fu-hsi is given as 2852 B.C. Evidently for these reasons some writers have spoken of Fu-hsi as the Chinese Noah. This opinion is confirmed by the Ya-chio Miao legend of Bu-i, who was beyond all doubt their Noah, and whom when speaking Chinese they call Fu-hsi." [66]

6 NOSU

The Nosu, a Tibeto-Burman language people, have lived in southwestern China since ancient times. Many old writings refer to the Nosu as "Lolos"; however, this is a pejorative term to them, of unknown Chinese origin.[67] When Edward Baber met them in the 1870s, he described them as a tall people, "taller probably than any European people," adding that "we never saw one who could be called, even from an English standard, short or undersized."[68]

Historically, the Nosu were sworn enemies with the Chinese, or the "sons of Han" as they called them. It was said that the Chinese regarded the Nosu "with some dread, as they credit them with powers of witchcraft."[69] Concerning their religion, this nation "fully recognizes a sovereign God, omnipotent, Creator of all things," wrote Legendre, "but he has not thought of building a temple to Him, nor of worshiping Him under any image whatever." Their religion was rather concerned with the appeasing of evil spirits which had the power to do them harm.[70]

We possess multiple impressive Flood traditions from the Nosu people. Samuel Clarke heard the following account from them in the late 1800s:

> "Some of the No-su, but not all of them, have a legend of the Creation, but all of them have a legend of the Flood. They manifestly trace their genealogy from Noah. They say a certain man had three sons. He received warning that a flood was to come upon the earth, and the family discussed how they should save themselves when this calamity came upon them. One suggested an iron cupboard, another a stone

65. Clarke, *Among the Tribes in South-west China*, pp. 54-55. The tradition adds that these initial two children "were born mute and without arms or legs. These they cut in pieces, and the pieces turned into men and women." (Ibid.) This graphic detail at the end of their Flood tradition is somewhat common in China and Southeast Asia. I think it is a distorted memory of the confusion at the Tower of Babel, and the division of mankind that occurred from there.
66. Clarke, *Among the Tribes in Southwest China*, p 59.
67. Edward Colburne Baber, *Travels and Researches in Western China (*London: J. Murray, 1882, p. 66.
68. Baber, *Travels and Researches*, pp. 66-67.
69. A. Henry, "The Lolos and Other Tribes of Western China," *The Journal of the Anthropological Institute of Great Britain and Ireland, vol. 33* (1903), p. 98.
70. A. F. Legendre, "The Lolos Of Kientchang, Western China," Annual Report of the Board of Regents of the Smithsonian Institution, 1911 (Washington: GPO, 1912), p. 578. This article was a translation from the French original in *Revue de l'Ecole d'Anthropologie*, vol. 20 (Paris, 1910).

> one, but the suggestion of the third that they should make a cupboard of wood and store it with food was acted upon. Thus the family was saved; but they say nothing about animals."[71]

It is possible these "three boats" are an echo of Noah's three dispatches of birds in search of dry land. Alternatively, it could be a memory of the fact that there were three sons aboard the Ark, which are Noah's three sons.

They say a certain man had three sons. He received warning that a flood was to come upon the earth, and the family discussed how they should save themselves.

According to Paul Vial (1855-1917), a French missionary who lived among them for 30 years, the Nosu possessed a Flood tradition which was well-known by all. This Flood put an end to the first world. So significant was this Flood that they even commemorated it in their weddings. How deep an impression must this Flood have left on their ancestors! Their tradition, which has amazing parallels with Genesis 7 and 8, went as follows:

> "The family of the venerable ancestors of the Gni (tribe of Gnip'a) was composed of four persons: three brothers and a sister. They were laborers, and were tilling their fields. Then one night, while they were resting, at midnight, came the venerable spirit Gninia. With a silver staff in his hand, he smashed and reversed the furrows. Angry, the elder brother said: "Strike him!" The middle brother said, "Chain him up!" The youngest said, "Let's question him a little. Why did you do this?" He answered, "You three brothers, it is useless to plow the earth. The time of the deluge has arrived. The water must submerge from heaven to earth, and from earth to heaven, all men must be drowned."

This "venerable spirit" that infiltrated their field evokes a memory of the Serpent menacing in the Garden — a memory which evidently seeped into their Flood tradition. It continues:

So significant was this Flood that the Nosu even commemorated it in their weddings.

> "The four of our ancestors, what did they do? The older brother shut himself up in an iron chest, and sank and drowned. The middle brother shut himself inside a copper chest, and sank and drowned. The youngest brother [who had prevented the older brothers from harming the messenger], with his sister, shut himself up in a wooden chest. The spirit said, "Take a chicken egg with you. As long as the chick does not sing, do not open the trunk door. As soon as the chick will sing, open the trunk door." They floated through the flood and came to a stop, entangled in the branches of an oak tree halfway up a rock on Mount Moutou (or Mouto). How were they to go down from there? There was no way, neither to climb nor to ride down. But then there appeared a branch of bamboo, by which they were able to climb down the mountain. From this time we have worshiped the bamboo as spirit (ancestors)."[72]

We see they remember the mountain of the Ark's landing. And so ingrained was this Flood in the mind of the Nosu, according to one Mr. Henry, that "nearly all legends begin with some reference (like our 'once upon a time') to Du-mu [their Noah] or the Deluge."[73] And regarding the content of their tradition, Henry wrote:

The youngest brother, with his sister, shut himself up in a wooden chest … They floated through the flood and came to a stop, entangled in the branches of an oak tree halfway up a rock on Mount Moutou

> "The legend of the Deluge runs that people were wicked, and Tse-gu-dzih [a deified patriarch] to try them sent a messenger to earth, asking for some blood and flesh from a mortal. All refused but Du-mu [their Noah]. Tse-gu-dzih then locked the rain-gates and the waters mounted to the sky. Du-mu was saved with his four sons in a log hollowed out of the Pieris tree; and there were saved otters, wild ducks, and lampreys."[74]

---

71. Clarke, *Among the Tribes in South-west China*, pp. 129-130.
72. Paul Vial, *Les Lolos: Histoire. Religion. Mœurs. Langue*. Écriture (Shanghai: Catholic Mission, 1898), pp. 61-65, 8-9.
73. Henry, "The Lolos and Other Tribes of Western China," p. 105.
74. *Ibid*. For another Flood tradition from the Nosu, see: Chen Qinghao and Wang Quigui (eds.), 《雲南民間故事集3》, *Collection of Yunnan Folk Tales, vol. 3*, 中國民間故事全集, *Complete Collection of Chinese Folk Tales, vol. 9*, (Taipei, 1989), pp. 543-546.

"Toiling in the Field" Flood Stories

What is the meaning of this "toiling in the field" theme which recurs in East Asian Flood stories, exemplified here in the Nosu account? If only Genesis had some parallel:

"Cursed is the ground because of you; in pain you shall eat of it all the days of your life; thorns and thistles it shall bring forth for you; and you shall eat the plants of the field. By the sweat of your face you shall eat bread, till you return to the ground, for out of it you were taken; for you are dust, and to dust you shall return." (Genesis 3:17-19 LSB)

7 YINUO NOSU

The Yinou Nosu (or Yinou Li) live in the Daliangshan ("big cold mountains") area of southern Sichuan. Paul Hattaway obtained an unpublished study of the Nosu living in this area, which preserves their tradition of the Flood. This tradition tells that the youngest of three brothers heeded a warning that was given about a coming Flood. He prepared a wooden boat, escaped the global Flood, and the boat landed in the mountains of Tibet:

> "Because the eldest [brother] was undisciplined, God sent a messenger to the sons to warn them of the flood. The oldest wanted to kill the messenger. The second son bound the messenger and asked him questions. The third politely asked him why the flood was coming. … The youngest son, named Dum, built a boat out of wood in 20 days. Twenty days later the rains came. It rained seven days and nights and flooded the whole earth. The two older sons died. The boat landed in the snowy mountains of Tibet. Dum had three sons who populated the whole earth."[75]

But who is the intruder in the field? "Now the serpent was more crafty than any beast of the field..." (Genesis 3:1)

8 DALIANGSHAN NOSU

The Daliangshan ("great cold mountains") Nosu live in the area of Xichang in China's Sichuan Province. One Father Martin, who met them in the 1890s, was privileged to hear their account of the Flood:

> "When man, increasing and multiplying, had invaded the entire world, then burst forth the deluge. On all sides the water gushed forth, from mountains, rivers, clouds, and fields. All mankind died except one brother and his sister of the ancient line of Omou. They cut down a tree, the sap of which is very commonly used in China as varnish, somewhat resembling our fig tree, and built an ark in which they took refuge. Then the ark floated on the water over all the land. The waters having at last receded, the ark rested on Olou Mountain. The brother and sister having thus escaped the catastrophe that destroyed all other human beings, joined in marriage and bore numerous children. From the two older ones, the first were of the Sifan type (an aboriginal race of the Far West very near Tibet), the second the Lolo type, and the youngest the Chinese type."[76]

Du-mu was saved with his four sons in a log hollowed out of the Pieris tree; and there were saved otters, wild ducks, and lampreys

An ark prepared beforehand. The ark grounded on a mountain. The survivors repopulated the earth. And if that was not enough, the next event they tell is a memory of the Tower of Babel:

75. "The History and Culture of the Nosu Yi People of the Liang Shan." Unpublished paper (1985). As quoted in Paul Hattaway, *Operation China: Introducing All the Peoples of China* (Carlisle, UK: Piquant, 2000), p. 415.
76. Legendre, "The Lolos Of Kientchang, Western China," *Annual Report of the Board of Regents of the Smithsonian Institution*, 1911 (Washington: GPO, 1912), pp. 579-580.

"Fearing a new deluge they undertook to build a very high house. A Pou Ouosa (a deity) tried to dissuade them from this work, but they would not listen even to his threats. But when the workman on top of the structure said: 'Bring a beam,' and the one who was below sent up a stone, then, no longer understanding one another, they separated. The Sifan emigrated toward the north, the Lolo to the east, and the Chinese to the south."[77]

I would add that there is internal evidence to authenticity here, in the details that correspond to those of other Tower of Babel traditions from China and Southeast Asia.

They undertook to build a very high house. A Pou Ouosa (a deity) tried to dissuade them from this work, but they would not listen … no longer understanding one another, they separated.

9 ZHUANG

The Zhuang are a people group of southern China numbering about 17 million, making them the largest of the 55 minority people groups officially recognized by the Chinese government. A Zhuang informant named Luo Shunda narrated several oral traditions, including this account of the Flood:

> "In ancient times, the ancestors said that a flood covered the entire earth. At the time when the flood covered the whole earth, only two relatives survived: a woman and a man. The pair of relatives were left upon a piece of dry ground. How they had floated to that piece of land, the two surviving relatives did not know, but everyone else was dead."[78]

Next, the text continues into an "incestuous union" element, which recurs in China and Southeast Asia. This is a distorted memory of the "tests" that Noah performed, sending birds on a series of flights over the flooded earth in search of dry land. We analyze this variant further in Appendix B. The tradition continues:

In ancient times, the ancestors said that a flood covered the entire earth. At the time when the flood covered the whole earth, only two relatives survived.

> "The surviving pair thought: "Now everyone else under heaven is dead, we are the only ones left, what should we do?" The pair thought about what to do. Then the aunt [woman] said: "Alas, how can two relatives be husband and wife?" The survivors brought a millstone to throw down from opposite sides (of the valley). The aunt threw down the lower millstone. The man threw the upper millstone down the mountain. (The two millstones) rolled down from the mountain peaks. The place where man's stone landed was right on top of the bottom stone, causing the two stones to be perfectly stacked on each other. The woman's millstone fit underneath, and even after rolling down the hill several times, the millstones were perfectly aligned, top upon bottom. "There's nothing for it, we two relatives have to become husband and wife," (they said)."[79]

Creation Story According to the Zhuang

Notice the parallels with Genesis 1-2 in the tradition that follows. The Bible and the Zhuang tradition describe the same events:

> "In the beginning there was no sky and there was no earth, everything was chaos, and the sky and the earth were covered in darkness. Then the sky and the earth were divided by Pangu—he took the sky in his hands, stretched it out, separating the sky from the earth. … After the sky and the earth had been separated, he created humans. When he began to create people, he used tools. When he first created people, he formed them out of yellow clay. He formed people out of yellow clay, and as soon as he set them down, they could walk."[80]

77. *Ibid.*, p. 580.
78. Eric C. Johnson et al., *Yunnan Zhuang Folktale Collection* (Kunming, China: Yunnan Nationalities Press, 2016), pp. 203-206. This version was also previously published in 2000, in a Chinese work which, translated, is *Babao Customs and Legends.*
79. *Ibid.*
80. *Ibid.*, pp. 194-196. Previously published in 2000, in the Chinese language work, *Babao Customs and Legends.*

10

BOUYEI

The Bouyei (previously called Chung-chia) are a people group closely related to the Zhuang. They speak a language of the Thai-Kadai family, which dominates much of Southeast Asia and southeastern China. The linguist David Holm met with Bouyei tribal authorities and priests in the late 1990s, and even obtained written copies of their cosmological account. This carefully preserved text contains a memory of the Flood:

> "Fuyi created a flood that reached to the sky,
>
> He created rain and clouds.
>
> At that time the Earth below was flooded all over,
>
> The world under the sky was completely inundated.
>
> The only ones left alive were Fuyi and his younger sister,
>
> The two of them, brother and sister, played man and wife.
>
> The two of them, brother and sister, played husband and wife."[81]

Like many versions of Southeast Asia, they refer to a buffalo sacrifice that was required to make the Flood subside.[82] This has strong parallels to Noah's famous sacrifice in Genesis 8.

Carabao (Asian buffalo in the wild)

In another Bouyei version, the young siblings who escaped the Flood are named Daekdou and Dadaeu. Their father's name was Bobwk. In return for helping the thunder god Dubya, who was imprisoned, he granted them the means to survive the Flood. The advance warning and instructions given to the siblings remind us of God's warning and instructions given to Noah:

> "When Bobwk was out at the market one day, Dubya persuaded the children to give him a drink of water. His strength returned, Dubya broke free, and as he left he pulled out a tooth and gave it to the children, telling them to plant it immediately, as a great flood would happen in the next few days. The tooth, when planted, grew into an enormous gourd, in which Daekdou and Dadaeu took refuge during the flood. When the waters finally receded, they looked everywhere for other signs of life, and finding none, sat down and cried. Their crying moved the Morning Star in heaven, who told them that they were the only survivors left on earth, and that they should become man and wife and repopulate the world."[83]

The tooth, when planted, grew into an enormous gourd, in which Daekdou and Dadaeu took refuge during the flood.

Unwilling to marry their sibling, the Morning Star proposed that they perform a test, each starting a bonfire separately. Their columns of smoke intertwined, and they took this as a sign that they should marry.[84] Again, this is a parallel to Noah's tests involving the raven and the dove.

81. David Holm, *Killing a Buffalo for the Ancestors: A Zhuang Cosmological Text from Southwest China* (DeKalb, Illinois: Northern Illinois University Center for Southeast Asian Studies, 2003), pp. 124-126.
82. *Ibid.*, p. 126.
83. *Ibid.*, pp. 193-194.
84. *Ibid.*, p. 194.

Sacred and Common Narrations

Not all stories are equal. David Holm, an expert linguist on the Zhuang, Bouyei, and other Tai-language people groups of China and Vietnam, provides perspective on the different classes of stories among the Zhuang:

"In Zhuang society myths are circulated and handed on from generation to generation in a number of forms. They circulate as prose tales, told most often in non-sacred contexts and often embroidered upon to suit the taste of the audience or the story-teller. The telling of such tales is not confined to any particular occasion, nor to any particular group of people, such as priests, who are recognized as having specialist knowledge. Then there are versions commonly called "ancient songs" which are orally transmitted sacred songs, very often many thousands of lines in extent. These are sung as major festivals and life-cycle rites, usually by older men well known in the locality for their command of the repertoire and their fine singing voices; such men may or may not be boumo or ritual masters, but often are. These versions of the myth may take as long as seven days to perform, and while they may be performed in abbreviated fashion if circumstances demand, they cannot be freely altered. Finally there are the written versions of the myth as performed by the boumo, the sacred scriptures. The texts in these cases are the most fixed of all and only intended for recitation in the sacred context of a ritual performance. … Often all that is needed is the mere mention of a particular theme (such as "the dog ate the rice"); that is sufficient to trigger off the rest of the story in the minds of the listeners."[85]

11 JINO

The Jino are a numerically small tribe (about 22,000), living in about 46 villages in southern Yunnan Province. A Jino creation story tells that "in primeval times, there was only water. Then two pieces of ice exploded, the heavier one descended and became Earth, while the lighter one ascended and turned into Heaven."[86] Regarding the Flood, Paul Hattaway summarized the Jino tradition in his great ethnographical survey of the tribes of China:

"One link between the Jino and the Bible is the Great Flood. Every Lunar New Year in February, the Jino celebrate by dancing around a large ox-hide drum. For centuries the Jino have orally passed on from generation to generation a story about how the human race perished in a huge flood. Their ancestors were able to survive because they found shelter in a huge drum. Being directed by a god, they received ten calabash seeds that sprouted and produced all the races in the world."[87]

The human race perished in a huge flood. Their ancestors were able to survive because they found shelter in a huge drum.

In 1986, another recording of the Jino Flood tradition in an older Chinese-language work was found by two professors, Gou Xu and Xu Kun, of Yunnan Normal University. Together with Lucien Miller, they translated this into English.

"At that time, there were a twin brother and sister, Mahei and Maniu, who lived with their parents. Seeing that the flood was rising higher and higher, and that all of humankind was on the brink of extinction, the parents felled a big tree, hollowed it out, and covered both ends with cowhide to make it into a big wooden drum in which grain and seed

85. Ibid., pp. 194-195.
86. Wang Xianzhao, "Minority Creation Myths: An Approach to Classification," in *China's Creation and Origin Myths*, eds. Mineke Schipper, Ye Shuxian, and Yin Hubin (Boston: Brill, 2011), p. 200.
87. Hattaway, *Operation China*, p. 234.

could be stored. A string of tinkling brass bells was attached to the drum from the outside. 'Now climb on in and flee for your lives! Remember, don't come out before the water from the flood dries up. Keep an eye on the flow of the water by looking through the hole you cut with this knife. And after you take a look, stop it up tight with the beeswax. When you hear bells tinkling, you'll know for sure that your drum has touched ground, and the water has gone down. Then you can break open the drum and come on out.' Manhei and Maniu did exactly as their parents told them."[88]

The parents felled a big tree, hollowed it out, and covered both ends with cowhide to make it into a big wooden drum.

Those tinkling bells, by which they knew the Flood was over, correspond to Noah's dove that returned with a freshly plucked olive leaf in its beak (Genesis 8:11).

12

DERUNG

"Great snow-covered mountains, mountainous subtropical jungles, and dense rainfall have kept the Rawangs in almost total isolation, not only from other tribes, but even from their relatives in adjoining valleys," wrote the linguist Hpong Sarep.[89] In northeastern Burma they are known as the Rawang or Dulong, and in southwestern China as the Derung or the Trung.

What is most unique about the Derung is their chant or ballad, called a Mangrong, which has allowed them to preserve their ancient traditions and migration accounts so carefully. Linguist Hpong Sarep adds that "The contents are set in rigid and unchangeable sequence, exact correctness being of utmost importance, so that later generations cannot change the facts."[90]

The mangrong (chant) containing their Creation and migration story was narrated by one of their elders, a man named Rawang Bezi Dui. First, he reiterated: "This does not come from me, it was told by the damshas and the very old men of long ago. I simply tell what I heard from them."[91] His narration on Creation included the following:

> "Dameu [God] created a pair of human beings, a man and a woman. They were also called Masuce (the first children) and Tongmangce (ancient children). They were moved from Ameu Adam [God plain] to Tane Adam [human plain]. Therefore, the names Masuce and Tongmangce were changed to Tanece (human children)."[92]
>
> "Tane Adam [human plain] was the world, the earth. In this world, although Dameu, the creator, created everything that exists, the earth was still half dark and not bright. Because of its incompleteness, they (the humans) held a meeting with all the animals to discuss the matter. The Big Frog started (saying) "If there is to be darkness, let there just be darkness, if there is to be light, let there just be brightness."[93]

This [chant] does not come from me, it was told by the damshas and the very old men of long ago. I simply tell what I heard from them.

88. Lucien Miller, Gou Xu, and Xu Kun, *South of the Clouds: Tales from Yunnan* (Seattle: University of Washington Press, 1994), pp. 68-69. For a similar narration, see: Chen Qinghao and Wang Quigui (eds.), 《雲南民間故事集2》, *Collection of Yunnan Folk Tales, vol. 2,* 中國民間故事全集, *Complete Collection of Chinese Folk Tales, vol. 8* (Taipei, 1989), pp. 491-497.
89. Hpung Sarep, "A Study of the Morphology of Verbs and Nouns in the Sinwal Dialect of the Rawang Language," *Linguistics of the Tibeto-Burman Area*, vol. 19, no. 2 (1996), p. 94. See also: Robert and Betty Morse, "Oral Tradition and Rawang Migration Routes," *Essays Offered to G. H. Luce by his Colleagues and Friends in Honor of his Seventy-fifth Birthday*, eds. Ba Shin, Jean Boisselier, A. B. Griswold, vol. 1 (Ascona, Switzerland: *Artibus Asiac*, 1966), p. 195.
90. Sarep, "A Study of the Morphology of Verbs and Nouns in the Sinwal Dialect of the Rawang Language," p. 96.
91. Randy J. LaPolla and Dory Poa, *Rawang Texts* (2001), p. 3.
92. *Ibid.*, p. 20. "Adam" is just the English transliteration of their word for "plain." I do not attach any significance to the fact that this word coincides with the biblical name Adam, as this can happen when names are transliterated.
93. *Ibid.*, p. 22.

The part of the sacred chant touching on the Flood follows. The Flood started due to an enormous corpse blocking the drain of the earth's waters:

> "They said to each other, "Let's make it flow away in the river," they said, and so everybody agreed. When they threw it [the corpse] in the water, it blocked the river drain and then the river began to flood. The water began to rise, and covered the earth, it covered all the mountains. The humans were all killed. At that time, two humans called "Mushungshice" (leftover ones) kept going uphill until there was only a small bit of the mountaintop and they were perched on top of land the size of a shazol hat surrounded by water."[94]

The Derung have a memory of Noah's dove, which they replace with a rooster that crowed to make the sun return.

It is noteworthy that this theme of "Flood caused by a blocked drain" is the same as we find among the Han Chinese. The Chinese Classics known as the Shu King and Shi King ascribe the Flood to a blockage and lack of drainage of the Yellow River. In other East Asian and Austronesian tribal versions, there is a blocked drain as well. The story is one and the same.

The Derung also have a memory of Noah's dove. They replace it with a rooster that crowed to make the sun return.[95] Robert and Betty Morse, who spent several decades with the Derung (or Dulong) people of Myanmar beginning in the 1940s, mention a Flood tradition as well.[96]

The Derung have a stunningly detailed migration story in their sacred tradition. First, they remember their ancestors descending from the mountain of the Flood and settling on a plain–reminiscent of Genesis: "It happened as they journeyed east, that they found a plain in the land of Shinar and settled there." (11:2 LSB) And in the Dulong version:

After the Flood, the two human beings came down from the mountain, settled on a plain, and there the humans procreated.

> "The perching place of the humans was an area the size of a shazeul hat, a kangla hat, left by the death epidemic (floods). When the nine suns appeared at the place where the two humans (who survived the plague) were, the water of the flood that caused the destruction started to recede, it is said. Then the two human beings went to the east and west to look for humans, but when they could not find any, they came down from Sangban Kwinzu (people migrated mountain), it is said. They passed down many steps of mountain ranges, and on Shanzing Adam (procreation plain) they built a house themselves and lived there. On this plain the humans procreated."[97]

And if that weren't enough, they remember the Tower of Babel event which happened next:

94. *Ibid.*, p. 55.
95. *Ibid.*, p. 28. "After collecting the amount to buy the sun, they said, "Let's go to call the sun." Everyone asked to go gave various reasons for not going, and were not willing to go. It was only the rooster who was willing to go." After adorning himself in gold, the rooster went to the sun. "The rooster cried out "Kang kar o ee..." Then he stepped up one level after another upward (higher and higher) and shouted to the sun from Ameu-azing. (God's place). "Oh, Anang the sun! Anang the sun! brighten up the lower plain, Tane-adam." At this call, the sun promised to come down and said, "I will, call me and I'll meet with you." The rooster then came back. From that time on, the rooster has called forth the sun."
96. "Extracting from such accounts, which the writer has been attempting to record on tape, transcribe and translate bit by bit, and putting the material back in proper sequence, we find the Rawang history starts with stories and legends of creation, and an account of a flood from which there were only two survivors." Robert and Betty Morse, "Oral Tradition and Rawang Migration Routes," *Essays Offered to G. H. Luce by his Colleagues and Friends in Honor of his Seventy-fifth Birthday*, eds. Ba Shin, Jean Boisselier, A. B. Griswold, vol. 1 (Ascona, Switzerland: *Artibus Asiac*, 1966), p. 202.
97. *Ibid.*, p. 61.

"When the Shazingce (children of Shanzing Plain) began to multiply, they said, 'Let's build a sky supporter stone house [tower] that the flood water can't reach.' When (the stones) were stacked, they fell down and scattered all over, and then the people came to not understand each other's speech, so they split up from there. When they came down from the Shazing Plain they came down nine (tongmang) ancient steps. They then came down nine namsue steps. They came down these steps, and when they crossed these steps, (somehow namsue tree was slippery so) they slipped down, and when this happened, one cried out 'akga' and became Rawang. One cried out 'agalo' and became Jinghpo, and one who cried out "Alae" became Lisu, and since that time all the different languages of people have existed and been spoken. But in damsha words the "longgung chuem" (stone trunk house) is what is talked about."[98]

They said, 'Let's build a sky supporter stone house [tower] that the flood water can't reach.' When (the stones) were stacked, they fell down and scattered all over, and then the people came to not understand each other's speech, so they split up from there.

This tradition is by no means an outlier. It has parallels with the Miao and other versions from southwestern China and Southeast Asia. And I want to be emphatic on this point: It is no longer tenable to dismiss Tower of Babel traditions as "missionary influence." They are simply too many, too well-attested, and too consistent, as we will see in this book. It is time to acknowledge that the Tower of Babel account in Genesis is genuinely and widely attested in traditions found all around the world, in the same way that Noah's Flood is attested in Flood traditions from all around the world!

Finally, after Babel, their tradition goes into a detailed account of their migration. They attribute their own tribal name Rawang to a river they once lived along by the same name.[99] Some scholars believe they migrated from as far as Inner Mongolia to their present location.

Chinese Skeptics Left Speechless

Paul Hattaway's book, *Shandong: The Revival Province*, is a must-read about the progress of the Gospel in that part of China. In one account, we read:

"[Chang Zihua] shared the gospel with his employees and friends but was often met with resistance and ridicule. Once, a man mocked his faith and told him it was foolish to believe in an invisible God. For weeks the weather had been heavily overcast and rainy, and he challenged Chang to prove his God was real. "Pray to your God and ask him to make the sun shine through," the man demanded. "If it happens I will believe in him too."

Chang was perplexed by this unexpected challenge. Not wanting to put God to the test or disgrace his name in front of unbelievers, he asked God to reveal his will on the matter. After a time of fervent prayer, Chang was convinced that the Holy Spirit had revealed God's will to him, and he told the man, "Tomorrow at noon the Lord Jesus Christ will cause the sun to shine and you will know that he is the true god."

News of the unique showdown quickly spread throughout the local community, as the rain continued to lash down that day and throughout the night.

The next morning dawned with torrential rain still pouring down

98. *Ibid.*, pp. 70-73.
99. *Ibid.*, p. 76.

from the sky. Dark clouds completely filled the horizon. Many unbelievers in the neighborhood gathered to see what the Christian would do when his faith was shown to be fraudulent. At eleven o'clock the Changs looked out of their window to see the countryside still being saturated by a downpour. At 11:30 nothing had changed, nor at five minutes before noon. It had rained continually for days.

A large grandfather clock stood against the wall in the Chang home. At 11:59 a.m. there was still no sign of the sun. The man who had issued the challenge stood poised, ready to mock. Just before noon the clock began to chime: "Dong...Dong...Dong."

At the very moment of the last chime, at precisely twelve o'clock, the sky suddenly split open and rays of bright sunshine burst through the clouds, illuminating the drenched community. The locals were astonished, and acknowledged the Christian God was the one true God. A new respect was given to members of the Chang family, and their faith was admired."[100]

13 LISU

The Lisu people, whose name means "come-down people," migrated from the mountains of eastern Tibet into southern China and adjacent parts of Southeast Asia. The missionary J. O. Fraser mentioned that the Lisu people have a distinct memory of the Deluge, commemorating it in their wedding ceremonies.[101] During the first decade of the 1900s, Archibald Rose recorded it as follows:

> "In the beginning the Heavenly Lord was angry with the people and he chose out a pumpkin-grower and called him, saying, 'Take the seed of a gourd and plant it in the ground and wait for the fruit.' … And the man heard and did as he was bid, and his gourd grew daily till it became the greatest in the land. And the clouds gathered and the rain fell without ceasing and the water rose over the earth. Then the man took his younger sister and said, 'We will cut a hole in the gourd and hide ourselves lest we also perish in the flood.' And they were carried in the gourd for many days, now high, now low, as the waters rose and fell, till at last they reached earth once more, and, opening the fruit, they found all living things destroyed and they alone were left."[102]

A Burmese depiction of the Lisu people in the early 1900s

Another glimpse into the Lisu memory of the Flood comes from two professors in Yunnan Province. In an antiquated Chinese work, they found the following Lisu account:

> "In an ancient time, in a stockaded village of some ten thousand households, there once were a brother and sister whose parents died when they were still young. As they were without friend or support, they stayed in a shed made of wormwood branches near the village, and they lived just like the wild boar and wild ox.
>
> One day, as the brother and sister were passing time putting wild vegetables they collected into their earthen cooking pot, adding buckwheat flour, and stirring with a pair of wormwood chopsticks, a pair

The Lisu people commemorate the Deluge in their weddings.

100. Paul Hattaway, *Shandong: The Revival Province* (2018), pp. 196-197.
101. J. O. Fraser, "Work Among Aborigines in the Tengyueh District," *China's Millions*, vol. 21, new series (London: Morgan and Scott, 1913), p. 128.
102. Archibald Rose and J. Coggin Brown, "Lisu (Yawyin) Tribes of the Burma-China Frontier," *Memoirs of the Asiatic Society of Bengal*, vol. 3, no. 4 (1910), pp. 252-253.

of dazzling, golden-colored birds flew down from the sky and alighted on the top of their shed. These birds were able to speak human language. "What poor orphans you are!" the birds exclaimed. … You two have had your taste of suffering. You've experienced enough sorrow. But your bitter days have not yet passed. Greater sufferings are yet to come. A huge wave will flood the earth. Go quickly now and find a gourd to use for your shelter. And don't come out till you hear us birds singing, and we've alighted on the gourd and are calling you." Then the birds flew up into a cloud and disappeared.

> Others just laughed. "Why should we be afraid of some flood drowning us?

Hearing this terrible news, brother and sister were terror-stricken. … They gathered their wits and decided they should let the villagers know of this threat to the human race, so that others might avoid disaster. They called on one household after another. One family said these orphans were so starved they were talking nonsense, while another claimed that, because they had no parents to teach them better, they were mistaking their dreams for reality. Others just laughed after hearing their story, saying, "Even if what you say is true, we live in a house made of fir. It doesn't shake in the wind, or rock when the earth quakes. It has pillars of iron and walls of brass. Why should we be afraid of some flood drowning us?'"[103]

Their urgent admonitions to their neighbors, which were unheeded, correspond to Noah, who doubtless warned his contemporaries and was called "a preacher of righteousness" (2 Peter 2:5). The tradition continues:

"Brother and sister could do nothing but go home and pick out a huge gourd. They sawed off the top to make a cover so they could hide inside when the flood came… Ninety-nine days and ninety-nine nights passed by. Suddenly, a mountain breeze began to blow, there was a clap of thunder and a flash of lightning, and the rain poured down as dense as a hemp forest. The water in the rivers, puffing and blowing deep breaths, began climbing the banks, ruining crops and houses, sweeping away people and cattle.

Brother and sister had hidden away in their gourd, and they floated about the world riding the surging waves. From time to time, they could hear the gourd ringing as it humped against the bottom of heaven. On and on they floated, unable to tell from within the gourd whether it was day or night, or how much time had gone by. At long last, the crashing of the waves could no longer be heard, and the endlessly floating gourd came to a rest. Brother and sister dared not to climb out."[104]

Finally, we have the part about birds, in congruence with Genesis 8:6-12:

> The birds called. 'The terrible flood is over. There's no need to be afraid or worried any longer. … Brother and sister lifted off the cover of the gourd. Lo! They had floated to the top of a mountain.

"They waited for the singing of the birds. They waited, oh so quietly, for good news from two golden birds. By and by, they heard the joyous twittering of the golden birds. 'Come out quickly, you orphans!' the birds called. 'The terrible flood is over. There's no need to be afraid or worried any longer. … Brother and sister lifted off the cover of the gourd. Lo! They had floated to the top of a mountain. The flood had completely receded. The earth was quiet. They were ecstatic, yet afraid. They had escaped catastrophe, but they were the only survivors on earth."[105]

103. Lucien Miller, Guo Xu, and Xu Kun, *South of the Clouds: Tales from Yunnan* (Seattle: University of Washington Press, 2016), pp. 78-79.
104. *Ibid.*, p. 79.
105. *Ibid.*, pp. 79-80.

14 TAI KAO

The Tai Kao ("white Tai") live in southern Yunnan Province and adjacent parts of Vietnam and Laos. Their Flood tradition, similar to others from Southeast Asia, tells that "their ancestors emerged from a pumpkin in which they had taken refuge during a divinely decreed flood that drowned all the other inhabitants of the earth because of their wickedness."[106]

Their ancestors emerged from a pumpkin in which they had taken refuge during a divinely decreed flood that drowned all the other inhabitants of the earth because of their wickedness.

15 TAI MAO

The Tai Mao are known by several other names, including the Shan (or Chinese Shan), Dehong, Kang, Dai, and Dai Nua. They live in western Yunnan Province, Burma, and parts of neighboring Laos, Thailand, and northeast India. Paul Hattaway mentioned their Flood tradition:

> "The Tai Mao have long possessed an advanced culture. By the thirteenth century they had created a Tai calendar, written books explaining the eclipses of the sun and moon, and composed a number of poems, legends, and fairy tales. A Tai tale tells of a cataclysmic flood that long ago destroyed most of the people and animals of the world. Through intermarriage among the survivors, the people began to multiply so much that soon the land could not support the needs of so many people."[107]

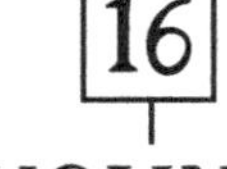

16 YOUNUO

The Younuo, or Yuno, are an offshoot of the Yao with their own language. They have a vague account of the Flood, which Paul Hattaway summarized as follows:

> "The Younuo have a flood legend. They claim the waters once rose up so high on the earth that they reached into heaven. Man then sounded a gong at the rooftop of the earth which woke the Thunder god. The Thunder god saw man's distress and came down to rescue them, causing the flood to end."[108]

17 NAXI

The Naxi people have lived around Lijiang in western China for about 1,000 years, but they are originally from western Tibet, like their distant relatives, the Mosuo (not to be confused with the Nosu).[109] The Naxi possess unique pictographic records, called Dongba, written by their priests long ago. Some of these Dongba refer to the Flood. The record called "The Descent of Man," or "Creation of the World," is narrated thus:

> "In ancient times, heaven and earth were in chaos and the Yin (female) and Yang (male) were commingling; trees walked, stones talked – everything was jerking and moving. … All people came to build up the holy mountain, to support firmly the sky above. When it came to the time [of] Congren Liwei, the tenth-generation ancestor of humanity, brothers began to mate with sisters and as a result heaven and earth were contaminated."[110]

Another Chinese tribe that remembers the number of generations from Adam to Noah! The sin involving marriage is strongly evocative of Genesis 6:1-4. And in another place, it is said the Flood was sent in judgment for a crime committed by men, as we read:

Naxi woman in customary dress

106. *Global Prayer Digest*, vol. 10, no. 4 (April 1991).
107. Paul Hattaway, *Operation China* (Carlisle, UK: Piquant, 2000), p. 495.
108. Hattaway, *Operation China*, p. 563.
109. Hattaway, *Operation China*, p. 395.
110. He Zonghua and Yang Shiku, *History of Naxi Literature*, (Xichuang: Xichuang National Minorities Publication, 1992), 130-31. As translated to English in: Archie Chi Chung Lee, "When the Flood Narrative of Genesis Meets its Counterpart in China." (18 November, 2018), pp. 10-11. Retrieved 20 March, 2023 from https://www.vanderbilt.edu/AnS/religious_studies/SBL2008/Lee.doc

"The heavenly gods sent a boar to flatten the cultivated land. Liwei's brothers caught the boar and wounded also the heavenly gods. Only Liwei helped to treat the wounds of the Yin god (female god) and the Yang god (male god). So the Yang god taught him the trick to escape the coming flood disaster by making a leather drum which will float on water. The flood covered the earth and only Liwei survived."[111]

When it came to the time [of] Congren Liwei, the tenth-generation ancestor of humanity, brothers began to mate with sisters and as a result heaven and earth were contaminated.

After the Flood, Liwei struggled to find a companion. Eventually, he married Qinghui (or Cunhongbaobai), the daughter of the God of Heaven. But before he could marry her, he had to pass a series of dangerous tests imposed by her father, such as milking a tiger and farming and harvesting in a short period of time. After a time in heaven, Liwei and his wife returned to earth. (It is possible this is an echo of the ascent of Enoch in Genesis 5:24, or the descent of angels chronicled in Genesis 6:1-4.) They also had three sons, who were unable to speak until their father made the required sacrifice to heaven to honor their heavenly ancestors. (Perhaps this inability to speak is the confusion of tongues at Babel in Genesis 11:1-9.) These three sons were the ancestors of the Tibetan, Naxi and Bai peoples.[112]

18 YAO

The Yao people live in the mountains of southern China and northern Vietnam. Of interest to our study is an ancient record of theirs, at least 800 years old, known as "King Ping's Charter." Copies of it survive in scrolls, folders, and books (with paper of silk, bamboo, or cloth), and even in tree bark.

Yao teenagers in traditional costumes

This Charter includes the ancient origin story of the Yao people and acknowledges the fact of the Flood. "The flood overflowed up to the sky for 7 days and 7 nights, on earth there were no people left except for Fu-xi and his younger sister." From this pair the world was repopulated.[113]

Yet why did the Flood happen? Another narration fills in the details:

"Long time ago, human beings broke heaven's laws. A higher deity (TianShen) punished the people. The deity sent a lower deity (LeiGong) to investigate."[114]

Next, a certain man and his wife trapped this deity (LeiGong), treated him terribly, and planned to eat him. However, their son, a young boy, secretly gave LeiGong some water and allowed him to escape.

"LeiGong returned to heaven and told TianShen of his experiences. TianShen was very angry at the way humans had treated LeiGong, so

111. *Ibid.*
112. Pedro Ceinos Arcones, *Sons of Heaven, Brothers of Nature: The Naxi of Southwest China* (Kunming: Papers of the White Dragon, 2012), pp. 237-239. See also: Michael Oppitz and Elizabeth Hsu, *Naxi and Moso Ethnography* (Zurich: Völkerkundemuseum Zürich, 1998), pp. 312-320.
113. Huang Yu, "Preliminary Study of the Yao 'King Ping's Charter," in The Yao of South China: *Recent International Studies (Paris: Pangu, 1991), p. 94.* Yu's primary source, translated from Chinese, is: *Editorial Committee of the Zhuang Autonomous Region, Investigations into the Society and History of the Yao of Guangxi*, vol. 2 (1983) and vol. 8 (1985).
114. Kendrick L Marr and Xia Yong Mei, "Benincasa hispida (Cucurbitaceae) the "Pumpkin" of Asian Creation Stories?", *Economic Botany*, vol. 55, no. 4 (2001), p. 575.

> he decided to flood the world. … LeiGong warned the small boy and his sister about the coming flood and sent the small boy some hulu seeds to plant. He told them to get into a hulu fruit when the flood came in order to escape. The whole world was flooded."[115]

Long time ago, human beings broke heaven's laws. A higher deity punished the people. … LeiGong warned the small boy and his sister about the coming flood.

Also, the Yao have a very old song in honor of their founder King Pan (or Pangu), which alludes to the great Flood. We see how deeply the knowledge of the Flood was woven into their history:

> "All the people in the world had been drowned by the flood …
>
> We brother and sister got married, …
>
> After being true husband and wife for a few years …
>
> On the seventh morning the flower entered her body …
>
> Those scattered on the green mountain became the Yao clans
>
> Those scattered below at the entrance of the cavern the Hundred Clans."[116]

19 PAI YAO

"The Pai Yao who inhabit Lian Nan district in Guangdong Province are an ancient ethnic group," wrote Xu Wenqing. While the Chinese government considers them part of the Yao minority, the Pai Yao (or Zaomin as they call themselves) consider themselves a remnant of a people group who migrated from the north.[117] Their Flood tradition is prototypically Chinese, but they replace the brother and sister with an aunt and nephew.[118]

20 TIBETAN TRADITION

Samuel Turner, a diplomat of the East India Company, wrote an early account of Tibet, from his expedition made in 1783. During his travels he recorded a Tibetan tradition of the Flood:

> "It is asserted that Tibet, in remote times, was almost totally inundated; and the removal of the waters that covered its surface, is imputed to the miraculous interposition of some object of their worship, whose chief temple is reported to be at Dorgeedin [Darjeeling]. … He, it is said, in compassion to the few inhabitants which Tibet contained, who in that age were little better than monkeys, drew off the waters through Bengal, and, by sending teachers among them, humanized the wretched race, who were subsequently to people it."[119]

Turner then commented: "In this belief of the Tibetans, which is too general to be totally rejected, it is not difficult to discover strong traces of the universal deluge, though the tradition, as might naturally be expected, is obscured by fable, and disfigured by a mixture of absurdity."[120]

Woman in Tibetan dress

---

115. *Ibid.*, p. 576.
116. Yu, "Preliminary Studies of the Yao 'King Ping's Charter,'" p. 95.
117. Nicholas C. T. Tapp, "Reflections on Fieldwork among the Yao," *Ethnicity and Ethnic Groups in China*, eds. Chiao Chien and Nicholas C. T. Tapp (1989), p. 226.
118. "In the beginning, a woman called Lo Shenqiao ate some soya beans a god had given her, and gave birth to seven brothers. These seven brothers wanted to eat the Thunder God's flesh; they lured Lei Gong, the Thunder God, to man's world and captured him, and imprisoned him in a granary. Afterwards Lei Gong was rescued by Fang the 16th and Shafang the 3rd. He flew back to the Celestial Court, and in a moment of anger, dug an opening to the river of Heaven, letting water drown the whole Earth, extinguishing all life on Earth. Only Fang the 16th and Shafang the 3rd, who were nephew and aunt, luckily survived. After the flood receded, when Heaven and Earth were in chaos difficult to discern, nephew and aunt then married." Source: Xu Wenqing, "Myths and Legends of the Lian Nan Ba Pai Yao," *The Yao of South China: Recent International Studies*, eds. Jacques Lemoine and Chiao Chien (Paris: Pangu, 1991), p. 406.
119. Samuel Turner, *An Account of an Embassy to the Court of the Teshoo Lama in Tibet* (London: W. Bulmer, 1800), p. 224.
120. *Ibid.*, pp. 224-225.

The Strong Man of Tibet

Tibet, known as "the roof of the world," has a reputation of great spiritual darkness, where demonic powers operate more openly than in most other parts of the world. Those who have read missionary reports from Tibet, or other reports by Western visitors, will know that there are many well-documented reports of supernatural occurrences which are plainly demonic and evil in source. Such forces seek to keep the people of Tibet locked in darkness, away from the saving knowledge of God in Jesus.

Most Western readers see the Dalai Lama as the leader and chief authority of Tibet. However, as Paul Hattaway writes in his unforgettable book, *Tibet: The Roof of the World*, "most Tibetans know that the real head of state of the Tibetan people is not the Dalai Lama but the State Oracle–an individual who is possessed by a demonic spirit called Nechung. Thubten Ngodup, a man who was born in Tibet in 1957, serves as the State Oracle and also has a seat as a deputy minister in the Tibetan government in exile."[121]

The Dalai Lama himself has acknowledged the real spiritual (and demonic) forces which govern Tibet. Hattaway explains that according to the Dalai Lama, "not only does a powerful demonic ruler exist over Tibet, but it is embodied within a man who holds a position in the government, and who is often consulted for guidance and advice!"[122]

To learn of this "Nechung Oracle" and his demonic influence over Tibet is startling indeed. However, as Christians, we need to be aware of the spiritual nature of the battlefield. "Our struggle is not against flesh and blood, but against the rulers, against the authorities, against the world forces of this darkness, against the spiritual forces of wickedness in the heavenly places." (Ephesians 6:12 NKJV)

With regard to Tibet, Hattaway's remarkable book records the history of church planting in Tibet and the steady but miraculous advance of the Gospel in this land of fierce spiritual opposition, along with many unforgettable stories. I strongly commend *Tibet: The Roof of the World* to all readers. Finally, we take courage in knowing that Jesus is stronger than any demonic power, for Jesus is the one who "binds the strong man," that is, the devil (Mark 3:27).

The Axi (or A-Hsi) are a subtribe of the Yi people, living in the mountains to the southwest of Kunming, the capital of Yunnan province. What is unique about this people group is how they preserved their most precious traditions–namely, in the form of ballads. "Though without any native literature the tribe has a rich mine of ballads which, handed down for many generations, contain the tribal myths wherein may be discerned the deep heart yearnings of men and women,

121. Paul Hattaway, *Tibet: The Roof of the World* (London: SPCK, 2020), p. 4.
122. *Ibid.*, p. 5.

a trustworthy account of religious and sacrificial customs, the manner of livelihood, and the habits of the tribe."[123] These ballads were often sung in alternating fashion by a young man and a young woman. Two of their most important ballads recount the stories of Creation and of the Flood.[124]

How these traditions reached us is also noteworthy. As W. H. Hudspeth wrote, "During World War II, a Chinese student, Mr. Kuang Wei-ran, driven to western China by the Japanese invasions, gathered the ballads from the mouth of a young A-Hsi man and after many corrections took the precious hoard which had been buried for thousands of years in the wilds of China and translated them into Chinese for the first time."[125] We have Mr. Hudspeth to thank for translating these into English.

The Axi people, though lacking writing, have carefully passed down their traditions in the form of ballads, sung in alternating fashion by a man and a woman.

Creation Tradition

The Creation account of the A-Hsi has general similarities with Genesis in regard to the creation of heaven and the earth. What is most striking, however, is the part about the creation of woman from man's rib:

"At the foot of a hill
In one place there was clay [yellow earth],
In a second place black coal
In yet another place, white mud.
T'oh-lo and Sha-lo
First took the clay
With which they made man's body.
Then, using the black coal and the white mud
They formed man's eyes.
T'oh-lo and Sha-lo
In this way created man.
After man was fashioned,
They proceeded to create woman.
T'oh-lo and Sha-lo
From man's body
Took out a rib
Added it to the woman's ribs
In this way woman was created.
Man and woman were now fashioned
But they couldn't move.
They were placed under the sun
And sunned for seven whole days
Whereupon they were able to move.
But they couldn't breathe.
The gods T'oh-lo and Sha-lo
Into their mouths
Blew a mouthful of breath
Upon which they were able to breathe."[126]

First Woman from First Man's Rib?

In what we just read above, this uncanny parallel with Genesis 2 might seem impossible to consider genuine. Frankly, I (Nick) questioned it initially too.

However, as I continued to encounter this detail in traditions from eastern Asia and the Pacific, tribes retelling the story of Creation and insisting

123. W. H. Hudspeth, "A creation Story of the A-Hsi," *Folklore*, vol. 70, no. 2 (1959), p. 398.
124. *Ibid.*, p. 398-399.
125. *Ibid.*, p. 399.
126. *Ibid.*, pp. 402-403.

that the first woman was created using a rib taken from the first man, I became more and more convinced of its authenticity. Many more instances of this belief are documented in this volume.

Further evidence in favor of the authenticity of this "rib" story comes from the high degree to which many tribes of Asia and the Pacific have a generally consistent storyline and consistent (and peculiar) narrative themes in their Flood and Creation stories. This lends support to their credibility. For more information about "rib" stories, see the Topical Index in the back of this book.

Flood Tradition

The A-Hsi tribe's Flood tradition, recorded in the 1940s and translated and published in the 1950s, also involves the first man and woman from the Creation account above. This first man and woman had ten children–five sons and five daughters. The eldest four pairs of children were married, in order of age, but the youngest son and daughter were too young to be married. Now, they all began to dig and toil and cultivate in a certain field. That is where we pick up the story:

> "They toiled until dusk, whereupon they went home to rest. However, the ground they had dug was land not allowed by the gods to be delved. Therefore, waiting until after they had gone home, a celestial god, taking the stretch of ground that had been dug up, covered it over with grass, wood and stones. The earth was made as it had been aforetime. They had worked for two days, panting, sweating. When they hastened back on the morrow, the earth was as though it hadn't been dug over. On the evening of the third day, all of them remained on the land they had delved, resolutely waiting and watching, to see who had dared to take what had been dug over"[127]

At last, they waited and saw that it was an old man! With his staff, he "was restoring the earth which they had dug over." The older siblings seized him and planned to beat him. But then the youngest children intervened, and implored their older brothers and sisters to do him no harm. "This is no other than a god. … Release him, be merciful to him." So the brothers and sisters paid attention, and set the elderly man free. Leaving, the old man said to them all, "You ought quickly to go home. In the near future, the Lord of Heaven is going to send a great flood. Each should quickly prepare something whereby to escape from the flood."[128]

> The old man said to them all, 'You ought quickly to go home. ... The Lord of Heaven is going to send a great flood.'

Acting on this word, the oldest son made a chest of gold, the second son a chest of silver, the third son a chest of brass, and the fourth son a chest of iron. The youngest son, by contrast, ran to a hill and asked the god Ko-tzu what to do. He was advised, "My good child, don't be apprehensive. Chests of gold, silver, brass and iron you cannot cope with. You simply make a chest of wood." So he made a chest of wood and took his youngest sister with him." When the chest was completed, heavy rain began to fall. Every day the heavens darkened; every day heavy rain became more copious; every day the flood increased … There was the sound of the collapsing of the hills, of the cracking of the earth." As the flood rose, the first through fourth pairs of siblings perished in their chests of gold, silver, brass, and iron.[129]

127. W. H. Hudspeth, "The A-Hsi Story of the Deluge," *Folklore*, vol. 71, no. 2 (1960), pp. 109-110. The text occurs in verse. I have simply reformatted it as prose to reduce length.
128. *Ibid.*, pp. 110-111.
129. *Ibid.*, pp. 111-112.

> "Only the fifth son and the fifth daughter, taking with them provision for a journey and seating themselves within the wooden chest, allowed the violent wind and rolling waves to blow them to a distant place. … The flood daily deepened! The water on the face of the earth as it rose became more violent. From the tops of the mountains it flowed into the void. It bumped against the base of heaven, kung–kung–kung it bumped three times. The Lord of Heaven then knew the water had reached the base of heaven!"[130]

It bumped against the base of heaven … it bumped three times. The Lord of Heaven then knew the water had reached the base of heaven!

This three times is the same number of times Noah sent a bird: first the raven, then the dove, then the dove again. The dove returned to him with a freshly plucked olive leaf in its beak, and Noah knew that the Flood was coming to an end. (Genesis 8:6-11)

There is even a reference to an old pine tree on the top of a hill, which stopped the wooden chest's drifting.[131] This is, no doubt, an echo of the Ark coming to rest on top of Mount Ararat.

The Sani people live in southwest China (Yunnan Province) and are closely related to the A-Hsi and Zhuang people groups. Though we have only fragmentary information on their Flood tradition, it appears similar to that of their A-Hsi relatives. They refer to a brother-sister pair, Asma and Ahei, who alone survived the Flood, and that theirs was the sole case in which incest was permissible.[132]

23 DONG

The Dong (previously known as Kam) are a minority people who have lived in southern China since ancient times. According to their tradition, the Flood took place during a fight between a personified "Lightning" and two humans: a brother named Zhang Liang and a sister named Zhang Mei.[133]

Lightning planned for Zhang Liang and Zhang Mei to drown in a great flood. Soon the mountains were submerged in water.

> "By then, torrential rain was falling. Lightning planned for Zhang Liang and Zhang Mei to drown in a great flood. Soon the mountains were submerged in water. Brother and sister survived by floating in the huge gourd that had grown from Lightning's tooth, but most other living beings were drowned. Many small creatures floating on the water or flying just above the surface begged to take refuge in the gourd. They promised to help Zhang Liang and Zhang Mei fight against Lightning, and were then welcomed on board.
>
> As the rain fell, the gourd floated up to the sky, until it reached Lightning's sky-home. On catching sight of Lightning, Zhang Liang shot at him with bow and arrows. At the same time, hundreds of hornets attached and stunk Lighting on the face. Lightning ultimately surrendered and agreed to release seven fireballs to reduce the flood."[134]

After the Flood, Zhang Liang and Zhang Mei resumed their normal lives. They each sought a mate, but finding none, they asked an eagle if there were any other humans on earth that they might marry. The eagle answered that no other humans

130. *Ibid.*, pp. 112-113.
131. *Ibid.*, p. 113.
132. B.B Vakhtin and R.F. Itsa, Эпические сказания народов южного Китая ("Epic tales of the peoples of southern China") (Moscow, 1956), p. 128.
133. D. Norman Geary et al., *The Kam People of China: Turning Nineteen* (New York: Routledge Curzon, 2003), pp. 215-216. Based on a translation of: Yang Guoren and Liao Zhengzhong, Minjian wenxue ziliao ji, di yi ji (*"Anthology of Folk Literature"*, vol. 1) (Kaili, China: 1981), pp. 1-11.
134. *Ibid.*, pp. 216-217.

had survived the flood, and advised them to marry each other, and this was the only way the human race would continue. "They were extremely reluctant to do so, and first conducted a special experiment, ensuring that they had the Sky's approval." After marrying, they eventually produced children who would form several people groups, each with their own language, including the Dong, Chinese, Miao, and Yao.[135]

Brother and sister survived by floating in the huge gourd … most other living beings were drowned.

In another version, a dog takes the place of Noah's dove.[136]

Magi from the East

Matthew's Gospel records that, when Jesus was born, "magi from the east arrived in Jerusalem, saying, 'Where is He who has been born King of the Jews? For we saw His star in the east and have come to worship Him.' And when Herod the king heard this, he was troubled, and all Jerusalem with him." (Matt. 2:2-3)

Where were these magi from? Matthew records that Herod later killed all the male children in Bethlehem who were two years old or less, "according to the time which he had carefully determined from the magi." (Matt. 2:16) But if these magi were from Babylon, Persia, or Arabia, would the decision to kill two-year-olds really be "according to the time" Herod ascertained from the magi?

Is it possible these magi were from a more distant nation like China? Is there evidence to support a Chinese identification of the magi? Do China's astronomical records also know of a "King Star" that was seen near the time that Jesus was born? To explore this most fascinating question, I highly commend to you the books "Shaanxi" by Paul Hattaway and "Faith of Our Fathers" by Chan Kai Thong.

"From the anthropologist's point of view," wrote Robert von Heine-Geldern, "the Wa on the border of Burma and India are without doubt one of the most important tribes of the whole of Southeast Asia. They alone have preserved in the center of Further India such ancient cultural traits as head-hunting, the erection of megalithic monuments, the use of the split drum, etc."[137] This nation, whose name means "mountaineer," was notorious for headhunting, believing that evil spirits held authority over them and required a human sacrifice to grant a good harvest.[138]

---

135. *Ibid.*, p. 217. The process by which they had these children was not direct, but involves our least favorite motif, that of "deformed flesh," which recurs in East and Southeast Asia, and which likely contains an echo of the Tower of Babel: "Soon after Zhang Liang and Zhang Mel had married, Zhang Mel gave birth to a grotesque son, without eyes, nose, arms and legs. With its one mouth it talked and ate. It was an abomination to its parents, and they chopped it up into pieces and scattered the pieces on the mountainsides. A few days later, Zhang Liang and Zhang Mel were astonished to hear the sound of babies crying on the mountain tops and in the ravines. When they climbed a mountain peak to have a look, they saw hordes of bouncing vivacious children everywhere they looked. Some of the children spoke Kam, some Mandarin Chinese, some Miao and some Yao."
136. "Among the northern Kam the story goes that there was once a great flood, and when the flood had subsided there was no rice seed to be found anywhere. A dog volunteered to go eastwards across a large river, to bring back some rice seeds from the heavily-guarded grain stores there. The dog was able to slip into a grain storehouse and roll around in the rice, so that the seeds clung to its fur. On its way home it had to swim across the river, and realizing that the water would wash the rice away, it held its tail high in the air as it swam. In this way, it came safely home with rice seeds clinging to its tail, enabling the Kam people once again to grow paddy rice." Source: Geary et. al., *The Kam People of China*, p. 114.
137. Robert von Heine-Geldern, "Research on Southeast Asia; Problems and Suggestions," *American Anthropologist*, vol. 48, no. 2 (1946), p. 158.
138. Paul Hattaway, *Operation China*, p. 534.

The Wa have a creation story known as Si Gang Li, which in their language means to emerge from a cave. This story tells of "the re-peopling of the earth after a devastating flood destroys most living creatures." As the name suggests, a small number of people survived inside a cave. After the Flood had ended, they came out and the survivors split up and gave rise to several tribes, including the Wa, the Han, the Yi, and the Dai.[139]

Another interesting version from the Wa people features a patriarch known as Ada Regan who anticipated the Flood and prepared a stone boat.[140]

> A Wa Flood story tells of a patriarch named Ada Regan who anticipated the Flood and prepared a stone boat.

25 KUCONG

The Kucong are a small tribe of southwestern China's Yunnan province and adjacent parts of Southeast Asia. The Chinese government has not yet recognized them as an official minority. Linguistically, they are related to the Lahu. The Kucong people's creation story, which is set to song, preserves a memory of the Flood which they say took place shortly after the creation:

> The Kucong Flood and Creation story is set to song.

"There was a family that had nine brothers and a little sister. Although the sister was very hardworking and she brought water to her nine brothers, they barely gave her any food. So one day, she left the house with an empty stomach. Then she cut a stick and made a staff out of it. Supporting herself with the staff, she walked to the bank of the Red River. That staff was very strange, however, and in just three days it grew until it became a large tree capable of reaching the sky."[141]

Many people groups of Asia have similar traditions of a cosmic tree that reached to the sky. I believe this to be a vague memory of the Tree of the Knowledge of Good and Evil (Genesis 2) mixed with a memory of the Tower of Babel (Genesis 11). The tradition continues:

"After three years the great tree covered the sky. At that time the little birds could no longer reach the peak of this tree, and the monkeys could not reach its last branches either. The land was completely dark, people had no way to live, everyone kept hoping that that tree would be cut down, but cutting that big tree was tremendously difficult. If a piece was cut off one day, the next day the wound was closed. In the end its secret was discovered, and after cutting for 99 days, the great tree that covered the sky was finally cut down."

> There was only a pair of siblings named Dansou and Danluo who lay down inside a huge gourd and escaped the disaster of the flood.

139. Mark Bender, "Echoes from Si Gang Lih: Burao Yilu's 'Moon Mountain,'" *Asian Highlands Perspectives*, vol. 10 (2011), p. 115.
140. "Ada Regan makes a stone boat in anticipation of a great flood. When the floodwaters cover the earth, he floats about accompanied by a cow and a calabash. After some time the cow becomes famished and eats the calabash. When Ada asks where the calabash went, the teary-eyed cow says it is within her. Ada asks her to give birth to it, the cow does so, and Ada plants it. After nine years and nine months the vines, leaves, and flowers soon cover the hillsides and valleys, but the calabash is nowhere in sight. Ada sends the cow, then an elephant, a rat, and an eagle to search for it, but all fail. Finally after a majestic dance, a peacock succeeds in finding the gourd hidden within sacred Caimu Mountain. Finally Ada takes action and opens the calabash with his knife." From: Wei Deming, *A Cultural History of the Wa Ethnic Group*, (Kunming: Yunnan Nationalities Press, 2001), p. 256. As translated to English in: Bender, "Echoes from Si Gang Lih," pp. 115-116. A similar version can also be found in: Chen Qinghao and Wang Quigui (eds.),《雲南民間故事集1》, *Collection of Yunnan Folk Tales*, 1, 中國民間故事全集, *Complete Collection of Chinese Folk Tales*, vol. 7 (Taipei, 1989), pp. 441-445.
141. Lei Bo and Liu Huihao, *A Brief History of Lahu Literature* (Kunming: Yunnan Nationalities Press, 1995), pp. 125-26. As translated in: Pedro Ceinos Arcones, "Dos Mitos de la creación de la minoría Kucong," 拉祜族文学史, *Chinaviva*. September 1, 2023. https://chinaviva.com/dos-mitos-de-la-creacion-de-la-minoria -kucong/

The destruction of that cosmic tree, however, resulted in a great Flood which burst from that very tree:

> "After a time there was a great flood, the water covered the entire earth. As the root of the great tree that had been cut down had been pierced by ants, the flood fell from the root of that tree, flooding the entire earth, and destroying the people who lived on the earth. There was only a pair of siblings named Dansou and Danluo who lay down inside a huge gourd and escaped the disaster of the flood. When the waters receded the two siblings married, having numerous children who are the ancestors of the Kucong, the Yao, the Hani, the Dai and the Han Chinese."

Criticizing Darwinism

> "When the Chinese paleontologist J. Y. Chen discussed some of these findings [the Cambrian explosion] at the University of Washington in Seattle more than a decade ago, he went out of his way to express doubts about the adequacy of Darwinism in accounting for what we see. The paleontologists in the audience ignored his doubts, and afterwards he asked a visitor why. The visitor told him it was very unpopular to doubt Darwinism in the U.S. He laughed and said: 'In China we can criticize Darwin, but not the government; in America, you can criticize the government, but not Darwin.'" (Journalist Tom Bethel)[142]

The Li are the native people of Hainan Island, the southernmost point in China. Their Flood story about the "big pumpkin" is truly stunning. It goes as follows. Long ago, there lived two brothers. The elder brother's name was Lao Dang, and the younger brother's name was Lao Ding. The wives of the two brothers were childless. One day, an old man with white hair and a grey beard came to the brothers. He gave instructions that they should plant a pumpkin in front of their door, and that "when the pumpkin blooms and bears fruit, the child will be born."

One day, an old man with white hair and a grey beard came ... He gave instructions that they should plant a pumpkin. ... After a hundred days, the pumpkin was as big as a house.

So Lao Dang and Lao Ding followed the old man's advice. They planted a pumpkin seed in front of their door, and they watered it and took care of it, hoping that it would grow quickly. But it took quite some time, for the pumpkin vine grew to great lengths, thousands of feet long, before it flowered and bore fruit. Finally, on the day the pumpkin bore fruit, both men's wives gave birth. The elder brother's wife gave birth to a son, named Lao Xian. The younger brother's wife gave birth to a girl, and her name was He Fa.

But that was not the last word on the pumpkin. Out of gratitude to the old man, the brothers continued tending to the pumpkin and it continued to grow. "After a hundred days, the pumpkin was as big as a house."

Then the flood began. It rained heavily, and did not cease raining for ten years. "The water flooded the entire earth. Fortunately, Lao Dang and Lao Ding dug a hole in the pumpkin in advance and put their children inside the pumpkin. They also drove cows, horses, dogs, cats, chickens, and other animals in with them." A mouse snuck inside as well.

---

142. Tom Bethell, *Darwin's House of Cards* (Seattle: Discovery Institute, 2017), pp. 136-137.

Fearing that water would leak into the pumpkin, the brothers sealed the hole of the pumpkin with beeswax. It is because of this that pumpkins today have a yellow-orange waxy color and are very smooth. As for the two brothers and their wives, they were not spared. The waters flooded their homes. All the animals on earth were swept away by the flooding. The big pumpkin also drifted with the waves until it drifted to Wuzhi Mountain.

Inside the pumpkin, the two siblings Lao Xian and He Fa grew up eating pumpkin flesh. The animals also fed on the pumpkin. "Ten years later, the heavy rain stopped. The waters slowly receded back toward the sea, but the big pumpkin was stranded on the top of Wuzhi Mountain."

Now the siblings wanted to know what the outside world was like, but there was no hole to climb out of the pumpkin. They asked several of the animals, in turns, to dig a hole through the pumpkin. First the horse, but it failed and lost its horn. The cow tried too, but failed and lost its upper teeth. The pig also failed, and its snout was flattened in the process. "Finally, the brother and sister asked the mouse to dig a hole. With its two sharp front teeth, the mouse succeeded in cutting through the pumpkin shell". To this day, it is said, horses no longer have horns, cows no longer have upper teeth, and pigs have short, flat snouts.

Before the sibling went out, they asked a rooster to go first. The rooster went out and immediately saw the sun, for it was dawn. "It flapped its wings happily and crowed loudly. It announced to the pumpkin that the world was a good place." Lao Xian and He Fa heard the rooster's crow and knew that everything was safe outside. Later they married and reestablished the human population.[143]

The parallels with Genesis are numerous. Another narration, although fragmentary, includes the theme found all over China that the siblings performed a series of tests which led them to marry.[144] This motif, and its parallels with Noah's tests involving the raven and dove, are analyzed further in Appendix B.

Lao Dang and Lao Ding dug a hole in the pumpkin in advance and put their children inside the pumpkin. They also drove cows, horses, dogs, cats, chickens, and other animals in with them. … the big pumpkin was stranded on the top of Wuzhi Mountain.

It flapped its wings happily and crowed loudly. It announced to the pumpkin that the world was a good place." Lao Xian and He Fa heard the rooster's crow and knew that everything was safe outside.

27 MULAO

The Flood tradition of the Mulao people of Guanxi is similar to other versions from southern China. It tells that there were two kind-hearted younger siblings who showed mercy to the thunder god, whom their evil elder siblings had trapped with the intention to kill and eat it. In reward for allowing his escape, they were given a tooth which, when planted, turned into a giant calabash gourd. The thunder god instructed them to tend to this plant, hollow it out, and fill it with rice in preparation for the coming calamity. The siblings followed these instructions.

Then came the Flood. "It rained continuously for three years and six months." It rained harder and harder, and the water rose higher and higher. The gourd floated upon the waters, and with a "thud" it struck heaven. An order was given

It rained continuously for three years and six months. … Everyone else on earth drowned, but the siblings floated in their gourd and landed on a mountain.

143. Chen Qinghao and Wang Quigui (eds.), 《廣東民間故事集》, *Collection of Guangdong Folk Tales*, 中國民間故事全集 *Complete Collection of Chinese Folk Tales*, vol. 3 (Taipei, 1989), pp. 345-349.

144. Chungshee Halen Lui, "Hai-nan-tao Li-ren wen-shen chih ven chiu" ("A study of Tattoo of the Li of Hainan Island"), *Bulletin of Ethnological Studies*, vol. 1 (Canton: 1936), p. 201. As quoted by Ho T'ing-jui, "A Comparative Study of Myths and Legends of Formosan Aborigines," *Asian Folklore and Social Life Monographs*, vol. 18 (Taipei: Orient Cultural Services, 1971), p. 276. The relevant text is: "Since they were brother and sister, it was impossible for them to marry and they dispersed east and west to seek mates. They met again without finding anybody. The same attempt was repeated and all failed. Aware of this trouble, the Thunder-god transformed himself into a human being, came down, and told the brother, "I came here as a witness. You two may become man and wife." The brother said, "Brother and sister cannot marry; otherwise, the Thunder-god would punish us." The Thunder-God said, "I am he. I will never punish you." But the brother still persisted that such a union was improper. The brother then again went out to look for a mate. The Thunder-god immediately disguised the sister by painting her face black. As a result, the brother met the sister without recognizing her, and he took her as a wife. From this union people multiplied and the present Li people descended."

in heaven to stop the rain, and the Flood subsided. Everyone else on earth drowned, but the siblings floated in their gourd and landed on a mountain. After three incidents (two animals that counseled them and one test), they agreed to marry.[145]

We will observe remarkable parallels between this Chinese Flood story and a New Guinean Flood theme.

On page 200 we will observe remarkable parallels between this Chinese Flood story and a New Guinean Flood theme. It is the same story. This presupposes an older account, which is older than both China and New Guinea. This is the Genesis record, which alone contains all the elements sufficient to account for these two traditions, and other traditions found all around the world.

28 TUJIA

The Tujia live in Hunan and neighboring provinces in southern China, where they are one of the larger minority groups in all of China. Their origin is uncertain, but they are at least in part the descendants of an ancient tribe known as the Ba people.[146]

Tujia Woman in Traditional Dress

Their impressive Flood tradition is very similar to that of the Mulao. It tells of the capture of the Thunder God (Lei Gong) by several children at the command of their evil and gluttonous mother. She and the other children planned to kill the Thunder God later and eat its meat, but first they wanted to fatten him up. So they imprisoned him in an iron cage and went up in the mountains to hunt with their dogs and hawks.

Only two people were left in the house with Thunder God: a young boy named Luo Zi and a young girl named Luo Mei. Lei Gong persuaded the children to give him a bowl of water, against the instructions they had been given. After drinking it, he escaped and went up into the sky.

> "Lei Gong found the Rain Mother again, cried bitterly, and demanded revenge: 'Please let it rain heavily for seven days and seven nights, so that the people of the world will be drowned. … Only Luo Zi and Luo Mei are good people. Let them remain safe.' So Lei Gong called for a swallow and gave it a gourd seed and said, 'Go quickly and give it to Luo Zi and Luo Mei.' The swallow nodded, picked up the gourd seed, and flew through the clouds and fog to Luo Zi and Luo Mei. He threw the seed to them.'"[147]

The gourd seed took root and grew rapidly. By the sixth day it was as big as a boat. On the seventh day, the girl picked it off the vine, and right then the sky changed!

"Please let it rain heavily for seven days and seven nights, so that the people of the world will be drowned. … Only Luo Zi and Luo Mei are good people. Let them remain safe."

> "Dark clouds rolled in, and the rain poured down like a bucket. It continued for seven days and seven nights. The floods submerged the villages and the mountains. There was a vast sea of water everywhere."[148]

The tradition notes that the boy did not ride inside the gourd with his sister, but floated along in a bucket, holding tightly to the gourd. Later, "the immortal god appeared to them and said, 'You two are the only ones left of the human race. Get married and have offspring.'" Luo Zi and Luo Mei were ashamed and

145. Chen Qinghao and Wang Quigui (eds.),《廣西民間故事集1》, *Collection of Guangxi Folk Tales, 2"*, 中國民間故事全集, *Complete Collection of Chinese Folk Tales*, vol. 5 (Taipei, 1989), pp. 395-398.
146. Chen Qinghao and Wang Quigui (eds.),《廣西民間故事集1》, "Collection of Hunan Folk Tales, 1", *Complete Collection of Chinese Folk Tales*, vol. 17 (Taipei, 1989), p. 335.
147. *Ibid.*, p. 347.
148. *Ibid.*, p. 347.

unwilling. But after three tests, involving millstones, bamboo sticks, and walking around a mountain, they understood that it was from God, so they agreed to marry. Still, they felt so guilty and ashamed that the boy's face turned red and the woman's face turned blue at that moment, and they said "we are ashamed before God." They continued, adding that they were ashamed before the ground, before their neighbors, and before each other. But finally, they came together, and from their offspring all the nations have their origin.[149] Here we cannot help but notice a parallel between "we are ashamed before God" and the shame resulting from Adam and Eve's sin in Genesis 3. These and other reasons (see Appendix B) lead us to conclude that there is a mixed memory of Adam and Eve in this and related Asian Flood stories.

Returning to the Tujia text, its narrator added that "Later generations respectfully call them Eunuch Luo Shen and Empress Luo Shen. In order to commemorate that they survived the flood and founded the human race, people built a dragon boat. There was a shrine on the boat, covered with red cloth, and two statues of gods were enshrined inside: one was a man with a red face and the other a woman with a blue face. This reproduces the appearance of the brother and sister when they got married."[150]

29 MAONAN

The Maonan people of northern Guangxi tell a Flood story which begins with a war between a benevolent god named Tu Tu and the evil thunder god. In the third battle, the thunder god was soundly defeated and imprisoned. Being a dragon, and one whose strength comes from water, he deceived two young siblings into giving him a drink of water (recall the Serpent who ensnared Adam and Eve, getting them to eat the forbidden food). Thus he managed to regain his strength and escape. As he departed, he gave the children two teeth which, when planted, grew into a massive gourd. Later, the Flood came.

"The weather suddenly changed, and it rained heavily for sixty days." These two siblings, Pan and Gu, were the only two mortals who escaped by taking refuge inside their giant golden gourd. "The flood carried Pan and Gu in their gourd to the top of the mountain," and "The flood lasted for three hundred and sixty days before receding." This length is a mere ten days short of the biblical 370 days. The siblings eventually married after confirmatory tests.[151]

Being a dragon, he deceived two young siblings into giving him a drink of water.

30 DAI

According to the Dai people of southwest China, there were originally seven suns in the sky. This caused excessive heat, so some young men shot six of the suns out of the sky. These upon crashing to earth caused fires on land and boiling water in the sea. To quell this disaster, the creator god named Yingba sent water upon the earth in excess, causing the Flood. Regarding this Flood, they tell:

> "He [Yingba] opened his divine mouth again and spat water towards the earth. The saliva that Yingba spat out suddenly turned into a downpour, covering the sky and pouring down toward the earth. The god Yingba did not eat or drink, but spat at the earth for a hundred days. So it rained heavily and continued for a hundred days and a hundred nights. As a result, the entire earth became a vast expanse of water. All the high mountains on the earth were submerged by the flood, but only one high mountain, named Pizahu Mountain, was not submerged. Half of the top of the mountain was exposed above the water. At this time, all kinds

The flood lasted for three hundred and sixty days before receding.

149. *Ibid.*, pp. 345-351.
150. *Ibid.*, p. 352.
151. Chen Qinghao and Wang Quigui (eds.),《廣西民間故事集1》, *Collection of Guangxi Folk Tales, 1*, 中國民間故事全集, *Complete Collection of Chinese Folk Tales*, vol. 4 (Taipei, 1989), pp. 257-265.

> of animals swam toward the mountain, but most of them had been drowned by the flood, and their bodies were floating all over the water … The water flooded the earth for a hundred days … After a hundred days, the heavy rain stopped and the flood slowly receded. A hundred days later, the entire earth returned to its original state. But by this time, there were very few people and animals who survived on the top of Pizahu Mountain."[152]

They also have a Creation story with noteworthy Genesis parallels.[153]

31 HANI

The Hani presently live in southern Yunnan Province, but their origins are to the northwest on the Tibetan Plateau. According to their traditions, they are an offshoot of the Nosu people.[154] Their creation story refers to a quarrel between the gods, as a result of which fire broke out in heaven and earth. Water was commanded to extinguish the fire, but this had the devastating result of flooding the entire earth:

> "The fireball was extinguished by the flood, and heaven and earth were saved, but the earth was submerged in a flood. No one escaped this disaster except two siblings, Zuo Luo and his sister Zuo Bei, who survived by hiding inside a gourd. Their gourd floated and drifted with the current for six years, until they reached the place where ten rivers converge. After the water fell, they walked out of the gourd and found themselves trapped in a mountain valley, and they settled in a cave which kept them safe from wind and rain."[155]

Zuo Luo and his sister Zuo Bei, who survived by hiding inside a gourd. Their gourd floated and drifted with the current for six years.

After this, they were disheartened by the discovery that there were no other human survivors on earth and no prospect for marriage. Brother-sister marriage was unthinkable, for Zuo Lou said, "Only pigeons from the same nest can form pairs. Brothers and sisters cannot marry." But a certain god urged them to marry. "He planted love in Zuo Lou's heart and cast love in Zuo Bei's heart." Still reluctant, they agreed to perform three tests: they threw leaves, threw wooden planks, and rolled millstones. The leaves landed on each other, the wood planks landed on each other, and the millstones rolled onto each other. Seeing that it was the will of heaven, they agreed to marry, and so repopulated humanity.[156]

They performed three tests, the results of which convinced them it was the will of heaven to marry.

---

152. Shen Zhengde (ed.), 西双版傣族民故事, *Folk Tales of the Dai Ethnic Group in Xishuangbanna*, (Kunming: Yunnan People's Publishing House, 1993), pp. 18-19.
153. "In the beginning when the heaven and the earth came into existence there was nothing in the world but bare land and vast ocean. All was in dreariness without any trace of human beings, animals, trees, flowers or grass. Then God king Yingba, the Creator, sent the saint couple Bu Sanggai and Ya Sanggai to the earth with a sacred gourd to create man and other living things because of their miraculous power and hearts of gold.
They cut the sacred gourd into halves. Hardly had they scattered the seeds upwards when the sky became heavily sprinkled with stars and alight with the shining of sun and moon, and no sooner had they spread the seeds downwards than the earth flourished with luxuriant vegetation, blooming flowers and aromatic fruit. However, the world was still without man and animals, whose lives had been absent from the sacred gourd seeds. The couple thought to themselves: as a place of fabulous abundance and extraordinary vastness, the earth should be ruled by a different kind of being … Thereupon they accomplished the creation of a man and a woman out of clay, and breathed life, soul and vitality into them. Purified by sunshine, moonlight, wind and rain, this clay couple finally came into life and began to walk about on the earth, and Bu Sanggai and Ya Sanggai gifted them with the ability to speak and to think. Their name was 'man.'" Source: Mineke Schipper, Ye Shuxian and Yin Hubin (eds.), *China's Origin and Creation Myths*, (Boston: Brill, 2011), p. 307.
154. *Atlas of Humanity*, "Hani People." Retrieved 13 July, 2024 from https://www.atlasofhumanity.com/hani
155. Chen Qinghao and Wang Quigui (eds.),《雲南民間故事集2》, "Collection of Guizhuo Folk Tales, 2," 中國民間故事全集, *Complete Collection of Chinese Folk Tales*, vol. 8 (Taipei, 1989), pp. 257-260.
156. *Ibid*., pp. 260-261.

32 ANONG

The Anong people are one of four sub-groups of the Nu nationality, along with the Nusu, Zauzou, and Dulong (Trung).[157] Their tradition of the Flood comes to us from Sun Hongkai's research among them, which began in 1960. "According to an Anong legend, long, long ago, there was a great flood. Among the ancestors of the Anong people, a brother and a sister hid themselves in a big gourd which protected them from the disaster. In order to continue the ancestral line of the Anong people, the brother and sister got married and had nine boys and seven girls. The first child was an Anong, the second was a Trung, and the rest were Han, Tibetan, Bai, Lisu, and Naxi. The Anong settled down in the Nujiang region, while the rest went to far away places to make a living. Because of this legend, the elders all believe the Anong are the indigenous people of the Nujiang region."[158]

Long, long ago, there was a great flood. Among the ancestors of the Anong people, a brother and a sister hid themselves in a big gourd which protected them from the disaster.

33 SHUI

The Shui people descend from the Luoyue, an ancient tribe that lived on China's southeastern coast, a few hundred miles east of the Shui's current homelands in Guizhou Province. The Shui Flood text is like many other Chinese versions in regard to its parallels with Genesis. It begins with "a pair of hard-working and upright orphans: a brother and a sister." After an unsuccessful search for food one day, they came across a magical axe near a spring of water. This turned out to be the Thunder God's axe, and it brought much success and prosperity to the orphans.

"Unexpectedly, three days later, an old man with white hair and a chest-length beard came to the brothers and sisters and asked them if they had picked up an axe." The children hesitated at first, then brought the axe to the man. The white-haired immortal man thanked the children, then gave them a shining golden tooth and instructed them to plant it. "The brother and sister thought the whole thing was very strange. But the immortal said they should do it, so they did so." Digging a hole, they planted the tooth in some fertile soil. This turned out to be a magical gourd vine, and it grew quickly.

> "On the ninth day, the gourd melon looked like a small barn with an orange-yellow hard shell. On the tenth day, the brother and sister went up the mountain to move the gourd, but it was too heavy and too big to move, so they had to leave the gourd on the slope. It happened that it rained heavily that night. One day, two days, three days, it kept raining. It kept raining for more than thirty days, and it never cleared up."[159]

At this point, the siblings abandoned their home (a cave) that had become soaked. Cutting a hole into the gourd, they took refuge inside. By the fourth month, the waters rose to the point that the gourd floated. By the fifth month, the mountains were covered, and by the sixth month the waters reached the sky (we can hear echoes of China's Shu King and Shi King). Still, the waters continued to climb higher, and the siblings cried out in panic. "When the immortal heard the cry of the brother and sister, he sent the water mouse to dig a drainage hole under the water. It took another six months for the flood to recede."

By the fourth month, the waters rose to the point that the gourd floated. By the fifth month, the mountains were covered, and by the sixth month the waters reached the sky.

After the Flood had ended, the white-haired immortal came to the siblings again and told them they must marry. After performing three tests (the first involving millstones and the second and third involving bamboo sticks) they agreed and came together in marriage.[160]

157. Sun Hongkai and Liu Guangkun, *A Grammar of Anong: Language Death Under Intense Contact* (Boston: Brill, 2009), p. 1.
158. *Ibid*. p. 3.
159. Chen Qinghao and Wang Quigui (eds.),《貴州民間故事集1》, "Collection of Guizhuo Folk Tales, 1", 中國民間故事全集, *Complete Collection of Chinese Folk Tales*, vol. 12 (Taipei, 1989), pp. 179-181.
160. *Ibid*., pp. 181-187.

34 GELAO

The Gelao people of Guizhou Province are one of the northern groups who speak a language of the Tai-Kadai family, which is prominent in Southeast Asia. They recount the Flood in the following terms; Long ago there were three brothers and a younger sister. The god Chege transformed himself into an old man, went down to earth, and spoke to the brothers as they were farming. He said, "The ants are all moving, and there is going to be a flood. Don't clear the wasteland. Don't plow the grass. Find a way to escape!"

The oldest two brothers responded to the old man harshly, and did not wish to be interrupted in their work. However, the younger brother, named Ayang, was of a different character. "He took a look and saw that this kind-hearted old man spoke very modestly and had good intentions to persuade his brothers not to plow, but to escape the flood." He pleaded with his brothers to listen to the old man, so they all listened. The old man instructed the younger brother to cut cedar wood, build a floating gourd-like vessel, and take his sister with him. He also told him to paint the "gourd," and take two baby chicks with him. But he instructed the other brothers, who had spoken to him harshly, to build vessels out of heavy woods which would not float.[161]

> The old man instructed the younger brother to cut cedar wood, build a floating gourd-like vessel, and take his sister with him. He also told him to paint the "gourd," and take two baby chicks with him.

When the Flood came, the older brothers sank in their vessels to the bottom of the sea and died. "Only the third child, Ayang, and his younger sister, floated on the water in their wooden gourd." After several weeks, the wooden vessel got stuck on a tree stump which was on top of a large cliff. As a result, there was no way down for the siblings.

What did they do to get down from this cliff? They found an eagle's nest next to their vessel and captured the three baby eagles, then made a deal with the mother eagle to release her babies in exchange for carrying them down by flying. First, they needed to make sure the mother eagle was strong enough to safely carry them down, so they gave her three tests carrying objects. She carried all three objects one after another. Then she carried the siblings down. Growing hungry, she demanded the boy give her the young chicks as food, and he agreed. Because of this, eagles now kill and eat chickens from time to time. Later, the god Chege reappeared to the siblings and advised them to marry in order to continue the human race. After performing a test, they understood it was the will of heaven, and they married.[162] Here we can detect a memory of Noah's raven and dove.

BAI

The Bai people live in Yunnan and Guizhou in southwest China. They say that Dragon King sent a flood in which it rained incessantly for seven years. "The sky collapsed and the earth cracked." Everything on earth was swept away and destroyed by the Flood. Only two siblings had been spared by the goddess Guanyin, who hid them inside a golden drum. The boy's name was Zhao Yupei and the girl's name was Tai Sanmei. After the Flood, Guanyin searched for the drum containing the siblings and it was found at sea. She enlisted the help of two birds, the duck and the eagle, who brought the drum to shore. But the two survivors still could not come out. Guanyin asked the woodpecker to peck and open the gourd, but it was not able. Then she asked the mouse to bite through the golden drum, and it succeeded. For this reason, mice and rats are always eating humans' food.

> The sky collapsed and the earth cracked. Everything on earth was swept away and destroyed by the Flood. Only two siblings had been spared by the goddess Guanyin, who hid them inside a golden drum. … She enlisted the help of two birds, the duck and the eagle, who brought the drum to shore.

Finally, Zhao Yupei and Tai Sanmei came out. Eventually they agreed to marry after three tests (involving smoke columns, wooden sticks, and grindstones) yielded a clear result.[163]

161. Chen Qinghao and Wang Quigui (eds.),《貴州民間故事集1》"Collection of Guizhuo Folk Tales, 1", , 中國民間故事全集, *Complete Collection of Chinese Folk Tales*, vol. 12 (Taipei, 1989), pp. 73-75.
162. *Ibid.*, pp. 75-82.
163. Chen Qinghao and Wang Quigui (eds.),《雲南民間故事集3》, "Collection of Yunnan Folk Tales, 3", 中國民間故事全集, *Complete Collection of Chinese Folk Tales*, vol. 9 (Taipei, 1989), pp. 11-17.

36 DE'ANG

The De'ang people of southwestern China have passed down a tradition of the Flood with an interesting twist. Long ago, there were only three people on earth: Tian Gong, his wife, and their daughter. It was a happy life, cultivating the land, but they were lonely. One day, Tian Gong took his tools and went to the mountain to chop wood. Then he saw a strong wind blowing, which blew a hundred leaves off a big tree. He looked up and said, "If only these leaves could turn into people, then we wouldn't be so lonely."

As soon as he finished speaking, the one hundred leaves turned into one hundred people, standing in front of him. There were fifty men and fifty women. Each of them took a family name, and each of the fifty men married one of the fifty women. Now there were 103 people in the world.

Well, all these new people on earth needed a house, so they went to a tree called "the living tree," cut it down, sawed it into planks, and built houses. They also needed fields to grow crops, so they cleared the mountainside. But there still was not enough food to eat. Then Tian Gong went up in the sky to God and asked for seeds. God gave him seeds of many grains, vegetables, and fruits, and he took them back to earth and distributed them to the people. They planted these, and the countryside filled with grains, melons, and fruits. Yet there was one gourd seed which Tian Gong planted on the seashore, and it grew to enormous size, with roots and vine extending into the sea. The gourd itself grew "as big as a hill," and it floated in the sea.

One day, a flood suddenly came upon the world. All the people hid inside the gourd, and they drifted upon the waters. They drifted for a long time, and one day they landed. Then there was a loud sound, a hole in the gourd burst open, and the 103 people came out. These became the ancestors of the De'ang, Han, Lisu, and many other ethnic groups that live today. After these people came out of the gourd, all the animals and plants were brought out as well.[164]

37 PUMI

According to the Flood tradition of the Pumi tribe of Yunnan Province, a long time ago there were three brothers who were clearing a forested plot of land. A crow went to the eldest brother and offered to reveal important news in exchange for the man's lunch. But the man cursed the crow, hit him with a stone, and drove him away. The next day, the crow flew to the middle son, and this one also spoke harshly to the crow, beat him, and drove him away.

On the third day, the crow went to the youngest brother, and he agreed to give the crow his lunch. So the crow said, "there is going to be a big flood this afternoon. You should run away." Later that day, a great flood burst out from the earth, ascending toward the heavens. Only the youngest brother survived, having been securely tied to the top of a very tall sacred tree. Later he threw a stick down which struck the earth, making a sound by which the boy knew that the flood had ended.[165]

> The crow said, "there is going to be a big flood this afternoon." … Only the youngest brother survived, having been securely tied to the top of a very tall sacred tree.

38 ACHANG

The Achang of southwestern China have an old tradition of Creation, followed by the Flood, which happened in this way: "Suddenly, one morning, lightning knocked down the big trees. Thunder knocked down the birds in their nests, and strong winds blew open the four sides of the sky. Heavy rain fell on the earth, and floods submerged all the villages. The earth turned into a flood again."

The mother earth goddess helped to repair the east, west, and north sides of the sky. Next, Zhapama (the first man) and Zhemina (the first woman) discussed what should be done about the southern direction, for "the surviving people

164. Chen Qinghao and Wang Quigui (eds.), 《雲南民間故事集3》, "Collection of Yunnan Folk Tales, 3", 中國民間故事全集, *Complete Collection of Chinese Folk Tales*, vol. 9 (Taipei, 1989), pp. 471-472.
165. Chen Qinghao and Wang Quigui (eds.), 《雲南民間故事集4》, "Collection of Yunnan Folk Tales, 4", 中國民間故事全集, *Complete Collection of Chinese Folk Tales*, vol. 10 (Taipei, 1989), pp. 503-510.

and animals were trapped on the hills," and "the floodwaters were still rising to the top of the mountain every day." Zhapama led his men to build a stone wall to block the flood, and a wooden door to block the winds. "The floods were subdued, the wind and rain were blocked, and the animals began to capture food and reproduce their offspring again. People returned to the plains from the mountaintops, rebuilt their homes, and restored peace and tranquility."[166]

39 BONAN

The Bonan are a small people group who have their roots in the Mongolian occupation of China several centuries ago. They seem to be of mixed Mongolian, Chinese, and Hui descent. The Bonan people have passed down a vague tradition of the Flood. The Flood is attributed to a rich, selfish man who shot a magical horse which had brought blessing upon the land. When shot, it roared in pain and "the earth-shattering road opened a large hole in Jishi Mountain." Waters poured out of this hole, destroying the world in their wake. Three men and three women survived, who founded the Mongolian, Hui, and Tibetan nations. They refer to a White Horse Temple which their people built "to prevent future generations from forgetting the happiness that this sacred horse brought to the people."[167]

40 BULANG

The Bulang people of Yunnan Province have a story called "Brother and Sister Marriage" which, as the name suggests, tells of a pair of siblings who had to marry because they were the only survivors of the Flood. They had four sons (and presumably four daughters) who gave rise to nations after the Flood. Regretfully, we do not possess the substance of this text.[168]

41 MONBA

The Monba of southwestern China (Monpa in India) have a vague account of the Flood. Their former habitation was destroyed, the mountains collapsed, and a remnant fled to the top of a mountain. There they suffered hunger and cold until a goddess named Chukisangmu dug a ditch which allowed the water to drain.[169]

166. Chen Qinghao and Wang Quigui (eds.),《雲南民間故事集5》, "Collection of Yunnan Folk Tales, 5", 中國民間故事全集, *Complete Collection of Chinese Folk Tales*, vol.11 (Taipei, 1989), p. 452.
167. Chen Qinghao and Wang Quigui (eds.), 甘肅民間故事集》, "Collection of Gansu Folk Tales", *Complete Collection of Chinese Folk Tales*, vol. 29 (Taipei, 1989), pp. 280-283..
168. Wang Xianzhao, 中国多民族兄妹婚神母探析, *Analysis of the Mythical Motif of Brother-Sister Marriage among Chinese Multi-ethnic Groups*, Institute of Ethnic Literature of the Chinese Academy of Social Sciences. December 6, 2010. Retrieved 11 July, 2024 from http://iel.cass.cn/ztpd/shyj/ssmzsh/201012/t20101206_2762700.shtml
169. Wang Shiyuan et al, 赫哲族, 巴族, 珞巴族, 基族 "Hezhe, Monba, Lhoba, Jinuo", 中國民族故事大系, *Chinese Ethnic Story Series*, vol. 16 (Shanghai, 1995), p. 298.

Consider the beautiful Rainbow Mountains of China's Gansu Province. Behold the knife edge boundaries between each color, that is, between each rock layer. Not one earthworm, not one erosional event or storm, not one tree root, not one burrowing creature disturbed these distinct layers before they were all deposited. Not one soil horizon formed. If these layers really were deposited one at a time over millions of years, where is the evidence of time? We know from flume experiments, however, that rapidly moving water is capable of forming such stratified "layer cakes." Yet this rock formation far exceeds (in breadth and depth) the scope of any local event. The Genesis Flood explains the rocks beneath the feet of China's people.

China's Rainbow Mountains

The Lhoba (or Luoba) people of southeastern Tibet have a Flood tradition which features a "brother-sister" marriage theme.[170] However, the substance of this tradition was unavailable at the time of publication.

The Qiang people, living in Tibet, are one of the earliest groups referred to in China's ancient historical records. They have a Flood account which tells that in ancient times, a mischievous monkey went to heaven and overturned a golden basin filled with water, which caused a flood on earth. After this disaster, only a sister and a brother were left on earth. They felt it was the will of heaven to marry because they rolled two millstones, which came together. They united in marriage and gave birth to a strange lump of meat, from which human children ultimately came.[171]

The She tribe of eastern China have a Flood tradition which is, in general, similar to many other Chinese versions. The Thunder God is captured, given water by two children, then escapes and causes the Flood.[172]

---

170. Wang Xianzhao, 中国多民族兄妹婚神母探析, *Mythical Motif of Brother-Sister Marriage among Chinese Multi-ethnic Groups*, (December 6, 2010). Institute of Ethnic Literature of the Chinese Academy of Social Sciences (IELCASS). Retrieved 11 July, 2024 from http://iel.cass.cn/ztpd/shyj/ssmzsh/201012/t20101206_2762700.shtml
171. Guan Jixin, *Qiang Literature*, (October 18, 2006). IELCASS. Retrieved 30 July, 2024 from http://iel.cass.cn/mzwxbk/gmzwxgl/200610/t20061018_2764291.shtml. Li Siying, *On the Inheritance and Evolution of China's Flood and Human Recolonization Myth* (June 30, 2022). IELCASS. Retrieved 30 July, 2024 from http://iel.cass.cn/ztpd/shyj/zggdsh/202206/t20220630_5415027.shtml
172. Liu Yahu, "南方民族洪水神的及意," "The Structure and Implications of the Flood Myths of Southern Nationalities" (April 23, 2009). *Chinese Folklore Society*. Retrieved 28 July, 2024 from https://www.chinafolklore.org/web/index.php?Page=2&NewsID=4519

Jeju Island, South Korea

KOREA AND JAPAN

Genetically, the Koreans and Japanese are mostly of Y-DNA (paternal) haplogroup O, that great lineage that dominates East Asia, accounting for the Chinese, Sino-Tibetan language speakers, and other nations of East and Southeast Asia. This is a lineage which I tentatively think goes back to one of Japheth's sons: either Magog or Tiras (Genesis 10:2). See page 270 for more on that.

A surprising discovery from this research is the presence of monotheism in ancient Korean and Japanese cultures, as we will see. This subject of primitive monotheism, and its pervasiveness among the ancient cultures of the world, was written about at length by Wilhelm Schmidt in his classic works, *Der Ursprung der Gottesidee* and *The Origin and Growth of Religion*. Yet ancient monotheism should not be too surprising if we remember that we are all descended from Noah, and that the worship of the true God was passed down by those who first repopulated the earth.

In addition to ancient monotheism, we find other witnesses to this God in the form of Flood traditions and other echoes of the early chapters of Genesis. Thus the Japanese have a memory of when the supreme God sent a Flood in judgment upon the world, but saved one man and his family, "locking him in a deep cave, before which he put a great shell, that the water might not run into the pit or cave." The minority Ainu people knew of the Flood, as well as the Ryukyu islanders. The Koreans recall the survival of a young man on a floating laurel tree. The memory of the Tower of Babel and the confusion of languages was also attested in Korea as recently as the 1600s. There are echoes of Babel and of the Garden of Eden in Japan as well.

All of this testifies to a shared origin, shared history, and shared Savior for the people of the East as well as the West. Promising a future salvation, which is now here, Scripture declared: "From the rising of the sun even to its setting, God's name will be great among the nations." (Malachi 1:11)

Tribes and Locations

45. Korea
46. Ainu
47. Okinawa
48. Miyako-jima
49. Hachijo-jima
50. Hateruma
51. Tarama Island
52. Japan

KOREA

The Koreans have long known of the existence of the supreme God in heaven. They called Him "Hananim" in their language. The name Hananim is related to the word "hanul" (heaven).[1] John Ross, a 19th century missionary, wrote that "the name Hannonim is so distinctive and so universally used that there will be no fear, in future translations and preachings, of the unseemly squabbles which occurred long ago among Chinese missionaries on this subject."[2] When the Bible was translated into Korean, Protestants chose the name Hananim for God.

In addition, the Koreans observed an annual sacrifice in which the king of Korea made offerings to Hananim on behalf of the nation. This took place every year at a sacred island near Pyongyang, where an altar was erected for this purpose.[3]

This holy sacrifice is reminiscent of Israel's annual Day of Atonement sacrifice, where the High Priest entered the most holy tabernacle to make atonement for the sins of the nation (Hebrews 9:7, Leviticus 16). However, Korea's sacrifice is certainly pre-Mosaic in origin, for the same reason that we find Noah and other patriarchs offering sacrifices to God several centuries before Moses.[4] Noah undoubtedly instructed his sons and descendants to offer sacrifices to God. We believe it is from this source that the sacrifices offered by many nations to God have their origin, even if these practices were corrupted over time.

Similar to the Korean sacrifice to God, we saw on page 45 that the Chinese had an annual "Border Sacrifice," which the emperor himself offered to God. The occurrence of this among both the Chinese and Koreans suggests that this practice predates the divergence of these people groups—likely taking us back to the time of Babel. The ancestors of the Koreans and the Chinese departed from Babel with a knowledge of the one true God, and an awareness that we owe Him a sacrifice. Yet these sacrifices were just a shadow of God's sacrifice, given to us as a gift, which makes us clean before God, as the Gospel teaches.

The King of Korea offered an annual sacrifice to the God of Heaven, on behalf of the people.

Jesus, the King of the Jews, and God in the flesh, offered Himself in sacrifice, once for all, and for all nations, to make perfect atonement and open up the way to God (Hebrews 9:11-12). God proved this by raising Jesus from the dead.

Tower of Babel

Speaking of Babel (Genesis 11:1-9), will we find any memory of that event in this far-east land of Korea? Indeed, Korean tradition speaks of the Tower of Babel. In the year 1668, a Dutch traveler named Hendrick Hamel met a group of Korean priests who did not practice Buddhism, but still held to the traditional shamanist religion of Korea.[5] These Korean shamans related to him an ancient tradition of what can only be described as the Tower of Babel:

> "They believe, by virtue of an old legend, that people originally had only one language. But the desire to build a great tower—by means of which they hoped to climb to heaven—caused the confusion of languages."[6]

The resemblance of the above passage with the 11th chapter of Genesis is unmistakable.

1. John Ross, *History of Corea* (London: Elliot Stock, 1891), p. 355.
2. *Ibid.*
3. Don Richardson, *Eternity in Their Hearts* (Ventura, California: Regal, 2005), pp. 61, 194. Richardson's source was a Mrs. John Tolliver, whom he interviewed in April 1978, at Three Hills, Alberta. Mrs. Tolliver was raised in Korea and heard various references to this altar during her youth.
4. See, for example, Abel's sacrifice in Genesis 4:4 and Noah's sacrifice in Genesis 8:20-22. Abel undoubtedly received his instructions on sacrifice from his father, Adam, who must have been taught this by God, possibly as early as the event of Genesis 3:21.
5. Buddhism arrived in Korea in approximately the 4th century A.D.
6. Ed. Abbé Prevost, "Bescriebung von Korea, der wehrlichen Tartaren und Tibet," *Allgemeine Historie der Reisen zu Wasser und Lande*, vol. 6 (Leipzig: Arkstee und Merkus, 1750), p. 602.

Flood

Regarding the Flood, the Korean tradition went as follows: The man who survived the Flood was known as the "son of the tree." An angelic being "used to come down from heaven and rest" on a big laurel tree. "She bore a son, whose father was the tree." When the Flood came, this tree became a floating vessel for the young man. (One version adds that the tree "foretold the boy when they would have a flood in [the] future. The boy told the villagers about the flood, but they did not believe it."[7]) The tree instructed him to "save animals, but not human beings."

Despite the warning, the young man saved another boy, in addition to various animals. "The rain stopped when they reached the summit of a mountain." There, upon the mountain, they met an old woman, with her daughter and her adopted daughter. The boy who was saved was crafty, and tried to cheat the tree's son out of marrying the woman's beautiful daughter. However, the son of the tree passed a difficult test and succeeded in marrying the young woman.[8]

In the above tradition, the echoes of Ararat are clear, but we may also detect echoes of other events in Genesis. The special tree sounds like the Tree of the Knowledge of Good and Evil (Genesis 3).The angelic being who came down and sired offspring sounds like Genesis 6:1-4. The tests imposed after the Flood correspond to Noah's tests involving the raven and dove, as we show in Appendix B. To find mixed memories of the Flood and other events of Genesis, such as the Garden of Eden, is not at all unusual. We saw many cases of the same in *Volume 1*, and this book is filled with them as well.

46 AINU

The Ainu had settled the northern part of Honshu (Japan's main island) prior to the Japanese. Over 1,000 years ago, the Japanese made war with them, and the Ainu were driven back to the northern islands of the archipelago, including Hokkaido, Sakhalin, and the Kurils. They are very distinct from the Japanese physically and linguistically. Their creation story, which they told to John Batchelor around the year 1880, is remarkably similar to that of Genesis 1:

An Ainu Man

> "In the beginning the world was a great slushy quagmire. The waters were at that time hopelessly mixed up with the earth, and nothing was to be seen but a mighty ocean of bare, sloppy swamp. All the land was mixed up with, and aimlessly floating about in, the endless seas. All around was death and stillness. Nothing existed in this chaotic mass and nothing stirred, for it was altogether incapable of sustaining life; nor were there any living fowls flying in the airy expanse above. All was cold, solitary, and desolate. However, the clouds had their thunder demons, the skies above their living creatures, and the Creator abode in the highest heavens with mighty hosts of subordinate deities.
>
> By and by the great God—the true God—determined to render the world inhabitable. He, therefore, made a water-wagtail [a type of songbird], and sent him down from heaven to produce the earth. When he descended and saw what a dreadfully shocking condition the elements were in, and how they were mixed up in confusion, he was almost at his wits' end to know how to perform his allotted task. But he thought of a way, for he fluttered over the waters with his wings, trampled upon the muddy

7. Im Seog-ye, *Yennal Iyagi Seonjib* (Gyohagsa, 1971), pp. 39-51. As quoted in: Choi In-hak, *A Type Index of Korean Folktales*, pp. 72-73.
8. Choi In-hak, *Chosen Mukasi-banasi Hyakusen* (Nihon Hoso Shupan Kyokai, 1974), pp. 64-67. Collected by In-hak in 1968. As quoted in: Choi In-hak, *A Type Index of Korean Folktales* (Seoul: Myong Ji University, 1979), pp. 71-72.

matter with his feet, and beat it down with his tail, till, after a very long time of fluttering, trampling, and tail wagging, dry places appeared, and the waters became the ocean. In this way the worlds were gradually raised, and made to stand out of the waters, and caused to float about upon them. Therefore, the Ainu call the world "Moshiri"—i.e., "floating earth," and hold the water-wagtail in great esteem, for was he not the angel of God? [9]

In the beginning God created the heavens and the earth. And the earth was formless and desolate emptiness, and darkness was over the surface of the deep, and the Spirit of God was hovering over the surface of the waters. (Genesis 1:1-3)

The Ainu also have a tradition that the first tree ever created was the "tree of evil." As John Batchelor summarized:

> "It is not supposed, however, that this tree was caused to grow, or was created in our sense of the word. But it is said to have been sent direct from heaven already grown and planted in a land called Wenpipok, wherever that may be.
>
> This tree is supposed to have been the origin of evil, or rather the means by which evil was brought into the world. I speak now not of moral evil, but physical; evil in the sense of causing bodily pain and suffering, but not evil in the sense of having brought sin into the world. The bark, not the fruit, is supposed to be the evil-causing agency."[10]

They know also of the Flood, as Batchelor wrote: "The Ainu speak of a great flood which took place many ages ago; all of the Ainu were drowned with the exception of a very few. How many were saved is not known."[11] Another legend of theirs contains a mixed memory of Noah's sending of birds (Genesis 8:6-12) and of Creation (Genesis 1).[12]

47 OKINAWA

The Ryukyu Islands are a chain of small islands to the southwest of Japan. Okinawa is probably the most famous of these islands. In the 1890s, Baptist missionaries inquired of the traditions of the Ryukyu people and were amazed to find among them a tradition not only of the Flood, but also a tradition of Adam and Eve. One Reverend Thompson writes:

> "It is a remarkable fact, and worthy of investigation, that they have among their traditions the story of Adam and Eve and of the deluge. Having no literature, their traditions are oral and handed down from father to son."[13]

The memory of "Okinawan Adam and Eve" lives on at Kouri Island, known as "Love Island."

Thompson did not provide details on these traditions of Adam and Eve and the Flood. However, there is a remarkable Adam and Eve story connected with the island of Kouri, a small satellite island of Okinawa in its northern part. Because of this story, Kouri Island is known as "Love Island":

> "Once upon a time, there was a young couple on an island. They were originally naked, eating rice cakes that fell from the sky, and lived happily every day. One day, they were overcome with anxiety, wondering, 'what if the rice cakes stopped falling from the sky tomorrow?', so they started saving the rice cakes little by little.

9. John Batchelor, *The Ainu and Their Folk-lore* (London: Religious Tract Society, 1901), pp. 35-36.
10. *Ibid.*, pp. 45-46.
11. John Batchelor, "Notes on the Ainu," *Transactions of the Asiatic Society of Japan*, vol. 10 (Yokohama: R. Meiklejohn & Co., 1882), p. 218.
12. Basil Hall Chamberlain, *Aino Folk-tales* (London: Folklore Society, 1888), pp. 8-9. "When the Creator had finished creating the world, and had returned to the sky, he sent down the cock to see whether the world was good or not, with orders to come back at once. But the world was so beautiful, that the cock, unable to tear himself away, kept lingering on from day to day. At last, after a long time, he was on his way flying back up to the sky. But God, angry with him for his disobedience, stretched forth his hand, and beat him down to earth, saying: 'You are not wanted in the sky any more.' That is why, to this very day, the cock cannot fly high."
13. Rev. R. A. Thomson, "Glimpses of the Liu Chiu Islands," *American Baptist Missionary Magazine*, vol. 79 (Boston: American Baptist Missionary Union, 1899), p. 518.

Eventually, the rice cakes stopped falling, and the couple desperately prayed to the sky for rice cakes to fall, but the sky god did not listen. Instead, they started fishing in the sea, where they learned the importance of life and work. When the couple went out to sea to fish, they saw dugongs giving birth, and came to understand the difference between men and women. Then they began to cover their lower bodies with cattail leaves. It is said that their descendants increased and became the ancestors of the people of Okinawa. It is said that from this legend, the island came to be called 'Love Island.'"[14]

48

MIYAKO-JIMA

Hokama Shūzen, an authority on the Ryukyu Islands, recorded the Flood tradition of the Miyako-jima people.[15] Even more interesting is their tradition of the origin of death, which has parallels with Genesis 3. This tradition, passed down from generation to generation, was recorded by the Russian scholar Nikolai Nevsky in 1926. And just like that biblical passage, a serpent figures prominently in this tradition:

Miyako-jima possesses a memory of the Fall (Genesis 3) involving man and a serpent.

"Long, long time ago it happened when the first people lived on this great Miyako, beautiful Miyako. The moon and the sun shining up in the sky were kind and tenderhearted, and wished to give men an elixir of longevity that they might preserve their natural beauty forever and ever. Accordingly on the night before the New Year festival (sicinu araju), they dispatched a messenger named Akara-zzagama to earth, to the island below. Akara-zzagama went on his way, carrying a yoke with two buckets on his shoulder. One of the buckets contained the waters of life (silimizi) and the other the waters of death (sinimizi). The moon and the sun sent him with a message saying, 'Pour out the waters of life onto men, so that they may die and rise to life again, and thus have long life from generation to generation; and onto the serpents pour out the waters of death, for they have no souls.' But Akara-zzagama was on such a long journey from the heavenly world that he felt exhausted and put the buckets down in order to give rest to his feet. While he was urinating by the roadside, a big serpent appeared from nowhere and poured onto himself the waters of life which had been prepared for men."[16]

What kind of serpent is this? It is none other than the serpent of Genesis–Satan himself, taking the form of a snake. But the story continues:

"Akara-zzagama's surprise was incomparable. He thought to himself, 'O no, what shall I do? How could I pour the little remaining fluid on men? There is nothing else for me to do but pour the waters of death on them.' Thus while weeping, he poured on men the waters of death.

14. "Kouri Island has an Okinawan version of the Adam and Eve legend." (February 26, 2014). Koury Island Guide. Retrieved 12 August, 2024 from https://www.kourijima.in/?p=7
15. "A long time ago, a long, long time ago, there were the Bunazee siblings. One fine day, the brother and sister went out to the fields to work. Suddenly from far off in the ocean, they saw a mountain-like wave ... The brother, concerned for his sister, [carried her] with great difficulty up a high hill. ... The tsunami swept away all life from the land. Resigned, brother and sister built a grass hut and pledged to be husband and wife." The sister gave birth to the ajikai mollusk at first, then to a human child. Gradually, the island became filled with people who descended from the sister and brother and honored them as the kami who regenerated the island." Source: Hokama Shūzen, "Okinawa in the Matrix of Pacific Ocean Culture," *Okinawan Diaspora,* ed. Nakasone R. Y. (Honolulu: University of Hawaii Press, 2002), p. 46.
16. Nikolai A. Nevsky, *The Moon and Immortality* (Tokyo, 1971), pp. 11-13.

Quite worried, Akara-zzagama ascended to heaven above to report on what had happened."[17]

Continuing, we detect a memory of the curse from Genesis 3:

> "In great anger the sun said, 'I initially hoped that men would renew their life and so never die, but you have destroyed my hope and brought my good intention to nothing. Your sin against men cannot be redeemed, so much so that as long as men live, and as long as Miyako is covered with greens, keep standing with the buckets on your shoulder forever and ever.' Consequently, to this day Akara-zzagama remains standing on the moon, shouldering a yoke with two buckets as punishment. What foolish beings men are! If they had been as shrewd as the serpents, men might have bathed in the waters of life, renewing their existence, but in fact, they were doused with the waters of death, and have since remained mortal. In contrast, from that time on the serpents always cast their skins, rejuvenating themselves, and therefore attain long life."[18]

49 HACHIJO-JIMA

Hachijo (or Hachijo Jima) is a small volcanic island located about 175 miles south of Tokyo. Like the Ryukyu people, the islanders of Hachijo spoke a Japonic language, and thus have some common history with the majority people of Japan. The Hachijo natives also knew about the Flood. A man named Gyofu Doi recorded the following tradition from them. While this is only a fragmentary narration, the parallels with the Genesis Flood are detectable.

The volcanic island Hachijojima

> "In ancient times, a tidal wave is said to have struck the island of Hachijo. It drowned all living beings except a pregnant woman named Tanaba, who escaped death by sticking to a wax tree. Surviving in a cave by the seaside, she brought forth a boy. Later they married and became the ancestors of the islanders."[19]

We will see that the Flood story of the Japanese on the main island (Honshu) also replaces the Ark with a cave.

50 HATERUMA

Hateruma is the southernmost of Japan's Ryukyu archipelago, located about 125 miles east of Taiwan. One of the foremost traditions of the native islanders was that of the Flood. It was told in the following terms, as recorded by Susuki Masataka:

> "It is said that in the past, many people lived peaceful lives on this island. One day, a rain of oil suddenly fell on the island, killing all living things. Fortunately, however, the two siblings escaped and hid in Mishukunugama [a famous cave on the top of a hill] and survived the disaster. After that, the two lived in this cave near the coast, until they became adults and became a couple."[20]

---

17. *Ibid.*
18. *Ibid.*
19. Gyofu Doi, "Hachijo jima no hito no hajime" ("The Origin of Man in Hachijo Island"), *Kyodo Kenkyu*, vol. 2, no. 7 (1914), p. 440. As translated into English in: Eiichiro Ishida, "Mother-Son Deities," *History of Religions*, vol. 4, no. 1 (1964), p. 46.
20. Suzuki Masakata, "Myths and Rituals of Hateruma Island," *Ethnological Studies*, vol. 42, no. 1 (1977), p. 26.

Reminiscent of the narratives of the Miyako islanders as well as those found across Taiwan, the story tells that in due time, the woman gave birth to her first child, but he looked like a fish. As a result, they moved away from the shore and built a hut on a mountain, but the second child also was not human in form. So they moved to another place, and at last gave birth to a human child, who was named Alamarinupa. From this male child the island was repopulated. These three attempts are like the three attempts of Noah to send a bird in search of dry ground when the Flood was coming to an end (Genesis 8:6-11).

Humanity's sins were so deep that a rain of oil poured out and all humans perished. Only a brother and sister were able to survive.

Other narrations of the Flood explicitly state that the Flood was sent in an act of divine judgment:

> "Humanity's sins were so deep that a rain of oil poured out and all humans perished. Only a brother and sister were able to survive by hiding under the Mishukunugama."[21]
>
> "As the number of humans on the ancient island increased, the people became corrupt. In their evil ways, they preyed on the weak and the strong alike. God became angry, hid his son and daughter, then rained oil on them."[22]

Tarama is one of the Ryukyu Islands of Japan, located toward the southwestern end of the archipelago. A vague memory of the Flood has been retold by the Tarama islanders, as follows:

> "The brother and the sister were working in the field one day when, suddenly, a large wave came upon them. The two ran up the hill and grabbed onto some fountain grass and were saved. Only these two siblings survived. Their house was swept away.
>
> The two got married, but the first to be born were a snake and a lizard. The next were a giant clam and a potato. Finally, on a third occasion, a human child was born. In this way, the village was repopulated."[23]

Beach at low tide, Tarama Island, Okinawa

21. *Ibid.*
22. *Ibid.*, p. 27.
23. *Folktales of Tarama Village*, edited by Tarama Village Office, 1981. As summarized in: Sogabe Kazuyuki et. al., *Reconsidering the Myth of Brother and Sister Ancestry* (Seijo University: March 1, 2007), pp. 8, 24-25.

52

JAPAN

I must confess, if there was a nation I was doubtful about ever finding the knowledge of the Flood, it was Japan. Far removed from biblical lands, vastly different in religion and culture, and historically opposed to Christianity (at least for political reasons), Japan seemed a daunting place to hope for any surviving memory of the events of Genesis 1-11. Secular authorities also assured me that Japan knew nothing of a global Flood. However, they would be proven wrong, as we can see. Japan certainly knows of Noah's Flood!

Izanagi and Izanami

The *Kojiki* and *Nihon Shoki*

We will begin with the recurring Flood story which we have already seen so many times in East Asia, which ends in a brother-sister marriage theme. That same story is found in Japan, most notably in the *Kojiki*. The *Kojiki*, which was completed in 712 A.D., is our earliest source on the history, mythology, and customs of the Japanese.

The *Kojiki* names Izanagi and Izanami as the brother and sister who married and established the human race. The difference is that in the Japanese version, the Flood event is not explicit. But originally it must have been there, according to the renown Japanese ethnologist Oka Masao:

> "Among Japanese myths we can find the story of the divine ancestors Izanaki and Izanami, the brother-and-sister pair who married and gave birth to numerous deities. This myth is a remnant of the flood myths often observed among the tribes of southern China and Southeast Asia. In these narrations humankind becomes extinct as the result of a flood that leaves only two survivors, a brother and a sister. Since they are siblings, they cannot wed. However, they conduct a magic ritual to remove the incest man, marry as non-kin partners, and bear offspring.
>
> In the Japanese myths, although the part with the flood has disappeared, the details of the story's content are exactly the same."[24]

The parallels with the "brother-sister marriage" Flood story which pervades East Asia are many. They are the same story, only that the Flood event has been scrubbed in Japan's version. Izanagi and Izanami also correspond to Adam and Eve, just as we will show in Appendix B that this "brother-sister marriage" theme bears a mixed memory of Adam and Eve and the Flood.

Yet the Flood is not altogether absent in the Japanese version. In fact, it seems to be implied. In *Volume 1*, Sections 3 to 4 of the *Kojiki*, we find that "Izanaki and Izanami, the final pair of the Seven Generations of the Age of Deities, stand on the celestial floating bridge, under which the ocean spreads broadly. They create Onogoro island, to which they descend and begin the process of procreating the different lands. In this scene they alone exist amid the ocean's broad expanse."[25]

Ninigi-no-Mikoto descends from heaven in a boat made of stone and lands on Mount Takachiho.

Not only this, but in both the *Kojiki* and the *Nihon Shoki* (a parallel text of the *Kojiki* written 8 years later) there is a distant memory of Noah. A deified man named Ninigi-no-Mikoto, the grandson of a goddess named Ameratasu, descends from heaven in a heavenly boat made of stone, and lands on Mount Takachiho.[26]

24. Quiros Ignacio, trans., "Studies on the *Kojiki*," no. 3 (March 2019), p. 2. Retrieved from https://kojiki.kokugakuin.ac.jp/wp-content/uploads/2019/05/f3a36cde05cb971b91fc0df9e883763b.pdf For the original, see: Basil Hall Chamberlain (trans.), *Translation of "Ko-Ji-Ki" or "Records of Ancient Matters"* (Tokyo: J. L. Thompson, 1932), pp. 21-22.
25. *Ibid*
26. *Nihon Shoki*, Book 2, Part 2. See: W. G. Aston (trans.), *Nihongi, Chronicles of Japan from the Earliest Times to A.D. 697* (London: The Japan Society, 1896), p. 70.

Ninigi's grandson named Jimmu becomes the first emperor of Japan.

Regarding these parallels to Noah and other Flood texts, no less an authority on mythology than Harvard's Michael Witzel observed that they were connected. He noted that Ninigi is parallel with Manu of the Indian Vedas, and Noah of Genesis, who both land on a mountain in a boat.[27]

More Garden of Eden Parallels

Next, let us turn to the Garden of Eden account recorded in Genesis 3. Japan also has a memory of this serpent and of this special tree! In particular, the eminent Chinese scholar G. Namjila has shown that a "Water of Immortality" tradition is widespread in the Amami islands, which are south of the main island of Honshu:

> "This version says, in the past human beings were young and immortal, for God provided them the wakamizu (water of rejuvenation). However, once man spilled the wakamizu by accident, and the wakamizu dripped on a cobra and a crape myrtle tree. Consequently, the cobra and the crape myrtle became revitalized and immortal since then, meanwhile man became mortal."[28]

Man spilled the water of rejuvenation on a cobra and a crape myrtle tree. ... Man became mortal.

The Flood and Monotheism

We have yet another witness in Japan to the knowledge of the Flood and of the events of Genesis. Around the year 1660, a Dutch ambassador named Van Zelderen was touring Japan with a group of government officials. Near modern-day Matsuyama, his Japanese interpreter directed his attention to a holy site in the vicinity:

> "Not far from Mettogamma [Matsuyama] (said the interpreter) lies an exceedingly high mountain, opposite to the island Moeko, on top of which stand several temples, which may be seen a great distance off at sea. In these temples the Bonzies worshipped that great God, which formerly not only created the sun, moon, and stars, but also the fifteen lesser deities which some ages since conversed upon the earth. The Prime God commanded the substitute gods that they should make a brazen egg, in which they were to enclose the four elements: water, earth, air, and fire, and also the four principal colors: red, yellow, blue, and green. Out of this egg the four elements and colors being tempered ran together, in such a nature that the visible world appeared. The world thus created, man was wanting. Not long after, a woman, growing in the shell of a calabash, had no soul, which the Chief God, pitying, made a steer come to the calabash, who through his nostrils blew breath into the calabash, which came to be a soul in the growing woman, who then coming forth, was familiar with the inferior deities."[29]

Mankind grew in wickedness ... The Supreme Deity secured one man and his family in a cave during the Flood

Certainly there are echoes of Creation in the above text. Next, the account immediately moves into the Flood:

27. E. J. Michael Witzel, Kazuo Matsumura (trans.), *Central Asian and Japanese Mythology*, (February 8, 2023), pp. 93-94. Retrieved from https://k-rain.repo.nii.ac.jp/records/1782
28. G. Namjila, "Water-of-Immortality Myths in Altaic and Japanese Cultures," *China's Origin and Creation Myths*, eds. Mineke Schipper, Ye Shuxian and Yin Hubin (Boston: Brill, 2011), p. 87.
29. Arnoldus Montanus, trans. John Ogilby, *Atlas Japannensis* (London: Tho. Johnson, 1670), pp. 477-478. I have brought antiquated spelling and grammar up to date for easier reading.

> "By [these] means mankind not only increased in number, but also in wickedness, differing more and more from their heavenly extract. Growing still worse and worse, mocking at thunder, rainbows, and fire, nay, they blasphemed the great God himself (whom when the interpreter named, he bowed his head to the ground) whereupon he called his inferior deities about him, telling them, that he resolved to destroy and ruin all things, kick the sun, moon, and stars out of the firmament, mix the air and water together, and make a round globe, in which the four elements should be resolved into their former mass. And chiefly he commanded the idol Topan to make thunderbolts to shoot through the air, and fire all the kingdoms with lightning, which was no sooner said, but it was done, the whole world on a sudden lying together like a heap of rubbish, so that none were saved, except one man and his family, that had entertained and duly worshipped the gods. The Chief and Supreme Deity took care in this general ruin for the innocent man, locking him in a deep cave, before which he put a great shell, that the water might not run into the pit or cave."[30]

Notice that the ark of Noah is replaced with a cave. For those who would question the authenticity of this Flood text, the text finds confirmation from previously cited texts from the Ryukyu Islands, which also say it was a cave.

As for this Noah-like figure, the tradition adds, "Moreover, the virtuous man got out of his cave, when the idol Canon called back the seas to their respective bounds, and Topan gathered the scattered thunderbolts together, and settled himself in the province Koejelang, where he got several children, which intermarrying grew into a considerable number."[31]

The tradition goes on to tell of a later rebellion by these descendants against the gods. "The inhabitants of Koejelang, joining their heads together, said, 'These are the gods which drowned our forefathers. Let us take revenge for so heinous a crime."[32] They sent the woods on fire, killing some of the gods. However, this did not end well for the rebel humans:

> "Yet seven of them [the lesser gods], getting up to heaven, complained of that execrable plot to the Chief God, who being exceedingly enraged at so great a piece of villainy, immediately commanded an angel, whom he empowered to punish them for their crime. The angel no sooner descended, but he drove the offenders out of the province Koejelang, to the boiling waters at Singock, in which they are continually tortured, without the least respite or cessation."[33]

...the stately chapel dedicated to the Creator of all things. In the middle of the temple is a great pot full of water, containing a great tortoise.

Is this not a memory of both the Tower of Babel and the Flood? Indeed. And no less striking is the reference to a "Chief God" who had created all the other gods.

Turning once more to the 17th century Dutch records, we find another reference to the worship of a supreme God. In particular, a majestic temple was demonstrated by the Japanese interpreter, which had been dedicated to the supreme Creator God:

> "Moreover, besides the ox-temple in Meaco, there is also to be seen the stately chapel dedicated to the Creator of all things, who is worshipped in a very strange manner. In the middle of the temple is a great pot full of

30. *Ibid.*, p. 478.
31. *Ibid.*
32. *Ibid.*, pp. 478-479. For another account, in which is described a temple dedicated to "the Creator of all things," as well as a memory of the Flood, see p. 279.
33. *Ibid.*, p. 479.

> water, surrounded by a wall, seven foot high from the ground, in the middle of which appears an exceedingly great tortoise, whose shell, feet, and head, stand in the water."[34]

We should not be surprised to find monotheism in Japan, for we have found it also in China and Korea. As for the symbols of pots filled with water and a great tortoise, this is probably a vague reference to the Flood, on account of parallels with memorials of the Flood in other cultures.[35]

A Chinese Flood Tradition in Japan

Finally, it is worth mentioning that the German scientist Engelbert Kaempfer, around the year 1691, also recorded a Flood account which was imported from the people of southern China and made its way to western Japan. This history features a patriarch named Peiruun, likened unto Noah, described as "a very virtuous and religious prince," who governed an island named Maurigasima, which no longer exists. His people, on the other hand, had become exceedingly wicked, so much so that they "incensed the gods to that degree, that by an irrevocable degree they determined to sink the whole island." However, Peiruun was spared. "This decree of the gods was revealed to him in a dream, wherein he was commanded, as he valued the security of his person, to retire on board his ships, and to fly [flee] from the island, as soon as he should observe, that the faces of the two idols, which stood at the entry of the temple turned red." He tried to warn the populace, but "he was only ridiculed for his zeal and care, and [he] grew contemptible to his subjects." These were, however, swallowed up when the Flood came. Replacing the slopes of Ararat with China's coast, the tradition concludes:

This decree of the gods was revealed to him in a dream, wherein he was commanded to retire on board his ships.

> "The king and his people got safe to China, where the memory of his arrival is still celebrated by a yearly festival, on which the Chinese, particularly the inhabitants of the southern maritime provinces, divert themselves on the water, rowing up and down in their boats, as if they were preparing for a flight, and sometimes crying with a loud voice, 'Peiruun,' which was the name of that prince. The same festival hath been by the Chinese introduced into Japan, and is now celebrated there, chiefly upon the western coasts of this empire."[36]

Conclusions on Japan

What shall we say in light of all the above? First, that Japan certainly has traditions bearing witness to the events of Genesis 1 through 11. That can no longer be denied. Second, that the God of the Bible is also the God of Japan. The God who told Moses that "I am the God of Abraham, Isaac, and Jacob," is also the God of Japan. This God told Abraham, and Isaac, and Jacob, "In your Seed will all the families of the earth be blessed," which was a promise of the coming Christ (Jesus), who is the Savior of the whole world. That blessing in Christ extends to all the families of the world, including Japan. "From the rising of the sun to its setting, the name of Yahweh is to be praised." (Psalm 113:3) May all the people of Japan believe in Jesus and be saved by Him!

From the rising of the sun to its setting, the name of Yahweh is to be praised. (Psalm 113:3)

34. Arnoldus Montanus, trans. John Ogilby, *Atlas Japannensis*, p. 279.
35. For more on this theme, see: John Francis Arundell, *Tradition Principally with Reference to Mythology and the Law of Nations* (London: Burns, Oates & Company, 1872), pp. 138-139, 260-262.
36. Engelburt Kaempfer, *The History of Japan, vol. 2* (London, 1727), Appendix pages 13-14.

Railay beach, Krabi, Thailand

SOUTHEAST ASIA

What could Southeast Asia possibly have to do with Genesis and the God of the Bible?" one might ask. "There are 5,000 miles separating Southeast Asia and Israel (the home of the Bible). They are worlds apart in religion and worldview. Southeast Asia is historically Buddhist, and does not believe in a Supreme God. And today, much of Southeast Asia is secular, under atheistic communism—Vietnam, Laos, and Cambodia in particular. Therefore, what do Jesus, the Bible, and Christianity have to do with the people of Southeast Asia?"

Tribes of the Region

53. Jarai (Vietnam)
54. Bahnar (Vietnam)
55. Karen (Myanmar / Burma)
56. Sedang (Vietnam and Laos)
57. Yi (Vietnam)
58. Thai (Thailand)
59. Lisu of Myanmar
60. Muong (Vietnam)
61. Kachin/Jingpo (Myanmar, India, and China)
62. Rakhine (Myanmar / Burma)
63. Burmese (Myanmar / Burma)
64. Lamet (Laos and Thailand)
65. Khang (Vietnam)
66. Laha (Vietnam)
67. Lahu (Myanmar, Thailand, and China)
68. Mang (Vietnam)
69. Nung (Vietnam and China)
70. Bru (Laos and Vietnam)
71. Pacoh (Laos)
72. Stieng (Vietnam and Cambodia)
73. Rengao (Vietnam)
74. Tay Pong (Vietnam)
75. Lawa (Thailand)
76. Co Lao (Vietnam)
77. San Chay (Vietnam)
78. Pa Then (Vietnam)
79. Giay (Vietnam)
80. Lao (Laos and Cambodia)
81. Isan (Thailand)
82. Thai Nghe (Vietnam)
83. Rade (Vietnam)
84. Koho (Vietnam)
85. Siyin (Myanmar and India)
86. Haka Chin (Myanmar and India)
87. Tawyan (Myanmar)
88. Tho (Vietnam)
89. Kim Mun (Vietnam)
90. Man Ta Pan (Vietnam)
91. Man Quan Trang (Vietnam)
92. M'nong (Vietnam)
93. Hmong in Vietnam
94. Hre (Vietnam)
95. Khmu (Laos, Thailand, and Vietnam)
96. Raglai and Cham (Vietnam and Cambodia)
97. Jakun (Malaysia)
98. Mantras (Malaysia)
99. Kelantan Tradition (Malaysia)
100. Salong (Myanmar / Burma)
101. Yao in Vietnam
102. Pu Peo (Vietnam)
103. Akha (Thailand and Myanmar)
104. Nyahon (Laos)
105. Viet (Kinh)
106. May (Vietnam)
107. Southern Vietnam Tradition
108. Mon (Myanmar)
109. Temuan (Malaysia)
110. Orang Seletar (Malaysia and Singapore)
111. Katu (Laos and Vietnam)
112. Tai Dam (Vietnam)

Much in every way. Prior to the arrival of Buddhism about 2,000 years ago, most tribes and nations of Southeast Asia had some level of awareness of a supreme God. Some of them called Him "Then" or "Tien." The knowledge of the one true God who created us was lost over time, as in all nations, but the memory of this God was not completely forgotten. Sacred traditions of these nations refer to an ancient Flood, and even a Tower of Babel event, which match the record of these events in Scripture. These point us to the God who created the world, and whose commands we have violated. Yet He is a God who pursues all of us.

Thus, the Jarai of Vietnam refer to "Father Drum" (their Noah), who survived the Flood inside a floating drum. In another text, they refer to the unlawful behavior of mankind which preceded the Flood. They recall a "tower of dispersion" as well, which collapsed at the time when their language was changed and the nations parted ways. The Bahnar tribe also remember this Tower, and claim that its architect was the eldest son of Bok Seugucur, their Noah. Concerning this Flood, they refer to an enormous floating drum in which pairs of animals were boarded, which was sealed watertight, and a chicken which announced the end of the Flood. The Karen tribe of Myanmar (Burma) remember the creation of the first woman from the first man's rib, as well as a Garden of Eden in which was a forbidden tree. The Sedang remember the promiscuous ways of mankind which prompted heaven to send the Flood, and the Yi remember a human pair who were spared. They floated in "a giant pumpkin, as big as a house," which landed at a mountain: no doubt a memory of Ararat.

The Thai people refer to Po Then, the God of the highest heavens, who sent the Flood but spared two children. Noah's raven is remembered as well. The Lisu people of Myanmar say the vessel was a giant hollow tree, which landed on a mountain, and that a rooster sang to announce the Flood's end. The Muong of Vietnam remember a forewarning which preceded the Flood, and they have an idea of Noah's sacrifice which he offered afterward. The Kachin people say that long ago they enjoyed "the pure worship of one supreme Being," living on a mountain called Mujai Singra Bum, before death entered the world. In their Flood tradition, two orphans survived in a great oval-shaped drum, which they exited after a cock crowed. The Lamet, Khang, and Laha peoples have their Flood stories as well, in which there is a vague memory of Noah's dove as well. In one version, the God of heaven, named Then, sends a sparrow to advise the surviving siblings to marry and reestablish the human race. The Nung people replace the Tower of Babel with a ladder. The Siyin and Tawyan remember this Tower and the confusion of languages.

"God spoke to Anha the chief," said the Bru people, "and told him that there was going to be a great flood. He commanded him to build a boat." According to the Stieng of Vietnam and Cambodia, the vessel was a raft, and according to the Rengao tribe it was a floating bed of straw. The Lawa have a memory of Noah's raven, and the Lao say a buffalo was sacrificed to the God of heaven after the Flood. The Rakhine, Burmese, and Viet people have their accounts of the Flood as well. Shall we cite the traditions of more than two dozen other tribes as well? To cite the words of the Apostle Paul again, God has not left Himself without witness in any nation on earth. (Acts 14:16-17)

The point is this: It is with the Holy Scriptures that these tribal traditions from Southeast Asia agree. Yet the God who inspired these Scriptures is the God who created us and to whom we must give an account. This same God inspired the promises in Scripture which foretold of Jesus, the coming Savior, who was God in the flesh, coming to redeem us back to Himself. These same Scriptures said that this message of forgiveness and new life in Jesus, for those who believe in Him, must be carried to all nations, including Southeast Asia. For it says, "In Him (Jesus) all the nations of the earth will be blessed," and "Rejoice, all coastlands." (Psalm 97:1-2) And as Jesus said, "Go and make disciples of all nations." (Matt. 28:18) This is very good news for all the people of Southeast Asia. And as Paul said, "Therefore having overlooked the times of ignorance, God is now commanding men that everyone everywhere should repent [change their ways, and believe in Him], because He has fixed a day in which He will judge the world in righteousness through a Man [Jesus] whom He determined, having furnished proof to all by raising Him from the dead." (Acts 17:30-31)

53

JARAI

"Some tribes have preserved the memory," wrote the explorer Henri Maitre, "transmitted from generation to generation, of the biblical facts which one finds, in the most diverse parts of the globe, among the most different cultures." Maitre adds: "The deluge, the tower of Babel, the dispersion of races, are known among certain [Southeast Asian] mountain tribes, which recount them in their own way, adapting events and characters to their primitive setting."[1]

That is certainly true of the Jarai people, of the Central Highlands of Vietnam. Consider what was recorded at the city of Pleiku, which was anciently the main settlement of the Jarai people. Here at Pleiku, in March of 1908, the French missionary Émile Kemlin and his companions were privileged to hear one of the Jarai people's most highly esteemed bards narrate several traditions of their history. One of these refers to the Flood and especially the Tower of Babel:

> "'It is here,' he told us, 'the center of the world! It is here, in fact, that after the deluge of our Father Drum [their Noah, who survived in a drum], that mankind so numerous erected the tower of the dispersion. It was so tall that it had to be stabilized with cords of rattan connected to the top.
>
> A herald went up on it to explore the sight of the universe. Once he climbed up, he cried out, I see a beautiful plain near the sea! I see another one in the west, near a large river!
>
> He could say no more, because at that very moment the tower collapsed and that unfortunate man fell to his death. In a hurry to reach these coveted lands first, the Annamites and Laotians had let go of all the ropes!
>
> The Bahnars and the Jarais, nonchalant by nature, were having fun biting sugar cane and had heard nothing. When they wanted to understand what was said, it was too late! Not knowing which way to direct their steps, they were forced to stay in their country.'"[2]

"After the deluge of our Father Drum [Noah], … mankind so numerous erected the tower of the dispersion."

So deeply impressed was that Tower on the memory of the Jarai people that the bard added: "Even now, we see the debris of one of the columns of that giant edifice. No one dares to touch it, because its complete disappearance would bring the end of the world!"[3]

Concerning the Flood, the tradition above mentions that their ancestor, "Father Drum," survived the Flood by taking refuge inside a drum. Another tradition tells that the debaucherous behavior of mankind incited a god named Yang to send a Flood. Only a brother and a sister survived, floating inside a great hollow trunk. Later the two married, since there was no one else on earth. They gave birth to children who became three races: first, the Jarai, second, the Lao, and third, the Viet.[4]

"Father Drum" survived the Flood by taking refuge in a floating drum.

1. Henri Maitre, *Les Jungles Moï: Exploration et Histoire des Hinterlands Moï du Cambodge, de la Cochinchine, de l'Annam et du bas Laos* (Paris: E. Larose, 1912), p. 27.
2. Émile Kemlin, "Au Pays Jaraï," *Les Missions Catholiques*, vol. 41 (1909), pp. 226-227.
3. *Ibid.*, p. 227.
4. Dang Nghiem Van, "The Flood Myth and the Origin of Ethnic Groups in Southeast Asia," *Journal of American Folklore*, vol. 106, no. 421 (American Folklore Society, 1993), p. 329.

54

BAHNAR

The Bahnar people are closely related to the Jarai tribe. We saw above that the Jarai have a tradition of the Tower of Babel. Do the Bahnar also remember that Tower? Indeed, they do. They even have a memory of its architect and leader (whom we know biblically to be Nimrod. See Genesis 10:8-12 and 11:1-9). In the words of Guerlach, a French priest who arrived in Vietnam in 1882, their tradition ran thus:

Traditional Bahnar dance

> "The architects of that time had grandiose projects: to build a structure whose roof would be lost in the black clouds of rain. The eldest son of our first ancestors was the director of the works and led his affairs smoothly. Everyone was put to work, so the work progressed rapidly. The frame was already in place. The eldest son, standing on the top, gave his orders in a resounding voice. He had (like the heroes of Homer) strong lungs and an iron throat. The sound of his voice sounded like the sound of the wind during a storm. So we could hear him easily. That very day, the director of works needed some rattan. He asked for some, but they brought him a beam. Dissatisfied, he threw the beam and cried out for rattan. Then someone handed him a rope. At that point, anger seized control of him. He began to beat up those men that he thought were mocking him.

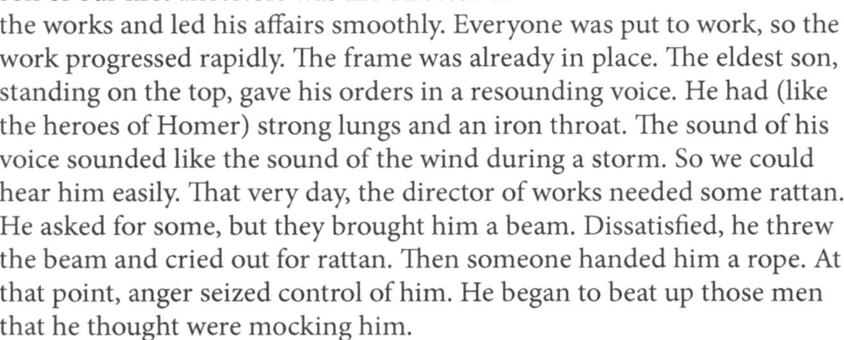

The men dispersed to all points of the globe. Some, speaking the Bahnar language, emigrated to the country of the Bahnars, others gave birth to the Sedangs, the Reungao, the Jarai, and so forth.

> Everyone burst out laughing, because we did not understand him, for the languages had been confused. Furious, the eldest son of Bok Seugucur jumped down from the roof, seized a strong club, and gave his brothers, sisters and grand-nephews a first-class beating.
>
> Such a striking conflict was not to everyone's liking. Also, to escape this whirlwind of beatings, the men dispersed to all points of the globe. Some, speaking the Bahnar language, emigrated to the country of the Bahnars, others gave birth to the Sedangs, the Reungao, the Jarai, and so forth. The eldest son remained with his parents and became the source of the Vietnamese people. This is why the Vietnamese are more intelligent and richer than the peoples of our mountains; they descend from the eldest son! Such is the origin of the different peoples, according to the native chronicles."[5]

We should note a few things: 1) the recurrence of a Tower of Babel tradition among not only the Bahnar but also their close relatives, the Jarai, confirms the antiquity and authenticity of the tradition. 2) In this tradition, the eldest son's father, "Bok Seugucur," is undoubtedly the man who survived the Flood inside a floating drum–Noah. 3) Whereas this tradition makes the chief architect of the Tower to be the son of "Father Drum" (Noah), we know biblically that this architect (Nimrod) was actually Noah's great-grandson.

The memory of Cain and Abel has left its mark on several Flood stories which have a "quarrel" element. Sometimes even the "two brothers" motif is present.

In regard to the Flood tradition that the Bahnar people told to Geurlach, it began with a notion of a quarrel between two creatures: a kite (bird) and a crab. I believe this is either a vague memory of Cain and Abel or of the protoevangelium in Genesis 3:15. ("I will put enmity between you [the serpent] and the woman, and between your seed and her seed. He shall bruise you on the head, and you shall bruise him on the heel." LSB) In favor of the "Cain and Abel" view, the Bahnar tradition refers to a "mark" on the crab, which could be the "mark" or "sign" that God placed upon Cain (Genesis 4:15). In any case, the tradition begins:

5. Jean-Baptiste-Marie Geurlach, "Moeurs et Superstitions des Sauvages Bahnars," *Les Misions Catholiques*, vol. 19 (Lyon: 1884), pp. 489-490.

> "Formerly, in the beginning, the kite took up a quarrel with the crab, and gave him a peck on the back so hard that his shell was pierced. We still see the mark of this famous pecking. The crab wanted to take revenge, but how could he draw out the kite who was hiding in the clouds?"[6]

We will see that many people groups have a "quarrel" element like this mixed in with their Flood story. This is not surprising, given the confusion of languages at Babel, and oral preservation of traditions. But we continue:

> "The crustacean made the waters of the sea and the rivers join together, so that they rose to the sky. All living things perished, except two persons, a brother and sister, who took refuge in a bass drum of enormous size."[7]

This "bass drum of enormous size" is Noah's Ark. There are still more parallels with Noah's Ark and the flight of the dove:

They brought with them a pair of each species of animals, and sealed up the vessel so that it floated on the water like a great boat. The flood lasted seven days and seven nights. At the end of that time, the brother heard a hen sing outside.

> "They brought with them a pair of each species of animals, and sealed up the vessel so that it floated on the water like a great boat. The flood lasted seven days and seven nights. At the end of that time, the brother heard a hen sing outside. Where did this chicken come from? It was sent by the spirits to advise our ancestors that the waters had receded, and that they could go out. As a captain exits his ship after everyone has landed, the Bahnar version of Noah released the birds from the giant bass drum. The other animals, seeing the door open, took advantage of it to find the best lands in which to dwell."[8]

We also have a summary of the Flood, and of the paradise before the Fall, from the narration that they told to the French scientist Henri Mouhot:

> "If you ask them respecting the origin of mankind, all they tell you is, that the father of the human race was saved from an immense inundation by means of a large chest in which he shut himself up; but of the origin or creator of this father they know nothing. Their traditions do not reach beyond the Deluge; but they will tell you that in the beginning one grain of rice sufficed to fill a saucepan and furnish a repast for a whole family. This is a souvenir of the first age of the world, that fugitive period of innocence and happiness which poets have called the golden age."[9]

The Lost Book, and Prophecies of a Future Salvation

When we come to Myanmar (Burma) and Southeast Asia, we would be remiss if we didn't mention a couple phenomena which played a part in the explosive advance of the Gospel among several tribes. The first was a tradition held by certain tribes about a "lost book." This book contained the knowledge of God, but at some point it was lost or destroyed. As a result, these tribes fell into great peril and adversity, and now had to appease certain demons who could do them harm.

> "That the Karens had, at some time in their history, a book which they afterwards lost, is a fact referred to in many of their

6. Guerlach, "Moeurs et Superstitions des Sauvages Bahnars," p. 479.
7. *Ibid.*
8. *Ibid.*
9. M. Henri Mouhot, *Travels in the Central Parts of Indo-China [Siam], Cambodia and Laos, vol. 2* (London: Murray, 1864), pp. 28-29.

traditions."[10] "Our fathers say the Karens once had God's Book, written on leather; and they carelessly allowed it to be destroyed."[11] In total, Don Richardson found 10 people groups with such a tradition, including: 1) Karens, 2) Kachin, 3) Lahu, 4) Wa, 5) Shan, 6) Palaung (De'ang), 7) Kui, 8) Lisu, 9) Naga, and 10) Mizo.[12] We can attest that these traditions have been found in several of the early ethnographic reports on various Southeast Asian tribes.

Yet they held to the strong conviction that one day, the true God would return the "lost book" to them, and they would worship Him once more and enjoy the favor of God. Some of these tribes had prophecies and visions of a white man coming to them, who would bring God's *Book* back to them. (This is no racial statement, this is simply what they foresaw.)[13] "Our prophets say that the white foreigners have the Book, and will in future time restore it to us,"[14] said the Karens. 'Karat Kasang [the Creator] once gave a book to our forefathers, but it was lost,' said the Kachin.[15]

The Lahu tribe said that the Creator, Gui Sha, gave his law written on rice cakes to their ancestors, but in a time of famine it was eaten. They longed for the day when God's law would be returned to them.[16] The Wa tribe, in the 1880s, had a prophecy that they took very seriously. They were convinced that the true God would soon send a white brother to them to restore their lost book from God. They even abandoned evil practices such as headhunting and spirit-appeasement, lest God should pass them by if He found them doing evil when He came.[17]

So certain were the Kui people, living on the border of Thailand and Myanmar, that they "actually built houses of worship dedicated to the true God in anticipation of the time when a messenger from God would enter such places of worship with the lost book in His hand to teach the people! No idols were ever placed in such places of worship, but Kui folk would 'gather and, in dim uncertain fashion, worship the great God above.'"[18] The Lisu people of southwestern China held the same promise, awaiting the return of God's book and a king who would rule them and protect them.

Therefore, when George Boardman, Francis Mason, Jonathan Wade and other missionaries (along with native Burmese missionaries) met these tribes, their listeners gave undivided attention to the message of Jesus. An amazing work of God was kindled in those days, and today there are hundreds of thousands of followers of Jesus among these tribal groups!

---

10. E. B. Cross, "How the Work of Christian Missions Began Among the Karens," *Baptist Missionary Magazine,* vol. 56 (Boston, 1876), p. 137.
11. Cross, "How the Work of Christian Missions Began Among the Karens," p. 138.
12. Don Richardson, *Eternity in Their Hearts* (Ventura, California: Regal, 2005), pp. 66-94.
13. On another occasion, in another place, it could have been a black missionary or a medium-brown missionary.
14. Cross, "How the Work of Christian Missions Began Among the Karens," p. 138.
15. Herman Tegenfeldt, *A Century of Growth: The Kachin Baptist Church of Burma* (South Pasadena, CA: William Carey Library, 1974), p. 46. See also: Ola Hanson, *The Kachins, Their Customs and Traditions* (Rangoon: American Baptist Mission Press, 1913), pp. 116-117.
16. Richardson, *Eternity in Their Hearts*, p. 77. See also: *Annual Report of the American Baptist Missionary Union*, vol. 91 (Boston, 1905), pp. 117-118.
17. Richardson, *Eternity in Their Hearts*, p. 78. See also Tegenfeldt, *A Century of Growth*, p. 46.
18. Richardson, *Eternity in Their Hearts*, p. 80.

55

KAREN

The Karens are one of the largest tribes in Myanmar (or Burma), numbering over five million. The Karens live in the mountainous region of eastern Myanmar, bordering on Thailand.

> "Among the interesting facts connected with the Karens," wrote Reverend Gilmore, "is the prevalence among them, when they first came in contact with Christian missionaries, of a number of traditional legends more or less resembling the narratives found in the early part of the book of Genesis." Writing in 1910, Gilmore added, "The existence of these legends was one of the factors which made possible the rapid success of the missionaries when they began work among the Karens 84 years ago."[19]

The existence of these legends was one of the factors which made possible the rapid success of the missionaries when they began work among the Karens 84 years ago.

Creation:

One of those earliest missionaries was Dr. Francis Mason, who met the Karens in 1830 and would spend the next 40 years or so among them. Among the amazing traditions that he heard from the Karens was this Creation story:

> "God created heaven and earth. The creation of heaven and earth was finished. … He created the sun, he created the moon, he created the stars. The creation of the sun, the moon and the stars was finished.[20]
>
> He created again (creating) man. And of what did he create man? He created man at first from the earth. The creation of man was finished.
>
> He created a woman. How did he create a woman? He took a rib out of the man, and created again (creating) a woman. The creation of woman was finished.…
>
> He created again (creating) food and drink. He created rice, he created water, he created fire, he created cows, he created elephants, he created birds. The creation of animals was finished."[21]

How did he create a woman? He took a rib out of the man ... The creation of woman was finished.

Garden of Eden:

Regarding the existence of an original paradise (the Garden of Eden), the tradition continues:

> "Father God said, my son and daughter, father will make and give you a garden. In the garden are seven different kinds of trees, bearing seven different kinds of fruit; among the seven, one tree is not good to eat. Eat not of its fruit. If you eat you will become old, you will die. Eat not. All I have created I give to you. Eat and drink with care. Once in seven days I will visit you. All I have commanded you, observe and do. Forget me not. Pray to me every morning and night."[22]

---

19. David Gilmore, "Karen Folk-lore II: The Fall of Man," *Journal of the Burma Research Society*, vol. 1, no. 2 (1910), p. 36. Edmund Cross, an early missionary himself, writes: "The gospel was not introduced to the Karens till 1827-8. Up to that time, so far as any record has been preserved, they were unknown to Europeans." Edmund Cross, "How the Work of Christian Missions Began Among the Karens," *Baptist Missionary Magazine*, vol. 56, p. 137. See also: L. P. Brockett, *The Story of the Karen Mission in Bassein* (Philadelphia, 1891), p. 24.
20. Francis Mason, *The Karen Apostle: Or, Memoir of Ko Thah-byu, the First Karen Convert* (Boston: Gould, Kendall and Lincoln, 1843), p. 112.
21. *Ibid.*, p. 113.
22. *Ibid.*, p. 113. Mason here translates the native words "Naukplau" or "Ku-plaw" as "Satan," and "Y'wah" as "God."

Then came the entrance of the devil–known to the Karens as Naukplau–and the temptation and the Fall. This tradition is set to verse:

A Karen Woman (1912)

> "Y'wah in the beginning commanded,
> But Nauk'plau came to destroy.
> Y'wah at first gave command,
> Nauk'plau maliciously deceived unto death.
> The woman E-u, and the man Tha-nai,
> The malicious fiend enviously looked upon them.
> Bot the woman E-u, and the man Tha-nai,
> The Serpent regarded with hatred.
> The great Serpent deceived the woman E-u,
> And what was it that he said to her?
> The great Serpent deceived them unto death,
> And what was it that he did?
> The great Serpent took the yellow fruit of the tree,
> And gave it to Y'wah's holy daughter;
> The great Serpent took the white fruit of the tree,
> And gave it to Y'wah's son and daughter to eat.
> They kept not every word of Y'wah–
> Nauk'plau deceived them. They died!
> They kept not each one the world of Y'wah,
> And he deceived and beguiled them unto death."[23]

Another early missionary, Edmund Cross, elaborates on this "Nauk'plau," the enemy of the human race:

> "It is necessary to allude to the belief of the Karens relative to the evil being by whom the man and woman first created were induced to transgress the commands of God. This evil being is variously designated in the Karen traditions, according to his influence on men, and his relation to the other stand of existence. His impersonation is sometimes male, and sometimes female. He is called Nauk'plau in allusion to his having tempted men to forsake God and then abandoned them to destruction, as the hen drives from her her weaned chicklings."[24]

Nauk'plau is the evil being by whom the first man and woman were induced to transgress the commands of God.

And Cross quotes the Karen tradition on how the devil himself was cast out of God's presence:

> "Nauk'plau at the beginning was just,
> But afterwards transgressed the word of God.
> Nauk'plau at the first was divine,
> But afterwards broke the word of God.
> God drove him out and lashed him from his place.
> He tempted the holy daughter of God.
> God lashed him with whips from his presence;
> He deceived God's son and daughter."[25]

23. Charles Forbes, *The Races of British Burma* (London: John Murray, 1878), p. 267. Mason, *The Karen Apostle*, pp. 116-117.
24. Edmund B. Cross, "On the Karens," *Journal of the American Oriental Society*, vol. 4 (New York: Putnam, 1854), p. 301.
25. Ibid.

Defense of the Authenticity of the Karen Traditions

How are we to account for the striking similarity between Genesis and these Karen traditions? Before one dismisses this as Christian teaching, there are several things that must also be considered:

1. The first woman's name, "E-u," is no derivation of the biblical Eve, as Mason and others have attested.[26]
2. The name "Thannai" is also used to represent man or mankind, among other tribes of northeast and Bengal. This testifies to the tradition's authenticity.[27]
3. As for the temptation by an evil serpent, the Karens are far from unique in possessing such a tradition. We will see in this book, just as we saw in *Volume 1*, that such traditions are widely diffused across the world.
4. The resemblance between the Karen name for God (Y'wah) and the Hebrew name Yahweh is coincidental, and not evidence of direct influence, for the following reasons:
    a. In reality, as affirmed by Macleod White, an early expert on the Karen mission, "Ouah" is a better rendition than Y'wah.[28] It is clear that "Ouah" and "Yahweh" are not the same name.
    b. On the authenticity and antiquity of this Karen word for God, Wylie's field expertise is uniquely helpful: "Ouah is the appellation given by all the Karens to the Eternal God, but with different adjectives attached. A Sgau Karen would say G'eha Ouah, "Lord God": a Pwo Karen might say this, but would be just as likely to say Moung Ouah, "the Honorable God", particularly if not acquainted with the Christians. A Mona Karen would say, Ouah Pado, "the Great God"; and a Taubeah would say L'Ouah Do, also "the Great God."[29] To see the name Ouah used among such a diverse and widely scattered set of Karen people refutes the idea that this word came about due to Christian influence.
    c. Again on the authenticity and antiquity of the Karen word for God, Charles Forbes noted that "the meaning of this word [Y'wah or Ouah] is 'to flow,' as a river or stream; and it is always coupled with 'Htoo,' which means 'perpetual.'[30]
5. There are many differences between the Karens' traditions and the Bible. That is true both for the traditions cited above, and their other traditions and religious beliefs. This confirms their originality.
6. The strongest parallels with Scripture possessed by the Karens are limited to Genesis 1-3. Therefore, if Christian (or Jewish) influence were the root factor, where are the Karen versions of the Exodus, the Virgin Birth, the Cross and Resurrection of Jesus, David and Goliath, or other famous stories of the Bible? And what kind of missionary only teaches about Genesis 1-3?

---

26. "Had it been a modern composition," Mason writes, "Adam would not have been Thanai; nor Eve, E-u, but A-wa, as written and printed by both Protestant and Catholic missionaries in Burma." Source: Mason, *The Karen Apostle*, p. 116.
27. Edward Dalton wrote, in his great ethnography of Bengal and parts of Burma: "Tha-nai or Tennai, is one of the words for mankind among the Hill Miris and Dophlas." Edward Tuite Dalton, *Descriptive Ethnology of Bengal* (Calcutta, 1872), p. 116.
28. Macleod White, *The Gospel in Burmah* (New York: Shelton, 1860), p. 202.
29. White, *The Gospel in Burmah*, p. 202.
30. Forbes, *The Races of British Burma*, p. 265.

7. Mason is not our only source for these traditions. We have the records of Edmund Cross and Jonathan Wade within a few years of Mason, confirming several of these traditions.[31]

8. I grant that Mason may have translated some words into overly biblical-sounding terms. However, word choice is a very different thing from actual missionary influence. As Forbes explained so clearly:

   > "However much they have Europeanised and embellished their native myths after their intercourse with the missionaries, there is not the slightest doubt that these existed among them prior to their earlier intercourse with Europeans. It was their very belief in these legends, as having been contained in those books long lost to their nation, that induced them to listen so readily to the teachers who suddenly appeared among them with a book, out of which they taught words so strangely agreeing with their own traditions. Moreover, these ideas are not found merely among the tribes that have received the Gospel, but everywhere among the heathen Karens, though in different degrees of completeness."[32]

There is not the slightest doubt that these traditions existed among them prior to their interaction with Europeans. (Charles Forbes)

The Flood:

Mason also heard allusions to their Flood tradition, though he never heard it in its entirety.

> "It thundered, tempests followed; it rained three days and three nights, and the waters covered all the mountains."[33]

> "Anciently, when the earth was deluged with water, two brothers, finding themselves in a difficulty, got on a raft. The waters rose and rose, till they reached to heaven; when seeing a mango tree hanging down, the younger brother climbed up it and ate; but the waters suddenly falling, left him in the tree."[34]

Tower of Babel:

Finally, Southeast Asia is full of Tower of Babel stories, and the Karens are no exception:

> "Oh children and grandchildren! Man had at first but one father and one mother; but because they did not love each other, they separated. After their separation they did not know each other, and their language became different; and they became enemies to each other and fought."

> "The Karens were the elder brother,
> They obtained all the words of God;
> They did not all believe the word of God,
> And became enemies to each other.
> Because they disbelieved God,
> Their language divided.
> God gave them commands,
> But they did not believe him; and divisions ensued."[35]

Their language divided. God gave them commands, but they did not believe him; and divisions ensued.

31. For more information, see: Ken Mason, *A Bibliography of Karenic Linguistics* (Chiang Mai: Payap University Department of Linguistics, 2004).
32. Forbes, *The Native Races of British Burma*, p. 268.
33. Mason, *The Karen Apostle*, p. 119.
34. *Ibid*.
35. Mason, *The Karen Apostle*, pp. 119-120.

56 SEDANG

The Sedang or Southern Mon-Khmer people live in southern Vietnam and adjacent parts of Laos. They have the following Flood legend, published by the Vietnamese ethnologist Dang Ngheim Van in 1972. This tradition alludes to both an original paradise and long lifespans in earlier times.

Mountainous region of Vietnam

> "Once upon a time, humankind was very numerous. People had more than enough rice and plenty of food. When rice matured, its grains automatically flew into homes and fish jumped from the water onto grills to be cooked. Human lifespans were so long that people became decadent. Men and women engaged in promiscuous sex and lived together outside of wedlock. Yang ("heaven") flew into a rage when he learned of this. He sent Bok Glaih to make thunder and rain and to cause a deluge that covered the whole surface of the earth, drowning all humanity.

Only one woman and a dog escaped, by climbing to the highest peak of Ngoc Linh Mountain."[36]

57 YI

Auguste Bonifacy (1856-1931), an officer in the French colonial infantry, spent his spare time as an ethnographer, writing many valuable works on the ethnic groups of Vietnam. He recorded the following Flood tradition from the Yi people of northern Vietnam:

> "In the beginning, the Man-zi and the M'ti (Thai) were at war. The former burned up all the villages of the latter, so that the latter prayed to Heaven for help. But a brother and a sister, Mni-ha and Tho-a, had not taken part in these crimes. They had taken refuge in a temple. Heaven advised them to enter a giant pumpkin, as big as a house, in which they stockpiled food. The flood came, and they sailed upon the waters. When they went down, the pumpkin stopped on the mountain Pia-ya, a resting place of spirits, where men no longer dare to live now."[37]

Yi tradition: The giant pumpkin stopped on the mountain Pia-ya, a resting place of spirits, where men no longer dare to live now.

Genesis 8:4 "The ark rested on the mountains of Ararat."

Notice the parallel with Mount Ararat in the above text. In the same way that Genesis records three dispatches of birds after which Noah learns that the Flood has ended, the Yi tradition refers to three signs that urged the brother and sister that they must marry.[38] Having married, they gave birth to three sons and three daughters. In time, these also married and gave rise to all the nations on earth. "These three united. The first is the ancestral pair of the

36. Dang Nghiem Van, "Ve truyen qua bau-me o Viet Nam [Myths of the Gourd-Mother in Vietnam]", *Tap chi Van hoc* [Review of Literature], vol. 3 (1972), pp. 50-61.
37. Auguste Louis Bonifacy, "Etude sur les coutumes et la langue des Lolo et des La-qua du Haut-Tonkin," *Bulletin de l'Ecole Francaise d'Extreme Orient*, vol. 8 (1908), p. 551.
38. Ibid. "The youths left the pumpkin and began to roam the mountains. A turtle stopped them and said, "Where are you going?" They said, "We are going to look for a wife and a husband." The turtle continued, "There are no more people on earth. You two marry." But they killed the turtle and flamed his shell to perform divination. But the divination told them: "Get married!" Then they wanted to return to their village, and they passed near the bamboo sticks which spoke to them, saying, "Where are you going?" They replied, "We are going to marry." The bamboo sticks responded, "Here, be united here." And they married."

Man-zi, the second that of the Mung [Phu La], and the third that of the M'ti (Thai). These three main races then produced the other races of the surrounding area."[39] On the number of pairs (3), we are reminded of Noah's three sons Shem, Ham, and Japheth, and their wives.

58

THAI

The Thai people, according to their own traditions, migrated from southwestern China to their present location.[40] We have much to report concerning this great nation, beginning with a Flood account which explicitly remembers the rainbow as a sign of God's promise in Genesis 9. "There was once a Flood in Siam," wrote a French missionary named Barthélemy Bruguière, who lived among the Thai and wrote an ethnographic report in 1829. "The god Phra-Phu-Thi-Chau placed a rainbow in the clouds, to reassure men against the fear of a new flood."[41] How remarkable to find the memory of this promise nearly 5,000 miles away in Thailand!

The god Phra-Phu-Thi-Chau placed a rainbow in the clouds, to reassure men against the fear of a new flood.

Concerning this Flood and Creation, Bruguière further summarized the popular Thai tradition:

> "From all eternity there existed a god called Phra-Hin. This god had a hen, and one day he felt like testing his power. He gathered some of the waste that his hen had made, and he formed two little dolls from it, which he brought to life. It was from this first man and first woman that the human race originated. The Flood came shortly after."[42]

Next, we have the reports of Antoine Bourlet, a missionary and ethnographer of the Society of Foreign Missions of Paris. He arrived in northern Vietnam in 1901. The Thai people told him their tradition of the Flood, which took place in the ancient past after mankind had multiplied prolifically:

> "[Mankind] soon became so numerous that Po Then, the Father of the highest heavens, anxious for his power, no doubt, resolved to destroy them. He sent the deluge upon them. For seven days and seven nights rain fell in drops as big as the fruit of the muoi [larger than an acorn]. The reservoirs of the earth opened, all the torrents overflowed, and the gulfs of water engulfed all the villages, all the tribes, and everything everywhere. … All the inhabitants of the earth perished. … There was a big gourd that looked like a basket to carry rice, and there was a big squash that looked like an attic. The young pair of children, Kap and Ke, made a hole and huddled in there: one in one vessel, the other in the other. And the water rose in a whirlwind in the air. It rose in whirlwinds to the sky, and the two children sailed together until they stopped in front of the house of the father Po Then."[43]

The young pair of children, Kap and Ke, made a hole and huddled in there: one in the gourd and the other in the big squash.

Do the Thai also have a memory of Noah sending birds (Genesis 8:6-12)? Yes. Some of the details have been lost, but the outline is still there:

> "[Po Then] sent to see who was thus whispering and talking in a low voice. The envoy went. He saw someone in the big bottle that looked like a basket, and someone in the big squash that looked like an attic. Then he came to report to Po Then of his mission."[44]

39. *Ibid.*
40. Charles Forbes, *The Races of British Burma* (London: John Murray, 1878), p. 41.
41. Barthélemy Bruguière, "Letter from Mgr. Brugiere, Bishop of Capse, to Mr. Gousquet," *Annales de l'Association de la Propagation de la Foi*, vol. 5, no. 25 (Paris, 1831), p. 102. Bruguière further wrote that the beliefs he cites are those generally held by the majority of Thai people (p. 100).
42. *Ibid.*, pp. 102-103.
43. Antoine Bourlet, "Les Thay," *Anthropos*, vol. 2 (1907), pp. 354-373, 612-632, 921-923.
44. *Ibid.* After the Flood, there is also an account of their attempt to fetch fire from the Spirit of the Sky, by sending various birds and animals to fetch it. (pp. 921-923) This fire fetching motif is highly connected to the "earth diver" motif, which is derived from a memory of the Flood (Genesis 6-8) and Creation (Genesis 1), as we have shown in *Echoes of Ararat* (*Volume 1*).

Po Then wanted to kill them, but the children begged for their lives and pledged to be good workers of the land. Po Then had mercy and let them live. This man and woman would eventually repopulate the world.[45]

The Red River Delta of Northern Vietnam

Bourlet is not our only source for the Thai Flood tradition. One Captain M. Cottes, who studied the Thai people extensively, recorded a tradition from those living at Tonkin, in the delta region of the Red River in northern Vietnam:

> "The Thai have a legend about their origin. In the distant past, the Buddha, being displeased with humans, resolved to annihilate them by burying them under water. Two orphans, a brother and a sister, honored Buddha according to their means; they found grace in his eyes. The Buddha told them to sow pumpkin seeds. From one of these seeds came a plant which grew up marvelously. It flowered after three days, and after six days yielded a pumpkin. After a month, this pumpkin could hold ten 'piculs' of paddy.

After having emptied it, the brother and sister put stores of cooked rice in it and took refuge there (like Noah in the ark). At once a torrential rain fell continuously for seven days and seven nights, which covered the whole earth and annihilated its inhabitants. The pumpkin floated, preserving the life of the brother and sister, and also the raven that accompanied them."[46]

That raven is a memory of Noah's raven and dove. And there is more:

> "When the waters had receded, the brother and sister left their shelter, and found that everything was dead around them. Their supply of rice was exhausted, but the crow took flight and found land where there were potatoes and roots for food. The seeds, left under the silt deposited by the water, sprouted and quickly produced fresh crops."[47]

The pumpkin floated, preserving the life of the brother and sister, and also the raven that accompanied them.

The pumpkin is said to have landed in Tonkin. The human couple later repopulated the world. They also succeeded in creating animals anew using a staff which they found by the corpse of an old woman who had eaten human flesh in the days prior to the Flood.[48]

The Vietnamese anthropologist Dang Nghiem Van collected over 300 Flood narratives across Southeast Asia. He states that this Flood story is present in virtually every ethnic group in mainland Southeast Asia. Here, it is usually a brother and a sister who survive the flood, and various ethnicities are afterwards created from seeds from a gourd. He writes: "In most versions of the tale, the protagonists who will escape the deluge receive some warning of the impending disaster and are counseled on how to avoid death."[49]

---

45. *Ibid.*
46. M. Cottes, "Sur Les Populations Thai du Tonkin," *Premier Congrès International des Études d'Extrême Orient: Hanoi 1902* (Hanoi: Schneider, 1903), pp. 118.
47. *Ibid.*, pp. 118-119.
48. *Ibid.*, p. 119.
49. Dang Nghiem Van, "The Flood Myth and the Origin of Ethnic Groups in Southeast Asia," *Journal of American Folklore*, vol. 106, no. 421 (1993), pp. 304-308.

The Flood tradition recorded from the Lisu living in Myanmar begins in the following way:

> "Just before the old world was destroyed, two orphans—a young man called Kywa-has and his sister Kywa-kyi-me—were living in a village high up in the Himalayas. One day they cut down trees in a new area to clear the land for cultivation because they had exhausted their old plot. After working the whole day long they went home, but when they returned the next day they found to their astonishment that the trees they had cut down were all alive and standing. They cut the trees down again and went back home at the end of the day, but the next morning they found that the same thing had happened."[50]

Don't just think of your own little area. The whole world's going to be flooded soon and all the people and all the animals, everything will be destroyed. You'd better think of a way to escape the flood.

A stranger trespasses in their garden. This motif likely comes from a mixture of the Flood memory and that of the Garden of Eden. We continue:

> "So that evening, instead of going back home, they hid nearby to find out what was going on during the night. Fairly soon they saw a wild cat and a viper arriving. These animals began to play, running and jumping among the trees that lay on the ground, and as they did this the trees they had jumped on stood up and were alive again, and soon all the trees were standing as before. The brother and sister started complaining. 'We're poor people,' they said. 'Why are you giving us such trouble?'
>
> 'Don't just think of your own little area,' said the wild cat and the viper when they heard this. 'The whole world's going to be flooded soon and all the people and all the animals, everything will be destroyed. You'd better think of a way to escape the flood.'"[51]

Next, the orphans are instructed to hollow out a very large tree trunk to escape the Flood:

They went to the trunk, got inside and sealed the openings. It rained and rained day after day, month after month, until the whole world was inundated. … When the waters receded, the tree trunk was left on a mountain top. Then they heard a bird singing.

> "'What can we do to escape?' asked Kywa-has and Kywa-kyi-me, now very frightened. 'Try boring a hole through a big tree trunk,' the creatures suggested. 'Put inside it all the things you want to save, and when the world is engulfed in three years, three months and seven days' time, get inside too and you'll be safe.'
>
> The creatures disappeared into the forest, and the brother and sister felled the biggest tree they could find. In seven months they had finished boring a hole through the trunk, and there they kept a rooster, a dog, their father's silver stick, their mother's silver comb and other household items, even needles. As soon as it began to rain, Kywa-has and Kywa-kyi-me went to the trunk, got inside and sealed the openings. It rained and rained day after day, month after month, until the whole world was inundated. The two inside felt their hollowed log being carried away by the rising water. When the waters receded, the tree trunk was left on a mountain top. Then they heard a bird singing, 'Si-si, si-si' outside and, as the log was remaining still, they lowered a needle through a tiny hole to test the depth of the water. They heard the plop of the needle and then silence so, thinking the water must still be high, they decided to stay inside. The next morning their rooster crowed 'The water's gone' instead of the usual 'It's morning now' at sunrise and 'It's evening now' at sunset. So they opened one side and looked through and saw the bird singing on a tree nearby.

---

50. Ludu U Hla, *Lisu Folk-tales*, no. 31 (Mandalay: Kyi-bwa-yei Press, 1968), pp. 119-135. As translated in: Gerry Abbott and Khin Thant Han, *The Folk-tales of Burma* (Boston: Brill, 2000), pp. 61-63.
51. Gerry Abbott and Khin Thant Han, *The Folk-tales of Burma* (Boston: Brill, 2000), p. 63.

> The dog too, restless and wanting to get out, began to bark. And the rooster crowed again, 'The water's gone. It's time to go outside.' So Kywa-has and his sister got out of the log and found themselves near a tree on the top of a mountain. There was nothing apart from the two trees left standing and the bird singing 'Si-si, si-si.'"[52]

Lisu Flood Story Featuring a Dog and a Rooster

The tradition goes on to tell how they reached the decision to marry. [53] In this "brother-sister marriage" narrative theme, which we explore further in Appendix B, we see an altered memory of the three test flights involving Noah's raven and dove (Genesis 8:6-12):

To this day, when the Lisu people hear the "nya-nisei" bird chirping during the rain, no matter how heavy the storm, they say that the rain is about to end.[54] How deeply this Flood was impressed on their cultural memory! No doubt they have passed this tradition down for over 4,000 years.

60 MUONG

Regarding the Muong people of northern Vietnam, Jean Funé recorded that "They have a legend about a flood from which a brother and his sister were saved, becoming the founders of the new race."[55] Another version tells that a magic turtle warned King Dit Dang about the coming Flood which covered all the high mountains nearly to their summits. Only when the king sacrificed a black buffalo did the waters recede. From bags of seed that escaped the Flood, the earth was replanted with trees and vegetation.[56]

Only when the king sacrificed a black buffalo did the waters recede.

Again, the presence of a sacrifice is easily explained by the biblical view which regards this as a memory of Noah's sacrifice, commanded by God before the Flood and executed after the Flood.

52. *Ibid.*, pp. 63–64.
53. "Some time later Kywa-has thought that although they were brother and sister they should marry, otherwise there wouldn't be any people left after they had died. He discussed the matter with his sister, who didn't agree at first. Then later, after a lot of pressure from the brother, who kept thinking about the future, she told him that it shouldn't be their decision. She would consent, provided that there were signs from the guardian nats [spirits] of the world that they should get married in order to produce children. So they called the nats to witness, asking for signs of approval of a marriage to prevent extinction. After paying respect to the nats they rolled two round bamboo trays down a hillside, and when they went down they found that one had landed on top of the other. Calling on the nats again they rolled down two mortars, which also ended up one on top of the other. They called on the nats a third time and rolled two frying pans down the hill, and once again the same thing happened. They took this to be a sign given by the nats to show their consent and so they got married." *Ibid.*, pp. 64-65.
54. *Ibid.*, p. 61.
55. Jean Funé, "Pioneering Among the Muong Tribe," *The Call of French Indochina and East Siam*, vol. 37 (Hanoi: Gospel Press, 1933), p. 12.
56. Pham Van Hung (2017), *Aspects of Philosophy in Mo Muong Hoa Binh,* PhD Thesis. Hanoi National University of Education, p. 110. See also: Huy Vọng Bùi, *Mộ Mường ở Hòa Bình* ("Muong Tomb in Hoa Binh") (Hanoi, 2016). Manh Hoang Quang, "Đại hồng thủy trong truyền thuyết của dân tộc Mường – Hòa Bình" ["Great flood in the legend of the Muong - Hoa Binh people"], July 14, 2022. Retrieved 12 January, 2024 from: https://spiderum.com/bai-dang/Dai-hong-thuy-trong-truyen-thuyet-cua-dan-toc-Muong-Hoa-Binh-1sSQS8OJV6vY

61

KACHIN / JINGPO

The Kachin people live in northwestern Myanmar and parts of adjacent India and China. In China they are known as the Jingpo (or Jingpho), and in India as the Singpho.

Jingpo women in traditional dress

Around the early 1850s, their most well-informed chief, the Bisu Gam, narrated a tradition of an original state when they were created and placed on a mountain called Mujai Singra Bhum. There they lived and enjoyed immortality, and they followed "the pure worship of one supreme being." However, "on their descending to the plains, they fell into the common lot of humanity," and "soon adopted the idolatries and superstitions around them." Their loss of immortality was tied to an act of disobedience against a prohibition from God not to bathe in a certain river called Ram Sita.[57]

Regarding their tradition of the Great Flood, or "Shan Shaing" as they called it, we have the following record from the Swedish missionary Ola Hanson, who met them in 1890:

> "The Kachin version of this almost universal story is the following. Sometime after Minggawn Wa had finished his created work and appointed dwelling places for the different races, he started to build a huge stone bridge across the Irrawaddy, the foundation of which can still be seen a few miles north of Myitkyina. His nine brothers, already mentioned, moved with envy because of the great achievements of their younger brother, determined to undo the work. So they came one day and said to him. 'Your mother is dead, return home.' This did not seriously trouble him, as he thought it would be easy to find a step-mother. Having failed the first time the brothers made a second attempt, saying, 'Your father is dead, come back.' This caused him great sorrow and 'his royal heart was filled with anger,' as he realized that no one could take the place of a father. He crushed in his wrath an adjacent mountain and returned home. Arriving at the palace he found both father and mother well and hearty. Realizing that he had been deceived, he determined to take vengeance on his brothers. He caused a great deluge intending to extinguish every form of life. The brothers, however, were not drowned, but were afterwards killed by a viper."[58]

In the above section we have, possibly, a vague memory of other events of Genesis such as the Tower of Babel (Genesis 11), Cain and Abel (Genesis 4), and the Serpent in the Garden (Genesis 3). Continuing, however, we come to the most important part of this Flood tradition. Here we have a clear memory of the Ark, the taking of animals, and Noah's dove:

> On the ninth day, they heard the needle ring against the stones, and the last cock crow. Then they knew that the earth was dry.

> "But all other human beings were killed except two orphans who escaped in a large, oval shaped drum. They took along nine cocks and nine steel needles. A needle was dropped and a cock let loose each passing day. On

57. Captain John Bryan Neufville, "On the Geography and Population of Assam," *Selections from the Records of the Bengal Government*, vol. 23 (Calcutta, 1855), pp. 7, 14.
58. Ola Hanson, *The Kachins, Their Customs and Traditions* (Rangoon: American Baptist Mission Press, 1913), p. 112. See also: Sir James George Scott, *Gazetteer of Upper Burma and the Shan States* (Rangoon, 1900), p. 417. A related version is recorded in: Charles Gilhodes, "Mythologie et religion des Katchins," *Anthropos*, vol. 3, no. 4 (1908), pp. 683-684.

the ninth day, they heard the needle ring against the stones, and the last cock crow. Then they knew that the earth was dry."[59]

Major C. R. MacGregor of the British Army also published a tradition from the Kachins in 1887. This preserves the detail of Noah plus seven other survivors, for a total of eight:

> "In the beginning there was a great flood, and all the wicked people who dwelt in the plains were drowned. This flood lasted for the eight ages of a man's life. In the ninth age Chirun and Woisin, two Nats, dried up the flood with their hair which was very thick and long. Modoi, the eldest son of Mutum, kept one family of seven people on top of a high hill, and they were not drowned."[60]

Modoi, the eldest son of Mutum, kept one family of seven people on top of a high hill, and they were not drowned.

According to Herman Tegenfeldt, it was two orphans floating inside of a drum who escaped the great Flood and afterwards repeopled the earth.[61]

Creation and Flood Stories Recited at Kachin Weddings

> "Lan Ke reported how creation myths were told in a wedding ceremony in 1974 in a Jingpo [Kachin] village, Yunnan province, southwest China. The ceremony continued from morning to night with feast, music, and dance. When evening came, the singing and dancing stopped, and guests went into the host's bamboo house. In the center of the house, people gathered and sat around a fire pit, then in a very solemn atmosphere, the Jaiwa (shaman) chanted an epic named Munau Jaiwa. This epic mainly consists of creation myths and flood myths. The myths tell that in remote antiquity a flood destroyed the world. Only a girl and her young brother survived by hiding in a wooden drum. They were married following the suggestions of the Mountain God. Then they gave birth to a baby which could not eat or sleep and cried all day. The Mountain God cut the baby into eight parts. Four parts became four men and the others became four women. Later they became the ancestors of some ethnic groups. Among them, the fourth one became the ancestor of the Jingpo people, who established the rule that from then on Jingpo people should not marry a sibling or a person with the same family name, but choose husbands and wives from certain other clans. This kind of myth told in rituals serves to confirm traditional history and remind people of the rules for marriage."[62]

59. *Ibid.*, pp. 112-113.
60. C. R. Macgregor, Military Report on the Khampti-Singpho Countries, 1887. As quoted in: Verrier Elwin, *Myths of the North-East Frontier of India* (Shillong, 1958), p. 20.
61. Tegenfeldt, *A Century of Growth*, p. 46. Tegenfeldt was a missionary in Burma from approximately 1941 to 1966. See also: Neufville, "On the Geography and Population of Assam," p. 15.
62. Yang Llihui and An Deming, "The World of Chinese Mythology: An Introduction," *China's Creation and Origin Myths*, eds. Mineke Schipper, Ye Shuxian, and Yin Hubin (Boston: Brill, 2011), pp. 49-50.

62 RAKHINE

The Rakhine or Arakanese have inhabited a 350-mile section of coastal northern Myanmar (Burma). Their language is closely related to that of the majority Burmese. They knew of the Flood, though unfortunately we have only a fragmentary reference to it. Sir Arthur Phayre (1812-1885), an early British expert on Burmese history, cited a "history of Arakan written by Maung Mi, a learned Arakanese Hsaya [monk]," from which we learn:

The chronicles of Arakan open with describing the emergence of the world from the water of a deluge.

> "The chronicles of Arakan [a province of Burma] open with describing the emergence of the world from the water of a deluge, and the appearance thereon of the beings who were the progenitors of the human race. The first kings reigned in Banaras, and to a son of one of these kings Arakan was allotted."[63]

How old is the name Rakhine or Arakan? Sir Phayre writes, "In an interesting paper on the oldest records of the sea-route to China from Western Asia by Colonel Yule, the author identifies the country named Argyre in Ptolemy [ca. 100-170 A.D.] with Arakan, the name being supposed to be derived from silver mines existing there. This name may be a corruption of the native name Rakhaing, from which the modern European form, Arakan, is derived. The word Rakhaing for the country is undoubtedly ancient, and would have been heard by the voyagers from whom Ptolemy derived his information."[64]

63 BURMESE

The majority Burmese people kept detailed records of their history, above all in the "Burmese Chronicles" ("Maja Rajaweng"), which date to at least the 1200s A.D. It should be borne in mind that the Burmese Chronicles are heavily influenced by Indian thought.[65] Nevertheless, there is a legend reminiscent of the origin of sin and death (Genesis 3), and perhaps also Genesis 6:1-4. As Sir James George Scott wrote:

There are suggestions of the forbidden fruit in the Burmese legend of the beginning of the world.

> "There are suggestions of the forbidden fruit in the Burmese legend of the beginning of the world. Although the general cosmographical system is taken from India and the Brahmans, it is believed that the first nine inhabitants who had descended from the skies were sinless and sexless, and lived on a kind of flavoured earth. Gradually, however, their appetites grew, and when they took to eating a particular sort of huskless rice which cooked itself, they became gross and heavy, and being unable to return to their blissful abodes, developed sex, and, after it, crime, because they had to work for their living."[66]

Lieutenant Colonel Phayre (1812-1885), who also was granted access to the Burmese Chronicles by the king of Burma himself, found reference to the Flood:

> "The history opens with announcing that, after a cycle of the great revolutions of the universe, wherein worlds are destroyed by fire, by water, and by air, had elapsed, the present earth emerged from a deluge. A delicious substance, like the ambrosia of the gods, was left by the subsiding water spread over the earth. The throne of Gautama first appeared above the water."[67]

---

63. Sir Arthur Purves Phayre, *History of Burma* (London: Trubner, 1883), p. 42. See also: Alexander Buxton MacMahon, *Far Cathay and Farther India* (London: Hurst and Blackett, 1893), p. 156.
64. Phayre, *History of Burma*, p. 42. The paper he cites is: Colonel H. Yule, "Notes on the Oldest Records of the Sea-route to China from Western Asia," *Proceedings of the Royal Geographic Society*, vol. 4 (London: Edward Stanford, 1882), pp. 649-660.
65. Sir Arthur Purves Phayre, "On the History of the Burmah Race," *Transactions of the Ethnological Society of London*, vol. 5 (London: John Murray, 1867), p. 13.
66. Sir J. G. Scott, "Indo-Chinese," *The Mythology of All Races*, vol. 12, p. 265. Scott, *Gazetteer of Upper Burma and the Shan States* (Rangoon, 1900), p. 524.
67. Phayre, "On the History of the Burmah Race," p. 13.

64 LAMET

The Lamet people are an isolated tribe of northern Laos and adjacent parts of Thailand. Very little information had ever been published about them until the Swedish ethnographer Karl Izikowitz visited them between 1936 and 1938. Their origin story recounts a global Flood which took place in the remote past:

> "[A mole] was in the habit of gnawing apart the traps set in the forests. One day the owner of some traps was digging in the forest, and he came across the mole, who had just gnawed apart his traps. Whereupon the mole said: 'If you do not kill me I will tell you how you can escape the deluge.' The owner of the traps promised then not to kill the mole. And the mole said that the man and his sister should make a big drum, and live in it during the deluge. But I shall remain in my hole in the earth, said the mole. The owner of the traps did as the mole told him, and lived with his sister in a big drum while the deluge lasted. When the waters had subsided, the brother and sister made a tube in order to find out if all the water had evaporated.
>
> When the earth was free of all the water, the brother and sister came out of the drum. They were the only two human beings left on earth. The brother had tried to find a woman he could marry, but in vain. The sister had also tried to find a man she could marry, but had had no luck. They did not know what to do. Just then there came a bird, the tiokok, who sang: 'You two should marry earth other.'"[68]

The mole said that the man and his sister should make a big drum, and live in it during the deluge.

Notice it was a bird that advised them to marry, just as it was a bird which provided the evidence to Noah that the Flood was over. After they married, the woman became pregnant and gave birth to a gourd, out of which came all the races of the earth.[69]

65 KHANG

The Khang people live in northwestern Vietnam, including the provinces of Lai Chau and Son La. The Vietnamese ethnologist Dang Nghiem Van summarized their Flood history. The Khang believed that a bamboo rat warned a brother and sister of the impending Flood. The pair enclosed themselves in a large gourd and survived the Flood, being carried on the surface of the waters. Afterwards, they realized there were no other survivors upon the earth, but they were unwilling to marry since they were siblings. After this, a sparrow advised them to marry, and with some hesitation they complied. In this way, according to the Khang, the world was repopulated after the Flood.[70]

Rice terrace field near Sapa, Vietnam

Why do so many tribes of Southeast Asia and China refer to an incestuous marriage, after the Flood, between a brother and sister? As we show in Appendix B, there is undoubtedly a connection between this variant and Genesis, particularly Noah's tests with the raven and dove near the end of the Flood. Many other variant themes also find their origin in the record of events found in Genesis 1-11.

68. Karl Gustav Izikowitz, *Lamet: Hill Peasants in French Indochina* (New York: AMS Press, 1979), p. 22.
69. *Ibid.*
70. Dang Nghiem Van, "The Flood Myth and the Origin of Ethnic Groups in Southeast Asia," pp. 330-331.

66 LAHA

The Laha (or La Ha) are a small tribe of northern Vietnam, numbering less than 10,000. Dang Nghiem Van summarized their Flood tradition, which is very similar to that of other Southeast Asia people groups, including the Thai, Lamet, Dong, and Wa. According to them, the earth-god feared that mankind was greatly multiplying, and would consume all the earth and its vegetation. So the god of heaven (named "Then") sent the Flood, but first allowed a mole to forewarn a brother and sister, so that humanity could survive. These hid themselves inside a hollow tree on a mountain, which allowed them to float and not drown. The god Then sent a starling bird, which counseled the siblings to marry each other and beget children in order to preserve the human race.[71]

They hid themselves inside a hollow tree on a mountain, which allowed them to float and not drown. A god sent a starling bird, which counseled the siblings to marry.

67 LAHU

The Lahu (no direct relation to the Laha) live in northern Myanmar (Burma), Thailand, and China. We have previously cited the Lahu as one of several Southeast Asian tribes with a tradition of a "lost book" which contained the knowledge of God, and who guarded the hope that God would one day restore this book to them.

Concerning God, they believed the following, as recorded by one Reverend Bate:

> "The Lahoo people attribute the creation of all things to a Being whom they call Ghusha. Again and again in their folk-lore they say 'If Ghusha had not created this, it would not be.' 'There is nothing that has not been created by Ghusha, his brightness shines in all the heavens, his glory shines in all the earth.'"[72]

Their Creation account also has certain parallels with Genesis.[73]

Concerning the Flood, what they told Reverend Bate is obviously similar to other tribes of the region:

> "In those early days two cultivators, CaPeh and CaNoo, robbed Ghusha by not making offerings of fruits of the harvest. Ghusha became angry and hid the sun and the moon; great darkness that covered the earth so they could not till the soil. … Ghusha then sent seven suns and seven moons which set the earth on fire and caused the water to boil until it reached to heaven. A brother and a sister entered a gourd and floated on the surface of the water. Ghusha lifted his head and looked from heaven but could not see man nor hear woman (in the gourd). So Ghusha sent a fly but it could not track man. Ghusha then sent a bee which found man, returned and reported to Ghusha that man was at the juncture of seven rivers and seven hills. Ghusha then sent a sparrow, it went to the gourd and pecked but could not open it. Ghusha then sent a mouse which succeeded in opening the gourd and freeing man."[74]

A brother and a sister entered a gourd and floated on the surface of the water. ... Ghusha then sent a mouse which succeeded in opening the gourd and freeing man.

Of the Flood, Antisdel adds that "Another tradition says that the men called C'Sheh and C'Va and two women Na Bi and Na Caw came out of the gourd. These multiplied and replenished the earth."[75]

71. Dang Nghiem Van, "The Flood Myth and the Origin of Ethnic Groups in Southeast Asia," pp. 330-331.
72. C. B. Antisdel, "The Lahoo Narrative of Creation," *Journal of the Burma Research Society*, vol. 1, part 1 (Rangoon, 1911), p. 65.
73. "After the creation of heaven and earth Ghusha took of the earth and created Man–Chaw Ti and woman–Va Si–and put "strength of earth into them" (that is imparted life). But man being without beauty was sorrowful, so he took looheh leaves and clothed himself. Then Adaw and Aga [creative underlings of Ghusha] gave him the seeds of silk and cotton, pieces of iron and of copper (for making implements)." Source: Antisdel, "The Lahoo Narrative of Creation," p. 67.
74. Antisdel, "The Lahoo Narrative of Creation," pp. 68-69.
75. Antisdel, "Lahoo Traditions Continued," *Journal of the Burma Research Society*, vol. 1, part 2 (Rangoon, 1911), p. 32.

Finally, they have some notion of the Tower of Babel:

> "There is a tradition of the confusion of tongues. Their 'Tower of Babel' was a pagoda. Then came the dispersion of the peoples."[76]

Regarding their migration, Antisdel adds, "The home of the Lahoo people at the time of the dispersion seems to have been [a place called] Mung Miehn. … The original home of the Lahoo is not known, but it probably was to the northwest, their traditions say they were three years coming to Mver Mehn Myi Mehn [in western Yunnan, China] and that they journeyed toward the rising sun and along the Mekong."[77]

68 MANG

According to the Mang people of northwestern Vietnam, the Flood occurred as follows: Long ago, the children of heaven became greedy. They asked for too much rain. The god of heaven ("Then") sent the Flood. A brother and sister survived, first on a raft, then when it sank, they climbed up a high mountain.

After the Flood, a crow appeared and counseled the siblings to marry and procreate. However, they did not heed the crow's guidance, and jumped into a fire and died. Heaven sent children down to earth, along with animals. These were the source of the ancestors of each tribe.[78]

Mang tribe: After the Flood, a crow appeared and advised the siblings to marry and procreate, but they would not listen.

Genesis: After the Ark landed, Noah sent out a raven, and it continually flew here and there.

69 NUNG

The Nung (or Nu) live in Lao Cai in northwestern Vietnam and in neighboring parts of China. Their Flood tradition, which Dang Nghiem Van collected, is similar to that of the Mang people. However, they say that the Buddha caused the Flood, and the surviving brother and sister floated inside a gourd. Like the Mang, they say it was a crow that advised the siblings to marry, in order preserve the human race. Their children founded the Chinese, Nung, and Thai races.[79]

Again, Genesis holds the key to explaining the origin of the "brother-sister marriage" narrative theme and other variants found globally. This is discussed further in Appendix B.

According to another version, the Flood was sent by the gods to destroy evil people and spirits. Only a brother and sister survived, who had taken refuge inside a cave at the top of a mountain named Neyamensilon.[80]

Finally, in another text from the Nung / Nu we have an apparent mixing of the Tower of Babel (Genesis 11) and Creation (Genesis 1). This tradition, called LaShan and CiShan, tells that after the Flood, the married brother and sister had erected a wooden ladder by which they had access to the people living in the sky, and that they produced iron for these sky people. Now there were ants on earth, and the brother and sister lived in harmony with the ants. However, one day the brother and sister laughed at the ants. This angered the ants, and they ate the ladder connecting the earth and sky, and these two have been disconnected ever since.[81]

After the Flood, the married brother and sister had erected a wooden ladder by which they had access to the people living in the sky.

76. Antisdel, "Lahoo Traditions Continued," p. 32.
77. *Ibid.*, p. 32.
78. Mac Dinh Di, Chau Hong Thuy, and Ly A San. *Truyen co Mang* ("Mang Folktales") (Hanoi: Nha xuat ban Van hoa [Culture Publishing House], 1985). As translated and summarized in: Dang Nghiem Van, "The Flood Myth and the Origin of Ethnic Groups in Southeast Asia," pp. 330-331.
79. Dang Nghiem Van, "The Flood Myth and the Origin of Ethnic Groups in Southeast Asia," pp. 330-331.
80. You Yanchun, *A Brief History of the Literature of the Nu* (Kunming, 2003), pp. 17-20. As translated in: Jinghua Huang, Chujing Yang, and Si Chen, "Spatial Imagination in Sacred Narratives of Mountain Communities in Western Yunnan, China," *Religions*, vol. 15 (2024), p. 12.
81. Jinghua, Chujing, and Si, "Special Imagination in Sacred Narratives of Mountain Communities," pp. 5, 10.

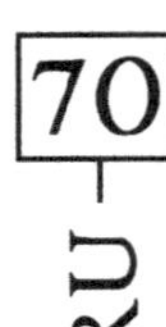

BRU

The Bru people group includes four main subgroups: the Bru Van Kieu, Tri, Mang Coong, and Khua. They live mostly in eastern Laos and adjacent parts of central Vietnam. Evangelization of the Bru began relatively late: around 1935. In 1942, a Vietnamese pastor named Bui Tan Loc arrived among the Bru, and recorded an amazing tradition of Creation and the Flood from them:

> "In the beginning God (Yuang Sorsi or Yiang Sursei) created a man and a woman. The man and woman lived together very happily. Every day they hunted wild animals and looked for fruit. Only one thing troubled them–they had no children. One day as they wandered in the woods God met them and he promised to give them children.
>
> God's promise was fulfilled, and the woman gave birth to eight sons at one time. Now they were more troubled than before, for as the children grew, they ate more and more until the parents were unable to support them. In desperation they took them to a high mountain and abandoned them.
>
> In the course of time one of the young brothers acquired a precious and beautiful sword having remarkable powers. When the handle was grasped securely rain would fall, and when the blade was held the sun would shine.
>
> One day the young lad who owned the sword became very hungry. He went about looking for food. On the bank of a river he saw a fig tree and a civet cat eating the figs. He went to the civet cat and asked for something to eat. But the civet cat said, "This is not your kind of food. If you want to eat these figs you will have to become a civet cat like me." So he brought out a civet cat skin and the boy put it on. He became a civet cat, eating figs and sleeping in the shade of the tree.
>
> The chief of that area was Anha. One day the youngest daughter of Anha was paddling a canoe along the river. She came to the place where the fig tree stood and saw the civet cat beneath it. She took the civet cat home as a pet, and the animal (or boy in disguise) was very happy to go."[82]

Now we come to the Flood itself:

> "God spoke to Anha the chief, and told him that there was going to be a great flood. He commanded him to build a boat. Although the chief tried to hire workers to help him make the boat, no one was willing, not even to escape a flood. When the boat was finished, Anha took his family into it. With him were his wife, four daughters, and two sons, eight people in all, plus the civet cat that the youngest daughter took with her. God commanded the civet cat to grasp the precious sword by the handle several times. A violent rainstorm followed. It rained for eight days and eight nights. The water rose destroying everything on the earth. The water rose up to the heavens, and the fish nibbled at the stars. The flood receded and the land dried off."[83]

God spoke to Anha the chief, and told him that there was going to be a great flood. He commanded him to build a boat.

The tradition goes on to tell that the boy removed his disguise and "lived thereafter with his wife, the youngest daughter of Anha."[84]

A Bru story recorded elsewhere attributes the Flood to a man that ate forbidden frog-flesh. In response, heaven sent the Flood, but first a frog warned three brothers and their sister of the impending disaster. They survived by floating on a raft and inside a great gourd. The three brothers later became gods, and one of them married his sister and perpetuated the human race, giving rise to many ethnic groups.[85]

82. Bui Tan Loc, "Creation and Flood in Bru Legend," *Jungle Frontiers*, vol. 13 (Christian and Missionary Alliance: New York, Summer 1961), p. 8.
83. *Ibid.*
84. *Ibid.*
85. Mai Van Tan, *Truyen co Van Kieu* [Van Kieu Folktales] (Hanoi: Nha xuat ban Van hoa Dan toc [Ethnic Culture Publishing House], 1978). As translated and summarized in: Dang Nghiem Van, "The Flood Myth," pp. 328-329.

71 PACOH (LAOS)

The Pacoh, who live directly south of the Bru, told the story of the Flood in this manner:

> "Following a great flood of the whole earth by the breaking up of the sky which holds the water back, only a woman and a dog were left alive as a result of having been put into a drum. After some time, because of loneliness and the need to repopulate the earth, the spirits permitted the woman and the dog to have eight children. Because of the dog parent, the Pacoh observed the totem taboo of avoiding killing or eating dogs."[86]

72 STIENG

The Stieng people narrated their Flood tradition to one Mr. Gerber, an assistant administrator in Thu Dau Mot, Vietnam:

> "God created mankind and the animals. Then there came a universal flood which destroyed all people except for a man and a woman from the mountainous regions, who got on a raft. Driven by the waves, they arrived at the edge of a sea (whose name is unknown). They survived. When the water went down, they married and gave birth to children."[87]

As the tradition continues, we see a connection either with the Tower of Babel tradition or the "lost book" tradition of Southeast Asia, or both:

God created mankind and the animals. Then there came a universal flood which destroyed all people except for a man and a woman.

> "Then God sent a master from heaven to instruct their children and to instruct them in religion. The master being himself a descendant of a deity. In those days, animals could speak like humans. The sons of the parents therefore took lessons from the master. But the eldest, believing himself to be wiser and more experienced than his brothers, neglected the study of religion and misplaced the books distributed by the master. This master, displeased by this, chased him [the elder son] away and kept his proud ones for whom he reserved a bright future."[88]

73  RENGAO

The Rengao people have a Flood tradition of a type that is rare in Southeast Asia, but common in both China and New Guinea. The Flood was unleashed due to the killing and eating of a sacred, magical pig by an evil king named Rok. The pig was "a spirit of the waters." The woman who had nurtured the pig survived, having fled to a high mountain. This tradition, evidently, was cited by both the Rengao and their neighbors the Jarai.[89]

Sapa Hoang Lien Son mountain range, Lao Cai Province, Vietnam

---

86. Richard Watson, April 1968 Transcribed Tape about the Pacoh for Navy Personal Response. As quoted in: Robert L. Mole, *The Montagnards of South Vietnam: A Study of Nine Tribes* (Tokyo: Tuttle, 1970), p. 113.
87. Louis Malleret, "Quelques Légendes des Moi de Cochinchine," *Bulletin de la Société des Etudes Indochinoises*, vol. 21 (1946), p. 63.
88. *Ibid*.
89. Émile Kemlin, "Alliances chez les Reungao," *Bulletin de l'Ecole Française d'Extreme-Orient*, vol. 17 (1917), pp. 72-73. On the Jarai, see: Émile Kemlin, "Au Pays Jaraï," *Les Missions Catholiques*, vol. 41 (1909), p. 227.

74 TAY PONG

The Tay Pong are a remote tribe of the Thai language group, living in the mountains of northern Vietnam. According to their tradition, when the Flood overtook the world, a brother and a sister survived by floating on a bed of straw. Debarking from their vessel once the Flood was over, they each sought a marital partner, but found none because there were no survivors. A god named Liep Loc ordered a rat to tell them that they should marry. They each threw stones, twice, and the results confirmed that they should marry. Eventually they gave rise to children who founded the Pong, Thai, and Viet races.[90]

75 LAWA

According to those of the Lawa people of northern Thailand, a brother and sister were warned of the coming Flood. They were able to survive inside a hollow tree on a high mountain. A crow (recall Genesis 8:7) appeared after the Flood and pecked open a gourd containing children. Some of these were eaten by a tiger, but those who survived gave rise to the Wa, Lao, and Han races.[91]

> A brother and sister were able to survive inside a hollow tree on a high mountain. A crow appeared after the Flood and pecked open a gourd containing children.

Another narration preserved a memory of the Tower of Babel, which they replace with a bridge: "The bottle cracked open and people came out from inside, and they crossed the bridge. However, the bridge broke and the people were scattered. This is how people began to speak different languages."[92] The recorder Obayashi himself noted the similarities with the Tower of Babel account, adding that there are other Southeast Asian peoples with traditions similar to the Tower of Babel, such as the Chin, Karen, Mikir, and Jarai.[93]

76 CO LAO

The Co Lao are a small tribe (numbering less than 2,000) that migrated from China into northwest Vietnam about 200 years ago. As recorded by Nguyen Van Huy during the 1980s, their Flood tradition runs thus: The god of heaven sent a great flood upon the earth to destroy its inhabitants, but not without first sending a messenger, who warned a brother and a sister. These escaped inside a floating gourd. A spirit from heaven later counseled them to marry, seeing as there were no other surviving candidates for marriage. The first tribes created through their union were the Yao, the Man, and the Co Lao.[94]

A San Chay woman

77 SAN CHAY

The San Chay, relatives of the Yao people of China, migrated into northern Vietnam around the year 1600. A French military officer named Auguste Bonifacy recorded their tradition of Creation and the Flood, sometime prior to 1905. This has remarkable parallels not only with the Genesis Flood account, but also with Genesis 1:

90. Dang Nghiem Van, "The Flood Myth and the Origin of Ethnic Groups in Southeast Asia," pp. 328-329.
91. Dang Nghiem Van, "The Flood Myth and the Origin of Ethnic Groups in Southeast Asia," pp. 330-331. See also: Obayashi Taryo, "Myths and Legends of the Lawa and Karen in Northwestern Thailand," *Ethnological Research*, vol. 29 (1964), p. 114.
92. Obayashi Taryo, "Myths and Legends of the Lawa and Karen in Northwestern Thailand," *Ethnological Research*, vol. 29 (1964), p.114.
93. *Ibid.*, p. 116.
94. Dang Nghiem Van, "The Flood Myth and the Origin of Ethnic Groups in Southeast Asia," pp. 332-333. The tradition was communicated by Nguyan Van Huy to Dang Nghiem Van in 1987.

"In the beginning, the sea and the earth existed together. They had not yet been separated. Before this, King Phun already lived, who knew the right way. He descended to the sea by borrowing the fins of the Ki-Lan (a magical creature), then returned to heaven. With his breath he created nine suns which set the earth ablaze. After this, Sich-Ca destroyed seven of the suns, in order to give light to the earth without burning it.

In the third year of the reign of Vinh-Chenh, a deluge of water covered the earth. More remained above the waters than the summit of the mountain Con-Lon. The trees, plants, people, and animals were destroyed. Only Phuc-Ili and his younger sister survived inside a pumpkin, and took refuge on the mountain. They alone remained on the surface of the earth."[95]

Only Phuc-Ili and his younger sister survived inside a pumpkin, and took refuge on the mountain.

After this comes a "brother-sister marriage" variant. They received signs, just like Noah received a sign that the Flood was over.[96]

78

PA THEN

The Pa Then (or Pa Hung), a tribe from the mountains of northern Vietnam, have a Flood story similar to the San Chay in general outline, but differing in the following part:

"Long ago, Bo (Thunder) entered a house with the intention of stealing. However, the owner saw him, was able to stop him, and shut him inside an urn. Trapped, Thunder called out desperately for fire. The owner's son, hearing his voice, uncovered the urn and Thunder escaped. As an act of gratitude, Thunder gave two of his teeth to his liberator. Once buried, these teeth produced a gigantic pumpkin. Thunder also closed the floodgates, which stopped the flow of water. Soon the waters rose, submerging the whole earth and drowning all men except for the owner's son, who had taken refuge in the pumpkin with his young sister. The waters then subsided, and the pumpkin came to rest on a mountain."[97]

Colonel Abadie also attested to their Flood tradition:

The waters then subsided, and the pumpkin came to rest on a mountain.

"They know the legend of the deluge, and that of the incest which followed, but with the following variant: the young sister had received eight beans from a spirit who had ordered her to eat one every year. However, she ate them all at once. So she gave birth to eight children who became the source of the 'Eight families', a name retained by the tribe."[98]

It is possible these "eight" ancestors are a memory of the eight survivors of the Flood in Genesis, but on this point we cannot be certain.

95. Auguste Louis Bonifacy, "Monographie des Mans Cao-Lan," *Revue Indochinoise,* vol. 2 (1905), pp. 922-923.
96. "They traversed it without finding any inhabitants. Then the black turtle told them to get married, but they struck the turtle and cut it into pieces. Yet the turtle came back to life and repeated the same advice for them. They would not listen to him and went into the forest. Immediately a tree told them to get married. But they took their knife and cut the tree. With its branches they lit two fires on the two banks of the river. The smoke from the two pyres rose above the river and joined, twisting in a spiral. They understood then that Heaven allowed their union." *Ibid.*, p. 923.
97. Auguste Louis Bonifacy, "Monographie des Pa-teng et des Na-e," *Revue Indochinoise*, vol. 10 (Hanoi, 1908), pp. 775-776. See also: Colonel E. Diguet, *Les Montagnards du Tonkin* (Paris: Augustin Challamel, 1909), p. 127.
98. Abadie, Les Races du Haut-Tonkin, p. 146. Etienne Lunet de Lajonquière, *Ethnographie du Tonkin Septentrional* (Paris: Ernest Leroux, 1906), p. 291.

79 GIAY

The Giay (pronounced "Zhay"), who live along the Red River in northern Vietnam, have a Flood tradition that is typical for Southeast Asia. Only two people survived the Flood–a brother and sister–by floating inside a gourd. After the Flood they finally married, and their descendants founded the various ethnic groups, including the Giay, Phula, and Tai.[99]

Laotian Man at a Temple

80 LAO

The Lao are the majority people group in the nation of Laos, making up nearly 55% of the total population. Nguyan Tan Dac recorded their version of the Flood:

> "Lord Then (God) ordered a flood to punish disobedient humans; three noblemen Lao escaped to heaven. When the waters receded they returned to earth with Then's gift of a buffalo."[100]

This "gift of a buffalo" offered to God is probably Noah's burnt offering (Genesis 8:20).

When the waters receded they returned to earth with Then's gift of a buffalo.

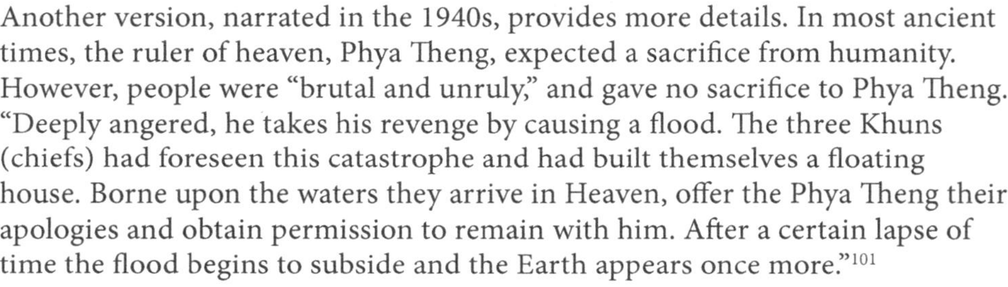

Another version, narrated in the 1940s, provides more details. In most ancient times, the ruler of heaven, Phya Theng, expected a sacrifice from humanity. However, people were "brutal and unruly," and gave no sacrifice to Phya Theng. "Deeply angered, he takes his revenge by causing a flood. The three Khuns (chiefs) had foreseen this catastrophe and had built themselves a floating house. Borne upon the waters they arrive in Heaven, offer the Phya Theng their apologies and obtain permission to remain with him. After a certain lapse of time the flood begins to subside and the Earth appears once more."[101]

81 ISAN

The Isan are a Lao-speaking people, approximately 22 million in number, living in northeastern Thailand. They possess palm-leaf manuscripts that are over 600 years old, containing their history and beliefs. The archeologist Louis Finot found this tradition of the Deluge in one of these manuscripts:

> "This happened in the early days of the world, when heaven and earth communicated. In heaven reigned Praya Then; on the earth, three chiefs: Khun Khet, Khun Kan and Khun Pu Lan Xon. These three governed a brutal and stubborn humanity. They were not yet civilized. Men lived by hunting and fishing. Praya Then wanted his share of their prey. He made claims on it several times, but the chiefs paid no attention. Irritated by this, Praya Then avenged himself by sending a deluge. The three chiefs, however, foresaw the disaster and built a floating house. Carried by the waters, they arrived at the entrance to heaven, where they offered their apologies to Praya Then, and got to stay with him.

These three governed a brutal and stubborn humanity. … Praya Then avenged himself by sending a deluge. The three chiefs, however, foresaw the disaster and built a floating house.

99. Dang Nghiem Van, "The Flood Myth and the Origin of Ethnic Groups in Southeast Asia," pp. 334-335.
100. Nguyen Tan Dac, "From the Laotian Story of the Gourd to the Deluge Legend of Southeast Asia," *Vietnam Social Sciences*, vol. 3 (Hanoi: 1985), 35-48.
101. Rene de Berval, *The Kingdom of Laos: The Land of the Million Elephants and of the White Parasol* (Saigon: France-Asie, 1959), pp. 379-380.

Example of a Palm Leaf Manuscript from Thailand.

> After a while the flood went down and the land reappeared. The three chiefs asked permission to return to the "country below" (muon lum). Praya Then made them present a buffalo, and then dismissed them."[102]

The three chiefs are probably Noah's three sons, and the buffalo offering is probably Noah's burnt offering to God in Genesis 8:20.

82 THAI NGHE

Dang Nghiem Van alluded to a Flood tradition of the Thai Nghe people of north-central Vietnam. We are not told exactly who or what caused the Flood, or who warned the surviving pair—only that a rooster had advised them that they should marry. They preserved the human race after the Flood, giving birth first to the ancestors of the Thai people.[103]

83 RADE

The Rade (also Rhade or Ede) live in the mountains of southern Vietnam, though they have a tradition that formerly they were islanders.[104] Around 1949, one B. Y. Jouin united the oldest and most knowledgeable tribe members to hear their historical traditions. They said there have been five epochs in history, and that in the third epoch a great Flood occurred.[105] Their tradition begins:

> "Here is the legend of Deluge. It is called 'Klei ea lip m'nuih dum', which word-for-word means, 'Inundation of the inhabitants of the past'"[106]

To summarize, a toad named Ae Dut went to heaven to beg water from Ae Die ("the Master of Heaven") because the earth has grown hot, dry, and waterless. In a possible echo of Babel, it says the toad "asked the Rade [people] to build a ladder to climb up very high, to reach the house of Ae Die." (We think this is

102. Louis Finot, "Recherches sur la littérature laotienne", *Bulletin de l'Ecole française d'Extreme-Orient*, vol. 17 (1917), p. 159.
103. Dang Nghiem Van, "The Flood Myth and the Origin of Ethnic Groups in Southeast Asia," pp. 330-331.
104. B. Y. Jouin, "Les Traditions des Rhadé," *Bulletin de la Société des Études Indochinoises*, new series, vol. 25, no. 4 (Saigon: 1950), p. 362.
105. Biblically, I would agree with the Rhade tradition. First, there was an original, perfect Paradise free of sin and evil. Second, there was the curse and the fallen state of the world that was created after Adam and Eve sinned. And third, there were the events immediately preceding the Flood and the Flood itself (Genesis 6-8).
106. *Ibid.*, p. 358.

a faint memory of the Tower of Babel.) Eventually, the Master of Heaven ordered his heavenly servants to grant the toad his request for water. However, not satisfied with two kettles full of water, the toad asked for seven kettles, which resulted in a deluge of rain that lasted seven days and nights:[107]

> "The rain then fell very heavily and everywhere. The water rose here and there. The Rhade had no place to take refuge. Many died. Others fled to the mountain. The only ones who escaped were a man and a woman—husband and wife. They placed themselves in a drum, with a pair of dogs. There was also a pair of buffaloes in another drum, a bull and a cow in a third drum, a pair of pigs in a fourth drum, and a rooster and a hen in a fifth drum. They tied the drums together.
>
> So the rising water lifted them up and they sailed upon the waters. Then they reached a mountain, and they came out of their drums and remained at the summit. They stayed on the mountain to wait for the water to subside, until it dropped enough that they could go back down and look for a place to settle and make a hut. Thus were men, dogs, oxen, buffaloes, pigs, and chickens able to multiply until now."[108]

The only ones who escaped were a husband and wife. They placed themselves in a drum, with a pair of dogs. They landed at a mountain.

The tradition adds several fanciful elements about how the Flood was ended, and of a hot stone which was thrown down from heaven to dry up the waters. "The Rhade people say that this stone must still exist at the bottom of the sea somewhere."[109]

84 KOHO

The Koho (or Co Ho), closely related to the Bahnar, live in the mountains of south-central Vietnam. Their origin story is very similar to the Bahnar version, and equally impressive. We have, first of all, the vague memory of Cain and Abel:

> "In the beginning of time, a bird (a kite) and a crab quarreled; the bird pierced the crab's shell with his beak. To revenge itself on the bird, who had flown away, the crab caused the oceans and rivers to swell to the sky."[110]

Next, the Flood:

> "All the creatures of the earth perished in the water except for two humans—a man and a woman—who, accompanied by a pair of every animal and bird, took refuge in a wooden chest.
>
> The flood lasted 7 days and 7 nights. Then the man and the woman heard a chicken clucking outside of the chest. Sent by the spirits (yang), the chicken told those in the chest that they could come out."[111]

Koho people

Perhaps most remarkable of all is their memory of Noah's incident of drinking too much wine:

> "Soon the couple had no more rice and were on the verge of starvation. when they heard a sound from the earth: it was an ant holding in its

107. *Ibid.*, pp. 358-360.
108. *Ibid.*, p. 360.
109. *Ibid.*, p. 361.
110. Jean Cassaigne, "Les Mois de la Région de Djiring," *Indochine*, vol. 4, no. 131 (1943), p. 12.
111. *Ibid.*

mandibles a gift from the spirits, two grains of rice. The man, destined to become the grandfather of the Koho group, planted the grains, and the next day a crop of gigantic rice covered the plain.

Some years later, the grandfather drank rice wine and fell into a stupor. When his eldest son saw him asleep naked, he began to mock his father. A younger son reproached his brother and covered his father with a banana leaf.

The grandfather awoke; and learning what had happened, he took away his eldest son's clothes and chased him into the forest. This eldest son founded the race of Montagnards (the Koho included) who have no clothes. The old man's other two sons became the ancestors of the Annamese [Vietnamese] and the Laotians."[112]

Then the man and the woman heard a chicken clucking outside of the chest. Sent by the spirits, the chicken told those in the chest that they could come out.

A Seven-Day Flood Duration?

Many Flood traditions found in Asia, as well as Austronesian Taiwan,[113] state that the duration of the Flood was seven days. This stands in stark contrast to the 370-day duration of the Flood in Genesis. If only Genesis contained a source where this idea of seven days could have come from:

> "For after seven more days, I will send rain on the earth forty days and forty nights" (7:4). "Now it happened after the seven days, that the water of the flood came upon the earth" (7:10). "You shall take with you of every clean animal by sevens, a male and his female" (7:2). "Then he waited yet another seven days; and again he sent out the dove from the ark" (8:10). "Then he waited yet another seven days and sent out the dove; but it did not return to him again" (8:12). "Also of the birds of the sky, by sevens, male and female, to keep their seed alive on the face of all the earth." (7:3)
>
> "In the seventh month, on the seventeenth day of the month, the ark rested upon the mountains of Ararat." (8:4)

And let us not forget that Creation in Genesis 1 was, famously, seven days and seven nights.

Therefore, if a group of people, after leaving Babel, were to forget the Flood's true length, "seven days" is the most likely substitute–even more likely than 40. To find "seven days" in wide occurrence is easily explainable from a position of Genesis truth. Finally, there are physical reasons why a length of 370 days is much more reasonable for a global Flood than seven days.

112. *Ibid.*
113. Valdis Gauss, *The Formosan Great Flood Myths: An Analysis of the Oral Traditions of Ancient Taiwan* (Edwin Mellen Press, 2022), p. 132.

85

SIYIN

The Siyin or Sizang are a tribe of the Kuki-Chin language group, living in the hills of western Myanmar (Burma) and neighboring parts of India. "There was once a great flood on the earth," as they told Major Rundall, "which drowned everybody except a few persons, who escaped by going up to the Kennedy Peak, on the Letha Range."[114]

Siyin chiefs 1900

Yet the most significant discovery among the Siyin people is a Tower of Babel tradition. A. C. Bateman, the Assistant Superintendent of Tiddim, heard this from them around the year 1900:

> "Many centuries ago all the Chins lived in one large village, somewhere south of Haka. They all spoke the same language, and had the same customs. One day, at a big council, it was decided that the moon should be captured, and made to shine permanently. By this means a great deal of unnecessary expense and bother would be saved in lighting. In consequence, the construction of a tower was begun, which was to reach to the moon. After years of labour the tower got so high that it meant days of hard marching for the people working on the top to come down to the village to get provisions. It was therefore, decided that, as stage upon stage was built, it should be passed up from below from stage to stage. Thus the people of different stages had very little intercourse, and gradually acquired different manners, languages, and customs. At last, when the structure was all but finished, the nat [spirit] in the moon fell into a rage at the audacity of the Chins, and raised a fearful storm, which brought down the tower. It fell from south to north. The people inhabiting the different stages were consequently strewn over the land, and built villages where they fell. Hence the different clans and tribes varying in language and customs. The stones and building materials which formed the huge tower now form the Chin Hills."[115]

The construction of a tower was begun, which was to reach to the moon. … The spirit in the moon overthrew their tower. Their languages were changed.

"Yahweh reigns, let the earth rejoice; Let the many coastlands be glad." (Psalm 97:1)

86

HAKA CHIN

The Haka Chin people, linguistic relatives of the Siyin, did not forget about the Flood, despite their general loss of historical traditions.[116] As one Lieutenant McNabb recorded among them:

> "The only really ancient tradition still extant amongst them is that of the flood. The flood they call 'Bwensokso.' Their story of it is as follows: Many hundreds of years ago there was a great and universal rain throughout the world, so that the rivers and the lakes and the sea rose and covered all the world with water, except some of the highest hills. The clouds then cleared away, and the sun shone so fiercely that all those who had escaped the floods died from the heat of it. Only two persons escaped, and they were a boy and his sister. They climbed up the highest hill, and on its summit hid themselves in a huge earthenware jar, which, being able to float,

114. Major Frank M. Rundall, "The Siyin Chins," *Royal Geographical Society Supplementary Papers*, vol. 3 (London: John Murray, 1893), p. 565.

115. Sir James George Scott, *Burma: A Handbook of Practical Information* (London: Daniel O'Connor, 1921), pp. 105-106. See also: Sir J. G. Scott, "Indo-Chinese," *The Mythology of All Races*, vol. 12 (Boston: Marshall Jones, 1918), p. 266.

116. As Lieutenant McNabb wrote, "They have no history, and but few traditions. … The few traditions that are still preserved amongst them are therefore oral. This lack of tradition and history is, I believe, greatly due to the want of separate respect and veneration with which the aged are treated amongst them. As soon as a man becomes old and decrepit, he is ousted by his son, who takes his place, and he no longer has a voice in the councils of the village chiefs. Thus the knowledge and experiences of the old, instead of being transmitted by them to the young, dies with them." E. B. Elly, *Military Report on the Chin-Lushai Country* (Simla: Government Central Printing Office, 1893), p. 86.

saved them from the waters, and also protected them from the heat of the sun. From these two, tradition runs, all the peoples of the earth are descended, but where the hill was they do not know."[117]

87 TAWYAN

The Tawyan (also Tawr or Torr) are a subgroup of the Tashon people of northwestern Myanmar (Burma). They have, like so many other people groups of Southeast Asia, a tradition of the Tower of Babel, which Sir J. G. Scott summarized thus:

> "The Tawyan have a variant of the tower legend. They set about building a tower to capture the sun, but there was a village quarrel, and one half cut the ladder while the other half were on it. They fell uninjured and took possession of the lands on which they were thus cast."[118]

88 THO

The Tho people live in the mountains of northwestern Vietnam near the border with Laos. Around 1920, the French Colonel Maurice Abadie led ethnographic field research of Vietnam's interior, in which he recorded this Flood story from the Tho tribe:

> "The god of heaven, having decided to drown the earth to punish mankind for their crimes, first chose to save two orphans from this disaster. These were a brother and a sister who, despite their poverty, observed the rites and gave the offerings. These orphans, having planted pumpkin seeds, obtained an enormous pumpkin and enclosed themselves inside it, taking with them provisions of cooked rice. Immediately after this, a rain lasting seven days and seven nights submerged the earth. All the earth's inhabitants perished, except the two orphans who landed on a mountain near their native country. The brother and sister came together in marriage and had three boys and a daughter, whose successive unions gave birth to the new human race. The ancestor, having traveled to China, was amazed at the fertility of this country, and he settled there and brought a couple of his children. These children became the ancestors of the Chinese. The other children who remained in Tonkin became the ancestors of the Tho."[119]

All the earth's inhabitants perished, except the two orphans who landed on a mountain near their native country.

89 KIM MUN

The Kim Mun people live in northern Vietnam and bordering areas of China, where they are known as the Lantien. The Flood tradition they recounted to Colonel Abadie is summarized as follows:

> "They believe in a deluge which drowned all people, except for a couple, Fou-Hai and his sister Fou-Hai-Muy, who floated inside a huge pumpkin. The legend adds that this pumpkin landed at the top of the Kunlun mountains."[120]

No doubt, these "Kunlun mountains" are a memory of the mountains of Ararat (Genesis 8.4). Continuing, they say that the surviving couple received a couple signs that they should marry, Fou-Hai married his sister and the world was repopulated from their offspring.[121]

117. Elly, *Military Report on the Chin-Lushai Country*, pp. 86-87.
118. Sir J. G. Scott, "Indo-Chinese," *The Mythology of All Races*, vol. 12, p. 267.
119. Maurice Abadie, *Les Races du Haut-Tonkin* (Paris, 1924), p. 58. See also: Etienne Lunet de Lajonquière, *Ethnographie du Tonkin Septentrional* (Paris: Ernest Leroux, 1906), pp. 148-149.
120. Abadie, *Les Races du Haut-Tonkin*, p. 122.
121. *Ibid.* The pair of signs advising them to marry were first from a turtle and second from a bamboo stick. See also: Etienne Lunet de Lajonquière, *Ethnographie du Tonkin Septentrional* (Paris: Ernest Leroux, 1906), p. 262.

90 MAN TA PAN

The Man Ta Pan are a subgroup of the Dao people of Vietnam and are few in number (approximately 1,000). They live in the northern mountainous regions of Vietnam bordering on China. According to Abadie, their Flood tradition was very similar to that of the Kim Mun (Lantien) people.[122] Regretfully, we lack further information.

Polystrate Fossils

Polystrate fossils are one "smoking gun" of the global Flood, falsifying the notion of millions of years. After all, if the sedimentary layers surrounding these vertically extensive fossils had been deposited slowly, over millions of years, then the fossil would not have remained intact long enough to be entirely buried, since it would have been exposed to the elements for long ages. For more on polystrate fossils, see the extensive field research of John MacKay[123] and Ian Juby.[124]

91 MAN QUAN TRANG

Another tradition of the Flood comes from a subgroup of the Dao people known as the Man Quan Trang ("Dao with white trousers"). Colonel Abadie learned that they still honored their ancestors Boc-Nhi and Sien-Muy, who survived the Flood in a floating vessel. He added:

> "The story of the deluge is told by their initiates with the following variant: Boc-Nhi and his sister [Sien-Muy], taking refuge in an enormous gourd, landed at the Kunlun mountains. They entered into marriage, after the incidents of the turtle and the bamboo which have been mentioned in connection with the Lantien tribe."[125]

Boc-Nhi and his sister [Sien-Muy], taking refuge in an enormous gourd, landed at the Kunlun mountains.

92 M'NONG

The M'nong people of Vietnam have this intriguing tradition of the first days of this world:

> "In those days everything was delightful. The animals lived together with man, and all could talk with each other. No one ever died. Only later, after a great catastrophe struck the world, did they lose their common language and begin to live separately."[126]

This "catastrophe," only vaguely described, seems to be a memory of the Tower of Babel. They also have a memory of the Flood (called the "Mang Ling"), recounted in their sacred chants. They say that a Flood broke out because the people committed incest. Rain fell for about two years without ceasing. A succession of sacrifices were offered, which proved ineffective. Then, after a period of two years, Mot Dlong and Mot Dlaang, their heroic ancestors, learned that they must sacrifice a buffalo. With prayer, they offered the buffalo sacrifice, and it was accepted. The rains stopped and the Flood began to subside.[127]

They have a memory of the Flood (called the "Mang Ling"), recounted in their sacred chants. They say that a Flood broke out because the people committed incest. Rain fell for about two years without ceasing.

This buffalo sacrifice which ends the Flood corresponds to Noah's sacrifice to God immediately after exiting the Ark. And just as the M'nong say that many different

122. Abadie, *Les Races du Haut-Tonkin*, p. 132.
123. https://creationresearch.net/exciting-research/polystrate-files/
124. https://ianjuby.org/about-polystrate-fossils/
125. Abadie, *Les Races du Haut-Tonkin*, p. 141. They add that "Sien-Mui had a pregnancy that lasted three years, after which she gave birth to a pumpkin, the seeds of which were thrown half into the plains, half into the mountains. It is from these mountain seeds that the ancestors of the Quan Trang people arose." (*Ibid.*) See also: See also: Etienne Lunet de Lajonquière, *Ethnographie du Tonkin Septentrional* (Paris: Ernest Leroux, 1906), p. 271.
126. "Man's Arrival," *Jungle Frontiers*, vol. 17 (Christian and Missionary Alliance, Summer 1963), p. 5.
127. George Condominas, trans. Adrienne Foulke, *We Have Eaten the Forest* (New York: Hill and Wang, 1977), pp. 229-230. The original French source: Georges Condominas, *Nous avons mangé la forêt* (Paris: Mercure de France, 1957).

animals were offered, Noah offered several types of animal sacrifices.

Hmong women, Sapa, Vietnam

93 HMONG IN VIETNAM

In China, this tribe is mainly known as the Miao people, but in Vietnam they are called the Hmong. Their Flood tradition is very similar to that of the Dong people of China. It tells that the thunder god sent a great Flood to destroy the inhabitants of the world. In gratitude for a previous favor done by the earth god, he first warned the earth god of his plan to flood the earth. A human pair, brother and sister, survived the flood by floating inside a white gourd.[128] No doubt, this gourd is a memory of Noah's Ark.

94 HRE

The Hre people live in central Vietnam and are related to the Bahnar tribe. Some have described the Hre language as easy to learn, adding that "frequently Hre [speakers] sound like Europeans."[129]

Long ago, they said, there was "a great flood which covered all the earth except for two mountains, the Goong Din, or East Mountain, and the Goong Dom, or West Mountain. On the Goong Din there remained 100 Vietnamese: the remnant of a people who lived in boats. On the Goong Dom only a woman and a dog remained, eventually mating." The Hre say that their ancestors came from this latter union. The Vietnamese, on the other hand, became more numerous than the Hre because of their greater number of survivors from the Flood.[130]

95 KHMU

For thousands of years, the Khmu (or Kammu) have lived in the northern area of Laos and adjacent parts of Thailand and Vietnam. They are the largest minority people group in Laos. They have an amazing Flood tradition which Henri Roux recorded, fittingly, near the remains of the village of Tau-pung. What was so special about this village? According to the Khmu, it was "the cradle of the many races of Laos," the center of their ancient settlement. It was also known to them as "Pumpkin Village," a term that recalls their ancient tradition of the Flood as well.[131]

The village of Tau-pung in Laos was known as "Pumpkin Village" in memory of the Flood.

> "Formerly, the people of Muong Sen say, a young man and his sister walking in the forest saw a "tocan" [that is, a spalax, a large blind mole]. They tried to catch it, but the rat escaped. The young siblings searched for him for two days and eventually found him at the bottom of a hole that the animal had just dug. The captured beast begged for mercy. His captors asked him for what purpose he had dug so deep into the ground.

128. Dang Nghiem Van, "The Flood Myth and the Origin of Ethnic Groups in Southeast Asia," *Journal of American Folklore*, vol. 106, no. 421 (Summer 1993), pp. 332-333. The original source is this Vietnamese-language work: Le Trung Vu, *Truyen co dan toc Meo* [Hmong Folktales] (Hanoi: Nha xuat ban Van hoa [Culture Publishing House], 1975).
129. Joann L. Schrock et. al. (American University), *Minority Groups in the Republic of Vietnam* (Washington: Department of the Army, 1966), p. 164.
130. H. I. Phillips, "Hre Creation Story," (unpublished research), pp. 1-3. As quoted in: Schrock et. al., *Minority Groups in the Republic of Vietnam*, p. 165.
131. Henri Roux, "Les Tsa Khmu," Bulletin de l'Ecole française d'Extrême-Orient, vol. 27 (1927), p. 177.

'I know,' said the rat, 'that a terrible cataclysm is going to occur, and I wanted to take shelter.' 'So what will happen?' 'I will tell you,' said the rat, 'but on the condition that you set me free.' The siblings released him immediately.

Then the rat said to them, 'In six days, a universal flood will occur. If you want to escape it, cut down a tree trunk. Hollow it out. Put some supplies in there. Hang it on a "Kurdoi tut" [a type of fig tree]. Sit inside and carefully seal it with beeswax.'

Six days later, a general flood arrived. Through a very small hole that they drilled, the two recluses noticed that the country was completely submerged. After a few days the water receded. The young people came out of their box. Nothing around them had survived."[132]

Next, the "brother-sister marriage" theme appears, which we analyze in Appendix B. Like the account of Noah's birds (Genesis 8:6-12), there are two attempts and then a bird gives them important information:

> In six days, a universal flood will occur. If you want to escape it, cut down a tree trunk. Hollow it out. Put some supplies in there. Hang it on a fig tree. Sit inside and carefully seal it with beeswax.

"The young man then said to his sister, 'We are now alone in the world. I will go one way, and you go the other. I will take as my wife the first woman I meet. You will take as your husband the first man you see.' They left and walked for a long time. They came to meet again. The brother then said, 'Perhaps we have not gone far enough to encounter new countries. Let us resume our journey and walk until we find inhabited lands.' Several days later, they met again. Their hearts then failed them and they fell into despair.

While they were sadly reflecting on their misfortune, the bird Togo arrived and advised them to stop their search there because, he said, they were the only two survivors of all people on the entire earth. There was only one path left for them: to marry each other. Otherwise, after the death of one of them, the human race would be doomed to disappear. The young siblings decided to follow the bird's advice."[133]

But instead of giving birth in the natural way, the woman gave birth to two large pumpkins. Out of these pumpkins came the founders of the Thai, the Lao, the Khmu, and other nations.

"As for the two pumpkins, they have now become two rocks," with cracks in them, from which the ancestral children are said to have emerged. The Khmu point to the site of these two rocks, where their ancient village of Tau-pung ("Pumpkin Village") was located. "Next to these two rocks there still remains the fig tree to which the first parents of the Khmu owe their life." The bird was also commemorated at a very old pagoda at this village.[134]

> The bird was also commemorated at a very old pagoda at this village.

132. Roux, "Les Tsa Khmu," p. 177. Another version tells: "Together they brought along wax to caulk it with and a needle to keep, and then they crept into the drum. The flood did come, indeed, and then, oh, how many years, how many months went by, I don't know. How many mountains and how many ridges the drum floated past, I don't know, nor how many villages or how many towns. It just floated along like that. The two of them inside took the needle and pricked a hole in the wax to look, but as the water trickled in they closed the hole again. The drum just floated along like that." Kristina Lindell, Jan-Ojvind Swahn, Damrong Tayanin, "The Flood: Three Northern Kammu Versions of the Story of Creation," *The Flood Myth*, ed. Alan Dundes (Berkeley: University of California Press, 1988), pp. 273-274.

133. Roux, "Les Tsa Khmu,", pp. 177-178. As for the identity of the bird, it was believed to be a malkoha cuckoo, if we may rely on another narration, recorded by Lindell, Swahn, and Tayanin, in "The Flood: Three Northern Kammu Versions," p. 274.

134. *Ibid.*, p. 178.

96 RAGLAI AND CHAM

The Raglai and Cham are two closely related tribes from southern Vietnam and Cambodia. From the anthropologist Jacques Dournes we possess a summary of their Flood tradition:

> "Going up again, we are at the top of Yapanang. We have risen five hundred meters. On the left, Mount Yaang-Lo, the local Ararat, at the top of which, says the legend, were deposited in a drum the two survivors of the great flood which covered everything.
>
> The sea had exceeded the surrounding mountains, except the Yaang-Lo, where the great drum landed, in which were the brother and sister from whom the Montagnards and Chams arose. The sea, which had risen twice to attack, had remained at the foot of the mountain. The white-headed lapwing had then said to him, 'I am old, spare my weakness, retire.' Saying this, it dropped a large stone into the sea, which caused it to withdraw. Before the inundation, it is still said, the summit of the Yaang-Lo inclined towards the Roglai country. Now its head bends toward the region of Drong."[135]

We see that they replace Noah's dove with the white-headed lapwing, and consider it the hero of the Flood.

A Cham woman in traditional costume

97 JAKUN

The homelands of the Jakun people in modern-day Johur, Malaysia were described as utopian forest lands, ideal for the cultivation of a wide variety of foods. The scientist J. R. Logan (1819-1869) met them in 1847 and heard their account of Creation and the Flood:

> "The origin of their country and race was thus related. "The ground on which we stand is not solid. It is merely the skin of the earth. In ancient times Pirman [God] broke up this skin, so that the world was destroyed and overwhelmed with water. … After Lulumut [a mountain] had emerged, a prau [sailboat] of pulai wood, covered over and without any opening, floated on the waters. In this Pirman had enclosed a man and a woman whom he had made. After the lapse of some time the prau was neither directed with or against the current nor driven to and fro. The man and woman, feeling it to rest motionless, nibbled their way through it, stood on the dry ground, and beheld this our world. … All mankind are the descendants of the two children of the first pair."[136]

In ancient times Pirman [God] broke up this skin, so that the world was destroyed and overwhelmed with water. ... He enclosed a man and a woman in a boat.

98 MANTRAS

"The Mantras are connected with one of those native tribes," wrote Father H. Borie in 1861, "remains of primitive races, who, in the peninsula as well as in the whole of Malaysia, were gradually driven back into the interior since the twelfth century, as fast as the Malays founded settlements on the coast. Since that period, these tribes have wandered about in the valleys, on the mountain sides, and everywhere where solitude reigns."[137]

135. Jacques Dournes, *En Suivant La Piste Des Hommes Sur Les Hauts-Plateaux du Viet-Nam* (R. Julliard: Paris, 1955), p. 18.
136. J. R. Logan, "The Orang Binua of Johore," *Journal of the Indian Archipelago and Eastern Asia*, vol. 1 (Singapore, 1847), pp. 277-278.
137. Reverend Father H. Borie, "An Account of the Mantras, A Savage Tribe in the Malay Peninsula," *Miscellaneous Papers Relating to Indo-China and the Indian Archipelago,* vol. 1 (London: Trubner & Co., 1887), p. 286. This article is a translation from a prior Dutch version published in 1861.

We have not recovered a Flood tradition from the Mantra people, although they almost certainly had one, given that we have found Flood traditions among their close relatives, the Jakun. What we have found from the Mantras is a vague memory of the Ark and the mountain (Ararat). They refer to the first man, known as Batin-alam, or "King of the Universe," who was created by God. This man "having built a beautiful and large ship, set sail for Rum. This ship, which sailed rapidly, possessed the wonderful privilege of sailing by itself." It came to anchor at a port where Malacca is now located. "In this ship were found all the things necessary for founding a colony," and "The Batin-alam's ship was not destroyed; it still exists, they say, buried under a mountain in the peninsula." On this point, Borie comments that "Evidently these are traditions, which have their source in the history of the Deluge."[138]

The Rock of Fire in the Strait of Malacca

99 KELANTAN TRADITION

Alfred Haddon, head of the Cambridge Expedition of 1899, heard a Flood legend from the Malay people of the state of Kelantan, which belongs to Malaysia. They explained how, in most ancient times, "a great Flood came down from the mountains, and overwhelmed the people that dwelt in the plains. And they were all drowned in that flood, save only some two or three menials who had been sent up into the Hills to collect firewood." Then there was great darkness because the sun, moon, and stars had been extinguished. "When light returned, there was no land but a great sea, and all the habitations of man had been overwhelmed."[139]

When light returned, there was no land but a great sea, and all the habitations of man had been overwhelmed.

100

The Salong (or Moken) people live on the Mergui archipelago, a group of islands off the west coast of Myanmar. "An interesting feature of this people," one missionary report noted, "is their pure monotheism, the confession of one Supreme Being, whom they name Tooda, and recognize as the creator of all things." And "there is also among them a distinct tradition of the deluge."[140] One visitor in 1853 described them thus:

> "The Salongs are a mild and timid race, are credulous and affectionate—and rarely quarrel, unless stimulated by intoxicating drinks. … They have many interesting traditions of a creation and universal deluge. They believe in future rewards and punishments in another state."[141]

138. *Ibid.*, p. 288.
139. Walter William Skeat, *Fables and Folk-tales from an Eastern Forest* (Cambridge: University Press, 1901), pp. 62-63.
140. "Tavoy Mission," *Baptist Missionary Magazine*, vol. 34, no. 7 (Boston: American Baptist Missionary Union, 1853), p. 269.
141. "State and Claims of Tavoy and Mergui," *Baptist Missionary Magazine*, vol. 34, no. 12 (Boston, 1853), p. 478.

The Salong people narrated their traditions to the Baptist missionary Judson Benjamin in the early 1850s. These traditions were described as bearing similarities to Genesis on Creation and the Flood. Regretfully, we possess no further details apart from this fragment:

> "After the deluge, of which the Salongs preserve a distinct and unique tradition, God came down from heaven, and assigned to the different nations and tribes of men their habitations and employments. He said to the Salongs, "You are foolish and disobedient. You must not possess gold, silver, domestic animals, houses nor lands. Go, be poor, and hunt fish in water seven fathoms deep."[142]

101 YAO IN VIETNAM

In the previous chapter, we encountered the Yao people in China. The Yao in Vietnam shared this Flood story with the Japanese anthropologist Matsmoto Nobuhiro in the mid 1930s:

> "Formerly there was a great flood which submerged all the world. All mankind drowned except for the Fu-I brother and sister, who escaped the flood by hiding in a gourd. After the water subsided, the two discussed whether or not they should marry. They agreed that if they burned incense and planted bamboo trees in different places and the smoke and tree-tops came together, they would marry; otherwise, they would not. They prayed to the heaven and burned incense and planted bamboo trees on separate mountains. Eventually the smoke and the tree-tops came together and they married. From them was born a leather bag from which ten boys and nine girls emerged. They became the ancestors of mankind."[143]

Yao woman in Sa Pa, Việt-Nam

102 PU PEO

The Pu Peo (or Qabiao) have a Flood tradition, according to which a god was angered at the fighting between two children (named Pe Si and Pe Say), an idea that has parallels with Cain and Abel. A brother-sister pair were forewarned of the coming flood, and were saved inside a floating gourd. Later they married, and they gave rise to the Lolo (Yi), Pu Peo, Thai, Viet, and Han Chinese peoples.[144]

A brother-sister pair were forewarned of the coming flood, and were saved inside a floating gourd.

142. Judson Benjamin, "Journal of Mr. Benjamin," *Baptist Missionary Magazine*, vol. 34, no. 3 (Boston, 1853), p. 84.
143. Matsmoto Nobuhiro, "Han-ko densetsu no ichi shiryo" ("A Datum Concerning Han-ko Legends"), *Essays in Oriental History Honoring Dr. Kato on his Sixty-first Birthday*, ed. K. Wada, p. 780. As translated into English in: Ho, *A Comparative Study of Myths and Legends of Formosan Aborigines*, p. 274.
144. Dang Nghiem Van, "The Flood Myth and the Origin of Ethnic Groups in Southeast Asia," *Journal of American Folklore*, vol. 106, no. 421 (Summer 1993), pp. 332-333.

103 **AKHA**

The Akha people living along the border area of Thailand and Myanmar (Burma) say that a great Flood ended the world's first age:

> "At that time a huge dung beetle went to the dragon and lied to him. "There are no people left on the earth." So the dragon caused water to appear on the earth for the first time. Then there was a flood for seven days and seven nights, and everyone died, except for a small boy and girl, brother and sister. They were riding in a giant gourd (some say), or a large drum (others say). The Akhas revere these two very highly to this day."[145]

Young Akha woman dressed in colorful traditional tribal costume

> They were riding in a giant gourd or a large drum. The Akhas revere these two items very highly to this day.

104 **NYAHON**

The Nyahon people number fewer than 10,000 and live in southern Laos. This tribe of the Mon-Khmer language family people knew of the Flood, but Barbara Wall could only record a passing reference to it in 1967:

> "Formerly, at the beginning of time, when heaven and earth were created, there existed a mother who was the mother of all. After the deluge, from which only a dog survived, this mother slept with it. She first gave birth to a son, who slept with his mother. From this union other people were born who mated amongst themselves. Thus the Nyahon, Lao, and other nations came to be."[146]

105 **VIET (KINH)**

The Viet or Kinh are the majority people of Vietnam, making up 85% of the national population. We have a vague memory of the Flood and of Noah's raven and dove in a text recorded among them. [147]

145. Paul W. Lewis, *Ethnographic Notes on the Akhas of Burma*, vol. 1 (1969), pp. 51, 56.
146. Barbara Wall, *Les Nya Hön: Étude Ethnographique d'une Population du Plateau des Bolovens* (Sud-Laos) (Ventiene: Vithagna, 1975), pp. 1-2.
147. "Formerly the crow and the pagoda cock were men and lived with the Saint. One day the Saint employed a hundred workers to build a boat. When this boat was built he sent the crow to the river to see if the water was high and if the boat could be launched. The crow, seeing a lot of shrimp and fish there, began to eat them and did not return home. The Saint, not seeing him return and tired of waiting for him, sent the pagoda cock to look for him. The pagoda cock soon found the crow. He said to him, 'There are a lot of shrimp and fish here, stay a little to eat with me, there's no hurry.' The pagoda cock listened to the crow and also began to eat. The Saint then sent the pigeon down the river to look for them. The pigeon saw them busy eating fish and shrimp; he said nothing to them but took a sheet of paper on which he wrote with his beak what he had seen and brought it back to the Saint. He was very irritated and launched his boat along. The crow and the pagoda rooster were afraid and did not dare to return. They went to stay in a house where a few people had written and left a little ink. The crow said to the pagoda rooster: 'I will rub my whole body with this ink and I will come home, this will make the Saint laugh and he will not beat me.' So he smeared his whole body with ink. The pagoda cock imitated him, but there was not enough ink for him and he could only blacken half of his body. He smeared the rest with red ink. This done, they returned home. The Saint laughed at their strange appearance and did not beat them. But when he embarked he chased them away and changed them from men into birds: the first into a crow and the second into a pagoda rooster. This is why the crow is all black and the pagoda rooster half red and half black." Source: Antony Landes, *Contes et Légendes Annamites* (Saigon: Colonial Printing Office, 1886), pp. 210-211.

106

MAY

In the mountains of central Vietnam's Quảng Bình province live the May people who speak a Vietic Chut language. The May people are fewer than 1,000 in number. Their Flood story runs as follows:

> "Once upon a time, the sky caused a flood, all the mountains were flooded, only the giant mountain of the god Cu Loong (man of heaven) was not flooded. Floodwaters swept away houses, trees, and people. Everything died. During that great flood, two siblings (a boy and a girl) used an eagle tree as a raft and drifted to Cu Loong mountain to survive.
>
> The water receded, and the two siblings stayed at Cu Loong mountain to make a living. A Buddha appeared and advised the two siblings to get married to continue the human race, but they refused. One morning, the younger sister was sweeping the floor, and the older brother was sitting and eating betel, accidentally throwing betel residue on the younger sister's thigh. The betel residue gave birth to an egg, giving birth to three children: the eldest was a May, the next was a Nguon person and the youngest was a Kinh person."[148]

Statue of Amitābha Buddha, Fansipan Mountain, Vietnam

107

SOUTHERN VIETNAM TRADITION

The French explorer Pierre-Paul Cupet (1859-1907) recorded a rather unique tradition from an unnamed tribe of southern interior Vietnam in the early 1890s:

> "In southern Annam the wild peoples tell of two very powerful sorcerers who had great influence through powerful talismans. One was master of fire, the other was master of water. The latter decided to take revenge on ill-minded neighbors, and did so by bringing a deluge. All the people died. Only he saved himself in a 'Tamtam' in which he floated on the waters for an immeasurable amount of time in complete solitude. None of his successors ever caused such a flood again."[149]

148. Phan Phuong, "Do-Ta Vong: Ngôi làng tiên cảnh." ["Do-Ta Vong: Fairyland Village"]. Báo Quảng Bình [Quang Binh Newspaper Website]. Retrieved 12 January, 2024 from https://baoquangbinh.vn/Multimedia/emagazine/202010/do-ta-vong-ngoi-lang-tien-canh-2181628/
149. Pierre-Paul Cupet, "Chez les populations sauvages du sud de l'Annam," *Tour du Monde* (1893), pp. 139-140. George Garland, Der Mythus von der Sintflut (Bonn: Marcus und Weber, 1912), p. 77. This may have some relation to a story recorded in China: "There arose a man named Gung Gung, wooly in body and red in hair, who believed himself to be a god because of his wisdom. He occupied the country on the Yangtze River and revolted against the divine princess. He called himself the spirit of water and used magic formulas to cause a flood that would cause the water of all the rivers to flood into their beds and cause great damage to the earth. Nü Wa ordered the Lord of Fire to subdue him. Gung Gung was defeated. Then in his rage he struck his head against Mount Imperfect and died. As a result, one of the pillars of heaven broke and the sky tilted to the northwest. But the earth fell into the depths in the area of the resulting opening in the southeast. Then Nü Wa melted five-/colored stones to repair the sky. She took the legs of a giant tortoise and positioned them as the four poles of heaven. But the flood led them away to the place where the earth had sunk into the depths. That is why to this day the northwest wind is so cold and all streams flow southeast into the great sea." Richard Wilhelm, *Chinesische Volksmärchen* (Jena, Germany: Eugen Diederichs, 1921), pp. 51-52.

108

MON (MYANMAR)

"Apart from any extinct aboriginals," wrote Gerry Abbott and Khin Thant Han, "the Mon were the earliest extant group to settle in the country, establishing themselves well before the southward migration of the Tibeto-Burman groups, from which they were ethnically and linguistically very different."[150]

Mon girls wearing traditional dress in Mawlamyine, Myanmar

The Mon people (also known as Talaing in Thailand) were first in Southeast Asia to embrace Buddhism, which was introduced from India, and which they staunchly adhere to today. But we must remember that they were not always Buddhist. Robert Halliday, who wrote an important history on the Mon in 1917, observed that "whilst Buddism is the acknowledged religion of the Talaings in general, there is a great deal in their beliefs that is to be traced to an earlier origin."[151]

Concerning this "earlier origin", we believe it is from this period that the Mon people have passed down their tradition of the Flood, which we will see below. While Indian influence is evident, there is also material here which is earlier, a relic of the time when the Mon lived with all other people at Babel:

According to tradition, there was an old world that preceded our current world. It happened that "More and more people had taken to behaving badly and they [the first man and woman] thought this could become a great problem, so they decided to wash the world clean." They accomplished this by preventing Manawthila, the elephant who supported Mount Meru, from breathing. As a result, there was no longer any vapor in the air. Even the sun and the moon suffered, and the old earth was destroyed, along with its inhabitants.[152]

After the evil people had been destroyed, the first couple let the elephant breathe again. "After holding its breath for so long it breathed mightily, and when it breathed out there was such a mass of vapour that torrential rain began to fall on the whole earth, inundating it until the flood rose as high as the abode of the Brahmas. After the rains there came a wind that blew and blew for months and years, drying up the water until the new earth, the present one, came into being. And then, before any living creatures appeared, the Brahmas who had once been human came down, settled and had families. It is from them that the early humans of this world are descended."[153]

Who were these Brahmas that repopulated the earth? The tradition says before they came to the new earth, they had escaped the destruction of the first earth by meditating and becoming Brahmas.[154] We find here a similarity with Noah and the seven others with him, for they too were granted escape from the global destruction–aboard the Ark–and they were the ones to repopulate the earth after the Flood (Genesis 7:23, 2 Peter 3:20). As we have seen in this chapter, this floating vessel which carried a small number of survivors during the Flood is attested to in the traditions of tribes and nations from all over Southeast Asia.

150. Gerry Abbott and Khin Thant Han, *The Folk-tales of Burma*, p. 376.
151. Robert Halliday, *The Talaings* (Rangoon: Government Press, 1917), p. 77.
152. Ludu U Hla, *Mon Folk-tales* (in Burmese) (Mandalay: Kyi-bwa-yei Press, 1968), vol. 4, no. 32, pp. 105-114. As translated in: Gerry Abbott and Khin Thant Han, *The Folk-tales of Burma*, pp. 60-61.
153. *Ibid.*, p. 61.
154. *Ibid.*

109 TEMUAN

The Temuan or Orang Temuan people live in southern peninsular Malaysia. They have a Flood tradition in connection with their most sacred site, Gunung Raja ("Royal Mountain"), located on the border of the states of Selangor and Pahang. A musician named Antares Maitreya began working with the Temuan people in 1992 and has preserved some of their traditions in songs. He found a Flood tradition from them:

> "Thousands of years ago, many Temuan people died because they had committed 'Celau' (the sins that angered god and their ancestors). Their god had sent a 'Celau' punishment in a form of a great flood which had drowned all the Temuan sinners that day. Only two of the Temuans, named Mamak and Inak Bungsuk, survived that day by climbing an Eaglewood tree at Gunung Raja (Royal Mountain)."[155]

Their god had sent a 'Celau' [sin] punishment in a form of a great flood which had drowned all the Temuan sinners that day. Only two of the Temuans survived.

The two survivors were able to calm the "Celau" storm by repeating a magic spell. From that place, the ancestral home of the Temuans, humanity was repopulated.

110 ORANG SELETAR

The Orang Seletar are the natives of Singapore island and the Straits of Johor area. According to one narration in 2011, their Flood tradition went like this:

> "The rain fell in torrents for 40 days and nights in Johore. The water level rose to the foot of Gunung Pulai [Pulai Mountain]. To counter the strong currents, the Orang Seletar tied their houseboats together. Unfortunately, the rope broke. Some of them were carried away by the currents and were lost."[156]

The rain fell in torrents for 40 days and nights in Johore. The water level rose to the foot of Pulai Mountain.

A related tradition was recorded in 2022.[157]

111 KATU

On several occasions, Dang Nghiem Van heard a Flood story from the Katu (or Co Tu) of eastern Laos and central Vietnam. However, only a fragmentary outline of it is available to us. It is said that one woman alone survived the ancient Flood by ascending a high mountain. Though she had no spouse, she became pregnant and gave birth to two children: a boy and a girl. When they had grown, they saw no choice but to marry. All the tribes and nations came from their descendants.[158]

---

155. "Akar Umbi" *Magic River*. Retrieved 11 November, 2019 from http://www.magickriver.net/akarumbi.htm. See also: Man Ess, *Kisah Lagenda Temuan* ["Temuan Legendary Stories"] (Blue Crystal Enterprise, 2011), p. 46.
156. Yvonne Young Ai Peng, "Be the Voice of the Voiceless Orang Seletar," INFO Johore Bar (January 2012), p. 55. http://johorebar.org.my/wp-content/uploads/2015/01/Page-55-56-Be-the-voice-of-the-voiceless-Orang-Seletar-by-Yvonne-Young.pdf
157. "In the times of the ancestors, (they) said (it) always stormed. Day and night it rained. (During) that time, (the rain) didn't stop. … They were looking for the same place. (They) looked for the same place. (Whether to) escape or not, the elders were at Mount Pulai. Stuck to each other at Mount Pulai, the elders found a shelter. (During) that time, the water was too fast. The water was too high. … When the water receded, (the boats) reached Singapore." Tan Zhi Xuan, "A Sketch Grammar of Seletar." Master's Thesis (Singapore, Nanyang Technological University, 2022), pp. 226-228. https://hdl.handle.net/10356/165162
158. Do Nhu Tuy, *Truyen co Cotu* [Katu Folktales] (Hanoi: Nha xuat ban Van hoa [Culture Publishing House], 1982). D. N. Van, "The Flood Myth," pp. 328-329.

112

TAI DAM

The Tai Dam or "Black Tai" are so named for the color of their attire, in contrast to their linguistic neighbors, the White Tai and Red Tai.[159] This tribe of northwestern Vietnam said that the Flood was sent after a dispute between mankind and the spirits (Taen), in which the later sent a drought to earth. The ancestral man, Pu Chao, performed a ritual or prayer asking for rain:

> "With such abundance was his request granted that a great deluge ensued, taking many lives. Saddened, a sympathetic taen [spirit] placed men, animals, and all their belongings on the great floating pumpkins, or bottle gourds, so that they would not perish in the flood. After the great floodwaters had receded taen let Tao Suong and Tao Ngern again return to earth. Tao Suong and Tao Ngern then took wives, becoming the progenitors of mankind."[160]

Tai Dam people at the market

159. Sumitr Pitiphat, "The Religion and Beliefs of the Black Tai, and a Note on the Study of Cultural Origins," *Journal of the Siam Society*, vol. 68, part 1 (Bangkok: Siam Society, 1980), p. 29.
160. *Ibid.*, p. 34.

Amis Folk Center, Chenggong Township, Taiwan

TAIWAN

Taiwan is considered by many linguists and archaeologists to be the springboard of Austronesian material culture and languages. Like other preliterate groups, the aboriginal tribes of Taiwan traditionally transmitted their mythology orally from one generation to the next in one of many mutually unintelligible Formosan languages. Of the conservatively estimated two dozen Formosan languages that were once spoken, 15 living languages survive including Amis, Atayal, Bunun, Kavalan, Kanakanavu, Rukai, Paiwan, Puyuma, Saaroa, Saisiyat, Sakizaya, Seediq, Thao, Truku, Tsou and Yami (a Batanic language).[1] The Flood traditions passed down by these tribes continue to serve as the basis for a number of rituals among Amis, Hla'alua, Kanakanavu, Sakizaya, Paiwan, Pazeh, Puyuma, and Truku.[2] Fifteen of the 16 officially recognized tribes have deluge stories. Additionally, the officially unrecognized Pazeh tribe's deluge myth is included herein. For a corpus of 220 Formosan deluge texts provided in full, see my (Valdis') work, *The Formosan Great Flood Myths: An Analysis of the Oral Traditions of Ancient Taiwan* (2022).

1. T. Shigeru, "Japanese Contribution to the Linguistic Studies of the Formosan Indigenous Languages," in *Austronesian Taiwan: Linguistics, History, Ethnology, Prehistory*, ed. David Blundell (Taiwan: Shung Ye Museum of Formosan Aborigines, 2009), pp. 71-100.
2. Valdis Gauss, *The Formosan Great Flood Myths: An Analysis of the Oral Traditions of Ancient Taiwan* (Mellen Press, 2022), p. 264.

Tribes of the Region

113. Amis	121. Puyuma
114. Atayal	122. Rukai
115. Bunun	123. Saisiyat
116. Hla'alua	124. Sakizaya
117. Kanakanavu	125. Tsou
118. Kavalan	126. Seediq
119. Paiwan	127. Truku
120. Pazeh	128. Tao / Yami

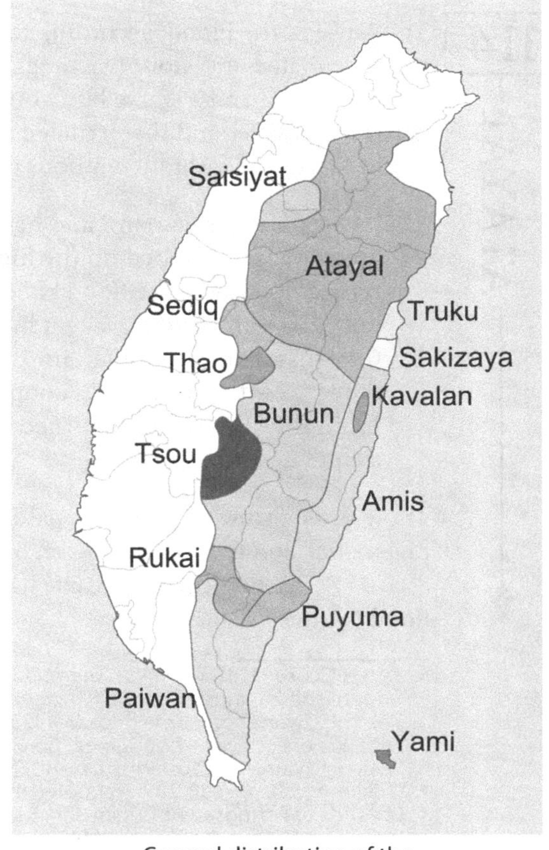

General distribution of the native tribes of Taiwan

113 AMIS

The Amis tribe inhabits part of the eastern coast of Taiwan. Around the year 1910, Japanese scholar Shinji Ishii studied and interviewed the Ami people and recorded many of their traditions. In three separate villages, they told varying accounts about the ancient Flood.

Black Bulbul

To summarize due to length, these accounts tell that in ancient times, a great flood destroyed all of mankind except for a brother and a sister, who escaped by floating in a wooden mortar. The pair landed on a high mountain and eventually, seeing no alternative, married each other and had children in order to preserve the human race.[3]

Another version, recorded by Japanese scholars Ogawa and Asai around 1920, adds a "fire fetching" motif. This is a recurring theme in Taiwan and Southeast Asia, and has clear parallels with Noah sending the raven and dove (Genesis 8:6-12) to see whether the Flood was going down. This narrative theme and its connection to Genesis is examined further in Appendix B.

> "After the deluge … one day people asked the tatachu bird to fetch fire from somewhere for them. The tatachu bird brought fire back, but it was extinguished when he dropped it in the sea. Next people asked a maggot to fetch fire. He successfully brought fire back, but it was extinguished soon. The brother and sister tried to strike the white stones together and they made fire. After that people could preserve fire from generation to generation."[4]

114 ATAYAL

The cause of the Flood, according to the Atayal people of Taiwan, was that "some people violated ancestors' teachings and committed incest. Ancestral spirits were irritated at last and a storm burst out one night." As another version tells, "A man married his sister and that irritated [the ancestral spirit gods] Utux". That may remind us of the forbidden unions of Genesis 6:1-4. The tradition tells:

> "It aroused the tsunami and had the whole land submerged in water. Some people climbed up the high mountain, Papak Waqa, to take refuge. However, the flood continued without subsiding. They threw a dog into water, but it was hit back by waves. The water remained. Then they threw an old woman into the sea but nothing happened. At last, they threw the incestuous couple into the sea and the water subsided. From then on, the land turned into how it looks today. There are [now] mountains and valleys."[5]

In ancient times, a great flood destroyed all of mankind except for a brother and a sister, who escaped by floating in a wooden mortar. The pair landed on a high mountain.

These three throws are clearly analogous to Noah's three dispatches of birds—a raven once and then a dove twice, before a favorable sign was received (Genesis 8:10-11). The element of sacrifice harkens back to Noah's burnt offering after the flood (Genesis 8:20).

---

3. James George Frazer, *Folk-lore in the Old Testament*, vol. 1, pp. 226-229. Shinji Ishii provided his unpublished manuscripts to Sir Frazer for his work. There is also a similar account, recorded by Yukichi Sayama sometime prior to 1923, in: Ho T'ing-jui, "A Comparative Study of Myths and Legends of Formosan Aborigines," pp. 268-269.
4. Yukichi Sayama and Yoshihisa Onishi, *The Myths and Traditions of the Formosan Native Tribes* (Tokyo: 1935), pp. 208-209. As quoted in: Ho T'ing-jui, "A Comparative Study of Myths and Legends of Formosan Aborigines," p. 319.
5. Provisional Committee for the Survey of Taiwan's Existing Customs by Taiwan Presidential Hall, *Report on Barbarians' Customs Volume One: Atayal Tribe*, pp. 22-45. As translated into English in: Poiconu, *Literary History of Taiwanese Indigenous Peoples*, p. 70.

115 BUNUN

The Bunun live in east-central Taiwan, between the Amis and the Tsou territories. Their Flood traditions have been recorded on multiple occasions, of which the following version is representative:

Bunun people in 1900

> "Long time ago, the flood happened suddenly as Bunun people were busy at work. They escaped to the mountains in a hurry. They climbed up the highest mountain—Jade Mountain. After the flood happened, all animals escaped to the mountains too. … As the food almost ran out, they had no choice but to catch and eat animals for survival. One day, the flood finally subsided, but Bunun people still did not dare
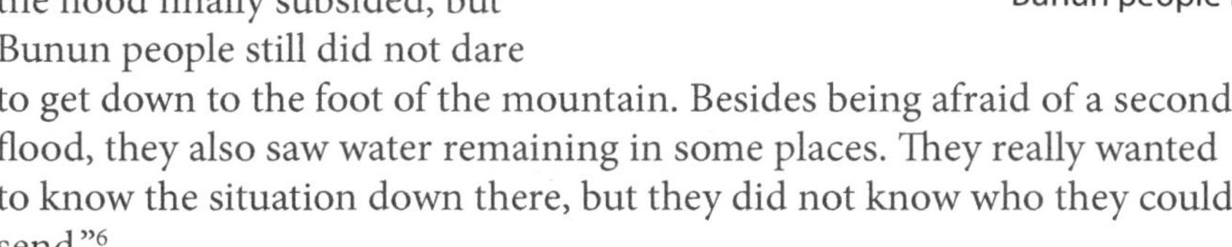
> to get down to the foot of the mountain. Besides being afraid of a second flood, they also saw water remaining in some places. They really wanted to know the situation down there, but they did not know who they could send."[6]

In what follows, note the similarity to Noah's sending the raven and the dove (Genesis 8:6-11):

> "They thought maybe they could ask birds to do them a favor, since birds have wings, so they asked a crow for help. The crow promised them to go down the mountain to take a look. However, as the crow flew to the foot of the mountain, it saw lots of corpses of dead animals from the flood. Therefore, it stayed there for food and forgot Bunun people's request. … Then they asked a frog, which was good at swimming, to have a look for them. The frog promised them and went down the mountain. When it got down, it found other human beings living there.[7] The frog held one piece of burning coal in its mouth and hoped to take it back. … It jumped into the water, but the burning coal was extinguished by the water. Though the frog brought back the evidence of people living at the foot of the mountain, Bunun people did not trust it, since they saw an extinguished coal. … Once again, Bunun people sent a black red-billed bulbul [a type of songbird] to have a look. The black bulbul agreed and flew to the bottom of the mountain to see if the frog told the truth about people still living there. It found out what the frog said was true, and so that Bunun people would believe, it decided to pick up the burning coal and take it back. It flew back to the mountain and showed the burning coal to Bunun people. Then all Bunun people went downhill happily."[8]

Then it came about at the end of forty days, that Noah opened the window of the ark which he had made; and he sent out a raven, and it flew here and there until the water was dried up from the earth. Then he sent out a dove from him, to see if the water was abated from the face of the land; but the dove found no resting place for the sole of her foot, so she returned to him into the ark, for the water was on the surface of all the earth. Then he put out his hand and took her, and brought her into the ark to himself. So he waited yet another seven days; and again he sent out the dove from the ark. The dove came to him toward evening, and behold, in her beak was a freshly picked olive leaf. So Noah knew that the water was abated from the earth. (Genesis 8:6-11)

6. Wu Zhen-yu, Bunun: Legends, Stories, and Early Customs (Nantou Yushan National Park, 1995), pp. 17-18. As translated into English in: Pasuya Poiconu, *Literary History of Taiwanese Indigenous Peoples*, vol. 1, trans. Wordsworth (Taipei: National Academy for Educational Research and Le Jin Books, 2012), p. 73.
7. Most Taiwanese Flood traditions clarify that it was on another mountain that human survivors were found.
8. *Ibid.*, pp. 73-74.

Is it by coincidence that the Bunun tradition and Genesis are in agreement? Certainly not. They remember the same event. The Bunun tradition replaces Noah's dove and olive leaf with a songbird and a piece of charcoal. Both are taken as a sign of hope, a proof that the Flood is ending. Noah's raven is the Bunun version's crow.

Another Bunun version puts it this way: "They sent flying birds to get fire twice, but failed both times. Finally, they sent kaipisi bird and got the fire."[9] One tradition adds: "Because of this it is forbidden for us to kill the kaipis[10] bird and the toad."[11]

It is also noteworthy that a giant serpent plays a role in the Bunun flood story. It blocks a river's course, and thereby causes the flood.[12] From global comparative analysis, there is good reason to believe this serpent is really the Serpent of the Garden of Eden.

> "Personal observation of the methods of narration has impressed me with the solemnity and seriousness with which aboriginal Formosan [Taiwanese] tellers relate their myths and legends. This is particularly true when material deals with their tribal ancestors or the origin of a cherished ritual. Before the interview started, there was always a libation or gift, accompanied by a brief prayer, made to their ancestors, even when the meeting took place in a local inn. … [The material] was never given lightly. The people were concerned that the stories be right and were reluctant to risk leaving out an ancestor's name or making any other deviation from tradition. If a deviation occurred, those around would confer and decide which they thought was the most accurate version. The people were also reluctant to rush through any of the narratives for fear of omissions and an atmosphere lacking seriousness. Furthermore, there was often a feeling that the stories should properly be told only at the time of the rituals or ceremonies associated with them."
>
> —Ho T'ing-jui,
> author of *A Comparative Study of Myths and Legends of Formosan Aborigines*[13]

116 HLA'ALUA

The Hla'alua, whose language is known as Saaroa, number only a few hundred today. This tribe lives in the mountainous areas of Kaohsiung in southern Taiwan. Their Flood tradition is similar to that of their neighbors, the Kanakanavu, in which a group of people and animals took refuge on Jade Mountain. Then, in need of fire to survive, the survivors sent animals to another mountain summit to retrieve it. In most narrations, the first animal, a goat, failed but the second animal, a muntjac, succeeded—again, a mirror of Noah's raven and dove.[14]

Hla'alua people

9. Yin Jian-zhong, *Documental Compilation and Research on Traditional Taiwanese Indigenous Myths and Legends* (Taipei: National Taiwan University, 1993), p. 112. As translated into English in: Poiconu, *Literary History of Taiwanese Indigenous Peoples*, p. 74.
10. Note that there are multiple spelling conventions for all of the Formosan languages.
11. Naoyoshi Ogawa and Erin Asai, *Myths and Traditions of the Formosan Native Tribes,* (Tokyo: Toko Shoin, 1935), pp. 591-592. As quoted in: Ho T'ing-jui, "A Comparative Study of Myths and Legends of Formosan Aborigines," *Asian Folklore and Social Life Monographs*, vol. 18 (Taipei: Orient Cultural Services, 1971), p. 316.
12. *Ibid.*
13. Ho T'ing-jui, "A Comparative Study of Myths and Legends of Formosan Aborigines," pp. 19-20.
14. "They had no fire [after the Flood]. They saw a fly rubbing its hands together, and with this in mind they imitated it, using wood. And when they rubbed sticks, there was fire. The people on the other mountain wanted the fire. They asked a goat to get the fire. The goat went after it. Before he reached home, his horns got hot and they hurt. He soaked them in water. He returned home, but had no fire. The mouse-deer took his place. He was able to return with the fire. They were all happy; they all petted him, and he gradually became smaller." Source: Naoyoshi Ogawa and Erin Asai, *Myths and Traditions of the Formosan Native Tribes*, pp. 702-703. As quoted in: Ho T'ing-jui, "A Comparative Study of Myths and Legends of Formosan Aborigines," p. 317.

117 KANAKANAVU

The Kanakanavu live in the Namasia District of southern Taiwan, near the linguistically related Tsou and Saaroa tribes. The Flood is attributed to a giant eel that blocked the drainage of water, eventually flooding the whole earth. Some took refuge on Mount Tanu'ung'incu.[15] Like other tribes of Taiwan, they tell of animals being sent after the Flood in search of fire.

> "They remained there [on the mountain after the Flood]. They stayed with the animals. They had no fire, so they could not eat. Being in this fix, it was decided that they should confer as to whom they should hire to go and get the fire. Only the goat could do this. He swam and went to Tanuungintau Mountain. There was fire there. The goat carried the fire back. He went to Nausurana Mountain. The people rejoiced. After that they cooked food."[16]

We can see it here that the "recovery of fire" theme is a memory of Noah's raven and dove. (We examine this theme more closely in Appendix B). How remarkable to find the memory of Noah's Flood in Taiwan, over 5,000 miles from Israel!

Kanakanabu: It was decided that they should confer as to whom they should hire to go and get the fire. Only the goat could do this. He swam and went to Tanuungintau Mountain. The goat brought the fire back. The people rejoiced.

Genesis 8:8,11: Then he sent out a dove … The dove came to him toward evening, and behold, in her beak was a freshly picked olive leaf. So Noah knew that the water was abated from the earth.

118 KAVALAN

The Kavalan people occupy the alluvial plain of the Lanyang River in northeastern Taiwan. They claim to have migrated to Taiwan from a mysterious island called "Sunasai," which, according to oral histories, was located to the south.[17]

Their migration story is inseparable from a memory of the Flood, perhaps mixed with Creation as well. Here is the tradition they narrated to a Japanese scholar named Shimizu Jun:

> "A long time ago, the land sunk in water. Nobody knew how the land sunk. Three siblings appeared from somewhere. They chiseled wood and made a boat. They floated on the ocean. They floated on the ocean for several days. They had not come to Taiwan yet. They had not arrived at the land of Taiwan. They saw the land, "Look! There is land here!" "Let's land here!" they were saying. The three ancestors landed in Taiwan."[18]

Women of Kavalan

The "three siblings" who "chiseled wood and made a boat" loosely correspond with the three brothers (Shem, Ham, and Japheth) of Genesis, who helped their father build the Ark.

15. Shigeru Tsuchida, "Kanakanavu Texts (Austronesian Formosan)," *Endangered Texts of the Pacific Rim* (Osaka: Osaka Gakuin University, 2003), pp. 71-91.
16. Naoyoshi Ogawa and Erin Asai, *Myths and Traditions of the Formosan Native Tribes*, pp. 732-733. As translated in: Ho T'ing-jui, "A Comparative Study of Myths and Legends of Formosan Aborigines," p. 317.
17. Utsurikawa Nenozo, Mabuchi Toichi, Tadao Kano,and Kokubu Naoichi, *Hundred-Year Dawn in Taiwan* (Taipei: SMC Publishing, 2005), pp. 78-79. As translated into English in: Poiconu, *Literary History of Taiwanese Indigenous Peoples*, pp. 111-112. Poiconu notes that the Ketagalan tribe have a similar migration story.
18. Shimizu Jun, *Collection of Kavalan Myths and Legends* (Taipei: SMC Publishing, 1998), pp. 218-220. As translated into English in: Poiconu, *Literary History of Taiwanese Indigenous Peoples*, p. 110.

119

PAIWAN

The Paiwan, who live in the mountains of southern Taiwan, were described by one 19th century author as "a turbulent and warlike people; fond of the chase … in disposition, they are proud and independent; in their habits, cleanly and neat."[19] In modern times, hunting remains an important part of Paiwan culture.

A Paiwan family house in Sandimen

The Paiwan tradition of the ancient Flood went like this:

> "In the ancient times, a flood happened and the water reached present Padain clan. Maybe it was because our ancestors cut the trees on Dawu Mountain and violated the taboo. They irritated the spirit and caused the disaster. All members climbed up Dawu Mountain … The flood lasted for five months without receding. Paiwan and Padain members killed boars, threw them into the water, and held Palisi (praying ceremony). For unknown reason, the flood subsided gradually and ancestors returned to their original habitat."[20]

All members climbed up Dawu Mountain … The flood lasted for five months without receding.

Note how the Flood ends. There is an animal sacrifice and a prayer ceremony. That is reminiscent of Noah's sacrifice to God after they exit the Ark.

Another narration, from the Jaqovoqovilje clan, adds that "two people, a brother and a sister, survived the Flood because they held on a huge tree."[21] Other Paiwan versions, however, say it was a tall grass, probably miscanthus, to which the siblings held tightly, and were not swept away by the Flood.[22]

Especially noteworthy, the return of Noah's dove with an olive leaf in its beak finds its echo among the Paiwan tribe, like other tribes of Taiwan: "A bird brought fire from somewhere and the wood beneath its feet began burning. In honor of this contribution, tribal people never kill such birds, even today. It is said this bird's beak turned red from holding fire in its mouth."[23] This prohibition is similar to that of the Mandan tribe of North America (see *Volume 1*), who forbade killing or harming the turtle dove on account of its having returned to the old man with a willow bough and willow leaves in its beak, a sign of the Flood's end.[24]

Paiwan traditions, like all Formosan mythologies, also contain references to a 'golden age' in the ancient past when "a piece of millet turned into a full pot of rice."[25] Such a 'golden age' reminds us of the Garden of Eden, before sin and the curse, in Genesis 3:17-19.

---

19. Surgeon General Charles Alexander Gordon, "Notes On The Ethnology And Ancient Chronology Of China" *Journal of the Transactions of the Victoria Institute*, vol. 23 (London: Victoria Institute, 1890), p. 178.
20. Provisional Committee for the Survey of Taiwan's Existing Customs by Taiwan Presidential Hall, *Report on Barbarians' Customs*, vol. 3, pp. 121-122. As translated in: Poiconu, *Literary History of Taiwanese Indigenous Peoples*, p. 86. Regarding the statements that they "cut the trees" and "violated the taboo" and irritated the spirit," it is added that Dawu Mountain was considered the "habitat of ancestral spirits," and that it was not to be entered, let alone to cut trees there.
21. *Ibid.*, p. 87.
22. *Ibid.*
23. *Ibid.*, p. 88.
24. Liguori, *Echoes of Ararat* [*Volume 1*], p. 86.
25. Poiconu, *Literary History of Taiwanese Indigenous Peoples*, p. 84.

120 PAZEH The Pazeh (or Pazih) people historically lived in the vicinity of Taichung in central Taiwan. Yukichi Sayama and Yoshihisa Onisha collected a Flood tradition from them around 1920:

> "In olden days our first ancestors came down from heaven. They lived in the central plain of Formosa and were very prosperous. After a long time there was a great flood which submerged the whole world and destroyed all men and animals except a sister, Sabongkashi, and a brother, Vanakushi. The two escaped the flood and drifted [in a floating vessel] to the top of the Tsupotsrariuts Mountain. After six days the water subsided, and they came down the mountain and stayed on the hill called Paladan."[26]

The two escaped the flood and drifted [in a floating vessel] to the top of the Tsupotsrariuts Mountain. After six days the water subsided, and they came down the mountain

Another narration is noteworthy, which was recorded in 1897 at the village of Liyu, in Miaoli County. It adds that "the couple predicted the coming of the flood," but says that the couple "escaped to the hilltop of Toopodararya."[27] A third version says that the flood occurred because "the people there were ill-behaved and spoke ill of others. God was enraged and then caused it to rain hard to wash the earth. The sea was full, overflowed, and inundated all lands." One couple escaped to Rariw Mountain.[28] In all these versions, there are clear echoes of the account found in Genesis.

Yu Shan (Jade Mountain), Taiwan

121 PUYUMA According to the Puyuma people of southeastern Taiwan, five siblings (three boys and two girls) survived the flood by floating in a rice mortar and landed at the mountain of Panapanayan, or Revoaqan in Taitung. Humanity was repopulated from the offspring of two of the survivors, who married after performing three tests.[29] In Appendix B we show that this "brother-sister marriage" variant involving three tests contains a memory of Noah and his three tests involving the raven and dove.

122 RUKAI The Capungan phratry of the Rukai tribe in southern Taiwan maintain that the reason for the Flood was humanity's failure to offer a prescribed sacrifice to a god named Tjavulung. Indignant, this god punished them with the Flood:

> "[The god called Tjavulung] told tribal members, "Why don't you kill boars as a sacrificial offering to salute my returning?" Tribal members refused, so the god man was irritated and said, "I will turn the world into an ocean." He stirred the land with his hands and a

26. Yukichi Sayama and Yoshihisa Onishi, *Seiban densetsu shu (Mythology of the Formosan Aborigines)* (Taihoku, 1923), p. 31. As translated in: Ho T'ing-jui, "A Comparative Study of Myths and Legends of Formosan Aborigines," p. 269.
27. Ino Kanori, *Pinpu Tribe Investigation Trip*, (Taipei: Yuan-Liou, 1996), pp. 132-133. As translated into English in: Poiconu, *Literary History of Taiwanese Indigenous Peoples*, pp. 109-110.
28. Paul Jen-Kuei Li and Shigeru Tsuchida, "Pazih Texts and Songs," Language and Linguistics Monograph Series, No. A2-2 (Taipei: Institute of Linguistics Academia Sinica, 2002), pp. 142-143. The source is a text recorded by Erin Asai in 1936 or 1937.
29. Poiconu, *Literary History of Taiwanese Indigenous Peoples*, pp. 94-95. See also: Josiane Cauquelin, *The Aborigines of Taiwan: From Headhunting to the Modern World* (New York: Routledge Curzon, 2003), p. 234.

flood happened suddenly. The world turned into ocean. Vuculj tribe climbed up Dawu Mountain while we, Drekai, climbed up Wutou Mountain."[30]

In other narrations, we find a vague memory of the sending of Noah's raven and dove, which they replace with a fly and a deer. "The people on the Katomoan [mountain] ordered the mouse-deer to fetch the fire, and he successfully brought it back."[31]

A Rukai Chief (ca. 1900)

The Serpent in Taiwanese Traditions

The Rukai have another story of the early days of the world with strong Genesis parallels, as we will see below. This appears to be a mixed, embellished memory of certain events of Genesis, including 1) the serpent and Eve in the Garden of Eden (Genesis 3:1-5); 2) celestial beings that abandoned their heavenly abode and mated with women on earth (6:1-4)[32]; 3) Enoch's ascent to heaven (Genesis 5:24); and 4) the destruction of the Tower of Babel (Genesis 11:1-9). To find these elements in this Rukai tradition is by no means an anomaly, for they are found all over the world.

> "Once upon a time, the sky and earth were connected with a very long stone staircase. Back then there was a family that had a very beautiful clay pot at their doorstep. After a while, out of nowhere, an egg and a hundred-pace [long] snake appeared in the clay pot. The snake curled around the egg to protect it. Later the egg hatched, and out came a beautiful girl. Locals believed that this girl was an incarnation of a goddess, and thus named her Megaigai. Megaigai grew into an extremely beautiful young woman. …
>
> One day a god in the sky named Gulele happened to see Megaigai. He was deeply attracted to her beauty and instantly fell in love with her. Gulele hurried down the stone stairs to earth and began to passionately woo the girl. The charismatic god eventually won the heart of Megaigai and the couple married. After the wedding, one by one Gulele's family began to climb up the stone staircase back to their home in the sky. Seeing this, Megaigai was worried that her husband would one day return to the sky as well. So she found an ax and destroyed the stone staircase. Gulele had no choice but to stay and live on earth forever, and the mortal world and the sky was forever separated."[33]

30. Poiconu, *Literary History of Taiwanese Indigenous Peoples*, p. 89.
31. Yukichi Sayama and Yoshihisa Onishi, *The Myths and Traditions of the Formosan Native Tribes*, pp. 331-332. See also: Poiconu, *Literary History of Taiwanese Indigenous Peoples*, p. 89.
32. In connection with this passage from Genesis 6, see Jude 6 and 1 Peter 3:19-20 and context.
33. Zhong, Zhi-cheng, "The Forgotten Creation Myths of Taiwan," trans. Deh I Chen. *Indigenous Sight*, October 23, 2018. Retrieved 3 March, 2023 from https://insight.ipcf.org.tw/en-US/article/28

123 SAISIYAT

The Flood is by no means absent in the traditions of the Saisiyat, who live in the mountains of northwestern Taiwan. The account they narrated around 1930 went as follows:

> "In the ancient times, human beings created by the god lived in the original land. Then a flood happened suddenly and human beings were dispersed everywhere without knowing what would happen. Then a man sat on a weaving machine and floated to Airubia Mountain."[34]

A man sat on a weaving machine and floated to Airubia Mountain.

Shigeru Tsuchida recorded a very similar tradition in November 1962 amongst the Marongarong Saisiyat. Again, we see the memory of Noah's ark coming to rest on Mount Ararat:

> "A long time ago this land was a hill. Later the sea rose and flooded the land, and all men were drowned in the sea.
>
> Thereupon an old man said, "How awful! We men will be all perished. Let us put a man on a pirogue [canoe] and set it adrift on the sea." "You (to the man) may go anywhere. (Wherever you may go) there will be a seed left in future."

The pirogue was driven away by water currents and came (at last) to Mt. Papak."[35]

An old man said, 'We men will be all perished.' He placed a man in a canoe and set it adrift at sea. … The canoe came at last to Mt. Papak.

124 SAKIZAYA

The Sakizaya live on the east-central coast of Taiwan in Hualien County. "The Sakizaya called the region (Hualien) Nararacanan, after raracan, an edible kind of shellfish".[36] In 2007 the Sakizaya tribe of Hualien became Taiwan's 13th officially recognized tribe. Prior to that, the Sakizaya had been considered to be part of the Amis tribe and had all but disappeared from history. This near disappearance is rooted in the Takubuwa Incident of 1878 (also called the Takobowan or Kaliawan Incident). The killing of a Qing businessman by a confederation of Sakizaya and Kavalan people in Kaliawan resulted in a major conflict between the Qing on one side and the allied tribes on the other side.[37] The overwhelming Qing response was so violent that both tribes had no choice but to abandon their burned down ancestral villages and blend in among the Amis tribe, where the Sakizaya remained in obscurity for over 100 years. The Sakizaya's century of anonymity resulted in "substantial losses in their identity, bloodline, and language," among other things.[38]

Regarding the memory of the Deluge, the following text is one of the few narrations we possess from the Sakizaya:

> "A long, long time ago, because of a major flood, siblings floated to Taiwan Island in a canoe and landed ashore in Yanliao, Hualien. They looked around and saw no one else... They had to get married and their children became the ancestors of the Sakizaya tribe.

34. Li Hui, "The Deluge Legend of the Sibling-mating Type in Aboriginal Formosa and Southeast Asia," *Chinese Ethnology Journal*, vol. 1 (1955). As translated to English in: Poiconu, *Literary History of Taiwanese Indigenous Peoples*, p. 71.
35. Shigeru Tsuchida, "Preliminary Reports on Saisiyat: Phonology," *Gengo Kenkyu (Journal of the Linguistic Society of Japan)*, vol. 46 (1964), pp. 51-52.
36. Cowsill, P. (2008). *Kiraya or Kira*, Taiwan. Retrieved 5 March, 2021 from http://patrick-cowsill.blogspot.com/2008/03/kiraya-or-kira-taiwan.html.
37. Chen I-chun, *The Making of Ethnicity in Postwar Taiwan: a case study of Kavalan ethnic identity*. PhD Dissertation (University College London. England, 2000).
38. Lin P. H., Tseng J. H., and Lin, P. C., "A study of applying Sakizaya Tribe's Palamal (the Fire God Ritual) into cultural creative products design," in *Cross-Cultural Design: 6th International Conference, CCD 2014, Held as Part of HCI International 2014, Heraklion, Crete, Greece, June 22-27, 2014, Proceedings*, ed. Rau P. L. P. (2014), p. 754.

The gods warned the Sakizaya people to work hard and worship the gods and ancestors devoutly, but after a long time of peace, the people gradually became lazy and angered the gods, so heavy rain fell, the river roared, and the leader of the Dargubay hurriedly led the people to Mt. Sha Po Dang to save their lives... a willing man and woman were sacrificed by being put in a rice sieve and pushed into the flood, but they were washed back to the shore by the flood. The priest shook his head and said, "God doesn't accept them!"

> At that moment, the heavy rain miraculously stopped, and the flood receded. ... A large marble rock was exposed... They call it "God's mark."

... at the moment of the extinction of the race, Dawa (the chief's daughter) walked up to the rice sieve and a boy named Namoh immediately followed her... In an instant, the two disappeared into the flood.

At that moment, the heavy rain miraculously stopped, and the flood receded... A large triangular piece of snow-white marble rock was exposed on the wall of Mt. Sha Po Dang. On the Qilai Plain, this sturdy rock wall can be clearly seen from every corner. The tribes call it Sipiledacay, or "God's mark" and everyone believed that it was a stone wall erected by the gods for Dawa and Namoh, witnessing their love and sacrifice for the tribe, and reminding the tribe to work hard, not to be lazy, and not to be disrespectful to the gods."[39]

Reminiscent of God's rainbow described in Genesis, the Sipiledacay stone is a reminder of the promise from God in Genesis 9:8-17.

125 TSOU

Our source on the Tsou tribe of interior Taiwan is Mr. Shinji Ishii, who spent years among the natives of Taiwan and shared his unpublished manuscripts with Sir James George Frazer:

Tsou children singing

"The Tsuwo [or Tsou], a tribe of head-hunters in the mountainous interior of Formosa, have also a story of a great flood, which they told to Mr. Ishii at the village of Paichana. When their ancestors were living dispersed in all directions, there occurred a mighty inundation whereby plain and mountains alike were covered with water. Then all the people fled and took refuge on the top of Mount Niitaka-yama, and there they stayed until the flood subsided, and the hills and valleys emerged once more from the watery waste. After that the survivors descended in groups from the mountains and took their several ways over the land as chance or inclination prompted them."[40]

Similar to the Bunun and other Taiwanese tribes, the Tsou have an element in their Flood traditions that is very similar to Genesis: the sending of birds on an exploratory mission after the Flood:

"As people arrived at Jade Mountain, the kindling was extinguished. They sent "kiuyisi" bird to find fire for them. It found fire and returned, but it

39. Tien Z. Y., *Myths, Legends, and the Fire God's Ceremony of Sakizaya* (Taichung, Taiwan: Morning Star Press, 2019), p. 24.
40. Beyer, "Origin Myths Among the Mountain Peoples of the Philippines," *The Philippine Journal of Science*, ed. Alvin J. Cox, Volume 8, Section D (Manila: Bureau of Printing, 1913), pp. 229-230.

flew so slowly that fire burned its beak. It discarded the fire because of the pain. Then people asked "uhngu" bird (a sparrow) to find fire. It flew fast and took fire back successfully, so people could use fire. To express their gratitude to the bird, people allowed it to eat grains in the farm."[41]

To express their gratitude to the bird, people allowed it to eat grains in the farm.

Some Tsou versions replace the birds with a goat (serow and muntjac) and/or a deer.[42]

126 SEEDIQ

The Seediq and the Truku tribes were recognized as split-offs of the Atayal tribe by the Qing, Japanese, and Kuomintang colonial regimes. However, it wasn't until 2008 that the Seediq tribe was officially recognized as an independent tribe by the ROC Government.

According to one Seediq text, the sea rose up and covered the land forcing the terrified people to retreat to the summit of Mt. Towaqqa. In desperation, they sacrificed an immoral woman to the deluge, but the flood did not abate. Next they set a young couple adrift on a small vessel. The young pair traveled to the end of the sea where they removed the debris that had blocked the water causing the flood to abate.

The Seediq Flood text directly parallels the Chinese Classics version, but is clear as to the Flood's global scope.

This young couple returned home and found their houses full of fish and planted the sweet potato seeds that they had saved. The plants bore much fruit and they prospered.[43]

127 TRUKU

During the early 20th century, the Japanese Empire once labeled the Truku tribe "the most hostile and barbarous savages."[44] This echoed a 1911 "Report on the Control of the Aborigines in Formosa," which concluded that "there is no such instance in other parts of the Empire, as in Formosa [Taiwan], where fighting is carried on all the year round under more dangerous and laborious conditions."[45] Of all the tribes that resisted Japanese colonialism throughout southeast Asia, the Truku are Taiwan's only tribe that held such naturally well defended mountainous positions that the deployment of a naval flotilla was required to subjugate them. The 1914 Truku War lasted longer than any other Japanese-Aboriginal engagement and required over 20,000 Japanese soldiers to defeat about 3,000 virile warriors over a nearly three-month-long campaign.[46]

The Truku story of the loss of immortality is connected with a snake, as in Genesis.

In agreement with the Bible, the Truku believe that mortality is a punishment exacted on humanity because humans were unable to keep their promises. In the beginning "A human being and a snake both came out of pig excrement. The human and the snake each agreed to help the other clean off his body. After the snake first cleaned off the human, the human neglected to clean off the snake in exchange."[47] Thus, it is the curse of the snake that ends mankind's natural state of immortality.

41. Pasuya Poiconu (Pu Chung-chen), *The Culture and Legends of the Tsou Tribe* (Taipen: Taiwan Publishing, 1993), pp. 128-130. As translated into English in: Poiconu, *Literary History of Taiwanese Indigenous Peoples*, p. 77.
42. Poiconu, *Literary History of Taiwanese Indigenous Peoples*, pp. 78-79.
43. Wu J., *Songs and Bonfires* (Taiwan: Jih-Tung Art Printing Co., 2019), p. 54.
44. Kim Kwang-Ok. "The Taruko and their Belief System." PhD Thesis (Saint Catherine's College, Oxford University, 1980), p. 55.
45. Bureau of Aboriginal Affairs, *Report on the Control of the Aborigines in Formosa* (Taihoku, Taiwan: 1911), p. 18.
46. Lee M. Y., "Culture and History Matter: Historical Trauma and Culture Protective Factors on Alcohol Use Among Truku Tribal People." PhD thesis (Seattle, University of Washington, 2017), p. 29.
47. Pu Chung-cheng, "The Connection between Myth and Social Change: a Truku Example," eds. Tu Kuo-ch'ing and R. Backus, *Taiwan Literature English Translation Series*, no. 24 (Santa Barbara: UC Santa Barbara, 2009), p. 136.

It is said that in ancient times, a great flood came and washed everything away. The people fled to the mountains. On the mountain top, the people built boats and filled them with all kinds of birds, such as chickens and ducks. They tried to convince an old man to join them, but he and his family refused to join them and stayed in their home.

After the flood receded, the tribes returned and found that everything was gone. First, they soaked a dog's tail in water and then wrapped rice and millet together in the dog's tail. When the millet was dry, they removed the seeds and planted them. This method of sowing is still used by the Truku people today.[48]

128 TAO / YAMI

128 Linguistically, the Tao/Yami language is Bashiic rather than Formosan.[49] As such, the Tao language is the only non-Formosan Austronesian language found throughout the native populations of the Taiwan archipelago, and the Tao tribe is the only tribe that is believed to have migrated north from the Batanes Archipelago (between Taiwan and the Philippines).

The Tao deluge text that is summarized below was published in 1981, which is less than 30 years after Orchid Island was introduced to Christianity. This text was narrated by elders of Iratay Village, one of six villages, each having its own unique deluge and origin stories.

In the beginning God created man to live in a garden. There was only one fruit that they were forbidden from eating. But when they did eat the fruit, God sent the people to Orchid Island upon the waves in wooden boxes.[50] Their children were crippled because of their incestuous parentage. Eventually, healthy people were born but their population remained small. The Tao immorality drew the ire of the gods. In due time, the gods caused a great flood to burst forth after a special white stone was lifted. The ocean grew bigger and bigger and covered the fields. The people were chased up to higher ground. So, they carried millet and salt to the highest mountain. After a year, the sea reached their houses, so they moved again. Every year they climbed higher. Finally, in the ninth year, the Flood stopped rising but most of the survivors had succumbed to famine.

> In the beginning God created man to live in a garden. But after eating the only forbidden fruit, God banished them to Orchid Island.

After eight more years, the ocean hadn't changed. One year later, in year 18, they found two mice and cast them into the sea. Finally, the ocean began to subside gradually. Only a few people survived.[51] A wide range of variety in motif is exhibited among the Flood myths of Orchid Island's six primary villages. For a compilation of 18 Yami Flood texts, see Gauss 2022.

---

48. Tien Z. Y., *Myths and Legends of the Truku* (Taichung, Morning Star Press, 2020), p. 59-60.
49. Rosa Enn, "Governance, Empowerment, and Environmental Justice – the Indigenous Tao of Orchid Island." (Doctoral Thesis, Universitat Wien, 2015), pp. 52-53.
50. D. Benedek, *The Songs of the Ancestors, A Comparative Study of Bashiic Folklore* (Taipei: SMC Publishing Inc., 1991), pp. 324-326
51. Liu B. X., *The Legend of the Ancestors of the Yami Iratay Tribe* (Taiwan: Institute of Ethnology, Academia Sinica, 1981), pp. 114-169.

Rocks formation of El Nido Palawan, Philippines

THE PHILIPPINES

The native peoples of the Philippines are primarily Austronesian in language and therefore closely connected to Taiwan and its tribes, from the previous chapter. They are a southeastern offshoot of that ancient people group which, paternally, is defined by Y DNA haplogroups O and N. This ancestral group traveled eastward from Babel, migrating across Central Asia on the north side of the Himalayas, and arriving in western China, from which they fanned across East and Southeast Asia.

As to a memory of the events of Genesis 1-11, they are well-attested in the Philippines, just as we saw in Taiwan. The Isnegs of Luzon have a tradition of a Flood which submerged the mountains, and of two siblings who boarded a banana tree raft, eventually landing at Mount Solo. They have notions of Creation and the Tower of Babel as well. The Talaandig people of Mindanao say that when mankind multiplied, they " transgressed the laws of their Creator." God "decided to clean the earth by means of a flood." A man survived on a mountain, along with a woman who floated on a drum, landing at another mountain. The Igorot tribe has a similar tradition, and this memory is so dear to them that they recount it at their weddings and holidays.

The Bukidnon people said that "a wise man had told the people that they must build a large raft. They did as he commanded and cut many large trees, until they had enough to make three layers." The Nabaloi recall a floating box, and the Subanon refer to a favored couple being rescued in a basket. A bird also figures prominently in many Flood accounts from the Philippines, a memory of Noah's dove.

These are just a few of the Flood stories recovered from the Philippines. They are more than sufficient to establish the fact that the echoes of Ararat resound even here, 6,000 miles from Israel!

Tribes of the Region

129. Isneg
130. Igorot (Luzon)
131. Talaandig (Mindanao)
132. Bukidnon (Mindanao)
133. Bontok (Luzon)
134. Ifugao (Luzon)
135. Ayta Abellen (Luzon)
136. Visaya
137. Atá (Mindanao)
138. Mandaya (Mindanao)
139. Tagalog (Luzon)
140. Subanon (Mindanao)
141. Higaonon (Mindanao)
142. Blaan and Tboli (Mindanao)
143. Itneg (Luzon)
144. Nabaloi (Luzon)
145. Luzon Tradition

129 ISNEG

"The Apayaos are courageous and lovers of freedom," wrote Lawrence Wilson in 1947 of this tribe in northern Luzon who call themselves the Isnegs. "The Spanish never did conquer them, and even we Americans had a difficult time establishing our benevolent government." Later, when America was seeking to liberate the Philippines from Japan, "the Apayaos volunteered, almost to a man, to assist in defeating the Japanese."[1]

The Isnegs narrated to Wilson a very interesting memory of the Fall (Genesis 3), mixed with the Flood. The tradition opens by describing the original paradise:

There was a time when the sky world was close to the earth and the people used to go there to trade.

> "There was a time when the sky world was close to the earth and the people used to go there to trade. These people were well-to-do, for Ewagan, the powerful, handsome, shining anito [spirit], was taking especial care of them. Through his magical powers it was not necessary for them to work. If a man wanted to start a new kaingin [garden or field], all that he had to do was to start his aliwa [a type of axe] in the place selected, and the aliwa would automatically cut down the vegetation. Or, if the kaingin needed cultivation, he just set the hoe in position and it would do the rest."[2]

But this happy state would not last forever. Songan, the leader of the people on earth, requested a celebration with the Ewagan and the sky people, who were superior in power. Ewagan agreed, but gave strict terms that had to be observed. On the third day of the celebration, a careless man committed a negligent act, bringing a poor beverage in a common vessel. "At this serious breach of etiquette, Ewagan became very angry, and all the people in the house were thrown into confusion, for they feared that Ewagan would kill them all."[3]

He did not kill them, but a grievous sentence was passed on them, which included that 1) Songan's powers were removed, 2) there was a famine on earth, 3) "a great flood should entirely devastate the whole world," 4) Songan would suffer defeats during enemy invasions, 5) "the rice, which hitherto had grown without the husks, would now have husks and the women were doomed to thresh it," 6) "the people of the earth should now have to labor for their daily needs", and 7) trade between the earth and sky ceased. The tradition concludes with a statement that "Then all the punishments specified in the agreement were carried out in full. To this day, life is hard for the people upon the earth."[4]

Their account of the Flood preserves the fact that the vessel landed on a high mountain. They say it was a raft instead of an ark:

All mountains were submerged. Two siblings rode a raft of wild bananas. They landed at Mount Solo.

> "There was, they say, a flood. All mountains, they say, were submerged. … The two siblings who rode a raft of wild bananas [or round logs] were lucky, as they were not drowned. … When the flood subsided, all the men were dead, only the two siblings were not drowned. They stayed, they say, on Mount Solo [a high peak in Luzon]: that is where they were stopped."[5]

The connections with Genesis extend still further. After the Flood, the Isnegs say an attempt was made to restore access to the sky. This Tower of Babel story is also similar to that of the Nung people of Vietnam and southern China. The strong man in this tradition seems to be Nimrod himself:

1. Laurence L. Wilson, *Apayao Life and Legends* (Philippines, 1947), p. 2.
2. Wilson, *Apayao Life and Legends*, p. 92.
3. *Ibid.*, pp. 92-94.
4. *Ibid.*, pp. 94-95.
5. Morice Vanoverbergh, "Isneg Tales," *Folklore Studies: Journal of Far Eastern Folklore*, vol. 14 (Tokyo: S.V.D. Research Institute, 1955), pp. 14-15.

"There was a woman and her son who lived together in a happy life. When the son grew to be a young man he was very strong. He planned to build a road going to the sky. The name of the son was Etkan. He was so strong that he was able to carry great, huge stones for the construction of his road leading to the sky. Etkan worked enough days to complete three rest houses. He planted betel leaf and betel-nut for the people to chew when they should go trading to the sky. One morning, the son told his mother not to bring his food until he had finished two more rest houses. After he had been working hardly three hours, the mother came with his food. But the son had not yet completed what he had told his mother. Then he became angry and kicked away the erected stones leading to the sky so that they were thrown to Nabuangan, Makaltog, and some parts of Katablangan. In these places we can still find the great, huge stones which Etkan collected for the construction of his road leading to the sky."[6]

There was a strong man who tried to build a road going to the sky.

Garden of Eden Traditions

Like the Isneg tradition above, many tribes all around the world have traditions of an original "golden age", described in terms similar to the Garden of Eden. Some nations also remember the long lifespans of the ante-diluvian people. For example, the Laotian elders refer to a time, "in the days when the earth was young and all things were better than they now are, when men and women were stronger and of greater beauty, and the fruit of the trees was larger and sweeter than that which we now eat, then rice, the food of the people, was of larger grain."[7] The Atayal and the Paiwan of Taiwan, among others, share similar traditions.[8] Many versions recall a temptation, a sin, and the fall from this initial, perfect state of life. Among these, the Pai-I of southwest China and the Paiwan of Taiwan attribute this curse to a taboo broken by a certain woman while cooking rice.[9] Although India is beyond the scope of this book, the Santal people have a similar story.[10] These things remind us of that fateful moment recorded in Genesis: "She took from its fruit and ate; and she gave also to her husband with her, and he ate." (3:6)

6. Wilson, *Apayao Life and Legends*, pp. 98-99.
7. Katherine Neville Fleeson, *Laos Folklore of Farther India* (New York: Fleming H. Revell, 1899), pp. 85-86.
8. Ho T'ing-jui, "A Comparative Study of Myths and Legends of Formosan Aborigines," pp. 111-112.
9. Ho T'ing-jui, "A Comparative Study of Myths and Legends of Formosan Aborigines," pp. 337, 340-341.
10. "When the Santals lived in Champa and Kiskus were their kings, the Santals were very simple and religious and only worshiped Thakur. In those days the rice grew already husked, and the cotton bushes bore cloth already woven, and men did not have to pick the lice out of each other's hair. Men's skulls grew loose and each man could lift off his own skull and clean it and then replace it. But all of this was spoiled by the misdeeds of a serving girl of one of the Rajas. When she went into the field for purposes of nature, she would at the same time pick and eat the rice that grew by her; and when she had made her hands dirty cleaning out a cow house, she would wipe them on the cloth which she was wearing. Angered by these dirty habits, Thakur Baba deprived men of the benefits which he had conferred on them. The rice began to grow in a husk and the cotton plants only produced raw cotton and men's skulls became fixed so that they could not be removed." Source: Cecil Henry Bompas, trans., *Folklore of the Santal Parganas* (London: David Nutt, 1909), p. 401.

130 IGOROT

The Igorot people achieved great understanding in astronomy and possessed a rich collection of oral literature, according to the anthropologist Otley Beyer.[11] Regarding the Flood, one explorer wrote that "there is a tradition among the Igorrotes of Northern Luzon, that after the deluge, people who had saved themselves in the hollow of a tree landed at a mountain called Kanlantan."[12] And in a tradition recorded around the year 1894, we read:

> "They preserve a tradition relating to their origin and beginning, after a great and dreadful flood which, a very long time ago, as their old people relate, covered the earth. All the inhabitants except a brother and sister were drowned. The brother and sister, though separated from each other, were saved, the woman on the summit of the highest mountain in the District of Lepanto, called Kalauitan, and the man in a cave of the same mountain."[13]

They preserve a tradition relating to their origin and beginning, after a great and dreadful flood which covered the earth.

Although they have forgotten the names of that ancient couple, Perez adds that "the memory of them lives freshly among the Igorots, and in their feats, or whenever they celebrate their marriages, the aged people repeat to the younger ones this wonderful history, so that they can tell it to their sons, and in that way pass from generation to generation the memory of their first progenitors."[14] We will make the case in Appendix B that this brother-sister pair are a memory of Adam and Eve.

131 TALAANDIG

The Talaandig are a highland-dwelling people in the province of Bukidnon, on Mindanao island. The Talaandig are approximately 100,000 in number, and are one of seven indigenous people groups from that province, along with the Bukidnon, Higaonon, Matigsalug, Manobo, Tigwahanon, and Umayamnon. Adolino Saway, a tribal elder of the Talaandig and the chief custodian of their oral traditions, has shared their amazing Creation and Flood story with the outside world:

When the generations of mankind multiplied, they transgressed the laws of their Creator.

> "When the generations of Balauy, Tibulun, Hinanglayan and Binanglayan multiplied, however, they also transgressed the laws of their Creator. This time, Magbabaya decided to clean the earth by means of a flood. Before the flood occured, Nabis ha Panggulu and his three children namely Nabis ha Andadaman, Nabis Lumbu Bulawan and Nabis ha Upak were instructed by Magbabaya to go up to heaven. His youngest son, Nabis ha Agbibilin, who was chosen to become the seed of the next generation, was instructed to climb to the top of Lumuluyaw mountain, also known as Dulangdulang, the highest peak of Kitanglad mountain ranges, in order to be saved from the calamity. Nabis ha

11. H. Otley Beyer, "Origin Myths Among the Mountain Peoples of the Philippines," p. 94.
12. Anon., "Rambles in Formosa," *The Japan Weekly Mail*, vol. 28, no. 7 (Yokohama: 14 August, 1897), p. 169.
13. Angel Perez, *Igorrotes: Estudio geográfico y etnográfico sobre algunos distritos del Norte de Luzon*, vol. 1 (Manila: 1902), p. 319. After the waters went down, the two discovered each other and married. "They say that from this brother and sister so providentially saved, all the Irogots that are scattered through the mountains originated." (*Ibid.*)
14. *Ibid.*, pp. 319-320. Also, Leslie Wolfe documented a related version: "The Igorots believe that once the earth was flat. Two sons of Lumawig, the Great Spirit, were very fond of hunting the wild hog and deer. In order to provide mountains, where these animals might live, they brought a flood upon the earth. Lumawig looked down from his place in the sky and saw only two persons, a brother and sister, were left alive on the earth and they were about to die from the wet and cold. Lumawig sent the dog and deer to get some fire. They had great difficulty in bringing the fire through the flood, but with the help of Lumawig they succeeded, and he built up a great fire which warmed the brother and sister and dried up the waters from off the earth, which became as it was formerly except that now there were mountains. The brother and sister married and had children, and thus the earth was repeopled." Source: Leslie Wolfe, "The Primitive Religions of the Philippine Islands." Master's Thesis. Drake University Bible College (Des Moines, Iowa, 1922), p. 23.

> Agbibilin followed the instruction and went up to Lumuluyaw while his father and his brothers went up to heaven."[15]

With these preparations complete, the Flood then began:

> The flood finally came and submerged the lowlands around Dulangdulang mountain. While the great flood was taking place, Nabis Lumbu Bulawan looked down through Kulaguwan, the door of the sky, and described to Nabis ha Agbibilin the merciful situation of the people on earth who were washed away by the strong waves. Thus, Nabis ha Agbibilin knew everything that happened during the great flood. The description given by Nabis Lumbu Bulawan to Nabis ha Agbibilin was delivered through a chant known as "sala", a poetic construction of phrases to describe the event. Talaandig song or chant known as "sala" originated from Nabis Lumbu Bulawan being the first person to deliver it.
>
> After days or months, when the flood finally subsided, Apu Agbibilin, as we address Nabis ha Agbibilin today being our great ancestor, went down from Mt. Dulangdulang and found a woman named Ginamayung who was saved on a "kalatung", a wooden Talaandig drum, at the opposite mountain which was later known as the mountain of Kalatungan. Through the instruction of Magbabaya, the two got married and were blessed with eight children: four males and four females.

Notice that a wooden vessel landed upon a mountain. Next, the patriarch gave instructions on how to marry so as not to commit incest in the future.[16] And finally, we can hear echoes of Noah's dealings with his sons, and of his proclamation of blessing over them, in Genesis 9:

> "Before Apu Agbibilin departed on earth, he gathered all his children and taught them all the knowledge and wisdom they need to survive on earth. His final instruction was delivered through the small jar of oil called "puti" which he gave to his eldest son …[17]

Our great ancestor went down from Mt. Dulangdulang and found a woman who was saved on a wooden drum at the opposite mountain.

BUKIDNON

132 The Bukidnon ("mountain people") of northeast Mindanao were a rather isolated tribe when the folklorist Mabel Cole spent time among them between 1912 and 1916. Notice in their tradition below that a "wise man" foresaw the Flood and instructed the people to build a "large raft":

> "A long time ago there was a very big crab which crawled into the sea. And when he went in he crowded the water out so that it ran all over the earth and covered all the land.
>
> Now about one moon before this happened, a wise man had told the people that they must build a large raft. They did as he commanded

15. Datu Migketay Victorino L. (Adolino) Saway, "Talaandig Flood Story." August 26, 2011. Retrieved 15 December, 2023 from https://talaandigsite.blogspot.com/2011/08/talaandig-flood-story.html. See also: Datu Victorino Saway, "The Legend of Mt Kitanglad," *Talamdan: the Official Publication of the Kitanglad Integrated NGOs, Inc.*, vol. 1, no. 1.
16. "When the children of Apu Agbibilin and Apu Ginamayung were old enough to get married, Magbabaya instructed them to let their children marry each other in order to multiply on earth. The marriage that was arranged by Apu Agbibilin and Apu Ginamayung became the origin of the incest law that is necessarily settled when a marriage is negotiated in the Talaandig community. During the marriage arrangement, Magbabaya specifically instructed Apu Agbibibilin to arrange the marriage alternately among his children and not to allow a brother and a sister who were born one after another to become partners in marriage." Source: Saway, "Talaandig Flood Story."
17. *Ibid.*

and cut many large trees, until they had enough to make three layers. These they bound tightly together, and when it was done they fastened the raft with a long rattan cord to a big pole in the earth.

Soon after this the floods came. White water poured out of the hills, and the sea rose and covered even the highest mountains. The people and animals on the raft were safe, but all the others drowned."[18]

About one moon before this happened, a wise man had told the people that they must build a large raft. They did as he commanded and cut many large trees, until they had enough to make three layers.

No doubt this "wise man" mentioned above is Noah. Another version was recorded by Alfonso de Guzman and Esther Pacheco. Important features in this narration are the landing upon a mountain, three lines of descent after the Flood, and a special serpent which we would identify as the Serpent of Genesis 3:

"Once upon a time, there lived a giant python at the 'pusod hu dagat' (center of the sea). It was so large that when it coiled its body, it filled the center of the sea. So much water was displaced and caused a flood at the bottom of the world. The water covered the land and killed everyone, except a widow named Gahemen. Gahemen survived by clutching on a piece of driftwood washed on top of Mt. Kimangki, the only dry spot, in Southeastern Misamis Oriental overlooking Kalabugao.

Gahemen survived by clutching on a piece of driftwood washed on top of Mt. Kimangki.

When the land had dried up, Gahemen gave birth to a son named Teheban. Teheban grew into manhood and married his mother. They had three sons: the eldest was Pabulusen, the middle was A-ayawa-en, and the youngest was Tataun-en. Each of the sons claimed a territory and became founders of groups."[19]

133 BONTOK

"The Bontoks are sometimes wrongly called Igorots," explained the anthropologist Otley Beyer. "They are a distinct people, occupying a part of the subprovince of Bontok. They are in some respects unique, and possess certain social institutions and traits which have not been found elsewhere in the Philippines."[20]

Concerning their Flood tradition, Beyer recorded:

"The sons of Lumawig [the creator] went hunting. In all the world there were no mountains, for the world was flat, and it was impossible to catch the wild pigs and the deer. Then said the elder brother: "Let us flood the world so that mountains may rise up." Then they went to inundate at Mabud-bodobud. Then the world was flooded. … all the people had perished. There were alive only a brother and sister on Mt. Pokis."[21]

How the siblings reached the mountain, we are not told. In the vast majority of Flood traditions of this type, it is by means of a floating vessel. In any case, the tradition continues:

"Then Lumawig looked down on Pokis and saw that it was the only place not reached by the water, and that it was the abode of the solitary brother and sister. Then Lumawig descended and said: "Oh, you are here!" And

18. Mabel Cook Cole, *Philippine Folk Tales* (Chicago: A. C. McClurg & Co., 1916), p. 125.
19. Rolando Esteban, Arthur P. Casanova, and Ivie. C. Esteban, *Folktales of Southern Philippines* (2011), pp. 21-22. The tradition continues with: "Pabulusen occupied the valleys formed by Libang and Maasam rivers and the lands in the vicinity of Sinakongan near Busilao River in Northeastern Agusan. He was the first datu of the place and his descendants became the keepers of power. A-ayawa-en settled in the area from the Pulangi River on the south to Tagoloan River on the north. His descendants became keepers of religious customs. Tataun-en, whose name means 'hungry' or 'famine,' lived in Agusan. Unlike the places of his elders brothers, Tataun-en's area was less blessed, so his people often experienced hunger."
20. Beyer, "Origin Myths Among the Mountain Peoples of the Philippines," p. 95.
21. *Ibid.*, p. 96.

> the man said: "We are here, and here we freeze!" Then Lumawig sent his dog and his deer to Kalauwitan to get fire. They swam to Kalauwitan, and the dog and the deer, and they got the fire."[22]

A memory of Noah's raven and dove (Genesis 8:6-12) is evident in the "recovery of fire" theme here, a topic which we explore further in Appendix B. The tradition tells that from this surviving pair all of the tribes of humanity arose.[23]

134 IFUGAO

134 The Ifugao people occupy the province by the same name in mountainous central Luzon. They have some memory of Eden, passed down by their ancestors from Babel:

> "... all of the people lived along a large river that ran through the central plain between the two great mountains. The period was something like a Golden Age, when things were much better than they are now. The people were demigods whose life was a happy one and their country a sort of Garden of Eden. To obtain rice, all that they needed to do was to cut down a stalk of bamboo, which was plentiful, and split open the joints which were filled with hulled rice ready to cook. Stalks of sugar-cane were filled with baiwax [an Ifugao rice drink], and needed only to be tapped to furnish a most refreshing drink. The river was full of fish, and the forests were filled with deer and wild hogs which were much easier to catch than those of the present day. The rice grains of that time were larger and more satisfying, and a handful of them was sufficient to feed a large family. But this Golden Age, like others, was not destined to last."[24]

Ifugao rice terraces, a tourist attraction in Luzon

As for the Flood, the Ifugao say that the Flood happened because people dug into the earth and struck water:

> "... they began to dig, and they dug for three days. On the third day the hole was very large, and suddenly they struck a great spring and the water gushed forth. ... Then the old men said: 'We must flee to the mountains, for the river gods are angry and we shall all be drowned.'

Then the old men said: 'We must flee to the mountains, for the river gods are angry and we shall all be drowned.'

22. *Ibid.*
23. "Lumawig awaited them. He said: "How long they are coming!" Then he went to Kalauwitan and said to his dog and the deer: "Why do you delay in bringing the fire? Get ready! Take the fire to Pokis; let me watch you!" Then they went into the middle of the flood, and the fire which they had brought from Kalauwitan was put out! Then said Lumawig: "Why do you delay the taking? Again you must bring fire; let me watch you!" Then they brought fire again, and he observed that that which the deer was carrying was extinguished." Then Lumawig swam and arrived and quickly took the fire which his dog had brought. He took it back to Pokis and he built a fire and warmed the brother and sister." *Ibid.*, p. 96.
24. *Beyer*, "Origin Myths Among the Mountain Peoples of the Philippines," pp. 111-112.

> So the people fled toward the mountains and all but two of them were overtaken by the water and drowned. The two who escaped were a brother and sister named Wigan and Bugan—Wigan on Mt. Amuyao and Bugan on Kalauitan. And the water continued to rise until all the Earth World was covered excepting only the peaks of these two mountains.
>
> The water remained on the earth for a whole season or from rice planting to rice harvest [about six months]."[25]

They struck a great spring and the water gushed forth. ... All the Earth World was covered except the peaks of two mountains.

In fact, many tribes say that the Flood burst forth from under the earth, which is in accord with Genesis 7:11, "on this day all the fountains of the great deep split open." To find this detail preserved should not be surprising, for many other details of the Genesis Flood have been preserved in traditions around the world.

Continuing, this oral history tells that after reuniting, "They descended the mountain and wandered about until they came to the beautiful valley that is today the dwelling place of the Banauol clan—and here Wigan built a house." (Notice the parallels with Genesis 11:2, "And it happened as they journeyed east, that they found a plain in the land of Shinar and settled there.") Later when the woman was pregnant, she was surprised by an "old man with a long white beard." This man, named Maknongan, assured the couple that they had done the right thing by marrying, that they must repopulate the world, and that they should offer sacrifices to the gods when they are in trouble.[26] Here we are reminded of the sacrifice which the old man himself offered after coming out of the Ark (Genesis 8:20). These details matching Genesis are significant.

135 AYTA ABELLEN

The Ayta Abellen are an isolated tribe of the Austronesian language family who live in the mountains of Luzon, in the provinces of Tarlac and Zambales. Roger Stone, who has produced valuable research on the Ayta Abellen language, also recorded a native tradition of the Tower of Babel from them. His source was a tribe member named Rodante Capiendo, regarded as one of the best Ayta Abellen storytellers. Capiendo learned this oral tradition from his father.

Stone told that "this recording was made immediately before Mr. Capiendo was told the account of the Babel story from the Book of Genesis," which is to say, he did not have a prior knowledge of this text.[27]

> "Back then, my father said something about the languages, why there are many languages and many kinds of people. What my father said, 'Back then, my son,' he said, 'at the earliest time, the people wanted to reach heaven. For they wanted to reach the skill of the Lord God but the Lord God, he disregarded it, [it] is said,' said my father, 'the Lord God disregarded.'
>
> Because of the length of time of their working, they made something good. The good which they did, they made a tower. There began the languages at the tower. For the tower, they raised and raised. The plan of the people who are making the tower, they wanted to reach the skill of the Lord God but the Lord God became angry it is said. 'It is said' I said because (this is) the word of my parents.
>
> Now, the Lord God became angry. 'This tower which was made over a long time period, one second only that I will tear it down," he said. Because of it being very tall, the Lord God did not like it. The Lord God tore it down in just one second. One second only, the tower was torn down. Now, the people who made the tower, they were shocked. Shocked. ...There it is said was the beginning of the many languages,' said my father. There it is said it began."[28]

The Lord God did not like the tower. The Lord God tore it down in just one second.

Tower of Babel stories are found all over the world, as we have seen thus far in this volume.

25. *Ibid.*, p. 112.
26. *Ibid.*, p. 113.
27. Roger Stone, *Analyzing Ayta Abellen Narratives for Peak, Participant Reference, Information Type and Fronting* (Summer Institute of Linguistics, 2007), p. 1. Retrieved from https://www.sil.org/resources/archives/52158
28. *Ibid.*, pp. 2-3.

136

VISAYA

The Visayans are from the Visayan island group, near the center of the Philippines between the major islands of Luzon (north) and Mindanao (south). On the existence of a Flood tradition from them, we have very early testimony, although it is a bare reference. In Thévenot's work, *Relations de Divers Voyages Curieux* (Accounts of Various Curious Voyages), published in 1663, we have a translation from an earlier Spanish manuscript from the Philippines. The author is one Dom Carlo del Pezzo. This account merely refers to the Visaya Flood tradition, but gives no details: "They believe in a first man, the deluge, and glory and punishment in another life."[29]

On the substance of their Flood tradition, we look to another source. Around the year 1910, a Visayan man narrated the following tradition, which his forefathers had passed down from generation to generation. Notice the "dove" and "crow", and other parallels with Genesis:

> "A long time ago, when Bathala, the god of the land, was peacefully ruling his dominions, he had many pets. Among these, his two favorites were the dove and the crow. The crow was noted for its bright, pretty plumage.
>
> One day Bathala had a quarrel with Dumagat, the god of the sea. Bathala's subjects had been stealing fish, which were the subjects of Dumagat. When Dumagat learned of this, and could get no satisfaction from Bathala, he retaliated. He opened the big pipe through which the water of the world passes, and flooded the dominions of Bathala until nearly all the people were drowned."[30]

His two favorites were the dove and the crow ... Dumagat flooded the dominions of Bathala until nearly all the people were drowned.

Now we come to the sending of the birds, with parallels to Noah's raven and dove:

> When the water had abated somewhat, Bathala sent the crow, his favorite messenger, to find out whether all his subjects had been killed. The crow flew out from the palace where the god lived, and soon saw the corpses of many persons floating about. He descended, alighted on one, and began to eat the decaying cadaver. When Bathala saw that it was late and that the crow had not returned, he sent the dove on the same errant, telling the bird also to find out what had become of the first messenger. The dove flew away, looking for any signs of life. At last he saw the crow eating some of the decaying bodies. Immediately he told the crow that the king had sent for him, and together they flew back to Bathala's palace."[31]

To hear such echoes of the Genesis Flood in the Philippines, 6,000 miles from Israel, is extraordinary. Yet it is exactly what we would expect if Genesis is true.

The tradition goes on to tell that the king rewarded the dove for its faithfulness but cursed the crow for its disobedience.[32]

29. Melchisédec Thévenot, trans., "Relation des Isles Philipines," in *Relations de Divers Voyages Curieux*, vol. 1 (Paris: Thomas Moette, 1696 [2nd edition]),, p. 2.
30. Dean Spruill Fansler, *Filipino Popular Tales* (New York: American Folk-lore Society, 1921), pp. 420-421.
31. *Ibid.*, p. 421.
32. "When the two birds arrived at the king's court, the dove told Bathala that the crow had been eating some dead bodies, and consequently had not done what he had been sent to do. Bathala was very angry at this disobedience. Without saying a word, he seized his big inkstand filled with black ink and threw it at the crow, which was immediately covered. Bathala then turned to the dove, and said, 'You, my dove, because of your faithfulness, shall be my favorite pet, and no longer shall you be a messenger.' Then he turned to the crow, and said, 'You, foul bird, shall forever remain black; you shall forever be a scavenger, and every one shall hate you.' So that is why today the dove is loved by the people, and the crow hated." *Ibid.*, p. 421.

Questions for Christians Who Question the Flood and Young Earth Creation

It is inevitable that critiques will come from our brothers and sisters in Christ who hold to old earth creation (OEC) or theistic evolution (TE). To these I ask the following questions. Questions such as these were very helpful for me to think through the consequences of my position, back when I was an old earth creationist:

1. Do you believe that Noah's Flood (Genesis 6-9) was global in scope? If not, can a local or allegorical flood be reconciled with the biblical passages? (e.g., Gen. 7:17-24, 10:32, Isa. 54:9, 1 Pet. 3:20, 2 Pet. 2:5, 3:6, Heb. 11:7, Matt. 24:37-39)
2. If the Flood was merely local or allegorical, why do tribes and nations all over the world have Flood traditions which match Genesis in both general outline and specific details?
3. Why does Paul logically connect Jesus with Adam in Romans 5 and 1 Corinthians 15? "As in Adam all die, so in Christ all will be made alive." (1 Cor. 15:22) What logic is there to Paul's connection of Jesus and Adam if Adam did not cause the entrance of death to the world because of sin?
4. The "law of sin and death" is defined in Romans 6:23 as "the wages of sin is death." Likewise, Romans 5:12 says "through one man sin entered into the world, and death through sin, and so death spread to all men, because all sinned." Do you agree that death entered the world when Adam sinned? The OEC and TE positions, however, teach that death was already in the world before Adam sinned (if he existed at all). How then can Paul say that death is the consequence of sin, if sin was already in the world? Does this not undo the entire logic of Paul's argument in Romans 5?
5. Can the law of sin and death be undermined without undermining the Gospel itself? Can the 3rd and 5th chapters of Romans be undermined without undermining the 8th?
6. If the sin and death problem of Romans 5 is only figurative, how can the atonement and salvation that Jesus offers be applicable to a figurative problem? Does a doctor at any time prescribe a literal remedy for a figurative illness? If the illness exists only figuratively, isn't the need for a remedy only figurative too?
7. Jesus said "from the beginning of creation God made them male and female," referring to the creation of Adam and Eve and their subsequent marriage (Mark 10:6). But how does He say "from the beginning of creation" if, according to OEC and TE teaching, mankind did not exist until billions of years after the world was formed?
8. Did Jesus have a wrong understanding of Creation and the Flood, based on his statements in Mark 10:6, Mark 13:19-20, Luke 11:50-51, Matthew 24:37-39, and Luke 17:26-27? If theistic evolution or old-earth creation is true, did Jesus know it? If not, doesn't that mean that Jesus taught some false ideas?
9. Was death originally present in creation, prior to human sin? In that case, isn't death part of that paradisical creation which God calls "good" and "very good" (Gen. 1:25, 1:31)? How can God simultaneously call death the "enemy" in 1 Corinthians 15:26 and "good" in Genesis 1?
10. How could God tell Adam the earth is now cursed and would produce thorns and thistles, as a result of Adam's sin, if there had been thorns and thistles all along? (Gen. 3:17-19) Wouldn't this declaration be utter nonsense to Adam?
11. If death, disease, natural evil, and suffering predate Adam and Eve, then who made them appear? Is it not God? But is God the author of evil? Perish the thought!
12. Why does Paul say in Romans 8:20 that the creation "was subjected to futility" and is in "slavery to corruption," if it was not subjected to futility and corruption in Genesis 3? If Paul is not talking about the moment when death and corruption entered the world, as a result of Adam's sin in the Garden in Genesis 3, what does this passage even mean? Are the statements "was subjected to futility" and "in slavery to corruption" without meaning?
13. Why does Luke see it as important to give a genealogy of Jesus that links him to Adam, as we see in Luke 3:23-38?

14. If the Genesis accounts of Creation, the Garden of Eden, and the Flood are figurative, at what point in Scripture are the historical narratives literal? Is it only figuratively true that hell is real, and that Jesus saves?
15. If the "days" of Creation are not 24-hour days but "periods of time," then are those "periods of time" out of order too? Doesn't Genesis 1:9-19 indicate that the earth existed before the sun was created? In that case, is the advocate of OEC or TE prepared to accept that the earth is millions of years older than the sun? Alternatively, if the order of events in Genesis cannot be relied upon, is there anything that we can be sure of in Genesis 1-3? Or how does the doctrine of scriptural inerrancy and authority apply to this passage if God cannot speak in a way we can understand in the very first page of Scripture?
16. If the "days" of Genesis 1 are not literal, 24-hour days, how are we to understand the contextual statements like "there was evening and there was morning, a second day" (Gen. 1:5, 8, 13, 19, 23, 31). What meaning do "morning " and "evening" have?
17. If the "first Adam" was not a literal person, doesn't this deprive Jesus of the title of "Second Adam"? (Romans 5, 1 Corinthians 15)
18. In what sense did Noah's Ark land in the "mountains of Ararat" (Gen. 8:4) if it was a local flood? Has a local flood ever lifted a boat to the top of a mountain?
19. Why did Noah require a dove flying and returning with a leaf in its beak to understand that the flood was ending (Gen. 8:6-11), if it was a local flood? How does this flight of the dove give new information to Noah in a local flood?
20. How is it not a broken promise which God made in Genesis 9:8-17 ("never again shall the water become a flood to destroy all flesh") if Noah's Flood was local in scope? There have been many locally destructive and deadly floods in history. Since God is no liar or breaker of promises, doesn't this require that God means there will never again be a global flood?
21. How could God tell the serpent in Genesis 3:14 that it shall now crawl on its belly, if snakes had crawled on their bellies all along? Doesn't this curse imply some anatomical change in the snake at the time of the Curse?
22. Why did God command Noah to take all kinds of birds into the Ark if it was a local flood? Have flying birds like ravens and doves ever been in danger of drowning and mass extinction in a local flood?
23. Genesis 1:30 seems to indicate that God created all animals to eat plants originally. But if this is not the case, and if carnivory and "nature red in tooth and claw" were part of that "very good" creation, why does Isaiah prophesy (in 11:6-9 and 65:25) of a time when animals "will do no evil nor act corruptly," "will not hurt nor destroy"? He adds that "the wolf and the lamb will graze together, and the lion will eat straw like the ox." (65:25) Isn't Isaiah judging the current state of nature as "corrupt"? Doesn't this confirm that there is a material difference between the "cursed" state of nature in Genesis 3 and the "very good" state in Genesis 1 and 2?
24. Who is the audience of Romans 1 who have beheld, "since the creation of the world," the evidence of God's attributes, existence, and power (1:19-20)? These same ones are "without excuse," according to verse 20, and they "suppress the truth in unrighteousness" according to verse 18. Is Paul not speaking of mankind? But Paul says this same audience has seen it "since the creation of the world." In what sense have people beheld God's evidence "since the beginning of the world" if, according to OEC and TE teaching, humans did not exist for over 99.9% of world history?

In the end, I came to see that a Christian position that embraces evolution, or pre-Adam death, lacks coherency. It is like pulling on a thread which will undo the entire garment. We cannot afford an incoherent Christian position. On the other hand, young earth creationism has this to its credit: by defending the straightforward teaching of the early chapters of Genesis, it thereby upholds the worldview that the entire Bible and the Gospel presupposes. The Bible offers a worldview and a Gospel that is fully coherent and strong. We can afford no other.

137 ATÁ

When the governor Edward Bolton met the Atá people, sometime approximately around 1900, he described their location as to the west and northwest of Mount Apo, which places them near the center of the island of Mindanao. The name Atá itself means "those up above" or "upland dwellers."[33] The Flood legend that Bolton heard from them went like this:

> "The greatest of all the spirits is Manama who made the first men from blades of grass, weaving them together until they resembled a human form. In this manner he made eight persons—male and female—who later became the ancestors of the Ata and all the neighboring tribes. Long after this the water covered the whole earth and all the Ata were drowned except two men and a woman. The waters carried them far away and they would have perished had not a large eagle come to their aid. This bird offered to carry them to their homes on its back. One man refused, but the other two accepted its help and returned to Mapuda."[34]

Mount Apo

There is good reason to conclude that this bird is derived from the memory of Noah's dove.

138 MANDAYA

The Mandaya tribe occupy the very mountainous eastern portion of Mindanao island. Our knowledge of their Flood tradition comes from one Melbourne Maxey, who spent many years among the Mandaya, prior to the publication of this text in 1913:

> "According to Mr. Maxey, the Mandays of Cateel believe that many generations ago a great flood occurred which caused the death of all the inhabitants of the world except one pregnant woman. She prayed that her child might be a boy. Her prayer was answered and she gave birth to a son whose name was Uacatan. He, when he had grown up, took his mother for his wife and from this union have sprung all the Mandaya."[35]

The water covered the whole earth and all the Ata were drowned except two men and a woman. They would have perished had not a large eagle come to their aid.

139 TAGALOG

The Tagalog, who are the majority people of Luzon, have a creation story with general parallels to Genesis.[36]

33. Fay-Cooper Cole, *The Wild Tribes of Davao District, Mindanao* (Chicago, 1913), p. 162. Cole's source, governor Edward Bolton, was murdered in 1906.
34. *Ibid.*, p. 164.
35. Cole, *The Wild Tribes of Davao District, Mindanao*, p. 173.
36. "When the world first began there was no land, but only the sea and the sky, and between them was a kite. One day the bird which had nowhere to light grew tired of flying about, so she stirred upon the sea until it threw its waters against the sky. The sky, in order to restrain the sea, showered upon it many islands until it could no longer rise, but ran back and forth. Then the sky ordered the kite to light on one of the islands to build her nest, and to leave the sea and the sky in peace.
Now at this time the land breeze and the sea breeze were married, and they had a child which was a bamboo. One day when this bamboo was floating about on the water, it struck the feet of the kite which was on the beach. The bird, angry that anything should strike it, pecked at the bamboo, and out of one section came a man and from the other a woman.
Then the earthquake called on all the birds and fish to see what should be done with this two, and it was decided that they should marry. Many children were born to the couple, and from them came all the different races of people." Mabel Cook Cole, *Philippine Folk Tales* (Chicago: McClurg, 1916), p. 187.

140 SUBANON

The Subanon people live in the mountains of the western part of Mindanao. They have a one-of-a-kind Flood story, which Myrna Promon recorded from them in 1993, with reference to their mountain known as Pinukis, or Mount Sugarloaf:

> "Now the reason Pinukis [Mount Sugarloaf] was so named was that when the enormous flood passed through, all the hills were covered with water. Pinukis was the only one not completely covered; the waves barely splashed back and forth over the very top of it. So it was said to have been scalped. Now there was a very large man. While the water was still high, this large man walked around on the surface of the water, of the water, carrying a basket.
>
> He picked up the people floating around and put them in his basket. But he said an incantation over them while he was putting them into the basket; he said, "It is not known which of these people has sinned. However, it will become evident which ones have sinned, because they will just fall through. Those who have not sinned will remain here in my basket." Because that basket of his had no bottom in it.
>
> Well, then the flood receded, he looked inside his basket. Only two people were left in it, a woman and a man. Then this large person said, "You two were the only ones without sin. So you two will now be the ones to populate the surface of the earth again." Now it is said that very large person was a giant."[37]

Then the flood receded, he looked inside his basket. Only two people were left in it, a woman and a man. Then this large person said, "You two were the only ones without sin."

The "giant" may be a memory of the "nephilim" in Genesis 6:4.[38]

141 HIGAONON

The name Higaonon means "people living in the mountains." The Higaonon people live in the mountains of north-central Mindanao. They are closely related to the Bukidnon and Manobo peoples. Francisco Demetrio heard a fragmentary reference to their Flood tradition:

> "Generally the survivors of the flood are a brother and a sister. There is another instant of a mother-son partnership. This was brought to my attention by Dr. Juan Francisco of U. P. [University of the Philippines] after I had written these pages. He says that the Flood-myth of the Higaunons of Magsaysay in northern Misamis Oriental tells of a mother and a son who survived the great flood."[39]

A second version says that only a pregnant woman survived the Flood, that is, with her son or sons still in the womb.[40] A third Higaonon version refers to "the occurrence of a great flood that forced them to go up the mountains to take shelter."[41]

37. Myrna Promon, "Pinukis," trans. Felicia Brichoux, (Summer Institute of Linguistics, 2002). Retrieved from https://www.sil.org/resources/archives/48638
38. For more on the subject of the "nephilim," see Dr. Tim Chaffey's book, *Fallen: The Sons of God and the Nephilim* (Burlington, KY: Risen Ministries, 2019).
39. Francisco Demetrio, "Creation Myths Among the Early Filipinos," *Asian Folklore Studies*, vol. 27, no. 1 (1968), p. 72.
40. "Various stories in Higaunon mythology relate that the Manobo came from the same female ancestor Gahomom ... even though the Manobo are considered "wild" and "without law" ... Gahomon, a pregnant woman, was the lone survivor of a great flood that occurred when something blocked the "pusud hu dagat," literally the "navel of the sea." Her children later became the ancestors of today's Higaunon and Manobo peoples." Oona Thommes Paredes, "True Believers: Higaunon and Manobo Evangelical Protestant Conversion in Historical and Anthropological Perspective," *Philippine Studies*, Vol. 54, No. 4 (2006), p. 526. Paredes's ultimate source, which is unavailable to me, is the unpublished notes of William E. Biernatzki, from his field research in 1978.
41. Phyllis Teanco, "The Indigenous Peoples (IPs) and their Ancestral Domain amid the pandemic: the Higaonon community as nature frontliners" (July 2021). Pre-print paper retrieved 18 November, 2023 from https://www.researchgate.net/publication/353513176_The_Indigenous_Peoples_IPs_and_their_Ancestral_Domain_amid_the_pandemic_the_Higaonon_community_as_nature_frontliners

142 BLAAN AND TBOLI

The Blaan and Tboli are closely related tribes, linguistically and geographically, living at the southern end of Mindanao. A very interesting Flood story has been found among the Tboli. Notice the divine warning that precedes the Flood, and a giant piece of bamboo as the vessel of escape:

> "In the T'boli origin myth, the god D'wata warns humans of a coming deluge. La Bebe, La Lomi, T'mefeles, and La Kagef hide inside a huge bamboo. After the waters recede, the four split their way out of the bamboo. La Bebe and La Lomi married, becoming the ancestors of the Christian Filipinos. La Kagef and T'mfeles also join and go on to produce 10 sons and daughters. Of these, Bou and Umen are the ancestors of the T'boli. The other 8 form couples; their descendants are the other non-Christian peoples of Mindanao, both Muslim and non-Muslim."[42]

Their relatives the Blaan have shared a creation story which has vague parallels with Genesis, but an important parallel on one point: the bird that was sent like Noah's dove during the Flood:

The god D'wata warns humans of a coming deluge. La Bebe, La Lomi, T'mefeles, and La Kagef hide inside a huge bamboo.

> "In the beginning there were four beings,and they lived on an island no larger than a hat. On this island there were no trees or grass or any other living thing besides these four people and one bird. One day they sent this bird out across the waters to see what he could find, and when he returned he brought some earth, a piece of rattan, and some fruit."[43]

This island surrounded by water is analogous to Noah's ark surrounded by water. The sending of a bird "to see what he could find," and which returns with "some earth, a piece of rattan, and some fruit" is clearly related to the account of Noah's dove returning with "a freshly plucked olive leaf in its beak" (Genesis 8:11).

143 ITNEG

The anthropologist Fay-Cooper Cole considered the Itneg (also known as Tinguian, but not to be confused with the Isneg) to have arrived at Luzon as part of a second wave of migration from the Indonesian Archipelago. Their ancestors "left their ancient home as a unit, at a time prior to the Hindu domination of Java and Sumatra, but probably not until the influence of that [Indian] civilization had begun to make itself felt."[44] Since that time, the Itneg have lived in the mountains of the Abra province of Luzon. Their Flood tradition is summarized as follows:

> "Learning of the plan [of the sea god to flood the world], Lang-an instructed her son to go up the highest mountain in the Cordillera with his household, to escape the great flood that was soon to come. And when it came, the flood filled up the valleys and plains, destroying crops and killing work animals. Then the floodwater surged up the mountain where Apo-ni-Tolau, his wife Humitau, and the warrior's household had sought safety. Humitau, who had lost her powers as a sea diwata (spirit) because she tasted her husband's mountain food, cried out to Tau-mari-u. Despite his anger, the lord of the sea took pity upon his favorite Humitau, and called back the floodwaters.
>
> But he vowed that thenceforth, he would sink boats and drown people in retribution for what Apo-ni-Tolau had done. After the deluge, Apo-ni-Tolau and Humitau came down the mountain, and had children who became the first people of the world."[45]

42. Jeneen Hobby and Timothy L. Gall, eds., *Worldmark Encyclopedia of Cultures and Daily Life*, vol. 4 (Pennsylvania State University, 2009), p. 963.
43. Mabel Cook Cole, *Philippine Folk Tales* (Chicago: McClurg, 1916), p. 141.
44. Fay-Cooper Cole, *The Tinguian: Social, Religious, and Economic Life of a Philippine Tribe* (Chicago: Field Museum of Natural History, 1922), pp. 235-236.
45. Damania L. Eugenio, *Philippine Folk Literature* (Quezon City, Philippines: University of the Philippines Press, 1989), p. 248.

That the woman Humitau suffered loss because she ate a forbidden food is most likely an echo of the first sin committed in the Garden of Eden, of which we find many traditions around the world. Mabel Cole (the wife of Fay-Cooper Cole) alluded to another Itneg narration of the Flood.[46]

Learning of the plan, Lang-an instructed her son to go up the highest mountain in the Cordillera with his household, to escape the great flood that was soon to come.

144 NABALOI

The Nabaloi live in the mountains of northwestern Luzon, in the province of Beguet. C.R. Moss collected many of their oral traditions between about 1910 and 1922, including the Flood tradition which follows. The Flood is attributed to a blockage of a river that drained the sea, which occurred when the woman guarding the drain fell asleep:

> "...The river became larger and larger until it had spread all over the land. All the people drowned but one brother and sister who had their box which they sailed. They were alive although there was no food. Then after a long time the river was cleared by an earthquake and became smaller. The box settled on Pulag [the highest peak on Luzon], where they built a house."[47]

At first, the siblings were unwilling to marry, but after receiving a sign, they married and produced offspring.[48]

145 LUZON TRADITION

The historian William Marsden shared an interesting Philippine tradition which has Flood and Creation parallels. Marsden's work was published in 1783, but he recorded this tradition some years prior to that. The tribal identity is not known, only that it is from the island of Luzon:

> "They believed that the world at first consisted only of sky and water, and between these two a Glede, which weary with flying about, and finding no place to rest, set the water at variance with the sky, which, in order to keep it in bounds, and that it should not get uppermost, loaded the water with a number of islands, in which the Glede might settle and leave them at peace. Mankind, they said, sprung out of a large cane with two joints, that floating about in the water, was at length thrown by the waves against the feet of the Glede, as it stood on the shore, which opened it with its bill, and the man came out of one joint, and the woman out the other. These were soon after married by consent of their God, Bathala Meycapal, which caused the first trembling of the earth; and from hence are descended the different nations of the world."[49]

Glede in Flight

46. "The Tinguian tale is as follows: Once in the very old times Kaboniyan sent a flood which covered all the land. Then there was no place for the fire to stay, so it went into the bamboo, the stones, and iron. That is why one who knows how [one] can still get fire out of bamboo and stones." Cole, *Philippine Folk Tales*, p. 103.
47. C.R. Moss, "Nabaloi Tales," *University of California Publications in American Archaeology and Anthropology*, vol. 17, no. 5 (Berkeley: University of California Press, 1924), pp. 233-235.
48. *Ibid.*, p. 235. "Then one day Kabunian came to cause them to marry, but they said, "We are brother and sister." They always slept in separate beds, but one morning when they awoke they were surprised to be in one bed. Finally they had twin children, a boy and a girl. Then many twins were born. They increased rapidly, and they are our ancestors."
49. William Marsden, *The History of Sumatra* (London, 1783), p. 259.

Island of Nuku Hiva, French Polynesia

OCEANIA

We come now to the islands of Polynesia, Micronesia, and Melanesia that are scattered across the largest ocean on Earth.[1] Do these islanders have any memory of the ancient Flood and of the other events recorded in Genesis 1-11? Indeed they do. In fact, the Polynesians and other islanders possess some of the most remarkable, well-preserved traditions to be found anywhere in the world. Their traditions tell of the Flood, the Tower of Babel, and Creation.

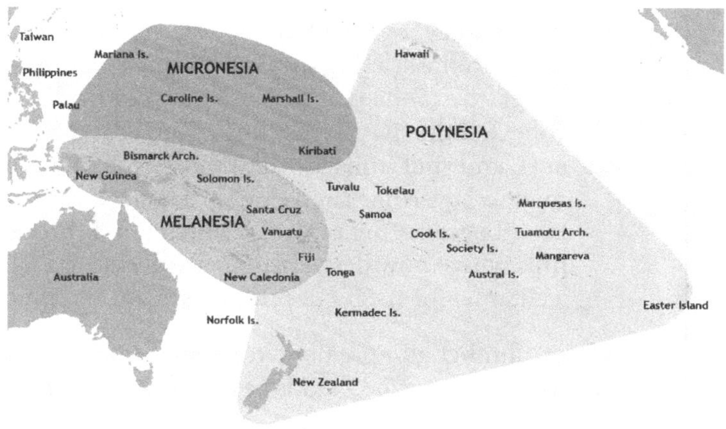

The Islands of Polynesia, Melanesia, and Micronesia

But in my mind, the most significant part of this chapter is a recurring story of the creation of the first woman from a rib taken from the first man. Not fewer than nine locations across the Pacific have yielded sacred traditions of the time that Eve was created! This is a revolutionary finding which confirms the witness of Genesis 2. Indeed, this story is found in various parts of the world, but nowhere with greater frequency than in the Pacific. Indigenous history continues to confirm the biblical record.

1. New Guinea, formally part of Melanesia, is reserved for the next chapter of this book. This is due to the incredible diversity of New Guinea and the large volume of material.

Tribes of the Region

146. Vanuatu
147. Lifou (Loyalty Islands)
148. Maori (New Zealand)
149. Tuamotu Archipelago
150. Admiralty Islands
151. Mo'orea
152. Makira
153. Tahiti and Eastern Society Islands
154. Raiatea and Western Society Islands
155. Hawaii
156. Yap (Caroline Islands)
157. Marquesas Islands
158. Samoa
159. Palau
160. Mangaia (Cook Islands)
161. Fiji
162. Kadavu
163. Aniwa
164. Erromango
165. Easter Island
166. Fakaofo (Tokelau Archipelago)
167. Nanumanga (Tuvalu)
168. Rakahanga (Cook Islands)
169. Nakanai (New Britain Island)
170. Tolai (New Britain Island)
171. New Britain Island Tradition
172. Chuuk

146

VANUATU

Vanuatu, formerly known as New Hebrides, is a group of small islands located about 1,200 miles northeast of Australia. The natives have a distinct memory of Noah's Ark, which they told to Robert Codrington sometime between 1863 and 1877:

People of Vanuatu

> "Where now in the centre of that island is the great lake, the Tas, there was formerly a great plain covered with forest. Qat cut himself a large canoe there out of one of the largest trees. While making it he was often ridiculed by his brothers, and asked how he would ever get so large a canoe to the sea. He answered always that they would see by-and-by. When the canoe was finished he took inside it his wife and brothers, collected the living creatures of the island, even those so small as ants, and shut himself with them inside the canoe, to which he had made a covering. Then came a deluge of rain; the great hollow of the island became full of water, which burst through the surrounding hills where now descends the great waterfall of Gaua. The canoe tore a channel for itself out into the sea and disappeared."[2]

We get another glimpse of their memory of the Flood from what the natives of Aneityum (one of the islands of the Vanuatu archipelago) told John Inglis in the year 1850:

> "They have the same traditions respecting the creation, the deluge, and some other great facts of universal history [as the eastern Pacific islands] ... [as a] consequence of the wickedness of the people, the gods were angry, and one of them sent a flood, which drowned all the people except a man and his wife that were saved in a canoe."[3]

And finally, note the native islanders' reaction when they heard the story from Genesis, which is so similar to their own traditions:

> "A native was one day listening to an oral translation of the flood, made by one of the Missionaries. He appeared particularly attentive, and at last said to the Missionary, "Stop! That is almost the same as our account;" and after detailing their tradition, he added, "But your forefathers have written an account for you, while ours only told it to their children: yours must be more correct than ours.""[4]

"Stop! That is almost the same as our account;" and after detailing their tradition, he added, "But your forefathers have written an account for you, while ours only told it to their children: yours must be more correct than ours."

Therefore glorify Yahweh in the east,
the name of Yahweh, the God of Israel,
in the coastlands of the sea.(Isaiah 24:15)

2. Robert Henry Codrington, *The Melanesians: Studies in their Anthropology and Folklore* (Oxford: Clarendon Press, 1891), pp. 166-167.
3. John Inglis, "Report of a Missionary Tour in the New Hebrides," *Journal of the Ethnological Society of London*, vol. 3 (1854), p. 61.
4. *Ibid.*

147 LIFOU

Lifou is the largest of the Loyalty Islands, a small archipelago almost 1,000 miles to the east of Australia. These islands were not discovered by Europeans until about 1803, and little meaningful contact with the natives until the 1840s.

In a work published in 1873, the missionary Samuel McFarlane wrote: "Many of the Lifuan traditions bear a striking resemblance to the records of sacred history."[5] These include traditions of the origin of sin and death, the Flood, and the Tower of Babel.

The Origin of Sin and Death (the Fall):

The Lifuans have, first of all, a memory of the original paradise:

> "The natives have no idea of the origin of the first man; they only know that his name was Walelimeme; that he had a wife and sons, and that he lived in peace amidst plenty. At that time there was not any sickness or death, and it was not necessary to work in plantations, because the food grew spontaneously and in abundance."[6]

Next, we come to their account of how immortality was lost. In this text we can see several parallels with the Garden of Eden. A memory of the actions of Noah, the old man, in Genesis 9 is mixed in as well: in particular, his drinking and his dealings with his three sons:

> "It appears that the sons of old Walelimeme had the power of changing themselves into birds, beasts, and reptiles at pleasure. On one occasion the eldest son, in the form of a rat, went on an exploring expedition, boring his way through the earth until he came to the residence of an old man, the chief of the lower regions. This old chief lived upon yams, of which there were not any at that time on Lifu. The Lifuan observed that the old man kept the yams for himself, and offered him other food; he asked to taste the yams, but was told that they were for the old chief alone, and that to take them would cost him his life. The son of Walelimeme, however, did not believe this, and watching his opportunity picked up a yam, and made for the surface of the earth again. On his way he tasted the yam and found it very good; on his arrival at home, he called one of his brothers and told him all; this brother tasted the yam and expressed his delight at the discovery of such excellent food. They then went to their father, who with the whole family tasted and were all equally pleased at the new discovery."[7]

The old chief was angry with them, and told them that as they had taken his yams, he would henceforth live upon human flesh. It was then that people began to die.

After this, they determined to go and steal a quantity of yams from the old chief below, and to plant them on earth. So they did, but they were discovered before they could escape. The sentence handed down is evocative of Genesis 3:

> "The old chief was angry with them, and told them that as they had taken his yams, he would henceforth live upon human flesh. Death should reign on Lifu in order to supply him with food. It was then that people began to die, as the Lifuans supposed, to supply the old chief with human flesh in exchange for his yams; … It was then that labour commenced, for having begun planting yams they found it necessary to cultivate every other article of food: nothing would grow

5. Samuel McFarlane, *The Story of the Lifu Mission* (London: James Nisbet & Co., 1873), p. 17.
6. *Ibid.*, p. 17.
7. *Ibid.*, pp. 17-18.

spontaneously as before, but weeds. Thus yams, their principal and much-liked food were introduced, but with them came labour and death."[8]

Nol's canoe was lifted by the waters and borne along by a current; it struck a high rock which was still out of the water, and split it in two.

The Flood:

Regarding their knowledge of the global Flood, McFarlane wrote:

> "They have a tradition substantially the same as the scripture account of the flood. It is that an old man named Nol (the name resembles Noah) made a canoe inland; the natives laughed at him for making it so far from the sea, declaring that they would not help him to drag it to the coast; but he told them that it would not be necessary, for the sea would come to it.
>
> When it was finished the rain fell in torrents and flooded the island, drowning everybody. Nol's canoe was lifted by the waters and borne along by a current; it struck a high rock which was still out of the water, and split it in two. (These two rocks are still pointed out by the natives; they form the heads of a fine bay on the north side of the Island.) The water then rushed into the sea and left Lifu "high and dry."[9]

How amazing it is to find a memory of this "high rock," which is Ararat, recounted by a nation on the opposite side of the world.

They also speak of a time when their forefathers assembled at a place near my station to erect a scaffolding which should reach to the clouds.

Tower of Babel:

Finally, the Lifou tradition of the Tower of Babel:

> "They also speak of a time when their forefathers assembled at a place near my station to build, or rather erect a scaffolding which should reach to the clouds. They had no idea of works in stone, hence their "tower of Babel" was raised by tying stick to stick with native vines. They labored on undaunted by the sad consequences of the discovery and stealing of yams underground; perhaps they anticipated a more agreeable issue to their explorations in the heavens. But alas for human expectations; before the top touched the clouds, the ground-posts became rotten, and the whole affair came down with a crash."[10]

The islanders were truly amazed when they heard the words of Scripture, which agreed with their traditions. This made them very receptive to the good news of Jesus:

These traditions had their weight in leading the people to embrace Christianity.

> "These traditions had their weight in leading the people to embrace Christianity. When the teachers arrived, they listened to the story of the fall, and said, "Yes, this is no doubt true, it is very much like what our fathers told us. They eat the forbidden yam, and death came among us, and we had all to work to provide food. Noah's ark was Nol's canoe, and the Tower of Babel was the ancient "ija" or scaffolding."[11]

8. *Ibid.*, pp. 18-19.
9. *Ibid.*, p. 19.
10. *Ibid.*, pp. 19-20.
11. *Ibid.*, p. 21.

148

MAORI

The Maori are the original people of New Zealand. The Maori have a class of priests responsible for meticulously guarding their sacred traditions. During the 1860s, one John White had earned their trust to the point that they narrated their traditions to him, including this Flood tradition:

> "Men had become very numerous on the earth. There were many great tribes. Evil prevailed everywhere. The tribes quarreled, and wars were frequent. The worship of Tane was neglected, and his doctrines openly denied. … But Para-whenua-mea and Tupu-nui-a-uta continued to preach until the tribes cursed them by saying, "You two can eat the words of history as food for you, and you can eat the heads of the words of that history." Then the two teachers were very much grieved."[12]

Mocked and scorned, the two men remained resolute, and they began constructing a giant raft. They "built a house on the raft, and put much food into it." Taking a few other people with them, they got onto the raft. The priest Tiu prayed that it would rain. So it rained in great torrents. "The water was now great, like an ocean, and the raft began to move about hither and thither. All men and women and children were drowned of those who denied the truth of the doctrines preached by Tane."[13]

Finally, after months adrift, they landed on dry ground at Ha-wai-ki.[14] They thought they would find survivors, but behold, everyone had drowned! Then, in a remarkable parallel to Genesis 8:20-9:17, they offered a sacrifice in worship, and a rainbow appeared in the sky:

They "built a house on the raft, and put much food into it." … The priest Tiu prayed that it would rain. So it rained in great torrents.

> "When they landed on the earth their first act was to perform ceremonies and repeat incantations. They performed these to Tane, to Rangi, and to Rehua, and all the gods. Sea-weed was the sacred offering given in place of slain sacrifice. … On the morrow, when they awoke, they produced fire by friction, and heated the [oven]. … then looking up, they beheld the rainbow and Rongo-nui-a-tau (great news of the whole year) in the sky; to which Tiu at once offered sacrifices."[15]

Another narration is similar, but in summary form:

> "In ancient history we are told that Tupu-tupu-nui-auta was the cause of the flood. He was the son of Para-whenua-mea. He asked for rain, and such torrents descended as produced a flood, which continued to rise until the plains, and hills, and the highest peaks of the mountains were covered by it; and all mankind, except those who had prepared a raft, and had taken refuge on it, perished in the water."[16]

All mankind, except those who had prepared a raft, and had taken refuge on it, perished in the water.

A third version is also similar. A God-fearing man named Puta was "commissioned to call on all the people of the world to believe in God. He built a temple in which to teach men how to become noble." However, it says "the tribes were rebellious," and they answered Puta, saying, "Your words are lies." Later, Puta "called to Raki to overturn the earth, and he struck the earth with his knife, and the earth turned upside down, and all the people of the world perished. Puta and his people alone were saved."[17]

12. John White, *The Ancient History of the Maori*, vol. 1 (Wellington: George Disbury, 1887), pp. 172-173.
13. *Ibid.*, pp. 173-174.
14. Not to be confused with Hawaii. Hawaii is merely named after this ancient homeland, Havaiki, to which many Polynesian traditions point back. The location of this Havaiki is unknown, but China is a possibility.
15. *Ibid.*, pp. 177-180.
16. *Ibid.*, p. 180.
17. *Ibid.*, pp. 169-170.

Creation

Regarding the creation, the Maori have passed down the following tradition. The parallels with Genesis 1 are evident:

> "Io dwelt within the breathing-space of immensity.
> The Universe was in darkness, with water everywhere.
> There was no glimmer of dawn, no clearness, no light.
> And he began by saying these words,
> That He might cease remaining inactive:
> 'Darkness, become a light-possessing darkness.'
> And at once light appeared.
> (He) then repeated those self-same words in this manner,
> That He might cease remaining inactive:
> 'Light, become a darkness-possessing light.'
> And again an intense darkness supervened.
> Then a third time He spake saying:
> 'Let there be one darkness above,
> Let there be one darkness below (alternate). …
> Let there be one light above,
> Let there be one light below (alternate). …
> A dominion of light, a bright light.'
> And now a great light preveailed.
> (Io) then looked to the waters which compassed him about,
> And spake a fourth time, saying:
> 'Ye waters of Tai-kama, be ye separate.
> Heaven, be formed.' Then the sky became suspended.
> 'Bring-forth tou Tupua-horo-nuku.'
> And at once the moving earth lay stretched abroad."[18]

We will hear from the Maori once more. John Nicholas recorded the statement below from them in 1814. This account refers to "the creation of man, and has been handed down from father to son, through all generations":

> "They likewise believe, which is more curious than all, that the first woman was made of one of the man's ribs, and to add still more to this strange coincidence, their general term for bone is Hevee."[19]

They likewise believe that the first woman was made of one of the man's ribs.

18. Hare Hongi (trans.), "A Maori Cosmogony," *Journal of the Polynesian Society*, vol. 16 (1907), pp. 109-114. The tradition was delivered to one Colonel Gudgeon by a Maori man named Tiwai Parsons, "some years ago," relative to publication in 1907. No doubt, the Maori man was concerned for his tribe's tradition to be preserved for posterity. Hare Hongi translated it to English. The editor adds, on p. 109, "It is interesting, as accrediting the great (and almost unknown) god Io with the creation of the Heavens and the Earth from Chaos, and as showing him to be the progenitor of the other gods of the Maori. The great god-creator Io, was so sacred in character that his name could, in former times, only be mentioned under circumstances involving the complete absence of everything of a contaminating nature; and, indeed, his very name is believed to have been unknown to all but the highest class of priesthood." And in evidence of the tradition's antiquity, he adds, "De Bovis has recorded a very similar cosmogony to this, from Tahiti, in which the Maori Io, is rendered as Ihoiho. It will be remembered that in the very fine Samoan "Chant of Creation" (J.P.S., vol. v., p. 19), Tangaroa takes the place of Io. Both accounts are no doubt based on the same original belief."
19. John Liddiard Nicholas, *Narrative of a Voyage to New Zealand, Performed in the Years 1814 and 1815, in Company with the Rev. Samuel Marsden,* vol. 1 (London: J. Black and Son, 1817), p. 59.

The first woman was created from a rib taken from the first man? The parallels to Genesis 2:20-23 here may seem impossible to believe. Yet as we will see in the following pages, this story is a recurring and well-attested one across many islands of the South Pacific.

Fakarava Atoll

149 TUAMOTU ARCHIPELAGO

The Tuamotus are an archipelago of small islands in the remote South Pacific. The natives have traditions with remarkable parallels to Genesis regarding Creation, the Flood, and the Tower of Babel.

At the island of Hao, the tradition that they told to the historian Eugene Caillot, between 1912 and 1913, went as follows. Note the similarity to how God created man and woman in Genesis 2:

When the earth was finished, he made the man, called Tiki, and his wife, Hina. Hina comes from a rib of Tiki.

> "We have three gods: Vateanukumauatua, Tane, and Tagaroa. It is Vatea who made the earth and the sky and all the things that are there. Vatea made the earth flat. The sky was adhering to it. Tane raised it, and Tagaroa kept it up and separate from the earth.
>
> The name of the land was Havaiki. When the earth was finished, he [Vatea] made the man, called Tiki, and his wife, Hina. Hina comes from a rib of Tiki. They slept together, and they had children."[20]

Next, their tradition contains a genealogy of ten generations of husband-wife pairs, culminating in a man named Rata and his wife Tepupura. It also tells that they had three sons, named Ataruru, Atamea, and Ataia.[21] This accords exactly with the ten generations from Adam to Noah, and the fact that Noah had three sons. As to the ten generations, remember that this detail is attested in a few texts and traditions from China.

Next, it has an account of a great Flood and the confusion of languages:

The Hao Islanders genealogy accords exactly with the ten generations from Adam to Noah, and the fact that Noah had three sons.

> "Men did evil on this earth and Vatea [God] was in a rage. He told Rata to build the canoe that would serve as a refuge. This canoe was named "Papapapa I Hunua" (flat land). It had to hold Rata and his wife, who was called Tepupura I Tetai, and their children, three of them, with their wives.
>
> Then the rain fell in torrents from the top of the space, that is to say, from the sky, and this earth was invaded by the waves. In the anger of Vatea, the gates of heaven were broken, the rain fell in great mass, and the wind was let loose. The earth was destroyed and submerged by the sea.
>
> Rata, his wife, and their three children, with their wives, had taken refuge in the hut (of the canoe); and six hundred and one epochs later, they came out when the waters had receded. They were then saved, as were all the birds and animals, the crawling creatures on the ground, and those flying in space, as well as their young.

20. Auguste Charles Eugène Caillot, *Mythes, légendes et traditions des Polynésiens* (Paris: Ernest Leroux, 1914), pp. 7-8.
21. *Ibid.*, p. 9.

> After that, this earth is filled with human beings. Atamea was the ancestor of Tetuhura, Ataruru the ancestor of Tetini (or Kokere), from whom descended Mutu. As for Ataia, he was the ancestor of Tuauki.
>
> Then the languages changed. He formed three: that of Tetuhura, that of Kokere, and that of Mutu, his descendant.
>
> At the time of the construction of the wall at Maragai, in the Havaiki land, we had, as in ancient times, only one language. But our ancestors told us to build the wall to reach the top of the sky and see Vatea. But he, being angry, broke the wall, drove away all those who built it, and then changed their language. Some had one language, others had another, and others still another language. Tetuhura, Kokere, and Mutu, the descendant, each had their own language, so that they could no longer understand each other, nor complete this wall, because of Vatea's anger."[22]

In the Havaiki land, we had, as in ancient times, only one language. But our ancestors told us to build the wall to reach the top of the sky and see Vatea.

The native islanders at Makemo told Caillot a very similar tradition. What's more, Kenneth Emory (1897-1992) found that this tradition had been recorded even earlier, in manuscripts written in 1853, on another island (Takaroa). However, Emory refused to believe this was anything other than "missionary influence."[23]

How should we respond to Emory's claim that this tradition must be the product of Christian teaching and missionary influence? Beyond what we have said in the Introduction, we have very good reasons, in the case of these particular texts, to affirm their originality:

1. The natives themselves insisted to Caillot that it was an ancient tradition that pre-dated the arrival of Europeans.[24]
2. This tradition was recovered in a relatively short time from the arrival of westerners (less than 50 years).
3. Caillot affirmed that the tradition contains many archaic words that they no longer know the meaning of, indicating its antiquity.[25]
4. There is clearly native material which conflicts with Genesis, such as many gods and a "wall" instead of a "tower."
5. Their genealogies give names which are not at all in the Bible. If Christian teaching were really the cause, we should find from Genesis such as Ham, Shem, and Japheth. But there is none of that here.
6. It is in agreement with other Polynesian traditions on many points.
7. If they got it from missionaries, where is the knowledge of other memorable biblical narratives such as the Exodus and the miracles of Moses, David and Goliath, the virgin birth, and the miracles of Jesus?
8. The Polynesians are known to have possessed very long genealogies, and meticulously preserved traditions.[26]

In summary, the reasons for accepting the authenticity of this particular tradition are strong. The reasons for rejecting it have more to do with a commitment to secular humanism. In any case, the reader can judge for themselves. The fact of the universal pervasiveness of the memory of Noah's Flood hardly depends on this one data point.

22. *Ibid.*, pp. 9-11.
23. Kenneth P. Emory, "The Tuamotuan Creation Charts By Paiore," *Journal of the Polynesian Society*, vol. 48, no. 1 (Wellington, NZ: The Polynesian Society, 1939), p. 19.
24. *Ibid.*
25. Caillot, *Mythes, légendes et traditions des Polynésiens*, p. 16.
26. See, for example: Percy Smith, *Havaiki: The Original Home of the Maori* (Christchurch: Whitcomb and Tombs, 1904), p. 23. John White, *The Ancient History of the Maori*, vol. 1 (Wellington: George Disbury, 1887), pp. iii-iv.

150 ADMIRALTY ISLANDS

The Admiralty Islands are an archipelago about 170 miles north of New Guinea. They probably possessed a Flood tradition, but we have not been able to recover it. What we have recovered, however, is a rather clear memory of the Tower of Babel. Josef Meier recorded this around the year 1900:

> "The Lohi people were one hundred and thirty. The chief of the Lohi was a man named Muikiu. He said to his people, 'Let's build a house going high in the sky!' So the men of Lohi began building the house. The structure was getting very tall. It was not far from reaching the sky itself. Then Po Awi, a man from Kali, came to Muikiu. He forbade him from building higher, and said, 'Who told you to build a house so high?' Muikiu said, 'I am the chief of this people, the Lohi. I said, let us build a house that goes high up to heaven. So we would do, if I had my way. But, my brother, it will be your way. We will build our houses low.' So Muikiu took water, and splashed it on his people. Then their language changed. Some went this way, some went that way. They were scattered. That is why each country has its own language."[27]

He said to his people, 'Let's build a house going high in the sky!' ... Then their language changed. Some went this way, some went that way. They were scattered. That is why each country has its own language.

151 MO'OREA

The people of Mo'orea, an island just a few miles west of Tahiti, also possessed a tradition of the Flood. William Ellis heard this from them around the 1820s:

> "The memorial preserved by the inhabitants of Eimeo [Mo'orea], states, that after the inundation of the land, when the water subsided, a man landed from a canoe near Tiataepua, in their island, and erected an altar, or marae, in honour of his god."[28]

This is reminiscent of Noah's burnt offering sacrifice to God, for we read that after exiting the Ark, "Then Noah built an altar to Yahweh and took of every clean animal and of every clean bird and offered burnt offerings on the altar." (Genesis 8:20)

Ellis also wrote more broadly of the consistent testimony to the Flood which he heard throughout the islands of Polynesia:

> "The principal facts are the same in the traditions prevailing among the inhabitants of the different groups, although they differ in several minor particulars."[29]
>
> "Traditions of the deluge, the most important event in the reference to the external structure and appearance of our globe that has occurred since its creation, have been found to exist among the natives of the South Sea Islands, from the earliest periods of their history."[30]

Regarding these traditions of the Deluge, Ellis says that "in one group, the accounts state, that in ancient times Taaroa, the principal god ... being angry with men on account of their disobedience to his will, overturned the world in the sea, when the earth sunk in the waters, excepting a few aurus, or projecting points, which remaining above its surface, constituted the present cluster of islands."[31]

"Traditions of the deluge, the most important event in the reference to the external structure and appearance of our globe that has occurred since its creation, have been found to exist among the natives of the South Sea Islands, from the earliest periods of their history." (William Ellis, ca. 1820s)

The memorial preserved by the inhabitants of Mo'orea, states, that after the inundation of the land, when the water subsided, a man landed from a canoe near Tiataepua, in their island, and erected an altar, or marae, in honour of his god.

---

27. Josef Meier, "Mythen und Sagen der Admiralitätinsulaner," *Anthropos*, vol. 2 (Salzburg, 1907), pp. 933-934.
28. William Ellis, *Polynesian Researches*, vol. 1 (London: Fisher, Son, & Jackson, 1831), p. 387.
29. *Ibid.*, p. 387.
30. *Ibid.*
31. *Ibid.*, pp. 387-388.

152

MAKIRA

Creation:

Mou'aroa (Shark's Tooth), Mo'orea

Makira, formerly called San Cristobal Island, is the largest of the Solomon Islands. The natives possess a very impressive tradition of the creation of the first man and woman, which they narrated to Charles Elliot Fox around the year 1905:

> "He [the god Hatiubwari] came down to the mountain Hoto (in one legend) and here he created men. It is curious that in almost all the tales the woman is created first. He took hard red clay and rolled this in his lands till it became plastic, he breathed on it and rolled it again, and then he formed a clay image, forming the head, legs, and arms. This red clay image he then placed in the sun, and by and by the heat of the sun caused it to live. It was a woman. Later, when the woman slept, Hatuibwari took a rib from her side, he added more red clay and moulded this also, and from this he made a man. This first woman and man had children and increased."[32]

Amazingly, they say that God created man from a rib taken from the woman! They remember the fact that God took a rib from the first person to create the other. They simply reverse the order of the man and the woman!

When the woman slept, Hatuibwari took a rib from her side, he added more red clay and moulded this also, and from this he made a man.

Fox himself gave his verdict, "I do not think there is any echo of Mission teaching in this myth. I never heard it from the coast, but first got it from an old man of probably the most inaccessible bush village, Bonibwaroto." And he added, "The old men of the Arosi bush, who are uninfluenced by Christianity, unite in considering these stories of the creation of the first pair (and of the flood) to be genuine native traditions, and I can see no good grounds for rejecting this evidence."[33]

I (Nick) fully agree with Fox, and would add that this rib tradition is found not only on Makira, but throughout the Polynesian Islands.

Flood:

The Makirans also have a remarkably well-preserved tradition of the Flood:

> "The first people who came to San Cristoval, so runs one Arosi story, came in the time of the great "Ruarua," a flood of waters from rain and oncoming sea combined, the Ruarua that according to some accounts

32. Charles Elliot Fox, *The Threshold of the Pacific: An Account of the Social Organization, Magic And Religion of the People of San Cristoval In the Solomon Islands* (London: K. Paul, Trench, Trubner & Co., 1924), p. 238.
33. *Ibid.*, pp. 238-239.

> covered the whole of San Cristoval, even the highest hills over 4,000 feet high! They came in a large canoe from Mwara (Malaita) … but originally from a country far to the north-west, whose name is known and handed down. … From this mysterious land the great canoe came to Mwara and thence to Arosi, a very large canoe, full of men, women, pigs, and dogs … until the canoe touched on the plateau inland, a place still sacred.[34]

Not only do they remember the Flood and the "very large canoe," but also the rainbow given as a promise by God:

> "I have already mentioned the tradition of this flood, which covered the highest hills of San Cristoval. The majority of the people of those days were drowned, and you may see them turned into stone pillars at Mwata, but some were saved in a very large canoe. The leader was Umaroa, and he had with him some others (Arara, Oha, Poro'ua, Waita, and Rabei, and some more) and pigs, dogs, and birds, two of each sort. They landed at Robwana, near Waimarai, and descended to the stream Wai abu (Sacred Water) to bathe, when an adaro [spirit] holding a bow came down to them in a rainbow (the usual adaro road) and told them where to live, after Umaroa had offered a sacrifice by the stream."[35]

They claimed that a rainbow continues to appear at their sacred place from time to time (there is no spray to cause a rainbow), as a sign of the first rainbow that appeared after the Flood.[36] Regardless of the truth of this claim, it shows what they believed about the Flood and God's promise, in agreement with Genesis.

They claimed that a rainbow still appears at their sacred place from time to time, as a sign of the first rainbow that appeared after the Flood.

"Andrew Lang very rightly observes that the personal bias of ethnological writers must always be taken into account in estimating the trustworthiness of their conclusions. There are some to whom the Bible stories seem to be anathema, and they unconsciously reject quite good evidence on no real grounds except their own bias." (Charles Elliot Fox, *The Threshold of the Pacific*, p. 238)

Tower of Babel:

Fox mentioned the existence of traditions with Genesis parallels from one of their clans, the Araha. These traditions even included a faint memory of the Tower of Babel:

> "They have further tales of the creation of man from red clay, of the coming of death, of a great flood, and of an attempt to build up to the sky."[37]

Regarding that attempt to build up to the sky, Fox heard this tradition in connection with a legendary village from ancient times, named Ba-eba-earo:

> "This is a legendary village near Heuru. The people divided themselves into two companies, and made a stairway with the object of climbing up into the sky; one company cutting the material and the other putting it together. They all climbed up together, but when very high the stairway fell and all were killed. They were not Masi or Kakamora, but ordinary people."[38]

34. *Ibid.*, p. 9.
35. *Ibid.*, p. 263.
36. *Ibid.*
37. *Ibid.*, p. 362.
38. *Ibid.*, p. 336.

153 **Flood and Tower of Babel:**

The natives of Tahiti and the Society Islands had their Flood tradition too, as they told to a missionary named John Orsmond:

> "Destroyed was Tahiti by the sea; no man, nor hog, nor fowl, nor dog, remained. The groves of trees, and the stones, were carried away by the wind. They were destroyed, and the deep was over the land." [39]

They made a stairway to climb up into the sky. ... The stairway fell and all were killed.

To summarize, this tradition tells that two persons, a husband and wife, took up their animals, and fled to a mountain called Pito-hiti. "They two arrived there. [Mount] Orohena was overwhelmed by the sea; that mountain, Pito-hiti, (alone) remained, that was their abode. There they watched nights ten [ten nights], the sea ebbed, and they two saw the little heads of the mountains in their elevation." From these two people, the world was repopulated.[40]

This tradition adds a notion that the wind carried great stones and trees into the sky, and that when the Flood began to subside, these fell dangerously from the sky. Perhaps this is a mixed memory of the wind that God sent to help end the Flood (Genesis 8:1) and the Tower of Babel (Genesis 11).

Creation, and Woman Created from Man's Rib

Amazingly, the Tahitians also have a persistent tradition of the creation of man and woman, which they told to William Ellis in the 1820s. "The first human pair were made by Taaroa, the principal deity formerly acknowledged by the nation. On more than one occasion, I have listened to the details of the people respecting his work of creation."[41]

> "They say, that after Taaroa had formed the world, he created man out of "araea," red earth, which was also the food of man until bread-fruit was produced. In connection with this, some relate that Taaroa one day called for the man by name. When he came, he caused him to fall asleep, and that, while he slept, he took out one of his "ivi," or bones, and with it made a woman, whom he gave to the man as his wife, and that they became the progenitors of mankind."[42]

Ellis found this so strikingly similar to Genesis that he wondered whether it was genuine. "Should more careful and minute inquiry confirm the truth of their declaration, and prove that this account was in existence among them prior to their intercourse with Europeans, it will be the most remarkable and valuable oral tradition of the origin of the human race yet known."[43]

Well, old Ellis would be thrilled at the discoveries that have come to light! We now possess confirming evidence in the form of similar traditions from many far-flung islands across the South Pacific. Stories of the creation of the first woman from a rib taken from the first man have been found not only at Tahiti, but also in New Zealand, Tuamotu, Makira, Hawaii, Erromango, Rapa Nui (Easter Island), Fakaofo, and the Chuuk Islands.

39. Ellis, *Polynesian Researches*, vol. 1, p. 387.
40. *Ibid.*, pp. 387-389.
41. *Ibid.*, p. 110.
42. *Ibid.*
43. *Ibid.*, p. 111.

Table 5: "First Woman Created from First Man's Rib" Traditions in Polynesia		
Location	**Relevant Text**	**Page**
Tahiti	"Taaroa one day called for the man by name. When he came, he caused him to fall asleep, and that, while he slept, he took out one of his "ivi," or bones, and with it made a woman, whom he gave to the man as his wife, and that they became the progenitors of mankind."	178
1New Zealand (Maori)	"The first woman was made of one of the man's ribs, and to add still more to this strange coincidence, their general term for bone is Hevee."	172
Tuamotu	"When the earth was finished, he [Vatea] made the man, called Tiki, and his wife, Hina. Hina comes from a rib of Tiki. They slept together, and they had children."	173
Makira	"This red clay image he then placed in the sun, and by and by the heat of the sun caused it to live. It was a woman. Later, when the woman slept, Hatuibwari took a rib from her side, he added more red clay and moulded this also, and from this he made a man. This first woman and man had children and increased."	176
Hawaii	"The body of the first man was made of red earth … and the spittle of the gods … and his head was made of a whitish clay … Afterwards the first woman was created from one of the ribs—lalo puhaka—of the man while asleep, and these two were the progenitors of all mankind."	182
Erromango	"Nobu [God] made a man and then, seeing that he was lonely, made a woman from a part of the man's body. As the children which the woman bore to the man grew to puberty they were sent to different parts of the island and there founded families."	191
Easter Island	"Lastly, Makemake impregnated some clay, and from it man was born. Makemake saw his creation and was pleased. Later, Makemake saw that things were not quite right—the man was alone. Makemake made the man sleep in his own house, and when he had fallen asleep, Makemake impregnated the ribs on his left side and woman was born."	192
Fakaofo	"The stone became changed into a man called Vasefanua. After a time he thought of making a woman. This he did by collecting a quantity of earth, and forming an earth model on the ground. He made the head, body, arms, and legs all of earth, then took out a rib from his left side and thrust it inside of the earth model, when suddenly the earth became alive, and up started a woman on her feet. He called her Ivi (Eevee), or rib, he took her to be his wife, and from them sprang the race of men."	193
Chuuk Islands	"The spirit came back and took a rib from the man's left side and made a woman out of it. Then he stuck his finger in the bleeding hole and dripped the blood onto the woman's head and limbs. He also blew into her nose and she lived."	196

As a result, we no longer have a reason to deny that this Creation account of the Polynesians is authentic, ancient, and aboriginal. This has major implications for anthropology, though not everyone in the field will be excited about it. Nor is it only in the South Pacific that we find such traditions, for we find them in North America, Greenland, South America, and beyond.

In short, the Tahitian Creation story is no anomaly or outlier. It is but one specimen of a very impressive set of historical traditions of the Creation, the Flood, and the Tower of Babel from the Polynesian peoples that inhabit the remote Pacific.

> We no longer have a reason to deny that the Creation account of the Polynesians is authentic, ancient, and aboriginal.

RAIATEA AND WESTERN SOCIETY ISLANDS

At Raiatea and the western Society Islands, the Flood tradition which Ellis heard went as follows: Long ago, a man went in his canoe and fished in sacred, forbidden waters. His hooks got caught in the hair of an underwater god, named Ruahatu, who "appeared at the surface of the water, and, after upbraiding him for his impiety, declared, that the land was criminal, or convicted of guilt, and should be destroyed."[44]

> "The affrighted fisherman prostrated himself before the god of the sea, confessed his sorrow for what he had done, and implored his forgiveness, beseeching him that the judgment denounced might be averted, or that he might escape. Ruahatu, moved by his penitence and importunity, directed him to return home for his wife and child, and then proceed to a small island called Toamarama, which is situated within the reefs on the eastern side of Raiatea. Here he was promised security, amid the destruction of the surrounding islands. The man hastened to his residence, and proceeded with his wife and child to the place appointed."[45]

The man and his family took their domestic animals with them in their escape. Next, we read:

> "They reached the refuge appointed, before the close of the day; and as the sun approached the horizon, the waters of the ocean began to rise, the inhabitants of the adjacent shore left their dwellings on the beach, and fled to the mountains. The waters continued to rise during the night, and the next morning the tops of the mountains only appeared, above the wide-spread sea. These were afterwards covered, and all the inhabitants of the land perished. The waters subsequently retired, the fisherman and his companions left their retreat, took up their abode on the main land, and became the progenitors of the present inhabitants."[46]

The sacred, forbidden place in this text seems to be a memory of the forbidden tree in the Garden of Eden, and the origin of sin and death which occurred there. We will find a similar tradition among the Valman people of Papua New Guinea on page 206. Also, this tradition has parallels with the Lifou story of the origin of sin and death. For all of these reasons, it seems that the people of Raiatea have passed down a memory of both the Flood and the Garden, but that these were ultimately mixed together.

44. Ellis, *Polynesian Researches,* vol. 1, pp. 389-390.
45. *Ibid.*
46. *Ibid.*, pp. 390-391.

William Ellis on the Evidence of Polynesian Flood Traditions

> "The memorial of a universal deluge existing in those communities by which civilization, literature, science, and the arts have been carried to the highest perfection, as well as among the most untutored and barbarous, preserved through all the migrations and vicissitudes of the human family, from the remote antiquity of its occurrence to the present time, is a most decisive evidence of the truth of revelation. The brief yet satisfactory testimony to this event, preserved in the oral traditions of a people secluded for ages from other parts of the world, furnishes strong additional evidence that the Scripture record is irrefragable."[47]

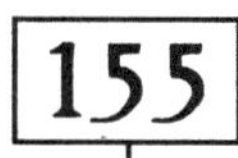

155 HAWAII

Captain William Shaler met the Hawaiian islanders in 1804 and recorded a remarkable account of the Flood from them. This account preserves a memory of Noah's dove:

> "I however learned, that they believe themselves to be the descendants of two persons called Mowee [Maui] and Henai, who escaped a universal deluge by flying to the summit of a remarkable high mountain of Owhyhee [Hawaii], called the Mona Koah. Here, when the waters began to subside, they say that a large bird, of singular shape and beauty, appeared to them, and gave them the laws and regulations they at present observe."[48]

When the waters began to subside, a large bird appeared to them and gave them the laws and regulations they at present observe.

Ellis recorded a similar version in 1822, and added that the Hawaiians attributed the Flood to the anger of a god.[49]

For another window into their Flood tradition, we turn to the writings of a native Hawaiian named David Malo (1793-1853). In his youth, Malo "was connected with the high chief Kuakini" and "was placed in an environment the most favorable to forming an intimate acquaintance with the history, traditions, legends and myths of old Hawaii." [50]

Well-acquainted, therefore, with the traditions of the ancestors, Malo wrote, "Long before the coming of the white people to Hawaii, the Hawaiians had heard about the deluge. The strange thing about it was that the Hawaiian kings did not know when this deluge, called "kai-a-ka-hina-lii", occurred, whether or not it was earlier than their arrival at the Hawaiian shores."[51]

Long before the coming of the white people to Hawaii, the Hawaiians had heard about the deluge.

They attributed the Flood to certain deities that lived in the sea. These retaliated after a king named Konikonia ran off with their daughter and

47. Ellis, *Polynesian Researches*, vol. 1, p. 394.
48. William Shaler, "Journal of a Voyage Between China and the North-western Coast of America, made in 1804," *The American Register: Part I for 1808*, vol. 3 (Philadelphia, 1808), p. 170. Interestingly, Shaler adds that "They have received by tradition the names of a line of sovereigns, including the present kind, whose number, allowing ten years' reign to each, carries back their political existence nine hundred years." (*Ibid.*)
49. "They said they were informed by their fathers, that all the land had once been overflowed by the sea, except a small peak on the top of Mouna-Kea, where two human beings were preserved from the destruction that overtook the rest, but they said they had never before heard of a ship, or of Noah, having always been accustomed to call it the "kai a Kahinarii (sea of Kahinarii)." William Ellis, *Polynesian Researches*, vol. 4 (London: Fisher, Son, & Jackson, 1831), pp. 441-442. And referring to traditions from Hawaii as well as Raiatea and Tahiti, Ellis wrote, "In each account, the anger of the god is considered as the cause of the inundation of the world, and the destruction of its inhabitants." Ellis, *Polynesian Researches*, vol. 1, p. 393.
50. David Malo and.N. B. Emerson (trans.), *Hawaiian Antiquities* (Honolulu: *Hawaiian Gazette*, 1898), p. 5.
51. *Ibid.*, pp. 307-308.

married her. This was forbidden to him, since he was from the earth and she was from the sea. She knew that a Flood was coming, and they fled to the tallest trees on a mountain. They built houses atop the trees, and the man took his family as well:

> "After ten days had passed Ka-hina-lii sent the ocean, and it rose and overwhelmed the land from one end to the other. The people fled to the mountains, and the ocean covered the mountains; they climbed the trees, and the waters rose and covered the trees and drowned them all. The ocean kept on rising until it had reached the door of Konikonia's house, but Konikonia and his household were not drowned, because the waters then began to subside; and when the waters had retreated, Konikonia and his people returned to their land."[52]

If Flood and Tower of Babel legends can no longer be denied as authentic, why should we be surprised if Adam and Eve stories join the ranks as well?

What do we make of this curious Hawaiian detail about a forbidden marriage? It is reminiscent of Genesis 6:1-4, which speaks of forbidden marriages in which fallen angels took human wives:

> "Now it came about, when mankind began to multiply on the face of the land, and daughters were born to them, that the sons of God saw that the daughters of mankind were beautiful; and they took wives for themselves, whomever they chose. Then the Lord said, 'My Spirit will not remain with man forever, because he is also flesh; nevertheless his days shall be 120 years.' The Nephilim were on the earth in those days, and also afterward, when the sons of God came in to the daughters of mankind, and they bore children to them. Those were the mighty men who were of old, men of renown." (Genesis 6:1-4 NASB)

We have one last Hawaiian tradition to relate. It concerns the creation of the first man and woman. As we have seen already in this chapter, the creation of Eve from a rib taken from Adam is well-represented in Polynesia. Hawaii is no exception.

Skeptics will protest that it is "missionary influence," but they will be wrong on this assertion, just as they have been wrong about Flood legends and Tower of Babel legends. Why should we be surprised if a nation that so carefully guarded their genealogies and historical traditions, as the Polynesians did, managed also to remember how the first man and woman were created? If Flood and Tower of Babel legends are authentic and found in large numbers (and can no longer be denied by secularists), why should we be surprised if Adam and Eve join the ranks as well?

Afterwards the first woman was created from one of the ribs—lalo puhaka—of the man while asleep, and these two were the progenitors of all mankind.

Now then, here is their tradition of human creation. Abraham Fornander summarized this, drawing on the consensus of old records and narratives which he had access to:

> "The body of the first man was made of red earth—lepo ula or ala-ca—and the spittle of the gods—wai-nao—and his head was made of a whitish clay—palolo—which was brought from the four ends of the world by "Lono." [One of the gods] When the earth-image of "Kane" [the supreme god] was ready, the three gods breathed into its nose and called on it to rise, and it became a living being.
>
> Afterwards the first woman was created from one of the ribs—lalo puhaka—of the man while asleep, and these two were the progenitors of all mankind."[53]

52. *Ibid.*, pp. 309-310.
53. Abraham Fornander, *An Account of the Polynesian Race*, vol. 1 (London: Trubner & Co., 1878), pp. 61-62.

Amazing agreement with Genesis. Of this first man and woman, Fornander added that "They are called in the chants and in various legends by a large number of different names, but the most common for the man was Kumuhonua, and for the woman Ke-Ola-ku-honua. Such is the general import of the Kumuhonua legend."[54] This fact is evidence of antiquity. And the fact of differences in the Hawaiian version as compared to Genesis, yet agreement with other Polynesian versions, is evidence of authenticity.

(The first man and woman) are called in the chants and in various legends by a large number of different names, but the most common for the man was Kumuhonua, and for the woman Ke-Ola-ku-honua.

YAP

156 The island of Yap, part of the Caroline Islands archipelago, is located about 800 miles east of the Philippines. Around 1896, an old chief named Toluk told his people's historical traditions to the explorer F. W. Christian. There is a memory of the Flood which, like the Hawaiians, they attribute to a forbidden union between a man and a spiritual being—possibly an echo of the mysterious Nephilim of Genesis 6:1-4. After the angel's mother killed her husband, she married another man, whom she warned of the coming Flood of wrath. He was instructed to build a house at the highest elevations in order to escape the Flood:

> "In seven days the vengeance of Loth [the angel's mother] would bring a high flood-tide to overwhelm the land. Meanwhile she counseled him to build a house on top of the highest hill to which they could withdraw, and bring with him some magic herbs with which certain rites or incantations were to be performed, which might avail against the inundation. He obeyed, and the two fell in to practicing spells and incantations. The wife looking out to sea at dawn of the fatal day exclaimed, "Behold the wrath of Loth." A typhoon was coming, sweeping down out of the north, bringing with it a terrible tidal-wave. It burst over the land. Nearly all Yap was covered under the raging flood, and all the people perished save one, a slave man in Unean, and the prudent couple."[55]

Male frigate-bird

There is also a memory of Noah's sending of the raven and the dove to search for land. However, they replace these birds with an albatross or a frigate bird:

> "Now the great spirit Yalafath, who sits musing in the sky, and takes a fatherly interest in the land of Yap, spake one day to his wife Mui-Bab, and said, 'I would know if the flood has destroyed the land as they tell me, and if any of the people has escaped death. Go down and see. Return and tell me.' And the goddess shot from the skies in the form of an albatross or, as some say, a frigate-bird, lighting on Tomil. And she saw how few were left to till the land now barren of food-bearing plants. Swiftly returning, she told Yalafath, the Giver of Good, of the hapless state of the people. And he sent down to nourish them the areca palm, the betel pepper, the banana, the plantains, the yams, and the water-taro. Therefore to this day, when they see the frigate-bird in the land of Tomil, they say, 'Lo, the sacred messenger of the mercy of Yalafath, Lord of the skies.'"[56]

To this day, when they see the frigate-bird in the land of Tomil, they say, "Lo, the sacred messenger of the mercy of Yalafath, Lord of the skies."

54. *Ibid.*, p. 62.
55. F. W. Christian, *The Caroline Islands* (New York: Charles Scribner's Sons, 1899), p. 283.
56. *Ibid.*, pp. 284-285.

How deeply ingrained the knowledge of the Flood was with the Yap Islanders. They also seem to have a memory of the Fall and the evil being who occasioned it:

> "The sister of Eliulap the first man, who was also a god, felt herself in labor, so she descended to earth and there brought forth three children. … And the world became very beautiful and her sons were happy and did not feel sickness or death, but at the close of every month fell into a slumber from which they awoke renewed in strength and beauty. But Erigeres, the bad spirit, envied this happiness, so he came to the world and introduced into it pain, age, and death."[57]

Erigeres, the bad spirit, envied this happiness, so he came to the world and introduced into it pain, age, and death."

157 MARQUESAS ISLANDS

The Marquesas are a group of very remote volcanic islands in the South Pacific, located 2,300 miles south-southeast of Hawaii. The natives had a "Chant of the Deluge," which they have preserved since ancient times. A former sailor named Thomas Lawson, who arrived in 1843, heard this Chant continually among them. Finally, he recorded it at the dictation of one of the oldest chiefs. Abraham Fornander has, very capably and faithfully, summarized this lengthy chant which can be read in its entirety elsewhere:[58]

> "The chant opens by saying that the Lord Ocean, Fatu-Moana, was going to overflow and pass over the dry earth, but that a respite of seven days was granted. It then speaks of the animals who were to be reserved from the Flood. It then speaks of a house to be built high above the waters; a house with stories, with chambers, with openings for light, stored with provisions for the preservation of the various animals. The animals then are fastened with ropes, tied up in couples, and, with one man before and one behind, marched off to this big, deep house of wood. Then the family enter, consisting of four women and four men. The men's names are given "Fetu-moana," apparently the father and master of the family, Fetu-tau-ani, Fetu-amo-amo, and Ia-fetu-tini."[59]

Marquesa islanders: "The Lord Ocean was going to overflow and pass over the dry earth, but a respite of seven days was granted."

Genesis 7:4 "After seven more days, I will send rain on the earth."

These "four women and four men" exactly accord with Genesis. Fetu-Moana, being the father of the other three, corresponds to Noah. The latter three men correspond, in some order, to Shem, Ham, and Japheth. We continue:

> "A turtle is then sacrificed; the family retires to rest amidst the din, confusion, and crowding of the confined animals. Then the storm bursts over them; the rain is pouring fearfully, and gloom prevails; all on earth is displaced and mixed up by the waters.
>
> The second part opens with a description of the waters retreating, and mountain summits and ridges reappearing, the grounding of the house, and the command of the Lord Ocean for the dry land to appear."[60]

Do they also have a memory of Noah's burnt offering, and of Noah's raven and dove? Let us read and find out:

> "The head of the family, encouraged by the sight, promises to sacrifice to the Lord Ocean seven holy and precious things and seven sucklings. Then a bird, called te teetina o Tanava—from its name apparently of a dark

57. Abbé Prévost (ed.), *Allgemeine Historie der Reisen zu Wasser und Lande,* vol. 18 (Leipzig: 1764), p. 395.
58. J. Linton Palmer, "Marquesan Tradition of the Deluge," *Proceedings of the Liverpool Literary and Philosophical Society,* vol. 31 (London: Longmans, 1877), pp. 281-290.
59. Abraham Fornander, *An Account of the Polynesian Race*, vol. 1 (London: Trubner & Co., 1878), p. 90.
60. *Ibid.*

colour—is sent out over the sea of Hawaii, but after a while returns to the vessel. The wind sets in from the north. On a second attempt the same bird alights on the sand of the shore, but is recalled to the vessel. Then another bird, called te Teetina o Mpepo, is sent out over the sea of Hawaii. It lands on the dry land, and returns with young shoots or branches it had gathered. The land is now dry, and the great ridges of Hawaii and of Matahou are fit to dwell on. In the third part reference is made to the debarkation of men and animals."[61]

Another bird returns with young shoots or branches it had gathered.

158 SAMOA

Samoa consists of a group of ten islands located about 2,500 miles east-northeast from Australia. Like their Maori counterparts in New Zealand, they had a priestly group responsible for carefully preserving their sacred traditions and beliefs. The missionary Thomas Powell, who arrived there in 1844, described how carefully these Samoan Falatel, or "history families," executed this duty:

High Chief and family, Samoa, ca 1914

> "The Samoans are very tenacious of their traditionary myths. This may partly account for their being so little known. There reside, on most of the islands of the group, one or more families who are the descendants of the hereditary keepers of these myths. … On the largest island of the Manu'a cluster of Samoa, there resides a family whose office it has been, from time immemorial, to guard these myths with sacred care, and, only on occasion of a royal tour, to rehearse any of them in public. They were taught to the children of the family with great secrecy, and the different parts of a myth and its song were committed to the special care of different members of the family; so that a young man would have the special care of the prose part, and a young woman that of the poetic part, while to the older members, and especially the head of the family, belonged the prerogative of explaining the meaning of the various allusions of the poetic lines. A single line would often bring out a lengthy piece of history."[62]

Powell was privileged to witness and record this priestly family narrating the Samoan history. This contains multiple parallels with Genesis. The following is a section of the poem which alludes to the Tower of Babel, which they called the "Forum of Confusion":

On the largest island there resides a family whose office it has been, from time immemorial, to guard these traditions with sacred care.

> "Descending, descending, first of all they came to the Forum of Confusion
>
> The Forum of Tranquility's the place where they enjoyed a calm and time of peace. …
>
> The errand this which brought the workmen down,

61. *Ibid.*, pp. 90-91.
62. Thomas Powell, "A Samoan Tradition of Creation and the Deluge," *Journal of the Transactions of the Victoria Institute*, vol. 20 (London: Victoria Institute, 1887), pp. 147-148.

> A clan of workmen as ten thousand known,
> With architect-in-chief but one alone.
> The rafter-breaking god came down, (with wrath inflamed and angry frown).
> Alas! My building all complete is scattered in confusion great!"[63]

Descending, descending, first of all they came to the Forum of Confusion."

Powell elaborated on this tradition, based on his interviews with the Samoan priests:

> "Tradition states that the architects from heaven built a splendid house for the king of Manu'a without first consulting [the creator god] Tagaloa. This was a violation of the injunction. Tagaloa therefore descended in great anger, destroyed the building and scattered the workmen."[64]

This is none other than the Tower of Babel. Notice it says they "descended" to the Forum of Confusion, just as Noah and his family descended from the mountains of Ararat and came to the plain of Shinar (Genesis 11:1).

In another part of their historical narration, there seems to be a mixed memory of both the Flood and Creation. It tells that the god Tagaloa assumed the form of a bird, called Turi, and flew over the water-covered earth in search of land. Finding none, he went about creating land, one island after another. "Tagaloa the Messenger [the bird] then returned to the heavens and reported the existence of those lands. Tagaloa the Creator then went on a black cloud to inspect them. He was much pleased and said, 'Ua lelei' i.e., 'It is good.' Then he stood on the tops of the mountains and trod them down so as to prepare them well for the habitation of man."[65]

The architects from heaven built a splendid house for the king of Manu'a without first consulting Tagaloa. ... Tagaloa destroyed the building and scattered the workmen.

A missionary named George Turner also heard an account of the Flood from the Samoans around the year 1840:

> "At one time the land was flooded by the sea, and everything died except some fowls and pigeons. The pigeons flew away, but the Moa, or fowls, remained and were made sacred by Lu, and not to be killed, and hence called the Sa Moa or preserve fowls of Lu."[66]

In another recording by Turner, we can hear the echoes of Genesis 1, perhaps mixed with the memory of Noah's dove (Genesis 8:8-12) and / or the time when "the Spirit of God was hovering over the fact of the waters" (Genesis 1:2).[67]

---

63. *Ibid.*, pp. 160-161.
64. *Ibid.*, p. 161.
65. Thomas Powell, "A Samoan Tradition of Creation and the Deluge," pp. 153-158.
66. George Turner, Samoa, *A Hundred Years Ago and Long Before* (London: MacMillan & Co, 1884), p. 11.
67. "The earliest traditions of the Samoans describe a time when the heavens alone were inhabited, and the earth covered over with water. Tangaloa, the great Polynesian Jupiter, then sent down his daughter in the form of a bird called the turi (a snipe), to search for a resting place. After flying about for a long time, she found a rock partially above the surface of the water. ... Turi went up and told her father that she had found but one spot on which she could rest. Tangaloa sent her down again to visit the place. She went to and fro repeatedly, and, every time she went up, reported that the dry surface was extending on all sides." George Turner, *Nineteen Years in Polynesia* (London: John Snow, 1861), pp. 244-245.

159 PALAU

On the Palau archipelago located about 550 miles east of the Philippines, it is said that long ago, the people committed a crime in killing a certain magical being. Seven gods came to investigate. They were received rudely, and they observed the people to be malicious and arrogant. So the gods sent the Flood to punish mankind. However, the gods decided to spare one woman, the only person who had shown them kindness. They "suggested to her that she prepare a raft and fasten it to a tree by means of a rope of forest slings." So the seven gods sent a tremendous flood that drowned all people, while the good woman Milathk floated aboard her raft. However, the waters climbed still higher, and as her rope was too short she died. The gods regretted this and brought her back to life. [68]

We see that they remembered the prophetic warning of the Flood, and the directive to construct a floating vessel. In another narration, recorded about 12 years earlier, in 1858, we have a memory of Mount Ararat or, in their terms, Mount Armilimui.

The good old dame, fast asleep on the raft, was borne on the face of the waters and drifted till her hair caught in the boughs of a tree on the top of Mount Armilimui.

> "The sea rose higher and higher, and flooded the islands, rent the mountains, and destroyed the abodes of men; and people knew not how to save themselves, and they all perished in the rising flood. But the good old dame, fast asleep on the raft, was borne on the face of the waters and drifted till her hair caught in the boughs of a tree on the top of Mount Armilimui."[69]

160 MANGAIA

Mangaia, the southernmost of the Cook Islands, is located about 3,000 miles east of Australia. The natives had an account of the Flood, which they shared with William Gill around 1872. This tells that in ancient times, the god Aokeu "caused the rain—his favourite element—to fall without the slightest intermission five days and nights in dreadful torrents." The waters rose and covered everything except the pinnacle of the mountain Rangimotia, which is called "the crown of Mangaia." But before it happened, Rangi, the first king of Magaia, had been forewarned of the catastrophe. So he retreated with his people to the mountain of Rangimotia. The waters climbed and climbed, and even reached the level of their feet, but then subsided to their original level. Thus the people were saved.[70]

Gill emphatically added, "This myth stands alone, no other achievement being attributed to Aokeu, which is a proof of its antiquity."[71]

Rangi, the first king of Magaia, had been forewarned of the catastrophe. So he retreated with his people to the mountain of Rangimotia.

Sacrifice to God:

From the remote past, the islanders of Manaia understood the need for an atoning sacrifice, just like Moses ordained for the nation of Israel. What they sought was a perfect sacrifice, which would appease the gods and grant protection for their people.

But an animal would not suffice. To the Mangaias, only a human sacrifice was acceptable. So they did. Volley Tangiiataua, a contemporary Mangaian, explained this requirement:

---

68. John S. Kubary, "Die Religion der Pelauer," *Allerlei aux Volks- und Menschenkunde,* vol. 1 (Berlin: Ernst Siegfried Mittler: 1888), pp. 53-54.
69. Karl Semper, *Die Palau-Inseln im Stillen Ocean* (Leipzig: Brodbaus, 1873), pp. 195-198.
70. William Wyatt Gill, *Life in the Southern Isles* (London: Religious Tract Society, 1876), pp. 80-83.
71. *Ibid.*, p. 83.

"Before Christianity our people used human sacrifices. The sacrifice had to be a young male without defect or blemish. This yearly sacrifice was offered for protection from evil spirits and gods. This human sacrifice had to be once a year on behalf of the whole island and the people."[72]

Before Christianity our people used human sacrifices. The sacrifice had to be a young male without defect or blemish. ... This human sacrifice had to be once a year on behalf of the whole island and the people.

Of course, God never authorized human sacrifice (Deut. 18:10, Jer. 7:31). Yet this practice by the Mangaians did serve as a "bridge" by which many Mangaians immediately responded to Jesus, the only One who could truly atone for our sins and make us right with God:

"The Tahitian missionaries were the chiefs and kings of Tahiti who were so excited about Jesus being the sacrifice for ALL the world that they wanted to tell others. The chiefs / kings of Mangaia accepted the Gospel. Many of the Mangaias became missionaries to Vanuatu, Papua, and Samoa. Many of the descendants were willing to go and be living sacrifices, not returning to Mangaia."[73]

161 FIJI

Charles Wilkes was the commander of the U.S. Exploring Expedition around 1840, when he traveled to the island of Fiji. The native Fijians narrated to him their memory of the Flood, in which eight people survived, the same number as in Genesis:

"They have a tradition of a great flood or deluge, which they call Walavu-levu. Their account of it is as follows: after the islands had been peopled by the first man and woman, a great rain took place, by which they were finally submerged; but, before the highest places were covered by the waters, two large double canoes made their appearance; in one of these was Rokora, the god of carpenters, in the other Rokola, his head workman, who picked up some of the people and kept them on board until the waters had subsided, after which they were again landed on the island. It is reported that in former times canoes were always kept in readiness against another inundation.

The persons thus saved, eight in number, were landed at Mbenga, where the highest of their gods is said to have made his first appearance. By virtue of this tradition, the chiefs of Mbenga take rank before all others, and have always acted a conspicuous part among the Feejees [Fijis]. They style themselves Ngali-duva-ki-langi (subject to heaven alone)."[74]

The Fijians have traditions of the Flood and the Tower of Babel, but they say they took place at Fiji.

The Wesleyan missionary Thomas Williams heard a similar Flood tradition in the 1840s, again with eight survivors:

"All [narrations] agree that the highest places were covered, and the remnant of the human race saved in some kind of vessel, which was at last left by the subsiding waters on Mbegga; hence the Mbenggans draw their claim to stand first in Fijian rank. The number saved—eight—exactly accords with the "few" of the Scripture record. … The highest point of the Island of Koro is associated with the history of the flood. Its name is Ngginggi-tangithi-Koro, which conveys the idea of a little bird sitting there and lamenting the drowned island. In this bird the Christians recognize Noah's dove, on its second flight from the ark. I have heard a

The persons thus saved, eight in number, were landed at Mbenga ... By virtue of this tradition, the chiefs of Mbenga take rank before all others.

72. Personal correspondence with Julie Von Vett, who obtained this tradition from Volley Tangliataua in writing in May 2023.
73. *Ibid.*
74. Charles Wilkes, *Narrative of the United States Exploring Expedition of the Years 1838, 1839, 1840, 1841, 1842*, vol. 3 (Philadelphia: Lea & Blanchard, 1845), pp. 82-83.

native, after listening to the incident as given by Moses, chant, "Na qiqi sa tigici Koro ni yali," "the qiqi laments over Koro, because it is lost."[75]

They also have a memory of the Tower of Babel, according to Thomas Williams:

> "Near Na Savu, Vanua Levu, the natives point out the site where, in former ages, men built a vast tower, being eager for astronomic information, and especially anxious to decide the difficult question as to whether the moon was inhabited. To effect their purpose, they cast up a high mound, and erected thereon a great building of timber. The tower had already risen far skyward, and the ambitious hopes of its industrious builders seemed near fulfilment, when the tower fastenings suddenly broke asunder, and scattered the workmen over every part of Fiji."[76]

The number saved—eight—exactly accords with the "few" of the Scripture record.

162 KADAVU

Kadavu is a small island located about 45 miles south of Fiji. One Captain William Campbell Thomson recorded a remarkable tradition from the islanders around the year 1890. This begins with a paradisiacal era, like the Garden of Eden:

> "The legend is as follows: At a remote period, or as the natives express it, 'Mamau' extending his hands into space, the god lived with the people in the village on the most friendly terms, giving them good fishing, good winds for their voyages, and fine seasons for their yams . This intimate and good feeling continued for some time, when the god called the people together and told them he was going away out of sight to sleep in a cave, but that they would be taken care of as before, and that they were to bring their offerings regularly and pass them into the cave."[77]

As for the ending of that original state, it happened in this way:

> "This duty was carried out strictly by those who had seen the god; but in course of time another generation came, who rather turned to ridicule the old stories of their fathers, and they began to neglect going to this cave. Then a little dove whispered into the ear of the god that the people were not so attentive as they used to be, whereat the god awoke and sent out another dove to tell them that he was very angry with them, and unless they returned to their former religion he should punish them. This caution they also turned to ridicule, with the exception of one family who went out of the village and lived apart, and continued to take up yams to the god to eat. In the meantime the town was fenced around and a deep trench dug behind, yams and figs brought in, and everything got ready to resist the god. Again the dove appeared and spoke to them without bringing them to a sense of their duty, and to show how little they stood in the awe of the god, they killed the dove with an arrow or spear, piercing its breast, and today they point to the 'mungi-tungi,' a species of dove with a red spot on its breast, as a proof of the truth of the story."[78]

Today they point to the "mungi-tungi," a species of dove with a red spot on its breast, as a proof of the truth of the story.

The last statement above is an amazing proof of the tradition's authenticity. Continuing, we read:

75. Thomas Williams, ed. George Stringer Rowe, *Fiji and the Fijians*, vol. 1 (Boston: Congregational Publishing, 1858), pp. 212-213.
76. *Ibid.*, p. 213.
77. William Campbell Thomson, "The 'Stone Age' in Australasia,' *Proceedings and Transactions of the Queensland Branch of the Royal Geographical Society of Australasia*, vol. 8 (Brisbane: Pole, Outridge &. Co., 1893), p. 81.
78. *Ibid.*

"The dove not returning, the god became very angry and shook the whole mountain of Mbukie Levu [Nabukelevu] and told the family beforementioned to get a big canoe built. The trees selected for this purpose were a long way inland, and much fun was made by the others who came to eat at the feast and help to build the canoe. By and by a big rumbling noise was heard, and the god turned over and shook all the island and came down to the village to find them in battle array, and heard defiance hurled at him from behind the palisading, so he just threw his club up and broke a hole in the blue above and the water poured down and all the people were drowned, save those in the canoe, who after a long time sailing about grounded on the top of the high mountain on the southward of the island."[79]

All the people were drowned, save those in the canoe, who after a long time sailing about grounded on the top of the high mountain on the southward of the island.

This high mountain that Thomson refers to is called Nabukelevu, but it is undoubtedly a memory of Ararat.

163 ANIWA

Aniwa is a very small island (about 3 square miles), which is part of the island country of Vanuatu. The missionary John G. Paton was powerfully used by God to reach Aniwa and the other Southern Hebrides islands with the Gospel, in the midst of great difficulty, personal suffering, and violent opposition from the natives who practiced cannibalism. His autobiography is riveting, and his escape from several attempts on his life is nothing short of miraculous.

The natives of Aniwa have a memory of the Serpent in the Garden of Eden, and the Fall. This is vividly illustrated by the following account from Paton, dating to the 1860s:

> "What a suggestive tradition of the Fall came to me in one of those early days on Aniwa! … One morning at daylight this Tupa came running to us in great excitement, wielding his club furiously, and crying, "Missi, I have killed the Tebil. I have killed Teapolo. He came to catch me last night. I raised all the people, and we fought him round the house with our clubs. At daybreak he came out and I killed him dead. We will have no more bad conduct or trouble now. Teapolo is dead!"
>
> I said, "What nonsense! Teapolo is a spirit, and cannot be seen."
>
> But in mad excitement he persisted that he had killed him. And at Mrs. Paton's advice, I went with the man, and he led me to a great Sacred Rock of coral near our old hut, over which hung the dead body of a huge and beautiful sea-serpent, and exclaimed, "There he lies! Truly I killed him."
>
> I protested, "That is not the Devil; it is only the body of a serpent."
>
> The man quickly answered, "Well, but it is all the same! He is Teapolo. He makes us bad, and causes all our troubles."[80]

He is Teapolo. He makes us bad, and causes all our troubles.

What does this statement mean, "He makes us bad, and causes all our troubles"? Paton continued: "Following up this hint by many inquiries, then and afterwards, I found that they clearly associated man's troubles and sufferings somehow with the serpent."[81] They attributed man's evil tendencies, and the suffering that is now in the world, with the Serpent—a clear memory of the Fall in the Garden of Eden.

Paton also heard from them a tradition of the Flood:

> "Far back, when the volcano, now on Tanna, was part of Aniwa, the rain fell and fell from day to day, and the sea rose till it threatened to cover

79. *Ibid.*, pp. 81-82.
80. John G. Paton, *John G. Paton, Missionary to the New Hebrides: An Autobiography Edited by his Brother* (London: Hodder and Stoughton, 1898), pp. 156-157.
81. *Ibid.*, p. 157.

everything. All were drowned except the few who climbed up on the volcano mountain."[82]

Matsinktshiki sailed on a volcano across to Tanna on the top of the flood.

The tradition continues that the evil god Matsinktshiki, becoming afraid of the rising floodwaters, broke the volcano off from the island of Aniwa and "sailed it across to Tanna on the top of the flood. There, by his mighty strength, he heaved the volcano to the top of the highest mountain of Tanna, where it remains to this day."[83]

We can see that they have replaced Noah's Ark with a floating volcano. And just like the Ark landed in the mountains of Ararat, the Aniwa islanders say it landed on top of the highest mountain of Tanna.

164

ERROMANGO

Erromango is another of the southern islands of the country of Vanuatu, located only 25 miles from Aniwa. The natives had a rather remarkable tradition of God's creation of man and woman, which they told to the ethnologist Clarence Humphrews sometime around 1920:

> "Another account says that the Nobu [God] made a man and then, seeing that he was lonely, made a woman from a part of the man's body. As the children which the woman bore to the man grew to puberty they were sent to different parts of the island and there founded families, although nothing is said of the presence of any women in the island, beyond the woman created for the first man."[84]

Nobu [God] made a man and then, seeing that he was lonely, made a woman from a part of the man's body.

Humphreys added that he thought this tradition was too similar to Genesis to be genuine, but three or four old men insisted to him that it predated Christian missionary teaching.[85] Indeed, looking at the tradition itself, and the natives' other traditions, there is no inherent reason to doubt its authenticity. As discussed on page 205, this tradition exists in many other parts of Polynesia as well.

165

EASTER ISLAND

What about Easter Island (Rapa Nui)? Does the memory of the events recorded in Genesis exist even here on the remotest inhabited island in the world?

Indeed, it does. Specifically, we have found a memory of God's creation of man, and the woman formed from the man's rib. The source for this was an old man named Pua Ara Hoa who, born around the year 1840, grew up prior to the arrival of Christian missionaries. This man has been considered the most important source of oral traditions from Easter Island, and it was he who compiled the 'Rapanui manuscripts.'[86] Prior to Hoa's death

Moai Statues at Easter Island

82. *Ibid.*, p. 158.
83. *Ibid.*, pp. 158-159.
84. Clarence Blake Humphreys, *The Southern New Hebrides: An Ethnological Record* (Cambridge: University Press, 1926), p. 186.
85. *Ibid.*
86. Paul Horley and Lilian López Labbé, "A new manuscript of Pua Ara Hoa 'a Rapu from the Archives of William Mulloy, Part 1: Description of the Manuscript," *Rapa Nui Journal*, vol. 28, no. 2 (University of Hawaii Press, 2014), p. 35.

Restored moai at Ahu Tongariki on Easter Island

around 1913, a young man named Arturo Teao Tori recorded many traditions from him, preserving them for us today.[87] Their Creation account went like this:

> "After a time, it occurred to Makemake [the Creator] to create a man in his own image, with a voice so he could speak with the Creator.
>
> Makemake impregnated some stones, but this did not work, as the waters that washed over them spilled into barren ground.
>
> Next, he impregnated water, but the seed he spilled produced only a shoal of tiny paroko fish."[88]

And now, we come to the signature parallel with Genesis 2:21-23, over 10,000 miles from Israel!

> "Lastly, Makemake impregnated some clay, and from it man was born. Makemake saw his creation and was pleased.
>
> Later, Makemake saw that things were not quite right—the man was alone. Makemake made the man sleep in his own house, and when he had fallen asleep, Makemake impregnated the ribs on his left side and woman was born.
>
> Makemake then said: Vivina, vivina, hakapiro e ahu ê!"[89]

Makemake made the man sleep in his own house, and when he had fallen asleep, Makemake impregnated the ribs on his left side and woman was born.

Finally, their migration story may contain a vague memory of Noah's Flood. But on this point we cannot be certain.[90]

87. Thomas Sylvester Barthel, *The Eighth Land: The Polynesian Discovery and Settlement of Easter Island* (Honolulu: University of Hawaii Press, 1978), pp. 297-298.
88. Sebastian Englert, *Leyendas de Isla de Pascua. Textos Bilingues* (Santiago, Chile: *Universidad de Chile*, 1980), p. 13.
89. *Ibid.* The last sentence is untranslatable. In a footnote, Englert writes: "The word *vivina* is unknown today; the sentence seems to refer to the death and decomposition of the human body (hakapiro, ahu)."
90. When a cataclysm and deluge destroyed King Hotu Matu'a's kingdom of Hiva, a holy man named Hau Maka dreamed of a new homeland for Hotu Matu'a's people. So, Hotu Matu'a sent seven young men in a special boat made of living wood to search for the new homeland. Upon landing on Easter Island, they planted crops and found the waters teeming with fish. Soon after, Hotu Matu'a arrived with two boats with his wife and his sister and her husband. Hotu Matu'a children divided the island amongst themselves and their population grew. Sebastian Roeling, *The Resilience of Easter Island: A Historical Ethnography* (Lulu, 2015), pp. 161-164.

166 FAKAOFO (TOKELAU ARCHIPELAGO)

The Tokelau Islands are made up of three atolls: Fakaofo (also known as Bowditch Island), Nukunonu and Atafu. According to oral tradition:

> "A canoe, containing three men and three women, sailing from Rarotonga got driven to the westward. They eventually landed on a reef which had a sand bank on it but no trees. This was Fakaofo, and here one man and his wife elected to stay, the others setting sail again and eventually reaching their home. Some coconuts which were in the canoe were landed with the man and his wife, and some they planted. By and by the woman died without children, so the man built himself a canoe and sailed to Nukunonu where he obtained another wife. The family of these two were the ancestors of the present inhabitants of Fakaofo."[91]

As we have seen previously, there are many islands in Polynesia where we have found traditions paralleling Genesis 2, telling that the first woman was formed from a "rib" taken from the first man. The island of Fakaofo is among this number as well. As George Turner heard from them:

He took out a rib from his left side and thrust it inside of the earth model, when suddenly the earth became alive, and up started a woman on her feet.

> "The natives there say that men had their origin in a small stone on Fakaofo. The stone became changed into a man called Vasefanua. After a time he thought of making a woman. This he did by collecting a quantity of earth, and forming an earth model on the ground. He made the head, body, arms, and legs all of earth, then took out a rib from his left side and thrust it inside of the earth model, when suddenly the earth became alive, and up started a woman on her feet. He called her Ivi (Eevee), or rib, he took her to be his wife, and from them sprang the race of men. To this day the children play on the sand at making models of men—body, hands, feet, head, and face, with holes for the eyes."[92]

The signature similarity to Genesis is unmistakable. That we should find this to be a recurring tradition on many islands of the South Pacific is even more stunning, another witness to its genuineness.

167 NANUMANGA

Nanumanga is a tiny island that belongs to the island nation of Tuvalu. George Turner of the London Missionary Society heard a Flood tradition from the natives during the 1840s or 50s, which he briefly mentioned:

A deluge is described also, and the serpent caused the waters to pass away.

> "Tradition asserts that the natives of this island came from Samoa in the canoe of Lapi and Lafai. The story is told here also of the union of the heavens and the earth, and of the separation, and the elevation of the former by the sea-serpent. A deluge is described also, and the serpent caused the waters to pass away. The serpent as the woman and the earth as the man united, and their progeny was the race of men. The first man was called Foelangi, and the first woman Telahi."[93]

91. William Burrows, "Some Notes and Legends of a South Sea Island," *Journal of the Polynesian Society*, vol. 32, No. 3 (September 1923), p. 152.
92. George Turner, Samoa, *A Hundred Years Ago and Long Before* (London: MacMillan, 1884), pp. 267-268. Regarding "Ivi," we previously saw among the Tahitians that this word means "bones."
93. *Ibid*, p. 288.

168 RAKAHANGA (COOK ISLANDS)

Rakahanga is a small atoll island located almost 3,000 miles east of Australia. The native people told this story to the early missionaries in the mid 1800s:

> "A king named Taoiau was on one occasion greatly incensed against his people for not bringing him the sacred turtle. The irate chief "awakened" all the mighty sea-gods upon whose good-will the existence of the islands—Rakaanga and Manihiki—depends, particularly a great divinity who sleeps at the bottom of mid-ocean, and who at the prayers of Taoiau rose up in anger like a vast upright stone. A dreadful hurricane began, and the ocean rose and swept over the entire island of Rakaanga. The few inhabitants of those days escaped destruction by taking refuge on a mound which was pointed out to me. This memorable event is known as "the overwhelming of Taoiau."[94]

169 NAKANAI (NEW BRITAIN ISLAND)

New Britain, off the eastern coast of New Guinea, is home to the Nakanai (or Lakalai) people. An elder of the tribe related their Flood tradition to members of the Summer Institute of Linguistics (S.I.L.), which was published in 1973:

> "At first God created men here on earth and each one did as he pleased. God saw how they lived and was not happy with them. He thought that their actions were not good.
>
> So our God thought of a way that he would be able to deal with them. He decided to make a man like Noah, not the Noah of the Bible, but a man from our legendary past.
>
> The first men were created by God at Romo near the Raga River in the Nakanai region. This village no longer exists, but we can see the remains of it even to this day. Every region had its origin at Romo, and in this man who was like Noah. Judgment and confusion too have their origin in this man. God made him intending to use him as a means of giving new life to the people of Romo.
>
> God revealed a way to that man. He sent him to the deep forest, and there he made a canoe. The people laughed at him and made jokes about him. They always made fun of him. They did not know that he was doing what God had told him to do. They kept on making fun of him and went on about their daily lives. They did not know that God had prepared a way for that man, that God would save his life, and that was why he was making the big canoe.
>
> God had told him that when the canoe was carved out, he should tie on the outrigger, try the canoe to see if it was a good size to sit in, and then see if it was all ready. Meanwhile God had readied the sea and the waters under the earth."[95]

God revealed a way to that man. He sent him to the deep forest, and there he made a canoe. The people laughed at him and made jokes about him. They did not know that he was doing what God had told him to do.

Then the Flood began in this way:

> "God also told him to dig up the opening of the spring of waters under the earth so that they could bubble forth and come out. He did this. Then he climbed into the canoe and went seaward. When the waters burst out, he paddled seaward.

Meanwhile God had readied the sea and the waters under the earth.

94. William Wyatt Gill, *Life in the Southern Isles* (London: Religious Tract Society, 1876), pp. 83-84.
95. Samuel Bubu, "The Great Flood," trans. Raymond Johnston, *Legends from Papua New Guinea,* ed. K. A. McElhanon (Ukarumpa, Papua New Guinea: Summer Institute of Linguistics, 1976), pp. 140-141.

The sea and the waters from under the earth covered all the villages. … Up until the present day, God has kept the human race going. You will see that many men from different places have customs that are similar to ours. The reason is that God made this man who caused the great flood, and he passed on our customs to all of us."[96]

God also told him to dig up the opening of the spring of waters under the earth so that they could bubble forth and come out.

170

TOLAI

The Tolai people live in the northeastern part of New Britain Island and the neighboring, much smaller Duke of York Islands. They tell the following account which, as we will see, is prototypically New Guinean. And although the "eel" in this story may seem benevolent, I think it is actually a vague memory of the Serpent, Satan himself:

Coral reef off the coast of New Britain

> Long ago, while fishing, the ancestors shot an eel and took it back to the village. But it was not a real eel. It was an old man who lived in the water. The next day, while the villagers were working in the gardens, an old man was told to clean the eel and prepare to cook it. But, speaking to the man, the eel asked for betel nut, betel pepper, and lime.
>
> Chewing the mixture, the eel said "Old man, do you think that I am an eel? I am not an eel. I am a man from long ago, from the time when the land had not yet risen. Men do not know anything about me. My skin is just like that of an eel. When the men cut me, you should go and stay at the base of a small coconut palm tree."
>
> When the villagers returned from the gardens, the old man begged everyone to return the eel to the river but no one listened to him. Instead, they cursed him and beat him up. As they cooked the eel, the river slowly began to rise. The water crested the banks, everyone was drowned. The old man stayed at the coconut tree and survived. Eventually, after everyone had died, the flood receded exposing their bones. Then the old man threw a green coconut into the water to see how deep it was.[97]

Do you think that I am an eel? I am not an eel. I am a man from long ago, from the time when the land had not yet risen.

96. *Ibid.*, p. 141.
97. *Wantok*, no. 72 (18 July, 1973), p. 4. As translated in: Slone, *One Thousand One Papua New Guinean Nights*, vol. 1, p. 14.

171 NEW BRITAIN ISLAND TRADITION

George Brown visited the island of New Britain from 1875 to 1880, where he met an unidentified people group. He wrote, "I have never found that they [the natives] could refer any farther back than to some event which had happened in their own lifetime, or in the lifetime of their fathers, such as the visit of some trading vessel or the name of some trading captain with whom they were acquainted."[98] However, they did preserve one historical tradition which contains a vague memory of the Flood.

According to the natives, there was a female creator, named Tabui Kor, who used to contaminate the food that she gave to her two sons, Tilik and Tarai. Meanwhile, she kept the best food for herself. When they discovered this, her sons snatched her food away. She became angry and sent a great flood. This was the origin of the sea.[99]

> Then the old man threw a green coconut into the water to see how deep it was.

172 CHUUK

The Chuuk Islands make up a small archipelago located about 800 miles north of New Guinea. Laurentius Bollig said that "Hardly any other group of islands in the South Seas was opened up to civilization as late as the Chuuk." Overlooked by the Spanish, who possessed the Caroline Islands (of which Chuuk is a part), Bollig added that "Chuuk was more or less terra incognita. Kubary stayed on the island from 1878 to 1879. It is probably through him that the first descriptions of the life and activities of the islanders reached Germany."[100]

With that introduction, we shall now hear another "rib" story. Bollig collected this from one of the older islanders who was well-informed on their traditions:

> "Semenkoror sent a man from heaven to earth. One of the heavenly spirits later met the man and asked him, 'Where is your wife?' He said, 'I don't have one.' Then the spirit said, 'If you had one, she would give birth and many people would be born on earth.' The spirit went away. The man fell asleep. The spirit came back and took a rib from the man's left side and made a woman out of it. Then he stuck his finger in the bleeding hole and dripped the blood onto the woman's head and limbs. He also blew into her nose and she lived. He [Bollig's source] described the expressions, 'Then she would give birth to a child,' as being related to this legend."[101]

> One of the heavenly spirits later met the man and asked him, 'Where is your wife?' He said, 'I don't have one.' ... The man fell asleep. The spirit came back and took a rib from the man's left side and made a woman out of it.

We now have nine separate occurrences of the "rib" story from Oceania alone. The genuineness and antiquity of this tradition, which so remarkably confirms Genesis 2, can hardly be denied any longer.

98. George Brown, *Melanesians and Polynesians: Their Life-histories Described and Compared* (London: MacMillan and Co., 1910), p. 352.
99. *Ibid.*, pp. 354-355.
100. Laurentius Bollig, *Die Bewohner der Truk-Inseln. Religion, Leben und kurze Grammatik eines Mikronesiervolkes* (Münster: Aschendorff, 1927), p. iii.
101. *Ibid.*, pp. 78-79.

Highlands of Papua New Guinea

NEW GUINEA

We come now to New Guinea, the world's second largest island after Greenland. This incredibly diverse island is home to about 1,000 living languages from about three dozen language families. New Guinea is therefore of tremendous interest to our study.

But there is an elephant in the room that we must address, based on the claims of secular anthropologists. The question is this: Are the peoples of New Guinea a prehistoric, stone age people? A people whose history predates anything in the Bible, rendering it irrelevant?

Tribes of the Region

173. Nimboran (Western New Guinea)
174. Iatmul (Papua New Guinea)
175. Parembei (Papua New Guinea)
176. Abelam (Papua New Guinea)
177. Sawi (Western New Guinea)
178. Biami (Papua New Guinea)
179. Mamberamo River Tradition (Western New Guinea)
180. Ali Island
181. Rumbiaks of Amberbaken (Western New Guinea)
182. Arapesh (Papua New Guinea)
183. Valman (Papua New Guinea)
184. Arso (Western New Guinea)
185. Dani and Yali (Western New Guinea)
186. Dao (Western New Guinea)
187. Horabi (Papua New Guinea)
188. Waropen (Western New Guinea)
189. Erave (Papua New Guinea)
190. Rangai (Papua New Guinea)
191. Fasu (Papua New Guinea)
192. Sepa (Papua New Guinea)
193. Kalauna (Papua New Guinea)
194. Foraba (Papua New Guinea)
195. Inanwatan (Western New Guinea)
196. Gavi (Papua New Guinea)
197. Jayapura (Papua New Guinea)
198. Dawawa (Papua New Guinea)
199. Huli (Papua New Guinea)
200. Jair and Kombay (Western New Guinea)
201. Pa (Papua New Guinea)
202. Kamoro (Western New Guinea)
203. Takia (Papua New Guinea)
204. Kire (Papua New Guinea)
205. Susure (Papua New Guinea)
206. Yimas (Papua New Guinea)
207. Porapora (Papua New Guinea)
208. Kembaran (Western New Guinea)
209. Orokolo (Papua New Guinea)
210. Kiwai (Papua New Guinea)
211. Muyu (Western New Guinea)
212. Risei Sajati (Western New Guinea)
213. Watut (Papua New Guinea)
214. Sawos (Papua New Guinea)
215. Morobe (Papua New Guinea)
216. Takai (Kar Kar Island)
217. Sentani (Western New Guinea)
218. Monumbo (Papua New Guinea)
219. Kilivila (Trobriand Islands)
220. Northeast Papua
221. Samo-Kubo (Western New Guinea)
222. Yapen Island
223. Mpur (Western New Guinea)
224. Sarmi Area (Western New Guinea)
225. Senggi (Western New Guinea)
226. Kimbe (Papua New Guinea)
227. Sobé (Western New Guinea)
228. Ipili (Papua New Guinea)
229. Siar (New Ireland)
230. Torres Strait
231. Ulau-Suain (Papua New Guinea)
232. Mejprat (Western New Guinea)
233. Tehit (Western New Guinea)
234. Amberbaken (Western New Guinea)
235. Nen (Papua New Guinea)
236. Biak Island
237. Manus Island (Papua New Guinea)
238. Madang Province (Papua New Guinea)

Is their history a denial of biblical Creation itself, and of the doctrine that Adam is a real person and the father of us all?

Or is their history altogether consistent with the Bible? Did their ancestors get off the Ark, just like ours? Do they know of Noah's Flood? Do they know of the Garden of Eden?

Now, if the secular, anti-biblical view is the correct one—that they are an ancient people whose history has nothing to do with the Bible, predating the biblical timeline by at least a factor of 10 or 20—indeed, refuting Genesis—then that theory can immediately justify itself by demonstrating that these jungle tribes know nothing of the events of Genesis 1-11. All the secularists have to do is demonstrate that authentic aboriginal stories matching Noah's Flood are not found in New Guinea.

That will not be happening. They do know of the events of Genesis, as we will see! They know these events because their ancestors were in that Garden, and were on that Ark! We are all brothers.

The Genesis Traditions of New Guinea

Now then, what do we learn when we examine the ancient traditions of New Guinea? First of all, we can quickly retire the false narrative that they know nothing of Noah's Flood. Simply put, New Guinea is the largest source of Flood and other Genesis-related stories of any nation or island contained in this book, with over 60 tribes or people groups represented in this chapter. Echoes of Ararat can be heard in all these stories, for the shared elements identify them as describing the same events as Genesis 1-11.

Thus, the Iatmul people say a man was instructed "to return home and build a wooden platform atop a tall coconut palm." Then he gathered his family, domestic animals, and possessions, and the Flood began." The rising waters nearly reached this man at the top of the tall coconut palm, until he threw gifts into the water and they receded.

The people at the ancient village of Parembei said the Flood was sent due to a sexual crime, and that their ancestor "built a ship and sailed the good people of the village away to safety." "Make a house on a tall coconut palm tree," was the warning given to two brothers, according to the Abelam tribe. "Take all the things you want, then climb tomorrow night." After the Flood had killed everyone, they threw coconuts down to discern whether the Flood still prevailed. When they heard one strike ground, they knew the Flood was over.

The late Don Richardson heard the Sawi tribe's version in his youth. "Long ago people were warned by a female spirit that water falling from the sky was about to flood everything. She urged them to prepare by lashing many dugout canoes together with very long vines and then building a big floating house atop the canoes." As for Noah's birds, "after many days, they released a series of birds, all of which returned except the last one."

According to the Arso tribe, a talking crocodile named Watuwe prophesied to a good man, "they will eat my flesh. Kwembo [God], however, will be very angry and a punishment will destroy the whole world with water." Watuwe directed him to take refuge at the top of Mount Sankria, which he did, taking four other people. All other life was destroyed in a global flood. Afterward, just like Noah with his raven and dove, "they sent down a kangaroo to see whether the ground below was yet dry, but the animal soon came back as it was still too wet." Then a small parrot was sent, followed by a pig. The latter stayed, which was "a sign to Towjatuwa and his people that they too could descend."

The Waropen people of West Papua say that two brothers survived the Flood in a boat with their children. In another narration, they say that a barbet bird and some crows were sent consecutively to search for land. A tribe known as the Fasu tell of an ancient Flood from which one couple escaped, having landed their boat on Mount Tipuria with a few animals. From the natives at Jayapura we learn that the first man's wife "was made out of the rib of Iria [the man] and the two of them lived together on the mountain Mer." They also have a certain memory of the Tower of Babel, as do the Trobriand Islanders right off New Guinea's eastern coast.

All the secularists have to do is demonstrate that authentic aboriginal stories matching Noah's Flood are not found in New Guinea. That will not be happening.

A Flood broke out, said the Nimboran tribe, after the first people committed a sin. "They built a house high above the ground but the water continued to rise until the house was destroyed and they floated on their ceiling beams upon the surface of the deluge. The entire earth was covered. They floated to the top of Kruabah Mountain." And the Pa tribe refer to a global Flood that destroyed all mankind "except for brother-sister couples who have a premonition of what is going to happen. They save themselves on a hastily built raft." The Porapora people refer to an ancestor named Bunara who built a large canoe on top of a mountain. When the people refused to help him launch it, he called down a flood. "He put all the available animals into his canoe and sailed out to sea."

"Back in the dawn of time," said the Samo-Kubo of West Papua, people committed a crime, and an unrelenting Flood was unleashed. "Finally, all the people climbed up the highest mountain they could find. But still the waters crept up. People everywhere were drowning." And, "Finally, two brothers built a raft. It was only a small raft. They climbed aboard. Soon, all the others tried to climb on, but the raft only held two. They sailed off, and left the others behind."

The Erave tribe refer to the unlawful killing and eating of a certain "snake-fish." A good man abstained, being forewarned in a dream against joining in the people's sins. That day, torrential rains began to fall and the earth was covered by a flood. The good man, his wife, and child climbed a coconut palm, taking a pair of chickens, dogs, and pigs, along with supplies. The tree grew taller at the rate that the waters climbed. Later, they threw coconuts down to test the water level. On the fourth throw, the sound alerted them it was safe to climb down. These repopulated the earth.

We can quickly retire the false narrative that the New Guineans know nothing of Noah's Flood.

The Sepa people's tradition is similar, involving a shape-shifting "snake-man" (no doubt a memory of the serpent of Genesis 3) who tells two girls what will happen. These warn the people, who scoff at them and kill and eat the snake anyway. Then the girls take their brothers and climb a very tall coconut tree, and "a flood came and destroyed them all and a big stone smashed the people." The Kaluana have a Flood tradition in which there is a memory of the Ark and Noah's birds, as do many other tribes. Among these are the Jair and Kombay, who remember the Creator sending a Flood to destroy sinners, but preserving two people in a bamboo tube. The Kire have a memory of the raven and dove, which they replace with a chicken and a bird which came from a leaf. Those living along the Mamberamo River have passed down a memory of a flood, the surface of which surpassed Mount Vanessa. Only a man and his wife survived, taking with them a pig, a cassowary, a kangaroo, and a pigeon.

But we have only scratched the surface. Let us continue and hear the echoes of Genesis 1-11 from New Guinea.

173 **NIMBORAN**

The Nimboran tribe of Western New Guinea[1] has preserved a memory of the construction of the Ark and the fact that it floated and came to rest on a mountain.

In the beginning, only Kasuitemu (male) and Bawa (female) lived on the earth with the animals. Kasuitemu convinced Bawa to have intimacy with him, which was not permitted for them. The next day the sky grew dark and the earth was covered with a torrent of rain and ashes. Then water started bubbling out of the earth and began to rise. They built a house high above the ground but the water continued to rise until the house was destroyed and they floated on their ceiling beams upon the surface of the deluge. The entire earth was covered. They floated to the top of Kruabah Mountain.

The waters began to abate, but very slowly. One night, a fiery being named Warikerang came down and visited Kasuitemu in a dream. Warikerang taught Kasuitemu to obey his commands and prophesied that the flood would dry up and that he and Bawa would have eight children. Warikerang visited the survivors many times and brought them many gifts and taught them how to live. And it happened that Bawa bore eight children who intermarried and repopulated the earth.[2]

They floated on their ceiling beams upon the surface of the deluge. The entire earth was covered. They floated to the top of Kruabah Mountain.

A second version says the survivors were two young siblings, and that they later married and repopulated the earth.[3]

174 **IATMUL**

In 1989, Eric Silverman collected and translated an important text from the Iatmul people who live along the Sepik River in Papua (eastern) New Guinea. Silverman considered this text to be an authoritative version of the Eastern Iatmul deluge tradition.

After an act of cruelty committed against the wife of a man named Wobowi, he takes counsel with "the largest and most powerful crocodile spirit," who is named Mendangumeli.

> "Mendangumeli agrees to help Wobowi exact retribution and tells Wobowi to return home and build a wooden platform atop a tall coconut palm. After building the platform and gathering his family, pigs, dogs, chickens, and possessions, Wobowi waits atop the coconut palm. After five days, it begins to rain. Two water lilies sprout in the grassy promenade outside the men's ceremonial house. Villagers are puzzled since these flowers normally grow in swamps and lakes. Curious, they pluck the lilies and two torrents of water shoot up from the holes in the ground, flooding the region. Mendangumeli tells Wobowi to spear and kill his deceitful cousin amid the rising water. He does so. The flood kills everybody from the community but Wobowi and his family. The village is destroyed. Still, the waters rise. Fearful of drowning, Wobowi throws shell valuables, pork, and betel-nut into the water in the hopes that Mendangumeli will accept these gifts and halt the flood."[4]

He tells Wobowi to return home and build a wooden platform atop a tall coconut palm. After building the platform and gathering his family, pigs, dogs, chickens, and possessions, Wobowi waits atop the coconut palm. After five days, it begins to rain.

1. The western part of New Guinea is typically called West Papua by Indonesians. However, for the purposes of this book, and to avoid confusion (West Papua is also the name of one of Indonesia's provinces on the island, the other being the much bigger Papua province), we will refer to the whole of Indonesia's territory (west of the 140th parallel) as Western New Guinea.
2. Kamma, *Religious Texts of the Oral Tradition From Western New-Guinea* (Irian Jaya) Part B, pp. 18-23.
3. Kamma, *Religious Texts of the Oral Tradition From Western New-Guinea* (Irian Jaya) Part B, pp. 23-26.
4. Eric K. Silverman, "The Waters of Mendangumeli: A Masculine Psychoanalytic Interpretation of a New Guinea Flood Myth--and Women's Laughter," *Journal of American Folklore*, vol. 129 (2016), p. 183.

The crocodile spirit Mendangumeli rescues Wobowi and his family, but requires the man pay with the cruel death of his daughter. We believe that this crocodile is actually a distorted memory of the Serpent from Genesis 3, which is Satan himself. And the death required by this creature may be none other than that which entered the world in Genesis 3, when Satan tempted our ancestors and they disobeyed God.

175 PAREMBEI

The Parembei are a sub-tribe of the Iatmul, living along the Sepik River in New Guinea. The center of their history is the village of Parembei, which is quite ancient and is adorned by stone monoliths.[5] The monoliths may date to the early period when the Iatmul and Sawos were a single people.

The ancestor Naua built a ship and sailed the good people of the village away to safety.

Laurie Bragge met the Parembei people in the 1960s. At a Parembei village named Kanganaman, the natives told him that the Flood was sent by God in response to a sexual crime committed by a man from a "haus tambaran" or spirit house in Kosimbit. "The lake beside the village flooded and drowned the people in hot water. The ancestor Naua built a ship and sailed the good people of the village away to safety. Naua had a brother called Masam, who was also responsible for settling of the people."[6]

It should be noted that "Naua" above, which resembles Noah, is also one of their clan names.[7] The name is ancient, and the resemblance to Noah seems to be coincidental.

176 ABELAM

The Abelam people make their homes in the Prince Alexander Mountains along the northern coast of eastern New Guinea. They have a Flood tradition which has parallels not only with the Genesis Flood, but also with the Garden of Eden. Although it is lengthy, we think you will find it to be one of the more memorable narrations in this book. It is also quite prototypical of New Guinean Flood texts, and has many points of continuity with other versions that we will read in this chapter:

> "Long, long ago, in the time of the ancestors, many people lived in a village in the Wosera area of East Sepik Province [Abelam People]. In this village, there was a masalai [spirit] woman named Ramingihan. This masalai dwelled with her child. One day, the men of the village wanted to have a festival, so they went hunting for lizards in the forest. They killed the lizards and used their skins for the hand drums that they would beat during the festival. ... they killed many lizards.
>
> The masalai woman's child was a lizard. The men killed this lizard too, and they carried it back to the village. Ramingihan, the masalai woman, had gone to another place in the forest at this time, so the men had not killed her. Poor Ramingihan arrived at the house and saw that her child was not there. She searched and searched, then she knew that the men of the village must have killed her child. Oh my, she was both troubled and furious. Quietly, she performed a small song and dance, then she turned herself into a dog. She walked and walked towards the village, then she saw them preparing the hand drums. She took a hand drum and saw that it was her child's skin.

5. Laurie Bragge, *A History of New Guinea's Sepik Region*, vol. 1, part 1 (Papua New Guinea Association of Australia, 2023), p. 230.
6. *Ibid.*, p. 231.
7. *Ibid.*, p. 190.

> She cried and walked back to her house inside the forest. Along the trail, she met two brothers who were breaking apart sago and taking the sago beetle grubs [for food]. The parents of the brothers had died, so they just lived by themselves. They hunted for their own food with their own strength. The ghost woman was still a dog. She went up to the brothers and they gave her some grubs. She ate some, then she waited for them."[8]

For this act of kindness, these men would be spared from the Flood:

> "The brothers thought that it was a dog from the village. They did not know that the dog was a ghost woman. It was nearly afternoon and the dog followed them to the village. They cooked the grubs, then when they were about to eat, the brothers were surprised to see the same dog sleeping by the house. They called out and the dog came up to them. They gave the dog some grubs, and they ate together. They ate, then the dog turned back into the ghost woman with long fingers and hair. Oh my, the two brothers were terrified and tried to find a way to escape."[9]

Make a house on a tall coconut palm tree inside the village.

Although they were initially terrified by her, she reassured them and gave instructions to survive the coming calamity:

> "However, the ghost woman told them, 'Don't be afraid of me. You gave me food and took care of me, so I can't ruin you. The people of this village killed my child, so I want to kill them. You must prepare something for yourselves. Then make a house on a tall coconut palm tree inside the village. Take all of the things you want, then climb tomorrow night when they are about to sing and dance.' After the masalai woman said this, she disappeared. In the very early morning, they awoke and did as the ghost woman had told them to do."[10]

The next day, the Flood broke out:

> "The villagers worked at cooking and gathering food. It was completely dark. They began beating the new hand drums, singing, and dancing. The brothers wanted to talk, but they shut their mouths because the villagers had never treated them well. The masalai woman heard the sound of the hand drums and the singing, then she arrived in the village. She turned into a dog, then she lay at the base of the coconut palm on top of which the two brothers were sitting. She lay there for a while, then she began to sing and dance to raise a flood. Before long, a woman went to the base of the coconut palm to throw away some garbage. The woman's leg missed and hit a big coconut leaf. Then the water shot up and began covering everyone. The people left the festival and the food, then they ran about. That night, the flood rose and killed everyone in the village. The masalai woman stood at the base of the coconut palm, jumping back and forth. She removed the water that would have swallowed the coconut palm. When it was nearly dawn, the two brothers descended.
>
> Oh my, the brothers were surprised to see that everyone in the village was gone. Only they were left, so they built a new village."[11]

They threw coconuts down from the top of the tree to discern the water depth. One day, they heard the coconut strike ground. Thus they understood that the Flood was over.

Another version says the surviving pair were a husband and wife. In any case, they threw coconuts down from the top of the tree on separate days to discern

8. Thomas H. Slone, *One Thousand One Papua New Guinean Nights*, vol. 2 (Oakland: Masalai Press, 2001), pp. 740-741.
9. *Ibid.*, p. 741.
10. *Ibid.*
11. *Ibid.*

the water depth. One day, they heard the coconut strike ground. Thus they understood that the Flood was over, and they climbed down the tree.[12] This is a parallel of Noah's tests involving birds, which we discuss in Appendix B. A third version says that snakes caused the Flood.[13]

177 SAWI

The Sawi live in the jungle of western New Guinea. They practiced both cannibalism and head-hunting when the missionary Don Richardson went to live among them in 1962. The Sawi elders shared their tradition of the Flood with Richardson:

> "Long ago people were warned by a female spirit that water falling from the sky was about to flood everything. She urged them to prepare by lashing many dugout canoes together with very long vines and then building a big floating house atop the canoes. She added a special instruction that the roof of the house must consist of more than just ordinary thatch because rocks would be falling from the sky with the water. Because rocks would punch holes through mere thatch, the roof had to consist of two layers: a lower layer made of slabs of thick palm bark under an upper layer of thatch so that both rocks and water would be deflected. Thus they were spared along with many animals and birds. Still afloat after many days, they released a series of birds, all of which returned except the last one. When at last the house rested on the earth, everyone was eager to rush outside, but the head man said, "Wait several more days. Everything is too wet." Later, the first food they ate back on the ground was fish they found stranded inside their homes that had been flooded."[14]

She urged them to prepare by lashing many dugout canoes together with very long vines and then building a big floating house atop the canoes.

Richardson also pointed out to me (Nick) that the Sawi, isolated in the depths of the New Guinean jungle, had never seen a vessel larger than a canoe. That they should have a knowledge of this great vessel, described so similarly to Noah's Ark is all the more remarkable.

178 BIAMI

The missionary Tom Hoey recorded this Flood account from the Biami people of Papua New Guinea in the early 1970s. They replace Noah's Ark with a tree that grew taller and taller as the waters rose:

> "Once a great flood came which covered the whole earth and wiped out everyone on earth except for the ancestors of the Biami people. Those ancestors climbed up into the Gobia Tree, … They took up into the tree their planting materials for crops, all their animals, their dogs and their pigs and everything else necessary for life. As the flood waters rose up on the face of the earth the people climbed further up the tree. They were safe in the branches of this tree because the tree grew up above the waters as the waters rose up.
>
> When the waters went down from the surface of the whole earth, the people were able to climb down the tree. The ground was very muddy, but eventually they planted their crops and their animals began to reproduce. They moved away from the tree and began to repopulate

Once a great flood came which covered the whole earth and wiped out everyone on earth except for the ancestors of the Biami people.

12. Thomas H. Slone, *One Thousand One Papua New Guinean Nights*, vol. 1 (Oakland: Masalai Press, 2001), p. 124.
13. Thomas H. Slone, *One Thousand One Papua New Guinean Nights*, vol. 2, pp. 559-560.
14. Personal correspondence with Don Richardson, 30 December, 2016.

the earth. Those who had climbed down out of the tree were the ancestors of the Samos, the Kubos, the Gobasis, and the Etoro."[15]

The Biami also have a creation story with interesting Genesis parallels, including the "breath of life":

> "At first the world was populated only by men. The first man in the world heard a small palm tree crying and crying. The man came to the small palm tree and it was put into his mind to begin to make a companion for himself. He took a knife and he carved the little palm tree into the shape of a woman. He carved all the woman' organs, and then he breathed the breath of life into the nostrils that he had carved in the palm tree. The woman became alive."[16]

As evidence of this flood, they refer to bones of drowned animals, which have been found on Mount Vanessa.

179 MAMBERAMO RIVER TRADITION

The Mamberamo River area of New Guinea is home to many little-known tribes. From one of these tribes, the German explorer Max Moszkowski (1873 – 1939) heard a tradition of the Flood.

The Mamberamo River

They spoke of a great flood which had been caused by the rising of the river. The waters even surpassed Mount Vanessa. Only one man and his wife escaped, together with a pig, a cassowary, a kangaroo, and a pigeon. The man and woman are the ancestors of all mankind after them, and the surviving animals are the ancestors of all the species that are now on the earth. As evidence of this Flood, they refer to bones of drowned animals, which have been found on Mount Vanessa.[17]

180 ALI ISLAND

Ali Island, which is less than one square kilometer, is located off the northern coast of New Guinea. The native people told a Flood tradition involving a special "talking eel," an unmistakable echo of Genesis 3:

The head of the talking eel warned the boy not to eat it and instructed him to tell his parents what to do.

> "The flood story had survived the test of time and has spread across the Sepik region, though the flood myth is also a universal one. The Ali Island version begins with the villagers killing a talking eel who had warned the villagers to remove the fish poison (Walamil) used to kill fish for a mortuary feast in the village. The eel was carved up and distributed among the villagers. The head part of the eel was given to a young boy. The head of the eel warned the boy not to eat it and instructed him to tell his parents what to do. The father planted the eel's head near a tall coconut tree, dug a hole near the tree so that the boy

15. Tom Hoey and John Mackay, "The Biami Legends of Creation and Noah's Flood," *Creation*, vol. 7, no. 2 (1984), pp. 12-13. Retrieved 15 November, 2018 from https://creation.com/the-biami-legends-of-creation-and-noahs-flood
16. *Ibid.*
17. Max Moszkowski, "Die Völkerstamme am Mamberamo in Holländisch-Neuguinea und auf den vorgelagerten Inseln," *Zeitschrift für Ethnologie*, vol. 43 (1911), pp. 340-341.

> and his mother can take shelter from the flood commanded by the eel. The flood destroyed the entire village, except for a neighboring village tribe known as Yini Parey, on the way to the feast, who were swept away by the flood on a breadfruit tree, ending up on a reef that became known as Ali Island. The boy's father had climbed the coconut tree as instructed by the eel. The boy and his mother remained sheltered in the pit near the tall coconut tree. The father, Kairap, ate coconuts to remain alive in the tree. To see if the flood had receded he threw three coconuts down from the tree. The first two coconuts sank into the water. The third coconut touched the hard surface of the earth. The smoke rising from the pit where the boy and his mother took shelter confirmed that the flood has subsided."[18]

To see if the flood had receded he threw three coconuts down from the tree. The first two coconuts sank into the water. The third coconut touched the hard surface of the earth.

Notice in the last few sentences the clear parallel with Noah's birds in Genesis 8:6-12.

181 RUMBIAKS OF AMBERBAKEN

We refer here to a clan known as Rumbiak, living at the village of Amberbaken. Their name probably derives from the Rumbiak people of Biak and Numford Islands, who engaged in trade with this village.[19] The tradition which they narrated in 1955 shows a rather clear memory of the rescuing of animals from the Flood. They have, however, replaced the Ark with a mountain, which itself is a memory of Ararat.

They built their house on the summit where nothing could fall on top of them. They gathered many kinds of animals and warned the other people that a deluge would soon come.

In the ancient times, a woman named Dwani lived on Pipaki mountain with her children. One day it happened that there were many terrible earthquakes. Dwani and her children ascended Pipaki and built their house on the summit where nothing could fall on top of them. They gathered many kinds of animals and warned the other people that a deluge would soon come and told them to join them on Pipaki. But no one heeded Dwani's call. Then, the deluge covered everything except the summit of Pipaki and everyone outside of Dwani and her children died.[20]

Pegunungan Arfak, the highest point in West Papua

18. Steven Edmund Winduo, "Reconstituting Indigenous Oceanic Folktales," *University of Hawaii Manoa International Symposium; Folktales and Fairy Tales* (2010), pp. 9-10. See also: Adam Amot, *The Great Flood, Legends from New Guinea: Book 2,* ed. Donald Stokes (1996), pp. 95-99.
19. Kamma, *Religious Texts of the Oral Tradition From Western New-Guinea* (Irian Jaya) Part B, pp. 172-173.
20. *Ibid.*, pp. 49-50.

ARAPESH

182 The Arapesh people live in the mountains of East Sepik in eastern New Guinea. Before considering the Arapesh Flood texts, recall that in Genesis 9:4 God admonishes Noah and his sons to abstain from eating blood. "But you shall not eat flesh with its life, that is, its blood."

With this in mind, it is interesting that the Arapesh tribe attribute the cause of the Flood to the consumption of blood.

We should also recall the admonition given by God to Adam and Eve in chapter 3, against the eating of fruit from a particular tree. Is it possible that the Arapesh remembered these two commands and merged them, identifying blood as that which was consumed and caused the Flood?

Only two people were able to escape, a man and a woman who found refuge on top of a mountain.

One day, the women of Lonem (Loneim Village, Mountain Arapesh People, East Sepik) went to their gardens to harvest taro. Meanwhile, their children went fishing at a taboo part of the river where a masalai (spirit) dwelled. The children did not know it, but a mudfish man had died there and his spirit remained in the water. The children caught his spirit and thought it was a real fish. They gave this dead fish to their mothers who took it to the village. They cooked the dead fish and when they cut it to eat, the fish was full of human blood. So they cooked it again in the fire but the blood did not dry up. Finally, they ate it with the blood and went to sleep.

That night, the water rose and flooded their village. The water went so high that it killed all of the people, dogs and pigs. The water covered everything in the village. Only two people were able to escape, a man and a woman who found refuge on top of a mountain.[21]

In a second Arapesh text, just one woman survived the Flood because she had refused to eat the blood of the eel killed by the other villagers.[22]

VALMAN

183 The Valman are a tribe of Papua New Guinea from the north coastal province of West Sepik. The Catholic missionary Christian Schleiermacher reported this Flood tradition from them, in an article published in 1900:

> "One day the wife of a very good man saw a big fish swimming on the shore. She called her husband. His name cannot be given by the Valman.[23] He could not see the fish at first. The woman laughed at him and pulled her husband behind a banana tree, so that he might peep at it through the leaves. He was terribly shocked when, after a long search, he discovered the monster. He quickly called his family—a son and two daughters—and forbade them to catch and eat the fish. The other men, however, with a bow and arrow and a rope as strong as the missionaries' wire, caught the fish and dragged it ashore. The good man admonished them not to eat the fish, but they did anyway."[24]

He quickly drove a pair of animals of all kinds up into the trees. Then he climbed up a coconut tree with his family.

The forbidden act thus committed, the Flood ensued. Notice the rescuing of animals before the Flood:

---

21. Slone, *One Thousand One Papua New Guinean Nights*, vol. 1, p. 60.
22. Roslyn Poignant, *Oceanic Mythology: The Myths of Polynesia, Micronesia, Melanesia, Australia* (London: Hamlyn, 1967), p. 92.
23. John Z'Graggen writes, in his analysis of New Guinea traditions: "The secrecy of myth is still alive in many areas, and in research some myths were told to me only on a mission station or plantation, or in a confidential way. I learned also that the myth is not so secret as the names of the characters. A myth with no names of the main actors is meaningless to the people." John Z'Graggen, "Topics of New Guinea legends," *Asian Folklore Studies*, vol. 42, no. 2 (1983), p. 264.
24. P. Chr. Schleiermacher, "Religiose Anschauungen und Gebrauche der Bewohner von Berlinhafen Deutsch Neuguinea," *Globus*, vol. 78, No. 1 (Brunswick, Germany: Druck und Verlag, 1900), p. 6.

"When the brave man saw this, he quickly drove a pair of animals of all kinds up into the trees. Then he climbed up a coconut tree with his family. No sooner had the wicked people consumed the fish than the water burst out of the ground with such force that no one could save themselves. Peoples and animals alike were destroyed. As the water rose quickly to the crown of the tallest tree, it also fell just as quickly. The brave man got off the tree with his family and planted new plants."[25]

No sooner had the wicked people consumed the fish than the water burst out of the ground with such force that no one could save themselves.

ARSO

184 Keerom Regency, directly east of Western New Guinea's largest city of Jayapura, is home to the Arso people. Their Flood tradition, narrated to P. W. Rombouts sometime prior to 1973, is quite compelling. Again there are elements of the Garden of Eden, including a prohibition to eat a certain food. In slightly abbreviated form, it went as follows:

"Long ago it was not possible to bring a child into the world by natural means. The womb had to be opened with a stone axe. The result of this operation, of course, was that the mother died." One day, a man named Towjatuwa,was fashioning a stone axe for this very purpose when he was approached by a giant crocodile named Watuwe who delivered a baby boy named Narrowra through the use of herbal medicine. Through this act, Watuwe taught mankind that women could live and become mothers rather than die in childbirth.

"Then the crocodile prophesied, 'When the child, Narrowra, grows up and becomes an expert hunter, the people will shoot me. They will eat my flesh. Kwembo [God], however, will be very angry and as a punishment will destroy the whole world with water. When you, Towjatuwa, and your son are offered my flesh to eat, you must refuse for anyone who eats it will perish.'" The crocodile directed the man to take refuge at the summit of Mount Sankria, adding, "There the jankwenk (the people from above) will tell you what to do next."

They will eat my flesh. Kwembo, however, will be very angry and as a punishment will destroy the whole world with water. When you, Towjatuwa, and your son are offered my flesh to eat, you must refuse for anyone who eats it will perish.

Sure enough, when Narrowra grew up, the prophecy came to pass. The men shot and killed the crocodile. They rejoiced and called for a celebration with the neighboring villages, for the death of this crocodile gave them meat in abundance.

Towjatuwa, however, abstained from the feast, just as he had been instructed. "Then he told [his son] Narrowra what they were to do. Narrowra went to fetch his friend Kunebuan, as well as his sister, Ubara, and the sister of Kunebuan, Membawa. The five of them set out for the mountain in Sankria." When they finally arrived at the summit, they met the Jankwenk [angelic beings].

"The jankwenk began to talk about the terrible punishment which would come to pass over the world as a result of the death of Watuwe. At the same time, they were told what was to be done after the dreadful punishment. All human, animal and plant life would disappear from the earth. Only that which stood on the Mountain of Sankria would survive the catastrophe. Their task was therefore to re-populate the devastated world with people, animals and plants." This would be done with seeds given them by the jankwenk.

Finally, the Flood broke out at the playing of the flute by four jankwenk. They "sounded a deafening noise" which was "a sign to the waters." "With thundering force the floods came. The water foamed and frothed. Trees were uprooted and dragged away. The clouds emptied the rain onto the earth with immense force. The water rose higher and higher. The force of the flood remained unbroken until all life was dead, all trees and plants uprooted. The Mountain Sankria was the only place where life remained intact."

The force of the flood remained unbroken until all life was dead, all trees and plants uprooted.

25. *Ibid.*

> "Slowly the water came to rest and the downpour lessened. After a few days the water began to subside. There was devastation everywhere. The only tree that still remained standing was a large ironwood at the top of Mount Sankria."[26]

The parallels with Genesis are amazing. But what about Noah's sending of the raven and the dove (Genesis 8:6-12)? Do the Arso have a memory of that as well? Let us continue reading to find out:

> "They sent down a kangaroo to see whether the ground below was yet dry, but the animal soon came back as it was still too wet. After a few more days of waiting, the lory (small, brightly coloured parrot) was sent. It too came back for it was not yet dry. After yet a few more days he sent down a pig. It stayed. This was a sign to Towjatuwa and his people that they too could descend and begin their designated tasks."[27]

They sent down a kangaroo to see whether the ground below was yet dry, but the animal soon came back as it was still too wet. ... After yet a few more days he sent down a pig. It stayed. This was a sign to Towjatuwa and his people that they too could descend and begin their designated tasks.

What we possess from the Dani and Yali people groups of the Central Highlands of Indonesian New Guinea are traditions about the origin of mortality. If you guessed that a serpent is somehow involved, you are correct. In these traditions, the serpent was tasked with delivering a message to mankind which would secure continual rejuvenation and eternal life, but the bird was tasked with delivering a message of mourning and death. As Kamma summarized:

> "In the interior of the main Island of New Guinea (Irian Jaya) where among others the Dani and the Yali-tribe are living, the snake is very important. The failing snake, in the race or match between the bird and the snake, causes death. The snake who failed was the same which later on caused the disaster of the landslides.
>
> ... (In primeval times) death was still unknown, it came as a fate to mankind. The possibility of a continuous rejuvenation was at hand. All the inhabitants of the mountains know about the fatal match between the Sibine-bird (hornbill) and the snake Kalije. These two kinds of animals were appointed to deliver their special message to the human being(s). The message of the bird in the Yali language was: 'Fong, fong' (meaning: morning-time, mourning-time). The snake's errand was to say: 'Nahamut, hahamut' (my skin, your skin): my skin will be the example for your skin."[28]

Because the bird was first in delivering his message, man has had to die ever since.

What do we make of this from a biblical standpoint? It appears they mixed the memory of the Serpent in the Garden and the memory of Noah's dove. We do not think it coincidental that these two creatures are involved, for the serpent and the bird keep showing up in story types all over the world that have shared features with Genesis, a fact which we explore further in Appendix B. Note well that the serpent and the bird (dove) are the only two creatures that delivered a 'message' to humans in Genesis 1 through 11:

> Now the serpent was more cunning than any beast of the field which the Lord God had made. And he said to the woman, "Has God indeed said, 'You shall not eat of every tree of the garden'?" (Genesis 3:1 NKJV)

26. P. W. Rombouts, "The Arso Version of the Story of the Flood," *Bulletin of Irian Jaya Development,* vol. 2, no. 3 (Jayapura: University of Cenderawasih, 1973), pp. 62-66.
27. *Ibid.*, p. 66.
28. Kamma, *Religious Texts of the Oral Tradition From Western New-Guinea (Irian Jaya) Part B,* pp. 122-123. Kamma adds that in the Dani language, the bird's message was 'rub your body with clay,' which represents mourning.

> And the dove came to him toward evening, and behold, in its beak was a freshly picked olive leaf. So Noah knew that the water was abated from the earth. (Genesis 8:11 LSB)

The key difference in Genesis is that it was actually the snake (Satan) that brought a message of death. The bird brought an object which was understood as a sign of life.

Preparing the Way for the Gospel in New Guinea

In the chapter on Southeast Asia, we saw that God had prepared many tribes for the coming Gospel. A similar thing took place in New Guinea, as the missionary Don Richardson wrote: "Among the Ekari, Damal, Dani, Ndugwa, and other tribes, more than one hundred thousand Stone Agers welcomed our gospel as the fulfillment of something their respective cultures had anticipated for hundreds of years. The Ekari called it aji. To the Damal, it was hai. To the Dani, nabelan-kabelan, an immortal message which one day would restrain tribal war and ease human suffering. The result: cultural fulfillment of the deepest possible kind. And it opened the door to faith in Jesus Christ for tens of thousands."[29]

186

DAO

The Dao people are a remote tribe of Western New Guinea, living in jungles surrounded by high mountains in New Guinea's Central Range. While we do not have a Flood story to report, there is a most interesting Creation story that they narrated to Donald Phillips. Distinct parallels with Genesis chapters 3 (the Fall) and 4 (Cain and Abel) can be seen here:

> "Our people believe that the very first humans on the earth were a mother and three sons. One day the middle son tried to commit incest with the mother and so the other brothers decided that they must kill him because of this evil act. They waited for just the right time when he least expected it. Then they shot him with their bows and arrows and killed him for his evil act. It was then that the two remaining brothers decided that in order that there would be more people on earth they needed to split their murdered brother's body in half and separate it into different sections from which new groups of people could be born.
>
> So, the older brother sent the younger into the jungle to gather the correct type of banana leaves in which to wrap the body parts. They would wrap the individual body parts of the murdered middle brother in these banana leaves after they had divided them into different groups according to types. After hours and then days the younger brother still hadn't returned with the appropriate leaves and so the older brother grew angry and impatient. He decided he would not wait any longer and in his frustration he grabbed his half of the murdered middle brother's corpse and carried it over next to a large

Some of the blood from the corpse dripped down into the ground next to that special tree which was next to that river. When it dripped down into the ground it seeped right into the mouth of a great evil spirit snake. For this very reason, even to this day we Dao people die.

29. Don Richardson, "Do Missionaries Destroy Cultures?" *Perspectives on the World Christian Movement*, eds. Ralph Winter and Steven C Hawthorne (Pasadena: William Carey Library, 2009), p. 490. For more information on what Richardson is referring to in regard to the Damal and Dani peoples, see his article, "Redemptive Analogy," also in *Perspectives on the World Christian* Movement, page 431.

special type of tree by the river. He then grabbed the closest large leaves he could find and began separating that half of the middle brother's body into different groups. Just then the younger brother returned with the proper banana leaves but it was too late, the older brother had started without him!"[30]

What happens next is most noteworthy:

"In his anger at the older brother the younger brother then grabbed his half of the corpse and carried it off into the highlands to divide the body by himself also. Because the older brother had not been patient and had used the wrong type of leaves, some of the blood from the corpse dripped down into the ground next to that special tree which was next to that river. When it dripped down into the ground it seeped right into the mouth of a great evil spirit snake. For this very reason, even to this day we Dao people die. It is said that if there had not been that disagreement between the two brothers and that blood had not gone into the great serpent's mouth next to that special tree, we would live forever!"[31]

Prophecies of a Coming Message from God

In 2003, Donald and Jennie Phillips sold their valuables and bought a one-way ticket to Indonesia, with no plans to return. Their mission was to find an isolated tribe of New Guinea that had never heard of Jesus, and to bring the Gospel to them. They learned of a remote jungle tribe known as the Dao people and went to live among them.

Unbeknownst to the Phillips, before they arrived, before they even thought about pouring their hearts and lives into such a dangerous and impossible task—God had gone ahead of them. God had prepared this people group in advance. As Donald Phillips later wrote:

"I looked at Apius [a Dao man] and said to the best of my ability, speaking very slowly: "Friend, when we built a house here you also built a house here. Why did you build a house here, but most of the other Dao people did not build here but only visit instead?" … He seemed to understand my question and got a kind of half smile on his face, almost a grin as he thought for a moment about his reply. After a few seconds he stretched out his arm next to him and held his hand about the height of his stomach if he would have been standing. "When I was about this high, just a young man, I woke up in the men's hut one morning and started cooking a sweet potato over the fire. My father was the last of the men in the house to wake up but when he woke he quickly sat up and said 'Wow! I had a really strange dream.' 'Well tell it to us' the other men said, because dreams are very important to us Dao people. My father continued on to say 'Oh, it was so strange. I saw pale skinned people hike up into our mountains. They hiked into our valley and somehow could speak our language. They said they had an important message for us and then they lived among us. Then after we had heard their message we became so close with these pale skinned people that they were like brothers and sisters to us, we became like family with them! And then I woke up! It was such a strange dream!' he said to the other men in the room." Apius explained.

30. Donald Scott Phillips, *Prophecies of Pale Skin* (Kindle Edition, 2013), Chapter 10.
31. *Ibid.*

Then looking up at my face and directly into my eyes, Apius continued. "Friend, when I saw you and your wife hike into our valley and I saw your pale skin, and then I saw you building a house here and trying to learn our language, and you told us you had an important message for us, bering the dream I decided I would do everything I could to help you learn our language as quickly as possible. I am here, living with you and helping you because I am waiting for the day I can hear your message. That is why I built my house here."

I could hardly believe what I was hearing. Apius was probably in his late thirties or early forties. His father had died years before we ever set foot into the Dao valley but from what Apius was saying, God had given his father a dream probably close to thirty years ago prophesying of our arrival in the Dao territory! … Even though they had been forgotten by the rest of the world, God had not forgotten about them. Over the next few weeks we would hear this same story from other Dao people as well. Apius' father was not the only man in the Dao tribe to have this prophetic dream. In fact, this wasn't just a dream to these people at all. It was a prophecy that foretold future events! And because of our pale skin and claim from the beginning to carry a "great message" they saw us as the fulfillment to this prophecy! Multiple men had experienced the same prophecy through dreams and passed it on to their children and clan also. God had been giving them these prophetic dreams to prepare them! He had been working out His plan here in the Dao valley. Before we had ever arrived here God's predetermined plan of having "people from every tongue, tribe, people and nation one day standing before his throne" as the Book of Revelation talks about, had been put into play!"[32]

Today, there is a thriving and growing Dao church, with native ministers taking the Gospel to other villages and their neighbors.

187

HORABI

The Horabi tribe's Flood account has a strong parallel to Genesis 3 regarding Adam and Eve and the forbidden tree. In the Horabi tradition, the woman disregarded the prohibition against taking water from a certain part of the river. She fetched water from the taboo area and gave it to her brother to quench his thirst from the midday sun. He unknowingly drank the taboo water and, when he arose to urinate at midnight found that his belly was rumbling in the same way as the water rumbles at the taboo part of the river. Then the flood came. They clambered onto the roof of their house but the water continued to rise. Then the woman approached the deluge, but the water shrank away from her. When the man approached the deluge, it took him away and the woman transformed into a bird and flew away.[33]

32. Donald Scott Phillips, *Prophecies of Pale Skin*. Kindle Edition, 2013. Chapter 8. Regarding the "pale skin" part, this is no racial statement. It is simply a description of what they foresaw. On another occasion, in another place, it could have been a black missionary or a medium-brown missionary.
33. Roy Wagner, *Lethal Speech: Daribi Myth as Symbolic Obviation* (London: Cornell University Press, 1978), p. 99.

188 WAROPEN

Waropen is an Austronesian language that is spoken in the Waropen Regency of Western New Guinea. We have several Flood texts published by G. J. Held in 1956. According to one narration, two brothers survived the Deluge in a boat with their children. After the waters subsided, they built houses to live in and the son of one brother married the daughter of the other brother and she conceived. These were the ancestors of the Waropen villages.[34]

Two brothers survived the deluge in a boat with their children.

In a second narrative, one day while in the jungle, Ibueri caught a snake and confined it in a bamboo joint. When he was away, the other villagers cooked and ate it. Thereon, the deluge came and everyone drowned. The corpses of the dead transformed into trees and animals. Only lbueri survived with his wife and daughter. They escaped the flood by using a rope to climb high into the mountains. They stayed there until the flood waters dried up. Then, Ibueri and his wife had a son and their children married each other and multiplied.[35]

A third tradition has a clear parallel to Noah's sending of the raven and the dove. It is said that some survivors lived by tying themselves to a tree while others were in canoes. As time went on and the waters failed to recede, they dispatched a barbet bird to search for land. Finding nothing, it returned. Next they released some crows. But, rather than search for dry land, the crows ate the corpses of the dead. Finally, they set the barbet out again. The barbet joined the crows and, being thirsty, they found a small creek and paid the old woman who guarded the creek in beads in order to stay there.[36]

189 ERAVE

The Erave people, living in the Southern Highlands Province of Papua New Guinea, have a fascinating Flood story. Long ago, many people lived in a village named Ipaiva. However, these people were bad. Among them lived a good man and woman with their child. One day while fishing, they saw a big fish that was like a snake. The good man told everyone that if they killed it, a big flood would come and everyone would die. However, the bad men ignored his warning and killed it. Then they took it to the village to eat. That night, the good man dreamt of a man who told him not to eat that fish because he would kill whoever did so. So the good man did not eat the fish.

The good man told everyone that if they killed the snake-like fish, a big flood would come and everyone would die. However, the bad men ignored his warning and killed it.

After the bad men ate, they cooked the medicinal part of the fish's innards. But it spilled into the fire and caused a deep black smoke to rise into the sky, causing torrential rain to fall.

The good people took two chickens, a cock and a hen, two pigs, two dogs, fire and some water and climbed a coconut palm. As the floodwaters rose, the palm tree also grew taller, rising to great heights in the sky. Later, they cast a new coconut down to the water three times, then the fourth time, it finally hit the ground. They knew that the flood had finished, so they left the palm. All of the people and animals on the ground had died; the flood had killed them. We are descended from these good people. And the animals also came from these survivors.[37]

The good people took two chickens, a cock and a hen, two pigs, two dogs, fire and some water and climbed a coconut palm.

34. G. J. Held, "De Zondvloed," in *Waropense teksten* (*Geelvinkbaai, Noord Nieuw-Guinea*) (The Hague: Martinus Nijhoff, 1956), p. 42-43
35. Held, "De Zondvloed," pp. 38-39.
36. Held, "De Zondvloed," pp. 41-42.
37. Slone, *One Thousand One Papua New Guinean Nights*, vol. 1, p. 134.

190 **RANGAI**

Situated in the Madang Province on the northeast coast of New Guinea, the Rangai tribe tells this tradition which involves a mixed memory of the Flood, the Serpent, and the Garden of Eden. We analyze this theme further in Appendix B:

The snake warned the children that if he was killed to take his guts and climb to the top of a coconut tree with fire.

Long ago, a giant python was discovered by some children who told the other villagers about it. They captured the snake and prepared to butcher it. Two girls and their brothers were appointed to guard the snake. The snake transformed into a young man and chewed some betel nut and spat it upon a banana leaf to prove to the other villagers that he was a man.

The snake warned the children that if he was killed to take his guts and climb to the top of a coconut tree with fire. The children told the villagers what had happened but no one believed them. So, when the villagers butchered the snake the children did as the snake man had told them..

Later that day, as the villagers began to eat, a storm broke out. The village was inundated by a flood and everyone died. Only the four children survived in the coconut tree. Then two masalai stones came and crushed the corpses of the other villagers. After this, two big chickens came down and swept all of the bones into the forest. Then the village was clean again and the two girls and their brothers came down from the coconut tree. The boys made a house and they all lived together there.[38]

191 **FASU**

According to the Fasu tribe of central Papua New Guinea, "the Fasu landscape emerged from flood waters as Mount Tipuria. A couple (one male and one female), caught in the floodwaters on their sago boat carrying various resources including sago palm shoots, pigs, tree kangaroos and garden produce, found refuge on Mount Tipuria and built a house and made gardens. They bore a number of children who, when grown, were married, each pair given a gift of either an important resource (sago palm shoots, pigs, tree kangaroos) or traditional knowledge (knowledge of fire-making, knowledge of hunting) by their parents. One couple, however, received secret knowledge that they took with them far away from Fasu land."[39]

A couple, caught in the floodwaters on their sago boat carrying various resources, found refuge on Mount Tipuria.

"He has not left Himself without witness" (Acts 14:16-17)

Don Richardson, a missionary to New Guinea, once wrote, "Has a culture been found that is lacking concepts that form redemptive analogies? A formidable candidate for this grim distinction was the cannibal Yali culture of Irian Jaya described in Lords of the Earth. If ever a tribe needed a Christ-foreshadowing belief that a missionary could appeal to, it was the Yali. By 1966, missionaries of the Regions Beyond Missionary Union (now World Team) had succeeded in winning about twenty Yali to Christ. Priests of the Yali god Kembu promptly martyred two of the twenty. Two years later, they killed missionaries Stan Dale and Phillip Masters, driving about one hundred arrows into each of their bodies. Then the Indonesian government, also threatened by the Yali, stepped in to quell further uprisings. Awed by the power of the government, the Yali decided they would rather have missionaries than soldiers. But the missionaries could find no analogy in Yali culture to make the gospel clear.

Another missionary and I conducted a much belated "culture probe" to learn more about Yali customs and beliefs. One day a young Yali man named Erariek

38. Slone, *One Thousand One Papua New Guinean Nights*, vol. 1, pp. 467-468.
39. Emma Gilberthorpe , "Pathways to Development: Identity, Landscape and Industry in Papua New Guinea," *Landscape, Power and Process: Re-Evaluating Traditional Environmental Knowledge* (New York: Berghahn Books, 2012), p. 212.

shared with us a story from his past. He said, "Long ago my brother Sunahan and a friend named Kahalek were ambushed by enemies from across the river. Kahalek was killed, but Sunahan fled to a circular stone wall nearby. Leaping inside it, he turned, bared his chest at his enemies, and laughed at them. The enemies immediately lowered their weapons and hurried away."

I nearly dropped my pen. "Why didn't they kill him?" I asked. Erariek smiled, "If they had shed one drop of my brother's blood while he stood within that sacred stone wall–we call it osuwa–their own people would have killed them."

Yali pastors and the missionaries working with them now have a new evangelistic tool. Christ is the spiritual osuwa, the perfect place of refuge. Yali culture instinctively echoes the Christian teaching that man needs a place of refuge. Ages earlier they had established a network of osuwa in areas where most of their battles took place. Missionaries had noticed the stone walls, but had never discovered their full significance."[40]

192 SEPA

The Sepa people hail from Manam Motu, a small volcanic island off the northern coast of Papua New Guinea. The Flood tradition told by the native islanders, like many others of New Guinea, involves a strange snake-man. In summary form, it tells that a strange snake appeared one day and then revealed its true identity to two young women while the other people were in the field. The snake transformed into a man, predicted that the villagers would kill and eat him, and gave the girls instructions to survive. The instructions were to take their younger brothers and climb a tree.

Men's house by the Sepik River, Papua New Guinea

Later that day, the villagers returned from the field and found the snake. "The two girls said to them, 'This is a man, let him go!' But the people said, 'You fell asleep and you are lying,' and added, 'That is good game to eat.'" So they killed the snake and ate it. Not long after, the Flood broke out. "A flood came and destroyed them all and a big stone smashed the people." But the girls and their brothers had climbed a very tall coconut tree and thus escaped. Later they threw young coconuts down (presumably to discern whether the earth had dried up yet). "And they descended and collected the bones of their fathers and mothers and buried them."[41]

---

40. Don Richardson, "Redemptive Analogy," *Perspectives on the World Christian Movement,* eds. Ralph Winter and Steven C. Hawthorne (Pasadena: William Carey Library, 2009), pp. 432-433.
41. Josef Schebesta, "Vier Sagen in der Sepa-Sprache (Neuguinea)," *Wiener Zeitschrift für die Kunde des Morgenlandes*, vol. 38 (1932), pp. 255-258.

193 KALAUNA

The Kalauna people live in the village by the same name, on the humorously named Goodenough Island, which is directly east of New Guinea.[42] They speak a Milne Bay language known as Iduna.[43] Michael Young met them in the 1960s and wrote an important ethnography on them, *Magicians of Manumanua*, in which we learn of this people's Flood story.

A flood came and destroyed them all and a big stone smashed the people. But the girls and their brothers had climbed a very tall coconut tree and thus escaped.

Their Flood story refers to an ancestral couple, Yaloyaloaiwau and Ninialawata, who were husband and wife. They had four children, including two boys named Kawafolafola and Wameya, and two daughters named Oyatabu and Kwavikwavi). When they grew up, the two brothers Kawafolafola and Wameya quarreled bitterly about food and who was the better gardener (we are reminded of Cain and Abel in Genesis 4). One night Wameya fastened up his house firmly and made it rain. The flood rose and carried away his house to the north until they were far enough away. Living separately from his brother, Kawafolafola found that his crops would no longer grow, and he stayed hungry for a long time.

One day Kawafolafola asked all the birds to fly to his brother for help. All the birds tried in turn, but they all gave up and flew back until finally, the small Kiki-kikifolu made it to Wameya's house. Then Wameya sent Kikifolu back with a basket full of soil which he dropped on the summit of Mt. Yauyaba while singing spells. It began to rain and thunder and the soil was spread by the rain all over Goodenough Island to Kikifolu. After that, it was possible to grow good food everywhere.[44] In this account, we can hear echoes of Noah's raven and dove.

Another tradition mentioned by Young has striking parallels to the Genesis account of Noah's shame (Genesis 9:20-25), as well as the Tower of Babel (Genesis 11):

> "In one set of such myths Kawafolafola is unuwewe [resentful] because his grandchildren laugh at his comic and futile attempts to eat: the food falls through the hole in his throat. He makes rain and creates a flood that scatters food and people, resulting in diverse customs and the babel of tongues."[45]

194 FORABA

From the Genaa clan of the Foraba people in eastern New Guinea, Roy Wagner recorded a Flood story in 1968. Although muffled and distorted, the echoes of Genesis can still be heard:

A long time ago, two male cousins named Genaa and Mube came to the area and made a small pool at the base of a tree. Then they went into the pool. Two other men who were very thirsty found the pool and, looking inside it, they saw Genaa and Mube. They took some grubs from the area and returned to their villages.

Evidently the eating of grubs from this place was not permitted, for the water in their stomachs soon began to rumble. Nevertheless, they shared the grubs with the other villagers and everyone except two young girls ate some. These girls had seen Mube surveying where he wanted to put a lake. In addition to abstaining, the girls ran to tell their parents but no one believed them. Instead, they teased the girls.

42. Goodenough Island was named after James Graham Goodenough.
43. David R. Lithgow, "Austronesian Languages: Milne Bay and Adjacent Islands (Milne Bay Province), *New Guinea area languages and language study*, ed. Stephen A. Wurm, vol. 2 (1976), p. 453.
44. Michael W. Young, *Magicians of Manumanua: Living Myth in Kaluana* (Berkeley, University of California Press, 1983), pp. 228-232. See also: Jerry W. Leach, The Kula: New Perspectives on Massim Exchange (Cambridge: Cambridge University Press, 1983), p. 391. For a related tradition, see pp. 179-182.
45. Young, *Magicians of Manumanua*, pp. 232-233.

The youngest girl took her little brother and fled to the summit of Mt. Misiro. From the summit, they heard the terrible sounds of crying and breaking trees from the village. In the morning, they saw that the village had been covered by a lake and that it was red with the blood of the dead. They made a fire to cook with and the lake water turned black from the charcoal from their fire. Then they made a boat and the brother went hunting around the edges of the lake. Meanwhile a bird visited the sister and told her to marry her brother. They got married and had many children and multiplied.[46]

A bird visited the sister and told her to marry her brother. They got married and had many children and multiplied.

In addition to the similarities with the Horabi tradition above, the bird that told the siblings to marry is an echo of Noah's dove. 8,000 miles of separation from the biblical lands was unable to extinguish this memory.

195 INANWATAN

The Inwantan people, living in the district by the same name in northwestern New Guinea, narrated their Flood tradition to Louren de Vries in 1994 or 1995. Uniquely, they attribute the Flood to the anger of a personified ceramic jar named Batúre. Batúre was injured by an incautious girl who threw fruit at him. This caused him to rush to the sea where he made the waters rise. Only one man with his children survived by slaughtering a dog and placing its dismembered corpse around his house. The children kept quiet and the dog's blood kept the water out of the house. Those without canoes turned into fish. Those with canoes kept their children quiet and drifted to different places. However, many of them transformed into flying foxes and flew away.[47]

A bird visited the sister and told her to marry her brother. They got married and had many children and multiplied.

196 GAVI

"I will tell thee now wherefore thou must never offer fish to a man of Gavi, be it never so large and good," wrote Annie Ker, referring to this village near the eastern end of the island of New Guinea.[48] In abridged form, the tradition goes as follows.

A long time ago, a man from the Gavi tribe found a lake that was teeming with fish. The next day, he took his fellow villagers to the lake to catch fish. They didn't know it but the lake was the home of the magic Abaia eel.

They caught more fish, prawns and eels than they could carry. Finally, the Abaia had enough and summoned all of the Water Spirits to the lake to punish the villagers. That night, dark rain-clouds filled the sky and rain fell in torrents. All of the Gavi villagers drowned except for one old woman who was a witch. She did not eat any of the fish from the lake. Knowing that the other villagers had eaten Abaia's fish, she knew that they would face consequences. She quickly climbed a tree with her two dogs and a torch. From time to time, she knocked the torch against the tree until the sparks fell which gave her a view of the flood waters.

Knowing that the other villagers had eaten from the magical Abaia eel's lake, she knew that they would face consequences. She quickly climbed a tree with her two dogs and a torch.

The deluge kept rising, and she remembered that one of her dogs had eaten a fish bone so she cast the dog into the flood, and the flood stopped rising. Periodically, she knocked sparks into the waters below and saw that they were receding. The next morning, she came down from the tree and saw that all of the other villagers were dead. Some of the children who had not eaten the fish had survived. She raised them and they multiplied. To this day, the Gavi do not eat fish.[49]

46. Roy Wagner, *Lethal Speech*, pp. 105-106
47. L. J. De Vries, *A Short Grammar of Inanwatan, an Endangered Language of the Bird's Head of Papua, Indonesia* (Canberra: Pacific Linguistics, 2004), pp. 96-101.
48. Annie Ker, *Papuan Fairy Tales* (London: MacMillan, 1910), p. 52.
49. *Ibid*, pp. 52-57.

197 JAYAPURA

The city of Jayapura is located on the Yos Sudarso Bay, historically known as Humboldt Bay. Due to Jayapura's prominence as a center for education, employment and transportation it is home to various ethnic groups. Therefore it is difficult to identify which tribe is the source of the following tradition. In any case, this creation account tells that the sun god (Tab) created the first man out of clay, and then created the first woman from one of the man's ribs:

> "First he [the god Tab] tried to make a human being out of clay, but he failed with clay from the upper layer. Clay of a deeper layer did not give good results either. Then Tab started to take blood-red coloured clay from the third layer and this time he succeeded. But the whole structure was only a shape. This form he had made had hands and legs, but not yet a nose, mouth, eyes, breath nor bones. Tab now made all these lacking members and organs out of different ingredients, such as: soft wood, the skeleton of a snake and the eyes of the primeval forest-cat.
>
> This accomplished, Tab spoke to this (structure): 'Child, your name is Iria, answer me.' And Iria said, 'Yes, Father.' Iria then got the instruction from Tab, to walk to the mountain Mér over the plain of Yotefa. He had to come back when Tab should order him to walk home again. And it happened just that way."[50]

Iria's wife was made out of the rib of Iria and the two of them lived together on the mountain Mér.

And now, we come to that critical element in this tradition:

> "Iria's wife was made out of the rib of Iria and the two of them lived together on the mountain Mér. Their first child was named Dohor, the second one Meach, both of them boys."[51]

In 1950, Kamma recorded another important text, with parallels to the Tower of Babel (Genesis 11). The ancestors found a stronghold on Inggoirosa Mountain where they could live without fear of attack by neighboring tribes. After their numbers had increased, the people became obsessed with obtaining the moon. So, they decided to erect a tower. Every member of the tribe regardless of age or sex worked together on the tower for many months. They divided into two groups: one to fell the bamboo timber and other materials required for the undertaking, and one group to fabricate the tower. At long last, they accomplished their mission and came within reach of the moon when the moon punished them by showering the tower with stones from the sky. This caused the tower to collapse. Those people fell into the sea transformed into sea creatures while those who fell to the earth transformed into land animals.[52]

The people became obsessed with obtaining the moon. So, they decided to erect a tower. ... The moon punished them by showering the tower with stones from the sky. This caused the tower to collapse.

50. Kamma, *Religious Texts of the Oral Tradition from Western New-Guinea* (Irian Jaya) Part A (Leiden: E. J. Brill, 1975), p. 81.
51. *Ibid.*
52. Kamma, *Religious Texts of the Oral Tradition from Western New-Guinea* (Irian Jaya) Part A, pp. 85-87.

198 DAWAWA

The Dawawa live in a remote mountainous part of Papua New Guinea's Milne Bay Province. In a forthcoming book, Martin and Beate Knauber will share the amazing and miraculous ways in which the Dawawa people came to faith in Jesus. Of interest to our study is their tradition of Creation and the Fall.

Now the Dawawa knew of a Supreme God called Mamaitsua. This is a compound word from "Mamai" and "Tsua," which literally means "birth-giving daddy" (not "father" but the term of endearment, "daddy"). He is the Creator. He is perfectly good and righteous and benevolent. Knauber found that all of the attributes of Mamaitsua correspond to the God of the Bible.

> The Dawawa knew of a Supreme God called Mamaitsua. This is a compound word from "Mamai" and "Tsua," which literally means "birth-giving daddy."

With regard to Creation, they held that Mamaitsua created everything at the beginning. He made two people, and he also made a tree. He planted this tree in the world, and he placed the two people there. At that time, there was a rope which hung down from heaven and connected to this tree. Whenever the two people wanted to be with God, they would climb the tree, then climb up the rope, and they would enjoy fellowship with God. Everything was good at this time, and there was no death or disease or decay. There was plenty of food. In a word, it was paradise.

However, one day the two people committed a certain error or crime. This left Mamaitsua very angry, and he cut the rope. People have lived apart from Mamaitsua ever since. The Dawawa understood that the only person who could restore that rope was Mamaitsua himself. He could not be appeased by magic, as they did with other spirits.

One day, the Knaubers introduced Jesus to the Dawawa people, explaining that He is Mamaitsua's Son. He was sent to restore that relationship with God. This analogy opened up their hearts and minds to hear about Jesus. It played a major role in their coming to believe in Jesus and being transformed by His power.[53]

> Mamaitsua created everything at the beginning. He made two people, and he also made a tree. ... At that time, there was a rope which hung down from heaven and connected to this tree.

199 HULI

The Huli are a large and historically powerful tribe of the Southern Highlands District. R. M. Glasse conducted fieldwork among them in the 1950s and heard reference to their oral history of an ancient Flood:

> "The man Huli [their ancient patriarch] begat many children by an unknown woman and they were the earliest settlers of the Tagari basin, cultivating not sweet potato but taro. Several generations later, the Tagari River inundated the entire basin, killing every living thing. For a time the land was empty. When the floodwaters subsided the deities re-created birds and possums, and they in turn gave birth to human progeny, the founders of the present parish groups."[54]

Also, an officer of the Department of District Services and Native Affairs in Papua New Guinea collected a Flood tradition from the Huli people sometime in the 1950s.[55]

---

53. Based on an audio presentation delivered by Martin Knauber at Calvary Chapel of St. Petersburg at following link, and based on personal correspondence with Martin Knauber in August, 2024. https://www.youtube.com/watch?v=YS8WQDU7vGk
54. R. M. Glasse, "The Huli of the Southern Highlands," *Gods, Ghosts and Men in Melanesia*, eds. P. Lawrence and M. J. Meggitt (Melbourne: Oxford University Press, 1965), p. 34.
55. "In the beginning everyone lived in the country as they do now. One day, while the women were sitting around the fire in their house, water started to come up through the fireplace. They were very frightened and ran outside and told their men. The men came and saw it, and found the water pouring out of the ground like a river. They were very frightened because quickly the water joined other rivers, and they began to rise and rise, and as they rose they covered all the low ground and then the mountains too, and everyone was drowned. Quite often nowadays when women are digging in the ground they find old ashes and stone axes. These belonged to the people who perished in the flood." Chris Ballard, "The Death of a Great Land. Ritual, History and Subsistence Revolution in the Southern Highlands of Papua New Guinea," PhD Dissertation, vol. 2 (Canberra: Australian National University, 1995), p. 325.

200 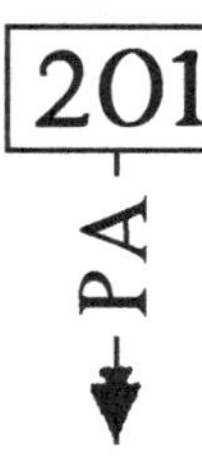

Two texts are reportedly shared by the Jair and the Kombay tribes of southwestern New Guinea. Both texts discuss a creator god named Tefafu who caused a global deluge to cover the earth with just two survivors preserved in a bamboo tube by Tefafu.[56] In one text, Tefafu caused the deluge to eliminate sinful people so that he could create perfect people anew. However, in the other text, Tefafu sent the deluge to destroy the perfect people, so that he could create evil and flawed people.[57]

What are we to do with this confusion? I (Nick) submit that they are mixing the Creation (Genesis 1-2) and Flood (Genesis 6-9) accounts. In the former, God creates perfect people and a perfect world. In the latter, God destroys disobedient, rebellious people. Both of the Jair / Kombay texts are correct in a sense; only they have conflated two events.

A creator god named Tefafu caused a global deluge to cover the earth. Two people survived in a bamboo tube.

201 PA

Pa or Pare is the name of a tribe and language of Papua New Guinea's Western Province. A man from this tribe narrated a quarrel story to Clemens Voorhoeve in 1967, which ends with a Flood.[58]

Two brother-sister pairs receive a premonition of the Flood, prepare a makeshift raft.

56. The creator god Tefafu found two humans who were born from lizard eggs. They married and filled the earth with their offspring. But they were not perfect: they had big ears, scaly skin, and other unsightly features. Moreover, they were disobedient and ignored Tefafu. Tefafu saw that they were not in conformity with his own likeness as intended. So, Tefafu chose a boy and a girl, placed them in a bamboo tube and destroyed the earth with a conflagration and subsequent deluge. Only the two in the bamboo tube survived. They got married and multiplied but the result was the same, so the annoyed god Tefafu placed two new children in a new bamboo tube and destroyed the earth with a second flood. Again, the result was not satisfactory so Tefafu sent a second conflagration and a third deluge. Two new children were chosen to survive in a bamboo tube. Finally, perfect people were created and Tefafu was satisfied. Tefafu allowed their offspring to multiply and fill the earth. The Jairs and the Kombays are descendants of those perfect people. Source: Kamma, *Religious Texts of the Oral Tradition from Western New-Guinea* (Irian Jaya) Part B, pp. 1-2.
57. In the beginning, the creator god Tefafu created handsome and perfect people. They were free of defect, sickness or any evil. This caused Tefafu to become jealous so he decided to destroy them all. He placed a brother and a sister into a bamboo tube and caused a global deluge. All of the people drowned except the two in the bamboo tube which Tefafu opened. Tefafu ordered them to get married and make offspring but the man rejected this as taboo. Tefafu assured them that it was OK for them to get married because there were no other humans on earth. Their children were no longer perfect. They had sickness, disease and were evil. This satisfied Tefafu. Source: Kamma, *Religious Texts of the Oral Tradition from Western New-Guinea* (Irian Jaya) Part B, pp. 2-3.
58. "But in Pa this is not the end of the story. The rain does not stop, but causes a flood which submerges the whole world, drowning every living being on it, except for two brother-sister couples who have a premonition of what is going to happen. They save themselves on a hastily built raft; first they are carried away with the current, but then they succeed in tying their raft to the top of an immensely tall tree reaching almost to the clouds. There they stay till the waters have receded. After some time two giants pass them; the first one comes from the mountains, the second from the sea. When the giants have changed places, the earth is again ready for habitation. The two young men now exchange sisters, marrying them, and they repopulate the earth. They are the ancestors of all the tribes living in the Nomad sub-district." C. L. Voorhoeve, "A Remarkable Chain Tale from New Guinea," *A Mosaic of Languages and Cultures: Studies Celebrating the Career of Karl J. Franklin*, eds. Kenneth A. McElhanon and Ger Reesink (Dallas: SIL International, 2010), p. 413.

202 KAMORO

The Kamoro people, living along the southern coast of Western New Guinea, have a vague tradition of the Flood which they told to Peter Drabbe in the 1940s. They attribute the Flood to the vengeance of two elderly women in response to the killing of their beloved bird, an osprey, by a man with a spear.[59]

203 TAKIA

The Takia people live on Karkar, a small island directly off the coast of eastern New Guinea. Their Flood tradition is prototypically New Guinean, being a mixed memory of the Flood and the Garden of Eden. It tells of a famed hunter named Nges Tamol, a widow, and her two children. According to the text, one day, the boy was sitting by a tree when he saw a giant python slither into a hole in it. The boy barricaded the hole and told the elders of the village what had happened. The next day, Nges Tamol, the boy, and the rest of the men from the village went to the tree and dug out the base of the tree encountering many snakes until they finally found the giant python.

Papuan men in folk dress

The hunters took the giant python back to the village, and when no one was looking it transformed into a man. The snake man told the old woman and her two children "Do not be afraid. I came to help you." He told them to save his head, middle, and tail when the men killed him. Then he transformed back into a serpent.

A giant python transforms into a man: "Do not be afraid. I came to help you."

The old woman did as she had been instructed, and that evening, the village was swept away in a tremendous deluge. The only survivors were the old woman and her two children. After the flood, the dismembered corpse of the snake transformed into a man again, and they all lived together and raised more children.[60]

The old woman did as she had been instructed, and that evening, the village was swept away in a tremendous deluge. The only survivors were the old woman and her two children.

59. The men, women, and children of the village got into their canoes, and there they slept in their canoes afloat. The floodwaters rose above the trees, so they fled toward the mountains. One mountain came to be underwater, so they fled to the next mountain. Then the highest mountains were covered, but they fled and came to the Pania district. The waters lowered, and some people drifted to different places. Still the floodwaters covered their old land. Then they determined to kill the man who had killed the osprey. They chased down his canoe, stabbed him with daggers and threw him into the sea. At that, the sea went down to its former place. As the water fell, it carried them off to the west. Source: Peter Drabbe, "Folk-Tales from Netherlands New Guinea (Continued)," *Oceania*, vol. 20, no. 1 (New South Wales: University of Sydney, 1949), pp. 71-73.
60. Slone, *One Thousand One Papua New Guinean Nights*, vol. 2, p. 774. See also: Colin De'Ath and Mary Mennis, "Merging Men and Nature: Myths of Melanesia," Oral History, vol. 9, no. 4 (1981), pp. 16-19.

204

KIRE

The Flood according to the Kire people of Papua New Guinea's northeastern coast went as follows. Long ago, two friends got into an argument, and a bitter quarrel ensued. The one who had been abused turned himself into a boar and consumed all his own jewelry. Finding himself in a garden, he began eating the taros and yams. An old woman spotted him, called all the villagers to help, and with difficulty they captured him and tied him to a log, planning to kill him shortly.

"You must not eat this pig. Otherwise you will die!" But the father became angry and shouted at the children, "You are lying!"

Prior to being killed, this boar turned himself back into a man and advised a girl and her younger brother, who had stayed behind during the daily hunt, that it was unlawful to eat him. "You are not allowed to eat me! Tell your parents not to eat me." Hearing the villagers returning, the children told the man to turn back into a pig lest he be discovered.

Later, "the children said to their parents, 'You must not eat this pig. Otherwise you will die!' But the father became angry and shouted at the children, 'You are lying!' The next day, the men went into the forest again to hunt. The pig turned into a man one last time and instructed the children that "If they cook me, take out my stomach and cut it open. Inside you will find decorative shells, beads, and bracelets." The people came back that evening, and the next day they killed and cooked the pig. The children took his stomach, went away and opened it, and found the promised jewelry. Then they came and confronted the whole village, "Where do you think we got the jewelry from?" And they warned the people not to eat the pig. But they would not listen.[61]

This flood covered the mountain and killed everyone who ate the pig. When the great flood came, the two children climbed a coconut palm tree.

Finally, the parents of the man came and discovered that the villagers had killed their son, despite their lies to the contrary. In their anger they caused a deluge:

> "This flood covered the mountain and killed everyone who ate the pig. When the great flood came, the two children climbed a young, low coconut palm tree. They took with them fire, a chicken, long yams, and a small tree. When the flood had destroyed all the people, the water subsided."[62]

We have, therefore, a forbidden food eaten, a quarrel, a discovery of guilt, a forewarning of the Flood, and supplies and animals taken by the survivors. Do we also have a parallel to Noah's tests involving birds? (Genesis 8:6-12) Let us read to find out:

> "The children wanted to know whether the ground was dry yet, so they threw down a young coconut, but the coconut disappeared in the mud. Then they threw down a yam tuber, and this also disappeared. Then they threw the chicken down, but the chicken went about eating all the corpses. Then they threw down the fire, and this dried out the ground. Then they threw down another unripe coconut, and it shattered when it hit the ground. They threw down a yam tuber, and it also burst. Finally they threw down a tree leaf, which turned into a bird. Then the two children climbed down from the tree."[63]

Finally they threw down a tree leaf, which turned into a bird. Then the two children climbed down from the tree.

Later, a bird advised them to marry, and they did so. Their progeny repopulated the earth.

---

61. Georg Holtker, "Aus dem Kulturleben der Kire-Puir am Unteren Ramu (Neuguinea)," *Jahrbuch des Museums Für Völkerkunde Zu Leipzig*, vol. 19 (Berlin: Akademie-Verlag, 1962), pp. 99-101.
62. *Ibid.*, pp. 101-102.
63. *Ibid.*, p. 102.

205 SUSURE

Susure is a village in Madang Province, northeastern Papua New Guinea, whose natives speak a language of the Adalbert Range group.[64] They have a Flood tradition which is similar to the Kire version above, except it is an eel, instead of a pig, that is mischievously eating taros in a man's garden. Then they captured this eel, which was named Mugagor. Next, he transformed himself into human form in the sight of an old woman and two of her children. Then he said, "When all your children are back in the village, you have to tell them that they must not eat me. If they eat me, I will destroy them all."[65] And the Flood happened in this way:

A magic eel is caught eating taros in a man's garden. Once captured, it transforms into a man and gives a warning about a flood.

> "Suddenly the water bird, called sumun, flew through the middle of the village and an orange fruit of a tree rolled like a ball through the middle of the village. Following the bird and the ball, the flood came right through the village, turned everything upside down and covered all the people who were cooking the eel. The flood drowned them all.
>
> As for the old woman with the two grandchildren, the water came to the coconut palm and rose higher, forcing the three to climb the palm. The water reached the lower palm leaves. The three wanted to find out the level of the water. So they took a very young coconut and threw it down. They heard the noise of the splash and the old woman said: 'Oh, my people, I have told you about this strange thing, but you were only concerned with eating the meat and now the flood came. It's your own fault.' She was talking like that while throwing 'drips' (green coconuts) into the water. After a long time one 'drip' fell down and did not make a splashing noise but fell onto the hard ground. Now the old woman said: 'It's all dry again, the water must have gone.' So the three came down and saw the bones of all the people."[66]

Their Creation story also has strong parallels with Genesis 1.[67]

206 YIMAS

The Yimas are a tribe living south of the Karawari River in central Papua New Guinea, just north of the New Guinea Highlands. An authority on the tribe's oral traditions named Stephen Mambi related this tradition of the Flood in 1985.

That night the younger one had a dream that a flood would come. The siblings prepared food and climbed to the top of two coconut palm trees.

Once, Yapalmay and Mampalmay had a brother named Yampwiukawi who they kept hidden in a clay pot. One day while they were farming, the other villagers killed Yampwiukawi. When Yapalmay and Mampalmay returned home, the other villagers invited them to eat a pig that they had killed but Yapalmay and Mampalmay went home first. They found that Yampwiukawi was missing and the knew what had happened. They were very sad.

That night the younger one had a dream that a flood would come. The siblings prepared food and climbed to the top of two coconut palm trees. Then the village flooded while everyone was still sleeping.

After a while, they threw a coconut down to see if the water was dried up yet, but it wasn't. Finally, they threw other coconuts down and found that the land was dry. Everyone in the village was dead so they went away in a canoe and went to Masindanai.[68]

64. Ernst Lehner, "Myths and Stories of Susure, North-East New Guinea," *Anthropos*, vol. 70 (1975), p. 739.
65. Lehner, "Myths and Stories of Susure," pp. 755-756.
66. *Ibid.*, pp. 756-757.
67. "Long ago in my area there was nothing but water, not a single tree grew. There was only water and the spirit called Tauar. This spirit arose from the water and saw nothing but water; so he pushed the water back to one side. This became the sea. Still the ground which appeared was wet and muddy and so the spirit thought: 'How can I get this ground to become dry?' So the spirit planted the trees and said: 'Here the fresh water for drinking should come out.' Again the spirit thought of something. He drew on the ground. Then he breathed into the drawing; and a man appeared. After having thought again, the spirit drew on the ground for a second time; breathed into it; and a woman appeared. The spirit said to them: 'You two will marry now.' After the man and the woman were married, the wife gave birth to many children." *Ibid.*, p. 741.
68. William A. Foley, *The Yimas Language of New Guinea* (Stanford: Stanford University Press, 1991), pp. 477-482.

207 PORAPORA

Sebastian Okim recorded this Flood account in East Sepik Province, writing in a mixture of Tok Pisin and English. According to author Martin Kerr who adapted and published this account, this is "perhaps the fullest deluge account written by a local person at the time", which was 1965.[69] We share it only in summary form.

The story begins with a quarrel between two brothers, Eprim and Bunara, contending over a woman named Osawa that both of them wanted to marry. The older brother Eprim prevailed in marrying her. However, one day while Eprim was away hunting, Bunara and Osawa secretly made love. Once he discovered this, Eprim tried to kill his brother but Bunara learned of his plan and escaped. After several episodes of violence and murders of family members and neighbors, we come to the section touching on the Flood:

> "From there [Madang] he [Bunara] ended up on a mountain called Sini where he set about constructing a large canoe. When it was completed he asked the local people on Sini to help him launch it. But these people refused. So thereupon Bunara brought rain and high tides. He put all the available animals into his canoe and sailed out to sea. From that time Bunara seems to have been lost."[70]

Bunara constructed a large canoe on a mountain. The locals refused to help. Bunara brought rain and high tides. He put animals into his canoe and sailed out to sea.

208 KEMBARAN

On the coast of Bintuni Bay in West Papua, the Kembaran elders told of "a Great Flood on Earth, many people died or stranded, but the ancestors of Kembaran were saved from tragedy because they were inside the earth."[71] This is one of those rare traditions in which the survivors found refuge from the Flood underground. We are not told what they did for air.

Once this earth was drowned. Only the tops of very high mountains were left.

West Papua woman cooks food

209 OROKOLO

The Orokolo live between the Purari and Vailala Rivers near the southern coast of Papua New Guinea. In 1880, the missionary James Chalmers met an older Orokolo man who told him several traditions, including one of the Flood.[72]

69. Correspondence between Martin Kerr and Valdis Gauss on November 23, 2023.
70. Reprinted with permission from Martin Kerr.
71. Adolina V. Samosir Lefaan, "Revealing The Leadership Characters of Women of Arfak Tribe, West Papua, Through Oral Literature," *Proceedings of The International Conference on Literature*, vol. 1, no. 1 (2019), p. 646.
72. "Once this earth was 'drowned,' only the tops of very high mountains left. Lohero and his younger brother were angry with the people about them, and they put a human bone into a small stream. Soon the great waters came forth, forming a sea, covering all the low land, forcing the people back to the mountains; the waters still increasing, the natives ascended until they had to take refuge on the tops of the very highest, and there they lived until the sea receded. Some went to the low lands; the others remaining on the ridges built houses and formed plantations." James Chalmers and William Wyatt Gill, *Work and Adventure in New Guinea, 1877 to 1885* (London: Religious Tract Society, 1885), p. 164.

210 KIWAI

The Kiwai are a people group who live in coastal southern Papua New Guinea near the Fly River. "One day long ago when the Másingára[73] people were working in their gardens close to the village," a certain man committed a wicked act which cannot be stated here. In consequence of this, the Flood was sent:

> "... the ground began to shake, a great flood rushed in from the sea, and the people were all drowned. After that the water went back. A certain great man escaped in a canoe and went to a place called Tümamópe. There he hid in a large drum."[74]

The ground began to shake, a great flood rushed in from the sea, and the people were all drowned.

At Ipisia, a village on one of the islands of the Fly River Delta, the following version was narrated:

> "In order to take revenge upon some enemies a certain Kíwai man once by means of sorcery caused the whole country to be flooded. He knew what was going to happen, so he embarked in a large canoe taking with him some dogs and pigs, plenty of food, and some young banana- and sago-trees for planting. One night the flood came rushing in and soon reached the floors of the houses. The people could not remain indoors but got into their canoes which they tied up to the roofs. The water floated away all the flooring, and as it rose higher, it carried away the thatches too. So the people shifted their canoes to the coconut palms and tied them to the tall trunks. But as the flood kept on rising, the ropes slipped higher and higher up the trees, and finally the people had to hold on to the leaves at the top. At last the leaves too were engulfed by the ever rising sea, and the canoes were swept away by the tide."[75]

He knew what was going to happen, so he embarked in a large canoe taking with him some dogs and pigs, plenty of food, and some young banana- and sago-trees for planting.

Finally, the Flood began to subside:

> "After a time the water began to abate and the tide floated the canoes back to the same place. There was a huge coconut-tree called Gágama, the crown of which first emerged from the water. The people held on to it, and gradually the water sank, and 'canoe he go down, tree he go on top.' After a time the people could touch the bottom with a pole, and at last the canoes stranded. As soon as the land was bare, the same man went and took away the bad 'medicine' which he had used for causing the flood. Only the posts of the houses remained, and the people at first had to sleep on the ground. The water had ruined all the plantations except the coconut groves. But the man planted a new garden and shared the crop with the people, and they built new houses."[76]

211 MUYU

The Muyu people live to the south of the central mountains in New Guinea, on the Indonesian (western) side of the island. Their Flood tradition refers to an ancestor named Kamberap who transformed himself into a pig and who also instructed the people to hold a celebration. During the feast, the people grew thirsty and found a drinking pool that formed near the stem of a Toromop tuber. The thirsty people pulled at all of the toromop plants to get more water which caused a flood. The people retreated but the deluge continued to rise. All were swept away in the deluge except seven people who were guarding the body of Kamberap.[77]

All were swept away in the deluge except seven people who were guarding the body of Kamberap, a shapeshifting pig-man.

73. Másingára is a village near the southern coast of Papua New Guinea.
74. Gunnar Landtman, *The Folk-Tales of the Kiwai Papuans* (Helsingfors: Finnish Society of Literature, 1917), p. 422.
75. Landtman, *The Folk-Tales of the Kiwai Papuans*, p. 356.
76. *Ibid.*
77. R. den Haan, "Het varkensfeest zoals het plaatsvindt in het gebied van de rivieren Kao, Muju en Mandobo (Ned. Nieuw Guinea)," *Bijdragen tot de Taal-, Land- en Volkenkunde ("Journal of the Humanities and Social Sciences of Southeast Asia")*, vol. 111 (1955), pp. 97-100. As translated in: Kamma, *Religious Texts of the Oral Tradition From Western New-Guinea*, Part B, pp. 3-7.

212 RISEI SAJATI

An informant from the village of Risei Sajati, in the Waropen area of the northern coast of New Guinea, narrated a tradition of the Flood around 1953. Freerk Kamma prefaced the tradition in this way:

> "According to the myths there existed in primeval times an enormously large village named Risei Sayati. But through the power and terrible anger of the Supreme Being against his creation on the face of the earth, this village split into two sections. The destruction meant here was certainly no other than the deluge of the time of Noah of the biblical history."[78]

The destruction meant here was certainly no other than the deluge of the time of Noah of the biblical history."

The tradition itself tells that in ancient times, the people lived in a large village named Risei Sayati (the same name as their current village). Some people made two rafts out of big mangrove trees and the deluge began. The rafts were separated and one landed at Wondama Bay where the survivors established Ambumi Village. The other raft remained anchored in place and the survivors rebuilt the village of Risei Sayati which still exists.[79]

213 WATUT

The Watut Flood story, colored by a memory of the Garden as well, begins with a woman who had an affair with a serpent. Similar to Genesis 3, it was no mere snake, but was a man who had the power to transform into a snake. Later, the ground was struck and a Flood burst out from the earth. Everyone was drowned except for a few young people. Two young men had taken refuge at the top of a coconut tree.

One day they ate a coconut and dropped the shell in the water. In their sight, the coconut shell began to drift toward a mountain. The young men climbed down, jumped into the water, and swam after the shell. It led them to a mountain where a couple girls had escaped the Flood. Each one married one of the girls, and they had many descendants.[80]

They dropped a coconut shell from the tree into the water. Following it, they arrived at a mountain where two girls survived.

214 SAWOS

The Sawos or Sos Kundi people live in the East Sepik Province of Papua New Guinea. Speaking a type of Ndu language, they are linguistically connected with the Abelam and Iatmul peoples. Their Flood story also contains a distorted memory of the creation of the first woman from a rib taken from the first man:

> "There was no ground, there was only water. There was only one man, and he had nothing at all. He appeared without cause between the clouds and the water. He saw something drifting on the water and wondered what it was. He took a piece of cloth material, which we call harrakain, and threw it down, and as it came down it turned into a pigeon. The pigeon landed on what the man had seen - it was land. This is the story of origin ...
>
> We use the word God, but in fact he was a big man and he gave rise to food and all things. His name was Ambusuatgu. The first man [Ambusuatgu] and the pigeon gave the land to a man who made a devil woman. He made her out of a piece of his own bone at Torembei. He decided to make her different from himself. He also

78. Kamma, *Religious Texts of the Oral Tradition From Western New-Guinea* (Irian Jaya) Part B, p. 26.
79. Kamma, *Religious Texts of the Oral Tradition From Western New-Guinea* (Irian Jaya) Part B, pp. 26-27. Kamma's source is a text recorded by one H. J. Teutscher not later than 1853.
80. Hans Fischer, *Watut: Notizen zur Kultur eines Melanesierstammes in Nordost-Neuguinea* (Braunschweig: Limbach, 1963), pp. 174-175.

made a man the same way. They lived at Mebinbit. At that place there was a small hole in the ground, which was made by the pigeon. They lived in this hole in the ground.[81]

Another narration concurs with the Arso version in saying that the Flood began at the playing of flutes by strange men. The tradition went like this: One day, almost the entire village went to catch fish in a certain pond, which must have been a forbidden place because of what happened next. Only three men abstained: a mute man and two other men. "Two men went on top of the spirit house and blew flutes. The poor mute man sat underneath the spirit house. Clouds thundered and the wind blew, and the rain came, but the two men who blew flutes continued. The water began to rise up to the holes where the posts of the spirit house were. The poor mute man ran up and told the two others with his hands that the water had risen to the base of the posts of the spirit house. However, they did not believe what the poor man had said, they just continued to blow their flutes. The water rose higher. The poor man ran up to talk to them again, but they did not pay attention to the mute man. The water continued to rise. It covered the spirit house, so the three men were within the flood. Now this place is called Seleapankraku."[82]

In the above version, we may detect a distorted account of Noah's sending of birds on repeated attempts. In this text, several attempts are made by the mute man to stop the Flood's advance. In Genesis 8, birds are released several times to see whether the Flood had sufficiently subsided yet. Indeed, there are many variants upon this account, as we show in Appendix B.

215 MOROBE

The following narration was recorded in the city of Lae, Morobe Province, in southeastern Papua New Guinea. Morobe Province is home to dozens of speakers of dozens of languages. As such, it is unclear which tribe this tradition comes from.

Aerial view of Lae in Morobe province, Papua New Guinea

> "Long, long ago, the people of a village went into the forest and cut it to make a new garden. After they cut the forest, they saw a big python lying on top of a tree." The people killed the snake and gleefully shared its meat among the whole village. Only an old woman and her little grandchild did not partake. For this mercy, they were spared by the other snakes that found out and determined to flood the world in revenge. "The snake told the little boy to take his entire family to the top of the mountain. This was because something would happen at night." What happened later that night was this: While all were sleeping–except for the boy and his family who had fled to the mountain–"the snake went to the middle of the village and broke the earth. Later the snake leapt again, and water shot up, breaking all of the houses. The people of the village were surprised, but they had no chance to flee. The water carried all of them away and only the little boy's family survived."[83]

The snake told the little boy to take his entire family to the top of the mountain.

81. Laurie Bragge, *A History of New Guinea's Sepik Region*, vol. 1, part 1 (Papua New Guinea Association of Australia, 2023), pp. 152-153.
82. Wantok, no. 217 (May 6, 1978), p. 15. As translated in: Slone, *One Thousand One Papua New Guinean Nights*, vol. 1, p. 112.
83. Wantok, vol. 999 (26 August, 1993), p. 22. As translated in: Slone, *One Thousand One Papua New Guinean Nights*, vol. 2, p. 873.

216 TAKAI

The Takai people live on the volcanic island of Kar Kar island, which belongs to Papua New Guinea and is located directly off the northeastern coast of New Guinea. Like so many others from New Guinea, their tradition contains echoes not only of the Flood, but also of the Garden of Eden:

Long ago, there was a giant masalai (spirit) eel that lived in a lake. One day, the women of the village found it while they were looking for food. They went back to their village and told their husbands about the giant masalai. The men sharpened their arrows and spears and the next morning they went to the lake to kill it. They took three young girls with them because the masalai eels like to see beautiful girls but they hide from men.

Long ago, there was a giant masalai (spirit) eel that lived in a lake.

When the eel saw the beautiful girls standing by the water, it surfaced. Then the men chased after it until they had the eel cornered. There, they killed it. Then they carried it back to the village, cooked it and ate it, having a big feast.

In the morning, a flock of birds circled the village then flew away. Soon after, the people heard thunder and felt a large earthquake. Everyone hid in their houses. The Earth broke apart and a big flood arose and carried their village out to sea. They drifted to the middle of the sea and became Karkar Island (Madang Province). The village is Dumad (Takai Tribe). Now, eating eel is taboo. They believe that if they eat eel, all the pigs would die.[84]

217 SENTANI

In the past, two villagers named Haboi and Wally met the Water god, named Dobonai, who lived on Mount Dobonsolo. Seeing that their water container was empty, Dobonai took them to a place with murky water. But when they refused to drink it, Dobonai took them to a clear water source where they filled their water carrier and caught a fish. Dobonai ordered them not to hunt any animals on their way back to their village. However, the prohibition was violated, and they hunted boars anyway. Then the water container spilled causing a flood that inundated their village. They had to cut down trees to make boats.[85]

Another text from the Sentani tribe is noteworthy for two reasons. First, it contains a "cosmic egg" motif, which is an altered memory of the separation of light and darkness, and the separation of the waters from the earth, both of which are found in Genesis 1. Secondly, it also contains a "world tree" motif, referring to a special tree by which people went up and down between heaven and earth. This is a mixed memory of the Tree of Genesis 3 and the Tower of Babel.

> "In primeval times earth and human beings did not yet exist. There was only darkness, utter darkness. The only existing object was an egg. Then the Northern wind blew (from heaven), touched the egg and broke the shell and out of the egg came a female being named Kani (earth).
>
> In the beginning heaven (the sky) hovered over the earth at a very close range. The first human beings could easily climb and descend to and from heaven by way of a huge banyan tree (yowake) with rattan and a rope made of the clouds."[86]

In the beginning heaven (the sky) hovered over the earth at a very close range.

84. Wantok, no. 550 (15 December, 1984), p. 23. As translated in: Slone, *One Thousand One Papua New Guinean Nights*, vol. 1, pp. 434-435.
85. "Storytelling Time! Here Are 4 Brief Folklore of Lake Sentani." *West Papua Diary*, 22 January 2023. Retrieved 18 April, 2023 from https://westpapuadiary.com/storytelling-time-here-are-4-brief-folklore-of-lake-sentani/.
86. Kamma, *Religious Texts of the Oral Tradition From Western New-Guinea* (Irian Jaya) Part B, pp. 52-53.

218 MONUMBO

The Monumbo are a small tribe on the northern coast of Papua New Guinea, numbering less than a thousand. Their tradition attributes the Great Flood to an evil spirit which had devoured a young woman:

> "The spirit in his house began to sing a magic song. Thereupon, a violent thunderstorm set in immediately. Many floods of water came down from the sky, and all humans and animals on earth drowned.
>
> Only a pregnant woman could crawl into a hole and was saved. One man remained alive because he had fled to a coconut tree. When the floodwaters had run off, the man climbed down from the palm tree and saw smoke rising from a hole. So he found the pregnant woman and took her to himself."[87]

One man remained alive because he had fled to a coconut tree. When the floodwaters had run off, the man climbed down and found the sole female survivor.

Another tradition is very similar to that of the Sepa people of Matam Motu Island, involving a strange snake that transforms into a man. The main difference is that the survivors, two little girls, took refuge under a large wooden bowl. (What they did for air, we are not told.)[88]

219 KILIVILA

The Kilivila people live on the Trobriand Islands, which are near the eastern tip of New Guinea. They have a tradition with remarkable parallels to the Tower of Babel, which was published in 1972:

Kitava Island, Trobriand Islands, Papua New Guinea

> "Long ago, in the Trobriand Islands, there was only one kind of people and they spoke only one language. One day, the men of one clan met together and decided to build a tower so tall that it would reach the clouds. They went to the forest and collected many kinds of trees and vines, then began to build this tower. They worked and worked until they came up to a cloud and then some of them climbed upon this cloud. When they climbed upon this cloud, the tower broke and fell down. The men were stuck on the cloud; they were tied together with the vines that they had used to build the tower. They tried to remove the vines but when they did this they twisted about.
>
> So now if you or I hear thunder, we are hearing these men inside the cloud trying to get rid of the vines entangled around their legs. The other clans of the island fell down with the tower to the ground. When they fell, they came down on all of the other small islands near their original island. These men started new villages at all of the places that landed. So now there are many other kinds of languages near this island."[89]

One day, the men of one clan met together and decided to build a tower so tall that it would reach the clouds. ... Now there are many other kinds of languages.

87. Georg Höltker, "Mythen und Erzahlungen der Monumbo- und Ngaimbom-Papua," *The Geographical Journal*, vol. 60 (St. Augustin, Germany: Anthropos-Institut, 1965), pp. 82-83.
88. Höltker, "Mythen und Erzahlungen der Monumbo- und Ngaimbom-Papua," pp. 83-84.
89. Slone, *One Thousand One Papua New Guinean Nights*, vol. 1, p. 4.

220 NORTHEAST PAPUA

Around the year 1905, the folklorist Annie Ker recorded a Flood tradition from some of the elders of an unspecified tribe of northeastern New Guinea. Although vague, the general outline of the Genesis Flood event can still be seen:

> "In the old days was a great flood, and the waters of the sea arose and covered the earth. The people of many lands were drowned, and still the sea rose, and rose, and rose, until the hills were covered. Then the [spirits] and the snakes feared for their lives, and hastened to the top of Tauaga, the highest of mountains."[90]

Then the spirits and the snakes feared for their lives, and hastened to the top of Tauaga, the highest of mountains.

Next the tradition tells that Raudalo, the king of the snakes, touched the rising waters with his forked tongue and thus made the Flood abate. Continuing, we read:

> "But Raudalo feared to depart lest the waters should rise again. He therefore took his dwelling in a cave of coral among the cliffs of Qarara, and remaineth unto this day, to keep guard over the sea. And when its waves are big and the people fear a flood, Raudalo comes forth from his cave, and repeats a charm which when the sea heareth, it is still and the people's fear melteth away."[91]

221 SAMO-KUBO

The Wycliffe translator Dan Shaw recorded a Flood tradition from the Samo-Kubo people of Western New Guinea, around the year 1970:

> "Many years ago, back in the dawn of time, someone made the lizards mad. They first made a lot of noise, then teased them until they couldn't stand it any longer, finally incurring the wrath of the Lizard Man. It began to rain. The rain poured down for days. The water began to rise, and still the rain came. Finally, all the people climbed up the highest mountain they could find. But still the waters crept up.
>
> People everywhere were drowning. It looked like the whole world was coming to an end. Finally, two brothers built a raft. It was only a small raft. They climbed aboard. Soon, all the others tried to climb on, but the raft only held two. They sailed off, and left the others behind."[92]

Back in the dawn of time, people made the lizards mad. ... incurring the wrath of the Lizard Man. It began to rain. ... Finally, two brothers built a raft.

222 YAPEN ISLAND

The people of Serui village on the island of Yapen (directly north of New Guinea) strangely attribute the Flood to the action of a whale, which acted on the behalf of a woman who had been mistreated:

> "When the whale started to spout the seawater it was not long before the whole area was flooded and the torrent overflowed the whole earth. Only four persons were saved by embarking in their canoe as fast as they could. One of the passengers was Dimaleitafi, and he gave the canoe the name of 'Yasi.'
>
> The canoe floated for a long time; they drifted hither and thither until the surface of the earth became dry again, 'and this happened exactly on the spot where now your house is built.'"[93]

90. Annie Ker, *Papuan Fairy Tales* (London: MacMillan & Co., 1910), pp. 30-31.
91. Annie Ker, *Papuan Fairy Tales* (London: MacMillan & Co., 1910), p. 31.
92. Tim F. LaHaye and John D. Morris, *The Ark on Ararat* (New York: Pocket Books, 1977), pp. 246-247.
93. Kamma, *Religious Texts of the Oral Tradition From Western New-Guinea* (Irian Jaya) Part B, p. 28.

223 MPUR

The Mpur people of Indonesian New Guinea have a tradition which attributes the Flood to some young children who unknowingly violated a taboo and ate a rat with red pepper. This offended Wabiton who, with her son Tumbi, transformed themselves into snakes and sent a deluge to punish everyone. All of the people died. After the flood, Wabiton and her son got married and the human race multiplied again.[94]

This offended Wabiton who, with her son Tumbi, transformed themselves into snakes and sent a deluge to punish everyone. All of the people died.

224 SARMI AREA

Freerk Kamma published a Flood tradition from the Sarmi area on the northern coast of New Guinea. Notably, this tradition features a demonic being who deceived a woman:

"In the time of the ancestors, a man named Wejasu and his wife lived near a well which was inhabited by a spirit. The spirit tricked Wejasu's wife by transforming into Wejasu and impregnated the woman." She gave birth to two children, one of which was reptilian: a crocodile. The crocodile child, whose name was Yarme, grew up as part of the family.

One day Yarme died of exhaustion from fighting a monster. When his true father, the spirit, found out, a Flood broke out. "At once, the skies darkened and rain fell in torrents. The spirit caused a great deluge to destroy the earth. Wejasu lead some people to safety by floating on a giant raft but they drifted far and moved many times meeting other survivors after the flood searching for a new home."[95]

225 SENGGI

Senggi is just west of the border between Indonesian and Papua New Guinea, on the north side of the Central Range. The tradition that K. W. Galis recorded from the locals around 1950 can be summarized as follows:

Once there was a man named Kungu. His brother-in-law stole Kungu's moon. Kungu's two wives also poisoned him but he survived. Kungu, for his part, did not take revenge. Later, his two nephews took revenge on his behalf, killing the brother-in-law and the two wives to avenge their uncle. Upon seeing what had happened and that the nephews were already gone, Kungu sent his children to live on the highest mountain peak. Kungu stayed behind and hollowed out the trunk of the great tree. Climbing inside the tree, Kungu begged the sago palm Bata to flood the earth. For forty days the deluge covered the earth and only Kungu and his children survived. His children populated the earth.[96]

Kungu stayed behind and hollowed out the trunk of the great tree. Climbing inside the tree, Kungu begged the sago palm Bata to flood the earth. For forty days the deluge covered the earth.

226 KIMBE

The town of Kimbe is the capital of the western part of the island of New Britain, which belongs to Papua New Guinea. Their Flood story went as follows: Long, long ago, there was a very old sorceress named Ramingain, who lived alone in the village. No one paid any attention to her. She was frail, blind, toothless and confined to her house.

One day, the people of the village held a feast, but no one remembered to invite old Ramingain. She was lonesome. On the last day of the feast, a young man and his sister heard Ramingain crying. They went inside her house and asked her what troubled her. Old Ramingain told them that she was sad because no one remembered her or involved her in the feast.

94. Jelle Miedema, "The Water Demon and Related Mythic Figures: The Bird's Head Peninsula of Irian Jaya / Papua in Comparative Perspective," *Bijdragen tot de Taal-, Land- en Volkenkunde*, vol. 156, no. 4 (2000), p. 748.
95. Kamma, *Religious Texts of the Oral Tradition From Western New-Guinea* (Irian Jaya) Part B, pp. 72-76.
96. K. W. Galis, Etnografische notities over het Senggi-gebied (onderafdeling Hollandia) (Government of Dutch New Guinea, 1957), p. 22. As translated in: Kamma, *Religious Texts of the Oral Tradition From Western New-Guinea* (Irian Jaya) Part B, pp. 16-18.

The brother and sister decided to stay with old Ramingain. All three of them ate together at Ramingain's house. Then, Ramingain told them that she was not happy with the people of their village, and that she would make black magic and kill everyone that night. Old Ramingain told the siblings to prepare a basket of food and to wait for her signal. She instructed them to climb a tall coconut tree with the basket to avoid the flood that would kill the other villagers.

Late that night, old Ramingain sang, calling out for the waters to rise underground where the people were singing, dancing and celebrating. … The siblings did as Ramingain had told them and before long the water covered all of the houses and trees. Old Ramingain's anger had killed them all.

She instructed them to climb a tall coconut tree with the basket to avoid the flood that would kill the other villagers.

Old Ramingain could not escape either. The water drowned her too. However, her masalai [spirit] protected the siblings. Eventually, the siblings came down from the tree and since they were the only survivors, they got married and had children.[97]

227 SOBÉ

The Sobé people live in the area of Bagaiserwar on the northern coast of New Guinea. Their Flood legend reminds us of the statement in Genesis 4:20-22 about the patriarchs Jabal, Jubal and Tubal-Cain, who made advances in agriculture, musical instruments and metalworking, respectively.

In the beginning there were four people. Sinef and Mensembrais could forge iron to make tools and weapons. Also, there was a woman named Fiayer and a man named Sigum who could wield great magic. Sinef and Mensembrais made a giant outrigger canoe and covered its deck with earth. Fiayer gave birth to many different fruits and nuts which they planted on the deck garden. She also caught two birds. The metalworkers made a magic cup and gave it to Mensembrais. Then Sinef ordered Sigum to stir the water which Sigum did. At once the water rose and daylight disappeared.

Sigum told Mensembrais to travel to the end of the world and to return because this would stop the deluge and bring back the sunlight. Then, Sigum ascended into the sky and gave control of the boat to Mensembrais and he became chief. The deluge covered the earth and people were washed away. The crew piloted the canoe as Sigum had told them and upon their return, the deluge subsided and the sun shone again. There they found that the other people had transformed into animals.[98]

The deluge covered the earth and people were washed away. The crew piloted the canoe as Sigum had told them and upon their return, the deluge subsided and the sun shone again.

228 IPILI

The Ipili people live on the southern side of New Guinea's Central Range, in the province of Enga. At the village of Tibinini, their tradition of the Flood was recorded, which features two orphans named Popaya-Akali-Lekeame and Lakeame. Leaving his sister with a good supply of water, one day Popaya-Akali-Lemeane left his sister to join a feast. After a time, Lakeame drank all of the water and went out in search of more. Finally, she found a pandus tree on Mt. Asenda. From the top of the tree, looking out she saw a flying fox stopper and removed it.

Suddenly the Silia River and Wataya River overflowed their banks. Even the mountains were flooded. Lakeme was stranded in the pandus so she asked a beetle to go to tell her brother about the terrible flood and where he might find and rescue her.

97. Slone, *One Thousand One Papua New Guinean Nights*, vol. 1, pp. 491-492.
98. Kamma, *Religious Texts of the Oral Tradition From Western New-Guinea* (Irian Jaya) Part B, pp. 58-61.

In a parallel to Noah's dove, the beetle went and found her brother at a feast. When he saw the strip of grass skirt that Lakeame had tied to the beetle's wing, he knew what had happened to her. He departed immediately to rescue her. Taking a branch for a torch and a shell he went down and created ditches for the flood to drain. In his unsuccessful attempt to save his sister, he created the Awaipa River, the Silia River and the Wataya River.[99]

In a parallel to Noah's dove, the beetle went and found her brother at a feast.

229 SIAR

The Siar people live on the island of New Ireland, a province of Papua New Guinea to the east of the main island. They have a Flood tradition which resembles certain other versions of New Guinea and South America, telling of a hidden water source (often at the base of a tree) which is discovered and, once opened, unleashes a great Flood.[100]

230 TORRES STRAIT

The Torres Strait area that separates New Guinea and Australia is dotted with many islands, in which a language known as Kala Kawaw Ya is spoken by the natives. A man named Nabaiya Yuwani narrated his people's tradition of the Flood in this language as a group of villagers listened along and Kevin Murphy recorded. The tradition went like this:

Once, there was a dani tree [strangler fig tree] in the forest at Komo. Many people lived in its branches, but, wanting to marry one of the beautiful girls who lived in the tree, a young man on the ground burned the tree down. The whole tree burnt leaving only a short stump behind.

Two brothers, Gwam and Muri, stumbled across the stump while they were hunting and they noticed that the stump had a heartbeat. They shot the stump with their spears and arrows causing the stump to rupture. Salt water came flooding out of it. The sea covered all the land. The brothers ran to find high ground and the roots of the tree burned and made the rivers and creeks and the sea between the islands, Kawa Island and Mata Kawa Island.[101]

231 ULAU-SUAIN

On the northern coast of Papua New Guinea, the Ulau-Suain are a people group who live at the village of Aitape. They have preserved the following tradition:

It is said that long ago, two masalai (spirit) men named Sumbriar and Runun lived on three mountains. One day, while arguing over food they agreed to stand on opposing mountain peaks, close their eyes, and point to the mountain of their choosing. Sumbriar peeked, and they both pointed at Mt. Sulkalia (in the middle). They left the mountains that they were standing on and met in the middle at Mt. Sulkalia. Then they began to sing and dance and call for rain causing a deluge to ensue. Mt. Sulkalia was cut in two. Runun was swept into the sea while the ground that Sumbriar stood on held fast.

After that, Sumbiar lived there and the place became known as Tumleo Island. Runun swam to You Island and to Karasau Island.[102]

---

99. Aletta Biersack, "Sacrifice and Regeneration among Ipilis: The View from Tipinini," (Eds.), *Fluid Ontologies: Myth, Ritual, and Philosophy in the Highlands of Papua New Guinea*, eds. L. R. Goldman and C. Ballard (Westport, CT: Bergin & Garvey. 1998), pp. 45-46.

100. In summary form: In ancient times, all saltwater was underground. An old woman covered the water hole with stone but she used the saltwater to cook vegetables. Now there were two brothers, Silik and Kambadarai, who seasoned their vegetables with urine. One day Silik tasted the old woman's vegetables and realized that it tasted better than his vegetables. So, he followed her, secretly, and observed how she removed the stone and drew saltwater from underground. Silik took some salt water and let his brother Kambadarai taste his cooking. Silik told him about the old woman. They went to get more salt water but when they arrived at the place, the saltwater began to boil up and soon everything was flooded. The old woman told them to dam up the water with stones. The way that Silik ran became the coast; The way that Kambadarai ran became the mountains of New Ireland. Many of the stones that they threw down became the islands in the region of Kavieng. Source: Roy Wagner, *Asiwinarong: Ethos, Image, and Social Power among the Usen Barok of New Ireland* (Princeton: Princeton University Press, 1986), pp. 24-25.

101. Kevin Murphy, "The cultural organization of social difference and relatedness at the border between Australia and Papua New Guinea." PhD Dissertation (October 2013: The Australian National University), pp. 187-188.

102. Slone, *One Thousand One Papua New Guinean Nights*, vol. 1, pp. 246-247.

232 MEJPRAT

The Mejprat people live in Bird's Head Peninsula, which forms the northwestern part of New Guinea. Their tradition of the Deluge went as follows: One day while fishing, a man's young son encountered a water spirit called Mos who told him, "In five days you must make a Sepiach Sif-feast." The child told his father the message and in five days he held the feast. Mos attended the feast but when the child saw Mos he cried out: "There it is again!" Mos wrathfully flung down his fruit necklace and water at once flowed from it, the skies darkened and everybody drowned. Among all the people, only a woman, her baby and her dog who lived high up on Tafajat Mountain survived.

Continuing, we find a vague memory of Noah's dove in Genesis 8: The flood stopped when the woman dropped some dirt into the water which fell in Mos's eye. In the darkness, the dog went into a hollow tree and came to a deserted swidden. When the dog came back, the woman saw charcoal and ashes from the swidden in its coat and she wondered where there was dry land. So, she took a long rope and tied it round one of the dog's legs and followed it to the swidden. The three of them stayed there until the child had grown big.[103]

233 TEHIT

The Tehit people in the Bird's Head Peninsula of Western New Guinea have a Flood tradition, of which we only possess a bare skeleton. It is said that a taboo was broken regarding the eating of a certain food, and this was punished by the Flood bursting forth from the earth and destroying the wrongdoers.[104]

The northwest tip of Bird's Head Peninsula in West Papua

234 AMBERBAKEN

The Amberbaken people live in a village by the same name, located not far from the northwestern tip of New Guinea. Their name comes from two words in the neighboring Biak-Numfor language, "Amber" (strange) and "baken" (body).[105]

The Amberbaken deluge story states that in the beginning, the earth was covered with darkness for seven days because the heavens collided with the Earth. The people scrambled to find safety but they were all killed in the cataclysm which included earthquakes and a deluge. All died except for a father named Sasui, his wife and their two children. After the inundation, Sasui searched far and wide and determined that there were no other people left on earth. So he instructed his two children to marry each other which they did. They had four sons, and some daughters who were the first to be born after the cataclysm.[106]

in the beginning, the earth was covered with darkness for seven days because the heavens collided with the Earth.

103. John-Erik Elmberg, "Balance and Circulation Tradition and Change among the Mejprat of Irian Barat," *Monograph Series*, vol. 12 (Stockholm: Ethnographical Museum, 1968), pp. 253-254.
104. Murti Bunanta, *Indonesian Folktales* (Westport, Connecticut: Libraries Unlimited, 2003), p. 128.
105. Freerk C. Kamma, *Religious Texts of the Oral Tradition From Western New-Guinea* (Irian Jaya) Part B (Leiden: E. J. Brill, 1978), p. 40.
106. *Ibid.*, pp. 40-46.

235 NEN

The Nen people live in a village called Bimadeben in southern Papua New Guinea. At this village, Mary Ayers reported that there were certain oral literatures which women were forbidden from knowing. The prohibition against allowing women to hear these stories was such that, it was warned that a great deluge would sweep across the land, and the earth would swallow up all the people, the land and everything in it. Kevin Murphy learned of similar taboos at Arufi and Serki which prohibited women from learning the men's stories. It was said that, if the women did hear the stories, a snake would fall from the sky and drill a hole in the ground, from which a deluge would spring forth and kill all of the people.[107]

It may be objected that these stories amount to a threat of a flood, not an actual affirmation that such a flood took place. However, 1) the featuring of a woman, a serpent, and a flood seems to imply a connection with Genesis, 2) this text contains elements in common with other New Guinean flood texts, which always affirm that such a flood took place, and 3) the conditional nature of these prohibitions does not preclude such a flood from having occurred. Could not these people believe that a violation would incur a flood for the very reason that such a flood did, in fact, occur in the past? Indeed, these stories imply a knowledge of Noah's Flood.

236 BIAK ISLAND

Biak Island is located directly north of New Guinea in the Cenderawasih Bay. Among the Biak Islanders, it is narrated that 3,000 years ago, the whole island of New Guinea was ruled by a great king named Manyova. But his subjects were wicked, so he caused a deluge to cover the whole earth. Only the summit of Sombunem Mountain remained dry. A sole man and woman, unknown to each other, escaped the deluge by climbing the mountain where they were fostered by Manyova. After the waters receded, the man and woman married and multiplied and lived under the protection of Manyova who provided for their every need. Eventually, their progeny dispersed across the earth.[108]

Another noteworthy version, told in the western part of the island (Supiori), contains a memory of the Ark and its landing upon a mountain. It says that in the primeval times the earth was covered by a deluge and the sun ceased to shine. Only one man escaped the cataclysm by floating on a pumpkin on the surface of the waters. He landed at the summit of Sombunem Mountain where he found a woman who had drifted there as well.[109]

Another text attributes the Flood to the action of a certain snake, and has a notion of the Ark.[110]

Only one man escaped the cataclysm by floating on a pumpkin on the surface of the waters. He landed at the summit of Sombunem Mountain where he found a woman who had drifted there as well.

107. Kevin Murphy, "The cultural organization of social difference and relatedness at the border between Australia and Papua New Guinea." PhD Dissertation (October 2013: The Australian National University), pp. 184-185.
108. Kamma, *Religious Texts of the Oral Tradition From Western New-Guinea* (Irian Jaya) Part B, pp. 29-33.
109. Kamma, *Religious Texts of the Oral Tradition From Western New-Guinea* (Irian Jaya) Part B, pp. 38-39.
110. "In ancient times an old man, Mandomaka, and a snake, Nawusoi (Ina-Wuso), are living near the source of a small river between Wasior and Sobei, where the snake lies tied to the original Anio Sara. When on one of his trips to the coast the old man is robbed by a boy he threatens him and says, 'If you do not bring me your sister for a wife within three days I will bring a dense darkness and a cloud-burst over you all.' The boy is so frightened that he says nothing to his parents, and old Mandomaka fulfils his threat. He curses the country, leaves in anger and never comes back. 'In this way that first time of security and well-being came to an end. Chaos and evil broke loose, caused by the snake Nawusoi, no longer kept in check by its partner.' The whole village is destroyed and the snake crawls away, dragging the Anio Sara with it. The Anio Sara runs aground on a big rock, but the building gets afloat again when two brothers appear, one of whom pierces the rock on which it is stuck. From the hole a deluge emerges. The other brother jumps on to the Anio Sara, and he sings and dances while floating on the big flood past all the Wandamen villages. ... Evidently Nawusoi, the snake, has vomited the flood and is itself lost in the deluge. At intervals during the wandering of the Anio Sara a number of beams have apparently come loose, so many that one is washed ashore at each village in Wandamen Bay. These become the main piles of their various Anio Sara." Freerk Ch. Kamma, *Koreri Messianic Movements in the Biak-Numfor Culture Area* (Hague: Martinus Nijhoff, 1972), p. 88.

237

MANUS ISLAND

A Flood tradition recorded on the Papua New Guinean island of Manus has remarkable parallels with the Garden of Eden, but the Serpent is an eel in this version. Again, it belongs to a recurring narrative theme in New Guinea which reminds us of Chinese Flood stories with a serpent-like "Thunder God."

> "They pulled it [the special eel] out of the water and cut it into pieces. All the people got some. The head of the Drusi went to the old woman but she didn't eat it. She put it above the fire to dry. When the woman slept the fish talked to her. It asked her for water and said that he was really a man in the shape of a fish [eel]. She gave him water. He told her that in the morning her grandson had to find a road to the mountains. He said that he would make a very big flood and destroy the village. He would get revenge. The woman told the villagers but they refused to listen. After they left for the mountains the flood came and destroyed everyone. Only the old woman and her son were saved in the mountains. The Drusi was a masalai [spirit] and could destroy people."[111]

The "eel-man" recurring theme in New Guinea Flood texts reminds us of the serpent-like "Thunder God" theme in Chinese Flood texts.

Does this not sound like the Flood stories that we find in China?

238

MADANG PROVINCE

Another tradition comes from a village called Dadami (the location of which is unclear), in Madang Province. It matches the prevailing theme of Flood stories found in New Guinea. It was a special python that turned back into a man, warned a young boy and girl, and allowed them to escape the Flood in tall coconut trees. "When the flood was over the children came down, built a house and were later married."[112]

111. De'Ath and Mennis, *Merging Men and Nature: Myths of Melanesia* (Boroko, Papua New Guinea: Institute of Papua New Guinea Studies, 1981), pp. 86-88.
112. *Ibid.*, pp. 101-102.

Padar Island, Labuan Bajo, Indonesia

INDONESIAN ARCHIPELAGO

Having covered New Guinea in the previous chapter,[1] we will now hear from the rest of the islands of the Indonesian archipelago regarding the Flood. Beginning with the Dusun people of Borneo, we are told that God warned a man named Muhgumbul in a dream of a coming Flood, instructing him to build a boat and take his family aboard. The Kiau people, a division of the Dusun, say it was a raft which carried the survivors. They insist it was a hen which returned from a flight and announced the end of the Flood. The Dyaks or natives of Borneo have a certain memory of Noah, whom they call Trow, who escaped the Flood in a giant wooden mortar, along with his wife and domestic animals. They replace the Tower of Babel with a ladder. The Sea Dyaks of the northwestern part of Borneo have not only a tradition of the Flood, but also of the Garden of Eden, in which the main difference is they replace the serpent with a dragon. The natives of Rote Island attach great importance to Mount Lakimola in their Flood account. They held an annual sacrifice here in memory of that event.

The Toraja people of Sulawesi replace the Ark with a feeding trough, and the Bare'e people point to fossil shells found on the tops of mountains as evidence of this Flood. The natives of Seram, in their Flood account, recall a bird which notified the survivors of the newly emerged land, and the Aoheng have a mixed memory of the Flood and of Babel. The Murut people replace the three flights of Noah's birds with three throws of coconuts to see whether the waters had dried up yet.

According to the natives of Flores, "Dooy, the forefather of their tribe, was saved in a ship from the great flood." The Solor islanders' tradition is similar, according to which "the earth burst and there was a flood of water." Two children survived in a tall coconut tree. The Ot Danom people of Borneo told that only a certain mountain peak called Boekit Arai "remained above the water, and extended a place of refuge for the few people who had been able to escape." In short, we see that 6,000 miles of separation from the land of Israel has done nothing to extinguish the knowledge of Noah's Flood.

Tribes of the Region

239. Dusun (Borneo)
240. Kiau Dusun (Borneo)
241. Dyak (Malaysia)
242. Iban (Malaysia)
243. Rote (Indonesia)
244. Toraja (Sulawesi)
245. Bare'e (Sulawesi)
246. Seram (Indonesia)
247. Aoheng (Borneo)
248. Batak (Sumatra)
249. Murut (Borneo)
250. Nage (Flores)
251. Solor (Indonesia)
252. Enggano (Indonesia)
253. Ot Danom (Indonesia)
254. Nias (Indonesia)
255. Timor
256. Kai Islands

1. The island of New Guinea is, of course, split between Indonesia and Papua New Guinea. The border runs along the 141st meridian east.

239 DUSUN

The Dusun historically lived in the coastal and near-coastal areas of northern Borneo, the third largest island in the world (after Greenland and New Guinea). Their chief enemies, the Murut, lived further inland.[2]

In 1959, the anthropologist Thomas Rhys Williams recorded many traditions from the Dusun people. Among these was a story about the loss of immortality, with Genesis 3 parallels:

> "The creation of the earth and man was at once, for God works at once. Man and the animals were created by God from the clay of the earth. First he created man, and then the snake, and then the lizard. They were called before God and asked the question, "Which of you will change your skins when you get old?"
>
> The lizard quickly said, "I" and God gave him the right of "Luhnuhnu." The snake answered as did the lizard, so God gave him the same right.
>
> Man could not speak because his mouth was full of rice flour. Thus, man is unlucky now and must die, rather than live forever as do the lizard and the snake."[3]

Thus, man is unlucky now and must die, rather than live forever as do the lizard and the snake.

Is it by chance that the Dusun people say the snake is connected with man's loss of immortality? Not at all. This is a theme found all over the world. The truth of Genesis 3 best explains the full range of such traditions that we find.

They also remembered the Flood. Their story began as follows:

> "Man began to live on the earth. There were many things to enjoy. Men laughed so much that after a while they forgot everything except enjoyment. They forgot the way between good and bad, and said things that were forbidden by God and hurt the feelings of others, offending them greatly. This offended God. He became "kohmous" (to be very offended at a person's behavior) with man. God could not become "ahtahgud" (angry) with man, for he had created man. Thus, fathers and mothers now cannot become angry with their children, for God the father treated man as his child and only became offended."[4]

Men laughed so much that after a while they forgot everything except enjoyment. They forgot the way between good and bad, and said things that were forbidden by God.

Such was the impetus for the Flood. Continuing, we can hear the memory of Noah and the Ark:

> "God sent a dream to a good man, named Muhgumbul, who had not enjoyed so much that he had forgotten. Muhgumbul dreamed there would be a great rain lasting for seven months and seventy days. In his dream he was told by God to make a boat of a whole trunk of a tree. This Muhgumbul did the very next day. When on the seventh day he had finished his task, he had a second dream. In this dream on the seventh night, he was told by God to go with his family into the boat. He was told to take all his food, and dogs and weapons and tools in the boat with him. God also told him to go about and tell the people that there would be a great rain. The next day Muhgumbul did as God told him. He took his family to the boat, and placed in it his dogs and weapons and tools. He then went and told the people, but they laughed at him and called him a fool. They enjoyed very much laughing at Muhgumbull and calling him a fool. They said to him, "How can you float a boat in the hills?" He left them laughing at him and went to the boat. He and his family built a hut in the boat and went to sleep."[5]

"They laughed at him and called him a fool. … They said to him, 'How can you float a boat in the hills?' He left them laughing at him and went to the boat."

2. Owen Rutter, *The Pagans of North Borneo* (London: Hutchinson, 1929), p. 31.
3. Thomas Rhys Williams, "Folklore Texts: A Tambunan Dusun Origin Myth," *Journal of American Folklore*, vol. 74, no. 291 (American Folklore Society, 1961), p. 69.
4. *Ibid.*, p. 69.
5. *Ibid.*, p. 70.

It cannot be overstated how similar this account is to Genesis. Undoubtedly this is Noah's Flood. Yet it occurs halfway across the world in Borneo. The tradition continues:

> "When they came awake they saw that it had been raining, such as they had not seen in their lives. The boat was floating high above the earth and no dry land was seen about them. This rain continued for seven months and seventy days, as the God had said in Muhgumbul's dream.
>
> This rain drowned all the people except the family of Muhgumbul. When the water began to go away, after seven months and seventy days, the boat began to settle to earth. Finally the water was gone and the boat came to rest under the tree called "Nuhnuk Arahahgong."[6]

This rain continued for seven months and seventy days, as the God had said in Muhgumbul's dream.

240 KIAU DUSUN

"The belief in a vast and devastating flood is certainly widespread," wrote Owen Rutter, "both among the North Borneo pagans and those of Sarawak."[7] From the Kiau Dusun (a division of the Dusun), the stunning account of the Flood that Rutter heard went as follows. There are several specific parallels with Genesis:

> "A long tumulus-like hill, about 150 yards long, 50 wide, and 75 high called Rindian, which stands in the middle of a plain near the Wariu River, is supposed to be the burial place of the Dusun ark, according to Kabong of Kiau. This was a bamboo raft onto which the Dusuns crowded with their livestock. One morning they were aroused by the cackling of a hen and found that she had flown from the raft and had laid an egg on the summit of Rindian Hill, which was protruding above the level of the water, and they realized with joy that the flood was beginning to subside."[8]

"The belief in a vast and devastating flood is certainly widespread, both among the North Borneo pagans and those of Sarawak."

In Southeast Asia and the Pacific, Noah's dove is often replaced by a hen or rooster, as we see in this version.

241 DYAK

The Dyaks (or Dayaks) are the native people of the island of Borneo. It is a general term which encompasses a variety of subgroups. A Scottish man named C.T.C. Grant recorded this account from the Dyaks during his tour in 1858. Their ancestor "Trow" can be identified with Noah:

> "Trow was a great man, and when the flood commenced proved himself to be so, for he procured a "lessong" (a large wooden mortar used for pounding patty), and made a boat of it, and taking the fair Temenjen [his wife], and a dog, a pig, a fowl, a cat, etc., he launched forth into the deep. After the flood subsided, Trow, having landed his stock and cargo, thought long and deeply, and after mature consideration seems to have come to the conclusion that to repeople the world many wives were necessary; so out of a log of wood he made one, and out of a stone he created another, and various other articles having been converted to a similar purpose, he married them, so that it was not surprising that ere many years he had a family of some twenty, who learned to till the earth and to lay the foundation of various Dyak tribes, including that of Tringus."[9]

---

6. *Ibid.*
7. Rutter, *The Pagans of North Borneo* (London: Hutchinson, 1929), p. 251. Sarawak is the northwestern part of the island of Borneo which belongs to Malaysia.
8. *Ibid.*
9. Charles Thomas Constantine Grant, *A Tour Amongst the Dyaks of Sarawak* (London, 1864), p. 68. As quoted in: Henry Ling Roth, *The Natives of Sarawak and British North Borneo*, vol. 1 (New York: Truslove & Comba, 1896), p. 300.

"Trow, then, is the reputed ancestor of the Tringus Dyaks," Grant adds.[10] Not only this, but they had a certain memory of the Tower of Babel, which Alexander Cameron heard from them:

At a very early period of Dyak history, a great ancestor of the Dyaks determined to construct a ladder by which he could climb up to heaven.

> "At a very early period of Dyak history, a great ancestor of the Dyaks determined to construct a ladder by which he could climb up to heaven. It is stated that he went on with his work, and got up pretty high, when suddenly one night a worm ate into the foot of the ladder, and brought it all down."[11]

IBAN

242 The Iban or Sea Dyaks are a subgroup of the Dyaks, living in northwestern Borneo. Their Flood tradition was recorded by one Archdeacon John Perham in the 1870s or 1880s. One of the most interesting things about their Flood tradition is how similar it is to certain South American versions, which we saw in *Volume 1*, including the Jivaro and Chamacoco. These tell that the Flood was connected with the eating the meat of a forbidden creature, typically a large snake:

> "Once upon a time some Dyak women went to gather young bamboo shoots to eat. Having got the shoots they went along the jungle and came upon what they took to be a large tree fallen to the ground, upon which they sat, and began to pare the bamboo shoots, when to their utter amazement the tree began to bleed. At this point some men came upon the scene, and at once saw that what the women were sitting upon was not a tree, but a huge boa-constrictor in a state of stupor. The men killed the beast, cut it up, and took the flesh home to eat. As they were frying the pieces of snake strange noises came from the pan, and at the same time it began to rain furiously. The rain continued until all hills except the highest were covered, and the world was drowned because the men killed and fried the snake. All mankind perished except one woman who fled to a very high mountain."[12]

All mankind perished except one woman who fled to a very high mountain.

A serpent. A forbidden food. A tree. We have here a mixed memory of the Garden of Eden and the Flood.

We will also hear from James Brooke, who met the Sea Dyaks in the 1840s. "Traditions, however–traditions of the Creation and Deluge–existed among them, distorted and degraded, of course, but yet bearing witness of the time when 'the whole earth was of one language and one speech.'"[13]

> "They would tell you of the woman who longed for the fruit of the assam-tree; but the tree was guarded by a dragon, and her husband dared not get it for her. When she asked for it herself, however, the dragon unfolded himself, and let her pick the fruit. Afterwards a child was born to her, whom the dragon seized one day and carried off."[14]

They would tell you of the woman who longed for the fruit of the assam-tree; but the tree was guarded by a dragon, and her husband dared not get it for her.

It is difficult to imagine a clearer reflection of the Garden of Eden. The story continues:

> "He was pursued by the woman and her friends, who found and killed, one after the other, seven young dragons, and then came to the body

10. *Ibid.*
11. Alexander Mackenzie Cameron, "Notes from Borneo, Illustrative of Passages in Genesis," *Transactions of the Society of Biblical Archaeology*, vol. 2 (London: Longmans, Green, Reader, and Dyer, 1872), p. 265.
12. Roth, *The Natives of Sarawak and British North Borneo*, vol. 1, p. 301. A similar Flood tradition was recorded in the 1890s. In this version, a woman, a dog, a rat, and a few other small animals survived. Charles Hose and William McDougal, *The Pagan Tribes of Borneo*, vol. 2 (London: MacMillan, 1912), pp. 144-147.
13. "The Rajahs of Sarawak," *Mission Life*, vol. 3, ed. J. J. Halcombe (London: Rivingtons, 1867), p. 130.
14. *Ibid.*, p. 130.

of the dead child. They seem to have made a feast upon the young dragons; as they were boiling them the water bubbled into these words:

'Gurok gurok, drowned be the bights [coasts],

Gurok gurok, drowned be the headlands,

Gurit, gurit, drowned be the hills."

And then for three days and three nights the rain poured down upon the earth. Everywhere the flood rose and rose, until there was nothing of dry land left, except a few high mountain-tops; and man and beast were drowned, save those who reached the mountains or were able to find ships. The former, they say, became Dyaks, the latter Malays."[15]

Was There Enough Room on the Ark?

Many people have raised objections that there was not enough room on the Ark for all the animals. However, genetically, it was not necessary to take every species aboard the ark. Only "a male and female of every kind" was needed, according to Genesis. In all likelihood, this "kind" was comparable to the "family" level of taxonomy, for there was no genetic need to bring every single species. As a result, there may have been as few as 1,500 animals aboard the ark, leaving plenty of space for storage and infrastructure. (For more information, see *Noah's Ark: A Feasibility Study* by John Woodmorappe.)

243 ROTE

Rote is a small island in the eastern part of the Indonesian archipelago, not far north of Australia. A translator named J. Fanggidaej, who translated several documents from Dutch into the local language, also collected several oral traditions from the islanders in the late 1800s. These included a Flood legend:

> "The ancients tell that in the early days, the sea rose above the earth, so that the animals and people were all killed. The vegetation and crops were destroyed without anything left. The water did not leave any piece of earth dry. Even the tops of the high mountains were covered by it, except the top of a mountain in Bilba called Lakimola, which the sea did not cover. A man with his wife and children had climbed on top of that mountain, Lakimola, and they did not die.
>
> After a period of several months the sea remained continuously rising, more and more, towards the top of that mountain."[16]

The ancients tell that in the early days, the sea rose above the earth, so that the animals and people were all killed.

Continuing, we also find a blended memory of Noah's post-Flood sacrifice, and of his sending of birds:

> "The people who were on the top of the mountain became very afraid, for they thought that it would not be long before the sea would reach them. That is why they asked the sea not to rise higher and higher.
>
> The sea therefore responded to the man: 'If you sacrifice to me an animal of which I cannot count the hairs (or feathers), then I will withdraw. Otherwise I will continue to rise.'

15. *Ibid.*, pp. 130-131.
16. J. C. G. Jonker and J. Fanggidaej, "Rottineesche Verhalen," *Bijdragen tot de Taal-, Land- en Volkenkunde van Nederlandsch-Indië*, vol. 58 (Hague: Nijhoff, 1905), pp. 427.

The man threw a pig into the sea, but the sea could count the hairs; then he threw a goat, a dog, a chicken, but the sea rose more and more. At last they threw in a cat. And the sea could not count the hair of the animal. So it ceased rising, and retreated to its place.

Then the sea eagle appeared and sprinkled some dry earth on the waters so that the land expanded. Then the man, woman, and children descended from the mountain to look for a place to live."[17]

So deeply convinced were the Rote islanders of the reality of the Flood that they offered an annual sacrifice of their harvested fruits to Mount Lakimola, made prayers for the next year, and would "celebrate with all kinds of dances as a sign of gratitude to [Mount] Lakimola."[18]

So deeply convinced were the Rote islanders of the reality of the Flood that they offered an annual sacrifice of their harvested fruits to Mount Lakimola, made prayers for the next year, and would "celebrate with all kinds of dances as a sign of gratitude to [Mount] Lakimola."

TORAJA

244 The Toraja people live on the island of Sulawesi, which is directly east of Borneo. A pair of Dutch missionaries and linguists who met the Toraja in the late 1890s published an ethnographic work which also contains this Flood legend from them:

"The Toradjas also have a story of a flood: In the olden times the sea once covered all the land (how and why this happened was not said). No one escaped this flood, except for a pregnant woman and a pregnant mouse, who floated in a pig trough. When the water had subsided and the earth had become habitable again, the woman saw a sheaf of rice hanging from an uprooted tree which was floating in the stream of water near where she stood. With the help of the mouse, which climbed the tree and pulled the rice from it, the woman was able to plant rice again. For this reason, the mice each year get their reward from the rice field."[19]

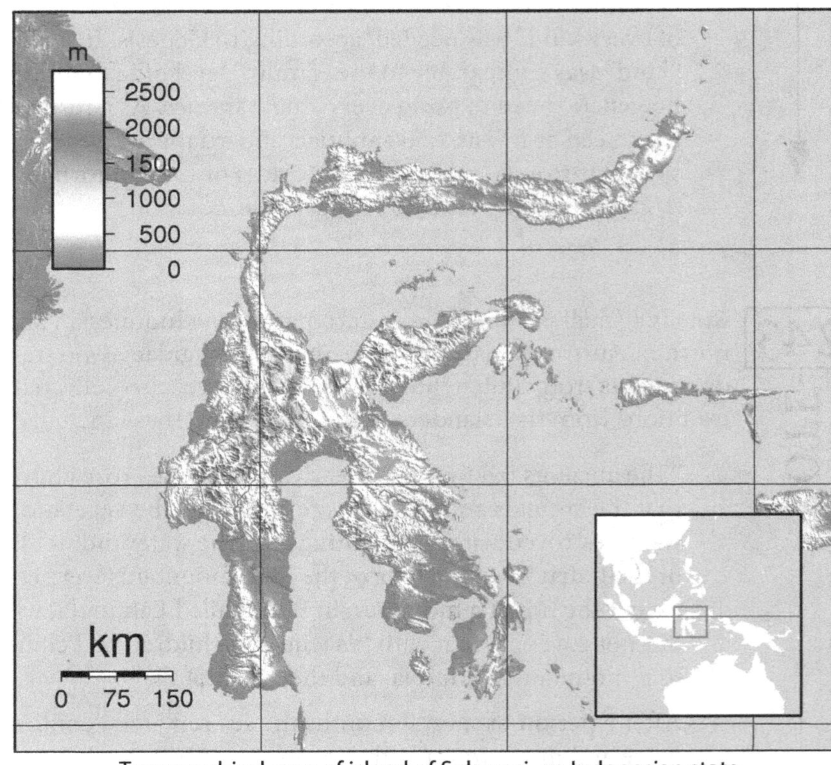

Topographical map of island of Sulawesi, an Indonesian state

In this detail of the mouse and sheaf of rice, there is a faint memory of Noah's dove and the "freshly plucked olive leaf." The woman later gave rise to two children, from whom the world was repopulated.[20]

---

17. Jonker and J. Fanggidaej, "Rottineesche Verhalen," pp. 427-428.
18. *Ibid*, p. 428.
19. Nicolaus Adriani and Albertus C. Kruijt, *De Bare'e-sprekende Toradja's van Midden-Celebes*, vol. 1 (Batavia: Landsdrukkerij, 1912), p. 20.
20. *Ibid*.

245 The Bare'e, another ethnic group of Sulawesi, narrate the memory of the Flood in this way:

BARE'E

> "The story of the Flood is also known to the Bare'e Toradjas. The water then covered the highest mountains, and as proof of this they point out that on top of mountain peaks 600 meters and higher, Neptune shells have been found. A pregnant woman managed to save herself in a pig trough, in which she floated upon the water. When the flood subsided and the woman was able to live again on the land, she gave birth to a son, and with this son she begot the present living human race."[21]

A pregnant woman managed to save herself in a pig trough, in which she floated upon the water.

246 The island of Seram is located between Sulawesi and New Guinea. The natives told a legend of the Flood to a government official of the Dutch East Indies named Petrus van der Crab during an expedition in 1860:

SERAM

> "They report in their traditions that, after a great flood of water, which overflowed the whole world, Mount Noesaku emerged."[22]

Only three people survived, having escaped to this mountain. Their names were Oeli Lima, Oeli Siwa, and Oeli Ase.[23]

Do these people, so far away from Ararat, have a memory of Noah's dove? Indeed, they do. The tradition continues:

> "By a bird, Marapati, they were told that other mountains had come out of the sea. On this note the three men took a pack of leaves from the aforementioned trees and went with them to different sides. Oeli Ase went to the newly-risen mountain and named it after his name (now Uliassers). Oeli Siwa went to the west, and Oeli Lima to the east. With the tree leaves they populated the newly visited regions."[24]

By a bird, Marapati, they were told that other mountains had come out of the sea.

247 The Aoheng live in the central part of the island of Borneo. The anthropologist Bernard Sellato recorded the following tradition from them during the 1970s or 80s. In this account we can hear echoes not only of the Flood, but also the Tower of Babel:

AOHENG

> "In those days, there was only one tribe of mankind, and everybody was speaking the same language, and everybody was living peacefully near the sources of the Mahakam River. There loomed Batu Mili, a straight rocky peak reaching up like the trunk of an immense tree whose canopy was lost in the clouds of the sky. And indeed, this tree-rock linked the earth of mankind to the heavenly realm of the gods.
>
> Every now and then a celestial but mischievous bear-dog descended from the invisible canopy of Batu Mili to sully the paddy that the womenfolk had spread to dry in the sun. After years of such unwelcome visits, the tribe assembled and decided to fell Batu Mili to prevent the creature's further forays. By the thousands they gathered at the foot of Batu Mili and built enormous scaffoldings to reach where the peak thinned up from its skirts. But Batu Mili was hard, solid rock and the people had only stone axes. It took them months, then years,

Every now and then a celestial but mischievous bear-dog descended from the invisible canopy.

21. Adriani and Kruijt, *De Bare'e-sprekende Toradja's van Midden-Celebes,* vol. 1, p. 247.
22. P. Van Der Crab, *De Moluksche Eilanden: Reis Van Z. E. Den Gouverneur Generaal Charles Ferdinand Pahud* (Batavia: Lange & Co. 1862), p. 212.
23. *Ibid.*
24. *Ibid.*, pp. 212-213.

wave after wave of men, cutting into the rock. As the years passed, the color of their skin changed. Those whose scaffoldings were built of white softwood became of a whiter complexion, and they are the ancestors of the Kenyah. Those who had built in red ironwood became our ancestors, as we Aoheng have a reddish-brown skin. And those who had built in bamboo are the ancestors of the Seputan, and their bodies are covered with the scabies, like the skin of the bamboo. From those times existed the various skin colors of mankind."[25]

Then they started speaking different languages. Soon they could not understand one another anymore. From those times existed the various languages of mankind."

It was when this "tree-rock" tower collapsed that the Flood occurred:

> "For a long time, they kept on hacking at the rock until one day the peak began to waver. The whole tribe withdrew to the plain and two men, Bovorok and Bovacang, the strongest and fastest of all, were chosen for the dangerous task of delivering to Batu Mili the final blows. They sharpened their axes a last time and prepared a light canoe, the bottom of which they made smoother with beeswax, then they climbed up the scaffoldings. When Batu Mili started to lean, the two men dashed down the skirts of the peak to the river, jumped in their canoe, and started paddling madly upstream to escape the falling mountain.
>
> The peak crashed down in a thunderous plangency that resounded for days. All the people were safe upstream, but the mountain was now lying across the plain, damming the river. Then the waters rose, higher and higher, and the people retreated to the mountains."[26]

As for the confusion of languages, this took place when the floodwaters still approached the highest mountaintop:

> "With the waters still rising and the rest of the world already submerged, they finally gathered on the narrow top of Diang Sara, the sole remaining dry mountain top. There were so many of them and not much to eat on Diang Sara, so they finally decided to eat the mushrooms that were plentiful there. But these made them sick, and then they started speaking different languages. Soon they could not understand one another anymore. From those times existed the various languages of mankind."[27]

They add an account of the migration of various people groups after the Flood, including themselves.[28]

> "Some might think that this myth, with its local versions of the Deluge and the Tower of Babel, reflects the influence of missionaries. They would be wrong," writes Bernard Sellato. "This same myth has been collected independently in various regions of Borneo with the same original details. There are, moreover, enough similar myths in other far-off countries so that there is no need to invoke influences due to the great monotheistic religions."[29]

"Some might think that this myth, with its local versions of the Deluge and the Tower of Babel, reflects the influence of missionaries. They would be wrong. This same myth has been collected independently in various regions of Borneo with the same original details."

Those who would deny the authenticity of Flood and Tower of Babel traditions should mark well Bernato's statement.

25. Bernard Sellato, *Hornbill and Dragon: Arts and Culture of Borneo* (Singapore: Sun Tree, 1992), p. 5.
26. *Ibid.*
27. *Ibid.*
28. "When the people on the top of Diang Sara saw that the water level was falling fast, they rushed to their canoes to take advantage of the swift flow to return to their land. Some canoes had been fastened with rattan rope, which could be cut with one easy blow of the sword, and these people were swept away, so far that they went across the seas, and they became the ancestors of the white people. When the bow-rope was of liana, it took some time to cut it, and the people on hoard those canoes went with the decreasing flow down to the coasts of Borneo, and they became the ancestors of the Moslem peoples. Those who had fastened their canoes with bark rope could not cut it and had to untie the knots. By the time they finished, the waters had receded and so they remained stranded in the central mountains. Those were our ancestors, and this is why we Aoheng still live here today. From those times existed the various tribes of mankind." *Ibid.*
29. Bernard Sellato, "Mythologie et Deforestation a Kalimantan," *Le Banian*, vol. 10 (Paris, 2010), p. 56.

The Dimensions of the Ark

Genesis records the dimensions of the Ark: 300 cubits long by 50 cubits wide by 30 cubits high (a cubit is about 1.5 feet). Did you know that these dimensions have been tested by naval and hydraulic engineers from South Korea, and have been found perfect for stability in violent waters?[30] That is an amazing fact which raises an important question: How did Moses know the perfect dimensions to record? Did he "make them up"? Was it a "lucky guess"? By no means. The internal evidence of Genesis indicates that Moses had a written record passed down from Noah. Noah, for his part, received the dimensions from God, who is the Author of physics.

248 BATAK

In 1887, the world traveler Joachim Freiherr von Brenner (1859 – 1927) met the Batak people of northern Sumatra (one of the largest islands of Indonesia). "When the earth became old and dirty," they told Brenner, "Debata [God] sent a great flood, "Dombang negri", which was to destroy all living things. The floods rose to the summit of the highest mountain, on which the last human couple had taken refuge."

When the earth became old and dirty, Debata [God] sent a great flood, "Dombang negri," which was to destroy all living things.

> "And when the waters reached their knees, the ruler of the earth feared that it might not be wise to destroy the whole human race. So he took a handful of earth, squeezed and kneaded it, tied it to a string, and laid it on the rising tides, so that the last pair could stand on it. This piece of earth grew in proportion as the people multiplied, forming the earth that exists today."[31]

Another account, recorded by the Dutch around the year 1780, has the Flood attributed to a serpent which supports the earth. When this serpent shook its head, the earth sunk in water. The daughter of the chief deity named Batara-guru descended to earth riding a white owl, and accompanied by a dog. "But not being able, by reason of the waters, to continue there, her father let fall from heaven a lofty mountain, named Bakarra, now situated in the Batta country, as a dwelling for his child; and from this mountain all other land gradually proceeded."[32] We find here a memory of Noah's dove.

249 MURUT

D. J. Prentice collected a Flood tradition from the Murut people of northern Borneo between 1965 and 1968:

> "A great flood covers the earth and destroys mankind, except for one man who climbs up a tall coconut palm (which, in some versions, grows higher and higher as the waters rise). When the flood recedes, the man throws down an old coconut on three occasions, to see whether it is safe to descend. The first two coconuts sink into the mud, but the third bounces, and the man climbs down."[33]

These three throws of a coconut are the three dispatches of birds (the raven once and the dove twice), after the last of which Noah knew that the Flood was over.

"The man throws down an old coconut on three occasions, to see whether it is safe to descend. The first two coconuts sink into the mud, but the third bounces, and the man climbs down."

These three throws of a coconut are the three dispatches of birds (the raven once and the dove twice), after the last of which Noah knew that the Flood was over.

30. Seon Hong et. al, "Safety investigation of Noah's Ark in a Seaway," *Journal of Creation*, vol. 8 (April 1994). Performed by Dr. Hong and other scientists at the Korean Research Institute of Ships and Engineering.
31. Joachim Freiherr von Brenner, *Besuch bei den kannibalen Sumatras* (Würzburg: Leo Woerl, 1894), p. 218.
32. William Marsden, *History of Sumatra* (London: J. M'Creery, 1811), pp. 384-385.
33. D. J. Prentice, "The Murut Language of Sabah," *Pacific Linguistics*, Series C, no. 18 (Canberra: Australian National University, 1971), pp. 241-242.

250 NAGE

The Nage people live in the central part of the island of Flores, which is east of Indonesia's main island of Java. In October 1910, an administrator of West Flores, a man named G. Beker, had the opportunity to observe an annual festival of the Nage. This festival also commemorates their Flood tradition, which tells:

> "Dooy, the forefather of their tribe, was saved in a ship from the great flood. His grave is under a stone platform, which occupies the centre of the public square at Boa Wai, the tribal capital. The harvest festival, which is attended not only by the villagers but also by people from far and near, takes place round this grave of their great ancestor. The people dance round the grave, and sacrifices of buffaloes are offered. The spirits of all dead members of the tribe, wherever they may be, whether in the air, or in the mountains, or in the caves and dens of the earth, are invited to attend the festival and are believed to be invisibly present at it. On this occasion the civil chief of the tribe is gorgeously arrayed in golden jewelry, and on his head he wears a golden model ship."[34]

At the annual harvest festival, all the people commemorate the Flood and the survival of their ancestor, Dooy.

Consider how seriously they took the Flood! How deeply that event was impressed onto the psyche of their ancestors, that they commemorated it in this way! And regarding this golden model ship, we are told:

> "The ship on his head, which is made of gold and has seven masts, represents the ship in which Dooy, the forefather, was saved when he escaped the flood."[35]

The ship on his head, which is made of gold and has seven masts, represents the ship in which Dooy, the forefather, was saved when he escaped the flood.

It is added, "In this miraculous way, Baluga Luomewona resolved the struggle of the mountains. But the strife itself has become proverbial and is used to this day when there is quarreling."[36]

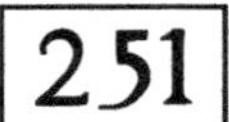

251 SOLOR

Solor is an island located about 360 miles east of Indonesia's most populous island of Java. The indigenous people, who speak a Malayo-Polynesian language, told their tradition about the beginning of the world to the ethnologist Paul Arndt (1886-1962). They related how "the earth burst and there was a flood of water." All people died except for two children sitting in the top of a tall coconut palm tree. The children were twins, a brother and sister. In the water below them were a snake and a deer, which protected the tree and the children in it from predators including crocodiles.

They threw a fruit down from the tree every day to see whether the earth was still wet. On the eighth day, the fruit fell on dry ground and split apart. Thus they discerned that the flood was coming to an end. Then the two children descended to earth. In the course of time, they saw how two grasshoppers mated. There they got the idea to do the same, and they became the progenitors of all mankind who have come after them.[37]

Again, these several throws of a coconut are the several flights of Noah's birds, the last of which conveyed a sign that the Flood was over. See Appendix B for more on this connection.

34. Sir James George Frazer, *Folk-Lore in the Old Testament*, vol. 1 (London: MacMillan, 1919), pp. 224-225.
35. G. Beker, "Het oogst- en offerfeest bij den Nage-stam te Boa Wai (Midden-Flores)," *Bijdragen tot de Taal-land- en Volkenkunde van Nederlandsch-Indie,* vol. 57 (1913), pp. 625.
36. *Ibid.*
37. Paul P. Arndt, "Demon und Padzi, die feindlichen Brüder des Solor-Archipels," *Anthropos*, vol. 33 (1938), pp. 4-6.

252 ENGGANO

Enggano is a small island in western Indonesia. O. L. Helfrich published a Flood tradition from the islanders:

> "One day, according to the story, the flood reached such a high altitude that the island was flooded by the sea, and every living creature drowned except for a woman. She owed her survival to her hair getting so tangled up in a tree that she could not be carried away by the stream and clung to that tree. Moreover, she swam very well. After the water had fallen back to the normal level, she climbed down the tree. She was very sad when she saw that she was alone in the world."[38]

Afterwards, with the help of a mysterious male figure who appeared, she resurrected people from corpses of those who had drowned. Thus the world was repeopled.

253 OT DANOM

The Ot Danom or "upriver people" live on the interior of the island of Borneo. Carl Schwaner (1817 – 1851) traveled across the interior of the island between 1843 and 1847, studying its natural resources and peoples. He recorded a Flood legend from the Ot Danom:

> "According to a tradition of the Ot-Danoms, a great flood took place on the island, in which many inhabitants lost their lives. Only the peak of the Boekit Arai, on the Mandai [River], a branch of the Kapuas River, remained above the water, and extended a place of refuge for the few people who had been able to escape. The waters covered the land for three months before they finally retreated and the ground became dry again."[39]

254 NIAS

The Nias people inhabit the small island by the same name, which is west of the island of Sumatra. One J.W. Thomas, a missionary who authored many works on the Nias people, recorded this legend around the year 1880:

> "The Nias people also speak of a great flood, which flooded their land long ago. The following is said of this: "In the past a quarrel had arisen between the mountains. Each of them wanted to be the highest. This strife vexed Baluga Loeomewona [the ancestor of the islanders], who went to his window and said to the mountains: "You mountains, I will cover you all!" And he took a golden comb and threw it into the sea, which instantly turned into a colossal lobster. It blocked the outflow of the water so that the water levels rose. This was followed by a torrential rain, and as a result of these two causes an enormous mass of water appeared, which rose higher and higher until all the warring mountains were covered except for two or three peaks. Only the people who had fled with their cattle to those mountaintops remained alive. All the others drowned.""[40]

38. O.L. Helfrich, "Nadere Bijdrage Tot De Kennis Van Het Engganeesch," *Bijdragen tot de Taal, Land- en Volkenkunde van Nederlandsch-Indië*, vol. 71 (Hague: Martinus Nijhoff, 1916), pp. 543-544.
39. C.A.L.M. Schwaner, *Borneo, Beschrijving van het Stroomgebied van den Barito*, vol. 2 (Amsterdam:Van Kampen,1854), p. 151.
40. L.N.H.A. Chatelin, "Godsdienst en Bijgeloof der Niassers," *Tijdschrift voor Indische Taal-land en Volkenkunde*, vol. 26 (Batavia: W. Bruining, 1881), p. 115.

255 **TIMOR TRADITION**

Regarding the Flood, the natives of the island of Timor said that in ancient times, "the men were evil, and were in constant war with one another, and made few sacrifices to the Creator." The Flood began in this way:

> "Very early in the morning, the sky was covered with black clouds and thunder began to rumble. Lightning flashed terrifyingly, crossing the sky. The rain began to fall, getting heavier and heavier, until it ran in waterfalls. The fields were flooded. The waters rose, rising higher and higher. Maupe said to his sister: 'Climb up that arequeira, and I'll climb up the coconut tree, so we don't drown.' The rain kept falling, whipped by the wind: the thunderstorms and lightning did not stop. The darkness continued, even though it was already time for daybreak. The waters kept rising, rising and rising.
>
> The two siblings had to climb up to the top of the trees to avoid being swept away by the torrent. Then they saw that two gigantic masses of water, one from the north, the other from the south, were rushing towards each other, swallowing everything and destroying everything. And they came together at the place where they were. Their terror was indescribable. 'It's all over!' shouted the two brothers.
>
> But what was their surprise when they saw that the coconut tree and the arequeira, as the waters increased, also grew, almost reaching the sky.
>
> For seven days and seven nights, the rain fell uninterruptedly, getting heavier and heavier. After this time, the waters began to recede, as did the arequeira and coconut trees, until they returned to their normal size. Fourteen days passed. When they were over, the two siblings came down from the trees."[41]

In ancient times, the men were evil, and were in constant war with one another, and made few sacrifices to the Creator.

The also say that "another consequence of their act [a sinful act in the most ancient past] was a climbing plant on earth that reached all the way to Heaven, the Seytaru. People could climb it and reach God. After that, it broke and no one can leave this world until they die."[42]

256 **KAI ISLANDS**

The natives of the Kai Islands, located to the west of New Guinea, undoubtedly had a Flood tradition, but only a fragment was still preserved when Johann Riedel met them. They referred to the time when "a heaven dweller, Parpara, sailed the sea of clouds in his boat to fish." He lost his fishing hook, and there was a certain quarrel with the fish below. Later, their ancestors "sent a dog down from heaven to earth, and when it came back up it had sand on its paws. Then they decided to descend themselves, but could only persuade their siblings, who descended with their four dogs and populated the earth."[43] They added that "the place that they came down to on earth was called Wuat, a place on Nuhujuut [one of the Kai Islands], which is still held in honor today."[44] Thus we have faint echoes of Noah's dove and of the descent from Ararat to the plain of Shinar (Genesis 11:1).

They sent a dog down from heaven to earth, and when it came back up it had sand on its paws. Then they decided to descend themselves.

41. Eduardo dos Santos, *Kanoik: Lendas e Mitos de Timor* (Lisboa: Serviço de Publicações da Mocidade Portuguesa, 1967), pp. 33-35.
42. *Ibid.*, p. 30.
43. George Gerland, *Der Mythus von der Sintflut* (Bonn: Marcus and Weber, 1912), pp. 65-66.
44. J. G. F. Riedel, *De Sluik-en Kroesharige Rassen Tusschen Selebes en Papua* (The Hague: Martinus Nijhoff, 1886), pp. 217-218.

Section IX

Twelve Apostles, famous landmark along the Great Ocean Road, Australia

AUSTRALIA

The Australians are said to be a prehistoric people, arriving on the last inhabited continent over 50,000 years ago, according to secular anthropologists. This obviously clashes with the biblical teaching that all of humanity traced back to Noah and the seven others with him on the Ark.

Sadly, many missionaries and churches in contact with these Australian tribes have embraced this secular, unbiblical view of history. They are content to teach that the Genesis Flood was local, if it occurred at all. But such teaching deprives the native Australians of their birthright as descendants of Noah and of Adam. By alienating them from their place in biblical history, it also alienates them from the Bible's promises, undermining the relevance of the Gospel to them. This message, which denies the Noahic Flood and the Book of Genesis, does a great disservice to our Australian brothers and sisters.

To those who deny the Flood, whether non-believing or Christian, I ask the following question: if the Flood recorded in Genesis is not true, why do the aboriginal Australians know of this Flood, as a fact of their history? Thus, for example, the Bunuba people insisted that "long, long ago, there was a great flood," sent by the god Ngowungun because humans committed a crime. A man survived in a canoe with his wives and a dog, landing on a mountain, to which he was guided by following a bird with a leaf in its beak. The Wunambal elders carefully guarded a Flood account which is quite similar. They added that God warned a man named Gajara, "If you want to live, take your wife, your sons and your sons' wives and get a double raft." Gajara was also instructed to take animals and long-lasting foods. They have

Tribes of the Region

257. Bunuba (Western Australia)
258. Wunambal (Western Australia)
259. Pitjantjatjarra (Central Australia)
260. New South Wales
261. Kurnai (Victoria)
262. Yuin (New South Wales)
263. Melbourne Area (Victoria)
264. Lake Tyers Area (Victoria)
265. Ngarrindjeri (Southern Australia)
266. Mount Elliot Tribe (Queensland)
267. Brabiralong (Victoria)
268. Gunditjmara (Victoria)
269. Ualarai (New South Wales)
270. Murrinh-Patha (Northern Territory)
271. Gwini (Western Australia)
272. Wiilman (Western Australia)
273. Boorong (Victoria)
274. Worora (Western Australia)
275. Gumbaynggirr (New South Wales)
276. Yolngu (Northern Territory)
277. Eora (New South Wales)
278. New South Wales Tradition
279. Turrbal (Queensland)
280. Warruwi (Northern Territory)
281. Yindjibarndi (Western Australia)

a memory of Noah's birds, the mountain landing, the sacrifice offered after the Flood, and the rainbow as well.

The Pitjantjatjarra people say that some people escaped the Flood in boats, and that they paddled to a mountain range. The Kurnai, like some tribes of Australia, say it was a bird (a pelican) which sailed a boat during the Flood and rescued some people. A second bird plays a role as well, like Noah's raven and dove. The Melbourne area natives narrated how, after a sin was committed, the god Bund-Jel sent a Flood which destroyed all people except for a pair who climbed a high tree on a mountain. All humanity descended from them.

> Christian teachers in Australia who compromise on Genesis deprive the native Australians of their birthright as descendants of Noah and of Adam.

The Ngarrindjeri refer to a flood which "swept over the hills with fury," and which lifted a man in his canoe to the top of a hill. The Mount Elliot tribe also recall this Flood in which "nearly all were drowned," and "only those who got on a very high mountain were saved." All the people would have been drowned, said the Brabiralong tribe, had not one of them "made a large canoe, in which he saved a great many." "Among the aborigines of the Portland district there is a tradition that a flood destroyed the whole human race with the exception of one man," and according to the Murrinh-Patha, after the Flood, "birds were sent out, and they returned with branches of tree bark."

The ancestor Wolaro prepared a canoe while the earth was dry, according to the Gwini of Western Australia. He gathered a few people, along with food and animals, and went in the canoe. After the Flood, a little bird plucked a leaf from a tree. "The water kept on rising, and finally even the mountain peaks disappeared. The world was one vast, flat sheet of water," we learn from a clan of the Wergaia tribe in Victoria. The people that drowned in the ancient Flood are today's sea creatures, claim the Worora tribe, and an old man's prayers to God made the Flood go down, told the Gumbaynggirr people. A large canoe was the vessel of escape, said the Eora people of the Sydney area, when the Flood covered the mountains and drowned all but two people.

257 BUNUBA

The Bunuba are a small tribe from the Kimberley region of Western Australia. Their Flood tradition was recorded by Howard Coate, an illustrious missionary, linguist, and anthropologist who spent over fifty years working among the aboriginal people groups, beginning in the 1930s. Coate's source was a Bunuba man named Jimmy Bird.

> "Long, long ago there was a great flood. It originated from the fact of some children who found the 'winking' owl in a tree and plucked out all its feathers. They forced a grass reed through its nose and treated the bird most shamefully. The bird flew without wings, into the heavens and showed himself to Ngowungu, the Great Father. Ngowungu became very angry and decided to drown the people.
>
> Later the people saw a small cloud rising which grew bigger and bigger till it spread all over the sky. The thunder began to roll and crash and the people were greatly afraid.
>
> With the rain and thunder was a terrible wind which broke great limbs off trees and rooted up others. During this terrible storm there was a noise above the awful crashes of thunder. This noise was coming from the north. The salt water, the sea, came pouring over the ranges from the north. The flood rose higher and higher till all the land was covered except the tops of two or three mountains."[1]

> The bird flew into the heavens and showed himself to Ngowungu, the Great Father. Ngowungu became very angry and decided to drown the people.

1. Howard Coate and W.H. Douglas, "Australian Aboriginal Flood Stories," *Creation*, vol. 5, no. 1 (1982), pp. 6-9. Retrieved from https://creation.com/australian-aboriginal-flood-stories Accessed August 21, 2018.

And in great similarity to Genesis, we read the following of the survivors and their vessel:

> "From further west a man and his wives with a dog were battling their way in a canoe when a bird with a leaf in its mouth flew in front of them showing them the way to Mt. Broome. They eventually reached Mt. Broome and landed there where some other survivors were.
>
> Then Djabalgari, the great left-handed man incised his little finger and let the blood trickle down into the flood waters. The waters began to go down and eventually disappeared off the country. All other people were drowned."[2]

A man and his wives with a dog were battling their way in a canoe when a bird with a leaf in its mouth flew in front of them showing them the way to Mt. Broome.

WUNAMBAL

258 "This is an old time story told by the earliest, profoundly knowledgeable elders," told an elderly man named Mickey Bungunie to Howard Coate. Indeed, this remarkable story goes back to the Genesis Flood, which it matches in many details. It is also quite similar to the previous text. Bungunie belonged to the Wunambal tribe from the Kimberley region in northwestern Australia. They are linguistically related to the Worora people, whom we will discuss later. Bungunie continued:

> "It came about that the earliest-time children living in those far-off days mocked, tormented and ill-treated the Winking Owl, Dumbi. They plucked out his feathers; they spat on him; they pierced him many times with grass spears, even thrusting a hole through his nasal septum. Up into the air they tossed him, jeering at him, 'Now fly!' But he fell down onto the ground with a thud. This they did again; and again Dumbi thudded to the ground. A third time those children threw him up into the air, but this time Dumbi continued to go up and up through the clouds out of sight and right on up to Ngadja, the Supreme One.
>
> 'What has happened to you?' asked Ngadja, the Supreme Being. 'What have they done to you?' The owl then presented his complaint to him, saying, 'The children mocked me; they held me in ridicule and persecuted me.'
>
> Ngadja, the Supreme One, was inwardly grieved and felt deep sorrow for him, so he gathered his followers together and held a council with them. Among the many followers of Ngadja gathered to this council meeting were Maguriguri [the sidewinder lizard], Windirindjal [another kind of lizard], the eel, the freshwater turtle, and the black goanna. 'Go,' said Ngadja, 'see where these people are; peer over the range and see if they are still camping in that same area, then come and tell me.' This he said to his followers for he was truly sorry that these children had mocked Dumbi.
>
> The first one to be sent was Maguriguri. He, the quick-legged one, ran to the place called Dumbey which is the range that lies across the country in that place. On returning he reported that they were all still there. Ngadja sent him again, saying, 'Go again to the same place; see if they are still there.' Maguriguri went to spy once more and returned again with the same report to Ngadja."[3]

Ngadja, the Supreme One, was inwardly grieved and felt deep sorrow ... He was truly sorry that these children had mocked Dumbi.

---

2. *Ibid*.
3. Howard Coate, "Aboriginal Flood Legend," *Creation*, vol. 4, no 3 (1981), pp. 9-12. Retrieved from https://answersingenesis.org/the-flood/flood-legends/aboriginal-flood-legend/

Next, a man named Gajara occupies the role of Noah. He is warned by God of the coming Flood, and is told to prepare and stock a vessel:

> "Ngadja, the Supreme Being, then instructed Gajara [who at that time was still a man], saying, 'If you want to live, take your wife, your sons and your sons' wives and get a double raft. Because of the Dumbi affair, I intend to drown everyone. I am about to send rain and a sea flood. Put on the raft long-lasting foods that may be stored,' he told him. 'Foods such as gumi, banimba, and ngalindja, all these ground foods.' So Gajara stored all these foods. He also gathered birds of the air such as the cuckoo, the mistletoe-eater, the rainbow bird, the helmeted friarbird and finches—those he took on the raft, and also a female kangaroo. Ngadja then said, 'All is ready now.' He thereupon sent Maguriguri to peep at the people for the last time. 'Ah!' the lizard said, gesturing in their direction. 'They all remain in one place!'
>
> Gajara gathered his sons as the crew, and his own wife and his sons' wives together. Ngadja the Supreme One gave Gajara some of his own foods. Then Ngadja sent the rain clouds down, shutting the clouds in upon them. The sea-flood came in from the north-northeast and the people were closed in by the saltwater flood and the tidal waters of the sea. The flood began to sweep all the living creatures together and was pushing them all along to one place, Dumbey. Here the waters were spinning in a whirlpool and the people were screaming as they looked for a way of escape. Ngadja whirled the flood waters and the earth opened, drowning and flattening them all. He finished them at Dumbey.
>
> Meanwhile, the flood carried all those who were on the raft with Gajara along on the current far away to Dulugun where the world ends and the waters flow over. That is where the flood had been taking him all the time, the place of the dead, where there is no land. The waters were rolling him this way and that way and spinning him around for a long, long time."[4]

The Supreme Being then instructed Gajara, "If you want to live, take your wife, your sons and your sons' wives and get a double raft. Because of the Dumbi affair, I intend to drown everyone. I am about to send rain and a sea flood. Put on the raft long-lasting foods that may be stored."

Does the Wunambal account also contain a memory of Noah's raven and dove? Indeed, it does:

> "At last, however, the flood-waters brought Gajara back in this direction. He sent some birds out from the raft, first the cuckoo. The cuckoo found the land and did not return to him. Gradually the waters were going down. The first land that Gahara sighted was the hilltop at Ngumbindji [Doubtful Bay]. 'Oh!' he said, 'I have found a hill!' and he was glad within himself. Then, as the waters continued to go down, he sighted Numbuzare [Mt Waterloo]. Later on, the other birds returned to Gajara and he sent them out again the following day. They arrived on the land and met Dumbi, the owl who said, 'Oh, you have returned already!' and invited them to stay. The land was already drying the waters up and the living creatures found a home and food. Soon in many places the owls were breeding."[5]

He sent some birds out from the raft, first the cuckoo. The cuckoo found the land and did not return to him. ... Later on, the other birds returned to Gajara and he sent them out again the following day.

They believe this Flood left a permanent impression on the earth's surface:

> "As the flood subsided Gajara noticed that it was leaving a water-mark like a painting along the hills. This is the flood spirit line, left there where the flood made it. The waters were taking him past Munduli [Montilivet] when he bumped into a rock. [Munduli is 'the tomahawk place' where they used to get stone for tomahawks.] Gajara was bumped off the raft with a splash and sank to the bottom. On the bottom of the sea he walked to the shore of the mainland."[6]

4. *Ibid.*
5. *Ibid.*
6. *Ibid.*

Do they even have a memory of Noah's burnt offering sacrifice to God? Do they remember the rainbow as well? Yes, on both accounts:

> "With regard to the kangaroo which they had taken with them on the raft and which was still with them when Gajara went down, and forced his way through the sea, and came out on the shore, they killed it after landing; and Gajara's wife Galgalbiri put it in the earth oven and cooked it with other foods. The smoke rose slowly until it reached through into the sky. Ngadja, the Supreme Being, said, 'Oh, what is that smell? Ah, they are cooking a good kangaroo! The marrow smells; I can smell the odour.' He could smell the steam and smoke rising from the female kangaroo as it was cooking and he was pleased.
>
> Ngadja, the Supreme Being, put the rainbow in the sky to keep the rain clouds back. The rainbow lies bent across the sky; he ties up the clouds behind it and the rain does not come. The rainbow keeps the clouds back and protects us so that the rainfall does not rise too high. Our people understand the significance of it. When we see the rainbow we say, 'There will not be any abnormally heavy rain.'"[7]

The rainbow keeps the clouds back and protects us so that the rainfall does not rise too high. Our people understand the significance of it. When we see the rainbow we say, "There will not be any abnormally heavy rain."

259 PITJANTJATJARRA

The Pitjantjatjarra are a tribe of the desert lands of central Australia. The missionary and translator Wilf H. Douglas was privileged to hear a Flood story from them around the year 1950. It is amazing that a tribe from a region where water is so scarce should have such a tradition about a great Flood:

> "Long ago, in the Creation country across the sea to the west, some people saw these red-legged birds strutting along with their heads moving up and down. Whenever the people approached them they moved forward always keeping the same distance between themselves and their followers.
>
> There were millions of these birds, and they were much taller than they are today. The men followed them to discover where they were all going. The birds walked east and eventually led the men to the coast of Australia. They stepped out of the sea where Fremantle is today, then turned north and walked up the coast. The men continued to follow them. When they reached the point just below where Port Hedland is now situated the great flood came.
>
> The sky opened and the water poured down in a great deluge. Many people were drowned, but some were saved on mangrove boats. They paddled towards the ranges in Central Australia, the Mardudjara people [now camped at Jigalong] leading the way. They were the first people to take dogs to the center of the continent. At last they reached the MacDonnell Ranges …"[8]

The sky opened and the water poured down in a great deluge. Many people were drowned, but some were saved on mangrove boats. … At last they reached the MacDonnell Ranges.

Notice, they landed on a mountain range, like Noah and his family.

7. *Ibid.*
8. Coates and Douglas, "Australian Aboriginal Flood Stories," pp. 6-9.

260 NEW SOUTH WALES TRADITION

John Henderson, writing around the year 1830, recorded a vague tradition of the Flood held by an unspecified group from New South Wales:

> "There is however a tradition, that he [a god named Baiame] once awoke, and having turned himself upon his side, the flood-gates of the salt-ocean were immediately thrown open, and the hills and valleys disappeared beneath the rolling waters. It is also reported, that when he next awakes, a similar catastrophe may be expected."[9]

The Kangaroo

Is the kangaroo an exhibit to evolution? Did the kangaroo evolve in Australia, along with other marsupials?

That view looked much better before the discovery of marsupial fossils in Europe, Asia, and North America. Not only that, but these fossils outside of Australia are conventionally dated to be older than those in Australia.[10] This animal once seemed so clearly and intuitively an exhibit to evolution and a denial of Genesis. But that turned out to be an illusion.

261 KURNAI

Robert Brough Smyth (1830 – 1899), as an official in the Board for the Protection of the Aborigines, collected information on the native peoples of Australia, at a time when this information was quickly disappearing. He published this in his work, The Aborigines of Victoria. This includes a Flood tradition of the Kurnai tribe of Victoria state in southeast Australia.

> "A long time ago, 'when father belonging to you and me been alive,' there was a very great flood; all the country was under water, and all the black-fellows were drowned except a man and two or three women, who took refuge in a mud island near Port Albert. The water was all round them. The Pelican, sailing about in his bark canoe, saw these poor people, and went to help them. One of the women was so beautiful that he fell in love with her. When she wanted to get into the canoe, he said, 'Not now—next time.' So that, ferrying the others one by one to the mainland, she was left to the last. She became frightened, and being a cunning woman, she wrapped a log of wood up in her 'possum rug,' laid it by the fire to look like herself, and then swam ashore and escaped. When the Pelican came back, he said, 'Come on now.' Receiving no reply, he became angry, and, going to the supposed woman lying by the fire, he gave her a kick, when he at once found out the trick that had been played upon him. Then he was very angry, and began to paint himself white, 'to look out fight' with the blackfellows. When he was half-painted, another Pelican came by, and not knowing what such a queer black and white thing was, struck the first Pelican with his beak and killed him. Before that, Pelicans were all black—now they are black and white, and that is the reason."[11]

A long time ago, 'when father belonging to you and me been alive,' there was a very great flood ... The Pelican, sailing about in his bark canoe, saw these poor people, and went to help them.

9. John Henderson, *Observations on the Colonies of New South Wales and Van Diemen's Land* (Calcutta: Baptist Mission Press, 1832), p. 147.
10. For more on this question, see: Jonathan Sarfati, *The Greatest Hoax on Earth? Refuting Dawkins on Evolution* (Atlanta: Creation Book Publishers, 2010), pp. 168-170.
11. Robert Brough Smyth, *The Aborigines of Victoria*, vol. 1 (London: 1878), pp. 477-478.

A very similar version was provided by one Mary E. B. Howitt (1866-1936):

> "There was a great flood which covered the land, and drowned the people, excepting a man and two women. Bunjil Borun, the Pelican, came by in his canoe, and took the man across to the mainland, then one woman, leaving the better-looking one to the last. She, being frightened, swam over to the land, having placed a log rolled up in her rug by the fire as if she were there asleep. Bunjil Borun discovering this, when he returned, became very much enraged and began to paint himself ready for fighting with the man whose wife had played him this trick. While he was doing this another pelican came up, and seeing a queer-looking creature, half-black and half-white, struck at it with his beak and killed Bunjil Borun."[12]

There was a great flood which covered the land, and drowned the people, excepting a man and two women. The Pelican came by in his canoe.

We have not only a global Flood but also a boat, two birds, and a quarrel reminiscent of Cain and Abel in Genesis 4.

> "Andrew Lang writing in the late 1800s presented his research on the religions of primitive peoples and found that the supreme god among these people was regarded as a fatherly figure, a creator, beneficent, and, the source of the moral code. As an example, Lang describes the beliefs of the Australian Kurnai tribe. The Kurnai refer to their god Mungnan-ngaur (meaning Our Father) as one who destroyed the earth by water but hence ascended to the sky where he remains. Mungnan is immortal, and his precepts include, listening to the older men, sharing with and living peaceably with friends, a prohibition of promiscuous behavior, and obedience to food restrictions."[13]

262 YUIN

A. W. Howitt recorded the Flood tradition of the Yuin tribe, who lived on the south coast of New South Wales:

> "Long ago Daramulun [the father] lived on the earth with his mother Ngalalbal. Originally the earth was bare and "like the sky, as hard as a stone," and the land extended far out where the sea is now. There were no men or women, but only animals, birds, and reptiles. He placed trees on the earth. After Kaboka, the thrush, had caused a great flood on the earth, which covered all the coast country, there were no people left, excepting some who crawled out of the water on to Mount Dromedary. Then Darantulun went up to the sky, where he lives and watches the actions of men. It was he who first made the Kuringal and the bull-roarer, the sound of which represents his voice. He told the Yuin what to do, and he gave them the laws which the old people have handed down from father to son to this time."[14]

After Kaboka, the thrush, had caused a great flood on the earth, which covered all the coast country, there were no people left, excepting some who crawled out of the water on to Mount Dromedary.

---

12. Alfred William Howitt, *The Native Tribes of South-East Australia* (London: MacMillan & Co., 1904), p. 486. For another Kurnai version, see: Andrew Lang, Custom and Myth (London: Longmans, Green and Co., 1893), p. 35. "In Gippsland there is a tradition of the deluge. 'Some children of the Kurnai in playing about found a turndun [bull roarer], which they took home to the camp and showed the women. Immediately the earth crumbled away, and it was all water, and the Kurnai were drowned.'"
13. Daniel R. Cote, "Original Monotheism: A Signal of Transcendence Challenging Naturalism and New Ageism." Doctoral Thesis. Liberty University (April 5, 2020), p. 34. The relevant section of Andrew Lang's work that Cote summarizes is: *The Making of Religion* (London: Longmans, Green, and Co., 1898), pp. 195-196. For more on Original Monotheism, I recommend Wilhelm Schmidt's work, *The Origin and Growth of Religion* (London: Methuen & Co., 1935).
14. Howitt, *The Native Tribes of South-East Australia*, pp. 494-495.

263 MELBOURNE AREA TRADITION

R. Brough Smyth presents a Flood tradition from an unspecified tribe, original to the Melbourne area in southeast Australia:

> "The doctors or priests say that the sea was created by Bund-Jel. The sea … has waters different from those that flow in the creeks and rivers, and very different from those that descend from the sky. … Many long ages past Bund-Jel was very angry with the blacks. Bund-Jel was very angry with all black people, because they had done evil and wicked things; and Bun-Jel [sent a deluge] many days on the earth, and all the black people were drowned, except such as Bund-Jel favored, and these were caught up with him and fixed in the sky as stars. One Koolin and one Baggarook-one man and one woman—who had climbed a high tree on a mountain, escaped the flood which Bund-Jel had made, and they lived; and all the people now existing are descended from these two."[15]

One man and one woman who had climbed a high tree on a mountain escaped the flood which Bund-Jel had made, and they lived; and all the people now existing are descended from these two.

Again we have divine judgment, a global Flood, a surviving remnant who ended up atop a high mountain, and subsequent repopulation.

264 LAKE TYERS AREA TRADITION

The Flood tradition of those living near Lake Tyers, in the southeast corner of Australia, runs as follows:

> "The Aborigines of Lake Tyers say that at one time there was no water anywhere on the face of the earth. All the waters were contained in the body of a huge Frog, … At length No-yang (the Eel) began to wriggle and distort himself, and the Frog's jaws opened. He laughed outright. When he laughed, all the waters came out of his mouth, and there was a flood. Great numbers were drowned in the flood. Many, very many, perished in the waters. The Pelican, who before the flood was a blackfellow, took upon himself to save the black people. He cut a very large canoe, and sailed among the islands which appeared here and there in the great waters, and he took the people into his canoe, and he kept them alive. By and by the Pelican had a quarrel with the people whom he had saved. He quarreled with them about a woman, and the Pelican was turned into a stone."[16]

The Pelican cut a very large canoe, and sailed among the islands which appeared here and there in the great waters. He took the people into his canoe and kept them alive.

265 NGARRINDJERI

The Ngarrindjeri occupy a part of South Australia between Cape Jervis and Lake Alexandrina. The missionary George Taplin lived among them beginning in 1853. They attribute the Flood to their supreme god Nurundere, and they remember the landing of the Ark on a high mountain:

> "Once when he [Nurundere] dwelt at Tulurrug two of his children strayed away into the scrub to the eastward, and were lost. Soon afterwards his two wives ran away from him. He pursued them, in company with his remaining children, to Encounter Bay, and there, seeing them at a distance, he exclaimed in anger, "Let the waters arise and drown them." So the waters arose in a terrible flood, and swept over the hills with fury, and, overtaking the fugitives, they were overwhelmed and drowned. At this time Nepelle lived at Rauwoke, and the flood was so great that he was obliged to pull his canoe to the top of the hill (that is Point Macleay); from thence it was transported to Wyirrewarre; the dense part of the milky way is said to be the canoe of Nepelle floating in the heavens. Then its owner, by using the same means as Wyungare had done, ascended thither also."[17]

The flood was so great that he was obliged to pull his canoe to the top of the hill, Point Macleay.

15. Robert Brough Smyth, *The Aborigines of Victoria, vol. 1*, p. 429.
16. Smyth, *The Aborigines of Victoria,* pp. 429-430.
17. George Taplin, "The Narrinyeri," *The Native Tribes of South Australia* (Adelaide: E.S. Wigg & Son, 1879), pp. 57-58.

266 MOUNT ELLIOT TRIBE

The Mount Elliot tribe were a cannibalistic tribe, living near Mount Elliot and Cape Cleveland in northeast Australia. James Morrill, who was shipwrecked in 1846 and held in captivity by the Mount Elliot natives for 17 years, heard their Flood tradition during this time:

> "They told me that their forefathers witnessed a great flood, and nearly all were drowned, only those who got on a very high mountain (Bibbiringda, which is inland of the north bay of Cape Cleveland) were saved. He understands them to refer to the flood mentioned in Scripture, especially as they say only a few were allowed to go up."[18]

They told me that their forefathers witnessed a great flood, and nearly all were drowned, only those who got on a very high mountain were saved.

267 BRABIRALONG

The Brabiralong or Brabrolung were a tribe of the Gippsland area, in the state of Victoria. John Bulmer, head of a Reservations in the Gippsland area, published a Flood tradition which is very similar to that of the natives near Lake Tyer.[19]

268 GUNDITJMARA

One Reverend Robert Hamilton referred to a Flood tradition of the natives near Portland, a city in southeast Australia. Geographically, we can identify this tribe as the Gunditjmara people. The nearby volcano, Mount Eccles (also known as Budj Bim), is held in great honor by the Gunditjmara. This mountain is also featured in their Flood tradition, as we will see below. In all likelihood, this is an echo of that original mountain, which is Ararat:

> "Among the aborigines of the Portland district there is a tradition that a flood destroyed the whole human race with the exception of one man, who was saved by one of the great powers taking hold of his long spear and drawing him up into the clouds from the top of a volcanic hill (Mount Eccles). On the flood passing away the man returned, and became the father of the new race of men."[20]

The nearby volcano, Mount Eccles (Budj Bim), is held in great honor by the Gunditjmara and is featured in their Flood tradition.

18. Edward M. Curr, *The Australian Race, vol. 2* (Melbourne: John Ferres, 1886), p. 450.
19. "The eel stood upon the tip of his tail, which so tickled the overgrown frog that he literally burst with laughing, and the water poured from him in such vast streams that there was presently a deluge, and all the Blacks would have been drowned, had not one of them, Loon by name, made a large canoe, in which he saved a great many. Why at the present day they call White men Loon, I cannot say. However, alas! For the ingratitude of human nature, those whom Loon had saved refused to give him a wife, in consequence of which he pipe-clayed himself in the orthodox fashion, and commenced hostilities forthwith. In this undertaking, however, he seems to have been worsted; at all events, all that is positively known is that he was transformed into a pelican, and that is owing to the pipe-clay that this been has always been so white about the head and breast." Edward M. Curr, *The Australian Race, vol. 3* (Melbourne: John Ferres, 1887), p. 548.
20. Rev. Robert Hamilton, "Australian Traditions," *The Scottish Geographical Magazine*, vol. 1, no. 7 (July 1885), p. 284.

269 UALARAI

The Ualarai, a tribe of eastern interior Australia, told the following Flood tradition to Katie Langloh Parker in the 1890s:

> "Mooregoo the Mopoke [a type of owl] had been camped away by himself for a long time. While alone he had made a great number of boomeranges, nullah-nullahs, spears, beilahmans, and opossum rings. Well had he carved the weapons with the teeth of opossums, and brightly had he painted the inside of the rugs with coloured designs, and strongly had he sewn them with the sinews of opossums, threaded in the needle made of the little bone taken from the leg of an emu. As Mooregu looked at his work he was proud of all he had done.
>
> One night Bahloo the moon came to his camp, and said: 'Lend me one of your opossum rugs.'
>
> 'No. I lend not my rugs.'
>
> 'Then give me one.'
>
> 'No I give not my rugs.'
>
> Looking round, Bahloo saw the beautifully carved weapons, so he said, 'Then give me, Mooregoo, some of your weapons.'
>
> 'No, I give, never, what I have made, to another.'
>
> Again Bahloo said, 'The night is cold. Lend me a rug.'
>
> 'I have spoken,' said Mooregon. 'I never lend my rugs.'
>
> Bahloo said no more, but went away, cut some bark and made a dardurr [hut] for himself. When it was finished and he safely housed in it, down came the rain in torrents. And it rained without ceasing until the whole country was flooded. Mooregoo was drowned. His weapons floated about and drifted apart, and his rugs rotted in the water."[21]

Fossil Bluff

Fossil Bluff in Tasmania is a testament to the global Flood. What kind of geological or meteorological forces could produce an 80-foot sedimentary layer of limestone, with evidence of violent and high-velocity flow, including fossilized crushed shells, bone fragments, and pebbles? Only the global Flood can explain the scale and the power to create such a massive deposit. Also, there are knife-edge boundaries between adjacent sediments, showing they were laid down quickly by moving water.[22]

21. Katie Langloh Parker, *Australian Legendary Tales: Folklore of the Noongahburrahs as Told to the Picaninnies* (London: David Nutt, 1896), pp. 68-69.
22. For more information, see: https://creation.com/fossil-bluff

270 MURRINH-PATHA

The Murrinh-Patha (or Murinbata) are a tribe from Australia's Northern Territory. They have a tradition of a Flood that took place back when people were "bird men." At that time, the sea suddenly invaded the land and began to threaten the mountains. Their leader, known as stone curlew man, led the people to escape to a mountain top. Those who did not make it turned into animals. Some men built a wall around the mountain to stop the Flood. Three times, the stone curlew man sent bird-men to search for land, but they returned without success. Then he cut off the first joint of a boy's finger, and the blood dripped into the sea. The waters began to recede at last. This time, birds were sent out, and they returned with branches of tree bark.[23] These birds are certainly a memory of Noah's dove and raven.

Three times, the stone curlew man sent bird-men to search for land, but they returned without success. ... Birds were sent out, and they returned with branches of tree bark.

271 GWINI

Around the late 1930s, Arthur Capell heard an account of the Flood from the Gwini (or Yeidji) people of northern Kimberley (Western Australia). It is said that their cultural hero Wolaro prepared a canoe while it was dry. He told some men and women to gather food and animals, and he put them in the canoe. Then he caused the Flood. After a while, a little bird went and plucked a leaf from a tree. The island rose and the sea water went down. Then Wolaro created the post-Flood world.[24]

Their cultural hero Wolaro prepared a canoe while it was dry. He told some men and women to gather food and animals, and he put them in the canoe. Then he caused the Flood. After a while, a little bird went and plucked a leaf from a tree.

272 WIILMAN

The Wiilman (or Wheelman) are a tribe from the southwestern tip of Australia, south of Perth. When Ethel Hassell moved into the territory of the Wiilman people in 1870, she was the first white woman seen by many of them.[25] A Flood tradition recorded by her or her husband went as follows. Notice the statement that the people at that time "were very big and strong in those days and could carry big rocks." This is reminiscent of the giants of Genesis 6:4:

> "Long ago, when my mother's mother was a baby, there was a period of great rains. It rained for days and days steadily. It rained so long that the moon got fat and round then thin again, then fat and round a second time, but it still rained and rained. The natives became very weary of so much rain. They were very big and strong in those days and could carry big rocks. Because of the rain all the rivers and creeks overflowed their banks and flooded all the low parts of the country. So much water went down the streams that the sand bars at the entrances of the rivers were broken and the sea came up and flooded the country. The natives had to move to higher ground but more water came and flooded their country and they had to move still higher. The waters continued to rise, however, and the natives were afraid that even the high country would be flooded. They decided, therefore, that they had better carry great rocks to the high places on which to build their huts. The men and women both proceeded to gather the great stones on the hill tops. Often some natives were drowned as they tried to carry the big rocks through the waters. Sometimes one, sometimes many had to drop the stones in order to save their lives. While this was going on the animals became tame and tried to follow them. Many of the animals sat on the great stones which had been dropped but the waters rose again and they had to swim away and search for other places. …

---

23. Roland Robinson, *The Feathered Serpent: The Mythological Genesis and Recreative Ritual of the Aboriginal Tribes of the Northern Territory of Australia* (Sydney: Edwards and Shaw, 1956), pp. 16-18.
24. Arthur Capell, *Cave Painting Myths: Northern Kimberley* (Sydney: University of Sydney, 1972), pp. 163-166.
25. Ethel Hassell and D. S. Davidson, "Myths and Folktales of the Wheelman Tribe of South-Western Australia," *Folk-Lore, vol. 45*, no. 3 (1934), p. 232.

At last a few survivors got to a big mountain. They had only a few big stones left. All the others had been lost when the other natives had been drowned. They piled all the stones together and climbed on top of them. They had practically nothing left."[26]

Later, a piece of ground appeared and grew slowly. Eventually, the kangaroos and the emus ventured onto this new land, and the surviving people followed them.

273 BOORONG

The Boorong are a clan of the Wergaia people in Victoria, southeastern Australia. Their version of the Flood was narrated as follows:

> "After the great flood, men and women became very numerous on earth. They were to be found everywhere. Wherever they went they did cruel and evil things to the animals that had been made to share the earth with them. … Long, long ago, before the great flood, the Nurrumbunguttias or spirit men and women lived on earth. They knew that the whole earth was flat, and that for long ages it had been dark, until Pupperrimbul, the Diamond Firetail, a little bird with a red patch on its tail, made the sun. Once that great ball of fire sailed across the sky it gave light and warmth. Even though the world was warm during the day, the Nurrumbunguttias were cold at night, and they did not like eating raw food, so they made fire to warm themselves and cook their food.
>
> Then came the flood. The water rose up quietly from the sea, until it was higher than the tallest gum tree. It was like a vast blue plain, with only the tops of the mountains standing up above it like islands. The water kept on rising, and finally even the mountain peaks disappeared. The world was one vast, flat sheet of water, and there was no place for the Nurrumbunguttias to live. Many of them were drowned, but others were caught up by a whirlwind which carried them off into the sky, where they became stars, and some, who were gods on earth, became the gods of the sky. Among them was Pund-jil. The Milky Way was made out of the fires that the Nurrumbunguttias had kindled when they were on earth. Slowly the flood waters receded. The mountain tops appeared again, and the spear heads of trees showed above the water."[27]

Long, long ago, before the great flood, the Nurrumbunguttias or spirit men and women lived on earth.

A diamond firetail bird stands on a tree branch

26. *Ibid.*, pp. 242-243.
27. Alexander Wyclif Reed, *Aboriginal Fables and Legendary Tales* (Sydney: A.H. & A.W. Reed, 1965), pp. 55-56.

274 — WORORA

The Worora are an Australian people group from Kimberley, which is the northernmost region of Western Australia. Howard Coate's source was a tribal authority named Albert Barunga, who narrated to him that unforgettable event as follows:

> "In ancient times the sea made the watermarks on the mountains and ranges. For example Mt. House, Mt. Waterloo, Mt. Hann all have these watermarks, they are right on top. The reason for this flood was men killed the old woman's third son, the one she loved."[28]

In ancient times the sea made the watermarks on the mountains and ranges.

The woman vowed to kill the people taking the life of her son. So she speared the "eye of the sea" several times, which at last caused a great flood.[29] The tradition adds that the people drowned at that time transformed into today's sea creatures.

275 — GUMBAYNGGIRR

The Gumbaynggirr (or Gumbainggir) people live near the eastern coast of Australia approximately midway between Brisbane in the north and Sydney in the south. Their memory of the Flood, which A.C. McDougall recorded in the late 1800s, went like this:

> "A great many years ago the sea broke over the land and flooded almost the whole earth. The earth floated and rose to the top and subsequently rose high on the water thus saving the ancestors of the Coombangree [or Gumbaynggirr] tribe from being drowned. When the water subsided the earth settled down in its usual position. During the time of the inundation one old warrior prayed to their Ulitarra (god) asking him to make the water go off the earth."[30]

During the time of the inundation one old warrior prayed to their god asking him to make the water go off the earth.

276 — YOLNGU

The Yolngu people of Australia's Northern Territory have a Flood tradition which, very interestingly, involves a serpent-man. This certainly evokes memories of that serpent from the Garden of Eden, Satan himself. It is one more example of Flood stories with an admixture of the Serpent from the Garden, just as we find them abundantly in New Guinea, and in China, the Americas, and occasionally in other parts of the world:

> "In the origin myths of a number of peoples, a great serpent associated with the rainbow is held responsible for the flood. This creature, which is believed still to exist (living in deep pools of water or in coastal whirlpools), occurs in the story of the Wawilak Sisters told by the Yolngu people of northeastern Arnhem Land."[31]

In the origin myths of a number of peoples, a great serpent associated with the rainbow is held responsible for the flood.

---

28. Coates and Douglas, "Australian Aboriginal Flood Stories," pp. 6-9.
29. "This sea travelled across like a range to them. The mountains sank beneath it. Then she finished them. They were drowned. While still there was no water, that is at the time when it disappeared, she picked up turtle and fish and took them up to the top of the hill at Nowulu. The place is called Nowulu, it's an island, that the place she climbed up to. Here she remained and dug for water right on the top. Then that one – the sea – was travelling and all the mainland was underneath it. That was the time it went back. That time it finished them; it drowned all those men. Only those who climbed right on top, over there, only those may be living. Then they returned this way. that was the sea that drowned all the men of that generation on the earth." (Ibid.) See also: Roy G. Willis, *World Mythology* (Oxford: Oxford University Press, 2006), p. 280. "According to the Worora of the Kimberleys of northwestern Australia, ancestral heroes known as the wandjina, caused a flood which wiped out the previous social order. The wandjina then dispersed, each to their own country, where they put up their paintings in rock shelters and created the new order of society."
30. A.C. McDougall, "Manners, Customs, and Legends of the Combangree Tribe," *Science of Man and Journal of the Royal Anthropological Society of Australasia*, vol. 4, no. 3 (April 22, 1901), p. 46.
31. Roy Willis, *World Mythology* (London: Duncan Baird, 1993), p. 280.

"The sisters went out from somewhere in the distant interior and travelled toward the northern coast of Arnhem Land. The younger sister was pregnant, while the elder had a child which she carried in a paper bark cradle under her arm. As they travelled, they hunted lizard, possum, and bandicoot, and gathered plants to eat. They named each species of plant and animal, as well as the places through which they walked."[32]

"... angering Yurlunggur, a semi-human python who lived there."

It is possible, in the above section, that there are faint memories of other events from the Garden of Eden, including Adam naming the animals, and the promise concerning Eve's future Seed, who is Christ Himself (Genesis 3:15). But on these details we cannot be certain. We continue:

"One day they met two men with whom they had intercourse, even though they all belonged to the same division of society. When the younger woman was ready to bear a son, her sister collected soft bark to make a bed. Unwittingly, the elder sister allowed her menstrual blood to fall into a waterhole, angering Yurlunggur, a semi-human python who lived there."[33]

Notice above that he is a "semi-human python." We continue:

"Yurlunggur created a storm and a great flood. The sisters sang songs in an attempt to drive the snake away, but he swallowed them and their sons as a punishment for polluting the well. When the flood had subsided, Yurlunggur, who had reared up above the waters, came down to earth, creating the first Yolngu initiation ground at the spot where he landed. The serpent then regurgitated the sisters and their sons, who became the first Yolngu initiates."[34]

277 EORA

The Eora are the native people in the area of what is now Sydney. Sadly, they were decimated by disease, and most of their culture has been lost due to Anglicization. They had a memory of the Flood, a fact first recorded in a letter from the wife of a Lieutenant John Macarthur, dated March 7, 1791. Her source was a close associate, the scientist and officer William Dawes (1762-1836), whom she mentioned to have heard a Flood tradition from them.[35] However, this mere mention leaves us with no substance as to their Flood account.

They are said to have a tradition of the deluge, when the water overtopped the Blue Mountains, and two men only escaped the devastation, in a kobou noe, or large ship.

But we do have one other source on the Eora people's Flood tradition. During the 1820s, two missionaries named Daniel Tyerman and George Bennet heard it from them. "They are said to have a tradition of the deluge, when the water overtopped the Blue Mountains, and two men only escaped the devastation, in a kobou noe, or large ship." With this all-too-brief summary, we will have to content ourselves. It is added that "they entertain some crude notions of a good spirit as well as an evil; but the former they disregard, and pay all their homage of fear–a fear which hath torment–to the latter."[36]

32. *Ibid.*, p. 281.
33. *Ibid.*
34. *Ibid.*
35. F. M. Bladen (ed.), "Appendix B: The MacArthur Papers," in *Historical Records of New South Wales,* vol. 2 (Sydney: Charles Potter, 1893), p. 505.
36. James Montgomery (ed.), *Journal of Voyages and Travels by the Rev. Daniel Tyerman and George Bennet*, Esq., vol. 2 (Boston: Crocker and Brewster, 1832), p. 266.

278 NEW SOUTH WALES TRADITION

John Henderson, writing around the year 1830, recorded a vague tradition of the Flood held by an unspecified group from New South Wales:

> "There is however a tradition, that he [a god named Baiame] once awoke, and having turned himself upon his side, the flood-gates of the salt-ocean were immediately thrown open, and the hills and valleys disappeared beneath the rolling waters. It is also reported, that when he next awakes, a similar catastrophe may be expected."[37]

Four Mile Beach in Port Douglas, Queensland, Australia

279 TURRBAL

The ancestors of the Turrbal tribe are the original inhabitants of the area where the city of Brisbane is located, in southeast Queensland (near the eastern tip of Australia). They have an account of the Flood very similar to the version above, which the polyglot James W. Fawcett recorded in the 1890s. This account would encompass not only the Turrbal, but also several of their linguistically related neighboring tribes.[38]

37. John Henderson, *Observations on the Colonies of New South Wales and Van Diemen's Land* (Calcutta: Baptist Mission Press, 1832), p. 147.
38. "The Turrabool speaking aborigines who inhabited the district of the Upper Brisbane River, in South Queensland, had a tradition regarding a spirit or unseen Being whom they called Budjah. This being was called Buddai (Buddha?) by another tribe. They believed him to be the common ancestor of their race, and described him as an old man of great stature. They stated that he had been lying asleep for ages with his head leaning on one arm, and the arm buried deep in the sand. A long time ago Budjah awoke, and the whole country was flooded with water. When it had subsided he fell asleep, and they believe that some day he will wake again and get up, and that on that occasion he will devour all the aborigines." J. W. Fawcett, "Australian Aborigines," *The Australasian Anthropological Journal*, vol. 1, no. 6 (May 31, 1897), p. 125.

280 WARRUWI

The Warruwi people live on the small Goulburn Islands just off the northern coast of Australia's Northern Territory. They have a tradition which combines a memory of the Flood and the Tree of the Knowledge of Good and Evil.[39]

The Paraburdoo iron ore mine in the Pilbara Region of Western Australia.

281 YINDJIBARNDI

We have a vague recollection of the Flood from the Yindjibarndi people of western Australia. This was recorded in the 1970s from a man named Gilbert Bobby, one of the foremost authorities on this tribe's sacred traditions.[40]

> Don't you know that tree's djang? If you cut it down a flood will come, and we'll all be drowned.' Crow took no notice of them, just went on cutting. At last the tree fell. From each side the sea water flowed in, filling the creek and flooding the country.

39. In the ancient past, a man named Mandulmandul used to feed the "bird-men," who lived at that time, from the fish that he daily collected in his net. "He would take what he wanted for himself, and give the rest to all the Bird people who assembled there. The good fish he gave to Djudjud, Seahawk Man, and Marwadi, Eagle Man; but to Crow Man, Guragag, he gave only the umbulnga—a species of inedible puff-ball fish. Old Crow would ask, 'Where's my fish?' Day after day he would be told, 'The umbulnga are for you.' At last, tired of this treatment, he went to a sacred djang paperbark tree and started to cut it down. When the other Bird Men saw what he was doing they called out in consternation, 'Don't you know that tree's djang? If you cut it down a flood will come, and we'll all be drowned.' Crow took no notice of them, just went on cutting. At last the tree fell. From each side the sea water flowed in, filling the creek and flooding the country. 'We'll die, we'll die!' cried the Bird Men. As the flood spread and the water became deeper, they changed their shape and really became birds. Beginning to fly, they identified themselves: 'My name is djudjud, seahawk,' 'My name is marwadi, eagle,' and so on. Crow called his own name, and added that he would continue to eat any kind of food at all— 'just as crows do today'. This is how the strait between the two islands was formed. In the middle, where it is rough and the waves are high, is the place where the drum net and the djang tree used to be. Mandulmandul 'turned himself into a rock, which is visible today at low tide. Source: Ronald M. Berndt and Catherine H. Berndt, *The World of the First Australians* (Sydney: Ure Smith, 1977), pp. 399-400. Originally published in 1964.
40. "Back when the earth was soft, a red-capped robin went out walking in Marduthunira country. He found a little stone lying there. He picked it up. He put it on his head and carried it right toward Robe River, leaving the ocean behind him. He took it as far as Robe River. That particular red-capped robin got up on Pannawonica Hill. He stood right on top. A certain man said, "Why did you bring that stone here? You brought the ocean with it!" That man was a native pheasant. He called out "Ocean go back!" He called out "Putput! Putput!" The ocean went right back to Marduthunira country. Pannowonica rose up to stand tall, after the native pheasant called out." F. J. F. Wordick, *The Yindjibarndi Language* (Canberra, A.C.T.: Australia: Dept. of Linguistics, Research School of Pacific Studies, Australian National University, 1982), pp. 251-253.

The Eurasian Steppe in early spring

NORTH ASIA

Those that deny the Flood have advanced a narrative that the knowledge of the Flood is absent in North Asia. "Flood legends are missing in North and Central Asia," wrote Richard Andree.[1] Flood traditions "are conspicuously absent from Eastern, Central, and Northern Asia," according to Sir James George Frazer.[2] They are "unknown in many parts of Asia," proclaimed Moriz Winternitz,[3] and "no trace of it exists among the Mongolian and Siberian populations," declared John William De Forest.[4]

These proclamations were very mistaken. In a stunning rebuke to these scholars, Walter Anderson said these claims are due to "ignorance of Russian- and Hungarian-language materials," rather than an actual absence of Flood traditions.[5] Indeed, we have found that the knowledge of the Flood is pervasive across northern Asia, from the Ural Mountains near the boundary with Europe, all the way to the Kamchatka Peninsula and the Bering Strait.

Thus, we will hear from the Turkic peoples that "Seven righteous brothers knew about the coming of the flood," and "The brothers built a carap (a ship), on which they took their animals with them, of livestock, birds, and reptiles, one pair at a time." So serious was this memory of the Flood that they offered an annual sacrifice in the spring to Jaik-Khan, "the Flood Prince."

Tribes of the Region

282. Altaian Turks
283. Mansi
284. Soyot
285. Mongolia
286. Ostyak
287. Nenet
288. Kamchadal
289. Tungus
290. Khaka
291. Shor
292. Chukchee
293. Orochi
294. Dolgan
295. Manchu
296. Hezhe
297. Oruqen
298. Nganasan
299. Khanty
300. Yakut
301. Sagai

The ancient texts of the Mansi people of western Siberia include a Flood account. They say the giants who lived on the earth at that time cut down a hollow poplar tree in order to build two boats, and they used ox skins for a roof. "Only one old man foresaw the coming Flood," said the Soyot people of eastern Siberia. "He sat down in it with a few people and with provisions, and thus escaped. This raft now stands in the high rocky mountains where it stopped. All other people and animals perished."

1. Richard Andree, *Die Flutsagen* (Braunschweig: Friedrich Vieweg, 1891), p. 34.
2. Sir James George Frazer, *Folk-Lore In the Old Testament*, vol. 1 (London: Macmillan and Co., 1919), p. 332.
3. Moriz Winternitz, "Die Flutsagen des Alterthums und der Naturvölker," *Mittheilungen der Anthropologischen Gesellschaft in Wien*, vol. 31 (1901), p. 305.
4. John William De Forest, "The Great Deluge," *Old And New*, vol. 6 (Boston: Roberts Brothers, 1872), p. 447.
5. Walter Anderson, "Nordasiatische Flutsagen," *Acta et Commentationes Universitatis Dorpatensis: B, Humaniora*, vol. 4 (Tartu, 1923), p. 5.

The Eurasian Steppe

The Mongolians are by no means ignorant of the Flood. In one of their accounts, an old woman predicted there would be a flood the following day, and instructed a young man to climb a mountain to escape it. And in another version, "a flood reached the sky and washed away all people, livestock, and birds. Only a young man escaped, whose name was Luoyue." This man had listened to an owl that told him to make a watertight bag from cowskin, in which he took refuge and escaped the flood.

The Ostyak or Ket people tell that "the water came so strongly that it flooded the whole earth up to the tops of the mountains." It was only on rafts or floating peat mats that people and animals survived, but they drifted apart and were separated. And concerning Noah's raven and dove, they have a memory of a great shaman named Doh who sent ducks and loons diving for earth. Only the third attempt was successful. The Nenet people's Flood account is similar, and they remember the Tower of Babel as well. After a stone tower was destroyed by the sky god Nun, "they wanted to talk to each other, but they could not. They were no longer able to understand each other." And their leader said, "Now let those people who speak different languages disperse throughout the earth."

The people of the Kamchatka Peninsula recall "a deluge and a mighty inundation of the whole country, which occurred not long after Kutka [God] had left them," and the Tungus people tell that "a long time ago, there was a big flood, even the mountains were submerged, and people in the world were drowned, leaving only a father and his daughter." The Turkic Khakas say that God "organized a flood to destroy the people who had stopped worshipping him," and that "the vessel on which a few people were saved remained after the Flood on the mountain Yzyk."

The god named Yayik-xan sent the Flood, which carried the raft to the top of a mountain, said the Shor people. The Orochi people, just north of Korea, remember this Flood and the sending of a crow and a raven. The Manchu people remember an old man who warned of the Flood—probably Noah himself. The Hezhe and Oruqen of eastern Siberia and northeastern China have their Flood memories as well, as do other ethnic groups of North Asia.

ALTAIAN TURKS

282 The Altaians, a people of Turkic descent and language, are an important link to the early Turks, that great nation that once dominated the Eurasian Steppe. The Altaians live in Altai Republic, which is located just northwest of Mongolia.

One of our sources on the Altaians is the Russian missionary Vasily Verbitskiy (1827-1890), who traveled to Altai around 1855 and wrote the earliest ethnography of the Altaians. Their sacred traditions include a jaw-dropping memory of the Flood and of an annual sacrifice, like the Chinese and Koreans:

> "Among some of the Altaic peoples the hero of the flood has also become the object of certain beliefs. As such he is often called Jaik-Khan ("the Flood Prince") and is prayed to as the intervener between the Over-god and man, and as the protector of man. In some places a white lamb is sacrificed to him annually in the spring. The sacrifice is carried out on a high mountain. He is also supposed to be the ruler of the dead, and as such is invited to the house-purification ceremonies forty days after a death, and begged to return the domestic animals, which the dead, according to the people, sometimes take with them. In the shaman rites also he is often spoken with and desired to convey the prayers."[6]

He is often called Jaik-Khan ("the Flood Prince") and is prayed to as the intervener between the Over-god and man, and as the protector of man. In some places a white lamb is sacrificed to him annually in the spring. The sacrifice is carried out on a high mountain.

When we compare with similar sacrifices, it is possible that this one was originally directed toward God, a ritual dating to pre-Babel times, but which was corrupted with the passing of the centuries.

We have another Flood tradition from the Altaians, published by Grigory Potanin in 1883. Potanin's source was one Father Postnikov, who probably recorded it a couple decades earlier:

> "Altaians believe that there was once a flood. The raft on which the ancestor of present day's humanity was saved, was preserved till this day. It stands on Mount Adygan (south of the village of Ulala, on the right bank of the Katun River). Whoever climbs this mountain will not return from there, but will die."[7]

The raft on which the ancestor of present day's humanity was saved is said to be at Mount Adygan.

In connection with this tradition, Holmberg adds, "In other places, tradition tells that on the site of the grounding of the ark, great nails have been found, believed to be remains of the vessel of the flood."[8]

Finally, the ethnographer Andrey Anokhin recorded the following Flood tradition from the Altai people:

> "The real earth is currently experiencing the second period of its existence. The Altaians attribute the beginning of the second period to the flood (jajbik), which they talk about like this. "The harbinger of the flood was a blue goat with iron horns (tamir mustu kök-takka). For seven days the goat ran around the earth and bleated furiously. There was an earthquake for seven days. The mountains burned for seven days. It rained for seven days. For seven days the hail fell with the storm. It snowed for seven days. After this, frosts set in.
>
> Seven righteous brothers knew about the coming of the flood. Of these, the eldest was Erlik, and another was Utgan. OIgan was gifted

6. Vasily Verbitskiy, *Altayskie inorodcy. Sbornik etnograficeskich statey I izsledovaniy* (Moscow, 1893), pp. 76, 103. As quoted in: Uno Holmberg, "Finno-Ugric, Siberian," *The Mythology of All Races*, vol. 4 (Boston: Archeological Institute of America, 1927), p. 365.
7. Potanin, Очерки северо-западной Монголии ("Studies of Northwestern Mongolia"), vol. 4, p. 208.
8. Uno Holmberg, "Finno-Ugric, Siberian," p. 366.

with divine abilities and was called nomchy (scribe). The brothers built a carap (a ship), on which they took their animals with them, of livestock, birds, and reptiles, one pair at a time."'[9]

Seven righteous brothers knew about the coming of the flood. … The brothers built a carap (a ship), on which they took their animals with them, of livestock, birds, and reptiles, one pair at a time.

And notice the memory of Noah's raven and dove, with which this tradition concludes:

> "When the flood ended, Oigan released a rooster (taka) from the ship, but he died from the frost. The second time, he released the goose (kas). The goose did not return to the ship. The third time, Olgan released a raven (cuskun). The raven also did not return back, because it found corpses and fed on them. ... Seven righteous brothers came out of the carap…"[10]

They add that this "carap" (ship) landed on Mount Yal-Monku, but some others say it was on Yjyk, near Kosh-Agach.[11]

Lastly, we have a story about the loss of immortality, in which is a clear memory of Noah's raven. This mixing up of the events recorded in Genesis is a common pattern around the world, due to the confusion of languages at Babel and imperfect oral transmission over the millenia:

> "When the first man was created by God Uligen, he was lifeless. In order to give life to this man, God Uligen dispatched a raven to Khudai in Heaven and asked him to bestow 'life' on the man. The raven received the 'life' from Khudai, took it in his mouth and flew back. The journey was so long that the raven became more and more tired, hungry and thirsty. He saw corpses of horses and camels on the ground again and again, but he restrained himself all the time. At last, he was too hungry to flap his wings any more. And at that time, he saw a freshly dead cow on the ground whose eyes were still bright. The raven could not help himself crying, 'Caw, caw, what bewitching eyes!' Hardly had his voice faded away, when the 'life' in his mouth dropped on to the coniferous trees, pine trees, and needle junipers on Earth. That is how these trees became evergreen."[12]

When the flood ended, Oigan released a rooster from the ship, followed by a goose, followed by a raven.

283 MANSI

The Mansi people, historically called the "Voguls," are a Uralic-language people group living in a region of western Siberia known as Khanty-Mansi Okrug. "The Vogul Genesis is made up of four texts," wrote Lucien Adam, who translated earlier material collected by Antal Reguly around the 1840s. "The first relates to the creation of the earth and man, the second relates to the creation of the giants and their fate, the third to the search for the daughter of a giant, and the fourth to the flood."[13]

"The Vogul Genesis is made up of four texts … The first relates to the creation of the earth and man, the second relates to the creation of the giants and their fate, the third to the search for the daughter of a giant, and the fourth to the flood."

Their Flood tradition, which involves giants, runs as follows:

> "After seven years of drought, the big woman said to the big man, 'It has rained elsewhere. How shall we save ourselves?' The other giants gathered in a town to hold council: 'What are we to do?'
>
> The big man replied, 'Let's cut an empty poplar tree in the middle and make two boats. We will then weave a rope five hundred fathoms long with willow roots. We will bury one of its ends in the earth, and we will attach the other to the front of our boats.'

9. A.V. Anokhin, *Материалы по шаманству у алтайцев ("Materials on Shamanism among the Altaians"). Сборник Музея Антропологии и этнографии при Российской Академии Наук ("Publications of the Museum of Anthropology and Ethnography of the Russian Academy of Sciences"* [MAE]), vol. 4, no. 2 (1924), p. 17.
10. *Ibid.*
11. *Ibid.*
12. Namjila, "Water-of-Immortality Myths," pp. 80, 82.
13. Lucien Adam, "Une Genèse Vogoule," *Revue de Philologie et d'Etnographie,* vol. 1 (Paris: 1874), p. 9.

'Let the man who has children get into the boat with his children, and let a covering made of ox skins be placed over them. Prepare food for seven days and seven nights and place it under the covering. Finally, put pots filled with liquid butter in each boat.'

Let the man who has children get into the boat with his children, and let a covering made of ox skins be placed over them.

Having thus ensured their own salvation, the two giants traveled through the villages, urging the inhabitants to build boats and weave ropes. Many did not know how to go about it. To these, the giants gave the necessary instructions. Others preferred to look for a place where they could find safety, but they searched in vain. The big man whom they addressed, because he was their elder, declared that he did not know of a place of refuge large enough for the people.

'Behold,' he added, 'we are going to be reached by the holy water, because already for two days we have heard the crashing of its waves. Let's get into the boats without delay!'"[14]

Having fled to their boats just in time, the violent waters advanced onto the land:

"Then the earth was submerged. Those who did not build boats perished in the hot water. The same happened to owners of boats whose rope was too short, as well as those who did not take liquid butter to facilitate the rubbing of the rope against the walls of the boat.

The water began to recede on the seventh day, and soon the survivors gained a foothold on the exposed parts of the ground. But unfortunately there were no longer any trees or plants on the surface of the earth. The animals perished, and the fish disappeared. On the verge of starvation, the men begged Numi Tarom to create fish, animals, trees, and plants again. Their prayer appears to have been answered."[15]

They had a snow-white raven. There was water everywhere on both sides of the house, but there was no earth.

Also, the Mansi have not entirely forgotten of Noah's dove. In another tradition, recorded by Bernat Munkacsi in approximately the 1880s, we can hear the echoes of Genesis 8:6-12:

"Tundra Hill's woman and old man were alive. They had a snow-white raven. There was water everywhere on both sides of the house, but there was no earth. The old man would not leave the house. He did not know how the outside world was shaped. While they were living like this, suddenly a noise came from the high heavens. The old man looked out the window: from above, out of the sky came an iron diving bird. To look for earth, he dove into the water. He searched all around, then he appeared, but he had found no earth. He caught his breath and dove back into the water. He searched here and there, and then he surfaced, again in vain. There was no earth.

He caught his breath a little and went under for a third time. When he surfaced, he breathed so hard that his throat burst. He had a piece of earth at the base of his beak. He swung himself up and rose into the sky."[16]

The parallels with the Noahic birds continue:

14. Lucien Adam, "Une Genèse Vogoule," p. 12. Lucien Adam was convinced of the authenticity and aboriginal character of these Mansi texts, for he wrote: "All these traits [the man kneaded with a mixture of earth and snow, Numi Tarom overseeing the cooking of a fish, wildlife becoming rare, and the hollow poplars transformed into canoes] are so many trademarks of the authenticity of which there can be no doubt." *Ibid.*, p. 13.
15. Lucien Adam, "Une Genèse Vogoule," pp. 12-13.
16. Oskar Dahnhardt, *Natursagen* ("Nature Legends"), vol. 1 (Leipzig: Drunk und Verlag, 1907), p. 63.

> "The woman and her old man lay down. When they got up in the morning, the earth was the width of a foot. The next day, when they got up, the earth had already reached as far as they could see. It had expanded so much; On the third day, when the woman and her old man looked out the window, there was no water; everywhere it had turned into earth.
>
> The old man said to his snow-white raven: "Just go, find out how big the earth has become!" The raven flew away, and was gone for a short hour. The earth had already become so big. The woman and her husband lay down. After they got up again, they sent the snow-white raven out again to find out the size of the earth. The snow-white raven only came home from its flight at midday. The earth had already become so big.
>
> On the third day they got up and said to the raven again: "Just go, see how big the earth has become!" He didn't return from his flight at all. So it was evening. At the time of laying down, he suddenly came home. Snow-white raven had turned black. The old man said to his raven: "You did something wrong on your flight!" The raven says: "What have I done? A person died, I ate from him, that's why I turned black!"[17]

The old man said to his snow-white raven: "Just go, find out how big the earth has become!"

284 SOYOT

The Soyot historically lived north of Mongolia and east of Lake Baikal in eastern Siberia. Though they now speak a Mongolian language, they originally spoke a language of the Uralic family.

Grigory Potanin (1835-1920), a Russian ethnographer and explorer of Inner Asia, recorded their Flood tradition in a work published in 1883:

> "One day she [the frog known as Alap that supports the world] moved. Ulu-Dalai (the great sea) became agitated, as if boiling, and overflowed its banks. Only one old man foresaw this circumstance and built a raft, strengthened with iron. He sat down in it with a few people and with provisions, and thus escaped. This raft now stands in the high rocky mountains where it stopped. All other people and animals perished."[18]

Only one old man foresaw this circumstance and built a raft, strengthened with iron. ... This raft now stands in the high rocky mountains where it stopped.

Where does China fit in the Table of Nations (Genesis 10)?

To the student of history, few biblical chapters are more interesting than Genesis 10, dubbed the "Table of Nations." This chapter has been called "the world's oldest ethnography." This detailed account finds broad confirmation from history and archeology.[19] However, an interesting and important question seems to remain unanswered: Where did the Chinese and the peoples of North Asia come from? From which of Noah's children and grandchildren have they descended?

I do not claim to know with certainty, but I offer my tentative thoughts. To answer this question, we must use the Bible, history, and genetics, including the paternally-inherited Y-chromosome data.

To begin with, it is important to note that two very different Y-chromosome haplogroups dominate East and North Asia. Therefore, we require not one but two different founders from Genesis 10. They are so different they must probably be from different sons of Noah.

17. Oskar Dahnhardt, *Natursagen*, vol. 1, pp. 63-64.
18. Grigory N. Potanin, Очерки северо-западной Монголии ("Studies of Northwestern Mongolia"), vol. 4 (Petrograd: 1883), p. 208.
19. See: Robert Dick Wilson, "The Date of Genesis X," *The Presbyterian and Reformed Review, vol. 1,* no. 2 (New York: Anson Randolph & Co., 1890), pp. 252-281.

The first haplogroup we are dealing with is O/N. This lineage is associated with China and most of East and Southeast Asia, including the Sino-Tibetan, Austroasiatic, Tai-Kadai, Finno-Ugric, and Turkic language families. The second male lineage is C. It is strongly associated with the Tungusic, early Japanese (Jomon), Mongolian (to a degree) and other small language families of Northeast Asia. C penetrates into Central Asia and south China, and is found in Melanesia, Australia, and even south India.

We must therefore take O/N and C separately. For O/N (including China), I like one of the sons of Japheth. Why Japheth? Because haplogroup O/N is relatively close to haplogroup R, and R corresponds to the Indo-Europeans, which are almost certainly sons of Japheth.

Biblically, Japheth is also an excellent candidate for O/N because he appears first in the list of nations in Genesis 10. Why does this matter? Because Moses has a pattern, in his organization of genealogies in Genesis, of dispensing first with the most secondary and peripheral members, in order to focus on the primary subjects.[20] Thus, Japheth's appearance first implies geographical remoteness from the Middle East, where Genesis was written. This would also fit well with the statements of Genesis 9:27 and 10:5 which imply that Japheth's descendants settled very distant lands.

But which son of Japheth? I think it is either Magog or Tiras. They are the most obscure. Scripture says very little about them. Their descendants are not listed. This implies rapid migration to distant places. After all, most of the grandsons of Noah listed in Genesis 10 are traced for an additional generation, or even further. Many are positively identified with particular nations. But that is not the case with Magog and Tiras. Presumably, that is because they quickly migrated to distant locations and thus could no longer be tracked.[21]

Whether O/N is Magog or Tiras, or possibly both, the path of migration appears to be a northeasterly route from Babel through Central Asia. Continuing on the northern side of the Himalayas, they eventually arrived in western China.

What about those belonging to Y-haplogroup C? Who is their ancestor? Whoever C is, he is closely related to haplogroups A, B, D, and E. Now A, B, and E are easily correlated with Africa. But that means they are correlated with Ham, for the Bible is clear that Africa is "the land of Ham" (Psa 78:51, 105:23, 106:22, 1 Chr 4:40). This, in turn, means that C must also be Hamitic!

How can this be? I think the Bible offers us a clue. There is one lineage to which Genesis 10 ascribes the first cities and the first kingdoms. There is one lineage which establishes settlements in East Africa, Mesopotamia, and Arabia in earliest times. That line is Cush (Gen 10:7-12).

Cush is, of course, a descendant of Ham. He is listed first, as the preeminent son (Gen 10:8). His descendants flew across the known world with a speed that would impress Genghis Khan or Alexander the Great. Therefore, it is not surprising if they also sent expeditions that would reach remote parts of Asia and the Pacific. Indeed, this is what the genetic evidence tells us regarding Y haplogroup C.

Therefore, I believe we have, in North and East Asia, a mix of Japhethic and Hamitic peoples. That is my working hypothesis. I am optimistic that the research of our creationist geneticists will yield further insights into these questions.

20. As Franz Delitzsch wrote, "It is the method pursued in Genesis, first to get rid of the collateral lines, in order afterwards to go on with the main line without interruption. Ham comes after Japheth not merely because he is the younger, but because through Canaan, Mizraim and Cush he borders more closely on Israel than Japheth does, for even within the three groups of nations the influence of this favourite progress from the more distant to the nearer prevails." Franz Delitzsch, *A New Commentary on Genesis*, vol. 1 (New York: Scribner & Welford, 1889), p. 302. Similarly, we can observe in Genesis that Moses dispenses with the line of Cain in Genesis 4, before focusing on the line of Seth. In 25:12-19, he dispenses with the genealogy of Ishmael's descendants, before focusing on Isaac. He dispenses with Esau's descendants (chapter 36) before focusing on Jacob's descendants (chapter 37 forward).

21. Some throughout history (including Josephus) have attempted to identify Tiras with the Thracians or Etruscans, or other peoples. However, there appears to be nothing in support of this other than phonetic similarity.

We come now to the Mongolian people, who forged a massive empire across Asia and eastern Europe 800 years ago. Do we have any connections between this great nation of North Asia and the Bible? Indeed, there are many.

The Mongolians have a creation story with parallels to the Garden of Eden, the eating of a forbidden food, and a curse.

Creation

We will begin with a text called The Bejeweled Summary of the Origin of the Khans. This history of the Mongol people was written in 1662 by a Mongol prince known as Sagang the Wise, or "Sagang Sechen." "A carefully prepared and generally accurate work, it is thus a very important source for information on Mongol history," wrote its modern translator, John Kreuger.[22]

The most noteworthy section of this text is a creation story with parallels to the Garden of Eden, the eating of a forbidden food, and the curse which resulted. This text describes an original utopia wherein people "lived to an incalculable age," and in which "they ate a pure food, samadhi."[23] At that time, they traveled by flight rather than on foot, and their bodies radiated with light. They were not humans at that point, but something like angels. This age, called "The time of the very first eons which have passed in original perfection," came to an unfortunate end:[24]

> "At a later time, one sentient greedy for tasty things, finding and eating a food called Butter of the Earth, and owing to everyone (then) consuming in like manner, the former food samadhi vanished. Eating this Butter of the Earth, their motion through the heavens disappeared, and they fell to the ground; the light in their bodies disappeared, and because it had become night and grown dark, the beginnings of ignorant sin (nisvanis) thereupon rose."[25]

Borhon Bagši sent a raven to carry the nectar of immortality to man's world, but he spilled it on a tree.

Thus they fell from their superior state and became humans. The text continues to tell that as people went on eating other types of impure foods, each food disappeared and they were infected by a new sin: sexual lust, jealousy, anger, murder and avarice.[26]

A similar account was recorded by the explorer and scientist Peter Pallas, who met with Mongolian-language peoples in the 1770s and was granted access to their genealogical records, holy writings, and traditions. According to Pallas, the Kalmyks (a Mongol people) remembered a "golden age" reminiscent of Eden, in which people enjoyed much longer life spans–over a thousand years.[27]

Yet another account of the loss of immortality exists in Mongolia. Interestingly, there are clear parallels with the failure of the raven in Genesis 8:7-12:

> "In the myth "Raven Spilled the Nectar of Life" prevailing in the area of Khalkha Mongolia, Borhon Bagši sent a raven to carry the nectar of immortality to man's world, so that human beings could become immortal. The raven was too tired en route, so he decided to have a rest on a spruce tree. A sudden cry of an owl nearby shocked the raven, and he spilled the nectar of immortality out of his beak. Hence, human[s] would age and ultimately die, but the spruce trees maintain their youth."[28]

22. Sagang Sechen, "The Bejeweled Summary of the Origin of the Khans," trans. John R. Kreuger, *The Mongolia Society Occasional Papers*, vol. 2 (Bloomington, Indiana: Mongolia Society, 1967), p. 4.
23. *Ibid.*, p. 10.
24. *Ibid.*, p. 11.
25. *Ibid.*, p. 10.
26. *Ibid.*, pp. 10-11.
27. Peter Simon Pallas, *Samlungen historischer Nachrichten über die mongolischen Völkerschaften*, vol. 2 (St. Petersburg, 1776), p. 30.
28. G. Namjila, "Water-of-Immortality Myths in Altaic and Japanese Cultures," *China's Origin and*

Namjila adds that a related story is told in the Inner Mongolia region of China, but that Borhon Bagši is replaced by a Khan.[29]

Regarding Mongol history, Pallas learned that "they place the first khan of the Mongols about 3,250 years before Tschingis [Genghis] khan. His name was Burudatshi, and they make him the son of a divine spirit called Tangri."[30] If we take the date for Genghis Khan's rise to the role of emperor as 1206 A.D., this would place their reputed ancestor of Burudatshi at about 2,045 B.C. This has interesting implications for the timing of their departure from Mesopotamia (Gen 10-11) and their arrival in North Asia.

More Echoes of Genesis

One Mongolian text refers to a great Flood in the ancient past. "As the world was forming and all creatures were multiplying, a great flood turned the world into chaos." This Flood was brought to an end by the goddess Mai Deer.[31]

An expanded version of this Flood story appeared in another publication:

> "Once upon a time the thriving world nearly came to an end altogether. It happened thus. At the very moment when heaven was about to form, earth to grow, and all creatures to reproduce themselves, the whole world was struck by a cruel catastrophe in the form of a torrential flood submerging and destroying all life in the universe. Ages later Goddess Mai Deer came down to the world for inspection on a snow-white sacred horse that shone brightly all over, to find on the blue waters only the top of Mount Sumeru, the highest mountain on earth leading to heaven. Then, suddenly, she caught sight of a group of people living in a cave near to the top of the mountain."[32]

Then, suddenly, she (Mai Deer) caught sight of a group of people living in a cave near to the top of the mountain.

This cave can be compared with the Ark's landing atop Mount Ararat. In evidence of the antiquity of this tradition, it is added that on three days a year, "the Oyrat Mongols sacrifice cattle and sheep to Mai Deer to receive her inspection."[33]

We are not done surveying Flood traditions from Mongolia. Another text says that only one man was saved, and that later he married a woman from heaven. "It is said that many years ago, a flood reached the sky and washed away all people, livestock, and birds. Only a young man escaped, whose name was Luoyue. Before the flood came, he listened to the old owl's report, killed the cow, made the cowskin into a watertight bag, got into it, and escaped the calamity."[34]

Before the flood came, he listened to the old owl's report, killed the cow, made the cowskin into a watertight bag, got into it, and escaped the calamity.

Creation Myths, eds. Mineke Schipper, Ye Shuxian and Yin Hubin (Boston: Brill, 2011), p. 80. Namjila's source is a Mongolian work which is inaccessible to me: D Tserensodnom, Mongol Ardyn Domog Ůligėr (Ulaanbaatar: Ulsyn Khėvlėliïn Gazar,1989), p. 81.

29. Namjila, "Water-of-Immortality Myths," p. 80. Namjila's source, inaccessible to me, is: D. Senggerincin, *A Collection of Mongolian Myths* (Hohhot: Inner Mongolia Education Press, 1990), p. 140.
30. Johann Gottlieb Georgi, *Russia: Or, a Complete Historical Account of all the Nations which Compose that Empire*, vol. 4 (London: J. Nichols, 1783), p. 183.
31. Ma Xue-Liang, Liang Ting-wang, and Zhang Gong-jin, eds., ("*Literary History of Chinese Minority Races*") (Beijing: Central Institute for Nationalities, 1992), p. 69. As translated to English in: Pasuya Poiconu, *Literary History of Taiwanese Indigenous Peoples*, vol. 1, p. 11.
32. Mineke Schipper, Ye Shuxian and Yin Hubin (eds.), *China's Creation and Origin Myths* (Boston: Brill, 2011), p. 293.
33. *Ibid*., p. 294.
34. Chen Qinghao and Wang Quigui (eds.), "Collection of Mongolian Folk Tales", *Complete Collection of Chinese Folk Tales*, vol. 36 (Taipei, 1989), p. 11.

And now we come to a featured Mongolian Flood story called "Heaven and Earth," which tells of a time when "people flocked to a mountaintop to avoid the water because the hero relayed predictions of a flood."[35] Namjil here summarizes this account, recorded in 1956 from an old Mongolian herdsman in Inner Mongolia:

People flocked to a mountaintop to avoid the water because the hero relayed predictions of a flood.

> "A lord in the human world and his entourage killed a ragged and poor tramp for no reason and robbed him of his golden goat. Furious, the God of Heaven decided to punish mankind with a flood and sink the wicked into the sea. After knowing this, the God of Earth wanted to save those innocent people, so he transformed into a poor old woman and descended into the human world to test people's conscience. The old woman first went to the house of the lord's housekeeper and another rich man's house, asking them to give her something to eat and then carry her across the river. But the housekeeper and the rich man drove her away. The old woman then turned to Arat, a poor young man, for help. The young man gave her the only bit of fried rice and sand grouse he had, then carried her across the river. At this time, the old woman disclosed her identity to the young man, predicted that there would be a flood tomorrow and the world would be flooded, and advised him to climb the mountain to escape the flood the following morning. Finally, the old woman warned Arat he could not leak the secret news to anyone, otherwise he would turn to stone. However, to save others, but at the peril of his life, the young man warned the villagers. They believed him and went to the top of the mountain early in the morning. At dawn, the great floods drowned everything. The villagers were saved, but the young man became a stone. Three days later, the flood receded, and the survivors came down from the mountain and began their new life."[36]

The old woman disclosed her identity to the young man, predicted that there would be a flood tomorrow and the world would be flooded, and advised him to climb the mountain to escape the flood!"

Finally, a Mongolian text known as Hailibu the Hunter is similar to the text above. The story tells of a hunter named Hailibu who sacrificed himself to let the people know of an impending Flood.[37]

Khan of Khans

> "God seems to have made the spiritual soil of Mongolia especially fertile for church planting," wrote missionary Brian Hogan, describing the advance of the Gospel in Mongolia. "The gospel continues to do its life giving and community-changing work. Churches continue to grow and reproduce. Conservative estimates state that the number of believers grew from just two in 1990 to over 50,000 believers in 2005. Mongolia has changed from a mission field to being a powerful mission force–sending out more missionaries per believer than any other nation on Earth. As in a previous age, Mongols again thunder off to the nations beyond their barren hills–this time under the leadership of the 'Khan of Khans'–King Jesus!"[38]

35. G. Namjila, *A Comparative Study of Altaic Mythologies in China*, trans. Wang Ruli (Salt Lake City: American Academic Press, 2023), p. 198.
36. Namjil, *A Comparative Study of Altaic Mythologies in China*, pp. 205-206.
37. "While they were hurrying away, the sky became overcast and it poured rain that whole night. The next morning, they heard a rumbling peal of thunder and a great crash which seemed to shake the earth to its very foundations. The mountains erupted, belching forth a great flood of water. Deeply moved, the villagers said, "Had Hailibu not sacrificed his life for us, we would have been drowned by the flood!" Afterwards, the villagers found the stone into which Hailibu had been transformed and placed it on the top of the mountain. Generation after generation, they have offered sacrifices to this stone in memory of Hailibu, the hero who gave his life to save others. People say that there is still a place called 'Hailibu Stone.'" John Elder and Hertha D. Wong, eds., *Family of Earth and Sky* (Boston: Beacon Press, 1994), p. 77. See also: John Minford (trans.), "Hailibu the Hunter," *Favourite Folktales of China* (San Francisco: New World Press, 1983), pp. 74-80.
38. Brian Hogan, "Distant Thunder: Mongols Follow the Khan of Khans," *Perspectives on the World Christian Movement* (Pasadena, CA: William Carey, 2009), p. 686.

286 OSTYAK

The Ostyak (or Ostiak or Ket) are a people group from western and central Siberia, some 2,000 east of Moscow. From the Yenisei Ostyak, or Kets, we have this Flood tradition which was collected by V. I. Anucin between 1905 and 1908, prior to the Russian Revolution:

> "The water began to rise strongly, the wind was blowing from the north. In the course of seven days, the water came so strongly that it flooded the whole earth up to the tops of the mountains. Everything was under water, only peat bogs surfaced, with forest growing on them. It was here that people and animals were saved. Then the evil North blew with such force that the waves were like mountains, and the North blew for seven days. Waves and storms broke the peatlands into pieces and scattered them in different directions very far away. Then the wind began to subside, and the waters died down. Being now far from each other, the people of each piece (which became the center of their land) forgot about the others, and so different lands and different peoples came to be."[39]

In the course of seven days, the water came so strongly that it flooded the whole earth up to the tops of the mountains.

There is a similar account which Antal Reguly heard among the Ostyaks during the 1840s. According to this version, the Flood lasted seven days and seven nights, and those who survived aboard rafts were separated from one another when the violent waters tore the ropes which had connected their rafts. Such an account, recorded among several subgroups of the Ostyaks,[40] has a certain echo of the Tower of Babel.

What about Noah's dove? Do the Ostyaks have any memory of this bird? Yes, in the form of an "earth diver" story, which we learned in *Volume 1* to be a mixed memory of the Flood and Creation. According to the Ostyaks, the great shaman Doh once sat upon the waters, exhausted, during a particular storm and then sent birds in search of mud with which to remake land:

> "Tired, Doh sat on his spirits, which looked like a swan, a loon, and others, but they also got tired, and the storm did not stop. Then Doh ordered the loons to dive into the water and get a piece of solid earth from the bottom. The loon dived unsuccessfully twice, but on the third time she got a lump of mud and brought it in her beak. Out of this mud, Doh made an island in the middle of the sea. After resting on it, he safely returned."[41]

The loon dived unsuccessfully twice, but on the third time she got a lump of mud and brought it in her beak.

287 NENET

P. I. Tretyakov recorded the customs and traditions of the Nenet people (previously referred to as the Samoyeds) who live in arctic northwestern Siberia. What he heard was a Flood story with the familiar "earth diver" twist, which is so common in northern Asia and the Americas.

> "About the worldwide flood, the Samoyeds tell the following legend. There was a great flood; seven people who were escaping in the boat were lifted by the water to the very sky, so that they could not get up without bending under the vault of heaven. Seeing the people that it was bad for them to come, they asked the loon to find them some

Seven people who were escaping in the boat were lifted by the water to the very sky, so that they could not get up without bending under the vault of heaven.

39. V. I. Anucin, "Очерк шаманства у енисейских остяков" ("Essay on Shamanism Among the Yenisei Ostyaks," *Сборник Музея антропологии и этнографии имени Петра Великого при Академии наук ("Sbornik Muzeya po Antropologii I Etnografii pri Akademii Nauk")*, vol. 2 (Petrograd, 1914), pp. 14-15. As traslated in: Uno Holmberg, "Finno-Ugric, Siberian," p. 366.
40. Bernard Munkacsi, "Die Weltgottheiten der Wogulischen Mythologie (III)," *Keleti Szemle*, vol. 9 (Budapest: 1908), p. 268.
41. V. I. Anucin, "Essay on Shamanism Among the Yenisei Ostyaks," p. 14.

> land; the loon dived into the water and after seven days brought up some earth, along with sand and grass. Throwing all these things into water, people began to ask God to arrange land for them. After that, the water subsided, the trees became visible, and the boat landed."[42]

A very similar version was recorded by the linguist Toivo Lehtisalo in the 1910s, which adds that the vessel was a raft, and that "the people took one of every animal on earth onto it."[43] We are not told what they did for reproduction.

Most significant of all is the Nenet people's memory of the Tower of Babel, and of Nimrod:

> "Once upon a time there lived people who spoke the same language. One day their leader looked at the sky and thought about how to get to it. He thought for a long time and decided to collect all the stones. 'We have so many people. We stack the stones one on top of the other and we will be able to reach the sky.' These people began to work, carrying stones. They worked for seven years.
>
> The news of this development reached heaven, where Num [the sky god] resides. He looked down from his tent and saw many people, like mosquitoes, carrying stones. Num looked and thought, 'If these people will work for seven more years, they will reach the sky.' Num told his sons about this. 'We must stop them with fire so they do not climb into the sky,' said Num. The sons struck the people and the stones with fire and destroyed the entire structure. Many people were crushed with stones.
>
> When the people and their leader woke up, they wanted to talk to each other, but they could not. They were no longer able to understand each other. The leader said, 'We built but did not reach the sky and cannot understand each other. Now let those people who speak different languages disperse throughout the earth. But you can't reach heaven like that.'"[44]

The informant added that the remains of that stone tower are the Ural Mountains.

When the people and their leader woke up, they wanted to talk to each other, but they could not. They were no longer able to understand each other.

The leader said, 'We built but did not reach the sky and cannot understand each other. Now let those people who speak different languages disperse throughout the earth.'

KAMCHADAL

288 In the far east of Siberia, on the Kamchatka Peninsula, we find a Flood tradition among the Kamchadales, which George Stellers recorded in the 1740s:

> "The Stalmenen [Kamchadales] also tell of a deluge and a mighty inundation of the whole country, which occurred not long after Kutka [God] had left them. A great many people drowned at that time. Some tried to save themselves in boats, but the waves had grown too large. Those who escaped had bound tree trunks together into great rafts, and took refuge there with their food and all their property.
>
> To prevent the rafts from drifting out to see, they tied large stones to long ropes and let them fall to the depths as anchors. After the waters had run off, their rafts grounded on the top of high mountains."[45]

---

42. P. I. Tretyakov, *Туруханский край, его природа и жители* ("Turukhansk Region, its Nature and Inhabitants") (Petrograd, 1871), pp. 201-202.
43. T. Lehtisalo, *Entwurf Einer Mythologie der Jurak-Samojeden* (Helsinki: Société Finno-Ougrienne, 1924), p. 11.
44. A. V. Golovnev, Кочевники тундры: ненцы и их фольклор ("Tundra Nomads: Nenets and their Folklore) (2004), pp. 98-99. This text was recorded in 1978. A similar version is reported in: Lehtisalo, *Entwurf Einer Mythologie der Jurak-Samojeden*, pp. 10-11.
45. "The Tungus from behind the Baikal describe it as follows: In the beginning was the earth, but then a great fire raged for seven years and the earth was burned up. Everything became sea. All the Tungus were consumed except a boy and a girl who rose up with an eagle into the sky. Having wandered for a time in the air, they descended to a place where the water had dried up. With them the eagle also descended to the earth." Source: George Wilhelm Stellers, *Beschreibung von dem Lande Kamtschatka* (Frankfurt, 1774), p. 273.

Uniquely, the Kamchadales also named Kutka as their Noah, saying that God (Kutka) once took human form. "The tradition of a universal deluge prevails," wrote the Russian naval explorer Otto Von Kotzebue, "and a spot is still shown, on the top of a mountain where Kutka landed from a boat, in order to replenish the world with men." So widespread was the acknowledgement of this Flood that the Kamchadales would say "that was in Kutka's day" to describe something that took place very long ago.[46]

So widespread was the acknowledgement of this Flood that the Kamchadales would say "that was in Kutka's day" to describe something that took place very long ago.

TUNGUS

289 According to the Tungus (or Evenki) people of east-central Siberia:

> "A long time ago, there was a big flood, even the mountains were submerged, and people in the world were drowned, leaving only a father and his daughter. The daughter said to her father, 'We have to carry on the family line!' So they married. Later, she gave birth to seven sons. Because they were their children, each son was given a surname, and they were told that they could marry within the same surname."[47]

Another account contains a vague memory of Noah's dove, replaced with an eagle.[48]

After the waters had run off, their rafts grounded on the top of high mountains.

KHAKA

290 The Khakas, or Abakan Tatars, are a Turkic people who live in a part of Siberia called Khakassia, located just northwest of Mongolia. Like certain other north Asian peoples, they insist that nails were found from this floating vessel:

> "Kudaj [God] organized a flood to destroy the people who had stopped worshiping him. During the deluge a big animal swam around for half a year. It never sank nor ceased to swim. Kudaj sent a big bird to him; he sat down on the other animal's horns and caused him to drown.
>
> The deluge was so great that the water approached the skies up to an axle-length. The vessel on which a few people were saved remained after the Flood on the mountain Yzyk, on the White Jus, in the Tajga. There one used to find very long nails from this vessel recently."[49]

The Shor people replace Noah's Ark with a raft and say it landed at a place called "Oyudun."

SHOR

291 The Shors hail from Kemerovo Oblast in south-central Siberia. They are considered to be descendants of different people groups of South Siberia, including Nenets, Yennisey, and Ugric peoples, who "were greatly affected by the Turks in the period of Turkic expansion northwards from the territory of central Asia."[50] They replace Noah's Ark with a raft, and say it landed at a place called "Oyudun":

46. Otto Von Kotzebue, *A New Voyage Round the World in the Years 1823-1826*, vol. 2 (London: Colburn and Bentley, 1830), p. 12-13
47. Manduhu, *The Mythological Stories of the Altaic Language Family in China* (Beijing: Ethnic Publishing House 1997), p. 303. As translated in: G. Namjila, *A Comparative Study of Altaic Mythologies in China*, p. 197.
48. Uno Holmberg, "Finno-Ugric, Siberian," p. 368.
49. Walter Anderson, "Nordasiatische Flutsagen," *Acta et Commentationes Universitatis Dorpatensis, B. Humaniora*, vol. 4, no. 3 (Tartu, Estonia: 1923), pp. 21-22. Anderson's source, inaccessible to me, is: N. I. Popov, "Kacinskije tatary Minusinskago okruga" ("The Catherine Tatars of the Minusinsk District"). Archive of the Russian Geographic Society, Saint Petersburg. Manuscript B IX 29, folio 21b.
50. D. M. Tokmashev, "Ethnolinguistic research of Siberian-Turkic folklore proper names based on Shor cosmogonical legends and myths," *Tomsk State University Bulletin*, vol. 2 (2012), p. 92.

"In a myth is a mountain with a four-edged apex and a lake on top of it. After the Great Flood a raft got stuck in that lake. They say the logs of this raft bob up [when] a war breaks out. This is the real geographical object in Mountain Shoriya in the middle flow of the Mrassu River."[51]

"Yayik-xan", according to their shamans, is the name of the god who caused the Great Flood. This is connected with the Turkic verbal stem "yay" meaning "flood" or "overflow."[52]

292 CHUKCHEE

The Chukchee people live in extreme northeastern Siberia, near the Bering Strait and Alaska. A tradition of theirs recorded in 1870 has the Flood story in the form of a snow storm. Given their arctic climate, the transformation of a Flood into a snowstorm is understandable.

> "Some said that the Good Spirit created different peoples in the beginning, while others claimed that in the beginning only one man and one woman were created, and all other people descended from these two.
>
> But over time, people became very evil. As punishment, the Good Spirit caused a terrible snowstorm to come over the previously undivided land. The wind of this storm not only killed most of the people and scattered the others widely, but it also tore the land apart and scattered it widely … from the scattered people the various nations were formed."[53]

Another Flood text recorded among them features a raven, a vague memory of its flight, and the need to create earth anew.[54]

293 OROCHI

The Orochi people live near the Amur region of Siberia, which is northeast of North Korea. This small ethnic group, less than 5,000 in number today, has preserved a rather remarkable tradition of the Flood, recorded by a Polish scientist named Stanislaw Poniatowski in 1914:

> "Once it was very good, but then there was such a great flood that it submerged everything. The people and the animals died. Only on one mountain were a brother and a sister left, along with some animals. They lived there for a long time, but they wanted to find out if there were other people. So they sent out a crow, telling the crow to return in seven years. They waited seven years, and ten years, and longer, but the crow did not return. Then they sent out a raven and told it to return in seven years. Seven years passed, and ten years, but still he did not return either. But then he returned and said that there were no people anywhere, only that in one place there were many dead human bodies, and they were being eaten by the crow sent earlier.
>
> Seeing that people could not be found, and unwilling to continue living in the way that they had been living, they decided to marry, and they had a son and a daughter."[55]

So they sent out a crow … Then they sent out a raven.

51. *Ibid.*, p. 96.
52. *Ibid.*, p. 96.
53. Baron Gerhard Maydell, *Reisen und Forschungen im Jakutskischen Gebiet Ostsibiriens in den Jahren 1861-1871*, vol. 1 (St. Petersburg, 1893), p. 618.
54. Waldemar Bogoras, *Chukchee Mythology, Publications of the Jesup North Pacific Expedition*, vol. 8, part 2 (New York: Stechert, 1910), pp. 151-154.
55. Stanislav Poniatowski, "Diary of an expedition to the land of the Golds and the Orochons in 1914" (in Russian), *История и культура Приамурья* ["History and Culture of the Amur Region"], vol. 5 (2009), p. 132. For a related tradition, see: V. A. Avrovin, *Орочские сказки и мифы* ("Orochi Tales and Myths") (Novosibirsk, 1966), p. 194.

294 DOLGAN

The Russian ethnographer A. A. Popov met the Dolgan people in 1930. He described them as a "small and backward tribe," and "one of the small tribes of the north, which are the subject of special concern on the part of the Soviet government pursuing the Leninist-Stalinist national policy."[56] Popov recorded a tradition from them which clearly resembles the Genesis account of Noah's dispatch of birds:

> "In ancient times, the earth was covered with water. When the water subsided, God sent the swan, saying, "Fly! See where the earth has appeared." So he sent the swan, and ordered him to return when he completed the task.
>
> The swan flew over the earth and saw a beautiful island. Arriving there, he sat down on the ground. His feet were covered with mud, and they became black. When he wanted to eat, his beak turned black also. It turned out to be dung [instead of an island]. That's why big Russian bosses do not like to eat swan."[57]

A Dolgan Woman

295 MANCHU

The Manchu people were once a powerful nation located in modern-day northeastern China and adjacent parts of Russia. This large ethnic group, over 10 million in number, have largely assimilated with the Han Chinese and lost their unique culture, but their tradition of the Flood has been recorded. It is similar to a version in circulation in Mongolia, which tells of an old man who sacrificed his own life to warn others of the coming Flood. This "old man" is reminiscent of Noah himself, who indeed warned people about the Flood (2 Peter 2:5):

When the water subsided, God sent the swan, saying, "Fly! See where the earth has appeared."

> "The old man Usurihan rescued a small loach [a fish] from the drying spring and put it into the river. The little loach turned into a young man, warned him of the news of the upcoming flood, and instructed him to avoid the disaster. Finally, the young man warned Usurihan repeatedly that spreading the news to others would end his life. However, regardless of his safety, the old man passed the news of the flood to the villagers so that they could be saved. Yet he himself rose up as a wisp of smoke and turned into the North Star hanging high up in the sky."[58]

A related version says that "the waters flooded the earth and threatened all human beings. Old Beile (the leader) transformed into a magical turtle that could absorb the water to save people from drowning. For this reason, Old Beile violated god's will and was turned into a stone turtle."[59]

The little loach turned into a young man, warned him of the news of the upcoming flood, and instructed him to avoid the disaster.

56. Andrej Alexandrovich Popov, *Долганский фольклор* ("Dolgan Folklore") (Leningrad, 1937), p. 5.
57. Popov, "Dolgan Folklore," p. 40.
58. Wu Bing'an and Li Wengang, "Selected Manchu Folk Stories" (Shanghai, 1983), pp. 19-20. As translated in: G. Namjil, *A Comparative Study of Altaic Mythologies in China*, trans. Wang Ruli (Salt Lake City: American Academic Press, 2023), p. 208.
59. G. Namjil, *A Comparative Study of Altaic Mythologies in China*, p. 208.

296 HEZHE

The Hezhe or Nanai people were called "sun watchers" because of their location in China's easternmost province of Heilongjiang and adjacent parts of Russia. Regarding the Flood, their tradition tells: "After an overwhelming flood, two siblings alone survived, being left at the foot of Solon Mountain and by the Naoli River." We are not told what caused the Flood or what kind of vessel the siblings survived in. Later, the birds of the forest made fun of the siblings for marrying, and the girl drowned herself because of regret.[60]

Vague echoes of Noah's birds, as well as Creation, are also found in an "earth diver" story which Berthold Laufer heard from them in the late 1890s.[61]

After an overwhelming flood, two siblings alone survived, being left at the foot of Solon Mountain and by the Naoli River.

297 OROQEN

During the 1600s, the Oroqen people fled southward from the invading Russians and now mostly live in northeastern China's Heilongjiang Province. Their tribal name means "people who live in the mountains," referring to the Khingan Mountains where they have lived and hunted for millenia.[62] Like virtually all Mongolic and Turkic ethnic groups, they have passed down a memory of the Flood. This tells:

> "The legend has it that a long time ago many families lived on both sides of a river under the Khingan Range. During a sudden rainstorm one night, all the land was flooded with boundless water in the twinkling of an eye, and most people drowned. Only one man and one woman survived. Later, they married and gave birth to five boys. These five brothers were the ancestors of the five surnames of the Oruqen people."[63]

All the land was flooded with boundless water in the twinkling of an eye, and most people drowned. Only one man and one woman survived.

And in another narration, they tell:

> "A long time ago, a disastrous mountain fire burnt all plants and trees and killed half of the human beings. After that, a big flood broke out, submerging the hillsides and flatlands. Only a man and a woman survived. They became husband and wife and gave birth to nine boys and nine girls. Later, the 18 brothers and sisters became nine couples, who multiplied the Oruqen people of the nine surnames."[64]

298 NGANASAN

The Nganasan people speak a Uralic language and live on the Taymyr Peninsula of north-central Siberia. Like several tribes of Siberia and North America, they have an "earth diver" story which contains a mixed memory of Creation and the Flood. Above all, the memory of Noah and the two birds in Genesis 8:6-12 is evident:

> "The earth existed a long time ago. There were a lot of people on earth. At first there was land. The water covered it. There were rivers and lakes. There were ducks. Ngangodya was a duck, and Noana was a loon.

60. Wang Shiyuan et al, "Hezhe, Monba, Lhoba, Jinuo", Chinese Ethnic Story Series, vol. 16 (Shanghai, 1995), pp. 11-12.
61. "In the beginning of the world there were only three men, called Shankoa, Shanwai, and Shanka. There were three divers and three swans. Once on a time [sic] the three men sent the three swans and the three divers to dive for soil, stones, and sand. The birds dived. For seven days they stayed under water. Then they emerged. They brought earth, stones, and sand, and they began to fly about, carrying the earth that they had brought. They flew all around the world. The earth originated when the divers flew, holding earth and stones in their bills. Mountains and plains arose. The divers flew about; and where they flew, rivers arose. Thus they determined the course of the rivers." Source: Berthold Laufer, "Petroglyphs on the Amoor," *American Anthropologist,* vol. 1 (1899), p. 749.
62. Chen Qinghao and Wang Quigui (eds.), "Collection of Heilongjiang Folk Tales", *Complete Collection of Chinese Folk Tales*, vol. 32 (Taipei, 1989), p. 95.
63. Sui Shujin, "Selected Oruqen Folk Stories" (Shanghai, 1988), pp. 370-371. As translated in: G. Namjil, *A Comparative Study of Altaic Mythologies in China,* p. 198.
64. Sui Shujin, "Selected Oruqen Folk Stories," pp. 6-7. As translated in: G. Namjil, *A Comparative Study of Altaic Mythologies in China*, p. 208.

Now the water has covered this land. Even the high ridges were covered. …The duck said to the loon, 'Loon, look for land under the water. How will we live without land? Find the land and bring it. Maybe the water will run out, maybe there will be land. Maybe someday a person will be here.'

'Okay, I'll go down.'

She was gone for three days. On the third day she came with her belly up, dead.

Now the duck dove and was gone for seven days. A week later she came back from the water. She brought a little grass, moss, and willow grass. And the duck said, 'I raised the earth up, the water will go down, and one day there will be a person here. Now only I know.'

Probably the shaman found the duck and learned all this from her."[65]

299 KHANTY The Khanty people, relatives of the Nganasans within the Uralic language family, had a similar tradition of the recovery of dry land after the Flood. Regretfully, we only possess a brief summary of it. However, the memory of Noah's dove can still be seen:

> "In Khanty mythology, according to one version of the Earth' origin, the latter was raised during the Deluge, as a red-cropped toadstool, by the bird Luli, species-wise a small lake loon."[66]

300 YAKUT The Yakuts are a Turkic-language people living north of Mongolia. We have a weak and mixed memory of Babel and the Flood from the Yakuts:

> "A long time ago, when there were still few people, the Yakuts say, they all lived together. One day a strong wind came and scattered people in different directions, and they found themselves completely without fire, because the fire they had produced had gone out. Then various birds began to bring fire to each clan separately. These clans began to consider them their deities. These birds included: swan, hawk, and eagle."[67]

301 SAGAI The Sagai live in the Khakassia Republic of Russia, slightly northwest of Mongolia. We only have a fragmentary tradition from this Turkic-language tribe, but enough to show a clear memory of Noah's raven:

> "Among the Sagai people, Kudai, having created 10 men and 9 women, calls all the birds in turn and offers to fly in search for a soul. Everyone refuses except for the raven. The later flies for "*mobu sug*," eternal water to revive a person. On the way he is tempted by carrion, screams and spills some of the water. As punishment for greed, the raven turns black and people lose immortality."[68]

We have seen traditions like this about the loss of immortality, which is a memory of Eden. In this case the memories of Eden and the Flood have been blended into one tradition.

---

65. Boris Osipovich Dolgih, *Мифологические Сказки И Исторические Предания Нганасан ("Nganasan Mythological Tales and Historical Traditions")* (Moscow, 1976), p. 50.
66. Tatiana Deviatkina, "Images of Birds in Mordvinian Mythology," *Folklore*, vol. 48 (2011), p. 145. The original source cited by Deviatkina was not available.
67. Dyrenkova, *Culture and Writing of the East*, vol. 4 (1929), p. 125.
68. N. P. Dyrenkova, *Culture and Writing of the East*, vol. 4, p. 123.

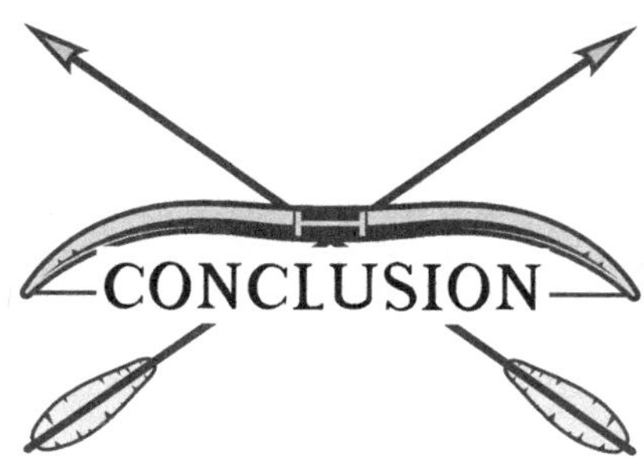

We have now heard from the tribes and nations of Asia and the Pacific. Their testimony has been unanimous. There can be no doubt that they knew of Noah's Flood. From China to Australia, from Polynesia to Southeast Asia, from Siberia to Taiwan and the Philippines, we hear essentially the same story over and over again. The general outline and the recurring details match Genesis. The Ark or "great canoe." Divine judgment of human evil. The forewarning. The favored few. The global Flood. The mountain of landing. The boarding of animals. The two birds. The sign that the Flood was ending. The exit and repopulating of the world. A sacrifice. There can be no doubt they are referring to the same event. This is a remarkable finding with massive implications.

But this leads us to a crucial question: How do we explain these Flood traditions? After all, we now see that Flood stories are universal. They are found in every far-flung corner of Asia and the Pacific that we've covered in this book, spanning nearly 10,000 miles. How did they get there? How did these Flood stories matching Genesis get to places such as China, Mongolia, Myanmar (Burma), Indonesia, Polynesia, New Zealand, and eastern Siberia?

Take some time to consider how you will answer that question. We each must answer it. With knowledge comes accountability. This is no idle question or vain debate. It has enormous implications for us. Why? Because according to the Word of God, in 2 Peter 3, Peter declares that how you respond to the knowledge of the Flood and of divine Creation will influence how you respond to Jesus. If you reject the Flood and biblical Creation, you will probably also reject Jesus as Savior and Lord. Why? Because if Genesis is false, then the New Testament and the message of Jesus are irrelevant.

I urge you, therefore, to answer this question very carefully and honestly. Do you believe that these hundreds of Flood stories reflect only a local flood or floods? You'd better be sure your position can stand up to scrutiny. Do you believe missionaries are responsible for these Flood stories? You'd better be sure your view can withstand cross-examination. However, I believe you'll find that these explanations do not hold up to scrutiny, for the reasons discussed more previously in this book (see the Introduction).

The only explanation that coherently and cleanly embraces all these Flood traditions is that the Flood recorded in Genesis actually happened. I know of no other explanation which can account for the breadth and the specificity and the force of this testimony from hundreds of tribes and nations matching Genesis. In the end, the truth of Genesis explains it easily. All other explanations require mental gymnastics and special pleading of the highest order. Not only this, but there is also vast scientific evidence that the Flood really happened (see Appendix D, as well as the introduction).

The High Antiquity of Genesis 1-11

In the end, one of the greatest evidences to the truth of the Genesis Flood (chapters 6-9) is this: *If we did not have the Genesis Flood text, we would have to reconstruct it, in order to explain everything else.*

What do I mean by that? We possess hundreds of tribal traditions of a global Flood, which differ in many ways, but which are inherently connected to each other and tell the same story. They must come from a common source, which raises the question: "What is that original, ancestral source which can explain all of them?"

It is none other than the Genesis Flood text, together with the Creation, Garden of Eden, pre-Flood, and post-Flood and Tower of Babel texts found in Genesis 1-11. Genesis 1-11 is the one corpus that can fulfill that role as the original ancestor, to explain all the other ones, because it has the elements (or motifs) to explain the stories that we find in China, New Guinea, the Pacific, Southeast Asia, the Americas, Africa, and everywhere else. Genesis fits the bill, and no other version does.

Consider all the recurring elements we have seen in this volume and the previous one. A great canoe, a forewarning, a divine judgment of mankind, a global Flood, a mountain landing, tests involving two birds, a sign received from the second bird, an exit and repopulation. A separation of earth from water, a woman created from man's rib, a moment of shame, a Garden of Eden, a forbidden food, a serpent, a curse. Two brothers, a Tower constructed, a confusion of languages.

Now please name the nation whose histories can account for these. I will wait.

Are the Sumerians and Babylonians the source of so many of these texts? That is not what the comparative analysis in Appendix A shows. These Mesopotamian texts cannot account for several recurring details in Flood traditions, whereas Genesis can. The Mesopotamian texts cannot account for many recurring elements found around the world, but Genesis can with its Garden of Eden text.

Will anyone argue that China's histories, as impressive as they are, are ancestral to the other Flood traditions that we find around the world? Why then do they lack many elements that show up in other versions, such as the raven and dove, the boarding of animals, the sacrifice after the Flood, and the Tower of confusion? Will someone argue the same on behalf of the New Guineans or any other nation covered in this book? What about Africa? Africa will be addressed in the next book, but there is no African historical corpus that provides the necessary substance to explain the recurring motifs around the world. Neither is it found in India or Europe.

Genesis 1-11 is the one body of texts that can account for the diversity of elements that we find around the world. It can account for Han China's stories. It can account for the Chinese ethnic minorities' stories, the Southeast Asia versions, the Pacific and Australian, and the North Asian versions.

A "brother-sister marriage theme" such as we find in East and Southeast Asia? No problem. Genesis explains it. An "earth diver" theme like we find in North Asia and North America? No problem. Genesis explains it. A "recovery of fire" theme like we find in different parts of the world? A shape-shifting serpent that warns of the Flood, such as we find in New Guinea? A special tree, and the dropping of fruits to test whether the Flood has ended? No problem. Genesis explains these as well. A mixed Garden of Eden and Flood story? A "world tree" theme, or a sacrifice offered to the waters? No problem. Genesis explains these as well.

One of the greatest evidences to the truth of Genesis 1-11 is this: If we did not have Genesis 1-11, we would have to reconstruct it, in order to explain everything else.

What This Means for Us

The Genesis Flood account, which has been doubted and dismissed for so long, is gaining new appreciation. We see that it was true all along, and its doubters were wrong. Consider, then, what this means.

First, it means that we can trust the Bible from the very first book (Genesis), beginning in the very first page. Second, it supersedes the atheistic, evolutionary, secular view of the world, and it establishes a God-centered, Bible-centered paradigm. Third, the Genesis Flood teaches us about God and about our relationship with Him. We see that He is a personal and present God who deals directly with His creation. He judges sin, but He also mercifully saved Noah and his family. He is almighty, He is all wise, He is all good. Furthermore, the Bible shows us that He takes no pleasure in the death and destruction of the wicked. Rather, He loves the world, and He wants people to turn from their sin and repent (2 Pet. 3:8, Eze. 33:11-12, Eze. 18:23). Even when the Ark was being prepared, He called out to the world, telling them they should repent, so that they too could escape the Flood (2 Pet. 2:5). Yet they would not listen.

But what about us today? God is not telling us to get in an Ark, nor to build one. However, He is calling us to put our faith in the One of whom the Ark was a foreshadow, which is Jesus (1 Pet. 3:20-21).

Repent and Trust in Jesus

The Apostle Paul, under the inspiration of the Holy Spirit, addressed a crowd of people at Athens who had never heard of Jesus before. He concluded with this word of exhortation: *"God is now commanding men that everyone everywhere should repent."* (Acts 17:30 LSB) Think about that statement: God is now commanding all people everywhere to repent. To repent means to change your mind and therefore your actions; to stop walking away from God and now walk toward God; to accept the truth about God; to confess your sin and your need for Him; to begin trusting Him and believing what He says. To repent also means to turn from pride, to turn from the devil's lie of "do what you want," and to acknowledge that God is on the throne, not self.

With that said, I have a question to ask you: Do you believe this statement of Paul? Is God now commanding all people everywhere to repent? Is that true? Is God really calling on everyone—including you—to repent?

That is an enormously important question, yet I understand it is also a difficult and uncomfortable question for many. We do not talk about God as much as we should. There is a tendency to keep discussions about God general, vague, and subjective. As for God's identity, people prefer a mysterious "higher power," a "force," or a distant God. A "force" or a distant God does not place any demands on our life. "The universe" does not ask me to repent.

But a clarion call like this from Jesus and the apostles—that God is personal, that He judges, that He calls us to repent, that He will change your life—this is a more challenging and demanding claim. And for many people, this claim is not easy to believe. "What gives you the right to say God wants me to repent? How do you know what He wants? Maybe He's a mystery. It's not clear-cut."

However, Paul anticipates that objection. Read the next verse, Acts 17:31. After saying God is now calling everyone everywhere to repent, he gives a reason. *"Because He has fixed a day in which He will judge the world in righteousness through a Man whom He determined, having furnished proof to all by raising Him from the dead."* (Act 17:31 LSB)

In particular, let's zero in on the last part of Paul's statement: "having furnished proof to all by raising Him from the dead." "God has given proof," Paul says, "of the coming judgment and the need for personal repentance and faith!" But you ask, "Proof? What proof?" "The fact that He raised Jesus from the dead," Paul says.

What a world-shattering statement! "Therefore," Paul says, "there is most certainly going to be a judgment, and God is now calling all people to repent."

You see, the resurrection of Jesus changes everything. It changes our assumptions about God, about our life, and about God's expectations for us. And I know that not everyone reading this believes that Jesus rose from the dead. But Paul is saying that God has given proof of it. Yet it is a proof which you must investigate for yourself.

Even the Athenians, Paul's audience, had to investigate it, because the resurrection of Jesus wasn't immediately obvious to them. After all, the Resurrection took place in Jerusalem, and they were almost 1,500 miles away in Athens. If they wanted to appreciate the proof, they had to inquire about Jesus' resurrection. They had to listen to the eyewitness testimonies. And God expects us to do the same today. That is part of seeking Him.

If you will search into it, you will see that it's true. Indeed, from all of my reading and study, it is true that God has given abundant evidence and proof to the resurrection of Jesus. However, you must check into it for yourself.

This, therefore, is the next step. If you do not yet believe in Jesus, you must investigate the facts about Him, His life, His teaching, His claims, and His death and resurrection. Read the Gospels. Do not reject the call of God in your life, which is for you to look into these matters, to believe, and to repent—to know Jesus as your Master and Savior. To be adopted as a son or daughter of God, through faith in Jesus. To receive the Holy Spirit.

To that end, if you are unsure about who Jesus is, what He came to do, and whether He really rose from the dead, see Appendix D for recommended reading.

As for Flood legends, the final word has not yet been written on this subject. In the next and final volume, we will explore the knowledge of the Flood in the remainder of the world, as we hear from the people of India, Africa, Europe, and the Middle East.

THE MYTH OF THE FLOOD MYTH

Refuting the Claim that Genesis Borrows from a Babylonian Source

This article is a reprint of an article I (Nick) wrote previously (April 29, 2022), which can be found on the Answers in Genesis website[1].

"Moses stole the flood story from the Babylonians." This year, many college freshmen will hear those words in lecture halls at universities across the nation. "Moses plagiarized an older flood story found in the Epic of Gilgamesh." Many college freshmen, weak in their faith and unequipped to deal with these objections, will be shaken by the words from their professors, who then proclaim, "The Genesis flood is nothing but a myth, borrowed from an earlier Babylonian source."

That argument is featured nowhere more prominently than in the book titled *The Flood Myth*, edited by Alan Dundes.[2] We will address that argument in this article.[3]

Is the Genesis flood account (in Genesis 6–9) merely a borrowed story or a fictional tale lifted from a neighboring nation? The way we answer this question has massive implications for how we see the Bible, and therefore how we view God and even ourselves.

We have, therefore, two very different positions before us concerning the Genesis flood. Only one can be true. Either Moses (the author of Genesis) is telling the truth, or Dundes and other secularists are telling the truth. To put it another way, there is a myth in *The Flood Myth*. It is only a question of whether the myth-teller is the one quoted (Moses) or the ones doing the quoting.

The Discovery of the Epic of Gilgamesh

Alan Dundes (1934–2005) declared that, after 1872, it was no longer possible for creationists to claim that we possess the original record of the flood in Genesis.

> "Before 1872, it had been possible to assume that all the other, various, flood myths reported from different areas of the globe were simply derivative from the biblical narrative. With the discovery of earlier Near Eastern flood myths—from Babylonia, for example—which seemed to be cognate with the Genesis version, a new tack had to be taken by the literalists."[4]

1. https://answersingenesis.org/the-flood/flood-legends/myth-flood-myth/
2. *The Flood Myth*, ed. Alan Dundes (Berkeley: University of California Press, 1988). More recently, the same arguments featured in Louise M. Pryke, *Gilgamesh* (Abingdon: Routledge, 2019), and Irving Finkel, *The Ark Before Noah* (New York, Anchor Books, 2015).
3. Other arguments made in *The Flood Myth* include: 1) 'The geologic record contradicts Genesis and supports Darwinian evolution', 2) 'There is not enough water to cover the whole earth', and 3) 'Flood legends can arise naturally, and are not referring to a global flood as depicted in Genesis. These legends lack the element of divine judgment spoken of in Genesis.' In response to #1 and #2, I recommend reading *Earth's Catastrophic Past* (2 volumes) by Andrew Snelling and *Carved in Stone* by Timothy Clarey. I have demonstrated that #3 is not true in this Volume and in the previous Volume. Amazingly, #3 is refuted in *The Flood Myth* itself, in the article by Hans Kelsen, titled "The Principle of Retribution in the Flood and Catastrophe Myths" (pp. 125-149). Kelsen rightly observes that it is present in the vast majority of flood traditions found around the world. For questions or objections about the feasibility of Noah's Ark, read *Volume 1* of *Earth's Catastrophic Past* by Andrew Snelling, and *Noah's Ark: A Feasibility Study* by John Woodmorappe.
4. Alan Dundes, *The Flood Myth* (Berkeley: University of California Press, 1988), 3–4.

Either Moses is telling the truth, or Dundes and other secularists are telling the truth.

What happened in 1872? An Assyriologist named George Smith published a translation of a large cuneiform tablet, found at the Library of Ashurbanipal in Nineveh. This tablet contained part of the Epic of Gilgamesh, an epic poem that dates earlier than the book of Genesis, and which contains an account of the flood with several specific similarities to Genesis.

In similar fashion, the anthropologist James George Frazer (1854–1941) proclaimed that for Christians who believe Genesis is true, "the difficulty has been greatly increased since modern research has proved the supposed divine original in Genesis to be not an original at all, but a comparatively late copy of a much older Babylonian or rather Sumerian version. No Christian apologist is likely to treat the Babylonian story, with its strongly polytheistic coloring, as a primitive revelation of God to man. … And if the theory of inspiration is inapplicable to the original, it can hardly be invoked to account for the copy."[5]

That is the claim made by Dundes, Frazer, and our other secularist friends, which we will now address.

Exposing Fallacious Reasoning

Is Dundes correct? Is Frazer correct, when he claims that modern research has "proved" that Genesis is not original at all, but a copy from the Babylonians?

Absolutely not. Our secular friends are very mistaken. There are several problems with their argument. I will list these problems now, and then we will discuss them further:

1. This argument relies on the post hoc, ergo propter hoc fallacy ("after this, therefore because of this"). In making this assumption, they do not account for the possibility that there is a document which predates both Genesis and the Epic of Gilgamesh (or other Babylonian cognates), to which Moses (the author of Genesis) had access.
2. They do not account for the fact that Moses lets us know he had sources.
3. Genesis itself provides strong internal evidence of the sources of Moses' writing: they are ancient sources from the patriarchs themselves, including Joseph, Jacob, Isaac, Abraham, and even Noah!
4. This argument is contradicted by historical trends from the ancient Near East, which point to simpler accounts giving rise to more complex, embellished ones—rather than the reverse. This points to Genesis as containing the original account, and the Epic of Gilgamesh as a later account.
5. This argument is contradicted by foreign flood traditions from across the world, which are ancient and original—yet they agree with Genesis rather than the Babylonian version.[6] Specifically, these foreign traditions agree with Genesis, and not the Babylonian version, on several particular points such as the sending of birds, the reason for the flood, and the type and shape of floating vessel.
6. Unlike the fictional Babylonian version, the Genesis account stands up to scrutiny, and finds confirmation from multiple fields of science, such as geology, naval design, and paleontology. This attests to its authenticity. After all, a false testimony will fall apart under critical cross-examination, but a true testimony holds up.

---

5. Frazer, "The Great Flood," in *The Flood Myth* (Berkeley: University of California Press, 1988), p. 120.
6. Secularists might not admit for a moment that these tribal flood traditions are genuine and independent of Christian teaching such as influence by missionaries. However, that denial can no longer be sustained in light of the evidence documented in this book and in the previous *Volume 1*.

What is the Epic of Gilgamesh?

What is the Epic of Gilgamesh? It is an ancient poetic work, fictional in nature, from a Babylonian source. This highly entertaining and dramatic story is about a strongman named Gilgamesh, who is two-thirds god and one-third man. Gilgamesh, after besting a rival demigod named Enkidu, develops a friendship with him. The two of them go on spirited adventures together, including fighting a fearsome forest monster called Humbaba. Later, his friend Enkidu falls under a curse and dies, and Gilgamesh becomes depressed at the loss of his friend. He then embarks on the "search for eternal life," and travels across the sea to meet Uta-napishti. The latter tells Gilgamesh how he once survived the flood, and how the gods gave him immortality as his reward. This flood account toward the end of the epic is where we find several parallels with the Genesis account.

Clay Tablet Containing Part of Epic of Gilgamesh

Further Observations about the Epic

Now it is clearly and readily apparent, upon reading the Epic of Gilgamesh, that it is full of myth and fictional drama. That is not in question. Our secular friends heartily agree to this. They insist it is from this fictional source that the Genesis flood is derived.

To fully appreciate how fictional and embellished the epic is—particularly for those who have not read it—let's take a moment and survey some examples that we find in the section about the flood:

- The gods said, "the uproar of mankind is intolerable and sleep is no longer possible by reason of the babel." That is, they sent the flood to destroy mankind because they were too noisy, and the gods couldn't sleep.[7]
- The flood is described in very figurative language. The storm clouds were so frightening that "even the gods were terrified … they fled to the highest heaven, the firmament of Anu; they crouched against the walls, cowering like curs [dogs]."[8]
- The "ark" of the epic was almost cube-shaped—120 cubits by 120 cubits, and seven decks in height (a very strange and instable design). And it was built in only three days.[9]
- The ship is complete with a captain and "tradesmen of every kind", in addition to Uta-napishti and his family. And it is launched into the sea before the flood begins.[10]
- The landing of the ship is described in poetic terms. "One day she held, and a second day on the mountain of Nisir she held fast and did not budge. A third day, and a fourth day she held fast on the mountain and did not budge…"[11]

7. *The Epic of Gilgamesh*, trans. Nancy K. Sandars (Harmondsworth: Penguin Books, 1962), p. 105.
8. *Ibid.*, p. 107.
9. *Ibid.*, p. 106.
10. *Ibid.*, pp. 106-107.
11. *Ibid.*, p. 108.

- After the flood, an argument ensued between the gods when they discovered that a remnant of mankind had escaped.[12]
- The gods "gathered like flies over the sacrifice," pleased by the delicious smell of the animal sacrifice that Uta-Napisthi offered.[13]
- Uta-napishti and his wife were granted immortality and became gods as a reward for surviving the Flood.[14]
- The whole flood narrative is full of dramatic, poetic, and emotional language.

Again, these examples are just from the epic's flood account. Many more examples of myth could be multiplied from other sections of the epic.

The point is this: we can see that we are clearly dealing with a mythical, fictional work.

The Genesis Flood Account

Now let's compare the epic's obvious myth and embellishment with Genesis chapters 6 through 9.

At this point, I encourage you to pick up a Bible and read this section. What you will find is that the Genesis flood account is amazingly simple, sober, and matter-of-fact. Yet it is detailed, with records of the exact calendar days when certain milestones occurred, detailed descriptions, and even measurements of the depth of water!

> "In the second month, on the seventeenth day of the month, on the same day all the fountains of the great deep burst open, and the floodgates of the sky were opened. The rain fell upon the earth for forty days and forty nights." (Genesis 7:11-12)

> "In the seventh month, on the seventeenth day of the month, the ark rested upon the mountains of Ararat. The water decreased steadily until the tenth month; in the tenth month, on the first day of the month, the tops of the mountains became visible." (Genesis 8:4-5)

> "Now it came about in the six hundred and first year, in the first month, on the first of the month, the water was dried up from the earth. Then Noah removed the covering of the ark, and looked, and behold, the surface of the ground was dried up. In the second month, on the twenty-seventh day of the month, the earth was dry." (Genesis 8:13-14)

The Genesis flood account gives the distinct impression of seriousness and credibility. It also reads like it is a journal written by Noah himself.

Whether you believe it or not is a separate question. But the character of the document is that it is simple, serious, and matter-of-fact, with a detailed and orderly record of events. The character is that of a journal.

Which Came First?

So here are the facts: We have a Genesis account which is sober, simple, and sounds historical, and the Epic of Gilgamesh which is poetic, full of myth, drama, and embellishment. Read the two for yourself, and that is what you will find.

Now then, the question is this: which came first? Consider the insightful words

12. *Ibid.*, pp. 109-110.
13. *Ibid.*, pp. 108-109.
14. *Ibid.*, p. 111.

of Kenneth Kitchen, a widely respected ancient Near East scholar and Egyptologist, who wrote:

> "The common assumption that the Hebrew account is simply a purged and simplified version of the Babylonian legend (*applied also to the Flood stories*) is fallacious on methodological grounds. In the Ancient Near East, the rule is that simple accounts or traditions may give rise (*by accretion and embellishment*) to elaborate legends, but not vice versa. In the Ancient Orient, legends were not simplified or turned into pseudo-history (*historicized*) as has been assumed for early Genesis."[15]

In evidence of this, Kenneth Kitchen cites as examples the legend of Sesotris in Egypt, progressive exaggerations in later traditions about the Hyksos kings of Egypt, the growth of traditions about Gilgamesh king of Uruk, and Enuma Elish.[16]

To put it in simpler terms, the rule we find is that historical accounts may give rise to legends, but legends do not give rise to history.[17] This clearly points to the Genesis account as the original, authentic version.

Think about that for a moment. We are being told by our secular friends that the Babylonian version is the source of the Genesis text. Yet the former is full of myth and embellishment, whereas Genesis is simple and sounds historical. And we have the clear testimony of history, both generally and in the ancient Near East specifically, which tells us that history may give rise to legends, but legends do not give rise to history. There is a "directionality" to myth. It goes in one direction. That direction is from simple accounts to embellished legends. This unmistakably points to Genesis as containing the original, and the epic a later derivative!

Dundes, Frazer, and their modern counterparts should know this. If it were any other document, I believe they would have no trouble telling us which one is more original and which one is a later development. Why do they fail when it comes to Genesis? I fear there can be only one reason: because of anti-biblical bias.

The Testimony of Flood Traditions from Foreign Nations

Now, you may ask, are there any other lines of evidence that would identify which account is more ancient? Yes, there certainly are. First, let us consider the testimony of hundreds of tribes and nations around the world who have traditions of an ancient global flood. The question we will ask is this: Do these other traditions agree more with Genesis or with the Babylonian account? After all, the two differ on many important points. For example, the sending of birds after the flood is very different in Genesis and the epic. Likewise, the reason the flood was sent is very different. The type and shape of the floating vessel are very different. The one they agree with should represent the older, more original one.

> The Epic of Gilgamesh fares very poorly when we compare it with flood traditions from other parts of the world, which agree with Genesis and not the Babylonian version.

The results are in. The comparison has been done. These foreign flood traditions agree with Genesis, and not the Epic of Gilgamesh. Let me be clear: they agree universally with Genesis. Not one tradition agrees with the Epic over against Genesis. Whenever these tribes say something touching on these areas of difference, they agree with Genesis and not the Epic:

15. Kenneth A. Kitchen, *Ancient Orient and the Old Testament* (London: Inter-Varsity Press, 1966), p. 89.
16. *Ibid.*
17. Jonathan Sarfati, *The Genesis Account* (Powder Springs, GA: Creation Book Publishers, 2015), p. 506.

- The account of birds: 42 to 0 in favor of Genesis
- The reason the flood was sent: 91 to 0 in favor of Genesis
- The shape of the floating vessel: 83 to 0 in favor of Genesis

Wherever the Epic differs from Genesis, it does so alone, and without support from other tribal traditions.

That is the exact thing we should expect if Genesis is true. But it is the last thing we would expect if the secular view were true.

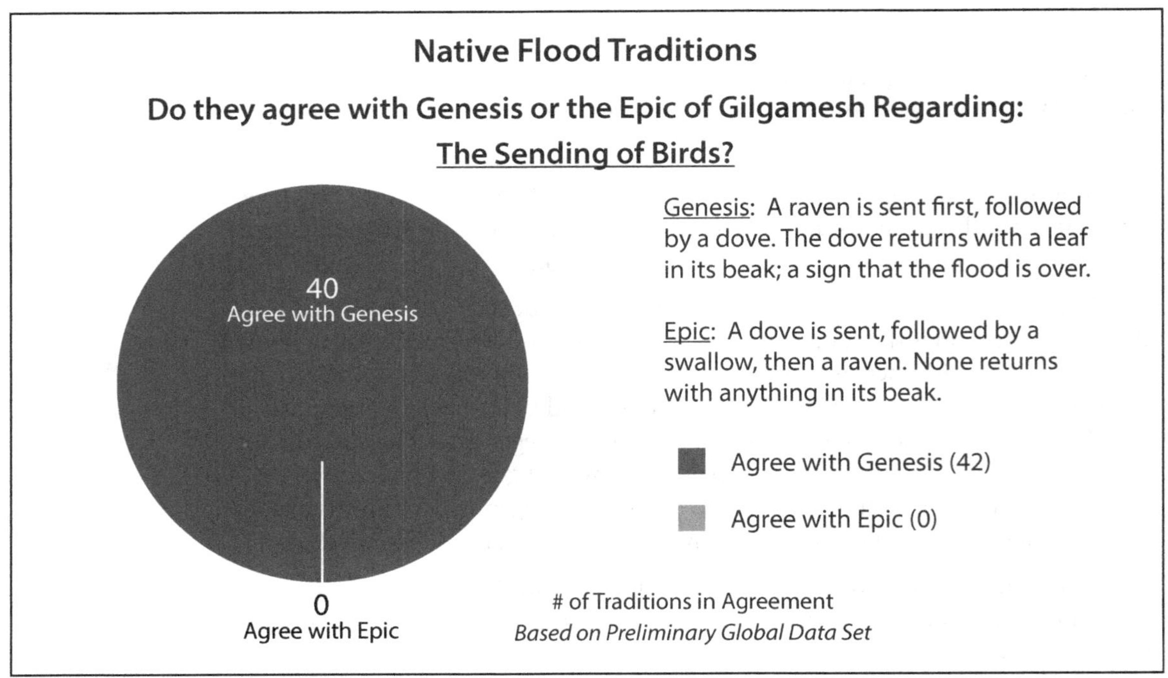

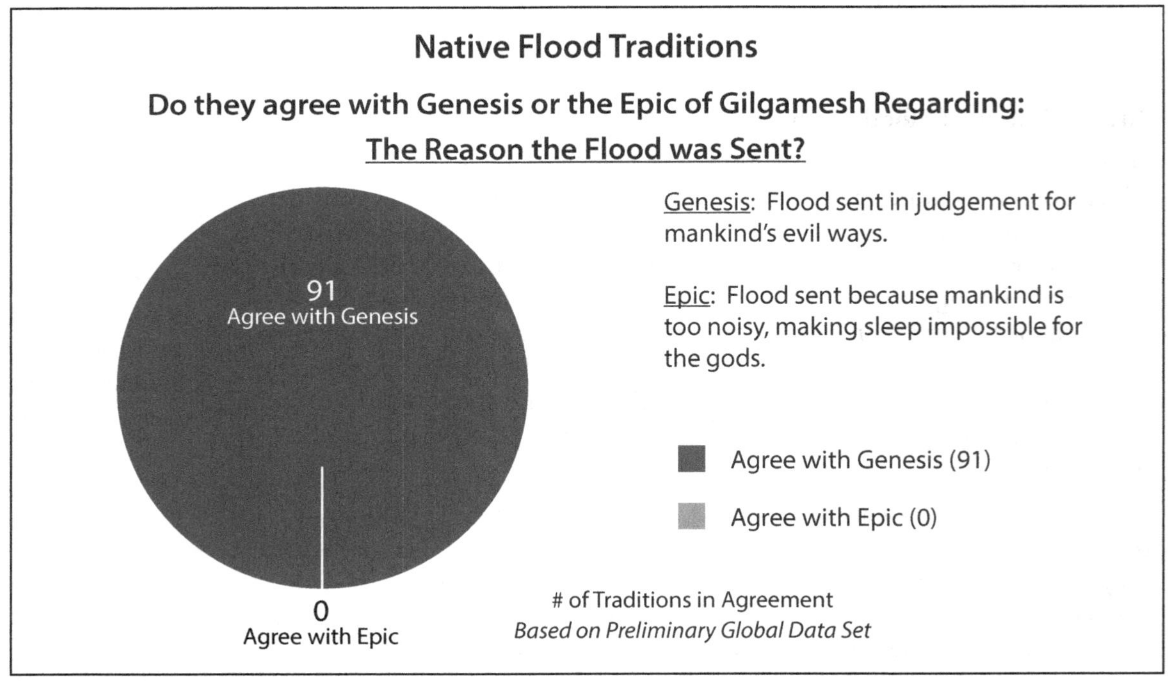

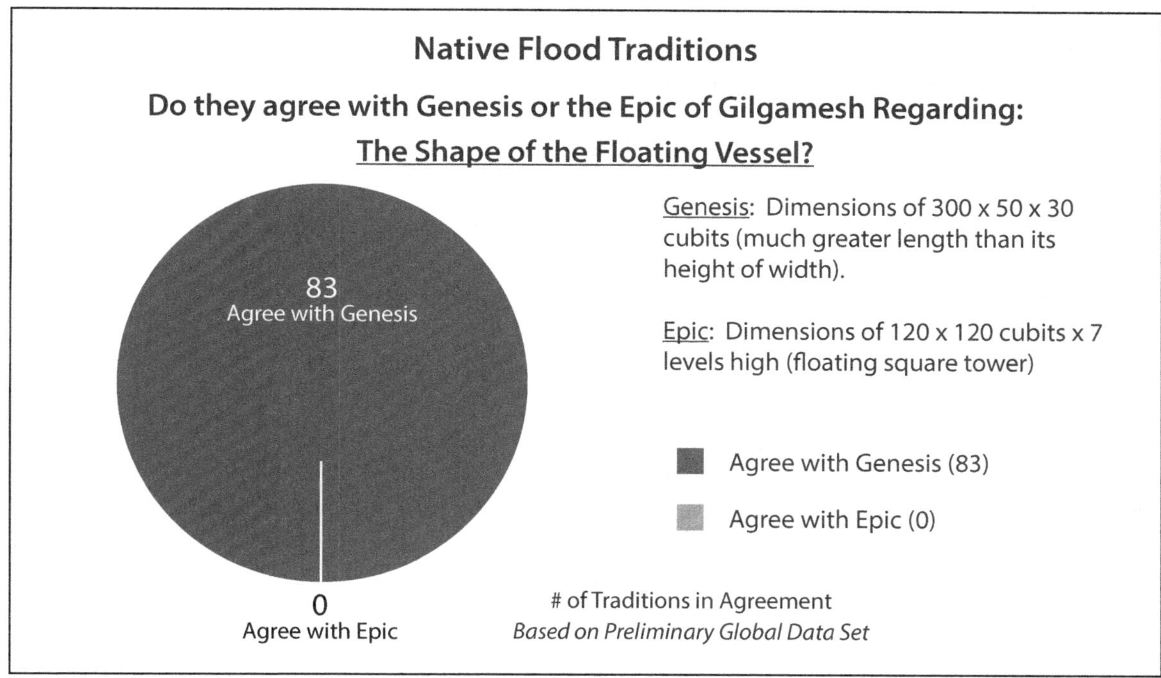

But Didn't Moses Plagiarize?

But wait, wasn't the Epic of Gilgamesh written several hundred years earlier than Genesis? Doesn't that prove—as Dundes and Frazer claimed—that Moses borrowed from the epic? Doesn't that prove that Moses copied the flood story from the Babylonians?

Wherever the Epic differs from Genesis, it does so alone, without support from other tribal traditions.

Absolutely not. Dundes and Frazer are committing the fallacy of post hoc, ergo propter hoc (before this, therefore because of this).

But there's more to it than that. After all, I would not imply that our secular friends are unaware of the post hoc, ergo propter hoc fallacy. They are well-educated. They are well-aware of this logical fallacy and its dangers.

The problem is this: they are borrowing a hidden premise. They are borrowing the idea that Moses claims he is not using sources. They borrowed that idea from somewhere, but not from the Bible, for it is not found there.

Think about that for a moment! They say Moses is borrowing. They are borrowing. They are doing the very thing of which they falsely accuse Moses. For this reason, I consider it a hypocritical argument. They are borrowing an unwarranted assumption—the assumption that Moses pretended he didn't have any sources.

Let's unpack this further. Do you remember the time the Sadducees tested Jesus with a riddle—a logic puzzle? They put before him the case of a woman who had been married to seven different men, one after another. "Whose wife will she be in the resurrection, since she had been married to all of them?"

Do you remember how Jesus answered them? He answered their logic puzzle with Scripture, exposing their faulty reasoning: "Have you not read in the book of Moses?" As he explained the meaning of the Scripture to them, he said, "Is this not the reason you are mistaken, that you do not understand the Scriptures or the power of God?" (Mark 12:24, 26)

Jesus exposed to them that they had a starting assumption, or premise, which was unfounded in Scripture. Therefore, they were arriving at false conclusions, because their reasonings weren't founded in Scripture. Jesus took great issue with both the Pharisees and Sadducees: they had built entire philosophies and traditions upon assumptions that were unsound, unscriptural, and ultimately immoral!

They say Moses is borrowing. They are borrowing. They are doing the very thing of which they falsely accuse Moses.

You have got to start with what God's Word says! Likewise, if you have a question about Scripture, you have to be willing to listen to Scripture's answer. If you want to criticize Scripture, you have to listen to what Scripture says. You cannot criticize Scripture based on an inaccurate understanding of Scripture. You cannot criticize Moses based on false presuppositions about Moses. As Jesus said to some of His objectors, ""I am not the one who accuses you. The one who accuses you is Moses."" (John 5:45).

Today, I can almost hear Jesus asking our secular anthropologists, liberal theologians, and other friends a similar question, "Have you not read Genesis, where Moses says, 'This is the book of the generations of Adam?'" (Genesis 5:1) If Moses refers to a book, why do you say he had no book?[18]

You cannot criticize Moses based on false presuppositions about Moses.

Have you not read in Numbers 21:14 (the fourth book of Moses), where Moses cites a "Book of the Wars of the Lord"? If Moses cites a book, why do you say he had no book?

Why do you claim for Moses something that he doesn't claim for himself?

Have you not read the 11 places in Genesis where Moses uses the Hebrew word *toledot*, which means genealogy or family record? He proceeds to cite genealogies and family records. If Moses cites records, why do you say he had no record?

Again, why are our secular friends claiming that Moses pretended he didn't have sources? How can they defend that? They cannot. At best, it is based on ignorance of Scripture. At worst, it is disingenuous. In either case, they are trying to paint Moses into a corner. They are trying to take a book out of Moses's hand, so that they can put another book in his hand (the Epic of Gilgamesh). They are trying to shut him off from all historical resources, so that they can make him dependent on a Babylonian myth. The whole argument is an unhistorical farce, and it needs to be abandoned immediately.

Sources from the Patriarchs, Including Noah

The truth is, Moses had access to ancient written sources, passed down by none other than Noah, Abraham, and the patriarchs themselves. How do we know this? From a great deal of internal evidence found in Genesis. This fact alone is sufficient to annihilate the notion of dependence on Babylonian texts. Moses used these patriarchal sources, under the divine inspiration of God, in writing holy and inerrant Scripture.[19]

They are trying to take a book out of Moses's hand, so that they can put another book in his hand (the Epic of Gilgamesh). The whole argument is an unhistorical farce, and it needs to be abandoned immediately.

In *Echoes of Ararat* (*Volume 1*), we surveyed in greater detail the wide array of evidence that Moses' sources were from the patriarchs themselves. In addition to

18. Notably, Jesus added: "If you believed Moses, you would believe me; for he wrote of me. But if you do not believe his writings, how will you believe my words?" (John 5:46-47)
19. The use of written sources by no means precludes the divine inspiration of Scripture. Luke, for example, opens up his gospel by saying that he obtained written sources, that he conducted many interviews with eyewitnesses of Jesus, and that he examined everything carefully to write an orderly and accurate account (Luke 1:1–4). Yet the Holy Spirit guided Luke through that process of his research and writing, to produce Scripture—of which Paul says "all Scripture is God-breathed," and of which Jesus says, "it is easier for heaven and earth to pass away than for one stroke of a letter of the Law to fail" (2 Timothy 3:16 NIV; Luke 16:17; see also 1 Timothy 5:17). In fact, very many books of the Bible are similar to Luke in this respect. Moses, likewise, lets us know he had access to such sources, and God worked through his pen as he wrote the inspired, inerrant account of Genesis and the other books of the Torah.

Genesis 5:1 and the 11 "toledot" statements in Genesis, the level of detail in Genesis—unnecessary detail, if Moses were "making it up"—which includes genealogies, lists of kings and chiefs, records of transaction amounts, detailed accounts of events, and more, only makes sense if we are dealing with eyewitness records and family memoirs.

Events in Genesis are told in a peculiar way that only the direct participants would have told them. We find highly personal, emotive accounts narrated in a way that only Joseph, Isaac, Jacob, and other patriarchs would have told them. For example, we read in Genesis 50:23 that Joseph, when he was very old, his great-grandchildren (the children of Machir, son of Manasseh) were born on his knees, and that he got to see his great-great-grandchildren (his son Ephraim's great-grandchildren).

This fact alone (that Moses had access to ancient sources from the patriarchs such as Noah, Abraham, and Joseph) is sufficient to annihilate the notion of dependence on Babylonian texts.

Why are these details in there? I submit to you that the form of Genesis only makes sense if we are dealing with family memoirs and ancient records from the patriarchs. Records which predate the Epic of Gilgamesh and other Babylonian cognates. Records which find vast confirmation from historical and archaeological evidence as well.[20]

Genesis is divinely inspired. It is God-breathed. Ironically, it is the humanity of Genesis that provides one of the best witnesses to its genuineness and historical reliability.

Genesis Withstands Scrutiny and Finds Confirmation in Science

Another sign of the authenticity of the Genesis account is that it withstands scrutiny and finds confirmation from multiple fields of science.

Genesis is divinely inspired. It is God-breathed. Ironically, it is the humanity of Genesis that provides one of the best witnesses to its genuineness and historical reliability.

First of all, the Genesis flood account truly stands out as the most historical, most trustworthy version to be found anywhere in the world. The Genesis flood text (chapters 6 through 9) is impressive in its sober, orderly, detailed account. It is truly superior to all of the flood legends that we find across the world, as amazing as many of those flood legends are. These flood legends reflect a memory of the great flood, but the account in Genesis is the autograph.

Second, let me call your attention to a very interesting pattern about flood legends: They localize the mountain where the ark landed. They say it was at some local mountain—Mount Rainier, Mount Denali, Mount Parnassus, some high mountain in the Himalayas, or some other local mountain.

Not so with Genesis. It would have been very convenient for the Jewish people to say that the ark landed at their greatest mountain, Mount Hermon. It says no such thing. It says the ark landed in "Ararat," located several hundred miles away, likely in Turkey.

These flood legends reflect a memory of the great flood, but the account in Genesis is the autograph.

That location is not the location you would pick if you were "making it up." Naming a mountain of disembarkation that is outside of a tribe's jurisdiction is nearly unheard of across global records. The fact that the Jewish scribes named a mountain outside of their nation as the place of disembarkation speaks to the great integrity with which they carefully preserved the historical record.

Third, Genesis also records some rather embarrassing details about Noah after the flood (see Genesis 9:20–23), showing us his human flaws. This is not the sort of thing you include if you are "making it up." That is very different from the embellishment that characterizes both the Babylonian epic and global flood legends. The epic says that Uta-napishti and his wife, as their reward for surviving the flood, were granted immortality and became gods.

20. In addition to Appendix B of *Echoes of Ararat* (*Volume 1*), see *Popular Handbook of Archaeology and the Bible* by Joseph Holden and Norm Geisler.

Fourth, consider the dimensions of Noah's ark: 300 cubits long by 50 cubits wide by 30 cubits high (a cubit is about 1.5 feet). Did you know that these dimensions have been tested by naval and hydraulic engineers, and they have been found to be the perfect dimensions for stability?[21] These dimensions gave the ark supreme stability even in the face of very powerful waves, which raged upon the earth during the flood.

Now that is an amazing coincidence. Did Moses just make a "lucky guess," which happened to be the optimal dimensions? No, he didn't guess. He didn't make it up. The internal evidence of Genesis indicates Moses had Noah's journal, with the dimensions given to Noah by God.

The Epic of Gilgamesh, by contrast, fails miserably in regard to the dimensions of the vessel. It gives dimensions of 120 cubits by 120 cubits, and seven decks high. This cube-shaped vessel, like the Epic itself, cannot be taken as credible. Such dimensions provide zero stability.

Fifth, geology actually confirms the flood. You won't be taught this in school, but the fact is the geologic record gives unequivocal, multi-faceted testimony confirming the Flood (see Tables 1 through 3 in the Introduction). The scriptural statement that "all the fountains of the great deep burst open" (Genesis 7:11) matches what can be seen all along the ocean floor, with these enormous mid-ocean ridges at tectonic plate boundaries encircling the globe. Plate tectonic forces were at work on a catastrophic scale during the flood. Plate tectonics were unknown before the 20th century, but Genesis referenced them.

We are also finding that the chronology of the flood, as recorded in Genesis 7–8, fits extraordinarily well with the fossil record and the geologic record. But on this point, I will refer you to the work of our excellent creationist geological and Bible scholars.[22]

In short, we have strong historical and scientific grounds to trust the Genesis flood account. In a court of law, the testimony of a false witness will be shredded apart in cross-examination. However, the testimony of a true witness stands up to cross-examination. The Genesis record stands up. Not only does it stand up, but it seems to be prophetically accurate, offering positive predictive value, as many of our creationist geologists are substantiating through modern research.

Appendix A Conclusion

Many of our college professors and teachers are trying to break the faith of Christian students by telling them that Moses stole from the Epic of Gilgamesh. But it is they who need to be taught that their assertions are fallacious on methodological grounds, contradicted by historical insights from the ancient Near East, contradicted by comparative study of flood traditions, and contradicted by the internal evidence of the two texts. An examination of this question confirms the truth, historicity, and authority of the Genesis record (see Table A-1).

---

21. Seon Hong et. al, "Safety investigation of Noah's Ark in a Seaway," *Journal of Creation*, vol. 8 (April 1994). Performed by Dr. Hong and other scientists at the Korean Research Institute of Ships and Engineering. Dr. Seon was not a creationist, but nevertheless, his research confirmed the seaworthiness of Noah's Ark.
22. On this point, see: 1) William D. Barrick and Roger Sigler, "Hebrew And Geologic Analyses Of The Chronology And Parallelism Of The Flood: Implications For Interpretation Of The Geologic Record", *Proceedings of the International Conference on Creationism*, vol. 5 (2003). 2) Andrew Snelling, *Earth's Catastrophic Past*. 3) Timothy Clarey, *Carved in Stone*.

Table A-1: Summary of Evaluation of the Argument that Genesis Flood Account is Dependent upon Epic of Gilgamesh (or other Babylonian Cognates)		
✓ = Can account for ✗ = Cannot account for		
Data Point	**Position** Genesis flood account is historically reliable and original, not dependent on Babylonian texts, but Moses had access to ancient sources passed down by the patriarchs	 Genesis flood account is not original and is dependent on the mythical Epic of Gilgamesh (or other Babylonian cognates)
Epic of Gilgamesh predates Genesis by a few hundred years	✓	✓
Historical considerations / directionality of myth (in Ancient Near East, the rule is that simple accounts may give rise to elaborate legends, but not vice versa)	✓	✗
Where Genesis and Epic differ, aboriginal flood traditions from other parts of world invariably agree with Genesis, not the Epic	✓	✗
Vast theological, worldview, and other textual differences pose enormous obstacles to Moses borrowing from the Babylonians	✓	✗
Genesis is the more sober, simple, historical-sounding, credible account	✓	✗
A wide array of internal evidence attests to the authenticity and reliability of Genesis	✓	
Genesis withstands cross-examination and finds confirmation from scientific investigation	✓	✗
Verdict:	The Genesis flood account is historically reliable and original, and is not dependent on the Epic of Gilgamesh or other Babylonian cognates. Rather, Moses had access to ancient sources passed down by the patriarchs.	

APPENDIX B

VARIANT FLOOD THEMES AND THEIR COMMON SOURCE

Early in the process of researching and preparing this book, one thing that struck me is that there are several Flood story variants that are quite different from the Genesis Flood text, even though they are describing the same event. Yet they are not isolated outliers, but recurring narrative themes found among several tribes.

The first variant that caught my notice was the "brother-sister marriage" theme, which is found so frequently in Flood stories from China, Southeast Asia, and Taiwan. "Where did it come from?" I asked myself. "How did these differences from the Genesis Flood account come about?"

Similar questions could be asked regarding many other types of Flood stories. Yet one of the most satisfying things, through the course of years of collecting and studying Flood traditions from all over the world, is that so many of these questions have been answered for me, and answered in a way that resounds for the truth of Genesis. These insights and observations were the inspiration for writing this article.

Earlier Insights from *Volume 1*

Volume 1, covering the aboriginal tribes of North and South America, was not without its unique Flood story variants. In *Volume 1* we showed that the "earth diver" variant consists of a mixed memory of the Genesis Flood and the Creation account found in Genesis 1. We saw that many strange "raven stories" are intimately connected with, and have their origin in, the memory of Noah's raven as recorded in Genesis 7. We saw that stories of a woman ravished by a serpent or sea monster—such as we find among the tribes of British Columbia and South America—contain a mixed memory of Noah's Flood and the temptation of the woman as recorded in Genesis 3.

Variants in *Volume 2*

Now in *Volume 2*, we will consider several of the recurring variants, which we will call "narrative themes," contained in this book. Specifically, we will discuss the following types:

- Brother-sister marriage (East Asia, Southeast Asia, and Austronesia)
- Recovery of fire (Globally scattered)
- Fruits dropped from tree of refuge (New Guinea, Indonesia, South America, and Australia)
- Forbidden snake meat eaten (New Guinea, Indonesia, South America, and Australia)
- Quarrel between two brothers causes Flood (Globally scattered)
- Fruit taken from tree or item taken from ground causes Flood (New Guinea, Indonesia, South America, Taiwan, and Australia)

Now I am contending that the truth of Genesis, and the events recorded therein, offers great explanatory power as to how these variants came about. It is an explanatory power which implies that the Genesis texts precedes all other tribal histories. Before proceeding, however, it is appropriate to take a few moments to explain the guiding principles in this comparative analysis.

The Impacts of Babel

In order to understand Flood traditions from a biblical perspective, one thing we need to consider is what happened directly after the Flood. In the 11th chapter of Genesis, we read about the Tower of Babel. The Tower of Babel is of unique importance, first, because that is where, according to our paradigm, the division of humanity into separate languages took place. That is where tribalization began. That is where migration and scattering began. That is where genetic differences in populations were cemented and would continue to accumulate. And importantly, that is where you could begin to develop traditions different from other nations, because of new linguistic barriers and the general isolation that ensued. Those unique languages would later become language families.[1] Some of those language families—like Indo-European and Semitic—would become massive in geographic scope through migration, population growth, influence, and/or conquest.

Let's consider the effects of Babel for a moment. What were the implications of linguistic confusion and isolation of the divisions of humanity? The following effects can be anticipated:

1. A loss of information. Elders and authorities who were experts on history now spoke different languages and were scattered.
2. The loss of information and historical details led to a lot of guessing, interpolating, and creating new details or stories in an effort to fill in the gaps of forgotten wisdom.
3. Some stories were mixed together. Once the basic structure of some stories is forgotten, and the division between one story and another is forgotten, it becomes very easy to blend one story with another, or to forget that a certain detail pertains to one event and not the other. An example would be a Flood story involving an evil serpent, or a Flood story involving a fruit taken from a forbidden tree.

The Elements Present in Genesis 1-11

Let's get a bit more microscopic and specific as we press toward a positive biblical model. This involves identifying the elements or components which comprise the historical narratives found in the early chapters of Genesis from Creation to Babel (Chapters 1 to 11). These are the raw ingredients, from the initial memory of the past, recounted to all the population by Noah, Shem, Ham, Japheth, and their direct descendants. These are the events that would orally and thus imperfectly be passed down. These are the details that a given population tried to remember and pass down, accurately or inaccurately, from generation to generation. This is the content that will be acted upon by the "entropy" of imperfect oral transmission over time. This content would even be impacted by, or fall casualty to, idolatrous beliefs and practices as a population started to worship false gods at a later date.

Based on a reading of Genesis, Figure B-1 distills the main elements and themes found in the Genesis records of Creation, the Garden of Eden, the pre-Flood world, the Flood, and the Tower of Babel. We will refer back to the numbered elements in Figure B-1 in the analysis which follows.

---

1. In addition to several dozen Tower of Babel / confusion of languages traditions around the world, there are several ancient histories from Mesopotamia which attest to this location and this event. For more information, see pages 272-273 of "*Volume 1*" (*Echoes of Ararat*) and: Charles Aling, "Cultural Change and the Confusion of Language in Ancient Sumer," *Bible and Spade* (Winter 2004), retrieved from https://biblearchaeology.org/research/chronological-categories/patriarchal-era/2567-cultural-change-and-the-confusion-of-language-in-ancient-sumer

Figure B-1: Elements Present in Genesis 1-11

Section 1: Creation (Gen. 1–2)

1A Create heaven and earth	1J stars, sun, moon	1S first marriage, bone of my bone, flesh of my flesh
1B formless, empty	1K fish, birds	1T Garden of Eden, paradise
1C darkness	1L land mammals	1U very good, no death
1D hovering over waters	1M man and woman	1V special tree, tree of life
1E light, seperate light and dark	1N dominion, stewards	1W forbidden tree, tree of knowledge of good and evil, forbidden fruit
1F sky, seperate waters	1O seven days, week	
1G earth, seperate earth and water	1P God creates man, dust of earth	
1H days, period	1Q breathes life into nostrils	
1I plants	1R woman created from man's rib	

Section 2: Garden of Eden and the Fall (Gen. 3)

2A Serpent	2F secret, hide, fear	2J Eve, mother of all living
2B forbidden fruit, forbidden tree, garden	2G God's judgment, curse, death, sin, evil, pain, thorns, thistles	2K cast out from Garden, paradise lost
2C temptation, woman sins, deceived, man sins	2H hard work, sweat, futility	2L ground, cultivate field
2D eyes open	2I enmity between man and serpent, kill serpent, bite foot, crush head	2M angel, flaming sword, tree of life
2E naked, ashamed, cover nakedness		

Section 3: Cain and Abel, Pre-Flood World (Gen. 4–5)

3A Two brothers	3D Cain cursed, mark / sign, exiled	3F hard work, pain, curse, seek rest / relief
3B sacrifice, offering to God	3E Enoch, taken up to God	
3C quarrel, rivalry, kill brother		

Section 4: The Flood (Gen. 6–9)

4A Angels came down to earth, took human wives, forbidden union	4J 8 survivors, 3 sons / 3 brothers	4Q sign, dry earth returning, knew flood was ending
4B giants, powerful	4K fountains of ocean, windows of heaven, open	4R exit Ark, open door, came down mountain, repopulated earth
4C man's evil, sin corrupt, violence	4L global Flood, ark lifted high, waters rise above mountains	4S altar, bonfire, burnt offering after Flood, animal sacrifice to God
4D God's judgment, destroy people, destroy earth	4M drowned, killed, people and animals	4T seasons, cold, heat, winter, summer
4E righteous man, old man	4N wind sent, wind dries earth, flood waters go down	4U promise, rainbow, God's bow in the sky
4F forewarned by God, prophetic warning, God spoke to man	4O Ark lands on mountain, fountains of sea close, windows of heaven close	4V Noah farmed, planted vineyard
4G construct Ark, wooden boat		4W drunk, uncovered, naked
4H bring pairs of animals, seeds, food	4P old man sends raven, raven fails, sends dove 1st time, sends dove 2nd time, dove succeeds, returns with an olive leaf in beak, olive tree	4X sons, covered, walked backwards, heads turned
4I 7 days		4Y sons, cursed, blessed

Figure B-1: Elements Present in Genesis 1-11		
Section 5: Tower of Babel (Gen. 10–11)		
5A Nimrod, mighty hunter 5B same language, all people together 5C build tower 5D brick, stome, tar, mortar	5E ascend to heavens, build high, pride 5F God displeased, construction stopped, tower broken	5G confused speech, many languages, many nations

Brother-Sister Marriage

The first narrative theme we will discuss is what may be called the "brother-sister marriage" or "incestuous marriage" or "tests required to marry sibling after Flood" theme, which is widely distributed across China, Southeast Asia, and even Austronesia.[2] As an example, consider the following text which occurs in the Khmu people's Flood story, presented previously on page 129. We pick up the story after the brother and sister emerged from the floating drum at the end of the Flood:

> 'What, what are we to do now? A woman wants to get a husband, and a man wants to get a wife. Let us go and make a search!'
>
> One of them went south and the other one went north. They searched and looked but there was nobody, looked and looked and the fact remained, however much they looked there were only they themselves, there was no one else but the brother and sister.
>
> They set out again, sought here and sought there and sought everywhere, but there was no one at all.
>
> There was a bird, a malkoha cuckoo there was, and it was cooking. 'Brother and sister, embrace one another.' 'Oh, that bird will make us marry each other," they thought, and thus they got married, they married each other."[3]

Now the first question we must ask is, what connection does this brother-sister incest story have to do with the Genesis Flood? A great deal. Contextually, this narrative theme almost always occurs within a Flood story. Not just any Flood story, but a global Flood with Genesis parallels. Parallels include a divine forewarning of the coming Flood, a floating vessel, landing on a high mountain, the survivors waiting to exit until they receive indication it is safe, and the absence of any other survivors on earth. The same event (the global Flood) is certainly in view. It is only a question of where this theme originated.

But what about the variation itself? What, if any, connection to Genesis does a story of brother-sister marriage have? To answer that, let's first map out the sequence of events, using our Khmu text above:

2. Examples in this book include, but are not limited to, texts from the Gha Mu, Magpie Miao, Zhuang, Bouyei, Kam, Li, Tujia, Shui, Yi of Vietnam, Lamet, Khang, Laha, Mang, Tay Pong, Nung, San Chay, Thai Nghe, Kim Mum, Man Ta Pan, Khmu, Yao in Vietnam, May, Puyuma (Austronesian Taiwan), and Nabaloi (Philippines). Research by Valdis Gauss has shown that at least eleven Austronesian tribes on Taiwan adhere to this incest motif within the deluge context (Gauss, 2022, p. 240).
3. Kristina Lindell, Jan-Ojvind Swahn, Damrong Tayanin, "The Flood: Three Northern Kammu Versions of the Story of Creation," *The Flood Myth*, ed. Alan Dundes (Berkeley: University of California Press, 1988), pp. 273-274.

1. The brother and sister each want to find a spouse, but marrying each other is abhorrent to them because incest is forbidden.
2. They conduct a search for partners. One walks north and the other walks south, but with no success (there are no other survivors on earth).
3. A second time, they set out in search for a mate, but with no success.
4. A bird advises them to marry.
5. They accept this counsel and decide it is best to marry. They do so, and humanity is restored from their offspring.
6. This, more or less, is the structure of the "brother-sister marriage" theme that we find so frequently in East and Southeast Asia.

Now then, what connection to Genesis does this narrative have? If only Genesis contained an account where two or three tests were performed, and then a bird convinced them it was now safe to do something:

Noah opened the window of the ark which he had made; and he sent out a raven, and it went out flying back and forth until the water was dried up from the earth. Then he sent out a dove from him, to see if the water was abated from the face of the land; but the dove found no resting place for the sole of its foot, so it returned to him into the ark, for the water was on the surface of all the earth. Then he stretched out his hand and took it and brought it into the ark to himself. Then he waited yet another seven days; and again he sent out the dove from the ark. And the dove came to him toward evening, and behold, in its beak was a freshly picked olive leaf. So Noah knew that the water was abated from the earth." (Genesis 8:6-11 LSB)

Indeed, the brother-sister marriage narrative is directly connected with the Noahic birds account in the 8th chapter of Genesis. To be specific, Table B-1 lists several parallels found in Genesis:

Table B-1: Common Elements between Brother-Sister Marriage and Noahic Birds Account (Genesis 8:6-12)	
1	It takes place directly after the Flood.
2	There is a first test or search (the raven's flight).
3	There is a second test or search (the dove's first flight).
4	The third action is successful (the dove finds and returns with an olive leaf) and persuades the human survivors it will be safe to do something (safe to exit Ark soon).
5	A bird or two birds are involved (a raven and a dove).

Is it merely "by chance" that this theme, found in East Asia, lines up with the Genesis text? Certainly not. And this correspondence is not limited to the Khmu text cited above. The Dong tradition refers to an unsuccessful first search by the siblings, an eagle that advises them to marry, and a special test that convinced them to marry. The Yi, Yao, Kim Mun, and Man Ta Pan people groups speak of a series of tests that persuaded the brother and sister to marry. The Mang and Nung people say it was a crow that advised the siblings to marry—clearly an echo of Noah's raven. The Khang say it was a sparrow, the Laha a starling bird, the Thai Nghe a rooster, and the Lamet a bird known as the "tiokok." Even when the bird is absent, other matching features of Genesis are present, not least of which the three tests and the sign received.

Think about the implications of what we have just seen. The "brother sister marriage" narrative theme, from China and Southeast Asia, is closely connected with the Genesis Flood from the Near East. This is a shocking discovery, but it should not be surprising if we regard the Bible as trustworthy.

Let's take a step back and consider this narrative theme more broadly and more globally for a moment. I have stated that some of its defining characteristics are the fact that birds are involved, that two or three tests were performed, and that a sign was received as encouragement to do something. It would become even more compelling if we found these factors in other story types around the world. Indeed, that is exactly what we find. In this book (*Volume 2*) and in *Volume 1*, we have found a large number of related narrative themes, as shown in Table B-2.[4] This is exactly what the biblical model predicts: that we would find many story types which correspond to the Genesis Flood, but with mutations upon one or more parts of the story.

Table B-2: Narrative Themes Connected with Brother-Sister Marriage
Themes involving birds with Genesis parallels:
1) Earth diver, 2) earth flyer, 3) raven is punished, 4) recovery of fire, 5) birds sent to notify survivors, 6) mark left on bird's tail after Flood, 7) rooster awakens the sun, 8) bird sent to get food, 9) bird plays a role in creation, 10) birds create post-Flood landscape, 11) bird cries or laments the effects of Flood, 12) bird sent to see if enemies are dead, 13) bird carries survivors out of Flood, 14) bird causes Flood to subside, 15) bird sprinkles earth on the sea, 16) bird with leaf in mouth leads survivors in canoe to land, 17) birds sent for supplies, 18) raven sent to give life to first man, 19) bird kills evil sea animal during Flood, 20) raven spills waters of immortality, 21) birds find land and settle, 22) bird sent from above to search or investigate Flood, 23) bird sent by survivors to ask for divine help, 24) bird sent to measure or survey earth, 25) bird warns man of Flood, 26) fruits tossed twice for bird to eat, 27) birds sent to gather building materials for vessel, 28) bird flew three times and complained of fatigue, 29) bird pilots boat to save drowning humans.
Themes involving two or three tests, and a sign received:
1) Fruits dropped from tree to test water level, 2) three attempts to give birth to human offspring after Flood, 3) fruits tossed twice for bird to eat, 4) tests required to marry heavenly woman, 5) water struck several times and subsides.

We have discussed the elements involving birds and tests, but what about the element of brother-sister marriage? Where did this idea originate? Within the text of Genesis 1-11, there are two candidates. The first is Adam and Eve, and the second is the forbidden marriages of Genesis 6:1-4 involving angels.

I think the true inspiration for this variant is Adam and Eve. They were closely related ("bone of my bone, flesh of my flesh", Gen. 2:23). She was taken from him, created from him. It could almost be said that they were siblings. Genetically, I think they were twin siblings, assuming that God took Adam's DNA and gave it to her.

Moreover, there is a heavy sense of moral wrongness and taboo in the brother-sister marriage theme. This seems to be a memory of the first sin itself, committed by this couple in the Garden! Was that not abhorrent and wrong to Adam and Eve, just like the thought of marrying their sibling? Hear Eve protesting to the Serpent, "No! We must not eat of that Tree!" Then hear the sister objecting to the thought of marriage, "No! We must not marry! That would be a crime."

4. Further analysis of these types to follow in a future publication.

And remember what happened to Adam and Eve after that fateful bite: they experienced shame over their nakedness in each other's presence. In their case, they felt shame after they ate from the Tree that God forbade (Gen. 2:25, 3:7). In the "brother-sister" case, shame hangs over the entire narrative until they finally decided to marry.

> Hear Eve protesting to the Serpent, "No! We must not eat of that Tree!" Then hear the sister objecting to the thought of marriage, "No! We must not marry! That would be a crime."

To give an example, consider the tradition from the Tujia people of China. Before the brother and sister agreed to marry, they said "we are ashamed before God" and "we are ashamed before each other." This is reminiscent of Genesis 3: "And the eyes of both of them were opened, and they knew that they were naked; and they sewed fig leaves together and made themselves loin coverings." (3:7, LSB) And again, "Yahweh God called to the man and said to him, 'Where are you?' And he said, 'I heard the sound of You in the garden, and I was afraid because I was naked; so I hid.'" (3:9-10, LSB)

To make this identification even more clear, recall what happens earlier in these Flood stories, especially those from the minorities of China. Do you recall the brother and sister talking to a dragon, the "Thunder God"? What were they talking about? The dragon was asking them to do something: to give him water.

Now, turning back to Genesis, what were Adam and Eve doing? Weren't they in the presence of the Serpent? Didn't the Serpent ask Eve to do something? (Adam was standing there also, according to Genesis 3:6!) Didn't he instruct Eve (and indirectly Adam) to eat a forbidden fruit?

Do you see the parallel? Could anything be more similar than this talking dragon and this talking Serpent? Is this not almost a perfect mixing of the Flood and Garden of Eden accounts? You could scarcely mix the Flood and Garden stories any better if you wanted to!

A final point can be made in favor of the Adam-and-Eve origin of this theme. I am arguing that we have here a mixed memory of Adam and Eve (Genesis 2-3) and the Flood (Genesis 6-9). It would help if we found other themes around the world where mixture is at work, combining the memories of Genesis 2-3 and Genesis 6-9. That is exactly what we find! We have the Flood stories of a bathing woman ravished by a serpent. We have Flood stories where something is stolen from a special tree. We have Flood stories with forbidden snake meat eaten. We have Flood stories where fruits are dropped from a tree. We have Flood stories involving a first woman.

> Could anything be more similar than this talking dragon and this talking Serpent? Is this not almost a perfect mixing of the Flood and Garden of Eden accounts? You could scarcely mix the Flood and Garden stories any better if you wanted to!

Now we cannot overlook the possibility that the forbidden marriages with angels in Genesis 6:1-4 are a factor as well. We should also mention the fact that close kin marriage was implicit and unavoidable in the earliest days recorded in Genesis. For example, Cain and Seth must have married their sisters.

However, I think the "Adam and Eve" memory is at least the primary inspiration for this story type from East Asia, based on the number of parallels between the two. In the end, we have an echo of Adam and Eve, mixed with an echo of the Flood. We can illustrate the transition which gave birth to this story type, as shown in Figure B-2. The next time you read a "brother-sister marriage" story from the peoples of East Asia, such as that of Izanagi and Izanami in Japan's Kojiki, remember Adam and Eve.

Figure B-2: Proposed Origin of Brother-Sister Marriage Theme

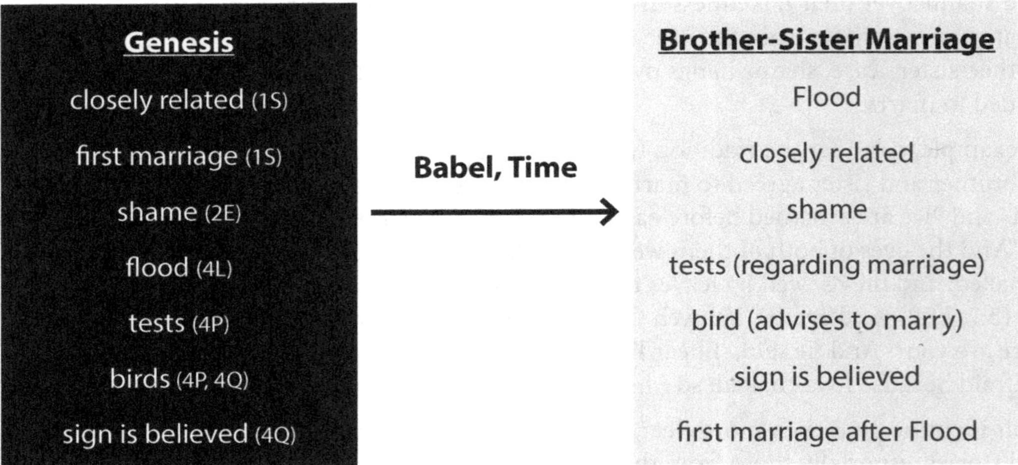

Note: See Figure B-1 for text elements and Scriptural references.

Recovery of Fire

The "recovery of fire" variant occurs most frequently in Austronesian Taiwan,[5] but also sporadically in the Philippines, Indonesia, South America, the southwestern United States, and parts of Australia.[6] It is possible that this variant arose independently in more than one part of the world. It normally occurs in a Flood tradition, toward the end, after the waters have begun to subside. The general outline of the recovery of fire story is as follows:

1. After the Flood, a surviving remnant of humanity lacks fire, so they suffer cold and darkness.
2. An animal, typically a bird, flies or runs to obtain fire. It fails on this first attempt, and returns with nothing.
3. Sometimes a second failed attempt is made.
4. A final and successful attempt is made, typically by a different animal than the first. The animal returns with a source of fire in its mouth or feet.
5. The surviving people can now use fire again. Often there is an expression of gratitude to the animal.

The "recovery of fire" theme is very easy to identify as closely connected with the Noahic birds account of Genesis 8. Little else is required but to read a few examples and compare it with Genesis. See Table B-3. Parallels include 1) when it occurs (right after the Flood), 2) that multiple attempts are made by animals, typically two to three attempts by birds, and 3) the final and successful flight involves an animal returning with a small object which brings hope and an indication of renewed life.

5. Eight fire origin motifs are found among nine Austronesian tribes on Taiwan. Gauss, *The Great Formosan Flood Myths* (2022), p. 220.
6. Examples in this book include, but are not limited to, texts from the Ami, Bunun, Hla'alua, Kanakanavu, Paiwan, Rukai, Tsuo, Igorot, Bontok, Itneg, Yakut, Andaman Islands, and Murinbata. Examples from *Volume 1* include texts from the Pomo, Paiute, Guaraní, Tacana, Arua, Caingang, Bororo, Mocovi, Achomawi, and Kaiwa.

Table B-3: Examples of "Recovery of Fire" Narrative Theme and Comparison with Noahic Birds Account
Genesis 8:6-11 (LSB): "Noah opened the window of the ark which he had made; and he sent out a raven, and it went out flying back and forth until the water was dried up from the earth. Then he sent out a dove from him, to see if the water was abated from the face of the land; but the dove found no resting place for the sole of its foot, so it returned to him into the ark, for the water was on the surface of all the earth. Then he stretched out his hand and took it and brought it into the ark to himself. Then he waited yet another seven days; and again he sent out the dove from the ark. And the dove came to him toward evening, and behold, in its beak was a freshly picked olive leaf. So Noah knew that the water was abated from the earth."
Amis (Taiwan): "After the deluge ... one day people asked the tatachu bird to fetch fire from somewhere for them. The tatachu bird brought fire back, but it was extinguished when he dropped it in the sea. Next people asked a maggot to fetch fire. He successfully brought fire back, but it was extinguished soon. The brother and sister tried to strike the white stones together and they made fire. After that people could preserve fire from generation to generation."[7] Mocovi (Argentina): "A very heavy rain had extinguished the Mocoví's fire and had made it impossible to light it again, for the sticks used for making fire were wet. While the Mocoví were pondering their dilemma, a vulture appeared in their country with a firebrand Sierra de La Ventana Mountains in its beak, from which all took some fire. The vulture was never to return to the boat, for he would have enough to do to find fire for the Mocoví. The tribe was extremely grateful for the favor. Although they hunt and shoot down all birds, not letting a single one escape, they never shoot at the vulture, not even the boys in sport."[8] Bunun (Taiwan): "They thought maybe they could ask birds to do them a favor, since birds have wings, so they asked a crow for help. The crow promised them to go down the mountain to take a look. However, as the crow flew to the foot of the mountain, it saw lots of corpses of dead animals from the flood. Therefore, it stayed there for food and forgot Bunun people's request. ... Then they asked a frog, which was good at swimming, to have a look for them. The frog promised them and went down the mountain. When it got down, it found other human beings living there. The frog held one piece of burning coal in its mouth and hoped to take it back. ... It jumped into the water, but the burning coal was extinguished by the water. Though the frog brought back the evidence of people living at the foot of the mountain, Bunun people did not trust it, since they saw an extinguished coal. ... Once again, Bunun people sent a black red-billed bulbul [a type of songbird] to have a look. The black bulbul agreed and flew to the bottom of the mountain to see if the frog told the truth about people still living there. It found out what the frog said was true, and so that Bunun people would believe, it decided to pick up the burning coal and take it back. It flew back to the mountain and showed the burning coal to Bunun people. Then all Bunun people went downhill happily."[9] Tsou (Taiwan): "As people arrived at Jade Mountain, the kindling was extinguished. They sent "kiuyisi" bird to find fire for them. It found fire and returned, but it flew so slowly that fire burned its beak. It discarded the fire because of the pain. Then people asked "uhngu" bird (a sparrow) to find fire. It flew fast and took fire back successfully, so people could use fire. To express their gratitude to the bird, people allowed it to eat grains in the farm."[10]

7. Ho T'ing-jui, "A Comparative Study of Myths and Legends of Formosan Aborigines," p. 319.
8. Robert Lehmann-Nitsche, "Mitología Sudamericana XII: la Astronomía de los Mocoví," vol. 2, *Revista del Museo de la Plata,* vol. 30 (Buenos Aires, 1927), p. 147.
9. Pasuya Poiconu, *Literary History of Taiwanese Indigenous Peoples*, vol. 1, trans. Wordsworth (Taipei: National Academy for Educational Research and Le Jin Books, 2012), p. 73.
10. "The Tsuo have an alternate narration of this Flood account where it is a goat and a deer rather than birds that are sent in search of fire. Land animals also replace birds in some other versions. Nevertheless, it is most often birds, and this is certainly the original sense, especially when we consider the preponderance of related themes where it is clearly birds (see Table B-2).

But what about the "fire" element? Does a fire have any place in the Genesis Flood account? Actually yes:

> Then Noah built an altar to Yahweh and took of every clean animal and of every clean bird and offered burnt offerings on the altar. And Yahweh smelled the soothing aroma; and Yahweh said to Himself, "I will never again curse the ground because of man, for the intent of man's heart is evil from his youth; and I will never again strike down every living thing as I have done." (Genesis 8:20-21, LSB)

I am suggesting that the "recovery of fire" narrative came about as a confused memory of the Noahic birds account and Noah's fire that he lit after the Flood to offer a sacrifice to God. I say a confused memory because, after Babel, people could have easily forgotten what Noah's dove returned with. Was it an olive leaf? Was it something else? Something of practical value to the surviving humans, especially in a world that was completely saturated?

They remembered a fire was lit after the Flood. They may have even thought of the initial dark, water-covered world of Day 1 of Creation (Gen. 1:2-4). In any case, once they forgot about the dove's olive leaf, it was plausible enough to conclude that fire—whether in the form of a burning stick or a hot coal or something else—was what the bird must have retrieved. Thus, the "recovery of fire" narrative was born. And it bears the signature of the Genesis Flood account, as do the Flood texts in which this narrative occurs. This is illustrated in Figure B-3.

Figure B-3: Proposed Origin of Recovery of Fire Narrative Theme

Genesis		**Recovery of Fire**
darkness (1C)		Flood
Flood (4L)	**Babel, Time**	darkness
bonfire after Flood (4S)	→	need fire after Flood
birds (4P)		birds
first attempt fails (4P)		first attempt fails
final attempt succeeds (4Q)		final attempt succeeds
bird returns with object (4Q)		bird returns with fire

Note: See Figure B-1 for text elements and Scriptural references.

Fruits Dropped From Tree and Forbidden Snake Meat Eaten

Part 1: Fruits Dropped or Thrown from Tree of Refuge

Next we will consider two closely associated themes, the first of which is "fruit dropped from tree." For this, we will head south from Asia to the island of New Guinea, which is ground zero for this theme. It is found also in Australia and certain islands of Indonesia, including Timor, Solor, and Borneo. Remarkably, halfway across the world, we also find the "fruits dropped from tree" story in South America![11] In many ways, the versions in South America are closer to

11. Examples in this book include, but are not limited to, Ali Island, Erave, Gavi, Kire, Manam Motu, Rangai, Tolai, Watut, Wedau, Yimas, Morut, Solor, and Melbourne area tradition. Examples from *Volume 1* include Pemon, Jivaro, Murata, Urarina, Tacana, Tupinamba, Guayaki, and Ipurina.

Papua New Guinea than those of Australia, which is a surprising finding with implications for future research.

The "fruits dropped from tree" theme forms part of a Flood story, always occurring at the end. Almost by definition, this theme occurs in a particular type of Flood story, one where a tall tree is the place of escape from the Flood.

The Flood stories in which this story type occurs are, in some ways, very different from those in Asia and other parts of the world, although they are linked to the same global Flood. It is also very noteworthy that this theme goes hand-in-hand with another theme, which we will discuss shortly: the forbidden snake meat eaten.

The typical sequence of the "fruits dropped from tree" narrative theme is as follows:

1. One or two people climb to the top of a tall tree to escape the Flood, usually after receiving a forewarning. They alone survive, and all other people drown.
2. Unable to see the water level, they throw or drop a fruit down from the tree to discern whether land has appeared yet. They hear a splash, indicating the earth is still covered by water.
3. After waiting for a period, they throw a second fruit. Again they hear a splash, indicating the earth is still covered by water.
4. After waiting again for some time, they drop a fruit. This time they hear the sound of the fruit striking the earth. They realize the earth is now dry and the waters have subsided.
5. The survivors climb down from the tree and resettle the earth.

First, can we establish that these stories are describing the same Flood as in Genesis? Yes, we can.

1. It is a global Flood. The length of time that passes and the fact that there are no other survivors indicates this is the same Flood described in Genesis, and no mere local flood.
2. It is no common tree that they climb, but is typically described as the tallest tree, and often a magical tree which rose in height at the same rate as the Flood rose. In other cases, it is a tall tree on a high mountain. In some versions, they float in a canoe and arrive at the treetop.
3. Other specific parallels with Genesis are present, including a divine judgment against evil, a forewarning given, parallels with the Noahic birds account, and parallels with the Garden of Eden. We will discuss the last two in the following pages.

Now you may already notice the parallels with the Noahic birds account. There are two or three tests, the first one or two are unsuccessful, and the third (or final) test is successful and is persuasive to the survivors that the Flood is ending. It also convinces the survivors to do something: to climb down the tree. We can illustrate this connection to Genesis with a few examples, as shown in Table B-4.

Table B-4: Examples of "Fruits Dropped from Tree" and Comparison with Noahic Birds Account	
Yimas (Papua New Guinea): "That night the younger one had a dream that a flood would come. The siblings prepared food and climbed to the top of two coconut palm trees. Then the village flooded while everyone was still sleeping. After a while, they threw a coconut down to see if the water was dried up yet, but it wasn't. Finally, they threw other coconuts down and found that the land was dry."[12] **Kire** (Papua New Guinea): A sister and brother were saved in a tree; to find out whether the water had subsided, they threw in a coconut, then a tuber of yam, both falling into the soft mud; then they threw the chicken, it began to eat the corpses; then they threw fire, it dried up the earth; they threw the coconut and yam again, they split; threw a leaf, it turned into a bird; brother and sister descended.[13] **Erave** (Papua New Guinea): "The good people took two chickens, a cock and a hen, two pigs, two dogs, fire and some water and climbed a coconut palm. In the flood the palm rose high into the sky. Later, they cast a new coconut down to the water three times, then the fourth time, it finally hit the ground. They knew that the flood had finished, so they left the palm. All of the people and animals on the ground had died; the flood had killed them."[14] **Pemón** (Venezuela and Brazil): The Makunaima, fleeing from the inundation, also sought places to climb up and shelter themselves. Chiké climbed up a palm tree called maripá, and his brother climbed a palm tree called warumá. They spent one winter atop the palm trees, feeding on the trees' fruits. … The Makunaima could tell that the waters were lowering from the distinct sound made by the discarded seeds from the fruits they were eating. When they knew that the seeds were not falling in water, they went down with caution, and went down little by little from the hills."[15]	Genesis 8:6-11 (LSB): "Noah opened the window of the ark which he had made; and he sent out a raven, and it went out flying back and forth until the water was dried up from the earth. Then he sent out a dove from him, to see if the water was abated from the face of the land; but the dove found no resting place for the sole of its foot, so it returned to him into the ark, for the water was on the surface of all the earth. Then he stretched out his hand and took it and brought it into the ark to himself. Then he waited yet another seven days; and again he sent out the dove from the ark. And the dove came to him toward evening, and behold, in its beak was a freshly picked olive leaf. So Noah knew that the water was abated from the earth."

Undeniably, this narrative theme, like so many others, is closely connected with the Genesis Flood account. This is evident even though Noah's raven and dove seem to be absent. Yet the birds may not be entirely forgotten, for we find a few versions around the world which do contain the element of birds:

1. The Urarina speak of three tests of the water depth. First, fruits were thrown and they struck water. Second, the father sent one of his sons down, and he turned into a heron. Third, he sent his other son down, and he turned into a "coro coro" bird. Finally, the father himself had to climb down.
2. According to the Kire people of Papua New Guinea, one of the objects thrown turns into a bird (See text in Table B-4 above).
3. The Chumash people of California say that acorns were thrown from the treetop into the water on two occasions, and the purpose was to feed a struggling bird.

12. William A. Foley, *The Yimas Language of New Guinea* (Stanford: Stanford University Press, 1991), pp. 477-482.
13. George Höltker, "Aus dem Kulturleben der Kire-Puir am unteren Ramu", Jahrbuch des Museums für Völkerkunde zu Leipzig, vol. 19 (1962), pp. 99-104.
14. Slone, T. H. (2001). *One Thousand One Papua New Guinean Nights*, Vol. 1 (Masalai Press), p. 134
15. Cesareo de Armellada, *Tauron Panton: Cuentos y Leyendas de los Indios Pemón*, 2nd edition (Quito: Abya-Yala, 1989), p. 55–56.

We will consider the question of how this variant arose in the following pages. But first, it is appropriate to introduce the "forbidden snake meat eaten" story, since it is so closely associated with "fruits dropped from tree."

Part 2: Forbidden Snake Meat Eaten

Now we come to one of most interesting narrative themes: that of the forbidden snake meat eaten. As mentioned above, this theme is closely associated with "fruits dropped from tree," often (but not always) occurring in the same Flood traditions. Geographically, it exists everywhere the "fruits dropped from tree" does—Melanesia, Australia, and parts of South America.[16] The general outline of the story runs like this:

1. A hunter or group of people hunt and kill a special snake.
2. Despite a prohibition against its consumption, meat from the snake is eaten.
3. A Flood is determined to be sent against the people in judgment for eating meat of the forbidden snake.
4. One or a few people, who did not participate in this violation, receive advance warning of this Flood and take shelter on the highest tree. Most frequently, this warning comes from the snake itself before it is killed.
5. A globally destructive Flood occurs and drowns all people except those sheltered on the high tree.

To illustrate this story in more detail, consider the examples in Table B-5:

Table B-5: Examples of "Forbidden Snake Meat Eaten" Narrative Theme
Jivaro (Ecuador and Peru) The Jivaro were about to have a festival, and they sent two young men to hunt food for the people. As they were hunting, their food kept disappearing while they were gone. They came to realize that their food was being stolen by the "pangi" — the great serpent, that is, the boa constrictor, which is the archdemon of their spiritual world. They found the snake and burned its hiding spot. Later, one of the two men ate the snake meat, which is forbidden since it is considered an evil demon. The man became struck with an unquenchable thirst, as he drank all the water he could find. Then he slowly turned into a monstrous snake, like the pangi. His companion returned and found him turned into a pangi. "Go quickly to save yourself. I no longer have power to respect you, but will only devour you. Go back to where our people are, and tell them what has happened. Warn them that the water is going to grow more and more, and that it will inundate the land. Tell them to go up on the highest hills, and upon the trees that grow on those hills. Otherwise, they will drown in the flood which will cover the earth. And you, put food in your canoe of palm wood, and with this go up to the highest hill. If the water covers even that hill, go up on the tallest tree of that hill to save yourself."[17]
Rangai (Papua New Guinea): "Long ago, a giant python was discovered by some children who told the other villagers about it. They captured the snake and prepared to butcher it. Two girls and their brothers were appointed to guard the snake. The snake transformed into a young man and chewed some betel nut and spat it upon a banana leaf to prove to the other villagers that he was a man. The snake warned the children that if he was killed to take his guts and climb to the top of a coconut tree with fire. The children told the villagers what had happened but no one believed them. So, when the villagers butchered the snake the children did as the snake man had told them. Inside the guts they found traditional adornments: the teeth of dogs and flying foxes. Later that day, as the villagers began to eat, a storm broke out. The village was inundated by a flood and everyone died. Only the four children survived in the coconut tree."[18]

16. Examples from this book (*Volume 2*) include Ali Island, Erave, Gavi, Kire, Lae Citi, Mpur, Napans, Rangai, Samo Kubo, Susure, Takai, Tolai, Valman, Watut, Wedau, Wewak, Yimas, and Wandjina. Examples from *Volume 1* include Jivaro, Miskito and Sumo, Murata, Urarina, and Andoque.
17. Rafael Karsten, *Mitos de los Indios Jibaros del Oriente del Ecuador* (Quito: Sociedad Ecuatoriana de Estudios Historicos Americanos, 1919), p. 4–6.
18. Slone, T. H. (2001). *One Thousand One Papua New Guinean Nights*, Vol. 1 (Masalai Press), pp. 467-468.

Iban (Borneo): "Once upon a time some Dyak women went to gather young bamboo shoots to eat. Having got the shoots they went along the jungle and came upon what they took to be a large tree fallen to the ground, upon which they sat, and began to pare the bamboo shoots, when to their utter amazement the tree began to bleed. At this point some men came upon the scene, and at once saw that what the women were sitting upon was not a tree, but a huge boa-constrictor in a state of stupor. The men killed the beast, cut it up, and took the flesh home to eat. As they were frying the pieces of snake strange noises came from the pan, and at the same time it began to rain furiously. The rain continued until all hills except the highest were covered, and the world was drowned because the men killed and fried the snake."[19]

Napans (New Guinea): "One day while in the jungle, [a man named] Ibueri caught a snake and confined it in a bamboo joint. When he was away, the other villagers cooked and ate it. Thereon, the deluge came and everyone drowned. The corpses of the dead transformed into trees and animals."[20]

The forbidden creature is typically but not always a snake. Yet several of the variants are also snake-like: an eel, a "snake-fish", a sea monster, or a dragon. This leads us to conclude that the original prototype was indeed a snake.

Now we come to the critical question: what relation does this story have with Genesis? If only Genesis had something to say about a snake that is associated with an eating prohibition:

> "Now the serpent was more crafty than any beast of the field which Yahweh God had made. And he said to the woman, "Indeed, has God said, 'You shall not eat from any tree of the garden'?" And the woman said to the serpent, "From the fruit of the trees of the garden we may eat; but from the fruit of the tree which is in the midst of the garden, God said, 'You shall not eat from it, and you shall not touch it, lest you die.'" And the serpent said to the woman, "You surely will not die! For God knows that in the day you eat from it your eyes will be opened, and you will be like God, knowing good and evil." Then the woman saw that the tree was good for food, and that it was a delight to the eyes, and that the tree was desirable to make one wise, so she took from its fruit and ate; and she gave also to her husband with her, and he ate. And the eyes of both of them were opened, and they knew that they were naked; and they sewed fig leaves together and made themselves loin coverings." (Genesis 3:1-7 LSB)

This passage from Genesis 3 very closely matches "forbidden snake meat eaten." Yet Genesis 3:1-7 says nothing about the serpent being killed, whereas this story insists that the serpent was killed. Does Genesis have anything to say about this serpent being killed? Indeed, we see the death of the serpent in the last line of this text, albeit speaking in the future tense:

> "And Yahweh God said to the serpent, "Because you have done this,
> Cursed are you more than any of the cattle,
> And more than every beast of the field;
> On your belly you will go,
> And dust you will eat
> All the days of your life;
> And I will put enmity
> Between you and the woman,
> And between your seed and her seed;
> He shall bruise you on the head,
> And you shall bruise him on the heel.'" (Genesis 3:14-15)

19. Henry Ling Roth, *The Natives of Sarawak and British North Borneo*, vol. 1 (New York: Truslove & Comba, 1896), p. 301.
20. Held, G. J. (1956). De Zondvloed. In G. J. Held (Eds.), Waropense teksten (Geelvinkbaai, Noord Nieuw-Guinea) Verhandelingen van het Koninklijk Instituut voor Taal-, Land- en Volkenkunde no. 20 (The Hague: Martinus Nijhoff, (pp. 28-44). p. 38

Alternatively, the idea that the serpent dies could have arisen in other ways: from the fact that death entered the world at that moment, or as a logical deduction if serpent meat is substituted for the forbidden fruit. In any case, this narrative theme is certainly connected with the Garden of Eden (Genesis 3).

The parallels become even more compelling if we consider that this same serpent shows up in several other story types. We have the "bathing woman ravished by serpent" stories[21], "serpent shot with arrow,"[22] "sea drain blocked by serpent,"[23] "serpent steals waters of immortality,"[24] and "serpent becomes a rainbow,"[25] "woman married serpent,"[26] and "snake causes Flood"[27] stories.

Connected with this body of traditions, we have found an ancient, pre-Columbian Aztec painting (Codex Vaticanus 3733), which reflects a memory of Eve and the Serpent. The woman named Cihuacohuatl was known as the "woman of our flesh" and the mother of the human race. Yet she was known as "serpent woman" and is "always represented with a great serpent", as we find her depicted here. She is also said to have "fallen from her first state of happiness and innocence."[28] Her twin sons, fighting, are also shown behind her.

Equally chilling is the fact that this serpent, in many of our "forbidden snake meat eaten" accounts, is no mere common snake. Rather, he is described as an archdemon or a spiritual figure in several traditions. The New Guineans describe him as "masalai" (spiritual) and a shape-shifter who can take the form of a man or a serpent. The Jivaro called it an "evil demon," the Miskito and Sumo described it as "some kind of spirit," and the Shuar say it was a spirit named Tsunki that took on the form of a serpent to influence humanity. Other Flood traditions containing an "arrow shot at creature" theme say it was a "spirit" that was shot and killed.

Equally chilling is the fact that this serpent is no mere common snake. Rather, he is described as an archdemon or a spiritual figure in several traditions.

Putting It Together (Fruits Dropped From Tree and Forbidden Snake Meat Eaten)

Let's put it together now. We have a body of tradition from New Guinea, Melanesia, Australia, and even South America, which conveys the following facts:

1. A hunter or group of people hunt and kill a special snake.
2. Despite a prohibition against its consumption, meat from the snake is eaten.
3. A Flood is determined to be sent against the people in judgment for eating meat of the forbidden snake.
4. One or a few people, who did not participate in this violation, receive advance warning of this Flood and take shelter on the highest tree. Most frequently this warning comes from the snake itself before it is killed.
5. One or two people climb to the top of a tall tree to escape the Flood, usually after receiving a forewarning. They alone survive, and all other people drown.
6. Unable to see the water level, they throw or drop a fruit down from the tree to discern whether land has appeared yet. They hear a splash, indicating the earth is still covered by water.

---

21. See, for example, the Kootenay, Lengua, Cashibo, and Mosetentribes in *Volume* 1.
22. See, for example, the Potawatomi, Acoma Pueblo, Menominee, and Bororo accounts in *Volume 1*.
23. See, for example, the Bunun and Kanakanavu texts earlier in this volume.
24. See texts from Japan and Taiwan's Dusun in this volume.
25. See, for example, the Murinbata text in this volume, and a Mundari (India) text: L. Nottrott, *Die Gossnersche Mission unter den Kolhs*, vol. 1 (Halle: Richard Mühlmann, 1895), pp. 59-60
26. See Watut in this volume, and Piros and Dorasque in *Volume 1*.
27. See Nanumanga, Kevasop, Manam Motu, and Barasana texts in this volume.
28. Alexander de Humboldt, *Researches Concerning the Institutions & Monuments of the Ancient Inhabitants of America*, trans. Helen Maria Williams, vol. 1 (London: Longman, 1814), pp. 195-196.

7. After waiting for a period, they throw a second fruit. Again they hear a splash, indicating the earth is still covered by water.
8. After waiting again for some time, they drop a fruit. This time they hear the sound of the fruit striking the earth. They realize the earth is now dry and the waters have subsided.
9. The survivors climb down from the tree and resettle the earth.

Does this sound familiar? Indeed, It has many common elements with the Garden of Eden and the Flood accounts in Genesis, albeit with some mixing and reassembling of the details. These include 1) a special serpent, 2) a forbidden fruit, 3) a special tree, 4) a human violation, 5) a prophecy or forewarning of a Flood, 6) a Flood global in scope, and 7) exploratory tests prior to debarking from the vessel or place of escape. We would be wrong to consider it coincidence that so many factors are present in both Genesis and this theme—especially as we see dozens of themes which also share so many elements both with this version and with Genesis. As for the mixing up of details, that is understandable and expected, given the confusion of languages at Babel and imperfect transmission of oral histories over thousands of years. Figure B-4 illustrates the origin of these themes.

Figure B-4: Proposed Origin of "Fruits Thrown from Tree" and "Forbidden Snake Meat Eaten" Themes

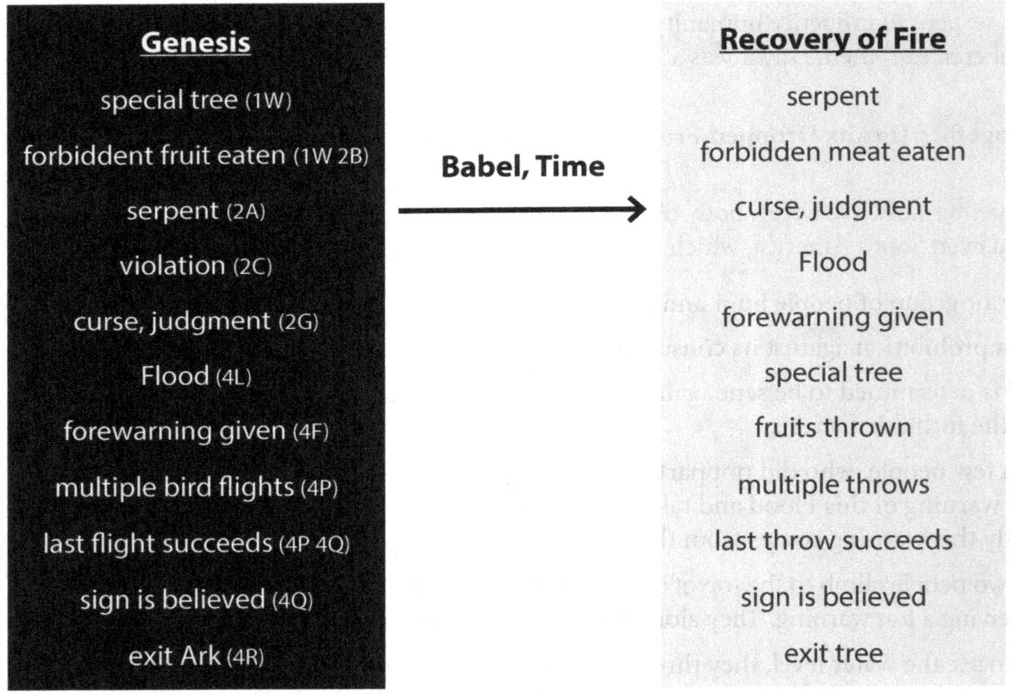

Note: See Figure B-1 for text elements and Scriptural references.

We continue to see the explanatory power of the biblical worldview! Dozens and dozens of narrative themes from cosmological traditions around the world can be directly accounted for if we begin with the Genesis record of events. We stare at a worldwide tapestry with an amazing variety of historical traditions, and Genesis can explain vast numbers of them, unlike any other historical text or tradition on earth. This is exactly what we should expect if the book of Genesis is true.

We stare at a worldwide tapestry with an amazing variety of historical traditions, and Genesis can explain vast numbers of them, unlike any other historical text or tradition on earth.

Quarrel between brothers causes Flood (Globally scattered)

A curious narrative theme that colors several Flood stories is that of a quarrel between two brothers. Unlike many other themes in Flood texts and other cosmological texts, it is very difficult to place this narrative theme in a particular geographical region. It is globally scattered. We find it in North and South America, Southeast Asia, southern China, the Philippines, Taiwan, Australia, New Guinea, and Polynesia.[29] Let us consider a few examples in Table B-6 below.

Table B-6: Examples of "Quarrel Between Brothers Causes Flood" Narrative Theme

Asian and Pacific Texts	North and South American Texts
Black Miao (China): "That catastrophe [the Flood] was in consequence of a quarrel between the two brothers A F'o and A-Zie."[30] **Kaluana** (Goodenough Island): "When they grew up, the two brothers Kawafolafola and Wameya quarreled bitterly about food and who was the better gardener. One night Wameya fastened up his house firmly and made it rain. The flood rose and carried away his house to the north until they were far enough away."[31] **Bidjandjara** (Australia): "The two brothers [Malgaru and Jaul] quarrelled. Malgaru went out hunting, but as soon as he was out of sight Jaul rushed to the waterbag. In a hurry to get at the water he jabbed at the taut skin with his club, making a hole in it. Water poured out. Malgaru came running back and tried to save the bag, but he could not stem the onrush of water. It spread across the land, drowning them both, and forming what is now the sea."[32] **Bahnar** (Vietnam): "Formerly, in the beginning, the kite took up a quarrel with the crab, and gave him a peck on the back so hard that his shell was pierced. We still see the mark of this famous pecking."[33]	**Wyandotte** (Ontario): There was a quarrel between two divine brothers, Sesta and Skareh. In the night Skareh stole all the earth's waters and held them in a giant bag in the sky. The people cried out for lack of water. Sesta, being concerned for the people's survival, took as an arrow a giant trunk of a pine tree, and shot it into the sky, piercing the bag. Yet now he had another problem, for the water spilled upon the earth and covered everything, even the hills.[34] **Maricopa** (Arizona): "The Brother met Coyote and called him brother, but Coyote would not reply. So a flood was sent to destroy Coyote and the earth and all its inhabitants. Small numbers were saved by clinging to trunks of trees that floated on the water. Coyote insisted the Brother should address him as Elder Brother. This was conceded."[35]

The stories are chasms apart in the details, but they share two elements: 1) a quarrel, fight, or contention that breaks out between two brothers in the ancient part, and 2) that this had some role in causing the Flood. The context of these stories also makes it clear that we are dealing with the same global Flood described in Genesis. And yet the Genesis Flood account (chapters 6 through 9) has nothing to say about a quarrel between brothers. How then are we to make sense of this narrative theme?

The observant reader will recall a text that is relevant to our discussion—not in Genesis 6 through 9, but in an earlier chapter. We are referring to Cain and Abel:

29. Examples in this book include the Black Miao, Bahnar, Pu Peo, Visaya, Tagalog, Kaluana, and Bidjandjara. Examples from *Volume 1* include the Wyandotte, Cree, Ojibwe, Miwok of Bodega Bay, Maricopa, and Secoya.
30. Samuel Clarke, *Among the Tribes of South-west China* (London: Morgan & Scott, 1911), pp. 43-44.
31. Young, M. W., *Magicians of Manumanua: Living Myth in Kaluana* (Berkeley: University of California Press, 1983), p. 228-232.
32. Berndt, R. M. & Berndt, C. H. (1977). *The World of the First Australians* (Ure Smith, Sydney), p. 401.
33. Guerlach, "Moeurs et Superstitions des Sauvages Bahnars," p. 479.
34. William Elsey Connelley, *Indian Myths* (New York: Rand McNally, 1928). Retrieved from: http://www.wyandotte-nation.org/culture/folk-lore-and-myths/indian-myths/.
35. Stewart Culin, "Games of the North American Indians," *Twenty-fourth Annual Report of the Bureau of American Ethnology* (Washington: GPO, 1907), p. 203–204.

> "So it happened in the course of time that Cain brought an offering to Yahweh of the fruit of the ground. Abel, on his part, also brought of the firstborn of his flock and of their fat portions. And Yahweh had regard for Abel and for his offering; but for Cain and for his offering He had no regard. So Cain became very angry, and his countenance fell. Then Yahweh said to Cain, "Why are you angry? And why has your countenance fallen? If you do well, will not your countenance be lifted up? And if you do not do well, sin is lying at the door; and its desire is for you, but you must rule over it." Then Cain spoke to Abel his brother; and it happened when they were in the field, that Cain rose up against Abel his brother and killed him." (Genesis 4:3-8, LSB)

The presence of a Cain and Abel element in Flood stories need not be surprising since it forms part of the corpus of historical knowledge possessed by those at Babel. Tribes and communities remembered the Flood, and they remembered Cain and Abel. But in some cases, they forgot where the boundary lay, and conflated them into one story.[36] This is well-accounted for by the view that takes Genesis as truth.

We should also take note that Genesis 4:15 says that God placed a "mark" upon Cain: "And Yahweh appointed a sign for Cain, so that no one who found him would strike him." (Genesis 4:15, LSB) The Hebrew word "oth," here translated as "sign," can be translated as mark, sign, omen, banner, or warning.

This may be what the Bahnar tradition refers to. "Formerly, in the beginning, the kite took up a quarrel with the crab, and gave him a peck on the back so hard that his shell was pierced. We still see the mark of this famous pecking."

Not every quarrel story involves brothers. Some involve a bird and a crab, like the Koho and Bahnar of Southeast Asia. Some involve a coyote or a raven, such as we find in the western United States. Some involve "the Great Hare" and a sea monster or serpent, such as we find in the midwestern states and in Canada.

However, there is another passage of Genesis that may be the inspiration for certain quarrel and fight stories, particularly those lacking the "brothers" element:

> "And I will put enmity
> Between you [the serpent] and the woman,
> And between your seed and her seed;
> He shall bruise you on the head,
> And you shall bruise him on the heel." (Genesis 3:15, LSB)

This fight between a man and a serpent—in which the serpent is ultimately defeated and killed—may be the inspiration for some of the versions alluded to above.

Item lifted from tree or ground causes Flood (New Guinea and Australia)

A curious theme appears in certain Flood stories from both Indonesia and South America.[37] Its most fundamental defining feature is that a forbidden item is taken or lifted. This error results in the Flood being unleashed, killing everyone on earth with the exception of a very small number of survivors. We will only survey this story briefly, but the core story is the following:

36. In other cases, such as the Aztecs, and the Dao tribe of New Guinea, they preserved a memory of Cain and Abel tradition, free of any mixing with the Flood or other stories.
37. Examples from this volume include texts from the Genaa, Horabi, Muyu, Tais of New Guinea, Yindjibarndi, and Muang. Examples from *Volume 1* include texts from the Ackawoio, Pemón, Wapishana and Taruma, Yabarana, Yuracare, Canella and Sherente, Kraho, and Yanomami. The Tao tribe of Taiwan's Orchid Island are included as well. It appears to be present in Africa too, which we will treat in the sequel.

1. There is an initial period of innocence and prosperity.
2. There is a prohibition against touching or lifting a special object.
3. Typically a magical tree is involved, which is the source of food or life.
4. A curious or covetous person violates the prohibition and removes something (typically from the tree). In some versions he cuts the tree.
5. Often a mischievous animal (a monkey) or a reptile is involved.
6. Water bursts from the special tree or other object. A globally destructive Flood ensues.
7. Divine judgment is explicitly stated or implied in the Flood.

Now if we begin with Genesis, all of these details can be accounted for. The tree that cannot be touched is the Tree of the Knowledge of Good and Evil, of which God strictly forbade eating its fruit. The mischievous animal or reptile is the Serpent (Satan taking the form of a snake). The divine judgment is the curse which took place in Genesis 3. And the Flood is Noah's Flood.

We would also note that this story is closely related to several other types, which include certain "special tree", "forbidden to cut down trees," and "forbidden snake meat eaten", and "hunting in wrong place" stories. This story, like so many others, can be well-explained from the view that Genesis records true history.

From the assortment of traditions below in Table B-7, the connections with Genesis can be clearly seen. The texts are only summarized here, but can be found in this *Volume* and *Volume 1*. Note that an African text is included in Table B-7 as well, which will be part of the eventual *Volume 3*.

Table B-7: Examples of "Item Lifted from Tree or Ground Causes Flood" Narrative Theme

Volume 1 **(N. and S. America)**	
Ackawoio (Venezuela and Guyana)	Initial innocence and harmony Animals made offerings to God who lived with them Magical tree in forest God deemed it best to chop it down, leaving only trunk Mischievous character (monkey) steals from tree Water burst from tree trunk, caused Flood Fruits dropped from tree to discern water level
Pemón (Venezuela)	Very similar to Ackawoio tradition above
Wapishana and Taruma (Guyana and Brazil)	Initial innocence and perfection God fed them from a magical tree that gave all kinds of food People discovered tree and indulged from it God cut down tree, which caused Flood Vague remnant of fruits dropped from tree theme
Yabarana (Venezuela)	Forbidden magical box opened A special sunbird flew out, cried out and caused a Flood Two people saved on a hill

Canella and Sherente (Brazil)	Warning given not to lift turtle Turtle is lifted Flood bursts out from under it Violator is carried by Flood to a tree
Kraho (Brazil)	Warning given not to lift turtle Turtle is lifted Flood bursts out from under it Pud rescues Pudlere by extending tree branch
Volume 2 **(E. Asia, Pacific)**	
Foraba (New Guinea)	Small pool of water at base of a tree contains grubs Hungry men come, eat grubs from pool These grubs were forbidden, stomachs rumble strangely Flood burst out
Horabi (New Guinea)	Man is thirsty His sister ignores prohibition against special water, gives to brother Man drinks taboo water, stomach begins to rumble strangely Flood burst out, woman turns into a bird
Muyu (New Guinea)	Very similar to Horabi and Genaa
Torres Strait	Special tree All kinds of people lived in it Someone burnt it down, left a stump only Tree trunk had a heartbeat Someone shot tree stump, water burst out, caused Flood
Pygmy peoples of Central African Republic	Chameleon heard noise coming from a tree Investigated strange tree. No water on earth at the time. Cut tree at the trunk with axe Water burst out, flooded earth
Yindjibarndi (Australia)	Stone lifted causes a Flood, reminiscent of Yanomami version from Brazil, bird (robin) does the action.
Warruwi (Australia)	Crow man disappointed with food (fish) given him In anger, decided to cut down sacred tree Other bird-men tried to stop him, warned a flood will come Cut tree down and caused Flood. Crow now eats carrion

Summary: Variant Flood Themes and Their Common Source

In short, if we are looking for a paradigm with broad power to explain the cosmological story types that recur in various parts of the world, we must look to Genesis. I truly believe that the smartest thing we can do if we want to reconstruct the oldest cosmologies of ancestral populations is to look to Genesis 1 through 11 and accept it. That is a costly and humbling decision, but it is also empowering.

I have put Genesis to the test while studying and exploring every ancient origin story I can find, and I have not been disappointed. Instead, I have repeatedly been amazed at the explanatory power of Genesis, whether it comes to "brother sister marriage" stories, or "fruits dropped from tree" or "recovery of fire" or "earth diver" or "woman ravished by serpent" or "forbidden snake meat eaten" or "world tree" or "brothers quarrel" or "fire flood" or "sacrifice offered to waters" or a wide number of other story types. This demonstrates the high antiquity, authenticity, and utter truth of the Genesis record.

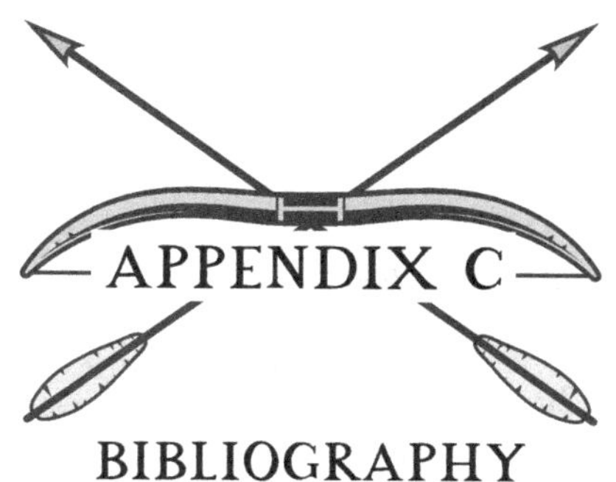

APPENDIX C

BIBLIOGRAPHY

Sources on China:

Arcones, Pedro Ceinos, "Dos Mitos de la creación de la minoría Kucong," *Chinaviva*. September 1, 2023. https://chinaviva.com/dos-mitos-de-la-creacion-de-la-minoria -kucong/

----------, *Sons of Heaven, Brothers of Nature: The Naxi of Southwest China* (Kunming: Papers of the White Dragon, 2012).

Atlas of Humanity, "Hani People." Retrieved 13 July, 2024 from https://www.atlasofhumanity.com/hani

B.B Vakhtin and R.F. Itsa, Эпические сказания народов южного Китая ("Epic tales of the peoples of southern China") (Moscow, 1956).

Baber, Edward Colburne, *Travels and Researches in Western China* (London: J. Murray, 1882.

Bender, Mark, "Echoes from Si Gang Lih: Burao Yilu's 'Moon Mountain,'" Asian Highlands Perspectives, vol. 10 (2011).

Biot, Edouard, *Le Tcheou-li: ou, Rites des Tcheou*, vol. 1 (Paris, 1851).

Brennecke, Stephen, "The Bronze Tree of Sanxingdui," *Journal of Creation*, Vol. 20, no. 2 (August, 2006). Retrieved from: https://creation.com/the-bronze-tree-of-sanxingdui-genesis-artefact Accessed 22 Feb. 2022.

Chan, Kei Thong, *Faith of our Fathers* (Shanghai: Publishing Group Orient, 2006).

Chen, Qinghao and Wang Quigui (eds.), "Collection of Guangxi Folk Tales, 2", "*Complete Collection of Chinese Folk Tales*", vol. 5 (Taipei, 1989).

----------"Collection of Hunan Folk Tales, 1", "*Complete Collection of Chinese Folk Tales*", vol. 17 (Taipei, 1989).

----------, "Collection of Gansu Folk Tales", "*Complete Collection of Chinese Folk Tales*", vol.29 (Taipei, 1989).

----------, "Collection of Guizhuo Folk Tales, 1", *Complete Collection of Chinese Folk Tales*, vol. 12 (Taipei, 1989).

----------, "Collection of Yunnan Folk Tales", 1, *Complete Collection of Chinese Folk Tales*, vol.7 (Taipei, 1989).

----------, "Collection of Yunnan Folk Tales, 2", *Complete Collection of Chinese Folk Tales*, vol.8 (Taipei, 1989).

----------, "Collection of Yunnan Folk Tales, 3", *Complete Collection of Chinese Folk Tales*, vol.9 (Taipei, 1989).

----------, "Collection of Guangdong Folk Tales", *Complete Collection of Chinese Folk Tales*, vol. 3 (Taipei, 1989).

Chock, Ginger Tong, *Genesis in Ancient China* (Honolulu: Eastward Garden, 2015).

Clarke, Samuel, *Among the Tribes of South-west China* (London: Morgan & Scott, 1911).

Eichler, Ranaan, "China is in the Bible," *Vetus Testamentum,* vol. 74, no. 1 (2023).

Fraser, J. O., "Work Among Aborigines in the Tengyueh District," *China's Millions*, vol. 21, new series (London: Morgan and Scott, 1913).

Geary, D. Norman et al., *The Kam People of China: Turning Nineteen* (New York: Routledge Curzon, 2003).

Global Prayer Digest, vol. 10, no. 4 (April 1991).

Graham, David Crockett, "Songs and Stories of the Ch'uan Miao," *Smithsonian Miscellaneous Collections*, vol. 123, no. 1 (Washington: Smithsonian, 1954).

Guan, Jixin, "Qiang Literature" (October 18, 2006). IELCASS. Retrieved 30 July, 2024 from http://iel.cass.cn/mzwxbk/gmzwxgl/200610/t20061018_2764291.shtml. Li Siying, "On the

Inheritance and Evolution of China's Flood and Human Recolonization Myth" (June 30, 2022). IELCASS. Retrieved 30 July, 2024 from http://iel.cass.cn/ztpd/shyj/zggdsh/202206/t20220630_5415027.shtml

Hattaway, Paul, Operation China: *Introducing All the Peoples of China* (Carlisle, UK: Piquant, 2000).

----------, *Shandong: The Revival Province* (2018).

Henry, A., "The Lolos and Other Tribes of Western China," *The Journal of the Anthropological Institute of Great Britain and Ireland*, vol. 33 (1903).

Ho, T'ing-jui, "A Comparative Study of Myths and Legends of Formosan Aborigines," *Asian Folklore and Social Life Monographs*, vol. 18 (Taipei: Orient Cultural Services, 1971).

Holm, David, *Killing a Buffalo for the Ancestors: A Zhuang Cosmological Text from Southwest China* (DeKalb, Illinois: Northern Illinois University Center for Southeast Asian Studies, 2003).

Huang, Yu, "Preliminary Study of the Yao 'King Ping's Charter,'" in *The Yao of South China: Recent International Studies* (Paris: Pangu, 1991).

Hudspeth, W. H., "A creation Story of the A-Hsi," *Folklore*, vol. 70, no. 2 (1959).

----------, "The A-Hsi Story of the Deluge," *Folklore*, vol. 71, no. 2 (1960).

Johnson, James J. S., "Genesis in Chinese Pictographs," *Acts & Facts*, vol. 44, no. 3 (2015).

Kang, C. H. and Ethel Nelson, *The Discovery of Genesis in China* (St. Louis: Concordia, 1979).

Kao, Lifeng, "Sacred Order: Cosmogonic Myth in the Chu Silk Manuscript", in *China's Origin and Creation Myths*, eds. Mineke Schipper, Ye Shuxian and Yin Hubin (Boston: Brill, 2011).

Kui, Shin Voo and Larry Hovee, "The Lamb of God Hidden in the Ancient Chinese characters," *CEN Technical Journal*, vol. 13, no. 1 (1999). Retrieved from: https://creation.com/images/pdfs/tj/tjv13n1chinese_lamb.pdf

LaPolla, Randy J. and Dory Poa, *Rawang Texts* (2001).

Lee, Archie Chi Chung, "When the Flood Narrative of Genesis Meets its Counterpart in China." (18 November, 2018).

Legendre, A. F., "The Lolos Of Kientchang, Western China," *Annual Report of the Board of Regents of the Smithsonian Institution*, 1911 (Washington: GPO, 1912).

Legge, James (trans.), "The Doctrine of the Mean," *The Chinese Classics*, vol. 1 (London: Trubner, 1861).

----------, "The Li Ki," *The Sacred Books of the East*, ed. F. Max Muller, vol. 28 (Oxford: Clarendon, 1885).

----------, "The She King," *The Chinese Classics*, vol. 4, part 2 (London: Trubner & Co., 1871).

----------, "The Shoo King," *The Chinese Classics*, vol. 3, part 1 (London: Trubner & Co., 1865).

Legge, James, *The Notions of the Chinese Concerning God and Spirits* (Hong Kong, 1852).

Liu, Yahu, "The Structure and Implications of the Flood Myths of Southern Nationalities" (April 23, 2009). Chinese Folklore Society. Retrieved 28 July, 2024 from https://www.chinafolklore.org/web/index.php?Page=2&NewsID=4519

Major, John S. et al., *The Huainanzi: A Guide to the Theory and Practice of Government in Early Han China* (New York: Columbia University Press, 2010).

Marr, Kendrick L and Xia Yong Mei, "Benincasa hispida (Cucurbitaceae) the "Pumpkin" of Asian Creation Stories?", *Economic Botany*, vol. 55, no. 4 (2001).

Medhurst, W. H., *A Dissertation on the Theology of the Chinese* (Shanghai: Mission Press, 1847).

Miller, Lucien, Gou Xu, and Xu Kun, *South of the Clouds: Tales from Yunnan* (Seattle: University of Washington Press, 1994).

Morse, Robert and Betty Morse, "Oral Tradition and Rawang Migration Routes," *Essays Offered to G. H. Luce by his Colleagues and Friends in Honor of his Seventy-fifth Birthday*, eds. Ba Shin, Jean Boisselier, A. B. Griswold, vol. 1 (Ascona, Switzerland: Artibus Asiac, 1966).

Nelson, Ethel, Richard Broadberry, and Ginger Tong Chock, *God's Promise to the Chinese* (Dunlap, TN: Read Books Publisher, 1997).

Oppitz, Michael and Elizabeth Hsu, *Naxi and Moso Ethnography* (Zurich: Völkerkundemuseum Zürich, 1998).

Paul Hattaway, *Tibet: The Roof of the World* (London: SPCK, 2020).

Rose, Archibald and J. Coggin Brown, "Lisu (Yawyin) Tribes of the Burma-China Frontier," *Memoirs of the Asiatic Society of Bengal*, vol. 3, no. 4 (1910).

Sarep, Hpung, "A Study of the Morphology of Verbs and Nouns in the Sinwal Dialect of the Rawang Language," *Linguistics of the Tibeto-Burman Area*, vol. 19, no. 2 (1996).

Savina, François M., *Histoire des Miao* (Hong Kong: Société des Missions Étrangères, 1924).

Schipper, Mineke, "Humanity's Beginnings in Creation and Origin Myths from Around the World," *China's Creation and Origin Myths* (Brill: Boston, 2011).

Shen, Zhengde (ed.),"Folk Tales of the Dai Ethnic Group in Xishuangbanna" (Kunming: Yunnan People's Publishing House, 1993).

Sun, Hongkai and Liu Guangkun, *A Grammar of Anong: Language Death Under Intense Contact* (Boston: Brill, 2009).

Tapp, Nicholas C. T., "Reflections on Fieldwork among the Yao," *Ethnicity and Ethnic Groups in China*, eds. Chiao Chien and Nicholas C. T. Tapp (1989).

Turner, Samuel, *An Account of an Embassy to the Court of the Teshoo Lama in Tibet* (London: W. Bulmer, 1800).

Vial, Paul, *Les Lolos: Histoire. Religion. Mœurs. Langue. Écriture* (Shanghai: Catholic Mission, 1898).

von Heine-Geldern, Robert, "Research on Southeast Asia; Problems and Suggestions," *American Anthropologist*, vol. 48, no. 2 (1946).

Wang, Shiyuan et al, "Hezhe, Monba, Lhoba, Jinuo"], "Chinese Ethnic Story Series", vol. 16 (Shanghai, 1995).

Wang, Xianzhao, "Minority Creation Myths: An Approach to Classification," in *China's Creation and Origin Myths*, eds. Mineke Schipper, Ye Shuxian, and Yin Hubin (Boston: Brill, 2011).

----------, "Analysis of the Mythical Motif of Brother-Sister Marriage among Chinese Multi-ethnic Groups" Institute of Ethnic Literature of the Chinese Academy of Social Sciences. December 6, 2010. Retrieved 11 July, 2024 from http://iel.cass.cn/ztpd/shyj/ssmzsh/201012/t20101206_2762700.shtml

Xu, Wenqing, "Myths and Legends of the Lian Nan Ba Pai Yao," *The Yao of South China: Recent International Studies*, eds. Jacques Lemoine and Chiao Chien (Paris: Pangu, 1991).

Sources on Korea and Japan:

Aston, W. G. (trans.), *Nihongi, Chronicles of Japan from the Earliest Times to A.D. 697* (London: The Japan Society, 1896).

"Kouri Island has an Okinawan version of the Adam and Eve legend." (February 26, 2014). Koury Island Guide. Retrieved 12 August, 2024 from https://www.kourijima.in/?p=7

Batchelor, John, "Notes on the Ainu," *Transactions of the Asiatic Society of Japan*, vol. 10 (Yokohama: R. Meiklejohn & Co., 1882).

Batchelor, John, *The Ainu and Their Folk-lore* (London: Religious Tract Society, 1901).

Chamberlain, Basil Hall (trans.), *Translation of "Ko-Ji-Ki" or "Records of Ancient Matters"* (Tokyo: J. L. Thompson, 1932).

Chamberlain, Basil Hall, *Aino Folk-tales* (London: Folklore Society, 1888).

Choi, In-hak, *A Type Index of Korean Folktales* (Seoul: Myong Ji University, 1979).

Eiichiro, Ishida, "Mother-Son Deities," *History of Religions*, vol. 4, no. 1 (1964).

Hokama, Shūzen, "Okinawa in the Matrix of Pacific Ocean Culture," *Okinawan Diaspora*, ed. Nakasone R. Y. (Honolulu: University of Hawaii Press, 2002).

Kaempfer, Engelburt, *The History of Japan*, vol. 2 (London, 1727).

Montanus, Arnoldus, trans. John Ogilby, *Atlas Japannensis* (London: Tho. Johnson, 1670).

Namjila, G., "Water-of-Immortality Myths in Altaic and Japanese Cultures," *China's Origin and Creation Myths*, eds. Mineke Schipper, Ye Shuxian and Yin Hubin (Boston: Brill, 2011).

Nevsky, Nikolai A., "The Moon and Immortality" (Tokyo, 1971).

Prevost, Abbé (ed.), "Bescriebung von Korea, der wehrlichen Tartaren und Tibet," *Allgemeine Historie der Reisen zu Wasser und Lande*, vol. 6 (Leipzig: Arkstee und Merkus, 1750).

Richardson, Don, *Eternity in Their Hearts* (Ventura, California: Regal, 2005).

Ross, John, *History of Corea* (London: Elliot Stock, 1891).

Sogabe, Kazuyuki et. al., ("Reconsidering the Myth of Brother and Sister Ancestry") (Seijo University: March 1, 2007).

Suzuki, Masakata, "Myths and Rituals of Hateruma Island", *Ethnological Studies*, vol. 42, no. 1 (1977).

Thomson, Rev. R. A., "Glimpses of the Liu Chiu Islands," *American Baptist Missionary Magazine*, vol. 79 (Boston: American Baptist Missionary Union, 1899).

Witzel, E. J. Michael and Kazuo Matsumura (trans.), "Central Asian and Japanese Mythology" (February 8, 2023).

Sources on Southeast Asia:

"Akar Umbi" *Magic River*. Retrieved 11 November, 2019 from http://www.magickriver.net/akarumbi.htm

"Man's Arrival," *Jungle Frontiers*, vol. 17 (Christian and Missionary Alliance, Summer 1963).

"State and Claims of Tavoy and Mergui," *Baptist Missionary Magazine*, vol. 34, no. 12 (Boston, 1853).

"Tavoy Mission," *Baptist Missionary Magazine*, vol. 34, no. 7 (Boston: American Baptist Missionary Union, 1853).

Abadie, Maurice, *Les Races du Haut-Tonkin* (Paris, 1924).

Abbott, Gerry and Khin Thant Han, *The Folk-tales of Burma* (Boston: Brill, 2000).

Antisdel, C. B., "The Lahoo Narrative of Creation," *Journal of the Burma Research Society*, vol. 1, part 1 (Rangoon, 1911).

Benjamin, Judson, "Journal of Mr. Benjamin," *Baptist Missionary Magazine*, vol. 34, no. 3 (Boston, 1853).

Bonifacy, Auguste Louis, "Etude sur les coutumes et la langue des Lolo et des La-qua du Haut-Tonkin," *Bulletin de l'Ecole Francaise d'Extreme Orient,* vol. 8 (1908).

----------, "Monographie des Mans Cao-Lan," *Revue Indochinoise*, vol. 2 (1905).

----------, "Monographie des Pa-teng et des Na-e," *Revue Indochinoise*, vol. 10 (Hanoi, 1908).

Borie, Reverend Father H., "An Account of the Mantras, A Savage Tribe in the Malay Peninsula," *Miscellaneous Papers Relating to Indo-China and the Indian Archipelago*, vol. 1 (London: Trubner & Co., 1887).

Bourlet, Antoine, "Les Thay," *Anthropos*, vol. 2 (1907).

Brockett, L. P., *The Story of the Karen Mission in Bassein* (Philadelphia, 1891).

Bruguière, Barthélemy, "Letter from Mgr. Brugiere, Bishop of Capse, to Mr. Gousquet," *Annales de l'Association de la Propagation de la Foi*, vol. 5, no. 25 (Paris, 1831).

Bui, Tan Loc, "Creation and Flood in Bru Legend," *Jungle Frontiers*, vol. 13 (Christian and Missionary Alliance: New York, Summer 1961).

Cassaigne, Jean, "Les Mois de la Région de Djiring," *Indochine*, vol. 4, no. 131 (1943).

Condominas, George, trans. Adrienne Foulke, *We Have Eaten the Forest* (New York: Hill and Wang, 1977).

Cottes, M., "Sur Les Populations Thai du Tonkin," *Premier Congrès International des Études d'Extrême Orient: Hanoi 1902*, (Hanoi: Schneider, 1903).

Cross, Edmund B., "How the Work of Christian Missions Began Among the Karens," *Baptist Missionary Magazine*, vol. 56 (Boston, 1876).

----------, "On the Karens," *Journal of the American Oriental Society*, vol. 4 (New York: Putnam, 1854).

Cupet, Pierre-Paul, "Chez les populations sauvages du sud de l'Annam," *Tour du Monde* (1893).

Dalton, Edward Tuite, *Descriptive Ethnology of Bengal* (Calcutta, 1872).

Dang, Nghiem Van, "The Flood Myth and the Origin of Ethnic Groups in Southeast Asia," Journal of American Folklore, vol. 106, no. 421 (American Folklore Society, 1993).

Dang, Nghiem Van, "Ve truyen qua bau-me o Viet Nam [Myths of the Gourd-Mother in Vietnam]", *Tap chi Van hoc* [Review of Literature], vol. 3 (1972).

de Berval, Rene, *The Kingdom of Laos: The Land of the Million Elephants and of the White Parasol* (Saigon: France-Asie, 1959).

de Lajonquière, Etienne Lunet, *Ethnographie du Tonkin Septentrional* (Paris: Ernest Leroux, 1906).

Diguet, Colonel E., *Les Montagnards du Tonkin* (Paris: Augustin Challamel, 1909).

Dournes, Jacques, *En Suivant La Piste Des Hommes Sur Les Hauts-Plateaux du Viet-Nam* (R. Julliard: Paris, 1955).

Elly, E. B., *Military Report on the Chin-Lushai Country* (Simla: Government Central Printing Office, 1893).

Elwin, Verrier, *Myths of the North-East Frontier of India* (Shillong, 1958).

Finot, Louis, "Recherches sur la littérature laotienne", *Bulletin de l'Ecole française d'Extreme-Orient*, vol. 17 (1917).

Forbes, Charles, *The Races of British Burma* (London: John Murray, 1878).

Funé, Jean, "Pioneering Among the Muong Tribe," *The Call of French Indochina and East Siam*, vol. 37 (Hanoi: Gospel Press, 1933).

Garland, George, *Der Mythus von der Sintflut* (Bonn: Marcus und Weber, 1912).

Gauss, Valdis, *The Formosan Great Flood Myths: An Analysis of the Oral Traditions of Ancient Taiwan* (Edwin Mellen Press, 2022).

Geurlach, Jean-Baptiste-Marie, "Moeurs et Superstitions des Sauvages Bahnars," *Les Misions Catholiques*, vol. 19 (Lyon: 1884).

Gilhodes, Charles, "Mythologie et religion des Katchins," *Anthropos*, vol. 3, no. 4 (1908).

Gilmore, David, "Karen Folk-lore II: The Fall of Man," *Journal of the Burma Research Society*, vol. 1, no. 2 (1910).

Guerlach, "Moeurs et Superstitions des Sauvages Bahnars," *Les Misions Catholiques*, vol. 19 (Lyon: 1884).

Halliday, Robert, *The Talaings* (Rangoon: Government Press, 1917).

Hanson, Ola, *The Kachins, Their Customs and Traditions* (Rangoon: American Baptist Mission Press, 1913).

Huy, Vọng Bùi, *Mộ Mường ở Hòa Bình ("Muong Tomb in Hoa Binh")* (Hanoi, 2016). Manh Hoang Quang, "Đại hồng thủy trong truyền thuyết của dân tộc Mường – Hòa Bình" ["Great flood in the legend of the Muong - Hoa Binh people"], July 14, 2022.

Izikowitz, Karl Gustav, *Lamet: Hill Peasants in French Indochina* (New York: AMS Press, 1979).

Jinghua, Huang, Chujing Yang, and Si Chen, "Spatial Imagination in Sacred Narratives of Mountain Communities in Western Yunnan, China," *Religions*, vol. 15 (2024).

Jouin, B. Y., "Les Traditions des Rhadé," *Bulletin de la Société des Études Indochinoises*, new series, vol. 25, no. 4 (Saigon: 1950).

Kemlin, Émile, "Alliances chez les Reungao," *Bulletin de l'Ecole Française d'Extreme-Orient*, vol. 17 (1917).

----------, "Au Pays Jaraï," *Les Missions Catholiques*, vol. 41 (1909).

Landes, Antony, Contes et *Légendes Annamites* (Saigon: Colonial Printing Office, 1886).

Lewis, Paul W., *Ethnographic Notes on the Akhas of Burma*, vol. 1 (1969).

Lindell, Kristina, Jan-Ojvind Swahn, Damrong Tayanin, "The Flood: Three Northern Kammu Versions of the Story of Creation," *The Flood Myth*, ed. Alan Dundes (Berkeley: University of California Press, 1988).

Logan, J. R., "The Orang Binua of Johore," *Journal of the Indian Archipelago and Eastern Asia*, vol. 1 (Singapore, 1847).

Maitre, Henri, *Les Jungles Moï: Exploration et Histoire des Hinterlands Moï du Cambodge, de la Cochinchine, de l'Annam et du bas Laos* (Paris: E. Larose, 1912).

Malleret, Louis, "Quelques Légendes des Moi de Cochinchine," *Bulletin de la Société des Etudes Indochinoises*, vol. 21 (1946).

Mason, Francis, *The Karen Apostle: Or, Memoir of Ko Thah-byu, the First Karen Convert* (Boston: Gould, Kendall and Lincoln, 1843).

Mason, Ken, A Bibliography of Karenic Linguistics (Chiang Mai: Payap University Department of Linguistics, 2004).

Mole, Robert L., *The Montagnards of South Vietnam: A Study of Nine Tribes* (Tokyo: Tuttle, 1970).

Mouhot, M. Henri, *Travels in the Central Parts of Indo-China [Siam], Cambodia and Laos*, vol. 2 (London: Murray, 1864).

Neufville, Captain John Bryan, "On the Geography and Population of Assam," *Selections from the Records of the Bengal Government*, vol. 23 (Calcutta, 1855).

Nguyen, Tan Dac, "From the Laotian Story of the Gourd to the Deluge Legend of Southeast Asia," *Vietnam Social Sciences*, vol. 3 (Hanoi: 1985).

Obayashi, Taryo, "Myths and Legends of the Lawa and Karen in Northwestern Thailand," "Ethnological Research", vol. 29 (1964).

Peng, Yvonne Young Ai, "Be the Voice of the Voiceless Orang Seletar," *INFO Johore Bar* (January 2012). http://johorebar.org.my/wp-content/uploads/2015/01/Page-55-56-Be-the-voice-of-the-voiceless-Orang-Seletar-by-Yvonne-Young.pdf

Pham, Van Hung (2017), *Aspects of Philosophy in Mo Muong Hoa Binh*, PhD Thesis. Hanoi National University of Education.

Phan, Phuong, "Do-Ta Vong: Ngôi làng tiên cảnh." ["Do-Ta Vong: Fairyland Village"]. Báo Quảng Bình [Quang Binh Newspaper Website]. Retrieved 12 January, 2024 from https://baoquangbinh.vn/Multimedia/emagazine/202010/do-ta-vong-ngoi-lang-tien-canh-2181628/

Phayre, Sir Arthur Purves, "On the History of the Burmah Race," *Transactions of the Ethnological Society of London*, vol. 5 (London: John Murray, 1867).

----------, *History of Burma* (London: Trubner, 1883).

Pitiphat, Sumitr, "The Religion and Beliefs of the Black Tai, and a Note on the Study of Cultural Origins," *Journal of the Siam Society*, vol. 68, part 1 (Bangkok: Siam Society, 1980).

Roux, Henri, "Les Tsa Khmu," *Bulletin de l'Ecole française d'Extrême-Orient*, vol. 27 (1927).

Rundall, Major Frank M., "The Siyin Chins," *Royal Geographical Society Supplementary Papers*, vol. 3 (London: John Murray, 1893).

Schrock, Joann L. et. al. (American University), *Minority Groups in the Republic of Vietnam* (Washington: Department of the Army, 1966).

Scott, Sir James George, "Indo-Chinese," *The Mythology of All Races*, vol. 12, p. 265. Scott, *Gazetteer of Upper Burma and the Shan States* (Rangoon, 1900).

Scott, Sir James George, *Burma: A Handbook of Practical Information* (London: Daniel O'Connor, 1921).

----------, *Gazetteer of Upper Burma and the Shan States* (Rangoon, 1900).

Skeat, Walter William, *Fables and Folk-tales from an Eastern Forest* (Cambridge: University Press, 1901).

Tan, Zhi Xuan, "A Sketch Grammar of Seletar." Master's Thesis (Singapore, Nanyang Technological University, 2022), pp. 226-228. https://hdl.handle.net/10356/165162

Tegenfeldt, Herman, *A Century of Growth: The Kachin Baptist Church of Burma* (South Pasadena, CA: William Carey Library, 1974).

Wall, Barbara, *Les Nya Hön: Étude Ethnographique d'une Population du Plateau des Bolovens* (Sud-Laos) (Ventiene: Vithagna, 1975).

White, Macleod, *The Gospel in Burmah* (New York: Shelton, 1860).

Wilhelm, Richard, *Chinesische Volksmärchen* (Jena, Germany: Eugen Diederichs, 1921).

Sources on Taiwan:

Anon., "Rambles in Formosa," *The Japan Weekly Mail*, vol. 28, no. 7 (Yokohama: 14 August, 1897).

Benedek, D., *The Songs of the Ancestors, A Comparative Study of Bashiic Folklore* (Taipei: SMC Publishing Inc., 1991)

Beyer, H. Otley, "Origin Myths Among the Mountain Peoples of the Philippines," *The Philippine Journal of Science*, ed. Alvin J. Cox, Volume 8, Section D (Manila: Bureau of Printing, 1913).

Bompas, Cecil Henry, trans., *Folklore of the Santal Parganas* (London: David Nutt, 1909).

Bureau of Aboriginal Affairs, *Report on the Control of the Aborigines in Formosa* (Taihoku, Taiwan: 1911).

Chen, I-chun, *The Making of Ethnicity in Postwar Taiwan: a case study of Kavalan ethnic identity. PhD Dissertation* (University College London. England, 2000).

Cowsill, P. (2008). *Kiraya or Kira, Taiwan.* Retrieved 5 March, 2021 from http://patrick-cowsill.blogspot.com/2008/03/kiraya-or-kira-taiwan.html.

Enn, Rosa, "Governance, Empowerment, and Environmental Justice – the Indigenous Tao of Orchid Island." (Doctoral Thesis, Universitat Wien, 2015).

Fleeson, Katherine Neville, *Laos Folklore of Farther India* (New York: Fleming H. Revell, 1899).

Gauss, Valdis, *The Formosan Great Flood Myths: An Analysis of the Oral Traditions of Ancient Taiwan* (Mellen Press, 2022).

Gordon, Surgeon General Charles Alexander, "Notes On The Ethnology And Ancient Chronology Of China" *Journal of the Transactions of the Victoria Institute*, vol. 23 (London: Victoria Institute, 1890).

Kim, Kwang-Ok. "The Taruko and their Belief System." PhD Thesis (Saint Catherine's College, Oxford University, 1980).

Lee, M. Y., "Culture and History Matter: Historical Trauma and Culture Protective Factors on Alcohol Use Among Truku Tribal People." PhD thesis (Seattle, University of Washington, 2017).

Li, Paul Jen-Kuei and Shigeru Tsuchida, "Pazih Texts and Songs," Language and Linguistics Monograph Series, No. A2-2 (Taipei: Institute of Linguistics Academia Sinica, 2002).

Lin, P. H., Tseng J. H., and Lin, P. C., "A study of applying Sakizaya Tribe's Palamal (the Fire God Ritual) into cultural creative products design." in *Cross-Cultural Design: 6th International Conference, CCD 2014, Held as Part of HCI International 2014, Heraklion, Crete, Greece, June 22-27, 2014, Proceedings*, ed. Rau P. L. P. (2014).

Liu, B. X., *The Legend of the Ancestors of the Yami Iratay Tribe* (Taiwan: Institute of Ethnology, Academia Sinica, 1981).

Pasuya, Poiconu, *Literary History of Taiwanese Indigenous Peoples*, vol. 1, trans. Wordsworth (Taipei: National Academy for Educational Research and Le Jin Books, 2012).

Pu, Chung-cheng, "The Connection between Myth and Social Change: a Truku Example," eds. Tu Kuo-ch'ing and R. Backus, *Taiwan Literature English Translation Series*, no. 24 (Santa Barbara: UC Santa Barbara, 2009).

Shigeru, T, "Japanese Contribution to the Linguistic Studies of the Formosan Indigenous Languages," in

Austronesian Taiwan: Linguistics, History, Ethnology, Prehistory, ed. David Blundell (Taiwan: Shung Ye Museum of Formosan Aborigines, 2009).

----------, "Kanakanavu Texts (Austronesian Formosan)," *Endangered Texts of the Pacific Rim* (Osaka: Osaka, Gakuin University, 2003).

----------, "Preliminary Reports on Saisiyat: Phonology," *Gengo Kenkyu (Journal of the Linguistic Society of Japan)*, Volume 46 (1964).

Tien Z. Y., *Myths and Legends of the Truku* (Taichung, Morning Star Press, 2020).

----------, *Myths, Legends, and the Fire God's Ceremony of Sakizaya* (Taichung, Taiwan: Morning Star Press, 2019).

Vanoverbergh, Morice, "Isneg Tales," *Folklore Studies: Journal of Far Eastern Folklore*, vol. 14 (Tokyo: S.V.D. Research Institute, 1955).

Wilson, Laurence L., *Apayao Life and Legends* (Philippines, 1947).

Wu, J., *Songs and Bonfires* (Taiwan: Jih-Tung Art Printing Co., 2019).

Zhong, Zhi-cheng, "The Forgotten Creation Myths of Taiwan," trans. Deh I Chen. Indigenous Sight, October 23, 2018. Retrieved 3 March, 2023 from https://insight.ipcf.org.tw/en-US/article/28

Sources on The Philippines:

Cole, Fay-Cooper, *The Tinguian: Social, Religious, and Economic Life of a Philippine Tribe* (Chicago: Field Museum of Natural History, 1922).

----------, *The Wild Tribes of Davao District, Mindanao* (Chicago, 1913).

Cole, Mabel Cook, *Philippine Folk Tales* (Chicago: A. C. McClurg & Co., 1916).

Demetrio, Francisco, "Creation Myths Among the Early Filipinos," *Asian Folklore Studies*, vol. 27, no. 1 (1968).

Esteban, Rolando, Arthur P. Casanova, and Ivie. C. Esteban, *Folktales of Southern Philippines* (2011).

Eugenio, Damania L., *Philippine Folk Literature* (Quezon City, Philippines: University of the Philippines Press, 1989).

Fansler, Dean Spruill, *Filipino Popular Tales* (New York: American Folk-lore Society, 1921).

Hobby, Jeneen and Timothy L. Gall, eds., *Worldmark Encyclopedia of Cultures and Daily Life*, vol. 4 (Pennsylvania State University, 2009).

Moss, C.R., "Nabaloi Tales," *University of California Publications in American Archaeology and Anthropology*, vol. 17, no. 5 (Berkeley: University of California Press, 1924).

Paredes, Oona Thommes, "True Believers: Higaunon and Manobo Evangelical Protestant Conversion in Historical and Anthropological Perspective," *Philippine Studies*, Vol. 54, No. 4 (2006).

Perez, Angel, *Igorrotes: Estudio geográfico y etnográfico sobre algunos distritos del Norte de Luzon*, vol. 1 (Manila: 1902).

Promon, Myrna, "Pinukis," trans. Felicia Brichoux, (Summer Institute of Linguistics, 2002). Retrieved from https://www.sil.org/resources/archives/48638

Saway, Datu Migketay Victorino L. (Adolino), "Talaandig Flood Story." August 26, 2011. Retrieved 15 December, 2023 from https://talaandigsite.blogspot.com/2011/08/talaandig-flood-story.html.

Stone, Roger, Analyzing Ayta Abellen Narratives for Peak, Participant Reference, Information Type and Fronting (Summer Institute of Linguistics, 2007).

Teanco, Phyllis, "The Indigenous Peoples (IPs) and their Ancestral Domain amid the pandemic: the Higaonon community as nature frontliners" (July 2021). Pre-print paper retrieved 18 November, 2023 from https://www.researchgate.net/publication/353513176_The_Indigenous_Peoples_IPs_and_their_Ancestral_Domain_amid_the_pandemic_the_Higaonon_community_as_nature_frontliners

Thévenot, Melchisédec (trans.), "Relation des Isles Philipines," in *Relations de Divers Voyages Curieux*, vol. 1 (Paris: Thomas Moette, 1696 (2nd edition).

Wolfe, Leslie, "The Primitive Religions of the Philippine Islands." Master's Thesis. Drake University Bible College (Des Moines, Iowa, 1922).

Sources on Oceania:

Barthel, Thomas Sylvester, *The Eighth Land: The Polynesian Discovery and Settlement of Easter Island* (Honolulu: University of Hawaii Press, 1978).

Bollig, Laurentius, *Die Bewohner der Truk-Inseln. Religion, Leben und kurze Grammatik eines Mikronesiervolkes* (Münster: Aschendorff, 1927).

Brown, George, *Melanesians and Polynesians: Their Life-histories Described and Compared* (London: MacMillan and Co., 1910).

Bubu, Samuel, "The Great Flood," trans. Raymond Johnston, *Legends from Papua New Guinea*, ed. K. A. McElhanon (Ukarumpa, Papua New Guinea: Summer Institute of Linguistics, 1976).

Burrows, William, "Some Notes and Legends of a South Sea Island," *Journal of the Polynesian Society*, vol. 32, No. 3 (September 1923).

Caillot, Auguste Charles Eugène, *Mythes, légendes et traditions des Polynésiens* (Paris: Ernest Leroux, 1914).

Christian, F. W., *The Caroline Islands* (New York: Charles Scribner's Sons, 1899).

Codrington, Robert Henry, *The Melanesians: Studies in their Anthropology and Folklore* (Oxford: Clarendon Press, 1891).

Ellis, William, *Polynesian Researches*, vol. 1 (London: Fisher, Son, & Jackson, 1831).

----------, *Polynesian Researches*, vol. 4 (London: Fisher, Son, & Jackson, 1831).

Emory, Kenneth P., "The Tuamotuan Creation Charts By Paiore," *Journal of the Polynesian Society*, vol. 48, no. 1 (Wellington, NZ: The Polynesian Society, 1939).

Englert, Sebastian, *Leyendas de Isla de Pascua. Textos Bilingues* (Santiago, Chile: Universidad de Chile, 1980).

Fornander, Abraham, *An Account of the Polynesian Race*, vol. 1 (London: Trubner & Co., 1878).

Fox, Charles Elliot, *The Threshold of the Pacific: An Account of the Social Organization, Magic And Religion of the People of San Cristoval In the Solomon Islands* (London: K. Paul, Trench, Trubner & Co., 1924).

Gill, William Wyatt, *Life in the Southern Isles* (London: Religious Tract Society, 1876).

Hongi, Hare (trans.), "A Maori Cosmogony," *Journal of the Polynesian Society*, vol. 16 (1907).

Horley, Paul and Lilian López Labbé, "A new manuscript of Pua Ara Hoa ‘a Rapu from the Archives of William Mulloy, Part 1: Description of the Manuscript," *Rapa Nui Journal*, vol. 28, no. 2 (University of Hawaii Press, 2014).

Humphreys, Clarence Blake, *The Southern New Hebrides: An Ethnological Record* (Cambridge: University Press, 1926).

Inglis, John, "Report of a Missionary Tour in the New Hebrides," *Journal of the Ethnological Society of London*, vol. 3 (1854).

Kubary, John S., "Die Religion der Pelauer," *Allerlei aux Volks- und Menschenkunde*, vol. 1 (Berlin: Ernst Siegfried Mittler: 1888).

Malo, David and N. B. Emerson (trans.), *Hawaiian Antiquities* (Honolulu: Hawaiian Gazette, 1898).

McFarlane, Samuel, *The Story of the Lifu Mission* (London: James Nisbet & Co., 1873).

Meier, Josef. "Mythen und Sagen der Admiralitätinsulaner," *Anthropos*, vol. 2 (Salzburg, 1907).

Nicholas, John Liddiard, *Narrative of a Voyage to New Zealand, Performed in the Years 1814 and 1815, in Company with the Rev. Samuel Marsden* (London: J. Black and Son, 1817), vol. 1.

Palmer, J. Linton, "Marquesan Tradition of the Deluge," *Proceedings of the Liverpool Literary and Philosophical Society*, vol. 31 (London: Longmans, 1877).

Paton, John G., John G. Paton, *Missionary to the New Hebrides: An Autobiography Edited by his Brother* (London: Hodder and Stoughton, 1898).

Powell, Thomas, "A Samoan Tradition of Creation and the Deluge," *Journal of the Transactions of the Victoria Institute*, vol. 20 (London: Victoria Institute, 1887).

Prévost, Abbé (ed.), *Allgemeine Historie der Reisen zu Wasser und Lande*, vol. 18 (Leipzig: 1764).

Roeling, Sebastiaan, *The Resilience of Easter Island: A Historical Ethnography* (Lulu, 2015).

Semper, Karl, *Die Palau-Inseln im Stillen Ocean* (Leipzig: Brodbaus, 1873).

Shaler, William, "Journal of a Voyage Between China and the North-western Coast of America, made in 1804," *The American Register: Part I for 1808*, vol. 3 (Philadelphia, 1808).

Smith, Percy, *Havaiki: The Original Home of the Maori* (Christchurch: Whitcomb and Tombs, 1904).

Thomson, William Campbell, "The 'Stone Age' in Australasia,' *Proceedings and Transactions of the Queensland Branch of the Royal Geographical Society of Australasia*, vol. 8 (Brisbane: Pole, Outridge &. Co., 1893).

Turner, George, *Nineteen Years in Polynesia* (London: John Snow, 1861).

----------, Samoa, *A Hundred Years Ago and Long Before* (London: MacMillan & Co, 1884).

White, John, *The Ancient History of the Maori*, vol. 1 (Wellington: George Disbury, 1887).

Wilkes, Charles, *Narrative of the United States Exploring Expedition of the Years 1838, 1839, 1840, 1841, 1842*, vol. 3 (Philadelphia: Lea & Blanchard, 1845).

Williams, Thomas, ed. George Stringer Rowe, *Fiji and the Fijians*, vol. 1 (Boston: Congregational Publishing, 1858).

Sources on New Guinea:

"Storytelling Time! Here Are 4 Brief Folklore of Lake Sentani." *West Papua Diary*, 22 January 2023. Retrieved 18 April, 2023 from https://westpapuadiary.com/storytelling-time-here-are-4-brief-folklore-of-lake-sentani/.

Amot, Adam, "The Great Flood, *Legends from New Guinea: Book 2*, ed. Donald Stokes (1996).

Ballard, Chris, "The Death of a Great Land. Ritual, History and Subsistence Revolution in the Southern Highlands of Papua New Guinea," PhD Dissertation, vol. 2 (Canberra: Australian National University, 1995).

Biersack, Aletta, "Sacrifice and Regeneration among Ipilis: The View from Tipinini," (Eds.), *Fluid Ontologies: Myth, Ritual, and Philosophy in the Highlands of Papua New Guinea*, eds. L. R. Goldman and C. Ballard (Westport, CT: Bergin & Garvey. 1998).

Bragge, Laurie, *A History of New Guinea's Sepik Region*, vol. 1, part 1 (Papua New Guinea Association of Australia, 2023).

Bunanta, Murti, *Indonesian Folktales* (Westport, Connecticut: Libraries Unlimited, 2003).

Chalmers, James and William Wyatt Gill, *Work and Adventure in New Guinea, 1877 to 1885* (London: Religious Tract Society, 1885).

De Vries, L. J., *A Short Grammar of Inanwatan, an Endangered Language of the Bird's Head of Papua, Indonesia* (Canberra: Pacific Linguistics, 2004).

De'Ath, Colin and Mary R. Mennis, *Merging Men and Nature: Myths of Melanesia* (Boroko, Papua New Guinea: Institute of Papua New Guinea Studies, 1981).

Drabbe, Peter, "Folk-Tales from Netherlands New Guinea (Continued)," *Oceania*, vol. 20, no. 1 (New South Wales: University of Sydney, 1949).

Elmberg, John-Erik, "Balance and Circulation Tradition and Change among the Mejprat of Irian Barat," *Monograph Series*, vol. 12 (Stockholm: Ethnographical Museum, 1968).

Fischer, Hans, *Watut: Notizen zur Kultur eines Melanesierstammes in Nordost-Neuguinea* (Braunschweig: Limbach, 1963).

Foley, William A., *The Yimas Language of New Guinea* (Stanford: Stanford University Press, 1991).

Galis, K. W., *Etnografische notities over het Senggi-gebied (onderafdeling Hollandia)* (Government of Dutch New Guinea, 1957).

Gilberthorpe, Emma, "Pathways to Development: Identity, Landscape and Industry in Papua New Guinea," *Landscape, Power and Process: Re-Evaluating Traditional Environmental Knowledge* (New York: Berghahn Books, 2012).

Glasse, R. M., "The Huli of the Southern Highlands," Gods, Ghosts and Men in Melanesia, eds. P. Lawrence and M. J. Meggitt (Melbourne: Oxford University Press, 1965).

Held, G. J., "De Zondvloed," in *Waropense teksten (Geelvinkbaai, Noord Nieuw-Guinea)* (The Hague: Martinus Nijhoff, 1956)

Hoey, Tom and John Mackay, "The Biami Legends of Creation and Noah's Flood," *Creation*, vol. 7, no. 2 (1984), pp. 12-13. Retrieved 15 November, 2018 from https://creation.com/the-biami-legends-of-creation-and-noahs-flood

Holtker, Georg, "Aus dem Kulturleben der Kire-Puir am Unteren Ramu (Neuguinea)," *Jahrbuch des Museums Für Völkerkunde Zu Leipzig*, vol. 19 (Berlin: Akademie-Verlag, 1962).

----------, "Mythen und Erzahlungen der Monumbo- und Ngaimbom-Papua," *The Geographical Journal*, vol. 60 (St. Augustin, Germany: Anthropos-Institut, 1965).

Kamma, Freerk C., *Religious Texts of the Oral Tradition from Western New-Guinea (Irian Jaya) Part A* (Leiden: E. J. Brill, 1975).

----------, *Religious Texts of the Oral Tradition From Western New-Guinea (Irian Jaya) Part B* (Leiden: E. J. Brill, 1978).

----------, *Koreri Messianic Movements in the Biak-Numfor Culture Area* (Hague: Martinus Nijhoff, 1972).

Ker, Annie, *Papuan Fairy Tales* (London: MacMillan, 1910).

LaHaye, Tim F. and John D. Morris, *The Ark on Ararat* (New York: Pocket Books, 1977).

Landtman, Gunnar, *The Folk-Tales of the Kiwai Papuans* (Helsingfors: Finnish Society of Literature, 1917).

Lefaan, Adolina V. Samosir, "Revealing The Leadership Characters of Women of Arfak Tribe, West Papua, Through Oral Literature," *Proceedings of The International Conference on Literature*, vol. 1, no. 1 (2019).

Lehner, Ernst, "Myths and Stories of Susure, North-East New Guinea," *Anthropos*, vol. 70 (1975).

Lithgow, David R., "Austronesian Languages: Milne Bay and Adjacent Islands (Milne Bay Province), *New Guinea area languages and language study*, ed. Stephen A. Wurm, vol. 2 (1976).

Miedema, Jelle, "The Water Demon and Related Mythic Figures: The Bird's Head Peninsula of Irian Jaya / Papua in Comparative Perspective," *Bijdragen tot de Taal-, Land- en Volkenkunde, vol. 156, no. 4* (2000).

Moszkowski, Max, "Die Völkerstamme am Mamberamo in Holländisch-Neuguinea und auf den vorgelagerten Insein," *Zeitschrift für Ethnologie*, vol. 43 (1911).

Murphy, Kevin, "The cultural organization of social difference and relatedness at the border between Australia and Papua New Guinea." PhD Dissertation (October 2013: The Australian National University).

Phillips, Donald Scott, *Prophecies of Pale Skin* (Kindle Edition, 2013).

Poignant, Roslyn, Oceanic *Mythology: The Myths of Polynesia, Micronesia, Melanesia, Australia* (London: Hamlyn, 1967).

Richardson, Don, "Redemptive Analogy," *Perspectives on the World Christian Movement*, eds. Ralph Winter and Steven C. Hawthorne (Pasadena: William Carey Library, 2009).

Rombouts, P. W., "The Arso Version of the Story of the Flood," *Bulletin of Irian Jaya Development*, vol. 2, no. 3 (Jayapura: University of Cenderawasih, 1973).

Schebesta, Josef, "Vier Sagen in der Sepa-Sprache (Neuguinea)," *Wiener Zeitschrift für die Kunde des Morgenlandes*, vol. 38 (1932).

Schleiermacher, P. Chr., "Religiose Anschauungen und Gebrauche der Bewohner von Berlinhafen (Deutsch Neuguinea," *Globus*, vol. 78, No. 1 (Brunswick, Germany: Druck und Verlag, 1900).

Silverman, Eric K., "The Waters of Mendangumeli: A Masculine Psychoanalytic Interpretation of a New Guinea Flood Myth--and Women's Laughter," *Journal of American Folklore*, vol. 129 (2016).

Voorhoeve, C. L., "A Remarkable Chain Tale from New Guinea," *A Mosaic of Languages and Cultures: Studies Celebrating the Career of Karl J. Franklin*, eds. Kenneth A. McElhanon and Ger Reesink (Dallas: SIL International, 2010).

Wagner, Roy, *Asiwinarong: Ethos, Image, and Social Power among the Usen Barok of New Ireland* (Princeton: Princeton University Press, 1986).

Wagner, Roy, *Lethal Speech: Daribi Myth as Symbolic Obviation* (London: Cornell University Press, 1978).

Winduo, Steven Edmund, "Reconstituting Indigenous Oceanic Folktales," *University of Hawaii Manoa International Symposium; Folktales and Fairy Tales* (2010).

Young, Michael W., *Magicians of Manumanua: Living Myth in Kaluana* (Berkeley, University of California Press, 1983).

Z'Graggen, John, "Topics of New Guinea legends," *Asian Folklore Studies*, vol. 42, no. 2 (1983).

Sources on Indonesia:

Adriani, Nicolaus and Albertus C. Kruijt, *De Bare'e-sprekende Toradja's van Midden-Celebes*, vol. 1 (Batavia: Landsdrukkerij, 1912).

Arndt, Paul P., "Demon und Padzi, die feindlichen Brüder des Solor-Archipels," *Anthropos*, vol. 33 (1938).

Beker, G., "Het oogst- en offerfeest bij den Nage-stam te Boa Wai (Midden-Flores)," *Bijdragen tot de Taal-land- en Volkenkunde van Nederlandsch-Indie*, vol. 57 (1913).

Cameron, Alexander Mackenzie, "Notes from Borneo, Illustrative of Passages in Genesis," *Transactions of the Society of Biblical Archaeology*, vol. 2 (London: Longmans, Green, Reader, and Dyer, 1872).

Chatelin, L.N.H.A., "Godsdienst en Bijgeloof der Niassers," *Tijdschrift voor Indische Taal- land en Volkenkunde, vol. 26* (Batavia: W. Bruining, 1881).

dos Santos, *Eduardo, Kanoik: Lendas e Mitos de Timor* (Lisboa: Serviço de Publicações da Mocidade Portuguesa, 1967).

Gerland, George, *Der Mythus von der Sintflut* (Bonn: Marcus and Weber, 1912).

Halcombe, J. J. (ed.), *Mission Life*, vol. 3 (London: Rivingtons, 1867).

Helfrich, O.L., "Nadere Bijdrage Tot De Kennis Van Het Engganeesch," *Bijdragen tot de Taal-, Land- en Volkenkunde van Nederlandsch-Indië*, vol. 71 (Hague: Martinus Nijhoff, 1916).

Hose, Charles and William McDougal, *The Pagan Tribes of Borneo*, vol. 2 (London: MacMillan, 1912).

Jonker, J. C. G. and J. Fanggidaej, "Rottineesche Verhalen," *Bijdragen tot de Taal-, Land- en Volkenkunde van Nederlandsch-Indië*, vol. 58 (Hague: Nijhoff, 1905).

Marsden, William, *History of Sumatra* (London: J. M'Creery, 1811).

Prentice, D. J., "The Murut Language of Sabah," *Pacific Linguistics*, Series C, no. 18 (Canberra: Australian National University, 1971).

Riedel, J. G. F., *De Sluik-en Kroesharige Rassen Tusschen Selebes en Papua* (The Hague: Martinus Nijhoff, 1886).

Roth, Henry Ling, *The Natives of Sarawak and British North Borneo*, vol. 1 (New York: Truslove & Comba, 1896).

Rutter, Owen, *Pagans of North Borneo* (London: Hutchinson, 1929).

Schwaner, C.A.L.M., *Borneo, Beschrijving van het Stroomgebied van den Barito*, vol. 2 (Amsterdam:Van Kampen,1854).

Sellato, Bernard, "Mythologie et Deforestation a Kalimantan," *Le Banian*, vol. 10 (Paris, 2010).

----------, *Hornbill and Dragon: Arts and Culture of Borneo* (Singapore: Sun Tree, 1992).

Seon, Hong et. al, "Safety investigation of Noah's Ark in a Seaway," *Journal of Creation*, vol. 8 (April 1994).

Van Der Crab, P., *De Moluksche Eilanden: Reis Van Z. E. Den Gouverneur Generaal Charles Ferdinand Pahud* (Batavia: Lange & Co. 1862).

von Brenner, Joachim Freiherr, *Besuch bei den kannibalen Sumatras* (Würzburg: Leo Woerl, 1894).

Williams, Thomas Rhys, "Folklore Texts: A Tambunan Dusun Origin Myth," *Journal of American Folklore*, vol. 74, no. 291 (American Folklore Society, 1961).

Sources on Australia:

Berndt, Ronald M. and Catherine H. Berndt, *The World of the First Australians* (Sydney: Ure Smith, 1977).

Bladen, F. M. (ed.), "Appendix B: The MacArthur Papers," in *Historical Records of New South Wales*, vol. 2 (Sydney: Charles Potter, 1893).

Capell, Arthur, *Cave Painting Myths: Northern Kimberley* (Sydney: University of Sydney, 1972).

Coate, Howard and W.H. Douglas, "Australian Aboriginal Flood Stories," *Creation*, vol. 5, no. 1 (1982). Retrieved from https://creation.com/australian-aboriginal-flood-stories Accessed August 21, 2018.

Coate, Howard, "Aboriginal Flood Legend," *Creation*, vol. 4, no 3 (1981). Retrieved from https://answersingenesis.org/the-flood/flood-legends/aboriginal-flood-legend/

Cote, Daniel R., "Original Monotheism: A Signal of Transcendence Challenging Naturalism and New Ageism." Doctoral Thesis. Liberty University (April 5, 2020).

Curr, Edward M., *The Australian Race*, vol. 2 (Melbourne: John Ferres, 1886).

----------, *The Australian Race*, vol. 3 (Melbourne: John Ferres, 1887).

Fawcett, J. W., "Australian Aborigines," *The Australasian Anthropological Journal*, vol. 1, no. 6 (May 31, 1897).

Hamilton, Rev. Robert, "Australian Traditions," *The Scottish Geographical Magazine*, vol. 1, no. 7 (July 1885).

Hassell, Ethel and D. S. Davidson, "Myths and Folktales of the Wheelman Tribe of South-Western Australia," *Folk-Lore,* vol. 45, no. 3 (1934).

Henderson, John, *Observations on the Colonies of New South Wales and Van Diemen's Land* (Calcutta: Baptist Mission Press, 1832).

Howitt, Alfred William, *The Native Tribes of South-East Australia* (London: MacMillan & Co., 1904).

McDougall, A.C., "Manners, Customs, and Legends of the Combangree Tribe," *Science of Man and Journal of the Royal Anthropological Society of Australasia*, vol. 4, no. 3 (April 22, 1901).

Montgomery, James (ed.), *Journal of Voyages and Travels by the Rev. Daniel Tyerman and George Bennet, Esq.*, vol. 2 (Boston: Crocker and Brewster, 1832).

Parker, Katie Langloh, *Australian Legendary Tales: Folklore of the Noongahburrahs as Told to the Picaninnies* (London: David Nutt, 1896).

Reed, Alexander Wyclif, *Aboriginal Fables and Legendary Tales* (Sydney: A.H. & A.W. Reed, 1965), pp. 55-56.

Robinson, Roland, *The Feathered Serpent: The Mythological Genesis and Recreative Ritual of the Aboriginal Tribes of the Northern Territory of Australia* (Sydney: Edwards and Shaw, 1956).

Smyth, Robert Brough, *The Aborigines of Victoria*, vol. 1 (London: 1878).

Taplin, George, "The Narrinyeri," *The Native Tribes of South Australia* (Adelaide: E.S. Wigg & Son, 1879).

Willis, Roy G., *Worth Mythology* (Oxford: Oxford University Press, 2006).

Wordick, F. J. F., *The Yindjibarndi Language* (Canberra, A.C.T.: Australia: Dept. of Linguistics, Research School of Pacific Studies, Australian National University, 1982).

Sources on North Asia:

Adam, Lucien, "Une Genèse Vogoule," *Revue de Philologie et d'Etnographie*, vol. 1 (Paris: 1874).

Anderson, Walter, "Nordasiatische Flutsagen," *Acta et Commentationes Universitatis Dorpatensis, B. Humaniora*, vol. 4, no. 3 (Tartu, Estonia: 1923).

Andree, Richard, *Die Flutsagen* (Braunschweig: Friedrich Vieweg, 1891).

Anokhin, A.V., *Материалы по шаманству у алтайцев* ("Materials on Shamanism among the Altaians"). *Сборник Музея Антропологии и этнографии при Российской Академии Наук* ("*Publications of the Museum of Anthropology and Ethnography of the Russian Academy of Sciences*" [MAE]), vol. 4, no. 2 (1924).

Bernard Munkacsi, "Die Weltgottheiten der Wogulischen Mythologie (III)," *Keleti Szemle*, vol. 9 (Budapest: 1908).

Bogoras, Waldemar, *Chukchee Mythology, Publications of the Jesup North Pacific Expedition*, vol. 8, part 2 (New York: Stechert, 1910).

Chen, Qinghao and Wang Quigui (eds.), "Collection of Mongolian Folk Tales", "Complete Collection of Chinese Folk Tales", vol. 36 (Taipei, 1989).

----------, "Collection of Heilongjiang Folk Tales", "Complete Collection of Chinese Folk Tales"], vol. 32 (Taipei, 1989).

Dahnhardt, Oskar, *Natursagen* ("Nature Legends"), vol. 1 (Leipzig: Drunk und Verlag, 1907).

De Forest, John William, "The Great Deluge," *Old And New*, vol. 6 (Boston: Roberts Brothers, 1872).

Delitzsch, Franz, *A New Commentary on Genesis*, vol. 1 (New York: Scribner & Welford, 1889).

Deviatkina, Tatiana, "Images of Birds in Mordvinian Mythology," *Folklore*, vol. 48 (2011).

Dolgih, Boris Osipovich, *Мифологические Сказки И Исторические Предания Нганасан ("Nganasan Mythological Tales and Historical Traditions")* (Moscow, 1976).

Dyrenkova, N. P., *Culture and Writing of the East*, vol. 4 (1929).

Elder, John and Hertha D. Wong, eds., *Family of Earth and Sky* (Boston: Beacon Press, 1994).

Georgi, Johann Gottlieb, *Russia: Or, a Complete Historical Account of all the Nations which Compose that Empire*, vol. 4 (London: J. Nichols, 1783).

Golovnev, A. V., *Кочевники тундры: ненцы и их фольклор* ("Tundra Nomads: Nenets and their Folklore) (2004).

Hogan, Brian, "Distant Thunder: Mongols Follow the Khan of Khans," *Perspectives on the World Christian Movement* (Pasadena, CA: William Carey, 2009).

Holmberg, Uno, "Finno-Ugric, Siberian," *The Mythology of All Races*, vol. 4 (Boston: Archeological Institute of America, 1927).

Laufer, Berthold, "Petroglyphs on the Amoor," *American Anthropologist*, vol. 1 (1899).

Lehtisalo, T., *Entwurf Einer Mythologie der Jurak-Samojeden* (Helsinki: Société Finno-Ougrienne, 1924).

Ma, Xue-Liang, Liang Ting-wang, and Zhang Gong-jin, eds., ("Literary History of Chinese Minority Races") (Beijing: Central Institute for Nationalities, 1992).

Maydell, Baron Gerhard, *Reisen und Forschungen im Jakutskischen Gebiet Ostsibiriens in den Jahren 1861-1871*, vol. 1 (St. Petersburg, 1893).

Minford, John (trans.), "Hailibu the Hunter," *Favourite Folktales of China* (San Francisco: New World Press, 1983).

Namjila, G., *A Comparative Study of Altaic Mythologies in China, trans. Wang Ruli* (Salt Lake City: American Academic Press, 2023).

Pallas, Peter Simon, *Samlungen historischer Nachrichten über die mongolischen Völkerschaften*, vol. 2 (St. Petersburg, 1776).

Poniatowski, Stanislav, "Diary of an expedition to the land of the Golds and the Orochons in 1914" (in Russian), *История и культура Приамурья ["History and Culture of the Amur Region"]*, vol. 5 (2009).

Popov, Andrej Alexandrovich, *Долганский фольклор* ("Dolgan Folklore") (Leningrad, 1937).

Potanin, Grigory N., Очерки северо-западной Монголии ("Studies of Northwestern Mongolia"), vol. 4 (Petrograd: 1883).

Sagang Sechen, "The Bejeweled Summary of the Origin of the Khans," trans. John R. Kreuger, *The Mongolia Society Occasional Papers*, vol. 2 (Bloomington, Indiana: Mongolia Society, 1967).

Schipper, Mineke, Ye Shuxian and Yin Hubin (eds.), *China's Creation and Origin Myths* (Boston: Brill, 2011).

Stellers, George Wilhelm, *Beschreibung von dem Lande Kamtschatka* (Frankfurt, 1774).

Tokmashev, D. M., "Ethnolinguistic research of Siberian-Turkic folklore proper names based on Shor cosmogonical legends and myths," *Tomsk State University Bulletin*, vol. 2 (2012).

Tretyakov, P. I., *Туруханский край, его природа и жители* ("Turukhansk Region, its Nature and Inhabitants") (Petrograd, 1871).

Von Kotzebue, Otto, *A New Voyage Round the World in the Years 1823-1826*, vol. 2 (London: Colburn and Bentley, 1830).

Wang, Shiyuan et al, "Hezhe, Monba, Lhoba, Jinuo", "Chinese Ethnic Story Series"], vol. 16 (Shanghai, 1995).

Wilson, Robert Dick, "The Date of Genesis X," *The Presbyterian and Reformed Review*, vol. 1, no. 2 (New York: Anson Randolph & Co., 1890).

Winternitz, Moriz, "Die Flutsagen des Alterthums und der Naturvölker," *Mittheilungen der Anthropologischen Gesellschaft in Wien*, vol. 31 (1901).

Wu, Bing'an and Li Wengang, "Selected Manchu Folk Stories" (Shanghai, 1983).

Miscellaneous Sources:

"Human-Like Tracks in Stone are Riddle to Scientists," *The Science News Letter*, vol. 34, no. 18, 29 October 1938.

Armitage, Mark and Jim Solliday, "UV Autofluorescence Microscopy of Dinosaur Bone Reveals Encapsulation of Blood Clots within Vessel Canals," *Microscopy Today*, vol. 28, no. 5 (September 2020). https://dstri.org/wp-content/uploads/2020/09/2armitage_MicroToday.pdf

Austin, Steven A. and J. D. Morris, "Tight folds and clastic dikes as evidence for rapid deposition and deformation of two very thick stratigraphic sequences," *Proceedings of the First International Conference on Creationism* (Pittsburgh: Creation Science Fellowship, 1986).

Bethell, Tom, *Darwin's House of Cards* (Seattle: Discovery Institute, 2017).

Catchpoole, David, "Grass-eating dinos: A 'time-travel' problem for evolution," *Creation*, vol. 29, no. 2 (2007). https://creation.com/grass-eating-dinos

Connelley, William Elsey, *Indian Myths* (New York: Rand McNally, 1928).

Culin, Stewart, "Games of the North American Indians," *Twenty-fourth Annual Report of the Bureau of American Ethnology* (Washington: GPO, 1907).

de Armellada, Cesareo, *Tauron Panton: Cuentos y Leyendas de los Indios Pemón*, 2nd edition (Quito: Abya-Yala, 1989).

de Humboldt, Alexander, *Researches Concerning the Institutions & Monuments of the Ancient Inhabitants of America*, trans. Helen Maria Williams, vol. 1 (London: Longman, 1814).

Dundes, Alan (ed.), *The Flood Myth*, (Berkeley: University of California Press, 1988).

Gould, Stephen Jay, "Creationism: Genesis vs. Geology,", in *The Flood Myth*, ed. Alan Dundes (Berkeley: University of California Press, 1988).

Hecht, Jeff, "Dino droppings reveal prehistoric taste for grass," *New Scientist*, Vol. 188 (2005). https://www.newscientist.com/article/mg18825274-400-dino-droppings-reveal-prehistoric-taste-for-grass/

Holden, Joseph M. and Norman Geisler, *The Popular Handbook of Archaeology and the Bible* (Eugene, OR: Harvest House, 2013).

Josephus, *Antiquities of the Jews, in The Works of Josephus*, trans. William Whiston (Peabody, MA: Hendrickson, 1987).

Karsten, Rafael, *Mitos de los Indios Jibaros del Oriente del Ecuador* (Quito: Sociedad Ecuatoriana de Estudios Historicos Americanos, 1919).

Kitchen, Kenneth A., *Ancient Orient and the Old Testament* (London: Inter-Varsity Press, 1966).

Lehmann-Nitsche, Robert, "Mitología Sudamericana XII: la Astronomía de los Mocoví," vol. 2, *Revista del Museo de la Plata*, vol. 30 (Buenos Aires, 1927).

Mortenson, Terry, "British scriptural geologists in the first half of the nineteenth century: part 1." *Journal of Creation*, vol. 11, no. 2 (1997).

Price, Paul, "How the Joggins polystrate fossils falsify long ages." https://creation.com/joggins-polystrate-fossils 16 Apr. 2020. Retrieved 27 Oct. 2021. Tasman Walker, "Chapter 5. The Geologic Record," ed. Robert Carter, in Evolution's Achilles Heels (Powder Springs, GA: Creation Book Publishers, 2014), p. 173.

Purifoy Jr., Thomas, "Why are fossil footprints curious evidence for the Flood?" Is Genesis History? https://isgenesishistory.com/fossil-footprints-curious-evidence-flood/ Retrieved 31 Oct. 2021.

Robinson, Philip, "Trilobite Conga Line vs Evolutionary Timeline," Creation, vol. 42, no. 3 (July 2020). Retrieved 30 October 2021 from https://creation.com/trilobite-conga-line

Roth, Henry Ling, *The Natives of Sarawak and British North Borneo*, vol. 1 (New York: Truslove & Comba, 1896).

Sandars, Nancy K. (trans.), *The Epic of Gilgamesh*, (Harmondsworth: Penguin Books, 1962).

Sarfati, Jonathan, *The Genesis Account* (Powder Springs, GA: Creation Book Publishers, 2015).

Schoolcraft, Henry R. and Thomas H. Benton, "Remarks on the Prints of Human Feet, Observed in the Secondary Limestone of the Mississippi Valley," *The American Journal of Science and Arts*, vol. 5 (New Haven, CT: S. Converse, 1822).

Seon, Hong et. al, "Safety investigation of Noah's Ark in a Seaway," *Journal of Creation*, vol. 8 (April 1994).

Snelling, Andrew, "Sedimentation experiments: Nature finally catches up!" *Journal of Creation*, vol. 11, no. 2 (1997).

----------, "The Carbon Canyon Fold, Eastern Grand Canyon, Arizona," Answers Research Journal, vol. 16 (2023), pp. 1-124. Snelling, "The Monument Fold, Central Grand Canyon, Arizona," *Answers Research Journal*, vol. 16 (2023).

----------, "The Carbon Canyon Fold, Eastern Grand Canyon, Arizona," *Answers Research Journal*, vol. 16 (2023).

----------, "The Monument Fold, Central Grand Canyon, Arizona," *Answers Research Journal*, vol. 16 (2023).

Thompson, Joanna, "This trilobite was equipped with a 'hyper-eye' never seen before in the animal kingdom." Live Science. Retrieved 30 October, 2021 from https://www.livescience.com/trilobite-eyes

Tomkins, Jeffrey M., "The Fossils Still Say No: Capping a Cretaceous Conundrum." (31 August, 2021). Retrieved 30 October, 2021 from https://www.icr.org/article/the-fossils-still-say-no-cretaceous-conundrum/

Vitaliano, Dorothy, *Legends of the Earth: Their Geologic Origins* (Bloomington, IN: Indiana University, 1973).

Wise, Kurt P., "The Fossil Record." Presentation at the Is Genesis History? Conference, June 19-23, 2017, Dickson, Tennessee. Retrieved from: https://youtu.be/wKuFQLkFW7o

----------., "Tracks but no Trilobites." (1 Oct. 2012). Retrieved 31 Oct. 2021 from https://answersingenesis.org/extinct-animals/five-tracks-but-no-trilobites/

----------, First appearances of higher taxa: a preliminary study of order in the fossil record. N.D. Unpublished study.

Witzel, E. J. Michael, *The Origin of the World's Mythologies* (Oxford: Oxford University Press, 2012).

Woodmorappe, John, "An anthology of matters significant to creationism and diluviology," *Creation Research Society Quarterly*, vol. 18, no. 4 (1982).

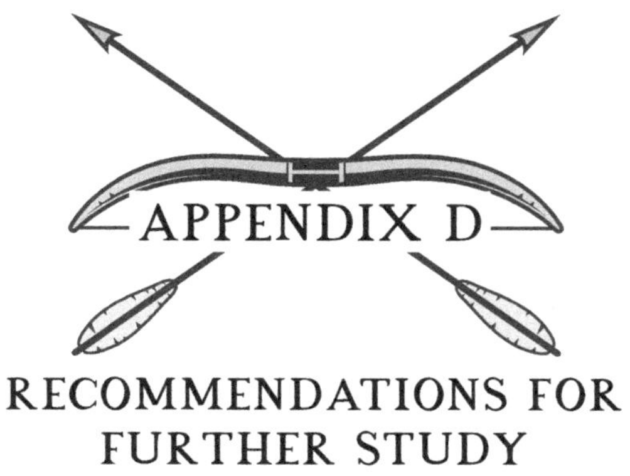

APPENDIX D

RECOMMENDATIONS FOR FURTHER STUDY

Evidence for Jesus and the Resurrection

The Case for Christ by Lee Strobel

I Don't Have Enough Faith to be an Atheist by Frank Turek and Norm Geisler

Forensic Faith by J. Warner Wallace

The Case for the Resurrection of Jesus by Gary Habermas and Michael Licona

New Evidence that Demands a Verdict by Josh McDowell

Geology

Earth's Catastrophic Past by Andrew Snelling (two volumes)

Carved in Stone: Geological Evidence of the Worldwide Flood by Timothy Clarey

Grand Canyon: Monument to Catastrophe by Steve Austin

Evolution's Achilles Heels edited by Robert Carter

Is Genesis History? (DVD and conference presentations)

Grand Canyon: A Different View by Tom Vail

The Genesis Flood by Henry Morris and John Whitcomb

Biology, Paleontology, and Genetics

Evolution's Achilles Heels edited by Robert Carter

Genesis Impact (book and DVD) by Dan Biddle

Contested Bones by Christopher Rupe and John Sanford

The Greatest Hoax on Earth? Refuting Dawkins on Evolution by Jonathan Sarfati

Replacing Darwin by Nathaniel Jeanson

Darwin's House of Cards by Tom Bethell

Ultimate Proof of Creation: Resolving the Origins Debate by Jason Lisle

Darwin's Black Box by Michael Behe

Icons of Evolution: Science or Myth? by Jonathan Wells

Signature in the Cell by Stephen Meyer

Genetic Entropy by John Sanford

An overview of the independent histories of the human Y chromosome and the human mitochondrial chromosome" by Robert Carter, Stephen Lee, and John Sanford. In Proceedings of the International Conference on Creationism, Volume 8 (2018).

Old Earth vs Young Earth

Refuting Compromise by Jonathan Sarfati

Coming to Grips with Genesis edited by Terry Mortenson

Searching for Adam: Genesis & the Truth About Man's Origin by Terry Mortenson

Other Flood-Related Resources

Noah's Ark: A Feasibility Study by John Woodmorappe

The Ark and the Darkness (DVD) by Dan Biddle

Answers to the Top 50 Questions about Genesis, Creation, and the Flood by Dan Biddle

Have You Considered? by Julie Von Vett and Bruce Malone

Biblical Archeology (on Genesis and other books of the Bible)

Popular Handbook of Archaeology and the Bible by Joseph Holden and Norm Geisler

Patterns of Evidence: Exodus (DVD and book) by Tim Mahoney

Patterns of Evidence: Journey to Mount Sinai (Two Parts) by Tim Mahoney

Unearthing the Bible by Titus Kennedy

New Evidence That Demands a Verdict by Josh McDowell

Scriptural Inerrancy

Defending Inerrancy: Affirming the Accuracy of Scripture for a New Generation by Bill Roach and Norm Geisler

Explaining Biblical Inerrancy by R. C. Sproul and Norm Geisler

Vital Issues in the Inerrancy Debate edited by F. David Farnell

Christianity and Liberalism by J. Gresham Machen

Flood Legends and Comparative Folklore

Echoes of Ararat: A Collection of Over 300 Flood Legends from North and South America by Nick Liguori

The Formosan Primary Anthropogonic Myths, Genesis, and the Creation of Man by Valdis Gauss

The Formosan Great Flood Myths (Vol. 1 & Vol. 2)

Flood Legends by Charles Martin

The Formosan 'Shooting the Sun' Myths: Aboriginal Oral Histories in Taiwan by Valdis Gauss

APPENDIX E

TOPICAL INDEX

Miscellaneous Topics

Rib Stories